mass
media
PROCESSES and EFFECTS

LEO W. JEFFRES
Cleveland State University

with
RICHARD M. PERLOFF

WAVELAND
PRESS, INC.
Prospect Heights, Illinois

For information about this book, write or call:

Waveland Press, Inc.
P.O. Box 400
Prospect Heights, Illinois 60070
(312) 634-0081

Dedication

To:

my parents,
Laurence and Edna Jeffres,
for their support all these years

Contents

4 THE AUDIENCE: Who's Paying Attention and Why?   119

5 MEDIA CONTENT AND PUBLIC PERCEPTIONS   165

6 SOCIAL EFFECTS OF THE MEDIA by Richard M. Perloff   201

7 POLITICAL EFFECTS OF THE MEDIA   247

8 ECONOMIC EFFECTS OF THE MEDIA   289

9 CULTURAL EFFECTS OF THE MEDIA   325

Preface

Comprehensive, up-to-date summaries of mass communication theory are difficult to achieve and even more difficult to focus. What seems elementary at one level requires elaboration at another. And the features which serve to elucidate with one style get in the way of those reading with a different purpose. No doubt this book will suffer from similar inadequacies which are a consequence of trying to serve several purposes. Nevertheless, this book tries to do just that. First, the book is designed to provide students with a comprehensive summary of the social science literature that attempts to understand mass communication processes — how the media operate, the relationship between media and the social context within which they operate, the audiences exposed to media symbols, the pattern of media content that permeates today's stimulating environment, and the various political, social, economic and cultural effects attributed to media institutions. An effort has been made to identify the basic concepts that are the building blocks communication scholars take for granted but which, left untouched, can mystify students. There also has been an effort to provide a minimum of descriptive material as context and historical background for understanding the social science generalizations that are the business of scholars. I hope this book is a useful vehicle for teaching mass communication processes to a broader than usual range of undergraduate classes. Most of the material has been presented in various class lectures and "pretested" in the preliminary edition. Secondly, the book was written to serve as a second text or useful reference for both graduate and undergraduate students. With that purpose in mind, there is an abundance of citations and references that can be used for "backtracking" and further probing by those interested in pursuing topics beyond the bounds of this book. An extensive index is also provided to improve the text's utility as a reference.

The book has been written and rewritten several times over the past half dozen years. Some of that activity may represent the author's somewhat compulsive desire to be inclusive, but it also stems from a major goal of the writing process. Though the author clearly began with a basic framework of chapters (introduction, society and the media, institutions, audiences, content and effects), the actual text emerged from an inductive style of searching the literature and letting the empirical research determine the resulting structure and content. More than a decade of social science journals was sifted for research on mass communication and mass media. Sorted into various piles and cross referenced, these were joined by the findings and perspectives elaborated in papers and text-length manuscripts. The summaries that followed, tentative or otherwise, are my own conclusions based on the literature. Certainly, other scholars will arrive at different conclusions, but they too have the burden of providing the evidence underlying their judgments. I hope the outline of my own logic and empirical evidence is sufficiently clear for students and scholars to make their own judgments. Since science is an open-ended process that can only produce tentative results, the book is not a "final statement" but necessarily represents a slice of time ending in late 1985.

The book is divided into two parts. The first half begins with an introduction to mass communication and some of the various perspectives employed to understand its processes. The mass media are placed in a social context — what is the relationship between mass media and society? Then media are examined at an institutional level — as industries, organizations, professional environments and collections of roles. Two additional chapters elaborate on the extensive audience research and the often inadequate literature concerned with patterns of media messages. The second half of the book focuses on effects, beginning with Richard Perloff's authoritative account of such social effects as violence and aggression among children, pornography, children's development as consumers, and learning of pro-social behaviors and various stereotypes. Next are political effects, with an emphasis on media consequences in election campaigns as well as longer-range contexts. This chapter could have been extended because it represents the major thrust of mass communication scholars working today and the topic is of such obvious significance to working democracies, but an effort was made to maintain a balance in chapter lengths. The economic effects chapter that follows concentrates on the influence of media advertising, and the final chapter integrates questions of cultural effects into an international context. These latter two chapters are not typically included in books about communication theory, but they represent the author's judgment that students facing an increasingly interdependent international environment need to pay attention to both topics. Writing each chapter was an education for the author as well as an opportunity to see "where the holes are." In some cases, little research has been done to provide even descriptive work. This is particularly true in the content chapter, where even basic frequency distributions are not available to tell us what film genre or other media content forms have been produced through the years.

Clearly there are omissions due to the limits on length and complexity. Probably the most significant is the literature on information-processing of media content. Secondly, given more time and room, the author would add a chapter devoted to systems concepts and models analyzing mass media at that level of analysis. In subsequent revisions updating the literature, such additions will be considered, but they are outside the scope of the current edition.

Finally, there are many people to thank for their direct and indirect contributions along the way. First is my co-author, Rick Perloff, for his excellent chapter on social effects. Secondly, my work began with an additional co-author, Marilyn Jackson-Beeck, who started the project in 1979 and asked me to join her. "Pun's" contribution survives in the opening pages of the introductory chapter and the basic structure of the book. Several others helped along the way, including Dennis Davis and Jack Suvak, whose efforts made the preliminary edition possible. The book has benefited greatly from various critiques, and I wish to thank Sharon Dunwoody, Robert Stevenson, Kent Middleton, Sidney Kraus, John Nichols, Jae-won Lee and Donna Rouner for their comments. None of these is responsible, however, for mistakes or the final judgments. The editors at Waveland Press also were most helpful and cooperative. Furthermore, I want to thank two graduate assistants, Melissa Spirek and Barry Pollick, for checking the list of final references, and graphics arts specialist John Ludwig for the cover design.

My current work is certainly not an achievement isolated in time. Rather, it is a product of my own interactions with others along the way, including my colleagues and students at Cleveland State University. I also owe a debt to colleagues and students at the University of the Philippines (Los Banos), where I spent 1983-1984 on a Fulbright. Furthermore, I am constantly amazed to find how useful my past associations as a graduate student are (the University of Minnesota and the University of Washington). And my interest in mass media began with Bert Cross at the University of Idaho many years ago. That interest was given practical form at the Lewiston *Morning Tribune*, which was a classroom filled with a host of talented journalists who had a high set of standards and broad perspective about their work. To all these people, named and unnamed, I extend my thanks.

Leo W. Jeffres
Cleveland, Ohio
February, 1986

1

Mass Communication Theory

This book investigates the nature of modern mass media of communication. Mass media today are the subject of much criticism because people fear or covet their potential power—and power attracts attention. Everyone from ethnic groups to cities and nations worries about the consequences of negative media images. A host of special interests seek to influence the media in campaigns designed to do everything from discouraging smoking and energy consumption to encouraging voting and economic growth. We will examine media development, structure and organization, content and audiences. We will also look at the effects of media and their relationships with other institutions. Our focus is on six mass media, including three types of *electronic* media (TV, radio, movies) and three types of *print* media (newspapers, magazines, books), each of which is attended to by millions of people.

So many people pay attention to these six media that we usually think of them as *mass media*. However, a definition of mass media requires an elaboration beyond this point. Any device that carries messages between people is a *medium*. This includes the telephone, telegraph, and bulletin board, but what makes a medium a *mass medium* is its ability to carry messages not just from one person to another but from one person to thousands or millions of others. For example, the President of the United States now can address the entire nation when he delivers a speech carried by television, something he could never do traveling from city to city. Because of television, every-one can watch and listen to him simultaneously. Indeed, the fascinating thing about mass media like TV is that they have liberated people from the normal constraints of *time* and *space*. For good or bad, they make it possible for people to share messages wherever they live, whenever they wish to do so.

Imagine for a moment what your life would be like without mass media. Without TV, radio, newspapers, magazines, books, and movies, you probably would have a lot more "free" time. However, an even more important difference in your life would show up in how you solicit and receive information. Without mass media, you would have to rely on people in face-to-face contact, as was the custom until the past several centuries. Instead of relying on expert reporters and media producers, most of whom are far away and unknown to you, you would turn to teachers, parents, friends, clergy and resident experts. These people would live in your own home or community. Without mass media you would be bound in space, geographically. Without mass media, your communication with these people would also be bound in time; you could talk with them only while they lived, while they were physically in your presence. Now with books, magazines, newspapers and other media, messages live on even when their originators pass away.

Most people grow up using several mass media on a daily basis which makes it difficult for them to appreciate the difference media make in their lives. A simple comparison between mass communication and interpersonal communication (that which occurs face-to-face) provides a useful illustration. Clearly, the major difference is the relationship between the *source* (who formulates messages) and the *receiver* (who translates messages from the source). In such face-to-face situations, both parties immediately influence each other. People *interact*. The words you hear as a receiver are chosen especially for you, so that you can understand them. The words are delivered to you when you are ready or willing to interact, at a pace that is more or less comfortable. You constantly provide nonverbal *feedback* to the source, through such nonverbal cues as nods and questioning looks. And you can talk back, in which case you become the source. Typically, you take alternate roles, sometimes turning your thoughts into words (as source), and at other times translating the source's words into thoughts (as receiver).

Contrast this with what happens when you watch TV. The relation-ship between you and the news anchorman is impersonal. When you turn the set on, the messages are not designed for you alone. You are unknown to the TV personalities and the people who produce TV shows, assuming you're like most people. In fact, some programs such as "The Little Rascals" probably were made before you were born.

And what if you don't like or can't understand messages from TV? You can talk back to the set all you want but the program goes on. In other words, there is *no immediate* feedback as there is in interpersonal communication. This makes you the receiver and only the receiver in most situations. On the other hand, you have a lot of freedom when you use mass media like TV. There is no obligation to pay attention, you can "tune out" whenever you wish, and you can choose various stories and programs. You can't be nearly so selective in your face-to-face discussions with friends, family and associates.

In order to contrast and summarize the major differences between mass and interpersonal communication, see the two diagrams in Figure 1-1.

Figure 1-1

Model Describing Mass and Interpersonal Communication

Interpersonal Communication	**Mass Communication**
Source — Message — Receiver	Sources - Messages - Receivers
└──────Feedback──────┘	└──(delayed feedback)──┘
single source	many participants as source
single receiver	many receivers
homogeneity	heterogeneity (diverse receivers)
immediate feedback	delayed feedback (if any)

In both, the basic elements are quite different. In mass communication, there are generally many sources and many receivers) and they may be quite independent of each other. The feedback which does occur (letters to the editor would be an example) is generally delayed and of a lesser "magnitude" than that which occurs in interpersonal communication. Furthermore, many of the mass communication messages have "lives" of their own once they are created, while the fleeting comments of interpersonal conversations have no such permanence. Secondly, the audience is more *heterogeneous* in mass communication; this is one of the features characterizing mass media—the audience must be sufficiently large that it can't be reached by any one person speaking or appearing at any one time. When the audience is that large it must include many kinds of people. Sources in mass communication are also numerous and diverse.

Consider, for example, the many sources involved in the latest edition of the *Reader's Digest*. Most of its articles are condensed by editors who work with material selected from other magazines and books. Their jobs are to shorten and to change the original author's work to make it fit the *Digest* format. The original source, meanwhile, relied on additional sources and material such as eyewitnesses, government authorities, documents and books. Once the *Digest* editors have finished their work, the condensed articles are processed further by artists who illustrate and make the text fit small pages. Later, technicians and craftspeople run the presses, pour the ink, and bind the magazine. Ultimately, finished copies of the *Reader's Digest* are delivered to homes and newstands through the aid of typists, computer programmers, letter carriers, and delivery services. Thus, there are many participants in the media organization that constitutes the "source" in this example.

In later chapters we will explain in detail how sources produce media messages and how these messages finally turn out. Here let us note the range of sources and participants involved. First, there are media managers who plan and coordinate media production and transmission. They must decide what will attract and maintain the audience and then translate that decision into products that may involve photographs, music, spoken words, written words, drawings and paintings, all of which necessitate the services of other experts. Experts work with media managers to produce articles, stories, films, videotapes and other "software" that express the media managers' imagination in concrete forms that can be transmitted by the machinery of mass media—such "hardware" as printing presses, TV transmitters or film projectors. Auxiliaries participate by operating the hardware at times when the audience is most likely to be attracted. Advertising agencies participate by coordinating the ad campaigns of different companies. In addition to helping determine how much money to spend and where to place the messages, ad agencies may actually produce the advertising copy or commerical film that later appears in the media. Agencies themselves employ people who do marketing research to find out consumer needs on which to base campaign decisions.

In all of the description so far, little notice has been paid to public participation. As noted, there is generally little audience feedback directly to media organizations, though there is abundant attention to audience needs and interests via such tools as the Nielsen ratings for television. However, audiences themselves are composed of active viewers, readers and listeners. If source behavior is more complex than the simple reflections of the work of a single individual, receiver behaviors are also a complex bundle of interests, media interests and gratifications. In later chapters we will describe audiences to mass media in greater detail. Here, let us note that people pursue media use in quite different manners. Books are generally sought out with considerable reflection while much TV viewing begins with the intention of "passing time." Furthermore, people differ from each other in how and why they use the media. People who live alone often find the radio or TV set a "noisy companion" that drowns out the silence while others avoid TV except for an occasional planned viewing of a documentary. Some people read the daily newspaper only for the sports content while those who are more print-oriented begin at page one and work their way through the entire paper. We also get quite different things out of our media behaviors. For example, some people use the opinion magazines and newspaper editorials as voter guidance at election time. Others read, listen or view to learn something about the "person" or personality. (For further information on this topic, see Wright, 1975).

Media Characteristics

Audience choices themselves are linked to media characteristics. Each mass medium has particular *qualities,* or attributes that lend themselves to particular types of appeal. Print media are strictly visual, appealing to sight. Thus, magazines and newspapers are designed to catch the eye, through color, pictures, headlines, drawings and typefaces. Messages transmitted by radio involve sound alone while TV and movies are based on both sight and sound. Thus, radio appeals to the ear with a barrage of music and sound effects while television and the cinema appeal to both senses with action-packed film accompanied by music and speech. In addition, some media may even appeal to the skin. Next time you're watching TV or are in a darkened movie house, take a look at the audience. You'll see people bathed in light. Noted media guru Marshall McLuhan goes so far as to say that TV and movies are *tactile* media producing a pleasant sense of all-over body stimulation.

A major characteristic distinguishing the print media from their electronic cousins until quite recently was *permanence.* Messages in print media can be saved whereas those transmitted by the electronic media must be consumed during their fleeting lifespan. This characteristic leads directly to another feature found in print media. Typically, electronic media are *nonindexable.* Unless you have an audio or video recorder, messages transmitted by electronic media are impossible to review. Until you've seen or heard something, you don't know what it is about and then it's too late to make a choice. In contrast, print media can be indexed by titles, headlines and captions so you can decide if and when to read specific material. In addition to indexability, permanence allows you the consumer to control the speed of message reception by altering your reading rate somewhere between "skim" and "study." With electronic media, you receive messages at the same speed they are transmitted, fast or slow.

Another feature that guides would-be media consumers is *scope* — whether a medium sends messages to a national, regional, or local audience. This factor also affects the types of messages sent and is affected by the means used to distribute mass media. Each of the six media studied here *can* have either wide or narrow scope but they tend to specialize thus avoiding duplication and high costs. National media generally include television, movies, books and magazines with TV reaching the largest audience most consistently. Most of its evening programs — "prime time" — are intended to appeal to one and all, young and old, across the country. Books, movies and magazines meantime exclude many potential consumers (for example, the illiterate and indigent) although they also tend to concentrate on the national audience. There are exceptions. City magazines have grown in popularity in recent years. A large portion of TV is also locally produced and locally directed. In contrast, except for papers like *USA Today*, the *Wall Street Journal* or the *Christian Science Monitor*, most newspaper and radio content is directed at the local audience. They may feature some messages that are the same as those found in other areas, but they tailor the product for their own area. Thus, radio stations and newspapers may vary in their dialect, ethnic and racial appeal. Indeed, it is hard for most newspapers to reach far beyond their own locale even when desired because of the need for timely distribution by trucks and other carriers.

Another way to classify mass media is by method of distribution. Basically, there are two ways to reach large, diverse audiences. Messages can be mass produced over and over or those messages can be presented once or a few times but to large numbers of people simultaneously. Print media (books, magazines, newspapers) typically produce multiples of the same product; movies are shown in theaters to many people cumulatively. In contrast, radio and TV are broadcast media which means that they seldom duplicate their messages but reach many when they transmit. Distribution and the element of permanence are obviously tied together; the new TV cassettes and TV record discs recently marketed are changing the situation. Here, the "broadcast" messages appearing on one's TV screen are distributed by record or cassette rather than carried "live" to millions of sets simultaneously.

When you decide to watch TV, read a book or listen to the radio, much of the time your decision will center around *content*. One major content is commercial messages. In the U.S., books and movies usually are not interrupted by commercial messages though some may be placed at the beginning or the end. In contrast, consider that commercial radio and most TV stations include a minimum of nine and one-half minutes of commercials per hour scattered within and between programs. As much as half of all newspaper and magazine content is advertising and your choice of medium is likely to be influenced by your interest in commercial messages almost as much as by articles, stories or programs. In some cases, the commercial messages are the main attraction for consumers. For example, homemakers turn to the food ads in their daily newspapers before the weekly shopping trip. Many people turn to magazine coupons to save money. On the other hand, commercial messages also constitute an annoyance when they appear but are not sought. If you do not wish to see TV commercials, you do have some options. You can turn to public TV or your own video recorder/player if you own one. There also are noncommercial public radio stations and some newspapers and magazines without ads.

Another content decision that consumers make when they turn to the media is the selection of message formats. Although the *themes* or *topics* in a medium may change somewhat depending on audience receptivity, there are basic *content structures* that tend to reappear through time. For example, there are fiction, non-fiction, biography, science fiction, and reference books. And there are horror movies, comedies, westerns, mysteries and dramas. Radio formats range from "beautiful music," to Top 40, jazz, soul, talk or all-news. Newspapers may be general, business, urban or suburban. Magazines run the gamut from general interest to photography messages and from fiction to special interests that include politics, jogging and chinchilla-raising. As for TV, there are situational comedies, soap operas, game shows, and police-detective shows.

There is an amazing variety in the topics and themes presented in the mass media but we also see these themes repeated across the different media. This occurs when a particular theme proves extremely popular, and, thus, commercially successful. An example is the movie *Star Wars* which prompted the TV series *Battlestar Galactica* and *Buck Rogers*. Those also stimulated an already strong interest in books about science fiction. Another example is the book *Roots* by Alex Haley which inspired two TV-mini series. Likewise, recording artists featured on radio tend to appear on TV along with newsmakers identified in print.

Generally, you can see that the mass media exist *symbiotically*, which is to say that they operate to the benefit of each other as some plants and animals do.

In the United States, mass media generally are run as businesses. They make money by selling either time or space. Electronic media such as TV and radio sell *time* to advertisers who hope that their commercials will be seen or heard when the audience tunes in to the programming. Similarly, print media such as newspapers and magazines sell *space* to advertisers hoping that their advertisements will be seen and read while receivers turn pages reading stories. The larger the audience, or the more "distinguished" the audience, the more money media can charge advertisers. In a sense, the mass media must deliver an audience to advertisers to remain in business themselves. This is a far cry from the interpersonal communication described earlier.

Other Perspectives on Communication

The preceding discussion of mass media is based on the most familiar model of communication which Fisher (1978) calls the "mechanistic model." It has also been identified by other names such as an "information model." In this perspective, an individual encodes a message that flows through a channel to another individual who decodes the message and may respond with feedback; the fidelity of the entire transmission is open to extraneous influence called noise. The locus of this perspective is the concept of channel — the connection between the receiver and the source. This is the perspective which has probably been used most often by mass communication researchers. It has produced an impressive display of studies which match components of the model or relationships between them. Though disparaged by some, this view of communication has been modernized and elaborated so that it continues to demonstrate a conceptual and research vitality. This is also the model most often assumed by social science disciplines other than communication as well as those in the humanities, other observers and critics.

However, this is not the only perspective of communication in use today. Scholars also are applying other perspectives in their study of both mass and interpersonal communication. Fisher's (1978) outline is a particularly useful one. In addition to the mechanistic perspective, he describes three others: the psychological, the interactional, and the pragmatic. We will briefly discuss these and how they fit into analyses of the mass media of communication.

The psychological perspective emphasizes the intrapersonal level and conceptual *filters* that affect the process of interpretation during encoding and decoding of a structured set of stimuli (such as media messages). This perspective focuses on the filters which operate in an

S-O-R-R model (Stimulus-Organism/filters-Response-Reinforcement). Using this model, we can look at how people selectively scan incoming messages for relevant cultural content, how attitudes affect both encoding and decoding of messages on such topics as politics, and how media credibility affects individual's consumption of media content. The psychological perspective probably has been the second most important source of inspiration for mass and interpersonal communication research. It is favored by those inclined to emphasize the behavior of individuals and how they react in complex environments. It is almost totally ignored by those who focus on macro levels of research. Its exclusion from the on-going debate about how to analyze communication impoverishes the dialogue. Use of the psychological perspective often results in ideological charges by Marxists and others that the researcher is favoring the "status quo" by emphasizing individual freedom and initiative. In response, those working at this level or within this perspective point out that the operation of macro-level systems rests on assumptions about human behavior and interaction. The evidence of questioning those assumptions is gathered by looking at the communication behavior of people individually and in groups. That includes media consumption, people's perceptions of media, individual uses of the media, human information processing of media content, and the impact of media on individuals. Subsequent chapters on media effects will include models prominently featuring the concept of "filter."

A third perspective is a view of human communication which developed from symbolic interaction. In this view, the "self" is seen as arising through communication and becomes known to us only through an internal dialogue with ourselves. The perspective is based on the view that people act toward objects on the basis of meanings the things have for them. Those meanings are derived from communication; the meanings are created, maintained and modified through communication. The locus of this perspective is "role taking," in which people align their behavior with others. We can use this perspective to look at how people's self concepts are developed through communication. An example particularly important for mass communication is the external images distributed by the media. In Chapter 5, we will review media images and stereotypes. People see much of their personal identity captured by their involvement in occupations or professions, as well as ethnic-religous and other group membership. Consistent with this perspective, many argue that the media have an impact on their personal identities by presenting negative or insensitive images that subsequently feed into interpersonal channels and evaluations.

Fourth, the pragmatic perspective conceptualizes communication as

a system of human behaviors observed as a pattern of sequential interaction. The most important unit is the interact or double interact (for
example, I ask a question, you answer equals one interact), and the
focus is on the system, not the individual. The interacts contain two
kinds of information: one pertaining to content and one pertaining to
relationship. The pragmatic perspective directs us to concentrate on
the sequential behaviors that link people to each other (Millar and
Rogers, in press). For example, what patterns of acts and interacts
reflect escalating conflict or harmonious relationships? Chopping up
people's interaction with the mass media, we might seek similar
behavioral patterns reflecting sustained media credibility. The pragmatic perspective is relatively new and has had virtually no impact on
mass communication research. However, that might change as new
technologies make mass communication more interactive and stimulate
researchers to conceive of mass communication in pragmatic terms.
The pragmatic perspective in particular and Fisher's set of
perspectives in general also should sensitize mass communication
researchers to use more "complete models" in their studies rather
than focusing on individual components (see Jeffres and Hur, 1983);
long-range programs of research are generally required for this to
occur.

Analyzing the Mass Media of Communication

If you and a friend walked into the CBS headquarters in New York
City or the newsroom of your local paper, you probably would agree on
what you saw and perhaps even on the significance of it. Scholars in
the same position might see different things or start from different
places in explaining the significance of the moment. For example, one
critic might point to CBS as merely a vehicle for the reproduction of
"mass culture," the place where the symbols of American society are
turned into cultural artifacts that mold the conscious thoughts of
Americans. Another critic might identify CBS as simply a reflection of
the capitalistic system, its TV programs reflecting the beliefs and
values of the dominant ruling class represented by CBS stockholders
and their representatives in management. A third observer might see
CBS as a group of coalitions jockeying for position in an uncertain
environment where no single person or group has control; CBS itself
would be but one source of symbols in a "pluralistic society." A fourth
person might see the network as an institution whose shape is molded
by the long-term consequences of audience behaviors tapped by such
measures as the Nielsen ratings. If these four individuals were
together, they might also disagree over what evidence would be accept-

able for verifying their statements or settling arguments over which one best represented reality. Clearly, how you evaluate the mass media of communication would vary according to the communication perspective being used as well as the overall philosophical perspective employed.

There are two central questions involved here. Each of these philosophical issues will be pursued briefly before we continue our examination of the mass media. First, where is the origin of "determinancy" (cause) located—in "society," in the pattern of symbols that form media content, or in people's behaviors as members of audiences? Secondly, how do we "know" what we "know"? In other words, what kinds of evidence are acceptable as the basis of our knowledge about mass communication?

These two issues represent classical struggles between different philosophical streams of thought about the nature of reality and the nature of learning. The first question represents the conflict between "idealism" and materialism." According to idealism, reality is the creation of the mind or spirit; as Dewey (1929: 108) noted, idealism is a tribute to the respect men pay to thought and its power. Materialism is a system of thought that explains the nature of the world as dependent on matter, or material things; thus, the origin of human consciousness is found in society and social arrangements.

Scholars tending toward one system of thought rather than the other reflect this in their investigations of mass communication. For example, George Gerbner's "cultivation theory"—examined in chapters six and seven—sees media images moulding society by the long-term presentation of relatively uniform versions of social reality. So, for example, by defining what is normal or deviant, the media cultivate similar definitions in the public. In the final chapter on cultural effects, we'll examine notions of "cultural imperialism" and its impact on indigenous culture; research in this area also fits into an "idealistic" orientation.

So many critics and researchers follow materialistic approaches that we have to segment them according to various schools or areas. Most of these are posed at the macro level and see influence occuring from the top down. For example, traditionally sociologists have seen people's behaviors as shaped by the social structure and meanings of a society; here we have research by Phillip Tichenor and his colleagues (1980) which looks at how a town's newspapers and other media reflect the size and diversity of its population. Papers in larger towns, for example are seen as distributing more conflict information than those in smaller towns because it is functional for such diverse communities. Also operating at this level, classical Marxists see media operations as determined essentially by economic forces (Murdock and Golding,

1977). Some variants of Marxism focus on how media operate in capitalist nations to support the ruling class (Garnham, 1983; White, 1983; Hall, 1977). At more micro-levels of analysis, researchers focusing on the individual have demonstrated how the behaviors, choices and perceptions of individuals operate to shape and set constraints on media institutions themselves. In later chapters we will look at how people's "cognitive filters" limit media effects, and how public choices and overt pressures alter media direction.

The second question focuses on evidence acceptable in our search for knowledge and certainty. It too reflects divisions. One is represented by "rationalism," the theory that reason alone, unaided by experience, can arrive at basic truth regarding the world. The other is "empiricism," the philosophical doctrine that all knowledge is derived from experience. Rationalism is associated with the concept of innate ideas and confidence in the intelligence of people. Here we find communication researchers that utilize semiology (the general science of signs) and focus on codes and underlying structures of media content, such as ethnic images and presentations of social classes. Though much of the work in this area consists of using the senses to observe media content, the traditional method for accepting evidence is clearly consistent with rationalism and traditions from the humanities. Identification of codes in media content is a product of rational analysis and interpretation. Disagreement over findings is a rhetorical issue, the basis of debate. In contrast, empiricism recognizes some a priori truths (logic and math) but requires that knowledge be derived from use of the senses and reflection (inner experiences). Most research falling under the category of empiricism today probably would fit more comfortably under the label of "dualism," a philosophical system that tries to explain phenomena in terms of both mind-and-matter principles (e.g., Immanual Kant). It is empiricism that accounts for the bulk of contemporary American mass communication research. It is also the basis for the scientific method and its constituent requirements that evidence allow for testability and rejection of hypotheses generated by critics and observers.

Research in mass communication today represents a clear interaction between these twin aspects of epistemology — the investigation of the nature of knowledge and the process of knowing. The interaction rests in part on an affinity with the notion of science as a body of knowledge but not as a process for achieving that knowledge. One might expect those who see influence stemming from our material surroundings to rely upon empirical methods of observation for detecting that influence; furthermore, those perceptions would allow for the acceptance or rejection of general ideas as experiments do. This is the essential linkage for empirical science.

However, Marxists and many others use an over-arching ideology for confirming observations rather than the reverse. For example, Jalbert (1983) demonstrates how media presentations are ideological by employing several analytical constructs that are illustrated rather than "confirmed" or "supported." Observations cannot disconfirm the ideology, as data do to hypotheses and questions do in scientific designs. By posing questions at the macro level and denying testability, these researchers shift to rational methods more consistent with the humanities and rationalism than with science and empiricism.

For some, the general assumption that determinacy is located in society and social relations remains, and the search for confirmation is found in the selection of ideologically-acceptable patterns from the infinite variety represented by media content. These are called "preferred readings." The methods used provide problematic results by placing the rules for evidence in rational rather than empirical domains, but proponents of these approaches insist on using deterministic language nevertheless, and that takes on a prescriptive tone.

Linking Media and Society
Where to Begin the Analysis, a Chicken-and-Egg Problem

Though we're talking about one relationship, there are two major links to be investigated: a) society→mass media, and b) Mass media→society. The first link is represented by the view that the mass media reflect society; the second link is the reverse: Mass media affect society. Clearly, at all levels today there is a belief that the mass media can and do affect our lives in important ways. Presidential candidates devote extensive time and money on mass media. At a more local level, disgruntled citizens call newspapers requesting that their names be omitted from reports about traffic accidents, fearing that the media coverage will damage their reputations. Unions and businesses both believe the media treat them unfairly while schools and organizations cultivate their publics through media campaigns.

At the same time, other observers argue that the mass media have relatively few effects and, instead, simply reflect the larger society. Journalists often argue that the media merely reflect society by holding a mirror up so we can see ourselves. In this line of argument, the media contain substantial portions of violence because much exists in the real world. In the political arena for several decades, some have argued that the media merely act as vehicles used by other forces of change in society with the media largely serving to speed up and magnify change.

Who's right? In part, the argument is the old "chicken-and-egg" problem. Which comes first? Does media coverage of candidates come first or are the media themselves manipulated by the candidates into presenting the pictures and stories they want? A simple "reflection" hypothesis would require that the media act as completely unoriginal, neutral vehicles rather than creative human organizations requiring decisions and professional judgments. For example, thousands of people in television and other media make decisions about how aggressive behaviors and other topics are presented; the "reflection" hypothesis would require that each person recognize his or her responsibility to present a picture of "reality" and know how to work so personal biases are kept to a minimum. We will argue that, though there may be considerable violence for media to "reflect," both news and fictionalized treatments of that topic may add to the way in which American media consumers process the information and are affected by it. At the same time, even if we could assume that the media act as neutral vehicles for passing on various content, the fact that they focus attention on problems can have an impact regardless of other institutions involved in the process.

Some of the disagreement over whether the media have independent effects centers on the "time frame" used to study such effects. In the short run, media effects seem more easily identifiable, but in the the long run such effects are more difficult to identify and may be ambiguous. This is particularly the case among those who argue for a more global view in which the question of effects itself is simply not pertinent; media form and content are simply part of a culture in which all parts are interdependent. Some also argue that media effects are minimal because the media themselves are affected by other institutions such as political and economic structures. Again, it's a question of where to start—with the egg that produced the chicken or the chicken that produced the egg.

Link 1: Media Reflect Society

The mass media can "reflect society" in a multitude of ways. Contained within this single linkage is not one but several issues. Some observers are interested in the media reflecting "culture" (norms, values), while others view media as one of several institutions (e.g., economic, political) operating according to normative philosophies consistent with the structure of society (e.g., capitalist, socialist). Furthermore, some look for the impact of "society" in the visible behaviors, perceptions and choices of the population. In summary, the media are seen as being affected by dominant social norms and values, by other social institutions and the dominant normative philosophy, or by public choices, behaviors and perceptions. We'll examine these briefly.

Culture — Media

Ignored by social scientists for several decades, the concept of "culture" has been revitalized in recent years. Culture is usually conceived as consisting of four kinds of symbols: values, norms, beliefs, and expressive symbols which include all aspects of material culture from stone axes to TV programs. Peterson (1979) outlines several current perspectives on culture. The first stresses our first link, the view that culture mirrors society. This perspective emerged in the decade following the end of World War II. Focusing on values and norms, this view says that culture mirrors society. Thus, we need to examine newspapers, movies, plays and other forms of expressive symbolism to understand better the less visible aspects of social relations. The utility of the concept that a single social system is mirrored by a single cultural system has been challenged on several fronts. Some researchers take into account less than the "whole society" suggested by the "mirror" hypothesis and some studies suggest that the "mirror" of society is "clouded" at best (Epstein, 1973). Some researchers have compared media content under the notion that the reflection hypothesis requires similarities in media surveillance of the environment. Thus, Luttbeg (1983) found little consensus among newspaper editors on what was the important news of the day in an analysis of a hundred daily U.S. newspapers. Atwater (1984) found similar uniqueness among local TV news coverage. Cline (1983) identified quite diverse pictures of Latin American presented in elite newspapers, and Martindale (1984) found newspaper gatekeepers making different decisions about covering the same political events. As articulated by Gramsci (1971), the notion of "media hegemony" refers to the dominance of a certain way of life and thought and how it is diffused through the public. This definition is "conceptually rooted" in Marxism (Altheide, 1984) or at least materialism. However, as Altheide (1984: 486) notes, this dominant ideology thesis has been uncritically accepted by many mass communication researchers and the "fit has not been a good one." He recommends looking at role relationships between journalists and their sources which we will do in Chapter Three.

Another perspective on culture (Peterson, 1979) focuses on how symbols may be used to perpetuate a fundamental split between dominant and dominated elements of society. The idea that culture is manipulated by or for the ruling classes comes from Karl Marx but the question of how class and status differences persist across generations has attracted many diverse researchers. Using this perspective, some have focused on the transmission of "class codes" through TV, museums, dialects, photography, journalists, intellectuals, education, etc. Summarizing a host of studies, Peterson (1979) concludes that a body of work does show how "economic capital is converted into cultural capital," a partial reflection hypothesis.

Society — Media

Those who have looked at "society" rather than "culture" as the force reflected by the media include not only Marxist-materialistic scenarios but also a "pluralistic model of power." This model does not assign continuing dominant influence to a single set of interests in contemporary western countries. It views power as manifest in the outcome of active conflict and competition among contending groups and individuals. Media organizations actively participate in this process when they focus on the diversity of debate and content. Clearly, this model is also consistent with some interpretations of the view that the media act as a mirror reflecting society. Thus, this view would argue that the media contain much of the conflict and divisiveness that stems from the competition among different interests. Rather than representing the values and ideas of their owners, the mass media are seen as interested arbitrators with a responsibility to at least try to represent the diversity of the country. Critics of the pluralistic view note that media pay more attention to the powerful than the powerless and give more credence to the views of the majority than to minorities. Some of these points will be raised again in the second chapter when the functions of communication in a democracy are discussed.

Media also reflect "society" and social forces in the materialistic perspective which states that all significant aspects of human life are determined by economic conditions. Marx's account is probably the most familiar and influential here. It presents history as a succession of dominant economic groups where the current manifestation of the class struggle is the capitalist exploitation of workers and where the inevitable consequence of the present situation is a revolution of the working class and rule by the dictatorship of the proletariat — the Communist party. Throughout this scenario, mass media organizations and their content reflect the ideas of the dominant capitalist class and are used to maintain their ruling position. In at least one sense the media are viewed by Marxists as a more modern "opiate of the masses" than religion. Thus, Marxists emphasize the relationships between communication entrepreneurs and the "capitalist class," and between ownership and control within communication industries. There is also attention to the ways in which mass media organizations process information and ideas so that the values and ideas of the elite are distributed to the public. Marxist literature as well as opposing viewpoints are voluminous and widely distributed. Among other things, critics note the divorce of ownership from management in modern corporations, question the assumption that media content "reflect" the "ruling class," and argue for a balance of interests that see power distributed among multiple sources other than just classes (Peterson, 1979).

The "reflection hypothesis" is also found in the view that practices and performances of mass media are largely defined by normative philosophies which express the relationship between media and society. Four major philosophies have traditionally been used to describe this relationship in the past (Siebert, Peterson and Schramm, 1956). We'll describe each briefly.

Authoritarian: The oldest philosophy of mass media, the authoritarian view places the media in the position of supporting policies of the state. However, though controlled by the government, through patents or licenses, for example, the media still function as private enterprise. When printing first emerged it was viewed as a threatening development and the government acted. In 16th century England Henry VIII declared all printing would be under crown control and used to support and advance the interests of the crown. Even the front pages of colonial newspapers such as Benjamin Franklin's "Public Occurrences" carried the phrase "Published by Authority," which recognized the relationship between government and the mass media of that day. However, long before the appearance of colonial newspapers, people were fighting to loosen official restrictions.

Libertarian: This philosophy is rooted in the ideas of Milton, Locke and others that people have the right to pursue truth which is best advanced when there is an "open market place of ideas." Libertarian philosophy values diversity and pluralism within society. This means that contrasting views should be allowed to emerge when they are present in a city, a nation, or other social context. It does not mean that each individual should entertain a pluralism of views. Emphasis is on the "potential" for individual expression and the absence of legal constraints and sanctions by the state. One of the first of many eloquent appeals against government restriction on communication was John Milton's *Areopagitica*. Protesting vehemently against the "chains that bind," Milton argued: "Give me the liberty to know, to utter and to argue freely according to conscience, above all liberties...who ever knew truth put to the worse, in a free and open encounter?" In Milton's arguments are clues as to what America's founding fathers had in mind when they drafted the first amendment to the U.S. Constitution, open discussion and debate, or open channels of communication. The *First Amendment* (still in effect today) says:

> Congress shall make no law...abridging the freedom of speech, or of the press; or the right of the people peacably to assemble, and to petition the Government for a redress of grievances.

One month before the U.S. Congress adopted the Bill of Rights, another document was adopted to form support for the Libertarian philosophy. The Declaration of the Rights of Man and Citizens in France asserted equality of all people, sovereignty of the people, and the inalienable rights of the individual to liberty, property and security. The libertarian press is regulated by members of society when they decide to support magazines or newspapers, for example. The media serve as the informational link between the government and the people. Thus, if information is restricted, then the people's right to be informed is denied. Today the media of many Western nations are largely based on this philosophy, though there have been constant challenges and revisions. When the Libertarian philosophy was formally added to the U.S. Constitution, mass media technology and distribution were very limited. There was no photography, no telephone, no TV and no radio. Few but the elite were able to read. As time went on the media became more accessible and literacy increased, but so did the size of media empires and the concentration of media ownership. Through the addition of new media there was increased diversity of voices, but many media outlets were owned by the same company or individual. Diversity of ideas was limited by the rise of broadcast networks, newspaper chains, and syndicates. Some of the challenges to mass media center on media responsibilities rather than media rights, which is the major concern of the third philosophy.

Social Responsibility: This philosophy places many ethical and moral restrictions on the mass media, stressing responsibility instead of freedom. Media today are major economic institutions, and few people can afford to start their own newspaper or TV station as an outlet for their opinions. The Social Responsibility philosophy requires media to offer opportunities for people's opinions to be heard. This philosophy emerged in a report of the Hutchins Commission on Freedom of the Press in 1947. The commission set out to answer the question of whether freedom of the press was in danger. It concluded press freedom indeed was endangered for three reasons: (1) the press had grown as a mass medium while the percentage of people able to express their ideas through the press had decreased; (2) the few people able to use the press had not adequately served the needs of society; and (3) those directly in charge have at times engaged in practices the public condemned. This mid-20th century view of the relationship between mass media and the government puts less faith in the Libertarian idea that truth will arise from the clash of ideas. The commission cited five main requirements for a socially-responsible press:

1. The press must give a truthful, comprehensive, and
   intelligent account of the day's events in a context
   which gives them meaning.

2. The press must provide a forum for the exchange of comment and criticism.

3. The press must project a representative picture of the constituent groups in the society.

4. The press must represent and clarify the goals and values of the society.

5. The press must provide full access to the day's intelligence.

Press reaction to the commission report was explosive. Since then discussions of mass media rights have given at least equal weight to media ethics and responsibilities. Indeed, many of the chapters in this book look at issues raised by the commission and others. Today, the American definition of "social responsibility" is still emerging. Numerous surveys have traced what seems to have been a general decline in the confidence Americans have in their major institutions. Yet Americans continue to place considerable confidence in key institutions, including the media (this will be discussed more in Chapter 5). However, generally positive attitudes are not always directly translatable into immediate support or approval on specific issues where there are cross currents of different attitudes. For example, a 1973 survey found that 43% thought authorities should be given the right to censor films, TV, radio and theater for unpatriotic or revolutionary content; 40% thought newspapers which preach revolution should be banned from circulation; and 43% favored government review of all protest meetings to be sure people weren't urging others to overthrow the system. However, 57% opposed banning meetings denouncing the president and only 27% favored the notion that no one should be allowed to have pornographic books, pictures, or movies in his possession (Harris, 1976). Similar patterns have been found in other national surveys where large percentages of adults thought newspapers whould be allowed to criticize police. Only one-third thought people should be allowed to make speeches against God or to publish books attacking the American system of government. In general, men, younger people (ages 21-29), and the college educated showed stronger belief in the two freedoms. Similarly, high levels were found for liberals, those high on mass media consumption, and those most active in the political arena. However, American beliefs in civil liberties were strongly tested by the Vietnam War and Watergate experiences; it is unclear how intertwined the beliefs are with those two situations. Another analysis (Zellman, 1975) showed that support for free speech and dissent has increased since studies made in the 1940's though it is more limited in concrete situations than for abstract principles. She argues that the relationship between support for abstract principles (such as freedom of the press) and behavior in real situations could be very tenuous and that few attempts are made to teach Americans to be true civil libertarians. According to one interpretation, diversity encourages an appreciation of the importance of civil liberties for democracy. Though the picture is far from settled, increased exposure through interpersonal communication and mass media seem to have a major part in producing this belief.

Communist/Marxist: In Communist philosophy, the media function to perpetuate and expand the socialist system. The media are instruments of the government and are owned and used by the state. Newspapers are permitted and are even, in some instances, encouraged to engage in self-criticism. For example, criticism of bureaucratic failures or factory inefficiency might be allowed, but such criticism is closely controlled. Marxists focus on the relationship between ownership and control of the media and the power structure in society. Lenin argued that the economic system determines society's legal and political institutions. The press serves the ruling class. In capitalist societies, mass media generally are owned by business interests, or capitalists, who use their media power to remain in control and to suppress other classes. When this elite is overthrown by the working class, it is logical to deny press access to the old elites. The concept of freedom takes on a meaning quite different from that in the previous two philosophies. Freedom means that the working class operating through society owns the means to produce or operate newspapers, radio stations, TV stations, etc. Though there are increasing divergencies in Marxist philosophy, the Soviet Union represents the major example of communist media practices. The mass media are viewed as agitators, teachers, and mobilizers of the public. Diversity of opinion is assuming a greater role in the Soviet Union today as coercion gives way to persuasion. The Marxist emphasis on ownership is translated into a network of controls and links between government officials, the Communist party, and media organizations.

Link 2: The Media Affect Society

Our second link reverses the flow of influence. Here the media are seen as affecting society. Again, the link is more complex than a single relationship would suggest. The media can affect "society" in a variety of ways ranging from effects on individual behaviors and perceptions to group relations and social institutions.

The issue of media effects has a lengthy history. For several decades scholars have debated whether the media have direct effects, specifically in the political arena. Starting in the earlier part of this century, observers often took what was considered a "maximum effects" view that the media were directly responsible for changing people's ideas, attitudes, and behaviors—shooting beliefs into people's minds almost as a doctor innoculates patients with a hypodermic needle. This approach has been called by several names—the "bullet theory," the "hypodermic needle" model, and the "Stimulus-Response" model (see Figure 1-2). The view stems from public fears over the power of mass media. Events of the Spanish American War and World War I reinforced beliefs that the media could shape events. One publisher, William Randolph Hearst, was accused of virtually starting the Spanish-American War. A new threat arose with the advent of radio, a medium which could leap over national boundaries and appeal directly to the masses without governmental interference. Each new medium has prompted similar questions about its potential use or misuse in the hands of people who want to affect the public—from radio and movies to comic books, television and the latest communication technologies.

Figure 1-2

The Hypodermic Needle Model of Mass Media Effects

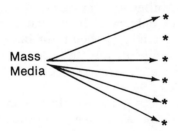

This model assumes that the audience members are all pretty much alike, responding to media in predictable, similar ways. Also, audience members are portrayed as being quite independent of each other. In a nutshell, the hypodermic model presents mass media as being very powerful.

The earliest scientific studies to focus on media influence came in the 1930's and 1940's. One group of studies focused on the impact of motion pictures on children. Published in the early 1930's, the Payne Fund studies concluded that children and adolescents copied many of their behaviors from actors and actresses (See Lowery and DeFleur, 1983: 31-57). Other studies also supported the view that the media can have powerful consequences, but it was a real life event which probably best illustrates this view. On Halloween evening in 1938, the CBS show *Mercury Theater of the Air* captivated listeners and convinced thousands that the United States was actually being invaded by creatures from Mars. Many people thought millions of Americans were already dead and they took to their cars to escape the advance of the Martians (Cantril, 1940). The panic produced by the show was seen as further evidence of media effects. The broadcast, narrated by Orson Welles, came just as European nations were setting the stage for World War II. That conflict prompted research into the impact of modern propaganda that used both radio and film as well as print media. Fairly sophisticated techniques of experimentation and measurement were already available; they were used to study effects of media directed not only by the enemy but also by the U.S. government at its own public. The U.S. government was concerned that the American public was ill-informed, and a series of films was produced to explain the nation's involvement in the international conflict. Researchers concluded that such films as *The Battle of Britain* and others in the *Why We Fight* series were only modestly successful in modifying opinions and general orientations, though they did increase factual knowledge. Most of these studies were experimental and were conducted in laboratory situations. The advantage of experiments is that they control outside influences so that you can see how media content affect particular behaviors being monitored. In real life settings, other factors which might account for the changes can interfere with the examination of any relationship. However, lab experiments are artificial and, thus, they cannot be directly transferred to real life situations.

One study which did focus on real life media use came when Professor Paul Lazarsfeld and his colleagues probed for media influences in the 1940 presidential election in Erie County, Ohio. They asked people whether their voting decision had been influenced by the media and were surprised to find little support for the view that media have direct effects. Instead, other people were identified, leading them to propose that influence moves from the media indirectly through people who are called "opinion leaders" to the less interested segments of the public. Voters reported little influence by the mass media primarily because they had made their minds up long before the campaign began. These researchers posited a new model of media effects in the political arena. This model depicted a *two-step flow of media influence* from the mass media (1) to opinion leaders (2) and thence to the general public (3). Media seemed to affect the public indirectly in subsequent studies where researchers found that opinion leaders (who constituted about 20% of the population) paid greater attention to the mass media campaign coverage and then used its knowledge to influence others' votes. Overall, the two-step flow model was comforting, if surprising to researchers, for it suggested that most of the public would be safe from foreign or domestic propaganda when and if it occurred. The model was also consistent with a philosophy which argued that the mass media should be independent of government interference.

Regardless of the accuracy of the two-step flow model in 1940, much has happened since then that forces us to raise additional questions. Radio was joined by TV in exposing a vastly expanded audience to news, commericals, programs and political "propaganda." A less educated and less interested segment of the public was exposed to media messages that were not mediated by opinion leaders and were not sought by those eventually exposed to them.

Shortly, another model combined features from both the hypodermic and two-step flow models. Called the *diffusion model,* it combines features from both of the previous models suggesting that, yes, media do influence the audience directly but interpersonal influence is also important.

Figure 1-3

The Diffusion Model of Media Effects

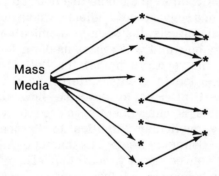

The diffusion model suggests that people are most directly affected by the media at the early stages of decision-making, making people aware and interested, but leaving to people the impact of trial and evaluation.

Since both the two-step flow and diffusion models suggest that mass media are not all-powerful, media theorists Joseph Klapper combined the two into an over-arching perspective known as *limited effects.* Unlike the hypodermic model, this perspective views the audience as active and involved. It asserts that personal preferences and opinions neutralize the effects that media would otherwise have. The audience is seen as interpreting messages selectively according to the principles of *selective exposure, selective perception* and *selective retention.* These principles say that people attend to messages with which they tend to agree and also recall such messages more readily. Klapper says that the effects of mass media, thus, are slight unless the audience is confused or forced to pay attention to propaganda such as occurs during brainwashing. Thus, the media are seen as reinforcing what already exists, whether it's a stereotype, a belief, or an opinion.

With subsequent election studies, the dominant view of media effects that emerged in the 1940s and continued into the next several decades was an "indirect effects model," also called "stimulus-inter-vening variable-response" model and by other names. Instead of asserting that the media have maximum consequences, the indirect effects model sees the media as one of a set of influences that include not only other people, but existing beliefs, feelings and information held by media consumers, and other environmental factors. Peterson (1979) is consistent with this view when he argues that the evidence is skimpy for the position that manipulation of mass media and other expressive symbols leads to political and economic power.

In general, the question of mass media effects has grown more complex rather than the reverse. Most researchers today would conclude that the question of whether or not mass media have effects is too simple a question. Certainly the media are not "all powerful," but neither does the evidence suggest that audiences have defensive filters that wash out all media effects. Instead, communication researchers have sought to identify how and when mass media affect individuals, groups and society. This recognition that the "effects question" is a complicated one has led to greater interest in what are called "process" models that attempt to describe how people decode messages and how this is subsequently related to various media effects. We will pay particular attention to "processes" in the chapters on social and political effects. The impact of advertising also is increasingly being viewed using process models. In addition, our discussion of audience behaviors will look at people's motivations and other aspects of media behaviors that often are part of approaches that emphasize process.

To complicate the situation, most recently a group of researchers headed by Professor George Gerbner has argued for a return to a more powerful and direct view of the media. They have tried to demonstrate that television in particular cultivates (affects) the norms and values of a society. Since the 1950s we have seen a steady expansion in the types of media effects being studied. Work by Gerbner and his colleagues is part of this stream of investigation and debate. One perspective on culture emphasizes that expressive symbols are the distinctive feature of humankind and represent the code for creating and recreating society from generation to generation. Since control is seen as existing in the expressive code itself rather than in other social arrangements such as those suggested by Marx, the mass media become the focal point of observers concerned with altering society.

Today mass communication researchers are asking how the media affect people and their institutions and under what conditions. Certainly the media are not alone but must compete with other sources of influence—peer groups, families, etc. In later chapters, we will examine the evidence for mass media effects in several arenas, starting with social effects and continuing to political, economic and cultural effects.

Summary

In this chapter we identified six modern mass media of communication and their characteristics. Mass communication was defined and contrasted with interpersonal (face-to-face) communication. Four perspectives on communication were described: mechanistic, psychological, interactionist, and pragmatic. We discussed how to analyze the mass media, focusing on two central questions: Where is the origin of "determinancy" (cause) located? How do we "know" what we "know"? These two issues were discussed as representing classical struggles between different philosophical streams of thought about the nature of reality and the nature of learning (idealism and materialism).

The relationship between media and society was discussed as two links: society→mass media, and mass media→society. The first link represents the view that media reflect society; the second link represents the converse view that media affect society. Our discussion of the first link considered the concept of "culture" and current views on how it is reflected in mass media. We also reviewed ways in which the media are seen as operating according to normative philosophies that include: Authoritarian; Libertarian, Social Responsibility; and Communist/Marxist. Our examination of the second link reviewed early views and research on media effects beginning with the hypodermic needle model and continuing to the two-step flow of media influence and the diffusion model. The issue of direct vs. indirect effects was discussed followed by recent interest in a more powerful media model.

2

Media and Society

Mass media do not appear overnight, of their own volition, for no good reason. Newspapers, radio and television have long histories of development and are the result of a variety of forces. Numerous economic, political, and social factors will be detailed in this chapter. With the appearance of each new medium, existing media have had to adapt during periods of uncertainty.

As far as print media are concerned, *literacy* is necessary before they can become popular. How has literacy affected the development of print media (newspapers, books and magazines)? Clearly there is another *chicken and egg* problem here. Which came first? Why should people learn to read unless they have interesting materials available? We know that some books, magazines, and newspapers must be available to stimulate people to read or to learn to read. We also know that newspaper circulation will be quite small unless the pool of literate people is large. Economically advanced countries with high literacy rates have near saturation of newspapers while poorer countries encourage literacy programs with weekly papers, pamphlets and wall sheets as part of their policy for catching up.

Education is the handmaiden of literacy. As such, it stimulates the growth of print media. In the United States, as elsewhere, the spread of mass education fed large numbers of readers into the audiences of print media. Inspired by the philosophy of Thomas Jefferson, this country introduced a mass education system (beginning in 1830) to prepare the population to become responsible citizens capable of selecting wisely from the media and equally capable of contributing to a "free marketplace of ideas."

During the first half of the 19th century, a popularization of print occurred in the United States. The growth of popular fiction and newspaper journalism had a profound impact, but Nord (1984) points out that *religion* also had a part to play. Nord argues that the missionary impulse lay at the foundation of this growing interest among the masses in learning how to read. The evangelical Christian publicists in the Bible and tract societies dreamed of a genuinely mass medium that would deliver the same printed message to everyone in the nation. To reach that goal, they helped to develop the modern printing and distribution techniques associated with the reading revolution of the 19th century.

Economic factors also are important to media growth, but not always in the way you might expect. Normally, the wealthier people and countries tend to have and to use the greatest number of mass media. Contrary to expectations, movies flourished and radio boomed during the Great Depression of the 1930's. Often the radio was one of the last things Americans gave up as their standard of living fell. Inexpensive entertainment and news bulletins seems to help people through the hard times.

A third factor affecting media growth is *technology*. The printing press clearly had to develop for books and newspapers to be widespread. The components that go into a radio or TV set had to be invented before radio and TV could be used by more than a few tinkerers. Technology itself is a response to social needs as well as a phenomenon that stimulates other social developments like mass media. Printing can be traced back a thousand years to Asia. Johann Gutenberg introduced movable type to Europe around 1440, yet the first newspapers were not successful until more than a hundred years later. In England, the crown saw that the printing press was the source of potentially upsetting power, so it licensed the press and brought it under greater government control. The licensing system didn't stop until the latter part of the 17th century, and then only as a result of political and economic pressures. Public opinion had become a force to be reckoned with, due to the growth of libertarian political philosophy. The monarch began to be ruled by public consent which could be influenced by printers and publishers. This forced the crown to be more respectful of publishers.

Radio, the first broadcast medium, faced quite a different reception from government during its early years. Almost every component of radio was separately patented in more than one country making it almost impossible to put the parts together without ending up in court.

Thus, radio was stymied until World War I when urgent military needs for improved radio systems led to the suspension of all patent disputes while various people cooperated with each other. Still, after the war many patent disputes remained; no one had sufficient patents to make a complete system. Within a three-year period (1919-1922) a series of cross-licensing agreements were made and, finally, the new medium took off. The chaos in radio also provoked a generally reluctant private sector to seek government intervention and this led to the formation of the Federal Communication Commission and licensing of radio stations. In the early stages, radio was not yet a mass medium because its primary audience consisted of amateurs (similar to ham radio operators today). The most recent media technologies have faced a similar situation. The same cassette or video disc will not play on all cassette or disc machines and this has let to questions about which system would survive in the long run. Technological competition can create reluctance on the part of a public not wishing to be caught with obsolete, noncompetitive technology. VCR's have moved beyond this stage and are now growing rapidly but the newest technologies continue to face this dilemma (AM stereo radio, computer software packages, etc.).

Urbanization and immigration also affect the development of mass media since large numbers of people are necessary to support a TV station or a daily newspaper. Thus, urbanization promotes the gorwth of mass media so that countries and regions which are most heavily populated tend to have more newspapers, radio stations, TV stations and movie theaters. Similarly, as immigrant groups move into various regions, they tend to develop mass media in their own languages. For example, there are Czech, Polish, Portuguese, Slovene, Lithuanian, Urdu, Yiddish, Arabic, and Carpatho-Russian newspapers right now in the United States.

The earliest book was "published" (actually, written by hand) on leathery, dried animal skins by Saxons living in what we now call England. The oldest printed book still surviving today was printed in 868, in China, letter by letter. Efforts at book production continued at a slow pace until the development of the printing press centuries later. With the printing press came mass production and a chance for a profitable new industry centered then on local bookbinders shops. In America early book publishing was quite limited, most of it consisting of Bibles, blank ledgers, account books, and custom-ordered books. Diversity of content and book distribution increased after independence. Thus, we see how printing technology and a restrictive political climate affected the growth of this medium.

The growth of libraries and mass education in the United States gave a big boost to book publishing. The McGuffey *Reader* was an illustrative case. The *Reader* was published as a series of elementary school texts in the 19th century; it eventually had a circulation of more than 120 million copies. Today educational books still account for more than half of total book sales with textbooks alone accounting for more than 30% of sales. Shortly after mass education began in the United States, libraries also began. The first public library was founded in Peterborough, New Hampshire, in 1833. Further stimulation came from Andrew Carnegie, who gave more than $50 million for library buildings across the country in the early 1900's.

By the mid-19th century, a New York publisher started selling song books for 10 cents and then ventured into *dime novels* which became very popular. The dime novels told tales of adventure about American pioneers. During the 1870's and 1880's salesmen even sold books door-to-door. The salemen searched out newly urbanized, literate city dwellers offering books with plots featuring adventure, romance, scandal and crime. Fiction also got a boost from newspapers which serialized dime novels and stories by such famous writers as Charles Dickens.

One of the most significant developments in the book publishing industry was the distribution of *paperbacks* along with magazines shortly after World War II. Virtually overnight, the number of potential purchasers for a book was increased 10 to 20 times as books appeared at newsstands, drug stores, supermarkets, and variety stores throughout the United States. Today this is taken for granted, along with the numerous book stores and book clubs that have come into existence more recently.

Newspapers: Changing Audiences

Before there were newspapers in the form seen today, there were attempts to provide similar content through other means. In early Rome, there were daily written records of the Senate called *Acta Diurna*. Later, there were town criers calling out the news—"Ten o'clock and all's well." The first newspaper whose form was similar to those we know today was the London *Gazette* of Oxford, England which began in 1665. In the United States, the first continuously-published newspaper was the *Boston News-Letter* dating from April 1704.

Most of the early colonial newspapers contained news that was hardly exciting by today's standards. Mainly, it consisted of clippings from London newspapers published secondhand. There were no photographs or large headlines. Items included sermon notices, obituaries, and commercial news. Circulation in any event was limited since people were reluctant to pay for newspapers and the audience of

N. E.   Numb. 1.

The Boston News-Letter.

Publiſhed by Authority.

From **Monday** April 17. to **Monday** April 24. 1704.

London Flying-Poſt from Decemb. 2d. to 4th. 1703.

Letters from *Scotland* bring us the Copy of a Sheet lately Printed there, Intituled, *A ſeaſonable Alarm for* Scotland. *In a Letter from a Gentleman in the City, to his Friend in the Country, concerning the preſent Danger of the Kingdom and of the Proteſtant Religion.*

This Letter takes Notice, That Papiſts ſwarm in that Nation, that they traffick more avowedly than formerly, and that of late many Scores of Prieſts & Jeſuites are come thither from France, and gone to the North, to the Highlands & other places of the Country. That the Miniſters of the Highlands and North gave in large Liſts of them to the Committee of the General Aſſembly, to be laid before the Privy-Council.

It likewiſe obſerves, that a great Number of other ill-affected perſons are come over from *France*, under pretence of accepting her Majeſty's Gracious Indemnity ; but, in reality, to increaſe Diviſions in the Nation, and to entertain a Correſpondence with *France*: That their ill Intentions are evident from their talking big, their owning the Intereſt of the pretended King *James* VIII. their ſecret Cabals, and their buying up of Arms and Ammunition, wherever they can find them.

To this he adds the late Writings and Actings of ſome diſaffected perſons, many of whom are for that Pretender : that ſeveral of them have declar'd they had rather embrace Popery than conform to the preſent Government ; that they refuſe to pray for the Queen, but uſe the ambiguous word Soveraign, and ſome of them pray in expreſs Words for the King and Royal Family ; and the charitable and generous Prince who has ſhew'd them ſo much Kindneſs. He likewiſe takes notice of Letters, not long ago found in Cypher, & directed to a Perſon lately come thither from St. *Germains*.

He ſays that the greateſt Jacobites, who will not qualifie themſelves by taking the Oaths to Her Majeſty, do now with the Papiſts and their Companions from St. *Germains* ſet up for the Liberty of the Subject, contrary to their own Principles, but meerly to keep up a Diviſion in the Nation. He adds, that they aggravate thoſe things which the People complain of, as to *England's* refuſing to allow them a freedom of Trade, &c. and do all they can to foment Diviſions betwixt the Nations, & to obſtruct a Redreſs of thoſe things complain'd of.

The Jacobites, he ſays, do all they can to perſuade the Nation that their pretended King is a Proteſtant in his Heart, tho' he dares not declare it while under the Power of *France* ; that he is acquainted with the Miſtakes of his Father's Government, will govern us more according to Law, and endear himſelf to his Subjects.

They magnifie the Strength of their own Party, and the Weakneſs of Diviſions of the other, in order to facilitate and haſten their Undertaking ; they argue themſelves out of their Fears, and into the higheſt aſſurance of accompliſhing their purpoſe.

From all this he infers, That they have hopes of Aſſiſtance from *France*, otherwiſe they would never be ſo impudent ; and he gives Reaſons for his Apprehenſions that the *French* King may ſend Troops thither this Winter, 1. Becauſe the *Engliſh* & *Dutch* will not then be at Sea to oppoſe them. 2. He can't then beſt ſpare them, the Seaſon of Action beyond Sea being over. 3. The Expectation given him of a conſiderable number to joyn them, may incourage him to the undertaking with fewer Men, if he can but ſend over a ſufficient number of Officers with Arms and Ammunition.

He endeavours in the reſt of his Letters to anſwer the fooliſh Pretences of the Pretender's being a Proteſtant, and that he will govern us according to Law. He ſays, that being bred up in the Religion and Politicks of *France*, he is by Education a ſtated Enemy to our Liberty and Religion. That the Obligations which he and his Family owe to the *French* King, muſt neceſſarily make him to be wholly at his Devotion, and to follow his Example ; that if he ſit upon the Throne, the three Nations muſt be obiig'd to pay the Debt which he owes the *French* King for the Education of himſelf, and for Entertaining his ſuppoſed Father and his Famy. And ſince the King muſt reſtore him by his Troops, if ever he be reſtored, he will ſee to ſecure his own Debt, before thoſe Troops leave *Britain*. The Pretender being a good Proficient in the *French* and *Romiſh* Schools, he will never think himſelf ſufficiently aveng'd. but by the utter Ruine of his Proteſtant Subjects, both as Hereticks and Traitors. The late Queen, his pretended Mother, who in cold Blood when ſhe was Queen of *Britain*, advis'd to turn the Weſt of *Scotland* into a hunting Field, will be then for doing ſo by the greateſt part of the Nation ; and, no doubt, is at Pains to have her pretended Son educated to her own Mind : Therefore, he ſays, it were a great Madneſs in the Nation to take a Prince bred up in the horrid School of Ingratitude, Perſecution and Cruelty, and filled with Rage and Envy. The *Jacobites*, he ſays, both in *Scotland* and at St. *Germains*, are impatient under their preſent Straits, and knowing their Circumſtances cannot be much worſe than they are, at preſent, are the more inclinable to the Undertaking. He adds, That the *French* King knows there cannot be a more effectual way for himſelf to arrive at the Univerſal Monarchy, and to ruine the Proteſtant Intereſt, than by ſetting up the Pretender upon the Throne of Great *Britain*, he will in all probability attempt it ; and tho' he ſhould be perſuaded that the Deſign would miſcarry in the cloſe, yet he cannot but reap ſome Advantage by imbroiling the three Nations.

From all this the Author concludes it to be the Intereſt of the Nation, to provide for Self defence ; and ſays, that as many have already taken the Alarm, and are furniſhing themſelves with Arms and Ammunition, he hopes the Government will not only allow it, but encourage it, ſince the Nation ought all to appear as one Man in the Defence of literate, educated people was small. Benjamin Franklin altered that situation rapidly. He started the first chain of American newspapers, owned a series of printing plants, proposed the first magazine for the colonies, and was the first to suggest that advertising be sold to support papers.

Generally, the period before the Revolutionary War saw intense political struggles between the colonial press and the British government. There also were some Tory (pro-British) newspapers such as the Lion *Gazette*, which was eventually mobbed and later moved to British-held territory. The war had several consequences for the press: more readers, less government control and increased frequency (semiweekly papers). The next decade saw an extremely partisan press where mud slinging was common and criticism intensely personal. Even George Washington, though supportive of an independent press, failed to escape criticism. Some believe he declined to run for a third term because of vicious attacks during his second term. Thus, the antagonistic relationship between the press and the government in the U.S. dates back to the origins of the country. Presidents often begin their terms with harmonious press relations but the honeymoon usually turns to scepticism if not antagonism. Honeymoons have become increasingly shorter in recent years. Recent presidents were not the first to change their views once they had been subjected to criticism. Witness the following quotes from Thomas Jefferson who is widely cited for the comment that he would prefer a press without a government to a government without a press.

> ...our liberty depends on the freedom of the press, and that cannot be limited without being lost. (1786)
>
> No government ought to be without censors; and where the press is free, no one ever will. If virtuous, it need not fear the fair operation of attack and defense. Nature has given to man no other means of sifting out the truth, either in religion, law or politics. (1792)
>
> Indeed, the abuses of the freedom of the press here have been carried to a length never before known or borne by a civilized nation. But it is so difficult to draw a clear line of separation between the abuse and the wholesome use of the press, that as yet we have found it better to trust the public judgment, rather than the magistrate, with the discrimination between truth and falsehood. (1803)
>
> Were I the publisher of a paper, instead of the usual division of Foreign, Domestic, etc., I think I should distribute everything under the following heads: 1. True 2. Probable. 3. Wanting Confirmation. 4. Lies...at present it is disputable to state a fact on a newspaper authority; and the newspapers of our country by their abandoned spirit of falsehood, have more effectively destroyed the utility of the

press than all the shackles devised by Bonapart. (1813)

I deplore...the putrid state into which our newspapers have passed, and the malignity, the vulgarity and the mendacious spirit of those who write them...These ordures are rapidly depraving the public taste. (1814)

Jefferson became president in 1801 and was returned to office in 1804; note the corresponding change in views. It should be pointed out that he never advocated government control despite personal reservations about press performance during his term in office.

By 1833, newspaper costs were cut to a penny; the *penny press* was born. Benjamin Day was mainly responsible with his newspaper, the *New York Sun* (the motto: It shines for all). The low price attracted a large audience that included immigrants and the growing number of city dwellers. The *Sun* was such a success that it amassed a circulation of 30,000 in just two years. Not only did the penny press change the nature of the audience; it also changed the definition of news. Instead of dry notices, it featured street sales, police activity, sex and vice. The penny press also started to crusade with repeated attempts to influence the public on controversial public issues.

Two important editors with very strong and influential perspectives were James Gordon Bennett of the New York *Herald* and Horace Greeley of the New York *Tribune.* Bennett opened his own state, national, and international news bureaus and got the galleries of Congress opened to journalists. He was one of the first to use the telegraph to speed up newsgathering and he began the first successful Sunday newspaper. Greeley was something of a radical who supported the Westward movement, serious news reporting, and specialization (for example, hospital news, fire news, military news). Among Greeley's famous correspondents were the author Charles Dickens and political philosopher Karl Marx. Greeley made the editorial page what it is today. He publicly supported women's rights, socialism, abolition of polygamy, liquor control, and the death penalty. He was also the first to develop what has now become a major means of newsgathering — the interview. It is difficult today to imagine how news could be gathered without an interview; prior to Greeley's innovation, most news was based on reporters' personal observations and clippings from other papers.

With the Civil War in the 1860's, newspapers faced the problem of how to keep the public informed without giving aid and comfort to the enemy (within the same country, no less). Large elements of the population from both sides were opposed to the war; thus, there was continuous, outspoken criticism of both the North and the South. Pro-southern New York newspaper editors sometimes had to flee mobs whipped up by returning war veterans. The headline of one Wisconsin

THE  SUN.

Number 1.]   NEW YORK, TUESDAY, SEPTEMBER 3, 1833.   [Price One Penny.

The Sun was first published in 1833. Selling for 1¢, it heralded the "penny press" era. This was the first issue of the newspaper.

newspaper article on the draft said "Lincoln Has Called for 500,000 More Victims." President Lincoln also was accused of outright treason by some journalists.

For the first time, news collected by journalists could be transmitted so quickly by telegraph that it might affect the war since battles often continued for days. This meant that some news releases were censored. Strangely enough, today's style of newswriting can be traced to the telegraph. Until its use, journalists tended to write long essays like novelists or narrate events in order of occurrence as historians do. However, since telegraph lines often were cut (specifically to prevent the transmission of news), important items would miss publication if they were contained in the last part of the story. To reduce the possibility of losing transmission of the most important facts, some journalists started putting the most important ideas in the first paragraph, structuring the remaining information in order of declining importance. This style, still popular, is known as the *inverted pyramid*. The style of newswriting coincidentally made it easy to cut stories too long for newspapers' strict space requirements. Today readers take for granted that they will learn the most important features of a news story first—through the headline and the *lead* (first paragraph). The inverted pyramid consequently is convenient for readers as well as writers and publishers as it makes news items easy to read quickly. Following the Civil War, major changes in the press occurred. In the South, newspapers directed at Black audiences appeared; it was during the post-Reconstruction years through World War I that the Black press in the South exerted the most power and influence (Suggs, 1983).

After the Civil War, great new forces such as industrialization, mechanization, and urbanization were at work affecting newspapers. Changes introduced by the penny press and Civil War continued but newspapers were most affected by their new operating environments. Mechanization revolutionized the printing process and permitted newspapers to grow both in size (number of pages) and circulation (number of readers). With industrialization came more advertising and improved transportation systems which helped get urban newspapers to people living some distance away from downtown areas. Literacy increased rapidly since mass education had been in existence a number of years. Between 1870 and 1900, illiteracy declined from 20% to 11% of the population. The percentage of children in public schools rose from 57% to 72% during the same period. As more newspapers came into existence, competition between newspapers increased. The most intense competition was in New York City although other cities also had more than one paper vying for the same audience. This led to the rise of evening newspapers (attempting to reach a slightly different audience than morning papers). The competition also inspired the use of gimmicks to boost circulation at least temporarily. One such gimmick was Nellie Bly's famous trip around the world to see if she could beat the 80 days suggested by Jules Verne in the novel *Around the World in 80 Days*. Editors tended to sensationalize in the heat of competition, culminating in the era called *Yellow Journalism* (named after a comic strip character, "the yellow kid"). Though the common person was respected, there was almost complete disregard for ethics and social responsibility. Audiences were offered a heavy diet of sin, sex, and violence. This format by today's standards would be similar to *The National Enquirer* or confession magazines. Hearst is the name most often associated with yellow journalism; you may see his actions characterized by Orson Welles in the classic movie *Citizen Kane.*

In the latter half of the 19th century, concentration of economic power by a few men and corporate excesses attracted the attention of civic-minded editors and journalists. Editors strongly protested the accumulation of so much wealth by John D. Rockefeller, J.P. Morgan, Andrew Carnegie and others. The journalists who investigated these men and their fortunes came to be known as *muckrakers,* for they brought to light various misconduct (i.e., muck) with reports widely published in newspapers and magazines. One series on Rockefeller's company (Standard Oil) ran for two years in *McClure's* magazine; the author was Ida Tarbell. Lincoln Steffens wrote "The Shame of the Cities," attacking corruption in city and state government. Edward Bok of the *Ladies' Home Journal* shocked readers by proving that Lydia Pinkham, to whom women thought they were writing for advice, had been dead for 22 years. The years 1910-1914 mark the high point in the number of newspapers published in the United States — 2,600 dailies and 14,000 weeklies. Economic pressures brought on by World War I led to a period of consolidation.

Following the war, new papers began using two techniques in New York City — the tabloid style format (smaller size) and extensive use of photography. The 1920's are called a period of Jazz Journalism. They also represent a continuation of the emphasis on sex, crime and entertainment from the Yellow Journalism period, plus some of the crusading from the Muckraking period. Prohibition provided sensational copy as socialites were caught in speakeasy raids. Photojournalism focused on the glamorous and sexy Hollywood stars from the new medium of motion pictures. However, the 1920's were not all sex and sensationalism. By then Hearst had toned down his version of "yellow journalism," the *New York Times* was establishing a reputation as a quality newspaper and readers had access to the wit and criticism of such figures as H.L. Mencken and Walter Lippmann.

The 1930's and 1940's saw the rise of interpretive reporting, though there was considerable backgrounding of news events before this period. Two factors are usually offered in explanation. With the election of Franklin D. Roosevelt and the growth of government programs, people's lives were increasingly affected by external events which needed interpreting and more context for understanding. We also see the rise of modern scientific technology. Thus, journalists attempted to add "why" to their traditional questions of "who-what-when-where-how?" The view that difficult subjects such as science and economics couldn't be made interesting also was discarded. This led to more specialization and better editorial backgrounds for journalists. The second factor here was the appearance of a competing medium, radio, which could deliver the news faster than newspapers could, even with "special, midday editions." Losing this "newness," newspapers turned to greater depth in their reporting.

A development which started in the early 19th century continues to affect the development of newspapers (plus radio and other media) today. It was the *wire services* which provided the same news to media across the country. One wire service is the Associated Press (AP), a cooperative newsgathering organization owned by member news organizations (mainly newspapers). The second major wire service is United Press International (UPI), a commercial news service stemming from the 1958 merger of old wire services owned by Scripps (United Press) and Hearst (International News Service). In 1984, UPI entered Chapter 11 bankruptcy proceedings despite earlier efforts to reach profitability by reducing the number of employees and seeking pay cuts. In the last century the wire services influenced news writing by promoting the summary lead, inverted pyramid style, and political neutrality. Today, their decision as to whether a story deserves coverage is crucial because local editors tend to follow the wire

services' lead. In daily newspapers, wire service news is typically the common denominator supplemented by news and features from various other sources (see Emery and Emery, 1984). Prior to the growth of wire services, printers exchanged their papers postage free through the mails, a custom dating to the early 1700's. Editors often inserted stories because of their value to exchanges and thereby to distant audiences. In this process, the major papers in New York and Washington achieved a stature out of proportion to their modest circulations (Kielbowicz, 1982).

Magazines: Diversity and Specialization

Magazines are a relatively new mass medium compared to books and newspapers, yet today they far outnumber the older print media. In the United States alone there are more than 12,000 magazines with a total circulation of about 350 million copies. One of the first American periodicals was Benjamin Franklin's *General Magazine and Historical Chronicle*, which appeared only 10 years after the first such publication in England. However, only 16 magazines, each with an average life of just 10 months, were published in the United States before the American Revolution. In the latter half of the 19th century, modern national magazines multiplied, especially after the Civil War, when magazines finally freed themselves of the remaining English influence. Congress helped to spur the growth of magazines by providing low-cost mailing privileges. The last decade of the 19th century witnessed a wide range of new magazines representing specialized markets (audiences), such as *Popular Science, Scientific American, Home Arts, Babyhood,* and *Glass of Fashion.* Later, the muckrakers stimulated magazine readership with their exposes serialized in *McClure's, Colliers, Everybody's,* and other magazines. News magazines began with *Time,* founded by Henry Luce in 1923. Growth continued but by the 1950's, the huge circulations reached by general interest magazines such as *Life, Look,* and the *Saturday Evening Post* were in jeopardy. Compared to the cost of reaching the same size and type of audience by television, magazine ads were expensive. The magazine production process was too expensive to maintain by increased subscription and newsstand prices alone. For the past two decades the trend has generally beren towards specialized publications aimed at audiences ranging from apartment dwellers to joggers and antique collectors. Today one of the five magazines with the largest circulation, *TV Guide,* concerns another medium. Other top magazines are *Parade* (which accompanies Sunday newspapers) with 21 million circulation; *Reader's Digest* (about 18 million subscribers); *National Geographic* (11 million); and *Better Homes & Gardens* (8 million). Despite these huge circulations, advertisers often pay more for reaching wealthier readers. Thus, *Time* magazine has one of the highest advertising sales though it is not in the top five in terms of circulation. (See Wood, 1956; Peterson, 1964; Wolseley, 1973).

Radio

Today few people could build their own TV set, but most could easily put together a radio receiver as many hobbyists did in the early 1900's. In fact, both the telegraph and radio were developed much at the hand of non-scientists who recognized their commercial and practical value. A literature professor, Samuel Morse, was responsible for the first telegraph line strung between Washington, D.C. and Baltimore (a distance of about 40 miles). On May 24, 1844, the first telegraph message was sent in dots and dashes. It asked, "What hath God wrought?" Though the government had financed the line, it threw away its opportunity to control the patents and relinquished all its rights, which became the property of private corporations. The medium was left to private enterprise—a precedent that would be followed in the U.S. with the telphone, wireless telegraph, and home broadcasting. Never again was the federal government a serious contender for controlling rights to those media. Sound escaped from the wire when Guglielmo Marconi, another imaginative tinkerer, modified lab equipment he had seen and strengthened it to the point where he could send dot-dash messages up to about a mile through the air without the help of telegraph wires. Transmission of the human voice was the next step and that occurred on Christmas eve in 1906 off the Atlantic coast. A decade of refinements that included invention of the "vacuum tube" prepared the way for radio broadcasting.

Early radio stations were set up by radio set manufacturers who needed to maintain a market for radio tubes and equipment after World War I ended heavy military usage. Westinghouse was the first to start regular programming with radio station KDKA, in Pittsburgh. What was then called the "radio music box" caught on and the number of stations grew so fast that the manufacturers shortly fell behind on orders. Without government regulation or private agreements, however, the airwaves became a jumble of competing voices. Stations competed for the same spot on the dial, overpowering each other with stronger and stronger signals. As a consumer, you wouldn't necessarily know where to tune your radio to get your favorite station because its frequency might change. Because of this, many stations failed entirely, especially small stations. Technical arrangements were so confused that the radio industry itself pressured the federal government to initiate regulation. Finally, in 1927, Congress passed the Federal Radio Act and created the Federal Radio Commission (FRC, later changed to the Federal Communication Commission, FCC). Besides licensing uses of radio frequencies, Congress also stipulated that radio stations should serve the *public interest, convenience,* and *necessity* in return for using the public airways. So that radio stations' public service could be reviewed periodically, Congress decided that broadcasters would be given licenses renewable every three years.

How to support radio broadcasting was still in question, at the time. A few radio listeners sent money to radio stations, but people preferred to listen to what they could find rather than pay for specific radio content. Eventually, advertising was used to support radio but not without extended public debate. Even the Secretary of Commerce, Herbert Hoover, opposed commercials on radio saying: "It's inconceivable that we should allow so great a possibility for services, for news, for entertainment, and for vital commercial purposes to be drowned in advertising chatter." Nonetheless, the first commercial was aired in 1922 on station WEAF in New York. The advertiser was very subtle in his sales pitch though the message lasted a full ten minutes.

Radio networks soon began in order to cut programming costs for local stations. As network affiliates, the stations were in a position to receive and transmit high-quality live radio dramas, most produced in New York, featuring stage actors displaced from theaters due to movies' growing popularity. The first radio network (now also a TV network) was NBC, which managed two systems of interconnections between local radio stations (the red and blue networks). CBS was the second major radio network which began in 1927 as part of the Paley family's effort to sell La Palina cigars. CBS, under the direction of William Paley, successfully competed with the more established NBC luring away big-name personalities such as Bing Crosby and Kate Smith. ABC came into being when the government insisted that NBC divest itself of one of its two networks; the blue network was sold to Edward Nobel who enjoyed a fortune based on sales of Lifesavers candy. Other networks were also in existence, some still today, such as the Mutual Broadcasting System. The newest radio network is NPR (National Public Radio), an organization linking non-commercial radio stations. (See Sydney W. Head, 1976; Sterling and Kittross, 1978 for more on radio's development.)

Learning from the Past: Television

Television did not suffer the growth pangs that radio did. By the time TV sets were placed on the market, the technology was quite sophis-

ticated. TV also borrowed its financial base since people were already accustomed to commercials from radio. The regulatory structure of the FCC was adaptable to the new medium. Even the visual quality was not novel since motion pictures had provided the audience with some "visual literacy."

The first TV transmissions were in 1931, about 20 years before television became widely available as a mass medium. The Second World War held up TV's development since the war effort required parts and labor which would have gone into TV sets. The FCC approved home televisions in 1941 but when station license applications came pouring in, a *freeze* was put into effect. Station construction was banned from 1948 to 1952 while a master plan was worked out to avoid technical problems. The plan involved an option of one standard system for color TV transmission and allocation of both UHF (ultra high frequency) and VHF (very high frequency) signals across the country. The same networks which dominated radio also came to dominate television programming, though ABC did not fully enter the competition until the 1970's. Since it had started later than the other networks, it had fewer affiliates and thus a smaller audience and less advertising income to use in program production and development.

At first television productions were live, but "I Love Lucy" changed all that. The program, which you can still see as reruns today, was *recorded*. The 1950's has been called the "golden age of television" because it brought audiences great comedians such as Milton Berle, Jack Benny, and Sid Caesar, as well as a string of dramatic productions such as Playhouse 90 that received critical acclaim.

In the early 1960's, network news expanded from 15 minutes to a half-hour format that symbolized the growth of public affairs programming during a decade of racial unrest, spectacular space coverage and Vietnam war protests. Both the 60's and 70's saw TV programs focusing on social themes, ranging from feminism to homosexuality, ecology and government corruption. Though TV's three decades have been characterized as a "vast wasteland" of light entertainment, they've also given us broadcasts of the McCarthy hearings that first cast doubt on the legitimacy of the senator's "red scare," children's programming such as Sesame Street and Mister Rogers' Neighborhood, "live newscasts" made possible by electronic newsgathering (ENG—usually labeled as portable minicams), and the Watergate hearings that unveiled the Nixon coverup in the 1970's. (See Head, 1976, and Sterling and Kittross, 1978 for more on TV's development.)

Advertising — Both the Bread and the Wrapper

Advertising has the dual quality of being both communication content and major financial support for many mass media. It has had this distinction almost from the start. Publications of the 17th century regarded the desire to buy or sell something just as much news as other events of the week, such as reports from a battle. Most advertising was local until national markets developed along with improved transportation and growing industrialization. At first advertising agencies in the latter half of the 19th century simply purchased space from newspapers and then resold it to various clients. That role expanded as agencies took over planning functions as well as actual writing and illustration. Advertising appeared on the front page of newspapers when they consisted of only four pages, but with the expansion of newspaper size to eight pages in the Penny Press era, advertising volume grew and more ads were moved inside the paper. Many ads were for patent medicines. Along with the growth of advertising that accompanied the appearance of the "consumer society" came questions about the ethics of some advertising and its potential influence. Some magazines told readers that patent medicines they were giving to their children contained cocaine, morphine and alcohol. To combat mounting public criticism, the Associated Advertising Clubs of America was organized in 1905 to campaign for "truth in advertising. Yet as late as 1931, the Raladam case showed that the pre-

Indigestion Has No Terrors For Him

That salt-shaker is filled with **Pepsalt**.
It cures and prevents indigestion.

BARRY'S TRICOPHEROUS

FOR THE HAIR.

vailing principle was "let the buyer beware." The Raladam Co. manufactured Marmola as a cure for obesity; the product contained an
ingredient that produced harmful side effects in some unsuspecting
consumers. However, the U.S. Supreme Court said that the Federal
Trade Commission could not stop the product from being advertised
because the 1914 FTC act did not forbid the deception of consumers
unless the advertising injured competing business. Not until the
passage of the Wheeler-Lee Amendment in 1938 were consumers put
on a par with business.

A number of other ethical questions have been raised through the
years: Does/should advertising cause people to buy things they do not
need? Does advertising unfairly influence journalists' professional
decisions? Does advertising create conformity or influence elections?
Some of these questions will be brought up again in Chapter 8. (See
Boorstin, 1972, and Wright and Mertes, 1974 for more on advertising).
In any case, advertising has become an important institution that is
evaluated not just for its commercial value but also its aesthetic
content, popular acceptance, and professional standards. The 1985
Clio awards honoring the best in advertising attracted some 10,000
entries from over 40 countries, and some forecast that ad revenues
would hit $100 billion in 1986 (Dougherty, 1985).

Relationships Among the Media
Shifting Forms and Functions

The arrival of each new mass medium does more than simply enlarge
the number of people who can be reached. Each contributes a different
"quality," forcing existing media to find some strategy for competing
with the newcomer. What are the special "qualities" offered by each
medium? The key dimension along which we can array the print media
—books, magazines and newspapers—is their permanence. Though
permanence means the content and messages can be reviewed again
and again at one's leisure (time flexibility), this characteristic also
tends to sacrifice the major "quality" offered by radio—speed or
immediacy. Radio's speed literally stole newspapers' attempt to meet
the public needs associated with immediacy when it replaced special
editions of newspapers. For important, breaking news stories, people
would turn to radio. Eventually, they would turn to the newspaper and
later magazines and books for in-depth reporting and extended discussions or analyses, but radio was there first. The next visual
medium, television, combined the immediacy of radio with the visual
quality first introduced by cinema. Later radio, through the invention
of the transistor, would become "mobile," an added quality that would

be central to its adjustments as TV started to capture more of people's time. Cable TV is less a new medium than a technological improvement on an old one, but cable does have two special qualities. First, it expands the potential number of channels. Rather than be restricted to the 12 or so signals that can compete in the same air space, cable systems can deliver dozens with current technologies. The second feature is specialization, or targeting. Cable systems "de-massify" the audience in some instances by targeting certain programming to a particular geographic audience while another area receives different content. How do these peculiar qualities of mass media figure in their relationships with each other?

The introduction of a new mass medium does not mean that existing media will be replaced. Each new medium tends to supplement rather than supplant existing media. However, the survival means that older media must change their form and functions to continue. Some thought that radio would destroy the daily press and if not radio, then surely TV. At first, the wire services, particularly the newspaper-owned, coop, Associated Press, refused to provide radio stations with news because they were viewed as competitors. Eventually, the print media recognized they had lost the "immediacy" quality but still had permanence and greater detail. Thus, the daily press moved to provide more indepth news, more descrition, more background and more analysis, leaving to radio the immediate reporting of events.

Radio itself was subjected to competition when television started to spread throughout the U.S. Families rearranged their living rooms as TV stole radio's prime-time audience. Having been supplanted as evening entertainment, radio was forced to change both its format and its function. The radio dramas, "The Great Gildersleeves" and "Gangbusters," for example, were replaced by music and news. Radio competed for its audience by becoming a musical companion that could follow people everywhere, including the places where TV was excluded, particularly the automobile. Radio stopped trying to capture the entire family and concentrated on particular audiences. Like magazines, radio specialized in terms of both content and target audiences. The "all-news" and "all-talk" stations of the 1970's aimed for a different audience than middle-of-the-road musical formats or hard rock music.

Television had its most direct impact not on radio, which managed to retool fairly quickly, but on the cinema, which saw two decades of downturn before recouping somewhat in the 1970's. Television has the quality of "privacy" more so than the social cinema (or "live theater"), which requires viewing among an audience of strangers rather than the privacy of one's own home. TV was also cheaper, at least in terms of direct costs, so TV also captured the entertainment function during weekends and other times for many people. Motion pictures have tried several strategies: specializing (Black films, the youth market), and "demassifying" the audience by aiming not at whole families but segments which would be attracted by such things as pornography, wilderness films, and graphic violence. Special effects which would draw repeat visits from younger people also have proved an effective strategy. Television's impact on newspapers is more recent than on film, in part perhaps because TV actually provided little news until the 1960's. There is some concern that TV news has now expanded to the point where it is decreasing the amount of time spent reading newspapers. What will the newer media technologies bring? Newer technologies seem to be spreading more quickly through the American audience; thus, we have relatively little time to consider what we want from new media and how some of the potentially negative consequences may be avoided. We will return to this issue in later chapters.

Mass Media Around the World

Today almost no part of the globe is free from mass media. Except for a few island nations, every country has newspapers or magazines. Radio, after being transistorized, made cheap and portable, was the growth medium of the 1950's and 1960's world-wide. The past decade or so has seen TV antennas popping up in devloping nations, and cable TV has made greater inroads in Canada and some Western European nations than in the U.S. However, though there are similarities in media technology throughout the world, media organizations and practices vary from nation to nation. Partly, the differences can be traced to distinctive philosophies of the media described in the first chapter of this book, but there are many arrangements that are peculiar to individual countries and cultures.

Print Media

The United States press system is very decentralized (i.e., local) with few newspapers that are national in scope. This also is the situation in West Germany. A strong regional press is based on individual cities that play major roles of specialization: Munich — culture; Frankfurt — finance; Hamburg — publishing. However, most Germans read daily papers which are actually "side editions" of papers from larger towns differing only in title and a few pages of local news and advertisements. Switzerland also has strong local press traditions. However, most other countries of Western Europe have the reverse, most daily papers emanating from one city, usually the nation's capital. This has

TV antennas on top of the Eiffel Tower in Paris.

started to change as the provincial press increases in importance. The number of newspapers and newspaper readers varies greatly around the world. France has 15,000 registered publications with a total circulation of 7 million, yet the French read relatively few daily newspapers compared to Germany or Scandinavian countries. Sweden and Norway have among the highest newspaper readership rates in the world. In Norway some 450 copies of daily papers circulate for every 1,000 people. For a single city, Hong Kong has an amazing number of papers offering readers some 50 different titles. The highest circulations for individual newspapers are found in the Soviet Union., Great Britain and Japan. The Ashai Shimbun of Japan has a circulation of more than 5 million. Contrast this with Botswana. This small country has a population of 735,000 and high illiteracy; its largest daily paper is a bulletin produced by the government which distributes 12,500 copies free of charge. There were hardly any newspapers when independence was granted so the government established a newspaper printed in two languages and staffed by government workers who were required to be as neutral as possible.

We will examine a representative sample of print media systems before looking at differences of organization and structure, control by regulations and laws, and cultural-ethnic patterns.

U.S.S.R.

There are no privately-owned papers in the Soviet Union. Most papers are published by such groups as factories, trade unions, youth groups, the government and the Communist party. The press is organized along geographic lines. At the national level is the all-union press which carries messages of government and party authorities. Provincial papers translate these policies for particular regions and groups while the local print media further relate party directives to daily activities. Newspapers also are organized to serve particular audiences. Thus, there are party papers at all levels: union publications, military papers and special papers for the youth. The State Committee on the Press of the Council of Ministers officially governs the press, but ultimately the press at each level is subject to the direction of the Community Party Central Committee which confirms the appointment of editors. The system is characterized by its "planning," not only in its formal organization but also its content. Five-year plans and yearly goals are translated into specific media objectives. Thus, news is defined less in terms of current events or situations than by social goals set by government and Communist party officials. For example, national TV devoted a program each month to the activities of workers on a Siberian pipeline; the program was a deliberate attempt to reinforce, or reward the workers, regardless of whether anyone watched or not. The media operate under the Marxist-Leninist philosophy that they act as arms of the government and the party, but this does not mean there is no criticism in newspapers. When the centralized economic system fails to accomplish its purposes, the mass media are used to exhort the workers to improve their performance. This takes the form of specific articles or letters to the editor criticizing the management of a factory.

Great Britain

The British press system has three main characteristics. One is a great contrast in circulation and content between the quality and popular press. The former is illustrated by "The Times of London," the paper often characterized as representing the British establishment. The latter is also called the "tube" press after the subway system because it is aimed at commuters. A second feature is the existence of large chains; at times only four publishers have controlled 70% of daily newspaper circulation. A third characteristic is the concentration of newspaper circulation in the national dailies and Sunday papers of London. These national dailies in recent years have suffered circulation declines, however.

Japan

The unique situation here is that the largest newspapers are considered the highest quality. The largest newspaper is Asahi Shimbun, considered one of the best. The Japanese system features the concentration of ownership found in England, with fewer than a half dozen chains accounting for half of the daily newspaper circulation. One unique feature is that newsgathering at government ministries is accomplished through press clubs. Reporters not belonging to such groups have little access to officials.

Argentina

Latin America's contribution to our sample represents the Spanish-language press of the continent. Argentina's newspapers have a long history of involvement in the nation's political life. Some papers have contributed officials and presidents to the nation. In recent years the papers have been subjected to severe political pressure. Before the country's return to democracy, violence was used as a means of controlling the media — sometimes by the government and other times by insurgents of the left or right.

Language plays both a divisive and a unifying function in societies. The Arab press has had strong ties to Arab culture being closely bound to the Arabic language. The version used in papers is a modified form of classical or literary Arabic universally understood by educated Arabs. The press is still heavily cultural in content. Most of its content is not created by professional journalists but rather by educated Arabs who write poetry, plays and stories. Linguistic divisions are best represented by the dual-language system of Belgium and the tri-lingual system of Switzerland. The entire media system of Belgium is duplicated in Flemish and in French. In Switzerland, some 69% of newspapers appear in German, 25% in French, and 5% in Italian, with 1% in Romansh. The canton of Grisons provides an extreme example of Swiss pluralism; school books must be published in six different languages including not only German, French and Italian but also Romansch, Grisons and Ladin. Europe does not have a monopoloy on linguistic divisions. Many, if not most, developing nations of Africa and Asia have several languages. Some rely on the use of English and French at the national level. Thus we find strong English-language newspapers in India (a former British colongy) and the Philippines (previously a U.S. colony), and French-language papers in the Ivory Coast (former French colony). Malaysian newspapers historically have been patterned along linguistic and political party lines. Ethnic and linguistic divisions led to race riots in May, 1969. Though the government is dominated by Malays, the economic power of the Chinese is greater. A third group is the Tamil people who immigrated from India. English-language papers seem to be holding their own, and Bahasa Malaysia papers are growing. Language policies favor the Malay language and encourage its incorporation in papers serving Chinese or Tamil groups as well. Singapore's concern with language takes two directions; one is a campaign to get people to speak Mandarin rather than other Chinese dialects (Kuo, 1984) and the other is to encourage the use of English for economic reasons.

Attitudes towards particular media content and what constitutes news also vary considerably around the world. In France there has always been more public distrust towards display advertising (as opposed to classified ads). In Norway there is much concern for culture and history and support for the view that newspapers should educate the public on such matters. Finnish papers devote much space to foreign news but also maintain a local, small-town character. They give almost no space to such things as crimes, divorces, and sex scandals, the last a staple of the "tube" press of Great Britain. The Swedes have a deep interest in current history and theology. This content is reflected in newspapers while stories of crime, trials, divorce and suicide are considered more personal matters that are not the public's business. The Mediterranean countries of Western Europe have tended to place more emphasis on literary events and used a style of writing more akin to the "essay format." The Chinese have contributed what may be considered a print medium in its own right—the "tatzepao," or wall poster. Though the government of the People's Republic of China seems to have restricted its use recently, the wall poster in the past has provided an inexpensive means for the public to contribute their views for public distribution. Anonymous in the past, posters now must be signed, thus restricting their function as a voice of dissent. Cultural traditions in Mexico until recently meant that the press refrained from criticizing the president while he remained in office; however, once out of office, officials were torn apart. The restraint while in office stems in part from professional pride and social pressures encouraging self restraint. More recently, newspapers have accepted official encouragement to criticize the national government and the president himself.

The status and credibility of journalists and their profession also vary. In Italy journalists have fairly high status in the social structure while in the Arab world prestige of the press is relatively low. In many developing countries, journalists must work at more than one job to earn a living and this subjects them to pressures from special interests for favors. With such practices usually come dependence and lower credibility.

How are the media related to society and governments? In almost all communist nations the press system is tightly centralized through governmental and party controls and an absence of "private" owner-ship. In East Germany, for example, papers and magazines are licensed at the national level by a press administration office. Most licenses are held by political parties, mass organizations such as factories, youth groups and unions, and cooperative publishing houses. Overall guidance is provided by the department of agitation of the party central committee. This is the group which draws up broad five-year plans based on estimates of social development. More specific plans are provided to editors as a framework for their own quarterly plans, which are then submitted for approval to the department. Actual weekly and daily plans are the responsibility of the newspapers themselves. The first two pages and local news pages are exempt from this framework and planning. However, conformity is still ensured by daily directives on the emphasis and content that shapes news presentation. Journalists in East Germany are seen as members of a profession playing a vital role in building socialism; thus, they are required to undergo special training. With this structure and organiza-tion, little censorship is needed in Eastern European nations where the most powerful papers and those with the largest circulations are the Communist Party daily followed by the government paper.

One Communist maverick whose press system diverges significantly from the Soviet model is Yugoslavia, an ethnically-diverse federation of six republics (Bosnia and Herzegovina, Croatia, Macedonia, Montenegro, Serbia, and Slovenia). The socialist system is based on a philosophy where the press is viewed as being owned by society which is distinct from the government. Newspapers and other media units are run as enterprises operated by councils with profits shared by employees. There is competition among papers to some extent. Publishing houses, no longer dependent on the state budget, must rely on independent sources of financing. The main requirement is that the enterprise operate profitably. Each workers' council decides what and how much to produce, selling price, etc.

There is tremendous diversity in non-communist countries. In some cases private ownership of newspapers is characterized by a high con-centration of ownership, as was noted in Britain. In West Germany, media baron Alex Springer's share of the daily newspaper market is about 27% while his nearest rival controls 3%. This is a drop from an earlier high of 40%. There is also growing concentration of press ownership in the United States, Sweden and Japan.

The press of Western Europe has always been quite politically partisan—more so than the American press in recent years. In France, for example, journalists ally themselves with one of the six unions which most closely reflects their political outlook. French readers also expect politics in journalism as a national phenomenon.

The French government has attempted to ensure a diversity of voices with a program of taxes and other subsidies for the press. However, the partisan press in recent years has tended to decline.

There are other patterns of ownership and press-government relations. In Norway, the press is independent and there are few commercial chains. Most large papers are owned by corporations with shares divided among individuals and political parties. Egypt's newspapers at one time were all owned by the Arab Socialist Union, an umbrella organization for the country's three political parties. They were all run by rival corporations and formal censorship was rescinded in 1974. Editorial boards of papers and magazines were appointed by the secretary general of the union, then President Sadat. The Ministry of Information decides what's printable and how stories are to be angled. Many African papers are government run. The African press was born and developed under imperialism and molded in the Western tradition; for two centuries it paralleled the press of Europe and North America. But a "purging" of major Western influences has occurred leaving only South Africa with the basic European press system. Another model is provided by Peru where the government took control of all newspapers with circulations of 20,000 or more for several years. The papers were to be turned over to different social, educational, professional and religious groups but the mechanism for transfer proved to be difficult to set up.

Media control generally is accomplished through a maze of laws and regulations. Most of them are restrictive but some were enacted with the intention of preserving diversity in the press. In Sweden there is a long tradition of press freedom and newspapers not only have the right but the duty to furnish the public with papers. Stoppage of publication through strikes or lockouts is a violation of law. Disputes are settled by negotiation or arbitration. Sweden also had the first national press council (1916). In Belgium, the title of professional journalist is protected by law and may only be used by those gainfully employed in journalism as their main job. In France, working journalists need professional identification cards issued by the government. France provides tax exemptions, newsprint subsidies and tax reductions for journalists and newspapers. Sweden also provides press guidelines. In West Germany, public authorities of "lands" (states or regions) are legally obliged to provide information to the press. There and in Austria journalists can refuse to disclose their sources of information in court. In Germany newspaper employees can refuse to testify; however, there are restrictions on the press to protect the morals of youths.

In Latin America, the "colegio" has been installed in several countries but not always with the same intent. Colegio laws typically require new journalists to have a professional university degree and government license to practice. Employers can be punished for hiring anyone else. Bolivia's adoption of the colegio system in 1972 seems to have been motivated by economic goals in order to gain minimum wages and satisfactory working conditions while restricting workers at a time when unions were quite weak. The colegio also has been seen as an attempt to achieve enough solidarity among journalists for policing their own ranks and fending off government interference. In Mexico, economic needs lead to the creation of Pipsa, a combined private-government corporation which is the sole agency for importing and distributing newsprint, the lifeblood of newspapers. Though the potential remains, so far Pipsa has not been used to favor or punish particular newspapers.

Some laws are directed more at maintenance of the government itself or at potential threats from outside the country. Finland's laws make it an offense to endanger the country's relations with its neighbors, a not so subtle reference to the Soviet Union. Another European democracy, Switzerland, has a similar law. Though freedom of the press is proclaimed in an article of the Swiss Federal Constitution, publicly insulting a foreign state, an international organization or one of their representatives is punishable by a fine or prison. The law is an attempt to protect the country's long tradition of neutrality. In South Africa, though the law protects journalists in many ways, they are liable when it comes to "racial and other sensitive areas." Not so subtle controls include censorship in Brazil. Prior to its suspension in 1978 for public affairs newspapers and magazines, censorship "was the center pole holding up the tent of control over the Brazilian media." After the overthrow of Chile's President Allende in 1973, newspapers were closed or suspended within a matter of days. Later self-censorship was substituted for direct controls.

Broadcasting

More than 150 countries have radio broadcasting and over 115 have television, 60 in color. There also are close to a billion radio sets and some 400 million TV sets around the world. The bulk of those sets are found in the industrial countries of North America and Europe with the United States having almost a third of all TV sets.

There is growing pressure on governments or private enterprises to alter broadcasting systems in one way or another. Some groups demand more public participation, others want more local programs, and some seek more (or less) advertising. At the same time, there has been a growth in the exchange of TV programs between countries but rising fears about the impact of foreign programming on national beliefs, values, and images. Minority ethnic groups within countries worry about their ability to withstand the dominance of national media systems. A survey of radio and TV around the world shows the diverse ways national broadcasting systems have been organized in response to different cultures and situations.

Ownership and control are often so intertwined that they're difficult to separate. A simple division into capitalism, with its private ownership, and socialism, with governmental ownership, is not only imprecise but misleading. In Italy the government owns most of the stock in the broadcasting system and held a monopoly until the mid 1970's. Then, after a period of confusion, private, over-the-air broadcasting was ruled constitutional. In Sweden most radio and all TV broadcasting is controlled by Sveriges Radio (SR), a corporation invested with monopoly rights and supervised by a board of governors. The radio industry has a third of the shares in the SR corporation, and the press and Swedish News Agency the rest, an arrangement to ensure independence of broadcasting from both government and commercial interests. West Germany's broadcasting is government owned and operated but not at the national level; the system is divided into nine regional stations assigned to the individual "lands" or states. When Portugal ended its long Salazar dictatorship, some radio stations were nationalized and the new constitution stipulated that television could not be privately owned. Japan's broadcasting system includes both commerical, privately owned stations and the national, Japan Broadcasting Corp. (NHK), which is a strange amalgam of public and private enterprise. Set up under Civil Code as a "private, juridical person," NHK began with "accumulated funds" and operates under a national honor system of sorts. Under the British and Dutch broadcasting systems, the facilities for national TV are government owned and made available to program companies or groups. Explicit ownership, regulation and operational control are distinct and separate. Most radio and TV systems in the Arab world are monopolies under direct government supervision. Government monopolies also are found in developing countries — Malaysia, Nigeria, and Ghana, for example, and in Communist nations where Yugoslavia's worker coop system provides the greatest deviation. Argentina has a three-dimensional radio system of 88 private commercial stations, 36 state commercial stations and 24 state noncommercial stations. When Juan Peron was overthrown in 1955 the military government took over many licenses and invited applications but handed only three back to the private sector. Since that time, they've lost money. The country also owns the physical properties of five TV stations in the capital city of Buenos Aires. In neighboring Chile the military junta inherited radio and TV stations following their takeover in 1973, but it minimized its role of proprietor of the media and ordered them to stand on their own feet financially.

Support for broadcasting comes from a variety of sources. Some 38 countries rely completely on advertising while an additional 42 depend on both advertising and license fees paid by consumers each month or annually. About 20 countries support TV and radio systems through government budgets and there are various other combinations of support elsewhere. When Switzerland first began TV after a long national debate in the late 1950's, support included not only license fees but also two million francs a year from newspaper publishers as long as commercials were not broadcast. The paper's subsidy was withdrawn by agreement when the number of licenseholders reached a sufficiently large figure. However, it was clear that the population was too small to rely on license fees and commercials began. Malaysia also has a combination of license fees and advertising for TV and radio but a 50% surcharge is imposed for each showing of imported advertisements on TV.

The size of license fees and how they're collected also varies widely. In West Germany, each set owner in 1978 paid $5 a month for television and a third more for radio. The British pay their license fees through the Post Office; the annual color TV license was raised to $71 and the black-and-white TV license raised to $22 in 1985. The Japanese Broadcasting System employs an army of collectors who not only collect the fee but also provide an expert and regular audience survey service at the same time. The Japanese system in which the public pays the fee has shaky constitutional foundations and is based largely on the expectation that consumers will be honorable and the collectors persuasive.

Who actually runs the day-to-day operations of TV and radio stations and who is in charge of broadcast programming? The answer varies. Even among countries with the same system of ownership or financial support, actual control and organization often differ considerably. In the U.S., the private broadcasting sector is regulated by the Federal Communication Commission which assigns frequencies and implements some controls to see that the stations operate in the public interest, convenience and necessity. Actual programming decisions are centered within the three TV networks at the national level and individual stations at the local level. Public broadcasting in the U.S. is kept at arms-length from national political influence with most programming emerging from a few large stations or state-wide broadcast systems. We'll discuss the U.S. system more in the next chapter.

Similar dual systems of public-private operation and government regulation are found in some European countries as well. In Great Britain the public broadcasting sector is centralized in the British Broadcasting Corp. (BBC) which is an independent government authority headed by a board of governors appointed by the queen and operated under a director general and professional staff. Thus shielded from direct political pressures, the BBC produces a full range of news and entertainment programs and conducts its own audience research. The private broadcasting sector is operated through 13 TV regions with individual program-producing companies. These companies are issued franchises for six-year periods by the government regulatory agency, the Independent Television Corporation (ITC), which also has authority over the amount and content of advertising. The ITC rents its own transmitters to the program companies. Britain added a third TV "network" in 1982 following years of debate and study; this system is independent of the BBC and ITV companies.

In France since 1975, production and operation of both radio and TV have been handled by seven companies endowed with relatively autonomous management. All of the program-producing companies have precise obligations spelled out in annual reports including prescriptions on morals, violence, language, advertising, and political balance as well as general programming obligations. In South Africa, one of the last industrialized nations to start television, TV is a state-controlled monopoly governed by a board of the South African Broadcasting Corp. In Italy the Christian Democratic Party has dominated the state-run Radio-Television Italiana since World War II. Austria's broadcasting system is characterized by an autonomous public corporation which has a legal monopoly on broadcasting. After 1976 the monopoly on radio broadcasting held by Sveriges Radio in Sweden was broken and the country divided into 24 local districts each with its own management staff and transmission time.

The Dutch system is unique in its control and organization. Called the "ultimate in pluralism," Dutch TV is similar to a quota system. Though the facilities are government-owned, air-time is split among social, political and religious groups which provide a variety of programming, both news and entertainment. By law any group can qualify for some air time once it achieves a minimum number of members. Each group also publishes a weekly program guide that contains advertising. Revenue from the advertising and a share of funds from license fees support the programming of companies. The amount of air time is prorated on a sliding scale based on group size. Since the late 1960's, both TV and radio have had commercials but they're separate from programs and handled by the Ministry of Culture.

In the South American nation of Colombia, a TV monopoly held by Inravision provides both an educational service and two commercial signals. It adopted an old Latin American commercial radio practice of selling blocks of time to independent producers and adapted it to the government system. Inravision calls for bids from private groups which have to describe their programs thoroughly, pay an application fee and deposit funds for four months of production. Some of the bids are then accepted to provide national programs. West Germany is unique in its reliance on self-regulating regional stations operating independently of central government supervision. Control of broadcasting rests within each of the nine states of the federalist system. Although state governments do not control content or budget, they do decide on the policies for radio operations. Broadcast organizations are run by councils composed of representatives from various segments of German society, administrative boards and station managers — a three-level control arrangement that has provided a national TV network more responsive to viewers' needs than many others. The top three regional broadcast organizations, Hamburg, Munich and Cologne, account for some 65% of the viewing audience and much of the national programming. There are two German TV networks, one a cooperative with income and programming coming from the regional stations, the other a national TV channel that complements the states' networks.

There are many features of broadcasting systems unique to specific cultures. Malaysia's media are conditioned by national policies on morality, belief in God, and respect for the constitution. Afghanistan's constitution until 1978 guaranteed the right of the people to public broadcasting. And Brazil's radio stations since the mid 1930's were required to air a low-key propaganda program from 7 to 8 nightly. The first ten minutes were allotted for the president, the next 20 minutes for ministeries and the last 30 for congress and the courts. Ratings were so embarrassingly low that the government attempted to curtail the program but congressmen were reluctant to give up their part. It has been popularly known as "The Hour of Silence" rather than "The Voice of Brazil" since unhappy listeners opt to turn off their radios. In Austria, a distinctive feature of radio is its wide use for passing on messages about such things as lost or stolen property, theater and cinema programs, meetings and sports events, personal greetings, requests for witnesses to accidents, religious, educational and charitable announcements. In Switzerland, there has been a question in German-speaking areas about whether standard German or Swiss German should be used in broadcasting. In the same country, as in many other western European nations, there are radio programs for foreign workers from Turkey, Spain, Greece, etc. In East Germany a series on TV called "The Black Channel" is aired every Monday evening presenting selected extracts from Western German TV as examples of misleading propaganda or illustrations of the inequities of capitalism. In Italy, independent radio stations with small budgets have appeared. Unable to afford correspondents, they use the so-called "token reporter," a private citizen who simply proceeds to the closest phone booth to call the station; he is then put on the air to report a story.

In China, untrained "barefoot journalists" have been used to report the news. The attempt to involve audiences is also illustrated by a story which notes that a Canton TV station had trained amateur film makers to fill a third of the station's requirements. In Africa, the "bush telegraph," or communication with drums, paved the way for the spread and effectiveness of radio as a medium. India has a long tradition of using radio forums to provide group listening and discussions for educational purposes. Japanese TV features "hard-hitting" dramas in which the characters are all frantically concerned about reaching a certain goal. There are dramas about businessmen trying to succeed; schoolboys attempt to win a football match; students rack their brains to pass an exam. The theme is always dedication to something that is almost, but not quite, impossible. In Nigeria the village square remains a powerful center for news and gossip and is a strong competitor for broadcasting and other media as sources of information. Opinion surveys in the U.S.S.R. have showed that the most popular shows are films, quiz programs, variety shows and sportscasts with a preference for less economic news and more attention to every-day topics. In 1984, one of the biggest hits on Moscow TV was a KGB spy serial in which Soviet agents battled American spies around the world in the manner of Ian Fleming's Agent 007. In East Germany morning TV programs are largely repeats for shift workers or adult educational programs. Both China and the Soviet Union have "wired-diffusion" radio systems where programs are fed over wires to sets in public places providing for more control as well as an efficient use of resources. So there is much diversity in broadcasting around the world. (See Martin and Chaudhary, 1983, Merrill, 1983, and Head, 1985 for more on other countries' media systems.)

Challenging Concepts of Social Control

The four major philosophies described in the first chapter remain as cornerstones of many mass communication systems. But there has been growing dissatisfaction that the typology of only four philosophies is too restrictive and does not adequately describe what exists in the world today. The arguments come from several directions. Many, like Altschull (1984), for example, argue that independent media cannot exist because they necessarily reflect the larger social order. He argues for a schema with an economic base and provisions for three types of environments: the market economy, the Marxist society, and "advancing" countries (for economically developing countries in the Third World). From Marxists come challenges that private control has produced private monopolies where few citizens have any access to the channels of mass communication in capitalist countries. For example, most televised air time in the U.S. is accounted for by only three network organizations. Almost 85% of West Germany's newspaper circulation is produced by only 16% of the papers. Another criticism comes from Europe's "New Philosophers," who have asserted that 19th century philosophical systems are out of date and Marxism is an obsolete ideology that inevitably leads to totalitarianism. These young philosophers, lapsed Marxists for the most part, are reminders of the impact felt by Solzhenitsyn's unveiling of the Gulag Archipelago (a string of Siberian camps for dissidents) and the invasion of Czechoslovakia in 1968.

But perhaps the most significant impact in the long run will be the objections from developing countries that the Western concepts of "freedom," private ownership and national development don't go together as the major philosophies suggest. Emerging nations in Latin America, Africa and Asia do not have the political stability of the U.S. or European nations, nor the traditions of civil liberties developed over centuries. At the same time they are faced with the need to plan and to mobilize the population for national economic and social goals. One such goal is unity among ethnic and racial groups often related only by conflict and past differences. If "freedom" of the media and free speech mean that this unity will not be achieved and critics will scuttle development programs, then such "freedom" is a luxury that the government, and by implication, society, cannot afford. Thus, the view of many leaders in increasing numbers of developing nations is that the mass media must be harnessed to work as a partner in national development. The "harness" represents a different definition of the relationship between the mass media and society (See Hachten, 1981).

One proposal would alter the four major philosophies to account for the differences in developing nations. Ralph Lowenstein offers a two-tiered system that separates ownership and philosophy of a given press system (Merrill and Lowenstein, 1971). Three types of press ownership are offered:

1. Private—ownership by individuals or nongovernment corporations; supported primarily by advertising or subscriptions;
2. Multiparty—ownership by competitive political parties; subsidized by party or party members;

3. Government—owned by government or dominant government party; subsidized primarily by government funds or government-collected license fees.

The characteristic separating the three types of "ownership" is the source of financial support which Lowenstein believes indicates important operational characteristics of the press. For example, a privately-owned media system most likely gets its financial support from advertising and subscriptions. Thus, we would expect such a system to be responsive in part to the needs of those chief sources of revenue. The second tier is philosophies. Here, Lowenstein retains the authoritarian and libertarian philosophies in the same basic form given earlier. However, the Soviet-Communist philosophy has been abandoned to make way for "Social-Authoritarian."

1. Authoritarian—government licensing and censorship to stifle criticism and maintain the ruling elite;

2. Social-Authoritarian—government and government-party ownership to harness the press for national economic and philosophical goals;

3. Libertarian—absence of governmental controls, except for minimal libel and obscenity laws, assuring a free marketplace of ideas and operation of the self-righting process;

4. Social-Libertarian—minimal governmental controls to unclog channels of communication and assure the operational spirit of the Libertarian philosophy;

5. Social-Centrist—positive governmental controls to harness the press for national economic and philosophical goals.

The "social responsibility" term has been abandoned as ambiguous. In its place are two new concepts of philosophy which pay some allegiance to the spirit of libertarianism but recognize that modern society and technology have restricted the marketplace of ideas and some societal interference is necessary to unclog the "choked" channels (e.g., regulations of the U.S. airwaves by the Federal Communication Commission). Lowenstein moves a step further to suggest applying his typology by medium within each country. Thus, one philosophy may relate newspapers to society, while two philosophies are needed to describe the situation for broadcast media. England provides an example:

Print Media
    Ownership: private
    Philosophy: Social-Libertarian

Television:

> Ownership: government
> Philosophy: Social-Centralist; Social-Libertarian

Radio:

> Ownership: government
> Philosophy: Social-Centralist

Lowenstein believes that his typology helps describe movements of national media systems. If a nation moves in the direction of Social-Libertarianism, for example, it attempts to maintain the idea of a privately-owned media system while assuring the operational spirit of Libertarianism via self regulation and government regulation. The aim of both Social-Centralism and Social-Libertarianism is to assure pluralism of voices though there is a limited number of channels. Emphasis on government control of information reflects movement towards Social-Authoritarianism.

Lowenstein's revision of the original four theories of the press is one of many, and new ones seem to appear with increasing regularity. Picard (1982/83) suggests aligning the approaches along a libertarian-authoritarian continuum rather than devising descriptive categories. One of the most useful efforts is provided by William Hachten (1981), who looks at media philosophies as clashing ideologies that represent differing perceptions about the nature and role of news because of their divergent political philosophies and historical traditions. His five concepts of the media include:

1. the authoritarian concept (where the media exist to support the state or authority and diversity is wasteful or irresponsible);

2. the Western concept (found in a handful of Western nations sharing such characteristics as protection of individual civil liberties, high economic and educational levels, a competitive democratic political system, sufficient private capital for media support, and an established tradition of independent journalism);

3. the Communist concept (similar to the Marxist system described previously);

4. the Revolutionary Concept (where the media are used to subvert the government or wrest control from alien rulers); and

5. the Developmental Concept (where the mass media are seen as important instruments for nation-building.

The latter two concepts are particularly useful when separated out from the others. The Revolutionary concept of the media is a relatively short-lived one because it addresses what is inherently an unstable situation. It applies equally to such situations as clandestine "self-publishing" in the Soviet Union, the use of audio cassettes in the revolution of Ayatollah Khomeni, the use of pamphlets urging opposition to colonial rule, or mobile radio stations sponsoring revolutions to overthrow governments of the left or right. Once independence or power is achieved, however, the revolutionary philosophy is found wanting because it addresses a situation that no longer exists. At that point, the Developmental concept is brought to the foreground. This concept holds that all instruments of mass communication should be mobilized by the central government to aid in the great tasks of nation-building: fighting illiteracy and poverty, building a political consciousness, and assisting in economic development. When the private sector is unable to provide adequate media service, the government has the responsibility. For some, the developmental concept is a rejection of the Western concept, but the debate is likely to continue for some time.

Describing the philosophical foundations of national media systems is not an idel task of little importance. Indeed, the characterization of governments and social systems is part of the continuing world-wide struggle between different philosophies and ideologies. This intudes upon the American system, as well, for developing nations are dissatisfied with the pictures of their countries that appear in U.S. media. Essentially, the objections are an extension of the logic for the Social-Authoritarian philosophies. Local newspapers and radio stations are operated in a program of "development journalism." Yet the media of the U.S. and other nations contain little of this "good news" about development in Africa, Asia, and Latin America. Thus, since this may hamper progress, international news media also must be made to serve developmental objectives. Certainly this view assumes that mass media can have major effects in social, economic and cultural development. We will return to these issues in subsequent chapters.

"Freedom" and "democracy" are two of the most popular ideas in the world today. Both terms appear in constitutions of countries with widely different practices. "Freedom" in some places refers to government ownership, in others it means citizens can say what they want without being thrown in jail; in all places, freedom has limits. In almost all nations, mass media are crucial to the exercise of power and the expression of opinions and ideas. Thus, the notions of freedom, democracy, and mass media communication are intertwined. Debate in the past couple of decades has emphasized "media responsibilities to society." One prominent critic sees this shift from emphasis on freedom to responsibility as reflecting a loss of faith in democracy itself. John Merrill (1974) notes that the stress on responsibility naturally leads toward control and restrictions on mass media. He believes that pluralism should be the objective of American sociey and that means diversity of information and ideas but not necessarily the "number" of media units operating. When a government "forces" libertarianism to work by producing pluralism, the country no longer has libertarianism but control, he argues. The problem is how to define "responsibility." Who is responsible to whom? In a pluralistic society with diverse political ideologies and conflicting ways of life, there can be no single concept of media responsibility, Merrill argues. Thus, to talk about media responsibility to society in a libertarian, pluralistic country is a contradiction.

The relationship between mass media and the government is the essential ingredient in the debate between different philosophies. But that link is not a one-way flow of influence. Davison (1965) notes that many of the characteristics associated with democracy depend on free access of all groups to the channels of communication—as both senders and receivers. One of these is the non-violent competition for political power. Communication is also essential for the government's reliance on persuasion rather than force to accomplish its domestic policies. And access to media channels is essential for those ouside the government who want to influence its actions and policies.

Society has three chief instruments which can be used to encourage or to prod the mass media to responsible performance (Schramm, 1973). One is the government and its various regulatory bodies at the national, state and local levels. The Federal Trade Commission, for example, is responsible for examining fraudulent advertising appearing on television. Local ordinances may affect the distribution of sexually-explicit films. Second, the media themselves, their personnel and associations, engage in activities that lead to self-regulation. Journalists ban together in their guild (a union), The Society of Professional Journalists (Sigma Delta Chi), a professional association, and other groups that affect media performance. Third, the general public, individually through pressure and collectively in organizations like media councils, influence the mass media. In one city, for example, a local radio TV council successfully pressured a TV station to shift the adult program "Mary Hartman, Mary Hartman" from early to late evening.

Summary

Mass media do not appear ovenight but have long histories that illustrate the impact of a variety of factors—growth of education and literacy, economic variables, technology, urbanization and immigration. In this chapter, we looked at the growth and development of newspapers, magazines, radio, television, and advertising. We identified the ways that existing media are affected by each new arrival on the scene. New media force those in existence to change their form and function to survive but they do not supplant them. We also surveyed mass media systems around the world—both print and broadcast media. Then we discussed challenging concepts of social control and applied them to different media systems. In the next chapter, we will take a look inside the media industries and organizations and note how people work within the media.

Inside the Media
Industries, Organizations, People

The mass media occupy a curious position in the lives of Americans as well as citizens of other countries. Together with interpersonal communication, mass communication represents the "cement" that is necessary for organizing social units ranging from families to ethnic groups, and from organizations to cities and countries themselves. Any form of interdependence—the distinguishing characteristic of social units—requires communication in the "formative" stage as well as subsequent periods of maintenance. Without such communication, we have aggregates with common interests or groups of left-handed people sharing a characteristic but not forming a social unit.

Communication is not only the "cement" linking us into patterns called businesses, clubs or families; it is also patterned. In interpersonal communication classes one studies communication patterns that take place in marriages, small task groups and large-scale organizations. But much of the "communication cement" that connects (or disconnects) us occurs through patterns that represent mass media organizations.

Mass media organizations are many and varied, and are themselves patterned through additional organizations such as TV networks. This highly organized system constitutes one of the most important institutions of modern nations, one that many fear threatens the stability of other institutions. What are the characteristics of the mass communication institution and how is it "related" to other institutions such as the family, government or the economy?

Institutional processes are organized, systematized and stable. In organization, roles are specified and relations between them delineated; for example, reporters and editors occupy roles with certain expectations of their behaviors and relationship. The relevant tasks to be performed in media organizations are specified and the media remain in existence beyond the life of any individual participant.

The mass communication institution is complex. In the last chapter we showed some of the connections between mass media and the political and economic institutions. Here we will elaborate on those connections in our dicussion of the industries. We also will describe the diverse organizations and levels of patterns that make up the institution. Clearly, there is no way we can specify all of the actual or potential patterns relating to mass communication. Thus, we need to ask what patterns are meaningful and what empirical evidence exists that relates the patterns to each other and verifies their existence. This last task underlies the fact that we are always concerned with people and their relationships. Thus, our attention will not be eternally fixed at high levels of abstraction but will shift to the people who fill media roles, their backgrounds and career paths. Since the institutions remain while individuals pass on when their contributions are over, there have to be processes for teaching people how to fill particular roles. This "socialization" process is the link between individuals and their responsibilities, and the media organizations and institution.

Different Scenarios on Where to Begin

Where do we begin in evaluating mass communication institutions? Certainly that differs according to one's perspective. Let's take the recent controversy over music videos and their potential impact as an example. An industry supporter might look at the entertainment industry which produces these videos as merely a vehicle for the reproduction of "mass culture," the place where the symbols of American society are turned into cultural artifacts that subsequently mold the conscious thoughts of Americans. A critic might see MTV (Music Television) as a reflection of the capitalist system — images used by the dominant classes to occupy the youth of the country while keeping them pliable to the interests of the moneyed class. An outside observer might look at the entertainment media as a set of coalitions jockeying for position in an uncertain environment where no one person or group has control. When scholars look at media institutions, they too often begin with different starting points in explaining what they see as significant.

In the rest of the chapter we will examine mass media industries and organizations and the people that work in them. Much of the information presented will help you in evaluating the usefulness of the orientations presented in Chapters One and Two.

The Institution, The Industries

When Dan Rather delivers a one-minute story about inflation in America, he is supported not only by a vast collection of microphones, cables and other hardware but also by an entire support system of people. It's not just you and Dan Rather engaging in a little friendly conversation, one in which you are the silent partner. Rather himself is a member of a complex organization — CBS, the journalistic profession, and a far-flung industry of mass media. Broadcasting isn't the exception, either. Though the author wrote this book, his "conversation" with readers would not take place without book editors, a publisher, and a distribution system. Mass communication is characterized not by the actions of isolated individuals but by the co-operative efforts of organizations, professions, and groups of skillful people integrated into loosely defined industries. This doesn't mean that the contributions of individuals are not significant or even para-mount in many instances, but it does mean that we need to look at the context in which media people work.

Mass media serve a host of functions for individuals and society, as we noted in the first two chapters. They provide entertainment, pass on traditions, coordinate activities and act as a "watchdog" over the government. Some of these functions also are shared by other institu-tions. New generations learn about their heritage not only from the mass media but also from their parents, schools, and churches. Often media and schools are considered to be part of what is termed the knowledge industry. The U.S. is now an information-based economy with about half of the gross national product accounted for by information sectors that include mass media, education, advertising, libraries, research firms, computers, and communication equipment manufacturers. The information sector has grown from a low of 5% of the U.S. labor force in 1860 to about 50% today. The U.S. has become the dominant supplier of information resources to the world, particu-larly to developing nations. One aspect of this is the sale of U.S. media products like TV programming, feature films, books and magazines. In this multi-billion dollar system you find Barbara Walters, your instruc-tor, records, books and billboards, all competing for your attention. This emphasis on information and knowledge is the chief charac-teristic of the Post-Industrial society. Schramm and Porter (1982: 131) note that the knowledge industry is organized along these lines:

Multipliers of Messages—the mass media, newspapers, magazines, books, films, radio, TV.

Carriers of Messages—telephone, telegraph, postal service, satellite systems.

Information Suppliers for Individual Needs—libraries, abstract services, data banks, computer service, etc.

Manufacturers and Maintainers—printers, technicians to install media services, manufacturers of printing, electronic equipment.

Special Service Suppliers—news agencies, writers, performers, artists, etc.

Economic Support Agencies—advertising agencies and departments, etc.

Administrative Support Agencies—legal counsel, public relations, financial services, etc.

Personnel Support—unions, trade associations, training services.

Data-Gathering Services—opinion research centers, audience research services, etc.

Education—schools and colleges, home-study opportunities, special schools for industry, military, etc.

Source: Fritz Machlup, *The Production and Distribution of Knowledge in the United States.*
Copyright © 1962 by Princeton University Press.

However, the mass media are viewed not just as a component of the knowledge industry, but also as prime sources of inexpensive entertainment by most Americans. Even here media compete for audiences against other opportunities that range from dancing to sports and from hobbies to picnics. Thus, media also are part of what is called the "leisure industry." Indeed, television alone consumes about a third of our free time according to a study by researcher John Robinson of the University of Maryland. Thus, media are located in two of the largest growing industries of modern times. The fact that mass media serve such diverse needs and interests plays a part in their growth and place of importance in American lives.

Just how big are the mass media? A study by Sterling (1975) found that the number of media outlets increased by nearly 270% in the past half century or so. The increases were due primarily to the fact that the number of broadcast stations grew by more than 1,000% while the daily press dropped nearly 20% in units. Since 1950, with the introduction of FM and TV services, media outlets and voices have increased at a faster rate than population growth primarily because of the available broadcast channels. The growth of low-power TV stations and other broadcasting outlets in the 1980's means a continuation of this trend. In 1985 more than 500 stations with limited signals were either licensed or under construction, and the FCC plans eventually to license about 4,000 such stations (Saddler, 1984). Table 1 provides us with some figures that sketch changes in media industries. Despite the decline in the number of newspapers over the years, the number of cities in the U.S. with a daily paper has actually increased, though the number of cities with two or more separately-owned dailies has declined. Most cities have a local newspaper monopoly. Despite competition from television, rising costs of newsprint and problems faced by some metropolitan afternoon dailies, the daily newspaper industry looks economically healthy (Radolf, 1983; Huenergard, 1983; Consoli, 1983). Overall newspaper employment has continued to rise in recent years. Many publishers have changed the content and appearance of their papers to attract new readers. Many have used a marketing approach to target information at specialized audiences. A good example is the national daily paper, *USA Today*, published by the Gannett chain. Though daily newspaper circulation has not kept pace with general population growth, advertising in the same papers has often exceeded the growth of the economy. The growing magazine industry also has become increasingly specialized. Production of so-called specialty magazines has jumped dramatically as publishers divide their marketplace into small, lucrative pieces. According to one count, there were 137 computer-oriented magazines in 1982, compared to 42 in 1977 (Schmid, 1984).

Though we tend to talk about the American press as if it were a rather homogeneous collection of newspapers, we need to recognize the long history of diversity among both audiences and organizations. The roots of Black newspapers go back 150 years to Cornish and Russwurms "Freedom Journal," begun in 1827. The Black press has traditionally been a weekly press. From 1866 to 1905 the Black press saw more than 1,200 papers begin, 70% in the South. Most had small circulations. The Black press united with Black churches to campaign for social justice. Another growth period occurred from 1905-1976 with the migration of Blacks from the South to northern industrial cities.

The first American Indian newspapers, the "Cherokee Phoenix," was published in 1828. One of the primary tasks of the early native American papers was educational. The past quarter century has seen a sharp increase in the availability of Spanish-language publications, and growth was particularly strong in the 1970's. Foreign-language papers continue to flourish in the U.S. and a recent sample illustrates this: Czech, Polish, Portuguese, Slovene, Lithuanian, Urdu, Yiddish,

Table 3-1

The Mass Media Industries: Numbers and Sizes

Books

Number of New Books and Editions:	12,069 (1960)
	36,071 (1970)
	53,380 (1983)

| Number of New Editions | 2,943 (1960) |
| | 7,359 (1981) |

| Number of Book Publishers: | 936 (1963) |
| | 1,120 (1972) |

| Number of Book Clubs | 57 (1963) |
| | 198 (1975) |

| Number of Libraries in United States: | 19,076 (1960) |
| | 29,044 (1983) |

Recording

Total Number of Domestic Records/ Tapes (in millions)	533 (1975)
	684 (1980)
	578 (1983)

Number of Phonograph Titles Issued:	6,157 (1955)
	8,909 (1960)
	11,559 (1967)
	9,701 (1970)
	9,048 (1976)

Sources:
Sterling & Haight (1978); *Statistical Abstract of the United States* (1985); *Bowker Annual of Library and Book Trade* (1984)

Magazines

Total Number of Periodicals:	5,880 (1945)
	8,422 (1960)
	10,688 (1982)
	10,809 (1984)

Number of Weeklies:	1,269 (1945)
	1,580 (1960)
	1,672 (1982)

Number of Monthly Periodicals:	3,025 (1945)
	4,113 (1960)
	4,078 (1982)
	4,429 (1985)

Top 10 Magazines (1982 Circulation):
- *Reader's Digest*
- *TV Guide*
- *National Geographic*
- *Family Circle*
- *Woman's Day*
- *Better Homes & Gardens*
- *McCall's*
- *Ladies' Home Journal*
- *Modern Maturity*
- *Good Housekeeping*
- *AARP News Bulletin*

Sources:
Sterling & Haight (1978); *Magazine Fact Book* (1982); *Magazine Newsletter of Research* (August, 1984); IMS/Ayer Directory (1985)

Radio

Commercial Radio on Air	5 (1921)
	618 (1930)
	765 (1940)
	2,867 (1950)
	4,306 (1960)
	6,889 (1970)
	8,556 (1985)

Commercial AM Stations:	2,086 (1950)
	3,456 (1960)
	4,292 (1970)
	4,785 (1985)

Commercial FM Stations:	20 (1940)
	781 (1950)
	850 (1960)
	2,597 (1970)
	3,771 (1985)

Number of FM Educational Stations:	2 (1941)
	48 (1950)
	162 (1960)
	413 (1970)
	1,194 (1985)

Number of Stations affiliated with radio networks:	1977	NBC -- 236
		CBS -- 266
		ABC -- 1,546
		Mutual -- 755
		Total: 2,803

Sources:
Broadcasting Yearbook (1985); Sterling & Haight (1978)

Newspapers

Number of Dailies:
1,749 (1945)
1,772 (1950)
1,763 (1960)
1,748 (1970)
1,745 (1980)
1,688 (1984)

Morning Dailies:
322 (1950)
312 (1960)
334 (1970)
458 (1984)

Afternoon Dailies:
1,450 (1950)
1,459 (1960)
1,429 (1970)
1,257 (1984)

Number of Sunday Papers:
549 (1950)
563 (1960)
586 (1970)
783 (1984)

Number of Weekly Papers:
16,227 (1910)
10,972 (1930)
9,661 (1945)
8,174 (1960)
7,612 (1970)
7,704 (1985)

Daily Circulation (in millions)
53.8 (1950)
58.9 (1960)
62.1 (1970)
63.3 (1984)

Weekly Circulation (in millions):
20.97 (1960)
27.86 (1970)
48.99 (1985)

Sources:
Editor & Publisher Yearbook (1984, 1985); ANPA Facts About Newspapers (1985); miscellaneous others

Television

Commercial TV Stations on Air:
610 (1967)
802 (1982)
907 (1985)

NBC Affiliates:
205 (1967)
214 (1983)

CBS Affiliates:
191 (1967)
202 (1983)

ABC Affiliates:
141 (1967)
207 (1983)

Number of Cable TV Systems:
400 (1955)
1,325 (1965)
5,000 (1983)
6,600 (1985)

Cable Reached 43% of TV Households (1984)

Low Power TV:
215 VHF (1985)
121 UHF (1985)

Number of TV Stations:
2 (1941)
98 (1950)
559 (1960)
862 (1970)
1,079 (1983)
1,206 (1985)

Number of Educational TV Stations:
2 (1954)
44 (1960)
185 (1970)
277 (1983)
299 (1985)

Number of VHF Stations:
474 (1960)
581 (1970)
654 (1985)

Number of UHF Stations:
85 (1960)
281 (1970)
552 (1985)

Sources:
Broadcasting Yearbook (1985); Broadcasting Magazine (June, 1985)

Film

Number of New Films Released:
344 (1930)
497 (1941)
425 (1950)
203 (1963)
267 (1970)
182 (1975)
395 (1983)

Number of Theaters:
15,000 (1923)
18,631 (1948)
12,699 (1972)

Number of Outdoor Theaters:
820 (1948)
6,000 (1961)
3,730 (1969)
3,801 (1975)

Number of Non-Theatrical Films Produced in United States
7,740 (1958)
10,670 (1965)
15,050 (1976)

Number of Made-for-TV Films shown:
1 (1965-1966)
43 (1969-1970)
149 (1972-1973)
180 (1973-1974)

Sources:
Sterling & Haight (1978); International Motion Picture Almanac (1985)

Arabic, and Carpatho-Russian. In addition to the ethnic press, we have a diverse religious press; for example, American Catholicism has a membership of 50 million and a press circulation of some 25 million.

The Economic Support Structure

The economic support structure for mass media tends to be the place where all controversies over media performance ultimately end. If TV isn't doing the job some critics say it should, it's because there is too much power concentrated in the hands of the networks. And, while businessmen point with dismay to anti-business biases in the media, other critics fear what growing chain ownership of newspapers and TV stations will mean for "diversity of voices" in the media. Some believe that economic ownership by corporations and elites also involved in business and industry will inevitably lead to fewer differences being aired in the public media. In contrast, others argue that the availability of more economic resources may lead to an improved media performance. Still others note there is only a weak connection between ownership and what appears in the media. What is the economic support structure for mass media and how is it important?

Ownership and the Support Structure

Generally we can describe the economic support of the mass media as falling along a continuum ranging from direct to indirect consumer support. As Figure 3-1 shows, at one end we have 100% direct support through consumer purchases. Here we find the book industry which derives most of its revenues from public purchases at stores or through book clubs. At the other end is the broadcasting industry where most of the support is indirect through either advertising (mediated through businesses that add advertising costs to the product purchase price) or institutional support such as that given by private foundations or the government.

Government regulation has been strongest at the "indirect" end of the continuum, where reactions to consumers may be delayed more often. Legal ownership of mass media varies along the continuum. In Chapter Two we noted how additional patterns are found in other countries. However, toward the direct end, most media units are held in the private, profit-making sector. Most books, magazines and newspapers are commercial enterprises that must maintain a profit to continue publishing. There are exceptions. University presses are sometimes subsidized to permit the publication of scholarly works that would not appear otherwise, and *Harper's* magazine in 1980 remained in existence only because it obtained the support of a private foundation. Before that, the profit margin was too small for its owners to

Figure 3-1
Media Support Continuum

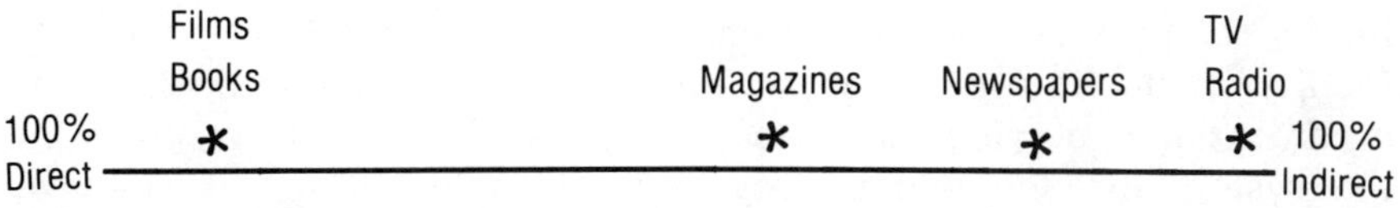

	Films			TV
Films	Books	Magazines	Newspapers	Radio
100%	*	*	*	* 100%
Direct				Indirect

Direct support comes in the form of subscriptions or purchases, while indirect support comes either through advertising or foundations, etc. Magazines, for example, get about half of their support from subscriptions/retail sales and half from advertising, while newspapers get about two-thirds of their revenue from advertising. The new technologies (e.g., cable, VCR's) are changing the continuum and will continue to do so.

continue their support. Government itself is represented in book and magazine publishing through the huge U.S. Government Printing Office. Some small neighborhood newspapers in large cities operate largely on the basis of volunteer efforts aided marginally by funds received through government and other channels. Moving toward the indirect end, we find that most TV and radio stations are profit-making concerns owned by private individuals or corporations. Furthermore, the major TV and radio networks, cable TV systems, and TV/film production companies are commercial enterprises. However, we also have a substantial non-commerical segment here.

Public broadcasting began in 1967 when there were 112 educational/non commercial TV stations and several hundred unrelated radio stations licensed primarily to universities and other nonprofit entities. The TV stations were served by National Educational TV (NET), a national production center funded by the Ford Foundation which provided five hours of nationally distributed programming weekly. By 1985 the system had grown to more than 300 TV stations in all major markets and served more than two thirds of the population through the Public Broadcasting Service (PBS), which provides 26 hours of programs weekly. Stations are licensed to more than 150 different institutions, including state agencies (35%), universities (30%), community nonprofit corporations (27%), and school boards and libraries (3%). National Public Radio serves a network of more than 200 public radio stations with about 40 hours of nationally-distributed programs weekly. These stations are licensed to universities (65%), communities (20%), and public schools, libraries, and state and local municipalities (15%). Three national institutions with responsibility for public broadcasting have been established: the Corporation for Public Broadcasting, the statutory body through which congressional appropriations to licenses are administered; the Public Broadcasting Service (PBS) organized by CPB in 1970 to operate the interconnection service to all public TV licenses, and National Public Radio, set up to initiate programs and to serve the interconnection facility for public radio licenses. PBS has grown from an engineering organization to playing a significant role in programming and planning the system through which programs are selected and funded by stations via the Station Program Cooperative (SPC).

The major form of support for media at the indirect end is advertising. An analysis of figures from the 1940's to the mid 1970's shows that advertising accounted for a growing share of newspaper revenue. U.S. advertising in 1947 was estimated at $4.26 billion, compared to $20.6 billion in 1971. Though the newspapers' share of advertising expenditures dropped from 52% in 1947 to about 27% in 1984, this still amounted to $23.7 billion (Coen, 1985). In general, financial analysts rate newspapers as significantly more profitable than the average of American industries. For example, a 1976 survey of American business gave the following annual rates of return on stockholder equity over the preceding five years: Knight-Ridder, 14.3%, Gannett, 16.5%, Times-Mirror, 15.2%, Washington Post, 15.5%, and the New York Times, 12.6%. The median for all 859 companies surveyed was 12.7%. All figures are after taxes. The TV industry also is highly profitable. However, when compared with other U.S. industries, it is only "average-sized," about the same as canned fruits and vegetables or the manufacture of paperboard boxes. It amounts to about 4% of after-tax household incomes for the average TV household.

How important is advertising as a "subsidy"? Do TV commercials pay their own way? In every medium the consumer contributes to information dissemination through the purchase of a stamp, magazine, newspaper, radio or TV set. There's also a subsidy attributable to advertising. Callahan (1978) compared advertising and circulation revenue with advertising/editorial content for print media. He also compared revenue and costs of receiver purchases and repair with advertising information and recreational content for broadcast media. For direct mail, revenue and costs were also examined. Compared to newspapers, electronic media offer far more noncommercial information as a percentage. In 1982, U.S. District Court ruled that the National Association of Broadcasters code was in violation of antitrust law (Maddox and Zanot, 1984). Until then, the code limited commercial TV time to 18 minutes an hour for non-prime time TV and 9 minutes, 30 seconds an hour for prime time. The same general procedures are still being followed independently, though there is advertising pressure. So, while about 60% of newspaper space is advertising, 12% of TV time is commercials (including both prime time and other time periods). For the period examined, advertising accounted for 77% of total newspaper revenue, the remaining 23% being the price to the consumer via subscriptions and newsstand sales. Compare these with the 38% of space accounted for by editorial content and 62% accounted for by advertising content. Thus, advertising in print media subsidizes information dissemination if we assume production costs for the two types of advertising/editorial content to be equivalent. Without advertising the 10 cent newspaper would have cost 43 cents at that time. For the period, advertising was 49.1% of magazine revenue, consumers paying 50.9%. Magazine content was 53% advertising and 47% editorial. Thus, the subsidy was minor over the 15-year period of the study. Adding up advertising revenue, and costs of radio set production and repair, we find that the consumer paid 36% and the advertiser 64%. Since 18 minutes of the radio hour are commercials, 30% is advertising and 70% other content. So there again is a subsidy of other content. For TV, advertising was 43% of all expenditures but accounted for only 25% of air time, thus providing a subsidy for noncommercial content.

Concentration and Diversity

"Diversity" is a goal of those who believe that American society should strive for a representative diversity of ideas on issues. However, though we might find general support for diversity and tolerance in the American public, how that diversity is to be achieved is another matter. The battle over what ideas and images should appear in the media is ultimately a battle over control. Private owners argue that efforts by intellectual elites to impose a "balanced picture" on media producers undermines the independence from governmental interference that is the basis for that diversity. And social critics point out that newspapers owned by the same corporation represent fewer views and ignore less powerful segments of society such as minorities and women.

Abel (1984) found in a study of some 1,900 TV and radio stations that 70% of the AM and FM stations and 90% of the TV stations had one or more female owners, though the average ownership held by women in other fields was only 12-25%. Other critics note that efforts by intellectuals to promote "cultural" fare and other images would reduce the satisfaction of the mass consuming audience if implemented. Bruce Owen (1978) argues that diversity as a government regulatory goal may be irrelevant for consumer interests. Who defines diversity is the key. For a consumer, there may be as much "diversity" within tradi-tional TV program types as in more innovative programs, for example. The major force behind the domination of diversity and fairness as broadcasting goals has been the desire of groups who want more of their kind of programming or more of the type *they* think people ought to see. Thus, debates over diversity are debates over control.

Diversity as a goal is not merely a matter of philosophical or legal niceties. It is grounded in the lessons of experience. First, a free flow of ideas is essential to political liberty and is essential in developing ideas of potential value to society. The notion of diversity in communication is not new; the challenge is in implementing diversity. Viewed as communication systems rather than industries, the major function of mass media is to circulate ideas which have consequences for every aspect of society. The circulation of ideas is an evolutionary process. From an enormous variety of possibilities, some ideas are introduced into the system; some are developed or modified as they circulate and some are deleted. Writers introduce ideas but so do producers and directors, networks and advertisers, and local outlets. Public officials may introduce ideas when they give speeches, hold press conferences, or generate interest to attract coverage. Members of the public who normally serve as audiences may also introduce ideas when placed before microphones and cameras in the studio or on the streets.

Certainly ideas enter social discussions in many ways and from many sources, but the mass media are chief among these. Many fear that the diversity of ideas will be reduced if there is concentration of economic power. Concern over media ownership stems from a fear that those who own, if not control, the media's activities will also be among the other economic and political elites of society. A "pluralist elite structure" is thought to require media elites to be sufficiently autono-mous from other elites in society (government, business, industry, edu-cation, religion, etc.) to provide a detached perspective on their activ-ities and to present a critical account of the behaviors of other elites.

Ben Bagdikian (1979) outlined the dimensions of growing control of information organizations in the U.S. by a relatively small number of national and transnational corporations. The top 20 corporations in newspapers, magazines, broadcasting, books and movies each controlled at least 50% of the sales in each area, and many were among the top 20 in more than one area. A recent study of the 290 directors of the 25 largest newspaper companies showed that there were thousands of interlocks with institutions that the papers covered (Dreier and Weinberg, 1979). Many directors sat on the boards of regional, national, and multinational business corporations, boards of chambers of commerce, hospitals, universities, charities, and foundations. Some held high federal office or served in state or local government. Most of the directors were white and male. There were no Blacks and only 15 women. There were 38 direct interlocks with the 50 largest banks and more than 100 direct ties with universities. Almost every one of the newspaper companies had directors on the boards of the local United Way or Chamber of Commerce. A study of Canada's elites showed similar socioeconomic characteristics of the directors of elite media organizations and those heading major corporations (Baldwin, 1977). However, there was less actual interlocking of directorships than predicted. The actual overlap was largely accounted for by ownership of media units by larger firms such as conglomerates. Otherwise less than a fifth of the elites also were economic elites.

Though newspapers have reported sweeping indictments of interlocks in other industries, they've been less forthcoming in self-analysis, though there certainly are exceptions. *The Lewiston Morning Tribune* (Idaho) presented its own readers with potential conflicts of interest represented not only by the publisher's ties but also reporters' and editors' (Tate, 1978). We'll return to this again later in our examination of how ownership affects internal operations of the media.

Sterling (1975) looked at trends in daily newspaper and broadcast ownership from 1922 to 1970, finding a 270% increase in the total number of outlets and voices because of the growth of broadcasting that occurred while the number of newspapers decreased. The number of media voices (total number of stations and newspapers) increased by 185%. Voices refers to the number of different ownership units within a market, regardless of how many stations or papers were owned by each. The increases were due primarily to the fact that the number of broadcast stations grew by more than 1,000% while the daily press dropped nearly 20% in units. So concentration of print media ownership increased. Since 1950, with the introduction of FM and TV services, there has not been increased concentration of media ownership. In the top 100 metropolitan areas, media concentration actually declined slightly because of the growing number of independently-owned broadcast stations. From peaks of 30 to 35 years ago, newspaper control of broadcasting outlets and voices has declined so that only a rather small percentage of broadcasting stations is controlled by the press. However, group and conglomerate company control of stations has grown slowly since 1950 with about a third of all stations so owned. During this period, media outlets and voices have increased at a faster rate than population growth primarily because of the available broadcast channels. However, trends suggest increasing concentration in the future unless cable TV and such new technologies as low-power TV change the situation. After peaking in 1940 (because of ownership of a major proportion of AM stations), and 1950 (because of similar early domination of FM and TV stations), press control has declined sharply whether one examines outlets or voices. The actual percentage of broadcast outlets and voices controlled by newspapers in the market area is not a menacing factor.

Table 3-2
Chain-Ownership of U.S. Mass Media

Percentage of Pay-Cable Subscribers served by Top 8 Distributing Companies in the U.S. (1976)	36.8%
Percentage of Commercial TV Stations Owned by Groups (1976)	58.0%
Percentage of Movie Theaters Owned by Top 4 Companies (1972)	12.5%
Percentage of Sales of Film Equipment in U.S. by Top 4 Companies (1972)	59.0%
Percentage of Magazine Revenue Accounted for by Top 8 Companies (Subscription, Sales . . .)	
—All Periodicals (1972)	33.0%
—Farm Periodicals	55.0%
—Specialized Business, Professional	40.0%
—General Peridocals	56.0%
—Other Periodicals	45.0%
Percentage of Daily Newspaper Circulation Accounted for by Chain-Owned Dailies (1978)	72.2%
Mean Number of Dailies per Chain (1978)	6.5
Percentage of Bookstores in U.S. Operated by Multi-Unit Chains (1972)	18.8%
Percentage of All Book Publishing (Shipments) Accounted for by:	
— 8 largest firms (1978)	27.0%
—20 largest firms (1978)	55.0%

Sources: Various, including Sterling & Haight (1978), Compaine (1979).

Concentration in Broadcasting

A recent study by Larson (1980) compared the concentration levels in the TV station industry with those in some other U.S. industries. The largest 20 owners in TV were used to measure concentration of control in TV. Television stations are viewed as the sellers of the industry's product and the advertising agencies and advertisers the buyers. He notes that the TV industry is often labeled an oligopoly where the largest 20 owners produce or control 75% of the product while the 8 largest have a share that either exceeds one third or one half, depending on high or low concentration. Measures of seller concentration included weekly "circulation," station income, and advertising revenues. In none of the "seller categories" was there concentration in the TV industry. For most measures of concentration, the TV industry was less concentrated than most selected industries, especially for seller variables. The measures support the conclusion that the TV station industry does not have high seller and buyer concentration. But, when consideration is given to an "additional" measure (the networks, program and advertisement sales), the industry was found to be highly concentrated. The Westinghouse petition in 1976 alleged that the networks had gained increased control over broadcast revenues and enlarged their percentage of network broadcast programming. Others have questioned the networks' market share of programming and broadcast revenues. Using 1982 information, Howard (1983) found that about 79% of all TV stations were licensed to group owners. The first multiple-station licensee in TV was the DuMont Broadcasting Co. which operated three local TV stations before starting the DuMont network. When the FCC established its multiple-ownership rules in the early 1950's, they were designed to restrict the size of individual groups; limits were 7 TV stations, including no more than 5 UHF. In 1985 the limit was raised to 12 stations as long as the group doesn't reach more than 25% of the nation's TV homes. The local stations owned by networks are important economically; in 1985, NBC made more profit from the five local TV stations it owns (in New York, Chicago, Cleveland, Washington and Los Angeles) than it did from the enire NBC TV network (Television Digest, 1985). In a recent breakdown (Howard, 1983), only three groups reached as many as 15 million homes weekly (ABC, CBS, and NBC owned-and-operated stations), while three other groups reached between 9 and 15 million homes weekly (about 15-20% of the nation's households). Thus, despite the fact that a few groups can reach large numbers of viewers, most broadcast chains have modest reaches.

Network power in programming markets is the subject of much debate. Manning and Owen (1976) conclude from their study that "network power is not based on advertising or the supply of television programs, which are nearly competitive. The major sources of their dominance are the technological economies of scale in simultaneous networking and their bargaining position relative to stations in the largest TV markets. Only about 9% of all U.S. advertising expenditures, or 15% of national advertising expenditures, go to network TV. There are a number of additional substitutes such as spot TV advertising, network and spot radio, national magazines, direct mail, and newspapers. Advertisers can purchase access to network audiences by sponsoring an entire program or series of programs or, more commonly, purchasing "participations" or partial sponsorship of programs selected by the network. Today, sponsorship of entire programs is quite rare except for special events or high culture categories. Generally, advertisers buy a package of commercial minutes spread over numerous programs throughout the year with the price dependent on audiences.

Looking at program markets and syndication, one study found a significant change in the relative shares of the three sources of network programming during the 1960's and 1970's: local production, the three networks, and the syndication market. Networks' production of entertainment series in the 6-11 p.m. time period fell from 29.5% in 1968 to 15.7% in 1975. The series' hours supplied by advertisers directly dropped from 33.4% to 3.0% while the proportion supplied by individual series packagers rose from 36.4% to 80.7%. Hollywood has dominated the supply to the networks of packaged prime time TV series since the early 1960's, in part because of restrictive reuse fees charged by the American Federation of Television and Radio Artists (AFTRA) for taped programs. Individual shares of major companies have usually ranged from 3 to 12% with most prime time series supplied by small companies. For several years there has been a trend toward original programming for the syndication market, but previously that was largely in the area of game shows and magazine programs; that is now expanding to include comedy and drama aimed at independent stations, cable systems and other operators (Gendel, 1985). Syndication has been a less important source of programming than the networks; station expenditures on syndicated programs range from 17 to 20% of network program expenses in the 1960's. Manning and Owen (1976) suggest that network affiliates are affiliates because network programming as a whole is more profitable than syndicate material.

There is a long history of ties between the film and TV industries in the U.S. In the late 1920's, RCA organized RKO Pictures to launch its own sound film system in competition with AT&T. More recently, broadcast ownership in the film field has involved other aspects. In the mid 1970's, ABC owned 278 theaters in 11 southern states. Cable TV systems also have been acquired by film companies such as Warner Communications. "Hollywood" — the complex of about a dozen important production/distribution companies — not only keeps half of the non-Communist world's theaters supplied with films but also takes 90% of the theatrical distribution revenue in America and gets half of what the U.S. TV industry pays others to provide programs. More and more film producers in Europe also have turned to the TV industry for support via production of feature films; we've also seen contributions from the networks to the national film aid funds and network co-production of films or commissions to private sector film companies.

The decline of Europe's film industries has coincided with the rise of TV over the three decades, but public service broadcasting has kept the European film heritage alive.

The Print Industry

Newspaper statistics for the past half century are illuminating. The number of newspaper chains went from 55 in 1930 to 167 in 1978 and the pace of concentration appears to be quickening. In 1982 some 26 different groups owned 10 or more daily papers; the number owned by Gannett grew to 86 in 1984—double the 1971 figure (Pierce, 1983). The number of daily papers published decreased considerably during the period from 1930 to 1945 and then remained relatively constant until the early 1980's when a considerable number of papers stopped publishing. At the start of 1985, there were 1,688 daily newspapers in the U.S.

The number of cities with a daily newspaper has increased (to 1,534 in 1985), but the number of cities with directly competing newspapers published by different publishers has decreased from several hundred to a handful (28 cities in October, 1982). Recently there has been a reversal of the trend showing decreasing numbers of cities with competitive newspapers. However, the growth is not in large cities where several notable deaths of papers have occurred recently, but rather in small daily communities. This can be traced to financial feasibility at the grass roots level, less expensive printing methods and sufficient advertising potentials.

National newspaper circulation rose from about 40 million in 1930 to a peak of 63 million in 1973, dropping slightly and then recovering a bit. The percentage of total daily circulation accounted for by the smallest 25% of newspaper firms has increased slightly over the years while the percentage accounted for by the largest quarter has decreased slightly. Average circulation of papers with no direct competition is somewhat above 20,000 while the mean for those with direct competition is more than 200,000. Thus, only a few larger cities have been able to afford multiple dailies. Population, location and market size seem to account for the ability of a city to support competing papers (Hagner, 1983).

The chains with the most papers in 1984 were Gannett, Thomson, Donrey and Freedom Newspapers, Inc. The top four chains by circulation accounted for 25% of all daily newspapers sold in the U.S. About a third of newspaper chains have only a few papers; the average is about six but the figure has been rising. One study showed that the largest chains in terms of number of papers contolled 4.1% of the nation's papers while the largest chain in circulation held about 6% of the total circulation (McIntosh, 1977). Members of the larger chains are mainly smaller newspapers.

Antitrust laws have demonstrated a weakness in their failure to slow the accumulation of newspapers by chains. As long as paper purchasers avoid acquiring a paper in competition with one they already own, they can generally assume immunity from antitrust attack. The established rule of thumb is that newspapers do not compete in the same market unless their circulation areas overlap. Antitrusters consider the prime competition among papers to be competition for advertising and only secondarily for circulation. In 1984, there were more than 150 newspaper groups and 69% of all dailies (with 79% of the circulation) were owned by groups (Browning, Grierson, and Howard, 1984).

Obsessed with the growth of chains, observers have overlooked a modest but important trend at the other end of the press spectrum, the neighborhood and community press. Typically couples in their 20's and 30's have avoided rigid politics and poured everything into small, workable community papers with intensely local, even personal coverage. In 1979 the editors of such a paper, the *Point Reyes Light* in northern California, received the Pulitzer Prize (Eisendrath, 1979). Estimates of the number of local papers range from dozens to scores; nobody knows for sure since such papers don't worry about state press associations. At the same time, neighborhood papers are appearing in many of the country's largest cities including New York City, Boston, Cleveland and Minneapolis-St. Paul. Thus, the same technology that costs large dailies millions of dollars to introduce has dropped the costs for starting new papers (Gaziano and Ward, 1978).

Magazines represent perhaps the closest approximation possible to "pure competition." A large percentage is separately owned; editorial and creative processes do not benefit from economies of scale or significant fixed costs; and there is specialization of taste among consumers. The American publishing industry itself is highly decentralized, operating in an unpredictable market and organized along craft rather than bureaucratic lines. Publishers themselves are affected by literacy levels, habits of book purchasing, libraries, copyright regulations, and bookstores that operate on exceedingly narrow margins. For example, a busy bookstore grossing $100,000 a year has an inventory of 8-10,000 books worth $30-35,000 and receives net profits of some $15,000. In 1982 there were some 50,000 book titles published in the U.S. (Grannis, 1983).

Cross-Ownership of Media

Loevinger (1979) notes that attacks on mass media recently have charged an "unholy influence" arising from cross-ownership between papers and broadcasting. But from 1950 to the early 1970's, there was a continuing decrease in such media cross-ownership and by 1974 the cross-ownership and media concentration ratios were at the lowest point that they had been since the beginning of broadcasting in the 1920's. In January 1975, the FCC barred new cross-ownership of TV stations and newspapers in the same markets (Compaine, 1979); several local TV-newspaper combinations were broken up but some were allowed to remain.

However, companies can own broadcast and newspaper properties in separate markets and here the trend is up. Howard (1983) found that 140 of the 420 TV outlets in the 100 largest markets were newspaper-related at the beginning of 1982; this 33% compares with 28% a decade earlier. Howard attributes this trend to existing media companies adding new properties to their broadcasting holdings, the growth of media companies with holdings in both publishing and broad-casting fields (such as cable TV), and the FCC's tacit sanction of news-paper ownership of broadcast properties in markets where publishers do not engage in the newspaper business.

Concentration vs. Exposure

Another way to look at concentration of media voices is to examine how many different voices or media outlets people are exposed to. The 1,688 daily papers in the U.S. are supplemented by some 7,700 weekly papers and more than 10,000 other periodicals. There also were about 12,000 broadcasting stations in 1985, including 10,511 radio stations and 1,479 TV stations, plus several thousand TV translators that extend the range of stations to remote areas and 6,600 operating cable systems serving some 15,000 communities. More than 97% of U.S. households can receive three or more TV stations and more than 90% receive four or more. Some 80% of all households can receive five or more.

Since 1922 the total number of media outlets (papers, broadcast stations) has increased much faster than the population. In a 1970 survey of 204 metropolitan areas of the country, the largest market was New York City, in which 610 media were available, with 519 of them originating in the market. There were 372 different owners. The smallest market was Glendive, Montana, with 36 media available to the public owned by 30 different owners:

> Considering the United States as a national media market, we have literally hundreds of competitors among newspapers and broadcasters alone, without considering national magazines, newsletters, and the innumerable other news and advertising media that proliferate beyond counting. To call this situation "concentration" is ludicrous in terms of economic analysis...No recognized economist or antitrust authority has

ever suggested that a market with dozens or hundreds of competitors, none of whom has as much as 10% of the market, should be considered "concentrated." The observable fact is that the mass media are daily engaged in vigorous competition for public attention, just as the politicians are engaged in competition for media attention (Loevinger, 1979).

Loevinger (1979) goes on to note Alvin Toffler's (1971) concern that America faces not a concentration of mass media voices but confusion arising from growing fragmentation and diversity.

In summary then, there are more chain owners of media units though the actual concentration of media voices has decreased in this century. We still need to consider what impact existing concentration has on media operations and performance.

Impact of Ownership and Concentration

How does "ownership" actually translate into media performance or content, and how does ownership concentration affect the media? Rather limited empirical evidence helps us answer these questions. Thrift (1977) examined 1,445 editorials in West Coast newspapers and found that they became less aggressive in their editorials once they were purchased by chains. Other studies of the effect of chain ownership or joint operating agreements have found little impact on editorial coverage (Wagenberg and Soderlund, 1976; Romanow and Soderlund, 1978; Browning, Grierson and Howard, 1984; Meyer and Wearden, 1984). Wackman and his colleagues (1975) found evidence that chains are not independent in their political endorsement editorial policies.

Though joint ownership of newspapers and TV stations in the same city is no longer approved, Gormley's (1976) earlier study of such situations found that common ownership tended to restrict the variety of news available to the public and that this was more noticeable in smaller cities. This occurred in part because reporters tend to cover stories that other reporters are covering. Contact between the two media units is necessary for this to occur; cross-ownership increases the potential for such communication by putting them in the same building and encouraging reporters to share carbons of stories.

How is ownership or legal control translated into policy and content? Certainly, intervention by owners in daily activities varies and generally is limited to major decisions or those with important financial implications. However, the potential for ownership interference is illustrated by the "Panax incident." The head of the Panax Corp., a chain of eight dailies, fired two editors who refused to run a shoddy article laced with innuendo and insinuations that President Jimmy Carter had encouraged staff members to sexual promiscuity, among other things. Some of the editors ran the stories on page one as requested but the others found the request that they print such material as front-page news unacceptable. The National News Council censured Panax and its head for "a gross disservice to accepted American journalistic standards." The censorship points out the limits of ownership control since owners are faced with pressure from the public and professional groups.

Reporters and editors learn what the newspaper's policy toward various issues are over time. The longer a staffer's employment by the paper, the better his prediction of that newspaper's policy (Kapoor, 1979). Another example of ownership control is found in the network-owned and operated TV stations, which accept a higher percentage of network programming than do those stations independently owned (Litman, 1978).

The impact of legal ownership is certainly not limited to commercial media. A survey of 125 public broadcast managers found that those who conduct on-air fund-raising were least likely to want to editorialize, apparently out of fear of offending potential contributors (Handberg and Meeske, 1978). Similar actions by management are suggested in a case that involved Stan Freberg who produced a satirical show deriding welfare and budgeting policies for the Public Broadcasting Service in 1980. A creature of the federal government and funded by Washington, PBS did not accept Freberg's program and a censor chopped out the offending segment and cut the program substantially. So legal custody can be implemented not only by chains but public managers as well. Indeed, the fears of government control by many are based on the belief that government sponsorship leads to timidity and the failure to criticize public policies.

If corporate ownership is translated into control over news and other media content, we would expect media coverage to be pro-business, some argue. A British study found much more unfavorable news about labor unions, but linked it to the strong element of conflict in such stories (McQuail, 1975). In the U.S., there is the feeling among business people that journalists are generally liberal rather than conservative and tend to be anti-business (Otwell, 1977). Research does indicate ignorance of business and how it works among both journalists and the public. Kahalas and Carper (1978) hypothesized that people who watch more TV would more likely have negative attitudes toward business, but they found no such relationship. On the other side, journalists worry about the professional loyalty of media chain managers. A *Los Angeles Times* staff writer argues that what distinguishes contemporary newspaper chain executives from their predecessors — men like William Randolph Hearst, Joseph Pulitzer and Col. Robert McCormick — is precisely their indifference to the promotion of a particular political cause or candidate. "Hearst and most other press barons of earlier generations used their newspapers to settle personal vendettas, to win political elections, to preach ideology, to start wars. The contemporary press lord tends to see his paper as a product, not a podium or a pulpit. That generally makes the papers more profitable, less colorful, and in theory at least, more responsible."

Media Organizations
They Come in All Shapes and Sizes

The media institution is composed of a variety of media organizations. Though you're probably most familiar with the national TV networks, we turn our attention first to the more "basic building blocks," TV and radio stations, the newspaper newsroom, and the movie studio. This is where most of the "media work" is accomplished, and we'll show how the structure of an organization tells you much about how it operates.

The Newspaper

Certainly newspapers of different sizes are organized in different ways, but the basic structure is the same in most. There are three major departments—business, mechanical and editorial. The "line chart" in Figure 2 shows that ultimate authority and legal responsibility lie with the publisher and, in large organizations, a board of directors answerable to stockholders. These were the people concentrated on in the last section. But let's look at the bulk of activities that take place below them.

Most news appearing in the paper is provided by staff reporters through the city editor, by national news agencies (AP, UPI) through the wire editor, and by out-of-town correspondents through the state news editor. The sports and social/living styles editors and their various assistants or reporters are sometimes subordinate to the city editor. Editorials are written by the editor and editorial writers. The stories written by reporters are edited by copyreaders and are eventually sent to the composing room. A makeup editor plans where the various stories are to be located in the paper—he makes up the newspaper, determining what pictures and stories go on page one and elsewhere. On some papers the makeup editor is also the managing or news editor. On large papers a board headed by the managing or news editor may make some of these decisions.

As the figure notes, there is a hierarchy in which editors supervise or oversee particular territory. Indeed, with the division of labor in newspapers, and other large organizations, there is the development of "territoriality." Editors-administrators-managers perform two major tasks: coordination of activities, and the resolution of disputes amongst those below. The chart also shows how "influence" may or may not be brought to bear from the outside, or inside. For example, in metro newspaper organizations, advertising and news editorial groups are physically separate and have virtually no contact. If a large advertiser wants to affect news coverage via its perceived advertising leverage, the influence may either be an informal contact outside channels (between the advertising department representative and reporter) or it can follow the organizational chart, in which case actual influence receives the approval or rejection of management. We can look at this process as one of gatekeeping.

In a study of AP managing editors in the U.S. and Canada, it was found that managing editors on larger papers were more involved as managers while those on small papers spent more time on editorial tasks. Most managing editors appeared to have "blank checks" as far as their newsroom role was concerned. About two thirds of the editors' time was spent on activities other than those dealing directly with the production of the day's paper (Trayes, 1978).

A national study of U.S. news journalists by Johnstone and his colleagues (1976) found dissatisfaction among journalists related to personal autonomy. They note that centralization in the news industry inevitably leads to organizational growth that affects the administrative structures. These factors underlie the so-called "reporter-power" movement which surfaced in a number of American news organizations a few years ago. At that time reporters sought more control over their activities and the final editorial product by seeking constraints on involvement by owners and publishers. For example, reporters want to feel free to pursue a story to its logical conclusion even if it embarrasses local elites in business, politics or labor; influential individuals from these and other areas may try to put pressure on media management when they dislike the way they are treated in the media.

Perhaps the most important structural feature of newspaper information-gathering is the "beat system" (Lacy and Matustik, 1983). Imagine that your group was asked to organize itself for reporting all the news in tomorrow's daily paper. If you scattered in all directions without any pattern to your efforts, you'd likely find some duplication and lots of significant events ignored. Newspapers cope with the uncertainty of news gathering by organizing reporters to cover geographic areas or topics. Gaye Tuchman (1978) calls this method of deployment the "news net." The net (or beats) produces daily features for the news organization written by reporters located in such locales as city halls, the police station, or school office. Freelancers are used

Figure 3-2
Example of Newspaper Organization

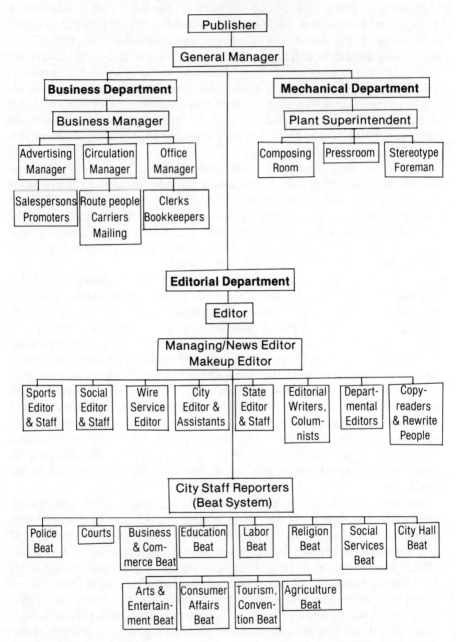

but tenuously. The "net imposes order on the social world" by assuming news will occur at certain places and not at others, thus creating a "news net" rather than a "news blanket." And there is a significant difference between the ability of a blanket and a net. The net today is intended for "big fish," with reporters placed at institutions where stories are expected to be found. The news net assumes: 1) readers are interested in occurrences at specific localities; 2) they are concerned with activities of specific organizations; and 3) they are interested in specific topics. At the national level, the news net concentrates on government offices in Washington, D.C., but here too there are huge gaps. Editors blame reporters and reporters blame editors for various holes in the net of Washington correspondents, including not just such neglected areas as the Agriculture Department or regulatory agencies but also the Pentagon and Congress (Thomas and Boyd, 1984). UPI correspondent Helen Thomas notes that there are fewer than a dozen reporters at the White House all day, though there are large numbers at daily briefings (Kiesel et al., 1978).

Television Stations

There are numerous differences between newspapers and TV stations in their organizational patterns though they also share many similarities. They are similar in that they both "turn out a product" for public consumption, both have sales or business marketing departments, both have technical departments, and so forth. But there are many differences too. The editorial or news department produces most of the locally originated content for papers but news provides only a small percentage of the content of a TV station. Thus, in TV stations you have more directors and managers at the same level as news director, and they also compete for the station's scarce resources. Another difference is the use of technology. Both media organizations increasingly are involved with sophisticated technology, but the technical component itself intrudes more visibly and significantly in the gathering of news and other content for television. When a TV reporter collects information for the news, he needs more than just a pencil and note pad; he is accompanied by a camera crew with its technical and logistical requirements.

A more significant difference between the two is in their staff deployment for collecting news. While newspapers use a beat system that encourages topic or area specialization, TV reporters tend to be generalists. For the most part, TV news reporters are dispatched to cover whatever events or situations need attention. Certainly you have specialists in sports, weather, or soft features, but the news organization itself does not reflect specialization by topic or area generally.

Thus, TV reporters on one story may interview the mayor, leaving immediately aftterwards to cover a house fire, or demonstration at the school board. An example of a TV station organization is found in Figure 3-3.

Figure 3-3
TV Station Organizational Chart

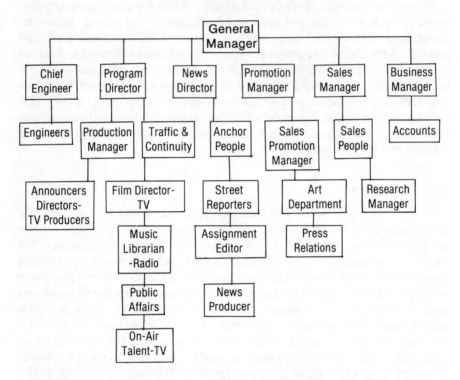

News is only one component of TV, so we need to look at the organization of entertainment too. A TV production team includes executive producers, the producer, director, story editor, and assistant director. The executive producers administer a producing company and are responsible for selling an idea to the network, haggling over the license fee, mediating union quarrels on the set, and coordinating the activities of the producer. The producer is assigned to each series by the studio and is answerable to the executive producer. The producer is responsible for a particular series and he guarantees continuity of characterization, setting, and plot. The director ordinarily is hired on a one-time basis and is a free-lance artist. A director analyzes the script for serious production problems, suggests actors to the producer, contributes to re-writing the script when necessary, and controls the actual filming. The story editor re-writes the original script to accommodate changes in character or locale dictated by the producer, increased or decreased budgets or network time periods, or errors in dramatic construction. He may author an entirely new script based on the writer's title or screen treatment. The assistant director is the lowest in the hierarchy of the production scheme. His duties involve blocking out the sequence of filming, arranging for extras and minor characters, directing background action, and making up cast-calls for shooting.

How does the structure of the TV station and production team affect the final product? Although there are assorted ways of looking at what is a complex process, one of the most interesting analogies is provided by Bantz and his associates (1980). They argue that the local TV news organization is best described as a factory in which the 6 p.m. newscast is churned out through a five-step process that begins with story ideation and moves through task assignment, gathering and structuring materials, assembly and presentation (see Figure 3-4). The sequence reflects an assembly-line approach which limits individual involvement in the organization and its product. The model also notes that the specialization, routinization and mechanization of TV news-work has four observable consequences: inflexibility, lack of personal investment in the product, evaluation of newswork in terms of pro-ductivity, and a mismatch between newsworkers' expectations and the reality of the news factory. "While the popular conceptions of tele-vision news usually encompass some image of the glamorous on-the-air news personality, television has an underlying structure little different

Figure 3-4
The News Factory Model

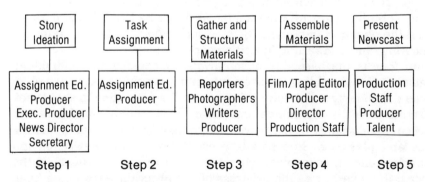

Source: Charles R. Bantz, Suzanne McCorkle and Roberta C. Baade, "The News Factory," *Communication Research* (January, 1980) 7(1): 53.

from any other organization that markets a product," Bantz and his colleagues note.

Five factors have tended to encourage routinization of newswork at media organizations: 1) the nature of news staffs—high mobility and specialization following growth in size; 2) technolgocial developments —portable video equipment and microwave transmission, the latter bringing live reporting into reality; 3) the impact of news consultants; 4) considerations of profit—news no longer loses money but makes considerable profit and thus rates strong management interest and 5) constraints on the organization's product where technical uniformity, visual sophistication, ease of understanding, fast pace and people-oriented stories produced in a minimum of time are emphasized under the demands of profit, consultants, producers, and technology.

The factory model divides tasks into chunks or pieces for different reasons than a typical assembly line. The size of the piece is related to the skill of the worker rather than the amount of time required to perform the task. Thus, an educated, experienced reporter has a larger chunk of the process than does a film editor.

The first step in the assembly line is producing story ideas and it involves two related activities: a) individual newsworkers and especially the assignment editor assess information flowing into the newsroom from various sources such as PR releases, other media, phone calls, etc.; and b) story ideas are examined during the daily story meeting of the assignment person, news director, early evening producer and executive producer. The story meeting functions as a meeting of management and supervisors to approve the day's work schedule, while narrowing the range of news inputs by committing the bulk of reporters' time.

Step two is task assignment by the assignment editor, followed by step three, gathering and structuring materials. At its simplest this involves rewriting a wire story but more often involves five related tasks: 1) obtaining any information the assigner had; 2) talking to someone on the phone or in person; 3) going somewhere to gather material; 4) shooting film or tape, and 5) writing copy.

Step four is the assembly of materials by constructing individual segments and assembling the segments into a newscast. Assembly of a segment is done by a film/tape editor who edits according to shot sheet instructions so it's a technical operation. The producer and director oversee the assembly of the newscast, going over the script, adjusting times and planning. Step five is presentation of the newscast, the producer remaining involved with the news product throughout the telecast and overseeing the progress of the program—watching time, dropping stories if necessary, informing the newscasters of any new information, etc.

Our diagrams of organizations so far seem to describe those who argue that newspapers, network TV and recording are best characterized as struggling political coalitions. Although public opinion polls recently have shown a concern over the power of commercial TV, this power is not wielded by a few people, owners or creative professionals. TV, for example, does not necessarily reflect the tastes and ideology of either the creators or those who control the channels of communication but represents a negotiated struggle between a number of participants that include: networks, the advertisers, the government — Congress and the FCC, the Courts and Justice Department, social critics and citizen groups, and program suppliers. One observer concludes that the prospect for more creative control at the inception level remains "dismal" because the content of drama depends on social and political conditions that exist outside the creative process. Figure 3-5 outlines some of these participants.

The struggle over TV content has not been between the audience, which may be satisfied with dramatic content, and the creators, but among elites who value access for both economic and social reasons. Herbert Gans (1974) notes that pluralistic societies have an ongoing struggle between "diverse groups and aggregates over the allocation of resources which is not limited to strictly economic and political issues but also extends to cultural issues." One struggle centers on control of TV drama.

Investigators have tried to explain popular drama as either a reflection of the creators' personalities or as a reflection of the economic values held by those controlling the communication channels. Both approaches provide only partial explanations of the complexities of the situation. Shanks (1976) notes that everyone in the TV networks is in the Program Department in his heart. "Wake the cleaning lady at 7 a.m. and she will tell you what to put in the schedule at 8 p.m. Saturday night or who to cast in the leads in a made-for-TV movie." Every TV show is at least indirectly affected by the planning, research, sales, and affiliates areas of a network — even though direct contact may not be there. Each network has several layers of bureaucracy; deal-making in TV is so complicated that series often go on and off the air before formal contracts are even signed. There are oral agreements and handshakes following considerable negotiation. A vice president of movies for TV at Columbia estimated that a fourth of all TV-movie deals fall through — not because of disagreements over creative content but over differences between lawyers for both sides. Of 100 presentations to a network, 30 pilot scripts are commissioned and 10 get orders with one series ending up on the air, according to one study.

Most American commercial TV drama is produced by a few major Hollywood production houses under contract to one of the major TV

Figure 3-5

Schematic Representation of the Mass Media as a Social System

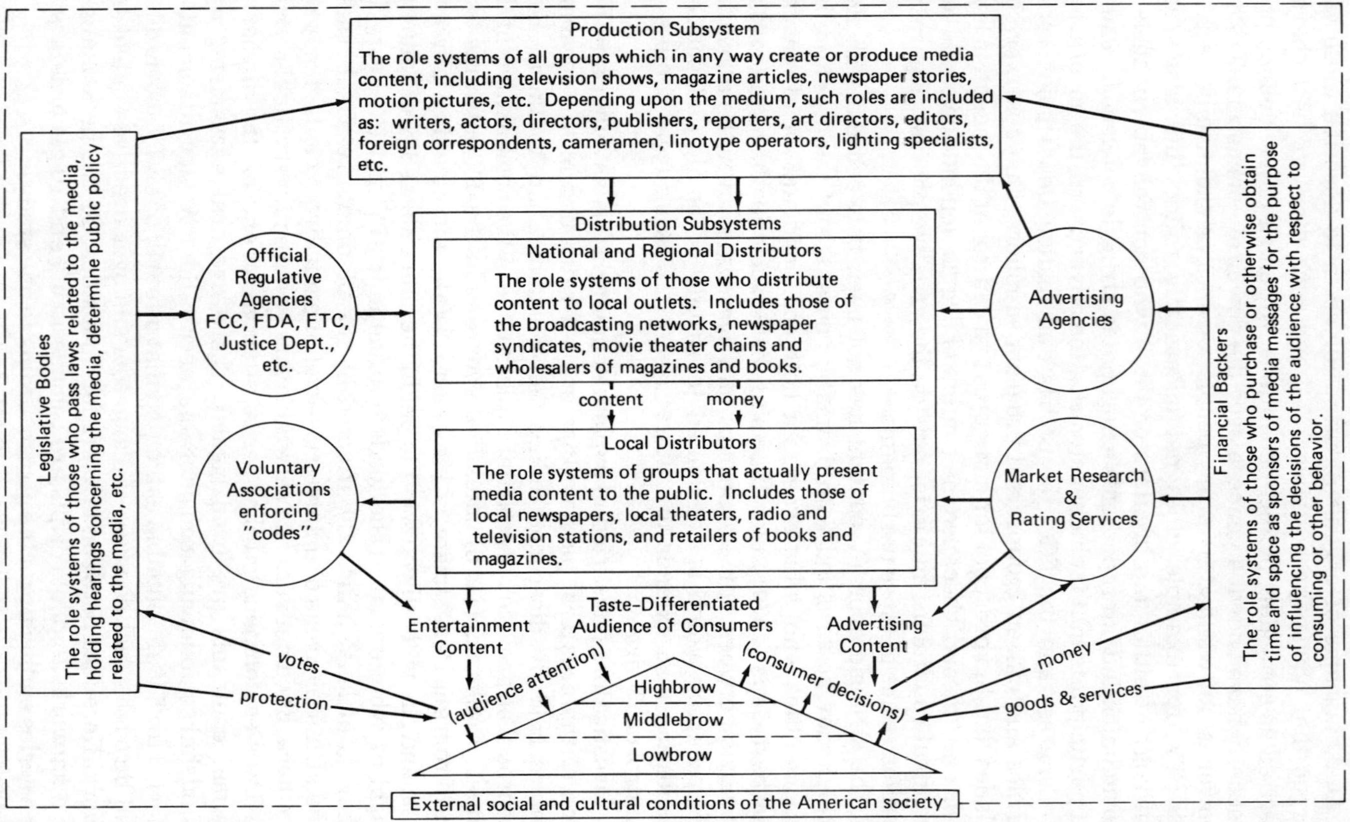

Production Subsystem
The role systems of all groups which in any way create or produce media content, including television shows, magazine articles, newspaper stories, motion pictures, etc. Depending upon the medium, such roles are included as: writers, actors, directors, publishers, reporters, art directors, editors, foreign correspondents, cameramen, linotype operators, lighting specialists, etc.
Legislative Bodies
The role systems of those who pass laws related to the media, holding hearings concerning the media, determine public policy related to the media, etc.
Official Regulative Agencies FCC, FDA, FTC, Justice Dept., etc.
Voluntary Associations enforcing "codes"
Distribution Subsystems
National and Regional Distributors
The role systems of those who distribute content to local outlets. Includes those of the broadcasting networks, newspaper syndicates, movie theater chains and wholesalers of magazines and books.
content
money
Local Distributors
The role systems of groups that actually present media content to the public. Includes those of local newspapers, local theaters, radio and television stations, and retailers of books and magazines.
Advertising Agencies
Market Research & Rating Services
Financial Backers
The role systems of those who purchase or otherwise obtain time and space as sponsors of media messages for the purpose of influencing the decisions of the audience with respect to consuming or other behavior.
Entertainment Content
Taste-Differentiated Audience of Consumers
Advertising Content
(audience attention)
(consumer decisions)
Highbrow
Middlebrow
Lowbrow
votes
protection
money
goods & services
External social and cultural conditions of the American society

Source: From *Theories of Mass Communication* by Melvin L. DeFleur and Sandra Ball-Rokeach.

networks. In 1960 control shifted from the advertisers, program, producers, and stations to the networks. Previously, advertisers and entrepreneurs made pilot films for series sold to individual agencies which then purchased TV time. One producer interviewed in 1967 complained that he had only three potential buyers for his productions while in the early days of TV there had been 30 or 40 possible buyers. By the mid-1960's, the networks had secured control of dramatic TV films. Since then relatively little drama has been made without approval and financing from the major networks. Because of a 1972 antitrust action against ABC, CBS, and NBC's alleged monopoly practices, Hollywood program suppliers have regained some power vis-a-vis the networks.

Networks claim that they are as dependent on the program suppliers as the suppliers are on them. With mutual dependency, each party blames the other for program content when criticism arises.

Many different kinds of citizen and pressure groups and even governmental agencies try to gain access to TV to present their particular points of view. Pressures on creative people and the networks are constant. Those concerned with TV violence have been the most active in pressuring for change in TV drama. Groups concerned with the portrayal of women and minorities from 1970 to the present also have been making a concentrated effort to obtain the attention of the networks, Congress and the FCC.

Within all organizations, decision problems are divided into smaller subproblems that are the duties of specialized decision makers. For example, a TV newscast is divided into shooting, film editing, copy writing, graphics creation, etc. This work is supervised and coordinated by higher-level gatekeepers. In this process individuals are organized into interest groups called subcoalitions. These often form along departmental lines as individuals and groups within the coalition make demands exacted as the price for joining or remaining in the coalition. Some of these demands will conflict. Earlier we noted the "territoriality" within newspaper editorial departments. A central problem in organizational theory is that the goals of individuals and groups within the system may conflict. In classical theory the solution to the problem of goal conflict is subordination—individuals giving up their individual goals and pursuing those of the organization. In the view of organizations as political coalitions, people are seen more as participants in the process of compromising rather than simply subordinating their desires for the assumed greater goal of profit or revenue maximization. However, this coalition model seems to apply equally as well to nonprofit systems as to commercial concerns. An analysis of the British Broadcasting Corporation showed that dispute over the goals of the organization corresponded to a struggle among subcoalitions of journalists vs. entertainment (Dimmick, 1979).

The Media People
Their Roles, Routines, Characteristics

Who are those people in the media and what are they doing? In this section we'll look at characteristics of the people that work in media organizations, their role perceptions and the patterns of behavior that make up their working days. One of the major roles is that of journalist and two major concepts will crop up in our discussion: objectivity and news. The first is the subject of much controversy; it demonstrates differences in how journalists and others perceive their roles. The second concept, "news," may seem elementary, but ask several of your friends to define it and you'll likely come up with little more than a list of examples.

The people and their roles clearly interact with the media organizations of which they're a part. Each individual has a personality that makes him or her unique. These personalities do not simply merge with the organizations, as the last section on coalitions demonstrated. New journalists, script writers, camera people, etc. are "socialized" into their roles in professions and organizations (see, for example, Burgoon et al., 1984). Part of this process occurs through informal settings over a beer after work while another part is institutionalized in schools or training sessions. Relationships with other people are among the most important things to be learned in the socialization process. For journalists it is the relationship with news sources that is so important.

Media Careers

People in the media are a diverse lot. Furthermore, those in news organizations are not mirror images of those on the technical side or in such fields as public relations or specialized media. And there is a pecking order within mass media. National networks and wire services, large city newspapers, major film producers all fall into the elite category while freelancers and media in smaller towns generally are less prestigious.

What do we know about "media people"? A national survey of more than 150,000 editors and reporters in the U.S. was conducted by Johnstone, Slawski and Bowman in 1971. Tables 3-3 and 3-4 summarize their findings. As noted, news journalists are concentrated in the two major centers of news — Washington, D.C. and New York City. There are more journalists in larger cities and they are generally younger than the U.S. civilian labor force, a fifth in the 25-29 age group. Only about 20% of journalists are female, compared to about a third of the labor force age 20 or older at the time of the survey. In another study, Ogan (1983) found that the percentage of women in newspaper management changed little from 1977 to 1982. Equal opportunity laws do seem to have had an impact in broadcasting, however, where the proportion of women has been rising more rapidly (Harwood, 1984). Wide differences between men and women's salaries have been noted in a variety of media areas including public relations, authors, advertising, editors and reporters, photographers and radio and TV announcers. A recent effort to update the Johnstone et al. study shows a dramatic increase in the percentage of women in broadcasting (26% in radio, 43% in TV) but no gains for Blacks or Hispanics (Weaver, Drew, and Wilhoit, 1985).

Table 3-3
Distribution of Media People

Number of Employees in Mass Media Industries in the U.S. (1976)

Book Industry	87,800	Newspapers	443,800 (1984)
Motion Pictures	218,000 (1983)	Radio, TV	157,400
Periodicals	69,900		

Index of Employment in Media Industries in U.S. (1976)   [1958 = 100]

Book Industry	134	Newspapers	122
Motion Pictures	102	Radio, TV	181
Periodicals	102		

Number of Employees in Weekly Newspapers, 1972:   65,100

Number of Editorial Employees in News Media, 1971:   69,500

daily newspapers	38,000	radio only	7,000
weekly papers	11,500	radio-TV	7,000
news magazines	1,900	wire services	3,300

Number of Radio, TV Network and Station Employees, 1976: 151,100

radio networks	900	all radio	86,300
AM and AM-FM		TV networks	13,800
stations	70,800	all TV stations	51,000
FM only stations	14,600	total TV employees	64,800

Number of members of:

Screen Actors Guild (SAG), 1976   32,434
American Federation of TV and Radio Artists (AFTRA), 1976   29,672

Number of employees in:

cable TV systems, 1974:	24,300
motion picture industry, 1975:	154,000
book publishing industry, 1975:	54,000

recording industry—
    manufacturing employees (1975):   17,800
    music stores (1972):   37,363

Occupational Distribution of Journalism Graduates in U.S. (1975):

Daily newspapers	16.8%	Public Relations	10.9%
Weekly newspapers	6.4%	Advertising	3.7%
Wire services	.9%	Magazines	3.3%
Television	4.7%	Radio	6.0%
Graduate School	6.4%	Teaching	3.7%
Other fields	24.0%	Traveling, etc.	7.7%

Geographic Distribution:

Northeast	36.3%	South	24.7%
North Central	22.7%	West	16.3%

Table 3-4

Characteristics of U.S. News Journalists

Age & Sex: Male, 79.7% ½ Female, 20.3%

Under 20	.7%	35-39	11.7%	55-59	7.0%
20-24	11.3%	40-44	10.5%	60-64	4.3%
25-29	21.1%	45-49	10.6%	65-69	2.0%
30-34	12.2%	50-54	8.2%	70 and older	.3%

Percentage of Women in News Media:

Radio	4.8%	Daily papers	22.4%	News magazines	30.4%
Television	10.7%	Weekly papers	27.1%	Wire services	13.0%

Ethnic Origins of Journalists:

	Percent Journalists	Percent U.S.		Percent Journalists	Percent U.S.
Anglo-Saxon	39 %	23.8%	Scandinavian	5 %	4.4%
German	17.5%	16.8%	Irish	13.6%	10.4%
French	4 %	1.5%	Black	3.9%	14.9%
Jewish	3.3%	2.6%	Italian	3.2%	4.1%
Polish	1.4%	2.1%	Other	9.1%	19.3%

Education of Journalists:

Some high school	1.8%	College graduate	39.6%
High school graduate	12.2%	Some graduate training	10.5%
Some college	27.9%	Graduate degree	8.1%

Where Journalists Start — First Jobs:

Television	5.2%	Weekly papers	14.1%
Daily papers	58.2%	Radio	15.5%
Wire services	4.6%	News magazines	2.3%

Career Paths Followed Most Frequently:

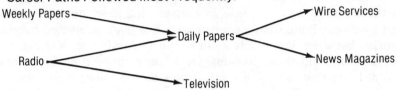

Membership of Journalists in Professional Associations:

45.3% belong to one or more journalism associations
15.7% belong to Greek-letter professional associations (e.g., Sigma Delta Chi)

Job Satisfaction among Journalists:

Very satisfied	48.5%	Fairly satisfied	38.6%
Somewhat dissatisfied	11.7%	Very dissatisfied	1.2%

Sources: Johnstone et al, 1976 and Gertner, 1985.

Anglo-Saxons are over-represented relative to the general population (39% vs. 24%) in the Johnstone et al. study, as are several other groups. Blacks are under represented (4% vs. 15%). More recently, observers have noted that the number of "lily-white newspapers" is declining, but the recent achievements at integrating the newspaper business may be threatened. The number of minority newspaper journalists has risen from 400 in 1968 to 1,700 in 1979, representing 4% of all professionals in the business. The number of minority journalism students also has grown, but two-thirds of the nation's dailies still have not hired a single minority news professional.

Minority journalists are concentrated on a small number of newspapers, with 38% employed by only 34 dailies. "There is a class issue as well as a race issue at work here, particularly at the more prestigious newspapers," Kotz (1979) notes. "Blacks and whites admitted to the newsroom tend to be those from prominent universities and those who appear to conform most closely to white middle-class standards." The 1978 survey reported that while twice as many minority students were enrolled in journalism schools as in 1972, they still were only 4.1% of all journalism degree candidates, and special programs are being cut back. If a study of major media markets in California is a guide, the percentage of minorities in both TV and newspaper newsrooms rose from 1979 to 1984; the percentage was higher in TV (Guimary, 1984).

Returning to our national survey of news people, we found younger journalists tended to have more education than older ones. Education was highest among those working for news magazines, followed by wire services and daily newspapers. Journalism and communication were the major areas of study in college, followed by English and creative writing. Education for journalists has been subjected to cross pressures between those advocating more training in writing and practical skills and those arguing for a more diverse or theoretical program. In another study of news broadcasters, news directors and editors in Ohio in 1978, Fisher (1978) found that 92% supported college preparation for work in broadcasting; half favored a major in journalism and a few less preferred a general liberal arts program. A national mail survey of commercial radio station managers found that 60% thought a radio newsperson should have college journalism training while 10% disagreed and the rest were neutral (Abel and Jacobs, (1975). Nearly 70% agreed that college campus radio experience was valuable for potential on-air personnel, while three quarters believed that there was no substitute for previous commercial radio experience and 70% felt a disc jockey's education was important even if he spoke well. The position of formal education was less important in British journalism training, by comparison. There the training was similar to the craft apprenticeship agreements employed by unions and industry in the U.S.

What are the career paths of journalists? Almost 81% of those graduating with journalism B.A.'s began in the news media. Daily newspapers were the first jobs of 58% of all those in the media, followed by radio (15.5%) and weekly papers (14%). The most frequent paths of job mobility are from weeklies and radio to dailies, from radio to TV and from daily papers to wire services and news magazines. There is relatively little movement between daily papers and television. The geographic flow of journalists within the U.S. has been toward the Northeast and its large population centers.

Once in the profession, relatively few journalists belong to professional associations (35%), and there were more social contacts with fellow journalists among TV and broadcasting than in print. Almost half of the journalists surveyed said they were very satisfied with their job, a figure comparable to the satisfaction of the labor force at large.

There is a generally-accepted notion that American daily papers are published by businessmen whose preferences for conservative and Republican policies are expressed in the editorial pages. Parsons' (1976) survey of almost 200 editors of large daily newspapers compared them with the electorate's partisanship. He found great over-representation among independents; 65% of the editors surveyed classified themselves as independents while only 35% of the electorate was in that classification. Democrats also were underrepresented: 21% vs. 41%. However, there was a tendency for editors who were Democrats to be more liberal and those who were Republicans to be more conservative. A recent national study of newspaper editors and the general public found substantially stronger support for capitalism and the American economic system among editors than found in the general public although support there was also very strong (Peterson et al., 1984).

Public relations is another major area attracting media people. Though we have no comparable national survey for describing promotional representatives, we have some statewide surveys. One survey of daily journalists and PR practitioners found the latter were more educated, a bit older, and better paid (Nayman, McKee, and Lattimore, 1977). Job appeal was given as the major reason for entering public relations by about 59% of those responding, while 20% said they entered because of salary and 21% because of the opportunity of advancement. Almost 90% considered public relations nearly or fully professionalized, and the things which were rated as most important included: having the opportunity for originality and initiative, having an influence on important decisions, freedom from continual, close supervision of their work, and improving their professional competence.

Professionalism and Role Perception

The novice reporter for your county weekly and a network TV anchor may seem to have little in common. One arrives on foot, the other in a limousine. They certainly have different audiences. But both may share the same role perceptions when they confront a public official with probing questions about corruption in office. Both are members of the journalistic profession which is an occupation applying systematic knowledge to preserve or extend some of the society's basic values. Both are expected to have specialized knowledge, skills and long-term higher learning. But knowledge and information-handling professions are subject to considerable controversy today. Critics from left and right, business and politics, academia and the general public question what roles journalists should attempt to play. In some respects, this controversy is an extension of that between different perspectives and interest groups cited earlier. However, despite the state of flux, there are areas of consensus.

First, what do we mean by role? A role refers to the rights and obligations, or expected behavior, of a person with a given status or rank in a group. In our case, we're interested in the rights and expected behaviors of people whose group is the journalistic profession or news organization and whose status is that of an information gatherer or processor. Our description ascribes the role in terms of function or use. This is where our controversy begins. Some focus on the journalists' uses or purposes (functions) for "society," others the uses for the organization. As our last section noted, there are conflicting obligations in all organizations. Journalists in large organizations may find their roles defined differently depending on which coalitions they belong to. And the "functions" or uses journalists perform for society could be many and varied, depending on who's making the list. In either case, the journalist is seen as being tied to the organization or to society, and this severely limits journalists' perceptions of autonomy. The key word is obligations.

How do journalists see their role? In the Johnstone national study, journalists were asked to rate the importance of a series of functions. At the top of the list was the investigation of claims and statements made by the government followed by providing analysis and interpretation of complex problems, getting information to the public quickly, discussing national policy while it's being developed, and staying away from stories whose factual content cannot be verified. The first item underlines the significance American journalists attribute to what is usually called their "watchdog function." In Great Britain, a survey showed that 57% of British journalists felt their role in society was that of an informant, while about a quarter felt their job was to entertain and a fifth to mediate between individuals and social institutions. Here we see agreement on what might be called a government watchdog function and an informant, gatekeeper function. This latter role as a gatekeeper that processes a variety of different types of information is often subdivided by observers into generalist and specialist. Culbertson (1978) notes that the press needs both specialists and generalists to act as an independent watchdog of society. "The specialist's knowledge of rules of evidence and the implications of data can aid sensitivity. The generalist's insistence on clarity can help understandability." Generalists apparently are preferred because they can write in lay language, express themselves briefly and avoid cooptation by the technical specialities which they must cover. Culbertson also notes that specialized journalists are harder to control in some cases because they may know more about stories than do their bosses. He says generalists and specialists must work within the same media institutions.

The "watchdog function" itself is often elaborated into subroles.

Sigal (1973) identifies several roles that journalists play which are essentially definitions of the relationship between journalists and the government. One is that of neutral observer trying to avoid involvement and not taking sides in disputes. Second is "participant" — either as an insider connected with government sources and influencing policy by reporting news, or as an outsider by active involvement, making news as well as reporting it (the ideolog is a variant here). Third is the "good citizen," who tries to weigh personal interests, the paper's interests, readers' interests, the national interest, and various sources' interests in deciding how to write and whether to publish a story. Fourth is the "adversary of the government," a long-established role that includes "gadflies" who persist for years as well as temporary adversarial relations more confined to specific topics or times. Two other roles, which are not limited to the journalist-government relationship, are the roles of "journalist as novelist" and the "precision journalist." The first uses the techniques of the writers of fiction to report on real events while the latter employs the information-gathering methods of the social scientist.

This watchdog function is not limited to Great Britain or the United States, although it is practically restricted to the democracies. In Holland, a critic argues that the main thrust of the muckraking journalist should be in awakening a pervasive distrust among the populace, one which sharpens people's perception of social reality.

But the journalistic role is not defined only in terms of functions performed for society but also includes those relating to organizations. Kumar (1975) notes that the British Broadcasting Company explicitly rejected the informality and personality in American broadcasting, emphasizing instead a "collective personality." Thus, the role of journalists is constrained by the immediate organization. The importance of the organization varies by role. A Colorado survey of public relations people and journalists showed journalists resigned themselves more to policy decisions in their organizations being handled by supervisory personnel while public relations people placed heavy emphasis on having an influence on important decisions within the organization (66% vs. 28%). The journalists were somewhat more dissatisfied than were the public relations people. Theoretically, the free-lance journalist who operates independently of any particular bureaucratic organization acts "solely" in his self interest (Nayman, McKee and Lattimore, 1977). A recent survey of newspaper journalists found self-direction and independence one of the top five criteria for a new job (Barrett, 1984). Other criteria were: personal interest and fulfillment, good salary, and opportunity to advance.

The potential for role conflict is a dilemma journalists and other media people face. Elliott (1977) notes, for example, the conflict

between demands of art and demands of journalists facing
professional goals as well as organizational struggles to survive. Those
too may end up as struggles between commerce (or survival, in the case
of governmental or nonprofit organizations) and professional
standards. These role conflicts often surface as dilemmas involving
distinctions between: high and low culture, professional or craft
standards and commercial judgment, self regulation and close bureaucratic control of the work situation, self motivation and financial
inducement, self-monitoring and serving an audience. The Glasgow
Media Group (1976), highly critical of TV news in Britain, argues that
TV news is patterned after the dictates of journalism rather than of
film "logic," a recognition of the influence of professional journalistic
roles across media. A Canadian, Laliberte (1976), notes that the
journalist is a specialized professional with neither more nor less
freedom than other professionals. He also argues that the more
internal pluralism and professional autonomy there appears to be in
the press, the more likely it is to be accompanied by conformity to the
prevailing social ideology. Rothenbuhler (1985) found that personnel in
the popular music industry were more sensitive to national industry-
wide criteria than they were to local contingencies. Thus,
professionals often work more for the respect of their colleagues than
for their audiences.

The journalist's role in the U.S. has changed through the years. Gaye
Tuchman (1978) argues that the changes are intertwined with the
growth of modern capitalism. The rise of the popular press and the
distribution of information to everyone challenged the right of the
mercantile elite to continue its political control. Thus, journalists perceived the public as a group to be protected as opposed to a group of
peers. Professional journalists tended to accept the idea that professionals are more qualified than their audience to determine the
audiences' own interests and needs. After World War I, professionals
argued that their impartial methods guaranteed a fair assessment of
occurrences, and, thus, guaranteed free speech.

How is this "professionalism" of journalists measured? An instrument developed by McLeod and Hawley (1964) has been used to show
that professional journalists generally are more concerned with
ethical standards, are more educated, are more critical of their own
employer, are more independent on the job, are less likely to take a non-
journalism job, and are less concerned with money and prestige. Using
a field survey of six TV markets in Wisconsin, one team of researchers
found that high professionals performed better than did the low professionals but those in the medium professional category performed
almost as well as those in the top category. High professionals also
were less likely than others to be willing to leave TV news for a higher

paying job. News directors were found to be slightly more professional than their staffs. High professionals made more money than low professionals, though there was little difference in education or age (Idsvoog and Hoyt, 1977). Values held by journalists may be universal in modern western democracies, Henningham (1984) suggests. He found that U.S. and Australian broadcast journalists held similar professional values as measured by the McLeod and Hawley instrument.

The social responsibility philosophy promotes service to society as the primary journalistic duty, while press philosopher John Merrill (1974) argues for an autonomous, individualistic inner-directed model of the professional journalist. A study of 35 daily newspaper journalists' value structures identified two types, an "inner-directed" high professional that emphasizes ambitions, independence and inner harmony, and an "outer-directed" one emphasizing an orderly society and helping others (Schwartz, 1978). The researcher suggests there may be a connection between professional orientation and journalistic performance which makes inner-directed high professionals more desirable because they have individual, managerial orientations, stress personal competence and personal satisfaction. Culbertson (1983) studied 256 varied news personnel from 17 papers and concluded that newspaper journalists could be characterized as falling into three distinct clusters which are consistent with the Johnstone et al. (1976) study and other research: traditionalists, interpreters and activists. The traditionalists emphasize local and spot news and downgrade interpretative and national-international material. Interpreters were somewhat inclined to downgrade local news and to upgrade national material. By contrast, activists were more cause-oriented and emphasized international copy. The groups held values that matched the descriptive labels.

News and News Values

"No news is good news," "All the news that's fit to print," "That's news to me." We have a plethora of cliches, slogans and folk wisdom dealing with "news," but seldom do we do a very good job of actually defining what we mean by news. In the last section we suspended judgment on defining news though we noted the importance of news and information in identifying the journalistic role. Regardless of the professional role assumed by the journalist, we have to solve the problem of deciding what is news.

News is the consequence of the human desire to know the state of the surrounding social and physical environment. News in general existed long before there was any institution—such as the mass media—for disseminating it. In the fifth century B.C., Sophocles wrote, "No man delights in the bearer of bad news." News is a valuable commodity of social exchange and the urgent need for news arises in all social organizations, from the family to complex bureaucracies. Recent information may be essential for maintaining social cohesion. Conflict or cooperation between groups may depend on news of the attitudes and behavior of interacting groups.

All news has some "basis in reality." In other words, news has some reference to real life, but that real life won't stand still. Even if we didn't disagree on how to look at it, we would have to decide on where to slice it up. In one sense the raw material of news is limitless, unpredictable and infinitely variable. Gaye Tuchman (1978) draws on her observational experience to look at how organizational routines make "news." She starts with the "glut of occurrences," or everyday happenings, which journalists recognize as news events by applying various criteria. Thus, Tuchman assumes that this stream of life consists of occurrences. Assuming that life consists of "occurrences doesn't help us get from "reality" to "news," however. Some people, like Altschull (1974), argue that news is a process like communication. News is what appears in a newspaper and a newspaper is something that contains news. Labeling news a process like communication simply begs the issue and attempts to ignore defining it by equating it with reporting (information-gathering process) or communication itself.

Efforts to define news often tend to dissolve into lists of events. Perhaps the best-known definition describes what is alleged to be an unmistakable news event: "When a dog bites a man, that is not news, but when a man bites a dog, that's news." If you made a list of "occurrences" that make the news, this novel situation might be on the list somewhere. List-making is a useful beginning in our attempt to move from "reality," or "occurrences" to "news." In the fast-paced routine of reporting, the journalist looks for various criteria in deciding if "occurrences" merit the title of "news." These characteristics are dimensions linking events and situations to members of the audience. The more characteristics contained in a single occurrence, the stronger the connection with your audience. Following is a list of such characteristics, though it certainly is not an exhaustive one. It is easy to find examples of specific stories in the news right now that contain these characteristics:

1. Timeliness and Proximity—both serviceable in measuring qualifications of the news; for example, a distant two-car accident with four dead is not news but the same accident in your home town is news to you. In foreign news, the rule of prox-

imity is applied: 10,000 deaths in Nepal equals 100 deaths in Europe equals 10 deaths in a distant state equals 1 death in your home town. And we could reverse the order for someone living in Nepal. (Luttbeg, 1983; Shapiro and Williams, 1984; Logan and Garrison, 1983).

2. Progress and Disaster—triumph and defeat, new inventions, natural disasters, rapid changes.

3. Eminence and prominence—big names make big news, even when what they do is trivial at times.

4. Conflict—most conflicts are newsworthy, especially public ones, but size and importance of people also are factors. (See Stone and Grusin, 1984, on TV as the bearer of bad news)

5. Novelty—the old adage about the "man biting dog" fits here, along with coincidences, unusual habits, novel ways of making a living, superstitions, etc.

6. Consequences—effects of government actions, inflation, expected results of other occurrences.

7. Human interest—here fall many stories with none of the above characteristics, but which are often viewed as having human interest because they affect people emotionally, striking old chords, etc., for example, the blind helping the blind.

Which characteristics are more important to you personally? Some of you may note changes that have occurred through the years. Recently, for example, there has been greater interest in "people" and the characteristic of prominence has taken on greater significance. There are also differences between the media. Utilizing its advantage of speed, radio emphasizes timeliness through its 5-minute newscasts every half hour or so. The list of characteristics above must be supplemented by a second list. This one does not contain characteristics that promote occurrences on their own merits but that contribute when combined with the characteristics in the first list:

frequency—the more similar the event's frequency is to the media, the more likely it will be reported; intensity of the event.

ambiguity—the less ambiguous the event, the more likely it will be noticed.

meaningful—based on cultural proximity (familiarity), and relevance (to audience).

consonance—this links expectations to the event; if a person predicts something will happen, he will more easily accept it; and, if one wants an event to occur, the same applies.

unexpectedness — the unexpected or rare make good news.

continuity — once an event is news, it will continue even if its intensity decreases.

composition — if an incoming story contrasts with other stories incoming, it more likely will be selected for balance.

elite countries — events concerning elite nations get more attention.

personal terms — events that can be seen in personal terms or the results of individual actions are more likely to become news.

negative consequences — the more negative its consequences, the more probable an event becomes news.

Both of our lists began with notions of time. And "time" is probably the one thing we would all use to distinguish which occurrences are news and which aren't. But the idea of time is hardly a simple one, as Roshco (1975) notes. For an item of information to be timely requires the conjunction of three things: recency, immediacy and currency. Recency, or recent disclosure, refers to the fact that "it was just learned" rather than "it just occurred." An example is the Dead Sea Scrolls which made news 2 millennia after they were written because they had just been discovered. And in 1985, news emerged when China disclosed 1,000 Muslims were killed in a 1975 rebellion kept secret from foreigners until the announcement. Immediacy depends on the interplay of communication technology and institutional practices of the media. It refers to "publication with minimal delay." For all-news radio, delay is much shorter than it is for newspapers. "In times past, when a single messenger might be the sole news medium for a report affecting the entire nation, immediacy was a matter of the time required for the courier to convey his message. In our age of multiple news media, much of the news is gathered by open exchanges between a news source and assembled reporters, so the immediacy with which news is reported depends upon the interplay between communication technology and the institutional practices of the media.

Currency refers to whether the information is relevant to present concerns. News is not an absolute; currency is as relative as the other aspects of timeliness. When editors and reporters exercise "news judgment" in assessing the "news value" of a report, they are applying their criteria of currency to the available items of recent information from which news is selected, constructed.

Immediacy links recent events and the media reporting them while currency links these events to segments of the public. Recency makes an item of information into an item of news; currency, which is based on audience interest, gives the news item its news value. So news as timely information implies the existence and interaction of a news source, a news medium and a news audience. A British observer notes that the time concepts employed by news people in the production of news are central to their occupation. Broadcasters emphasize events that occur within a given day and highly value those occurring within the most recent few hours while daily newspaper journalists deal with material that appears as "yesterday's news." Language also features the notion of immediacy; stories contain such words as upheaval, suddenness, unpredictability, etc. News stories which are still changing and unfolding are talked of as "breaking" stories. The general public and journalists tend to agree that one of the most important functions of newspapers is to provide a thorough and *timely* account of significant events, according to a national survey (Burgoon, Bernstein, and Burgoon, 1983). Journalists in many countries find it difficult to acquire knowledge about their publics (Donsbach, 1983), but a study of TV broadcast journalists in San Diego found they were quite successful in predicting public interests across a range of topics that included issues (e.g., economy, city council, education), unexpected events (e.g., robberies, fires), the weather and sports (Wulfemeyer, 1984).

So timely occurrences with particular characteristics are candidates for your daily news. But journalists, like other people, always have too much work to do and to cope they attempt to control the flow and amount of work to be done. In doing this, journalists utilize a number of additional definitions of news as short cuts. Called on to give accounts of diverse, unexpected events such as disasters on a routine basis, journalists classify events as hard vs. soft news, spot vs. developing news, and continuing news. Hard news refers to concrete, public events where reporters can report significant facts about topics of interest and consequence to their audience. Soft news refers to features which are generally less timely, often less concrete, and usually not immediately important to media consumers. Spot news refers to one-shot events while developing news refers to stories where facts are still emerging and the story is not complete. Continuing news refers to series of stories on the same subject based on events occurring over time. These definitions decrease the variability of events as raw material, but they are difficult to apply consistently over time.

It is this application of definitions that many critics focus on in their attempts to decide what's news. After all, if you and I don't agree on the significance of a particular event or how it was covered by the news media, we would probably argue not about our personal prefer-ences or the nature of the occurrence itself but about how it was covered. The reporter should have focused more on my "substance" than your "superficial generalizations." Observers have looked at this process in several ways.

Richard Carter (1967) looked at journalists as communicators and viewed communication as a process by which "situations are conveyed across time and space." Situations here are "occurrences." The basic purpose is to give the audience the opportunity to attend to a situation. There are two basic reportorial functions here: observation and description of situations. The standard of performance is "accuracy," the fidelity of the reported situation, and the criterion used by the reporter is "relevance." If a report is to be accurate, the relevant must be included and the irrelevant excluded. "Completeness" is a problem because what's omitted can contribute to inaccuracy. In Carter's view the observation function is achieved when the five W's + H (Who, What, When, Where, Why and How) questions have been answered. The description function is achieved when the most important value is placed first, the second most important second, etc. This is the "inverted pyramid" style of writing.

"News value" here refers to the relationship of readers to the situation and it implies the use of the criterion of "interest" and significance. Interest is the reader's likelihood of seeking out the situation, and significance is the likelihood of the situation affecting the readers. The six questions are derived from experience with probable news values: What — occurrences — are news; Who — people — are news; When — the timely is news; Where — that which is close is news; Why & How — the reasons and the manners of actions are news.

Time also affects the way we look at journalists and their news-gathering activities. Sociologist Robert E. Park (1940) almost a half century ago distinguished between "acquaintance with" a topic and "knowledge about" the topic. Whatever is known through acquaintance with" is likely to be concrete and descriptive while that known through "knowledge about" tends to be abstract and analytic. The former emphasizes facts while the latter deals in concepts. Though the two categories can be located along a continuum, they are distinct forms of knowledge, each having different functions in the lives of individuals. "Because news concentrates on describing signals rather than analyzing their significance, a reporter and a scholar examining the same events are usually concerned with different data," Roshco (1975) notes.

The process of gathering information and deciding what's news are the primary concerns of critics like Altschull (1974), who argues that there is no way news can be "value-free" because a series of value judgments have been imposed on the event along the way. This is the question of how the reporter relates to the occurrence, or final news product. Though there is more than a little controversy over how it's implemented, the norm of "objectivity" is still probably .the most commonly-accepted statement of the ideal relation journalists are expected to adopt.

Objectivity

Two politicians arguing about "unfair" coverage of their election campaigns are likely to lay blame at the feet of journalists who are forsaking their professional norm of "objectivity." Indeed, if you selected a dozen people at random in this country, a majority would probably tell you they want journalists to be fair and objective in their reporting of the news. Yet this concept of "objectivity" is one of the most controversial ideas not only in the newsrooms of TV stations and newspapers, but also in film production, academia and the offices of the myriad of elites who want to control the media. To make it even more complicated, many people aren't even talking about the same thing. Is the "objectivity" of documentary film makers the same as that of news journalists or that of social scientists? Though some suggest the debate over objectivity has ended (Hage et al., 1983), such an announcement may be a bit premature. Hackett (1984) suggests that rather than dismiss the concepts of objectivity and bias, researchers should make them the objects of investigation.

Definitions may be the last refuge of rascals and scholars, but it's the "semantic differences" that usually lead to misunderstandings and confusion. And that clearly is the case with "objectivity." The first distinction is between objectivity as "intention" and as "outcome." In one view, objectivity refers to the ability to interpret or view phenomena without having those views or interpretations unduly distorted by personal feelings; this view looks at the outcome. Another media philosopher, John Merrill (1974), argues that objectivity has nothing to do with the actual performance but with the intention of journalists not to let their personal feelings affect their reporting. Objectivity here is a goal one should strive for. In this sense, Clark Kent may be the most objective reporter in town because he scrupulously bends over backwards not to favor those candidates he likes with undeserving newspaper copy. In the Altschull sense, intention is irrelevant and Kent is a necessary failure because his coverage is incomplete and based on our mild mannered reporter's personal judgments. "So long as news reports are incomplete—and news reports cannot be other than incomplete—they can neither be fair nor accurate." In the Altschull scenario, then, the journalist is condemned to failure.

The second distinction centers around whether objectivity refers to any particular "relationship." In other words, if we're to decide whether our Clark Kent is objective, what do we look for? Do we try to determine Kent's intentions by comparing his performance with that of others or his own past record? Or do we compare Kent's performance with some external measure of "reality"? How do we go about this? Are we merely comparing our "objectivity" or perspective with that of Clark Kent's, and, if so, then is Altschull right—objectivity is impossible because of the differences in personal values, philosophies, the interference of human judgment.

Where does our notion of objectivity come from and how has it changed? The origins of objectivity in journalism are at best unclear. Furthermore, though we can describe the background of objectivity and more recent differences over its position, past factors favoring its elevation to an accepted norm may be irrelevant to its current functioning among journalists and others in the U.S. media system.

Though no society of journalists ever formally adopted "objective reporting" as a canon of their craft, it has become the accepted term for designating allegiance to the nonpartisan pursuit of factual accuracy.

As Blankenburg and Walden (1977) note, the roots of objective reporting are thought to be lodged in 19th century technology, industrialization and urbanization. The wire services are particularly credited with developing objectivity and teaching it to newspapers. Objectivity was consistent with providing concise, interesting, nonpartisan news accounts that reduced transmission costs and attracted readers. Media critic, Herbert I. Schiller (1979), traces objectivity's development in tandem with the commercial newspapers' assumption of a crucial political function—the surveillance of the public good. The commercial newspaper's presence as a new social institution was justified because news objectivity was grounded in the paper's defense of public good in a world of fact. Objectivity drew from the belief that the new technology—photography—affords an exact, accurate copy of reality. Later, with the development of public relations and the need of the newspaper industry to advertise itself, the paper's role as defender of the public good was questioned in the 1920's and 1930's. Sociologist Morris Janowitz (1975) notes that since World War I, journalists have increasingly come to consider themselves professionals and have searched for an appropriate model. The model selected can best be called the "gatekeeper" model which sought to apply the canons of the scientific method to increase objectivity and to enhance one's effective performance. This model emphasizes the sharp separation of reporting fact and disseminating opinion. "Under the gatekeeper concept of professionalism, journalists encountered institutional pressures and personal limitations in searching for objectivity and separating fact from opinion. But to the extent that they thought of themselves as professionals or hoped to make journalism into a profession, they had little doubt about standards of performance although there was much debate about their clarity and how to apply them."

Objectivity became the keystone of journalistic morality during the 1930's. Explicit codification by professionals of the techniques of journalistic objectivity occurred during the period leading up to the Second World War. However, the Canons of Journalism adopted by the American Society of Newspaper Editors in April, 1923, did not even contain the word "objectivity" but did use "impartiality." The whole of Canon 5 is: "Impartiality—Sound practice makes clear distinction between news reports and expressions of opinion. News reports should be free from opinion or bias of any kind. This rule does not apply to so-called special articles unmistakably devoted to advocacy or characterized by a signature authorizing the writer's own conclusions and interpretations." The distinction between news and opinion (or interpretation) in the Canons provides some support for the view that "objectivity" is tied to "intention" rather than "outcome." At the very least, the professional norm of objectivity among journalists separated intentional news gathering and reporting from all the other activities of the media. It should be noted too that the Canons spoke to newspaper journalists, and later radio and TV. It did not include magazine journalism, opinion media, or explicitly political media. Thus, the Canons argued that "objectivity" occupied an important place in journalism in its efforts to function within a pluralistic system, but it did not govern all journalistic roles.

After World War II, media criticism of an obsessively objective journalism grew along with a debate between advocates of objective detachment and those in favor of social responsibility in journalism. In 1943, AP General Manager Kent Cooper proclaimed that objective news was the "highest original moral concept ever developed in America and given to the world." In 1969 critic Andrew Kopkind argued that "objectivity is the rationalization for moral disengagement, the classic cop-out from choice making." Objective reporting has tended to mean a constrained form or style that emphasizes concrete, obtrusive and finite events rather than trends or other topics. However, reporters can "breach these structures in work labeled 'analysis,' 'investigation,' or 'interpretation.' Today you often see interpretation, where the reporter offers reasoned opinions based on facts. The exact boundary is hazy, yet tangible enough to press critics who call for interpretation as a needed alternative, and to devotees of objectivity who fear interpretation as a kind of creeping advocacy" (Blankenburg and Walden, 1977).

What happened to spread the change? Two phenomena following World War II stimulated the reappraisal of standard reportorial methods and news content: one technological and the other political. Television's arrival and McCarthyism together showed print journalism of the 1950's that ways were needed to respond to the increasingly complex world. By the early 1950's Sen. Joseph McCarthy's escalating accusations about the presence of communists in the federal government were reported under a ceaseless stream of large headlines and in the glare of television. This made at least some newsmen dissatisfied with what Elmer Davis labeled "dead-pan objectivity." Journalists were walking a tightrope between two great gulfs—on one side the false objectivity that takes everything at face value and on the other, the interpretive reporting which fails to draw the line between a reasonably well established fact and what the reporter or editor wishes were the fact. By the 1960's, the gatekeeper model of journalistic professionalism was questioned by some working journalists who recommended replacing the scientific method with the concept of the journalist as critic and interpreter.

"Objectivity" was criticized in various intellectual quarters (Christians, 1977). Outspoken academic social scientists became doubtful about their ability to be objective and claimed that the search for objective reality led to a retreat from personal and political responsibility. Some journalists also proclaimed that the task of the journalist was to represent the viewpoints and interests of competing groups, expecially those of excluded and underprivileged groups. Some, like Rivet (1976) in France, argue that journalism is a medium of action and the journalist is a political protagonist. Another way of changing the role avoided the personal involvement of preferences and values but assigned to reporters role-obligations comparable to those of scientific researchers. Journalists would be responsible for indicating the validity of the information they reported as well as for assuring the accuracy of the material attributed. Westerstahl (1983) argues that objectivity can be defined as adherence to certain norms or standards, and this consists of two major components: factuality and impartiality.

The debate over reportorial objectivity raised the question of what constituted adequate role-performance. Thus, we're faced with how "objectivity" is actually carried out. Perhaps the prime writing form used to implement objectivity has been "attribution"—"he said," "she stated," "the president told reporters." All statements of opinion, preferences, assessments, predictions, etc. are supposed to be attributed to identifiable sources. This may include both indirect quotes and those where quotation marks are used to indicate the "exact words" of the source. In a study by Culbertson and Somerick (1976) in three Ohio cities, almost 85% of those surveyed knew what quotation marks were designed to tell. Almost 40% said they notice bylines, which essentially attribute the article to a particular reporter. Of course, regardless of attribution, the reporter still has the responsibility for deciding what's included or excluded, and "objectivity" has had rather little to say about the problem except for "balancing" reporting with representative spokespeople from differing positions.

One way to "balance" is to represent a situation as a dichotomy of pros and cons, giving all or both sides their say. Gaye Tuchman (1972) argues that objectivity has become a "ritual" that stands between journalists and the public—including their critics. A position of objectivity is also used by doctors and lawyers vis-a-vis their clients, she notes. A ritual is a routine procedure which has relatively little relevance to the end sought in that particular situation. The ritual becomes more important when the goals are more vague.

What systematic evidence do we have that bears on reporters' objectivity? Starck and Soloski (1977) asked how a reporter's attitude toward the role of the press in society made a difference in the kind of story produced, finding that journalists with a participant bias tended to write stories of an analytic or interpretive nature and de-emphasized simple factual presentations. Martin, O'Keefe and Nayman (1972) found that editors' personal beliefs about campus demonstrations were not related to giving favorable or unfavorable coverage in their newspapers. Editors also were more correct in judging their readers' support for demonstrations than their readers were in judging their newspapers' viewpoints.

Others have looked at media "bias" towards groups like the Ku Klux Klan and similar extremist groups, finding that the media gave considerable attention to politically deviant groups (Monti, 1979) but used more negative terms to characterize them (Shoemaker, 1984). News coverage over time is more difficult to judge. Individual stories may be highly accurate, but a variety of factors affect what many observers may consider biased reporting. One observer, for example, notes the differential coverage of the races in the Rhodesian war that ended in 1979. As one major newspaper editor noted, the killing of whites provoked cries of outrage while black casualties on either side got relatively little attention. Coverage was hampered by government restrictions, racial segregation inhibiting movement, home office pressures for interesting stories, proximity of spokespersons of one side, and probably prejudice by some whites (Morris, 1979).

Numerous studies have tried to look at objectivity by gauging the "accuracy" of journalists. Accuracy has been defined to include not only correct or incorrect facts but also what sources consider problems of omission. Thus, reporters' work is examined for sins of both commission as well as omission. In a study of how accurate sources thought local TV news was, Singletary and Lipsky (1977) found that 65% thought the story was "entirely correct" and 31% "generally correct." Some 78% who noticed an error found only one, and 63% of the errors were what the researchers called "objective," e.g., wrong time, identification, description, etc., while 37% were "subjective," e.g., misleading statements.

Newsgathering, Newsmaking Practices

Daily newsgathering can be described as a combination of personal judgments and role performance. The latter consists of conventions and processes adopted consciously or unconsciously to reach professional goals. Some of these were noted in our discussion of organizational structure. Gaye Tuchman (1978) notes that journalists typify events as news according to how they happen. Events are classified according to how they fit in with practical tasks. Thus, soft news is usually controlled and seldom pertains to unscheduled events. Journalists also tend to focus on "concrete" occurrences that can be classified as "events," rather than treating ongoing processes or trends. This leads to a fragmented view of society, some have observed (Rositi, 1977). Journalists tend to rely upon authoritative sources in gathering news. Such sources tend to be more visible—in prominent positions (mayors, presidents, chairmen) and locations—and more observable—in the public arena. A recent content analysis of some 5,190 news stories appearing on network TV newscasts found a strong preference for use of established institutional sources, particularly those in the government, military, politics, business or professions (Whitney et al., 1985). Thus, not only do "occurrences" make news stand out, so do the sources. One way people stand out is through group affiliation which helps one gain access to the media. Whitney et al. (1985) also found a strong geographic dimension to TV news where a majority of the news comes from one state or city within a region, and cities which are media centers capture a disproportionate share of story datelines.

It is the relationship between journalists and sources that has special significance for our understanding of how the media operate. Some people act as news sources only once in their life, but a much larger percentage of information emerges from enduring links between journalists and authoritative sources such as the presidential press secretary, state legislators, professional spokesmen and the police chief. These long-term links between reporters and sources also connect their organizations (See Fico, 1984, 1985; Dunwoody and Ryan,

1985). Over time, both reporters and their sources benefit from the relationship. Viewed as an exchange, the reporter gets publishable information while sources get to highlight aspects of situations that are beneficial to them. Several researchers have found a symbiotic relationship between reporters and their sources (Miller, 1978; Davison, 1975; Rada, 1977). Culbertson (1975-76) notes that news executives frequently rotate beat assignments so journalists can't easily be coopted in their relationships with sources.

Summary

In this chapter we examined media industries, organizations and people. The media are part of larger leisure and information industries which have assumed growing importance in the American economy. Advertising is the major form of economic support for American media; it subsidizes the delivery of information and entertainment. The number of media units has grown tremendously in this century, but there has also been a growing concentration of ownership across the media. However, in terms of individual markets, the number of potential voices available is enormous in most cases. Ownership can and does have an impact on the operation of media organizations, sometimes illustrating the conflict between demands of the organization and those of the professional roles. We also examined the structure and operation of different media organizations, including a paper's newsroom and TV studio. Various models have been used to describe the newsmaking and production of entertainment in organizations. Lastly, we looked at media people, their roles, routines and characteristics. Among the chief roles of journalists is the "watchdog." Since news is the primary concern of journalists, its definition is a crucial task. We looked at various approaches to news and discussed the idea of "objectivity." The newsgathering process also was discussed briefly.

The industries, organizations and people produce a complex product but how is it received by the audience? In the next chapter we will look at media audiences and their characteristics.

4

The Audience
Who's Paying Attention and Why?

The mass media take a big slice of our daily lives — in many cases, more than any other activity except sleeping. Today, the media account for half of our free time and their importance has grown as people's leisure time has expanded through the modern era. Most Americans spend the bulk of their leisure hours inside their homes and almost half of this time is spent either watching TV, listening to the radio, or reading a newspaper or magazine. TV viewing itself is the favorite leisure activity of more than 40% of American adults. The television is on more than 7 hours a day in the average home, and most Americans spend at least 2-3 hours a day in front of a TV set, though the attention certainly varies.

Though most media consumption is viewed as a leisure activity, entertainment is only one of the bases for media's prominence in people's lives. Books are essential ingredients of educational programs and newspapers are used to obtain job-related information. In fact, it is this multifaceted nature of mass media that probably accounts for their success in maintaining large, diverse audiences. Media provide such a variety of content and serve such diverse purposes that they attract huge audiences. For example, the night that TV unveiled the person who shot J.R. Ewing on *Dallas* attracted 83 million viewers, or 53% of TV households in the U.S. alone. In this chapter, we will examine the audiences of mass media — who's watching, listening, reading. We also will explore the reasons people join media audiences.

What draws them there and how do people feel about the media? This chapter on media audiences is also a necessary stepping stone to our discussion of media effects in subsequent chapters.

How Big a Slice Do Media Take?

Virtually everyone today has at least some measure of "free time," but this was not always the case. We are now at the end of what one observer called the "Golden Age of Leisure." Since the Industrial Revolution in the 18th and 19th centuries, there has been a dramatic increase until the past two or three decades, when it began to stabilize (Mercer, 1977). Still, one national poll showed that half of the men and 43% of the women felt they did not have enough leisure time (Roper, 1980). How much free time do we have? If you ask people, you get quite different estimates that depend on how people define "free" or "leisure" time (Foxall, 1984). Survey researcher John Robinson (1977) has employed a diary method in which people across the nation described all of their activities from midnight to midnight for a particular 24-hour day. Using this information to estimate a week's activities, he found that people had an average of 38.5 hours "free" each week, which represents about 23% of the week's 168 hours. The rest of the week breaks down like this: 32.6% sleeping; 19.3% working for pay; 12.2% family care; and 13% personal care. Looking at it this way, the average person has 38.5 hours "free" once personal and family obligations are taken care of, work is done, and sleeping is subtracted.

In the rich, consumer society in which we live, an impressive array of activities compete to fill the 38.5 hours of free time we have each week. Media take about 47% while organizational activities fill almost 10%, our social life another 20%, recreation only 3.4%, and other leisure pursuits 19%.

How we spend our time varies considerably by age, as Table 4-1 suggests. The greatest amount of free time is available at the youngest and oldest ends of the age scale. While those age 18-25 have 50 hours free weekly, those age 56-65 have almost 42 hours free and those 46-55, 35.2 hours free.

We also see that media behaviors take an increasing share of leisure time as we move up the age ladder. Although the youngest age group spends the smallest portion of its leisure time on mass media consumption (remember that this group also has the most free time available), its actual media use of 18.5 hours weekly is only exceeded by the 18.8 hours of those age 46-55 and the 22.6 hours of those age 56-65. Now, let's take a look at each medium and how people distribute their "media time."

Table 4-1
Time Use and Leisure Activities by Age

Time Use	18-25	26-35	Age 36-45	46-55	56-65
Sleep	33%	32%	33%	33%	33%
Work for pay	16%	20%	20%	18%	12%
Family care	9%	13%	12%	14%	14%
Personal care	12%	12%	13%	14%	16%
Free time	30%	23%	22%	21%	25%

Total: 168 hours = 100%

Free Time

	18-25	26-35	36-45	46-55	56-65
Organizations	17%	11%	9%	9%	8%
Media use	37%	45%	49%	53%	54%
Social life	21%	23%	21%	15%	15%
Recreation	5%	3%	3%	4%	3%
Other leisure	20%	18%	18%	19%	20%
Total Hours: (100% =)	50.0	38.4	37.3	35.2	41.8

Source: John P. Robinson, *Changes in Americans' Use of Time: 1965-1975*, Cleveland: Communication Research Center, Cleveland State University, August, 1977. Used with permission.

Television. More leisure time is devoted to TV than to the other media combined. Yet TV use is elastic — TV viewing tends to be the time when people have nothing better to do. People give up watching TV when they've got other things to attend to. One-third of the audience deserts the average hour-long program before it's over (Brown, 1983a). However, though TV is readily abandoned to pursue more satisfying activities such as visiting friends, TV use still provides considerable satisfaction on a regular basis. On an average day, at least 80% of the populace watches television (Robinson, 1977). Pervasive TV use is a worldwide phenomenon and Americans are no more addicted to TV than are other people.

The spread of cable TV and videocassette recorders also is having an impact. People can now switch their viewing time (Levy, 1983; Levy and Fink, 1984) or watch other materials when nothing they like is available. VCR's are selling so quickly that some 50 to 60 million households may have them by the end of this decade. The sale of blank videotapes has risen at an even faster pace (Lachenbrush, 1984). These technologies are altering TV viewing patterns and may increase total viewing time or affect attention to news (Reagan, 1984; Webster, 1984; Henke et al., 1984; Becker, Dunwoody and Rafaeli, 1983).

Television's strong claims on the attention of the American public are attested to by the fact that on the average weekday, five-sixths (84%) of the adult population watches something on TV. According to Broadcasting Yearbook (1985), 25% of U.S. homes use TV in the morning (10 a.m. - 1 p.m.), 30% in the afternoon, and 63% during prime time (8-11 p.m. EST). And almost three-quarters of those watching TV see one or more news programs. News today is particularly important for TV stations because it is such profitable programming for commercial stations. But it's also a major interest of consumers. While 84% of all adults in a national survey in 1982 had watched TV the previous day, 67% had seen TV news and most of them had watched news from 5 - 6:59 p.m. when most local and national newscasts are offered across the country. (See Table 4-2.)

Table 4-2
Daily TV and News Viewing by Age Groups

	All Adults	Watched TV	Watched TV News	Watched TV but Saw No News
All Adults		84%	67%	17%
By Age: 18-24		83%	53%	30%
25-29		84%	64%	20%
30-34		85%	69%	16%
35-44		80%	62%	17%
45-54		80%	70%	10%
55-64		88%	75%	13%
65 +		89%	80%	10%

Source: Albert E. Gollin and Nicolas A. Bloom. *Newspapers in American News Habits: A Comparative Assessment.* New York: Newspaper Advertising Bureau, 1985. Survey conducted in 1982. Used with permission.

Viewing patterns showed a substantial amount of selective loyalty to local or network programs at various times of the day. (See Table 4-3.) Among the 67% who saw any TV news "yesterday," about one-half (47%) of the adult population watched only one type of newscast daily, and a network evening news program was the type seen most often. About one third of all daily television news-viewers watched only local newscasts and 37% saw only network news. The audience for television news in the morning is quite small. Nationally, only 21% of adults watched any TV news in the morning. Network news shows were seen by 15% (NBC's *Today*, ABC's *Good Morning America*, and CBS' *Morning News*) while local news was watched by 6%. The audiences for local and network news in the afternoon and evening periods were more nearly equal in size.

Table 4-3
Daily Viewing of Local & Network TV News

Viewing Patterns	Morning (Before lunch)	After lunch, up to dinner	After dinner	Total (All day)
Watched only network news	13%	10%	24%	25%
Watched any local news only	4%	9%	23%	22%
Watched network and local news	2%	3%	5%	16%
Cable	2%	1%	2%	4%
Total who saw TV news	21%	24%	50%	67%

Source: Albert E. Gollin and Nicolas A. Bloom. *Newspapers in American News Habits: A Comparative Assessment*. New York: Newspaper Advertising Bureau, 1985. Survey conducted in 1982. Used with permission.

Newspapers. From 68% to 80% of American adults read a newspaper on an average day (Bogart, 1981), but there is some evidence that the daily newspaper habit may now be in a period of decline. It shows up most vividly in per capita circulation figures, but also in national surveys of newspaper reading. A 1978 survey (NORC) found that only 57% of the sample said they read a newspaper everyday, down from 62% in 1977, 69% in 1972, and 73% in 1967. The major factor often cited for the decline is age. Robinson's 1975-76 diary study found that 90% of those age 66 or older had read a daily newspaper the previous day, compared with 51% of those age 18-24. The percentage of people reading a newspaper rose consistently with advancing age groups: 66% of those in the 30-39 group, 79% in the 50-65 group, for example. Newspaper use also does not appear to depend on how much free time people have available. (Robinson and Jeffres, 1979, 1981). The relationship between age and newspaper reading will be examined further in our discussion of media diets.

People read about one-fifth of the newspaper. Contrary to the belief of many, editorials are read just as often as other articles — 25% of the time. Content preferences seem to remain remarkably stable over time. Newspapers contain a wide variety of materials. Some may be of interest to a relatively small number of people — but they may have a strong loyalty to that feature of the paper. Almost all readers (92%) page through the full newspaper. Most (89%) read the paper at home. Studies indicate that people are attracted to an individual newspaper article by its subject rather than its design per se. A national survey of almost 2,000 adults in 1982 found that four out of ten people thought their major newspaper did a "very good job" in reporting on crimes, sports or inflation. Some 30-35% thought coverage was very good about other countries and unemployment. At the bottom, only 14% thought their paper did a very good job in reporting on pollution problems and 17-18% gave the same rating to reportage about personal health and neighborhood news (Bogart and Gollin, 1983).

Daily readership of morning and afternoon newspapers closely parallels their share of total newspaper circulation: 44% reading an afternoon paper, 36% reading a morning paper, and 13% reading one or more papers of both types (Gollin, 1978). As Table 4-4 shows, newspaper readership rises as we move up the age scale (Grotta and Babbili, 1983). While three quarters of those in the top age groups read a newspaper, less than two thirds of those age 18-24 read any newspaper (also see Hartman, 1983). Reading of morning and afternoon papers takes place throughout the day and is not restricted to the time of publication. Morning papers are frequently read in the late evening; afternoon papers are usually read the next morning. This delayed reading may reduce the incentive to read more than one type of daily paper. More than half of the national sample of readers read a paper two or more times, and 22% turned to a daily paper at least three times during the preceding 24 hours.

Clearly, the daily newspaper serves as an information source at various times of the day for many readers, rather than being picked up and read at one sitting. Reading takes place almost around the clock, peaking just prior to the onset of the work day and again at its close.

Table 4-4
Readership & Frequency of Newspaper Use

	Read any newspaper	Read any morning newspaper	Read any afternoon newspaper
All Adults	69%	36%	44%
By Age			
18-24	64%	32%	38%
25-29	58%	30%	37%
30-34	63%	35%	38%
35-44	68%	34%	45%
45-54	75%	43%	50%
55-64	76%	40%	48%
65 +	74%	36%	50%

Source: Albert E. Gollin, "The Daily Diet of News" (New York: Newspaper Advertising Bureau, 1978). Used with permission.

But at any hour between 6 a.m. and midnight, at least 3% of the adult population can be found reading a newspaper. Both morning and evening newspapers are read soon after they arrive but also at other times throughout the day.

Radio. Some 99% of U.S. households have at least one radio and 41% have six or more sets. The average is 5.5 radios per household (RAB, 1984). Some 38% of Americans listen to the radio at least an hour a day while another 21% listen for two hours, and 36% more than that. Despite the enormous impact of television in the 1950's, radio has continued to grow and prosper. Since its early development in 1920, it has achieved growth rivaling that of all other media. Radio is an especially strong medium among both the general population and specialized audiences. The overall radio listening audience is larger than the TV audience for a sizeable segment of the day. The highest audience measurement comes at approximately 8-9 a.m., then tapers off before climbing back up to a plateau between 3-7 p.m. These "highs" are commonly called drive-time when many people listen while commuting to or from work. Television begins to take over the audience after 8 p.m., but among younger people radio is the major mass medium.

A national survey in 1982 found that 67% of American adults recalled listening to the radio at least once the previous day. As Table 4-5 shows, radio listening declines with advancing age. While 72% of

Table 4-5

Daily Radio and Radio News Listening

	Listened to radio	Heard news on radio	Heard no news on radio
All Adults	67%	48%	19%
By Age			
18-24	72%	45%	27%
25-29	78%	52%	26%
30-34	73%	55%	19%
35-44	68%	50%	18%
45-54	63%	46%	17%
55-64	62%	49%	13%
65 +	53%	41%	12%

Source: Albert E. Gollin and Nicolas A. Bloom. *Newspapers in American News Habits: A Comparative Assessment.* New York: Newspaper Advertising Bureau, 1985. Survey conducted in 1982. Used with permission.

those age 18-24 listened to the radio on the previous day, only 53% of those age 65 or older listened. Radio news listening is closely linked with radio listening in general; we would expect this since exposure to radio is episodic and newscasts are frequent. Some 48% of U.S. adults hear radio news on an average day.

Radios are highly portable and readily integrated into diverse locations by our highly mobile population. For example, 95% of all cars, 67% of our living rooms, half of the kitchens and 7% of people's bathrooms have radios (RAB, 1984). Overall exposure to radio news broadcasts is similar to the average number of times a paper is read each day. As a whole, the average adult heard 1.2 news broadcasts while the average radio listener heard 1.75 broadcasts. Given the two media's contrasting styles of news presentation and the scope of their news coverage, there is little reason to suspect that radio and newspapers compete with one another in satisfying people's news appetite. The times of the day when people read the paper or hear the news on the radio also suggest a complementary relationship.

Movies. Film attendance in the U.S. has ridden a bumpy path since the 1930's when movie attendance was at its peak. However, in the past few years movie attendance has gone up significantly. A study for the Motion Picture Association of America (Mastroianni, 1980) showed that 118.9 million persons were moviegoers in 1980. The figure for theater admissions jumped 17% by 1983 reaching a number last achieved in 1961 (Gertner, 1985). Examining the public age 12 and older, we find that 23% went to a film at least once a month in 1983 while 32% went once every 2-6 months, 9% less than once every six months, and 36% not at all. The most frequent moviegoers are teenagers (age 12-17); that same year, 54% of them went to a theater at least once a month and another 30% went occasionally (once in 2-6 months). Only 12% said they never went to a film compared to 38% of adults age 18 and older who never went to films; among adults only 20% went to a film at least once a month and 32% at least once over a six-month period.

The bulk of motion picture admissions continues to be generated by movie-goers under age 40; they account for 87% of total yearly admissions (Gertner, 1985). The busiest days are Fridays and Saturdays and the peak months are July and August. Ticket sales in 1982 were projected by the Motion Picture Association at $1.17 billion, the highest in 20 years. The average admission price was $2.93. A national survey by Louis Harris in 1978 found that the average number of times people went to a movie was about 4 times per year; moviegoing in cities was twice the level of that in towns and rural areas.

Shaw House, home of Shaw Brother Studios in Hong Kong, one of the largest producers of Samurai films in the world.

What films do people go see? Though family films have been maligned as "box-office poison," 24% have been successful according to a study of 5,000 films rated during the first 11 years of the Motion Picture Association of America (1968-1979). While 27% of parental guidance films were successful, only 14% of movies rated R and 5% of X-rated films were financially successful. Persons under age 17 are not admitted to R-rated films without adult permission and no one under age 18 is admitted to X-rated movies. Some 70% prefer American films to foreign films (Gertner, 1985).

Books and Magazines. While newspaper usage was declining in Robinson's 1965-75 diary data, time spent reading books and magazines increased from 1.6 to 1.9 hours per week. National surveys by Mediamark Research (1984) show that 94% of American adults read magazines each month with the average person selecting 9.6 different magazine issues during that period. The heaviest reading

Movie set for historical films at Shaw Brothers, Hong Kong.

occurs among those with the following characteristics: age 18-44, college-educated, professional/managerial, household incomes of $30,000 or more. The highest readership occurs on Saturdays and during the winter months. Some 42% of the reading occurs after dinner but before going to bed. Another 5% actually occurs in bed before sleeping. There also are strong differences by age. For the three youngest age groups, the increases in book and. magazine reading closely parallel the drops in newspaper time that occurred during the same period. Specialty magazines and books seem to fulfill important functions for younger people. However, other reports show book use among youth to be quite limited (Brazaitis, 1984).

How strong is your own loyalty to a magazine? How do you use them? One survey indicated that three fourths of readers kept an issue of a magazine for future reference and an even larger percentage discussed an article or feature with another person during a six-month period. A national survey for the Magazine Publishers Association (1983) showed that the average adult reads each magazine purchased on more than three different days and college graduates read more magazines than less educated people. Younger people also tend to pay more attention to magazines as topics of conversation than do older people. While about two thirds of those age 18-24 had discussed a magazine article with someone in the past six months, about 40% of those age 65 or older had done so.

Daily Media Diets and News Diets. Are the media complementary items on people's media diets or are there trade-offs? If the former occurs, then TV viewing, for example, might stimulate newspaper reading. If the latter occurs, TV viewing might displace newspaper reading. We can envision various combinations of media substitutions or complementary use among radio listening, TV viewing, and newspaper reading. Furthermore, though attention to TV news might stimulate newspaper reading because people want details about some critical event on a given day, in the long run watching TV might reduce people's attention to newspapers. We also might find a pattern of complementary media use within one generation but evidence that substitution is occurring in another. These are the questions being raised by both scholars and media practitioners.

Robinson and Jeffres (1979) found support for their hypothesis that people who use one news medium are more likely to use another. In general then, we find that people who read newspapers also are more likely to watch TV news than are non-newspaper readers. Thus, the media complement each other at a single point in time. This relationship also tends to hold for all age groups so there is no tendency toward increased specialization or fractionalization in news media among those under age 30, as some have suggested. Such specialization would have indicated TV news was supplanting newspaper use among younger people.

The news media are quite competitive in attracting media consumers. As the amount of TV news has expanded in the past two decades and newspaper circulations have failed to grow as rapidly as the population, a host of researchers, observers and critics have focused on relationships between different media use. Though the question is certainly not settled, the empirical evidence is growing.

However, publishers and editors are concerned with trends and whether consumers are changing across time. Though TV and newspaper use may be complementary at a point in time, more subtle shifts may be occurring in the long run. For example, we might see TV displacing some print behavior across generations. This is the major reason newspapers are so interested in younger audiences. In an examination of several national studies, Robinson and Jeffres (1979) found that time devoted to the newspaper from 1965 to 1975 declined while time devoted to TV increased dramatically, particularly among older people. The same phenomenon applied to viewing TV news, the content one would expect would most directly compete with newspapers. Increased viewing was also found among younger people over the decade, but younger age groups also gave evidence of a "trade-off" between newspapers and other print media during that period. Reading of magazines, books, and other matter also showed increases over the decade. Gravitation toward more specialized print media is less evident among people aged 50-64 which could indicate a direct functional trade-off of newspapers for TV among this oldest group.

Certainly it is difficult to determine the exact nature of trade-offs between media activities unambiguously with the information now at hand. There also are signs of certain changes in media usage since 1975-76. The National Opinion Research Center (NORC) at the University of Chicago documented a 9% decline in the public's reported daily use of the newspaper between 1975 and 1978. Moreover, the NORC survey shows a pronounced "generation effect" — the tendency of the youngest adults to read newspapers at a lower rate than previous generations of adults at that stage in their lives. Between 1975 and 1977, the percent of 18-30 year olds claiming to read the newspaper daily dropped from 51% to 42% and those aged 31-43 from 68% to 60%. A greater decline was found among the younger age groups, particularly those aged 30-39. A study conducted for Scripps-Howard in 1982-83 found that 72% of a national sample of adults watch TV everyday compared with 70% who read a newspaper, so comparable figures tuned into each medium. However, it is still too early to gauge the relation of these reports to actual use of the newspaper or to circulation figures. Furthermore, newspapers are fighting back with research and efforts to satisfy readers.

We get a better picture of how people mix-and-match their media use by looking at people's daily news diets. Patterns of individual news consumption are formed by classifying each person into one of eight logically possible types, depending upon his or her daily use of one, two, or all three media, or no media (See Table 4-6). Using data from a national survey (Gollin and Bloom, 1985), we find one-quarter of all adults make use of all three kinds of news sources and another 23% combine newspapers and television into their daily diet. Some 8% both read a newspaper and hear at least one radio newscast; another 9% combine TV and radio newscasts. Some 11% only read a newspaper while 10% attend only to TV and 5% only to radio on a daily basis.

In the past two decades, a lively debate has developed over the importance of newspapers and television as news sources. The debate has been fueled by results of Roper polls conducted since 1959 and documenting an apparent rise of television as America's preferred news source. In the polls, people were asked: "Where do you usually get most of your news about what's going on in the world today?" Since 1959, TV has been the key source for a growing number of adults, rising from a base of 51% to proportions that have stabilized at about 65% since 1972. Newspapers, in contrast, have declined from a leading position, cited by 57% in 1959 to less than half in recent years. One national study sought to contrast the strengths of the two media —

TV's role as a medium of first exposure for big news stories and newspapers' varied role both as a back-up source and in providing desired additional details (Gollin, 1978). Respondents were asked:

> Some people feel that generally you can find out all you want to know about big news stories from TV news programs. Others generally want the additional details that newspapers give you on a big day. Which best describes the way you feel?

One-third of the respondents felt they got enough details from TV news while almost two-thirds preferred the additional details about big stories found in their newspapers. Looking first at TV news consumers, we find that exposure to TV news bore no relationship to people's preferences, contrary to what one might have expected. The groups that were most partial to TV news were those who stressed the quality of network news coverage and local news watchers who were attracted by the personality of the newscasters. The group least disposed to favor TV news consisted of network news watchers who did not actually seek the news itself. For example, the news appeared on a channel they were already watching, or their spouse wanted to watch the news. The links between news preferences and newspaper reading are much stronger. Those who read a daily newspaper were far more likely to have expressed a preference for newspapers than TV in meeting their needs for news. Non-readers were significantly more partial to TV news. Regular readers of newsweeklies — who were

Table 4-6
Individual News Consumption Patterns

Pattern of Exposure	1977	1982
Exposure to any news:	92%	91%
All three sources	25%	25%
Newspapers & TV	20%	23%
Newspapers & Radio	12%	8%
TV & Radio	7%	9%
Newspaper only	12%	11%
TV only	10%	10%
Radio only	6%	5%
Not exposed to news	8%	9%
	100%	100%

Source: Albert E. Gollin and Nicolas A. Bloom. *Newspapers in American News Habits: A Comparative Assessment.* New York: Newspaper Advertising Bureau, 1985. Survey conducted in 1982. Used with permission.

twice as likely to read both morning and evening papers daily and who consumed more radio and TV newscasts—were among the most partial to newspapers.

More people read a newspaper than watch news on TV, alone or in combination with other news sources. However, this does not mean that newspaper readership is always based on an interest in the news printed in the daily paper, any more than watching TV news necessarily signifies interest in what is being presented. This is the "why" question, and news is but one element in a mix of offerings by both media.

Origins of Media Behaviors — The Why Question

For several decades, people interested in mass media focused predominantely on potential effects. We'll bring this investigation up to date in the second half of the book. But the question of media effects itself necessarily involves an examination of audience behaviors. Recently there has been greater interest in trying to understand the determinants of media consumption patterns, particularly newspaper reading and television viewing.

However, the "why" question—"Why do people engage in mass media behaviors?—is hardly an easy one. In trying to dissect this question, we'll show how people ask the "why" question in different ways, depending on their interest, their assumptions, their perspectives. The question is posed at different levels, some focusing on specific *media use situations* (why you curl up with a book rather than TV on a cold winter night), some asking questions about *individual patterns* of media use (comparing, for example, a TV fan with a newspaper fan), and others seeking answers to the why question at even higher levels where they examine the impact of the *media system* or *social system* on people's media behaviors (seeking, for example, the impact of government regulation on content diversity and audience choices). Answers to the different questions, however, are not necessarily incompatible; indeed, one "why" question often leads to another. Furthermore, additional complexity is introduced when researchers asking questions at the same level disagree or use different approaches. We'll discuss each of these levels and different ways of viewing media audiences before we examine the research available.

Media Use Situations. One "why" question focuses on why people actually engage in media behaviors in specific situations. In other words, what leads one to read a newspaper, watch TV or listen to the radio at a point in time? What are the intentions that lead people to seek media or other activities, and are such intentions triggered by different situations (dinner, commuting, companionship with family, etc.)? Few researchers have systematically looked at situational determinants of media consumption, but we can all find examples in our own lives. If the newspaper doesn't arrive in the morning, many of us are at a loss during breakfast. Our "media situations" themselves form patterns that are more or less peculiar to individuals, which is the focus of other "why questions."

The Individual Level. "Why" do people use media differently and how do individual media consumption patterns develop? People asking this why question often locate the origins of TV viewing and newspaper reading within individuals, who are viewed as having at least a measure of responsibility for their own media use. But even this question is more complex than we might think. One "why" question seeks to identify the uses and gratifications that attract people to the media and hold them once they're there. This perspective tries to link more basic human needs with wants and wishes and with the gratifications people derive from media and the uses to which they put media. Here too we can find examples from our own lives. Most of us use the entertainment guides of newspapers to help plan our weekends; the constant background music from a radio may make us feel a bit less lonely or bored. However, our own patterns of media consumption are not created wholesale with no influence from our families. Indeed, we are socialized into a host of customs and behaviors. A variety of researchers have used the socialization perspective to understand how customs, beliefs, values, roles and behavioral patterns are passed along from one generation to the next. Certainly the family is a major socialization agent involved in teaching us how to think about the media and how to use them.

Others look at individual differences in media use patterns by focusing on personalities and individual characteristics. Are our media patterns linked to personality profiles? For example, compulsively curious people may be hyperactive information-seekers. Secondly, we can look at individual differences in terms of two other sets of characteristics, ascriptive factors that we inherit or carry around with us (for example, sex, race, ethnicity) and achievement-oriented factors such as education, income and occupational status. Research into personality and individual differences such as education and income is quite extensive, but more recently we have begun to ask how media use fits into life styles.

Media and the Social System. A third set of "why" questions locates the origins of media-use patterns outside the individual, though it doesn't claim that "everything" is determined by the "social system." This "structural/cultural" explanation either stresses the importance of such national/cultural factors as social stratification and economic equality, or it emphasizes the way that the national media system and availability of content constrain or affect people's media use patterns (see Webster and Wakshlag, 1983). This perspective suggests that such media consumption is "low involvement behavior" that is essentially unplanned. Thus, people are more or less acquiescing to nationally-laid plans beyond our individual control: we watch TV sitcoms because that's what the networks give us. Most of the literature that focuses the why question at this level is descriptive or anecdotal, though comparisons across time and comparisons of different countries will eventually provide more grounded explanations.

Defining "Media Use". Each "why" question paints a different picture of the mass media audience, but the differences concern not only explanations but definitions of "media use." People often speak of "media use" or "TV consumption" as if they were self explanatory, but they're not. Sometimes we use the terms to refer to the amount of time people spend engaging in particular media behaviors, but this captures only a single dimension of the complex behaviors labeled media use. Salomon and Cohen (1978) note that the idea of "television viewing" may refer to several different things: addiction to TV, the amount of content absorbed, or the decision-making behavior one performs in the service of personal gratification. Hill (1983) found three distinct but related dimensions to media exposure: frequency, activeness, and attentiveness during exposure.

Probably the most controversial element of media use is the extent to which people are active or passive. As Schramm (1973) notes, the audience is no longer viewed as simply a passive mass of individuals but rather as active entities who interact with the sender of the messages. From World War I to the 1950's, the audience was considered passive and took the label of "target" audience. But evidence from surveys and other research showed that the audience was not always responding as predicted. This led to the view that audiences may be divided into social categories — education, income, beliefs, etc. These categories of people would develop reference groups which they would use for comparing media content processed. So there was a dramatic shift in perspectives. The audience no longer was a passive, defenseless target but an active thing which had to be dealt with. Bauer (1973) wrote that "people actively seek out information for such diverse purposes as reinforcing or consolidating their existing opinions, preserving or strengthening their self-image, ingratiating themselves with other persons, or even for the solving of cognitive problems."

British researcher Jay Blumler (1979) notes that the concept of an "active" audience is not totally "ideology" free and should be converted into an empirical question and tested. In other words, some people prefer to think of the audience as either active or passive because it justifies their view of what the media system should look like. Blumler suggests that the viewer is active prior to exposure if he consults information about what is available, plans what will be consumed, has a prior expectation, or sets criteria as to what is preferable to consume. We might expect people to be active in some situations, inactive in others (Levy and Windahl, 1984).

In the following sections we will look at the evidence researchers have gathered to answer "why questions." First, we will look at media use situations. Then we will move to the individual level where we find the bulk of the evidence falling into two streams of research: social categories which look at the relationships between media patterns and two sets of factors (ascriptive characteristics such as race and ethnicity and achievement-oriented factors such as education and income); and uses and gratifications which refer to the ways in which people use the media and are gratified by that use. Two additional sections will look at media socialization—how individual differences in media use are passed on by the family, and life styles—which represent an integration of media use with other elements that make up patterns of daily activities.

Media Consuming Situations

What directs you to turn on the TV set rather than go visit a friend? And what leads you to read a book rather than go for a walk? Indeed, there is some question about how "active" people are in their media use. Do you consciously decide to watch TV because you're bored? Or do you plan your TV viewing in advance filling in the rest of your free time with other activities. As we noted earlier in this chapter, much of TV viewing appears to be "time filler," something done when other alternatives have been ruled out or are even less attractive. Clearly, not all media-use situations are the same for a particular person.

The Action/Motivation perspective pictures the individual as independent from society and free to develop behaviors that move him toward goals and maximize his personal growth (Grunig, 1979a). This perspective focuses on communication strategies for seeking, avoiding and processing information. Its basic assumptions are: individual freedom of choice to choose and interpret media experiences, motivated action as a function of orientations toward some future state, and conscious goals described by the individual as the most suitable objects of study. Instances of media use in this perspective are defined as individual information-seeking acts and individuals are assumed to be rational, goal-directed media users.

Another way to define this perspective is its emphasis on the conditions that activiate individuals to move toward or away from media situations. Psychologists generally limit use of the term motivation to "activation" of behaviors, reserving the direction of such behaviors to other concepts such as "learning." There is relatively little empirical research that focuses on initiating intentions or motivations that propel people toward or away from media use.

Minimally, then, a motivational analysis of media behavior addresses the conditions under which the behavior is activated, triggered, aroused, or instigated. So "activation" is concerned with the question, "Why does behavior occur?" while "direction" is concerned with the question, "Given the many forms behavior can take, why does it take this form?" The concept of motivation has been used considerably in the work of personality theorists (see Freud, Fromm, Sullivan, Horney). To predict behavior we have to measure more than just predisposition to respond, but also whether the situation is seen as one that engages the predisposition. This view of motivation calls for an analysis of conditions that activate media behaviors which fits with the need for both situation and personality variables as behavioral determinants (Unger, 1984).

How are media behaviors initiated? To what extent can we say people "actively" seek to engage in media behaviors? One researcher argues that people use media the same as they play tennis or eat food—to seek pleasure—and there's no need to pursue the question further. That doesn't tell us why some people in one situation decide to seek pleasure by watching "Dallas" on TV, but the next week seek pleasure by reading the newspaper at the same time. The question isn't that easily dispensed with. Rather than classifying all media use as "pleasure seeking," some observers recently have found it useful to distinguish between situations in which people seek media content and situations in which the process of reading, viewing or listening is central. Jeffres (1975) distinguished between "media-seeking" and "content-seeking." The first refers to situations in which you turn to the media because the act of consumption—reading, watching, listening—is more important than the content. You might, for example, turn on the TV because you're bored and the content is a secondary consideration; you may pick the "lesser of several evils" available at that moment. Again, you're driving across country on a long trip and turn the radio on to stay awake; you don't even know what is on but you need to "listen" regardless of the content. Certainly the poor reception or offensive content may lead you to consider other alternatives, but content is a secondary consideration. In content-seeking situations, you decide to use a medium *because* of the content. Here you rush home to find out "who shot J.R." or you anxiously wait for your favorite film director's latest work to arrive in town and plan accordingly. Some of our content-seeking aims at larger parcels than others—TV programs vs. the weather. The actual seeking of particular items may be called "information-seeking." How often do you pick up the newspaper to find out the outcome of a sports event, what's on TV (Gantz and Eastman, 1983), or what's for sale at the grocery store? Another type of media use might be called "non-seeking" (Jeffres, 1975) where the individual does not actively seek either content or media but is virtually sought out by other people or the media. Here you're sitting in the back of someone else's automobile and are "forced" to listen to the radio whether you want to or not. Or someone thrusts a magazine article in your face and solicits your cooperation.

The content/process distinction, also noted by others (Cutler and Danowski, 1980; Kelly, 1978; Csikszentmihalyi, 1975), is important for pragmatic reasons too. We might hypothesize that media-seeking, or a concern for process, is related to habitual use and patterns that are likely to continue over time. Thus, people who media-seek newspapers may be more likely to continue their reading for a longer period than those whose newspaper use is characterized as information seeking. An emphasis on "process" does not mean that people are not selective once reading or viewing has begun. Jeffres (1975) has elaborated this in terms of TV viewing and newspaper reading. His findings indicate that people who media-seek newspapers are more likely to start reading on page one while content-seekers are more likely to begin with other sections of the paper. Research conducted for the Newspaper Advertising Bureau (Gollin, 1978) found that 62% of Americans read a paper by going through the entire paper and reading whatever is interesting.

This is a complex area. It should be mentioned that some media behavior is done for negative reasons—for example, other people turn on the TV. Jeffres (1974; 1976) reports that 74% say they are content-seeking when they turn on the TV as opposed to media-seeking. Newspapers (66%) and radio (45%), on the other hand, are more associated with media-seeking. People just wanted to "listen to the radio" or "read the newspaper." A significant portion of radio use (19%) is non-seeking, that is, forced by circumstances.

We get another picture of people's activity from a 1977 national survey done for the Newspaper Advertising Bureau (Gollin, 1978). People who had a choice of news programs in the early evening were asked why they watched the program they chose rather than another available at the same time. The reasons they gave provide some clues for understanding the motives and habits that underlie TV news-watching patterns. Responses are classified into 20 categories that reflect either *perceived attributes* of the programs themselves (for example, style or content) or the *viewing situation* of the individual TV news consumer.

Three reasons stand out as prime justifications for people's viewing of either local or network news programs (see Table 4-7). First was attachment to a favorite newscaster and second was inertia — the choice of a channel taking precedence over the selection of a news show. The 20% of viewers who gave reasons of this kind attest to the importance of audience flow in building news audiences (also see Wakshlag et al., 1983). However, the use of remote control channel

Table 4-7

Reasons for Watching a Specific News Program

Reason	Viewed Network news	Viewed Local news
Style of Presentation	38%	25%
My favorite newscaster(s)	32%	18%
More entertaining	5%	6%
(more) Pictoral coverage	1%	1%
Content, Quality	21%	23%
Local coverage	5%	8%
Clear coverage	4%	2%
More informative	4%	4%
Weather reporting	3%	6%
National/World coverage	3%	*
Up-to-date coverage	1%	2%
Variety of coverage	1%	1%
News/Human interest specials	*	*
Viewing Situation	33%	43%
Habit	14%	13%
News on channel I was watching	11%	24%
Better reception on that channel	6%	3%
Spouse prefers/watches it	2%	3%
General	26%	26%
Like it better (no further specifics)	13%	11%
All other reasons	5%	7%
No particular reason	2%	5%
Don't know/no answer	6%	3%
	118%	117%

*Less than a half percent.

Source: Albert E. Gollin, "The Daily Diet of News" (New York: Newspaper Advertising Bureau, 1978). Used with permission.

selectors may reduce the tendency to watch a single station. The third specific factor mentioned by a substantial number of people was habit and 13% gave answers that stressed the routine nature of their news viewing.

Situational factors and the personal style of newscasters are the key considerations that underlie exposure to TV news. Based on these findings, how active are television news consumers on an average weekday in their use of TV as a news source? The answer seems to be "not very." The appeal of specific newscasters may betray an "active" orientation by those for whom this factor was important, but the other major reasons cited strongly suggest the news was being seen by a large percentage because the TV set was on. Rubin (1984) found that ritualized TV use was habitual, frequent and indicated a high regard for TV as a medium. Instrumental TV viewing, by contrast, was purposeful, selective and goal-directed.

Individual Media Patterns

Though most of my newspaper reading may be media-seeking, yours may be content-seeking for the most part. Thus, we have different patterns of media use, and here we turn to individual differences that may help explain such diverse patterns. In my household, breakfast may trigger newspaper reading while the smell of bacon and eggs may accompany *AM America* in your household. Situations may be quite similar, but the media patterns differ. How do we explain individual differences? One of the most prominent approaches has been called "social categories."

This perspective uses demographic categories to describe who uses mass media. It matches media consumption with such factors as: race, sex, income, education, occupation, religion, marital status, ethnicity and homeownership. This perspective is generally concerned more with description than explanation, but the social categories of media audiences provide us with "locator variables," those that help us find people exhibiting particular media consumption patterns.

Social Categories

Of all the potential social categories that help explain why people use the mass media, three have received the bulk of our attention because they seem to be the most significant: education, income and occupation. Sometimes the three factors are combined into "socioeconomic status" (SES) or used to figure "social class." SES may affect our media behaviors in many ways: total media use, greater use of one medium than another, or content preferences.

Is overall time spent with the media related to our powerful SES predictors? Robinson's 1975 diary study did not find any general increase or decrease in media use as one went up the educational ladder, though there was a small drop among those with college degrees. The two educational groups with the most and the least amount of free time available spent about the same proportion of that time with the media: those with some college education spent 42% of their 47.5 hours of free time with mass media while those with college degrees spent 45% of their 36.1 free hours weekly consuming newspapers, books, etc. Only a small percentage escape from all media on a given day. Who are these people? McQuail (1976) quotes Butler and Stokes (1970) as finding non-newspaper use in Britain associated with lack of education, low income, youth or extreme age, sickness, cultural isolation and alienation. On the other hand, Jackson-Beeck (1977) found that non-TV viewers are rare in the U.S., "not a meaningful population subgroup" and socially insignificant.

Education also is related to individual media use, though the differences are not always very large. As Table 4-8 shows, the higher your education, the more likely you are to have listened to the radio, read a newspaper or gone to a film. However, exposure to TV is similar among all education groups. More educated people are heavier readers of both morning and evening papers (Einsiedel, 1983) but the largest differences are for morning papers. College graduates turn to a newspaper more often during the day. They say they are less satisfied with what they get from TV news and want added details from newspapers. Robinson also found that the better educated spend slightly more time reading the newspaper, but they spent considerably more time reading magazines and books. While the average adult reads 1.13 magazines per day, a college educated person reads 1.37 (MPA, 1984).

Education affects not only the amount of time we spend with different media but also our content and format preferences (Mobley, 1984). The better-educated are more likely to listen to classical or easy-listening radio stations, the lesser educated to top-40 or country-western stations. The more highly educated also tend to prefer public broadcasting on TV more than less educated people, and they report more moviegoing (Peterson and Davis, 1978).

Income. Relationships between income and media use are similar to those discussed for education but there also are differences. Those with more income are less likely to have watched TV yesterday, but are more likely to have turned on the radio or to have read a paper. Income also interacts with age in affecting media use. Older people, especially those retired, were heavier daily viewers of TV and watched the news more often. Magazine readership rises with each income level and those in households with $40,000 or more annual incomes are a third

Table 4-8
Media Use by Education and Income

	Watched TV yesterday	Saw TV news yesterday	Listened to radio yesterday	Heard radio news yesterday	Read any newspaper yesterday	Go to movie frequently
All Adults	84%	67%	67%	48%	67%	20%
Education						
Not high school graduate	86%	72%	56%	37%	58%	10%
High school graduate	85%	64%	66%	45%	66%	21%
Some college	81%	66%	73%	55%	67%	{ 29%
College graduate	83%	69%	76%	61%	79%	
Income						
Less than $10,000	88%	75%	55%	42%	53%	
$10,000-$14,999	86%	68%	63%	45%	64%	
$15,000-$24,999	87%	67%	64%	45%	67%	
$25,000-34,999	82%	66%	76%	58%	74%	
$35,000 or more	80%	66%	76%	55%	77%	

Sources: Albert E. Gollin and Nicolas A. Bloom. *Newspapers in American News Habits: A Comparative Assessment.* New York: Newspaper Advertising Bureau, 1985. Survey conducted in 1982. Gertner, 1985. (Movie attendance = at least monthly). Used with permission.

more likely to read magazines than the average adult (MPA, 1984).

Occupation. If we look at occupations in terms of a ladder of status, we find increasing print media use with advancing status. Almost a fourth of managers and officials read both morning and evening papers — twice the figure for most occupational groups (Gollin, 1978). Blue collar workers read a daily paper less than those in white collar occupations or those who were not employed. Occupation and class also have been related to media use in other countries such as Yugoslavia (Dzinic, 1974) and Great Britain. In the latter, interviews with working and middle class adults found differences in how some news is interpreted by people from the two classes, but papers were the most important source of information on industrial relations for both groups, then TV, radio, and finally other media (Hartman, 1979). Two other British researchers studying a group of boys over two decades found that TV was a major home-based activity in the working class where it occupied a more central place in the home-based leisure compared with his middle-class counterparts (Himmelweit and Swift, 1976).

Achievement-oriented categories such as occupation are important because they point to social roles that require or create a desire for information about one's environment. However, some social categories are inherited or assigned to us. These "ascriptive" categories, also important for media use, include: gender, marital status, race, ethnicity and geographic designation.

Gender. Changes in sex roles in the U.S. today are likely to show up in changed leisure behavior in the future, but a study by Gentry and Doering (1979) found traditional gender differences in media use: males were more likely to go to X-rated movies, watch sports on TV and read sex-oriented magazines while females were more likely to watch TV soaps, read the society page in newspapers, and read home-oriented magazines.

Robinson's 1975 diary data show the total time spent with mass media is greatest among single housewives. Married housewives spent 7 hours less each week; some gender differences, thus, reflect occupational status. As Table 4-9 shows, only minor differences are found between the percentage of men and women who watched TV or read a newspaper "yesterday," but larger differences occur for radio listening. More gender differences emerge when we look beyond time spent with media to content and format preferences: newspaper content (Weaver and Mauro, 1978); magazine preferences (Sosanie and Szybillo, 1978); graphic design in advertising (Surlin and Kosak, 1975); radio formats (Lull, Johnson and Sweeny, 1978); and TV programs (Frank and Greenberg, 1979).

Race and Ethnicity. Attention to ethnic and racial differences in media use has grown in the past two decades. Robinson's 1975 diary data show that Blacks and whites spent about the same percentage of their free time with the media (44%). There also was no racial difference between the percentage of whites and non-whites who watch TV or TV news on an average day, as Table 4-9 shows. However, whites were more likely to listen to radio news and to read a daily newspaper on an average day. Surveys also show Blacks favor programs featuring Black performers (Allen and Bielby, 1979) but have newspaper reading patterns similar to those among the general population when SES is taken into account (Jackson, 1978). While Blacks have received some attention in the past two decades, other racial and ethnic groups in the United States only recently have come to the fore (e.g., Allen and Clarke, 1980). Surveys of Hispanics show that those who are more traditional are oriented toward Spanish-language radio (O'Guinn and Meyer, 1984) and TV programs, while non-traditionals — younger and more educated — prefer radio and TV programs in English (Dunn, 1975; Greenberg et al., 1983). White ethnic groups also are not homogenous media audiences. By providing news of the ethnic community and the mother country, ethnic media seem to meet needs not fulfilled by the metropolitan media. Czechs, Hungarians, Irish, Slovenes and other ethnics in one study (Jeffres and Hur, 1980) spent a considerable

Table 4-9

Media Use by Ascriptive Factors

Percentages of People Who:

	Watched TV yesterday	Saw TV news yesterday	Listened to radio yesterday	Heard radio news yesterday	Read newspaper yesterday
All Adults	84%	67%	67%	48%	67%
Gender:					
Male	84%	68%	70%	51%	68%
Female	85%	66%	63%	44%	66%
Race:					
White	84%	67%	67%	48%	69%
Nonwhite	86%	70%	64%	43%	56%
City/Area Population					
Non-metro. area	84%	66%	62%	47%	68%
50,000-249,999	86%	67%	68%	54%	65%
250,000-499,999	81%	62%	67%	42%	73%
500,000 or more	85%	70%	69%	49%	64%

Source: Albert E. Gollin and Nicolas A. Bloom. *Newspapers in American News Habits: A Comparative Assessment.* New York: Newspaper Advertising Bureau, 1985. Survey conducted in 1982. Used with permission.

amount of time with both ethnic and metropolitan mass media. Those who identify more strongly with their ethnic groups use the ethnic media more often (Jeffres and Barnard, 1982; Korzenny et al., 1983).

Other Ascriptive Factors. Religious affiliation affects exposure to some TV programs, particularly those with religious themes (Tanney and Johnson, 1984; Gaddy, 1984). Marital status is another important factor. For example, married people tend to be heavier newspaper subscribers. The size of a community and people's commitment to living there are also predictors of daily newspaper circulation. That commitment is expressed as homeownership and local involvement (Stone, 1977; Rarick, 1973; Jackson, 1981, Stone and Fortini-Campbell, 1981; Weaver and Fielder, 1983). People living in larger cities are more likely to read morning papers while radio news captures a larger percentage of people in smaller towns and cities. TV viewing does not seem to differ much by size of population. Other research shows that people living in rural areas are less likely to read daily papers regularly, primarily because of availability.

In summary, social categories are useful ways to locate members of media audiences in the larger environment. Media use is related to some of the characteristics in each of the two groups, ascriptive and achievement-oriented factors. The higher the education, the less likely one watches TV but the more likely one reads a newspaper or goes to films. Income and occupation are similarly related to media use. Traditional gender differences also have been found in media use. Men, for example, watch more sports on TV and women watch more soaps. Race appears to be unrelated to the amount of time spent watching TV, but whites are more likely to read daily newspapers than Blacks. Use of ethnic media has been related to group identification among a variety of different ethnics (e.g., Hispanics, Czechs, Hungarians). Other factors linked to some media behaviors are religion, marital status, and community integration.

Uses and Gratifications

A second approach to explaining people's patterns of media behavior is called "uses and gratifications." This perspective examines media functions from the view of the consumer; it seeks to examine the uses to which people put their media behaviors and the gratifications that people derive from media use. In general, researchers working in this tradition have provided us with lists of what people say attracts them to the media and holds them there. A second area of concern has been the question of whether different media or different content are "functionally equivalent"; in other words, people may relieve their boredom by either reading a book, watching TV, or visiting with friends. These behaviors may then be functionally equivalent.

The uses-and-gratifications tradition takes the audience member as the focus. According to this view, audience members can articulate their needs and the uses to which they put the media. The media also are seen to compete with other sources of need satisfaction. Uses and gratifications draws on research that goes back to the 1940's. Early studies looked at the functions of radio soap operas (Herzog, 1942), the use of the media to orient oneself to other people (Lasswell, 1948), and use of films for escape.

McQuail, Blumler and Brown (1972) present their view of the audience's relation to the media: "The audience member temporarily occupies a particular position in relation to what he is viewing, a position affected by a large number of factors, including those deriving from his personality, social background, experience, immediate social contact, and, of course, from the content itself. He brings certain expectations and responds in line with these, and he derives certain affective, cognitive and instrumental satisfactions."

McQuail and his colleagues have developed a typology of gratifications that starts with diversion—including escape from routine, problems and emotional release. Second are personal relationships which include vicarious (para-social) companionship and social utility such as conversations, family viewing, and viewing to meet the standards of a group. Third is personal identity which includes personal reference (self evaluation), reality exploration (ideas about personal concerns) and value reinforcement. Finally, there is the surveillance function (McDonald and Glynn, 1984).

Where do uses and gratifications come from? Dimmick, McCain and Bolton (1979) identify two sources. One is an individual's need structure, which itself may be affected by changes in one's physical tastes or socio-psychological states. As one grows older, for example, some needs increase while others fade in importance, and one's media use pattern will change to fit the new constellation of uses and gratifications that matches the underlying needs. A second factor which may alter one's uses and gratifications pattern is changes in the available media (Sparkes, 1983) and nonmedia sources of need satisfaction. Here, we may find a new media or leisure-time innovation such as cable TV, video discs, or jogging. These offer new avenues that compete with existing ones for fulfilling different uses and gratifications. Changes in media and other behaviors may result as a consequence.

People do not develop their pictures of the media and potential uses in a vacuum. The newer technologies offer us a clear example of this as businessmen try to figure out how to market videotext or interactive cable services. The general public will need to learn how the new services can be used and what gratifications can be derived from that use before they diffuse widely throughout the population. This will be a social process as individuals consult with friends and neighbors, experts and advertising messages. The actual application at a later time will involve matching the potential uses and gratifications with personal needs, but that will follow this general "public educational process." Lichtenstein and Rosenfeld (1984) support the notion that the decision to utilize mass communication channels has two parts. The first involves acquiring normative expectations about gratifications from different media; the second concerns individual decisions about how to seek gratifications within the defined environment. Thus, an individual makes decisions from among socially and culturally defined possibilities. Stanford (1984) found some support for this view. She concluded that general orientations to TV (e.g., TV's most important function is entertainment) give a better explanation of actual gratifications received from a particular TV program than efforts to link them to needs.

Needs and Uses/Grats. Five groups of "needs" were identified by Katz,

Gurevitch and Haas (1973) in Israel: 1) cognitive needs, such as the need to understand; 2) affective needs relating to strengthening aesthetic or emotional experience; 3) integrative needs related to strengthening one's confidence, credibility, stability; 4) needs relating to strengthening contact with family, friends and the world;, and 5) needs related to escape or tension release. Results of their survey showed that books cultivated the inner self while films and TV gave pleasure in the Israeli context. They also found TV the most diffuse medium and users applied it to a wide range of functions, whereas movies and newspapers were the most specific media.

We would not expect one's media pattern over time to be maintained unless the media behavior provided the expected uses and gratifications, i.e., met personal needs (Swanson, 1979). Evidence for this was found by Palmgren and Rayburn (1979), who concluded that uses and gratifications are better predictors of public TV viewing than such traditional social categories as education and income. We also have evidence from the print media (Wang, 1977; Atkin, 1973). Actual sources of media gratifications include: media content, exposure to the media per se, and the social context that typifies the situation, such as sitting in a darkened movie theater (Katz, Blumler and Gurevitch, 1974).

Uses/Grats Each Medium Provides. TV has been linked with such a broad range of uses and gratifications that many critics have feared it would lead to the "colonization" of virtually all leisure time (Robinson and Sahin, 1981). Rubin (1983) found two television viewer types. The first uses TV out of habit, to pass the time, and for entertainment; this model of audience use emphasizes the communication medium itself. A second type of TV viewer — the escapist viewer — uses TV to forget about personal problems and to get away from other people or tasks. Escapist viewing occurs at reduced levels.

TV's appeal to youth also is based on uses and gratifications. Rubin (1977) investigated differences among children, young teenagers and adolescents in their TV viewing behaviors and motivations to use TV. Six sets of reasons for viewing emerged: to learn, as a habit or to pass time, for companionship, to forget or for escape, for arousal, and for relaxation. Viewing to pass time was the prominent reason for viewing TV across all age groups. Though adolescents also seem to use TV for "information" or "entertainment," Wade (1973) found that media play a relatively small part in teenage lives. TV seemed to be a leisure option exercised when family communication was somewhat poor or clubs and hobbies insignificant. Radio and film also are favorite media of younger audiences, the former primarily because of its musical gratifications. The most frequently-cited use of radio by youths is to pass the time, as filler or background (Gantz et al., 1978). Relieving tension and sustaining a desirable mood also were mentioned by youths and others (Bryant and Zillman, 1984).

Reading itself is a gratifying experience for many people, yet 45% of U.S. adults do not read books at all according to the Library Association. However, at least a third of adults say they draw "creative satisfaction" from reading books. The print media that manage to attract and to hold larger audiences are newspapers and magazines. Of course, people read newspapers "for news," but they also are attracted by the advertising, comics, bridge columns, advice columns, etc. (Larkin and Grotta, 1979). Towers (1985) looked at newspaper readers' uses and gratifications and found three dimensions emerging: surveillance, diversion and interaction. Surveillance was more important for regular subscribers and readers while occasional weekday readers used it more for interaction.

Social Situations. Blumler (1979) sought to link people's social situations and their media-related needs. Factors representing social situations are grouped as follows: (1) normative influences on what people get out of the media, such as one's lifecycle position or place in the social structure; (2) compensators, which are sources of a need to compensate for the lack of opportunities and capacities, for example, lack of a phone, car or satisfying job; (3) facilitating factors which enable one to have a richer involvement with media content, such as organizational affiliation and frequent social interaction; and (4) subjective reaction or adjustment to one's situation indicated by satisfaction with one's work and leisure. Results show that newspaper gratifications tend to be linked to facilitating influences while TV uses and gratifications are connected to compensatory ones.

Individual Patterns. Particular needs and uses-and-gratifications will be more important for some people than others. What are these individual differences? For example, Lometti, Reeves and Bybee (1977) found that behavioral guidance was the most important media use for the college age group. The elderly provide an example of a social group whose use of mass media is linked to particular needs though the evidence is still not clear. Davis (1971) did not find support for the view that older adults use TV as a substitute for social involvement, but Hess (1974) found that TV viewing can substitute for face-to-face communication no longer available to the elderly. Three non-media sources of gratification — job, social activity, and solitary activity — were more important than the media in a study of elderly by Swank (1979). Examining the relationship between source dependence and life style, Swank (1979) found evidence that print media and radio use may facilitate interpersonal contact rather than function as substitutes for missing activities.

Are Media Functionally Equivalent? Are the media complementary in their uses—TV specializing in particular gratifications while newspapers serve other uses—or are the mass media functionally equivalent and interchangeable in their satisfaction of people's needs? After reviewing more than 100 studies conducted between 1955 and 1977, Weaver and Budeenbaum (1979) concluded that people value both newspapers and TV in complementary manners for knowledge and diversion as well as an adjunct to interpersonal communication. While TV is seen as fulfilling a general-surveillance function, papers are associated with information seeking, in-depth subject knowledge and election guidance. Only for escape is there a clear difference between newspapers and TV. Other studies find: paper subscribers using TV as a complementary medium (Grotta et al., 1975); TV and papers evenly split in satisfying the need to keep tabs on things while TV was favored for relaxing, killing time and being entertained (Weaver, Wilhoit, and Riede, 1979); people paid not to use TV turned to radio, magazines, newspapers, friends and associates for entertainment (Tan, 1977).

Environment. The environment in which the audience finds itself affects both people's "need structure" and the list of behavioral alternatives. Changes in geographic location may mean different facilities are available to meet people's needs. Kelly (1978) looked at leisure styles in three cities to examine factors that shape leisure choices. They found similarity in how activities were ranked in terms of importance: marriage intimacy, reading, and family activity lead all rankings while TV ranked no higher than sixth out of more than a dozen. Kelly concludes that similarities in leisure patters were striking and differences were explainable by the environment—climates, natural resources available, and community opportunities. New media technologies are important examples of the man-made environment that may expand or restrict leisure alternatives (Butler and Kent, 1983). Nordlund (1978) suggests that interaction with available media may lead to increased dependency on the mass media rather than other sources of "company" at times of loneliness.

Criticism. There has been a variety of criticism of the use-and-gratifications research tradition. One such criticism argues that the volume of work has produced little more than conflicting lists of "uses and grats." Others have pointed to conceptual confusion or asked where the uses themselves come from (Swanson, 1979). Some of this criticism is premature as researchers build on each other's work and extend our ability to generalize across time and situations. Rosengren (1974) attempts to provide a paradigm to avoid some ambiguities. Figure 4-1 contains basic human needs, motives and behaviors, individual characteristics, the structure of society and media structure, and uses-and-gratifications derived from media use. Another criticism noted by some observers is that the uses-and-

Figure 4-1

Visualized Paradigm for Uses and Gratifications Research

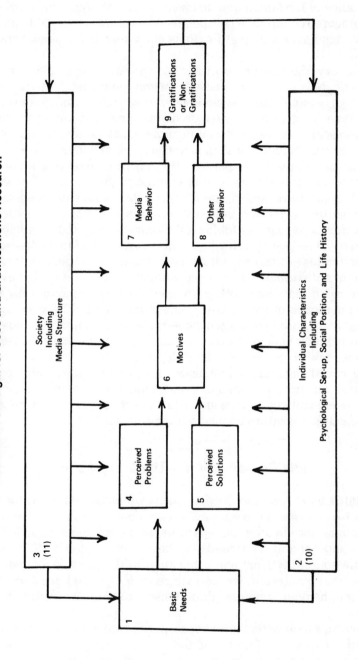

Source: Karl E. Rosengren, "Uses and Gratifications: A Paradigm Outlined," *The Uses of Mass Communications*, edited by Jay E. Blumer and Elihu Katz. Copyright © 1974 by Sage Publications. Reprinted by permission of Sage Publications, Inc.

gratifications perspective seems to emphasize stability and maintenance of the status quo. In its early days this may have been the case, but more recently the perspective has been elaborated to identify ways in which uses and gratifications change as one's need structure changes.

In summary, the uses and gratifications perspective has been used to understand how people view their media behaviors. Attributing a measure of activity to the audience, researchers have developed several typologies that tap various dimensions of meaning including: diversion/escape, coping with relationships (with family, friends, or via para-social communication with strangers), establishing and reinforcing personal identity (as a personality and role enactment), and surveying the environment (understanding the political, social, economic systems). Some have linked use of particular media to categories of needs (cognitive, affective, integrative, and escape) or particular uses and gratifications (e.g., watching TV to pass time is the dominant use for all age groups). Social situations have been linked to media-related needs. Individual differences have been found in people's patterns of uses and gratifications (e.g., college students use media for behavioral guidance more than many other groups). We also discussed the functional equivalence of media with some evidence that TV viewing and newspaper use both provide the same range of uses and gratifications but each medium specializes in particular functions (e.g., TV viewing for escape, newspaper reading for indepth knowledge).

While social categories and uses and gratifications help explain differences in people's media use, researchers using these perspectives generally have focused on the short-range. A longer view is provided by the literature on media socialization.

Media Socialization — The Longer View

"Socialization" refers to the process by which behaviors, values and customs are learned by each new generation. We learn many of our behaviors in the family; our parents serve as models or explicit teachers encouraging us to read or not to watch too much TV. Thus, we find some continuity from one generation to the next. We expect, for example, that children in homes with reading material are more likely to become heavier readers than those from homes without such material.

In a sense, socialization is a process that prepares one to take on the way of life of his or her family and the larger social groups one needs in order to perform adequately as an adult. How does this process occur? There appear to be three ways for mass media socialization: modeling, reinforcement and social interaction. Evidence of actual reinforcement is scanty. It seems that few parents bother to reward or punish their children for exhibiting media behaviors (Mohr, 1979). In a study of high school sophomores, Thorn (1978) found only 28% said their parents ever suggest or require that they not watch certain programs. In modeling, a child uses his parents' media pattern as an example for his own behavior. Presence of a newspaper in the home as a child means one will be more likely to read one as an adult (Einsiedel, 1983). Jeffres (1968) found that modeling is more likely to occur among teenage boys when they strongly identify with their fathers. Most of the attempts to use reward and punishment to influence children's media behavior come before adolescence (Lyle and Hoffman, 1971).

Evidence for learning through social interaction is more abundant. A series of studies by a group at the University of Wisconsin (McLeod and O'Keefe, 1972) show that the amount of time adolescents spend watching TV and the type of content viewed are affected by parent-child interaction. They characterized families in terms of two dimensions of parent-child interaction: "socio-oreintation," which focuses on child-parent relations, and "content-orientation," which focuses on child-concept relations. In families that stress only social relations (called "protective families"), adolescents spend the most time watching TV; they also prefer entertainment to news and public affairs programs. In homes with strong and varied conceptual development but low insistence on obedience (called "pluralistic families"), adolescents spend relatively little time watching TV and show relatively great interest in news and public affairs programs. The third type of home, "laissez-faire," is characterized by both low socio-orientation and low concept-orientation. In such homes, adolescents' TV viewing is moderately high but they seem disinterested in newspapers or public affairs programs on TV.

Much TV viewing or radio listening occurs as a family or group-activity. Chaffee (1972) notes the need to look at the interpersonal context in which media are actually used. Decisions to watch TV, or what to watch, may be the product of others' decisions or a family negotiation. Parents serve both as models as well as explicit teachers of their children in such situations. This group viewing also may create problems. For example, in a 1980 poll of adult women (Roper, 1980), 21% cited TV viewing decisions as a source of marital disagreement, more than twice the figure for politics and three times the number citing sex as centers for discord. And another survey which solicited kids' most commonly voiced complaints showed that more than a third complained about their parents not buying them things that they see advertised on TV. How do families solve conflicts over media use? Dimmick (1976) looked at the family communication patterns and how they relate to solving conflicts over TV viewing. The families that stress concept orientation solve TV viewing disputes via voting or compromise to a much greater degree than the other types. Some voting and compromise are evident in consensual families for all aged children and in protective and laissez-faire families with older adolescents age 15-17.

While parents are a major force in the socialization process, they are not the only force. There are many different agents of socialization. Peer groups and siblings also are important. Teachers, spouses, one's own children, work associates, friends, and neighbors may all serve to influence one's media pattern. The potential importance of various agents changes as the individual influenced matures and grows old. From early childhood to adolescence, the parents' influence wanes and the influence of peers and teachers increases. In adulthood, occupational peer groups, friends, spouses, and the various reference groups we adopt as bellwethers for our opinions should increase their power to influence media usage.

Adoni (1979) looked at mass media use and two of the primary agents of socialization, parents and peers. Studying 15-17 year-old students in Israel, Adoni found that teenagers who had strong ties with peers also made frequent trips to the cinema, theater and rock concerts. These media and situations provide opportunities for adolescents to reinforce social ties with their peers. Strong peer group ties also were found for those with frequent exposure to magazines, records and radio — the youth-dominated medium. Youths who had developed the highest degree of interaction with both parents and peers also were the most active media consumers. A decrease in almost all activities characterizes low interaction with both peers and parents. Book and record consumption seem to serve as substitutes for weak integration in these primary groups. Looking at seventh, eleventh, and twelfth graders in the U.S., Chaffee and Tims (1976) found that adolescents from socio-oriented families tended to vary their viewing patterns more in the direction of their parents than did those in families where this orientation was weak. Strong peer orientations were found to be associated with conformity to peer viewing norms when viewing with friends. Social learning was greatest when the child viewed with parents.

Families exert influence by making media available. Elliott Medrich (1979) found that the TV set is always on in more than a third of inner city families whether anyone is watching or not. Called "constant TV households," these families are ones where parents are less likely to control, regulate or monitor their children's viewing. The majority of children in such TV households were heavy viewers and could watch as much as they wished. The larger the household, the more likely the family will subscribe to cable TV for greater variety (Metzger, 1983).

The importance of mass media varies through the life cycle. Earlier we examined media use patterns for adults. Here we will look at childhood, adolescence and early adulthood.

Childhood. Mass media consumption begins very early in a child's life. TV is the first medium to occupy much prominence in most contemporary chidren's lives in the Western world. However, children's short attention spans mean early viewing is usually for brief periods. Preschool children are exposed to about 25 hours of TV each week. Children typically begin their TV viewing three to four years before entering first grade. Most children watch at least some TV every day and most watch for two or more hours per day. The amount of viewing increases during the elementary school years but there is no agreement on when peak viewing occurs. Comstock and his colleagues (1978) report that children age 2-5 watch TV 29 hours a week and children age 6-7 some 26.7 hours a week. Older studies show less viewing, suggesting there has been a general increase the past couple decades.

When children watch TV depends on their daily schedule. For pre-schoolers the largest amount of viewing occurs on weekday and Saturday mornings, decreases in early afternoon and rises in mid-afternoon until about 5:30 p.m., when it drops until increasing in early evening. After 8 p.m. it drops drastically as bedtime arrives. Children of elementary school age (6-11 years) spend most of their TV viewing time during prime time, followed by late afternoon and early evening hours.

Children's early preferences for TV content are animals, puppets, etc., but that begins to change by school age when situation comedies rank first in school-age children's preferences. Sitcoms remain popular into adolescence, but interest also grows in adult dramas, mysteries, variety shows, and crime shows. Children are not highly adventurous TV viewers, according to a study by Wakshlag and Greenberg (1979). Program popularity among children is related to program familiarity. The strongest predictor of program popularity for school children is whether a program is new or returning.

Gender differences are not important for the amount of TV children watch, but content preferences by gender begin to appear in elementary school. Boys seem to like adventure programs and girls prefer popular music.

Recent surveys suggest that mental ability is not related to TV viewing; recent research contradicts earlier work which linked socio-economic status to the amount of children's TV viewing (Lyle and Hoffman, 1971; Adler et al., 1978). However, the issue is far from settled and work continues. Greater TV viewing among Black children has been found even when socio-economic status was taken into account.

What about media other than television? Lyle and Hoffman (1971) found that fewer than half of first graders could recall when they had last seen a movie and only 46% reported listening to the radio the previous day. Less than half reported reading comics within the week and about a fifth listened to records the previous day. Radio grows in importance among older children. Lyle and Hoffman (1971) found that 72% of sixth graders had listened to the radio the previous day. Overall radio listening averaged about an hour a day for fourth and fifth graders. Low print use has been found among children, but by the sixth grade, a fifth of students read at least some part of the newspaper daily and a third read some portion several times a week. Comic book reading decreases between first and sixth grades, while use of other print media—newspapers, magazines, and books—increases.

Of course, what a child gets out of early media use is limited by the level of cognitive development (Wartella, 1979; Ward, Wackman and Wartella, 1977). Greenberg and Reeves (1976) found the perceptions of reality of TV among children increasing as the specificity of content increases. TV usage also was positively related to perceptions of reality while age was negatively related. Brown (1976) looked at usage and medium preference among a thousand school children age 7-15 in Scotland in 1972. They were asked which medium they used for different uses and gratifications. About a third of each age group said they used TV for mood control (sadness or unpleasantness) and at least 31% use TV for social purposes—so they can talk about TV with friends. At age 7, children peaked on TV usage for diversion, i.e., getting lost in a program, to alleviate boredom, to discuss subject matter with friends, and to stimulate thinking about various subjects. At age 9, two other information uses appear: using TV to find out about different people and places. Among 11-year-olds, the most important uses are to learn about different people, to be able to discuss TV with others, to relieve boredom, to get lost in viewing, and to stimulate thinking. At age 13, learning about different places and people, learning about things not learned in school, and talking about TV with friends are the most often mentioned functions of TV viewing. Thus, informational uses become more important with advancing age. In the early years, many children say they watch TV so they can join in conversations with friends about TV. This decreases as the children get older, with a rise in the selection of other media for social conversations. Similar switches are seen in media use to forget unpleasantness and when one feels sad.

Schramm, Lyle and Parker (1961) identified three major reasons why

U.S. children watch TV: passive pleasure of being entertained (such as living a fantasy); information-seeking; and social utility (as a subject to talk about with other people). More recent studies have downplayed the distinction between fantasy-seeking and information-seeking behaviors. Von Feilitizen (1976) suggests that the media in Sweden satisfy more than 30 functions for children age 3-15, including: habit, cognitive functions, entertainment, social functions, and nonsocial or escapist functions. Radio there was found to be functionally similar to TV. Books, comics and records served escapist functions. Books and newspapers served informative functions, and TV satisfied the most needs.

Adolescence. Adolescence, generally referred to as the period from age 12 to 18, is a time of searching and introspection in which the adolescent confronts the need to find a suitable place in an adult-dominated society. Early and mid-adolescence are periods of attempted escape from parental influence and often disassociation from others in the family. Late adolescence sees the development of self awareness shaped by environmental realities and a redefinition of personal values. As the adolescent's interests and activities extend beyond the home arena, TV viewing declines (Selnow and Reynolds, 1984). This process starts earlier in higher socio-economic status homes, though the differences are small; viewing patterns and program preferences are linked to emerging adult sex roles (Avery, 1979).

A 1980 Gallup survey of teenagers found that watching TV followed visiting friends as a favorite way to spend an evening. Some 24% said visiting friends was their favorite way to spend an evening, 15% cited watching TV, 12% going on a date, 9% going to movies, 8% playing or watching sports, 7% reading, 7% staying home with the family, and 7% going to a party. TV viewing was higher among boys than girls, younger teens (age 13-15) and those with blue-collar backgrounds. TV viewing in the U.S. and elsewhere reaches its peak at the beginning of adolescence and by the end of adolescence has declined by 10% or more (Comstock, 1975; von Feilitzen, 1976; Robinson, 1977; Cowie, 1981/1982). The major decrease comes in prime time and late afternoon viewing. Decreases are found for all content categories except public affairs and news programs, for which a modest increase is found for girls. News viewing and total amount of TV viewing were negatively related in a study of high school students. While news preference increases with age, overall TV viewing decreased in terms of general enjoyment and hours viewed (Prisuta, 1979).

Reported motives for using TV remain relatively stable according to one study. Both sixth and tenth graders watch TV for relaxation, entertainment, and relief from loneliness, at least in the United States (Lyle and Hoffman, 1971). Brown (1976) found that, for Scottish children, the use of TV for generating conversation topics, for diversion when feeling sad, and for forgetting unpleasant things declined from age 9 through 15, while the importance of peers and records in meeting these needs increased. Rubin (1979) found that teenagers seeking arousal prefer dramatic programs while habitual, escapist and companion-ship-seekers favor situation comedies. Habitual viewers also avoided news and public affairs programs. Adolescents are less likely to seek out TV when they are angry or hurt. Lyle and Hoffman (1971) found that two-thirds of sixth and tenth grade children said they study with the accompaniment of TV.

Though TV viewing declines during adolescence, other media use increases. There is a marginal increase in use of news-oriented print media in senior high school and it's greater among boys than girls (Weber and Fleming, 1983). Lyle and Hoffman (1971) found that almost all tenth graders had access to a newspaper at home. While younger children are attracted to papers by comics, in adolescence there is increased readership and interest in local news, sports, personal advice columns, and entertainment sections. Elliott and Quattlebaum (1979) found support for earlier findings that newspapers are found to be most useful by adolescents for learning about civic leaders, keeping an eye on government, keeping involved in important events, and finding information about daily life. Adoni (1979) found that teenagers who read newspapers also attach importance to political and voluntary activities; use of other media was not related to such values. Magazine reading also grows during adolescence, as does use of books. Sex-related content preferences also appear—boys preferring sports magazines and girls enjoying fashion magazines. Moviegoing during adolescence fluctuates, depending on availability of theaters and other recreation facilities in the community. However, moviegoing facilitates ritualistic dating behaviors and provides topics for peer groups. Radio listening grows dramatically during adolescence, and listening to music is a favorite way to relax, be entertained or fill a lonely void.

Himmelweit and Swift (1976) attempt to draw many of the socialization factors together in a longitudinal study which looked at media use by 13-14 year olds in 1951, then checked them again at ages 24-25 (in 1962) and ages 32-33 (in 1970). They note that ability, skills, role models, and opportunities provided by the home and school counted for a good deal in the crucial adolescent period when the basis for future taste was laid. Adolescent media taste was a strong indicator of adult media taste. Many of the middle and working class youths were from non-TV homes in 1951, so we have a tracing of media use from the pre-TV saturation period to today's media mix. They concluded that media formed part of the background rather than the foreground of the leisure life and interests of adolescents and young men.

As adolescents, the students were oriented to active leisure pursuits: only 14% mentioned reading as their favorite interest and only 5% cited radio, TV or the cinema. At age 24-25, media use was considerable and two thirds watched TV two or three evenings a week, 46% had been to the cinema in the past two weeks, 38% read two or more newspapers daily, 55% subscribed to periodicals and half read at least two books per month, yet the majority thought they spent little time on the various media; 54% thought so about reading, 62% about radio and 62% about TV.

Himmelweit and Swift concluded that the medium most readily available during a given period was most heavily used by those with the fewest resources. Thus, in the early 1950's, the heaviest cinema-going was found among those of low IQ and those from working-class backgrounds. In the early 1960's, heavy use of TV was related to low IQ and low education of parents. Heavy viewing of TV as an adult correlated with frequent cinema-going as an adolescent—pointing to the functional equivalence of media.

Age culture also affects people's tastes, so that different types of content appeal at different times of people's lives. In adolescence, the boys liked action pursuits and adventure content, but by early adult life tastes were more catholic and varied, and interest greater in the informative, nonfiction and the useful. Taste in part also reflects what the medium offers; thus, researchers believe the media "create as well as reflect taste." Tastes were found to be related to socializing experiences as well as personality predispositions and outlook on society, though the strengths of these influences vary across periods. Background and ability were the most important factors predicting "highbrow" preferences but personality also contributed. In the adult stage (age 24-25) tastes again were related to background factors such as education and occupation, and to personality predispositions and outlook on adult life. The researchers conclude from other analyses that a positive outlook orients the individual toward the varied, the demanding, and the factual. Conversely, poor adjustment, a sense of powerlessness, and an authoritarian outlook on society are associated with interest in strong stimulation within a safe, predictable, and stereotyped format.

At any one point in time, an individual's tastes in one medium are consistent with preferences in others; those who liked TV adventures also liked reading adventure stories in books. Adolescent media tastes predicted later media usage and taste almost as well as information about the subject's educational attainment, job level, outlook and personality predisposition as an adult. Predictions of media preferences at age 32-33 also showed significant influence from media habits, tastes and content preferences from earlier age periods.

In summary, media socialization refers to the process of passing on media behavior patterns largely through social interaction but also through reinforcement and modeling. The abundant literature on social interaction, for example, shows that particular styles of inter- personal communication within families can reduce the amount of time children spend watching TV and stimulate their attention to public affairs content. In addition to the family, peer group ties are linked to frequent movie going and listening to the radio. We also examined changes in media use patterns through the life cycle. Media consumption—particularly TV—begins very early in childhood, with the amount of time spent watching TV rising in elementary school and decreasing in adolescence. Print media use grows from comic books in the younger years to at least occasional newspaper reading in adolescence. Content tastes and the uses and gratifications associated with media behaviors also change through the life cycle, though one long-range study found tastes in adolescence predicting media prefer- ences in adulthood.

Communication and Life-Styles

How does TV viewing relate to housework, child care, household obligations, study, travel or personal care? In general, our attempts to explain people's media behaviors have failed to show how they fit into individual patterns of daily activities. The motivation/action perspective did look at alternatives considered in specific media-use situations, but it does not look at such relationships across time. Our look at individual patterns focused on social categories and uses-and- gratifications. The former are demographic categories that locate people in the physical environment, while the latter relate media to individual needs. Yet each media behavior is an activity that must compete with a host of other behaviors. For example, newspapers are products that compete with others in a consuming society.

As culture becomes more homogeneous with respect to language and custom, it may become more heterogeneous, or diverse, with respect to life styles, especially material life styles (Felson, 1976). The question is how to relate media consumption to other behavioral domains. Newspaper use is linked to social categories, reading is a leisure-time activity, and leisure pursuits may be connected with such obligatory behaviors as work. The perspective which seems to come closest in recognizing the need for looking at "interconnections" is the life-style perspective.

The U.S. has seen a proliferation of alternative life styles in the past couple decades, though people use the term in quite different ways. Zablocki and Kanter (1976) define life style in terms of shared preferences or tastes, where the people sharing a life style are a "collectivity that otherwise lacks social and cultural identity." Thus, people sharing a life style may not communicate with each other and may not share ascriptive characteristics such as ethnic background. In one sense, the term "yuppies" has been used in recent years to refer to a life style rather than a group based on social characteristics. People from quite different age groups have identified with the complex of product purchases (computers, sport cars), style preferences (modern, nontraditional), and personal goals (high achievement-oriented, self-development) that have generally represented "the good life" in advertising campaigns. People also differ considerably in their ability to match personal resources with the price tag accompanying this life style, but that doesn't stop them from trying. Contrast the "good life"/ "yuppies" life style with one which might fit well under the headings "back-to-nature" or "Mother Earth." The media use patterns that fit each would differ considerably.

Zablocki and Kanter point out that consumption behaviors alone are insufficient for identifying life styles, and we also have to examine the meanings that people attribute to their media use and other consumption behaviors. Levine (1968) defines life style as what "emerges from the mutual adaptation of parts of experience felt so intensely that their contacts and organization produce an emotionally gratifying whole." Mass communication scholars interested in how media use "interconnects" with other behaviors are concerned with how media content, the media consumption process itself, and the "meanings" attributed to media behaviors fit into different life styles.

Where do "life styles" come from? Perhaps the factor most often cited is social class or socio-economic status. Three basic types of economically-determined life styles are: (1) property-dominated; (2) occupation-dominated; and (3) income or poverty dominated. These three roughly correspond with conventional designations of the traditional upper class, upper middle through working classes, and the lower class or the poor. For example, the life styles dominated by property ownership are characterized by extended family and strong kin ties and occupation of their own insulated, territorially distinct social world, such as that found in private clubs and schools. In occupation-dominated life styles, life is shaped largely by selling one's labor for wages; one's feeling of self-worth tends to stem from measures provided by the work situation. The first indicator of identity is likely to be occupation or current job. Poverty-dominated life styles are also characterized by strong kinship and a reliance on family for a host of activities and support.

While life style has been related to social class and status, Zablocki and Kanter (1976) note that tastes and preferences are neither completely determined by economic status, as Marx implied, nor completely individualized. "Tastes are determined in part by relative position in the markets for wealth and prestige, in part by individual choice informed by education and experience, and in part by voluntarily chosen, collectively-held standards that determine life styles." The inadequacy of class as the sole economic factor identifying life style is underlined by the fact that it is often difficult to determine whether emerging patterns of consumption are attributed to the blurring of class boundaries or to the upward mobility of whole classes themselves as a society becomes more affluent.

Though economic position no longer dominates the definition of a life style for a growing segment of the U.S. population, the very rich and the very poor may still find their life styles more or less automatically given by their location in the economic system.

As Bell (1973) notes, one sign of the arrival of the post-industrial society was the relative independence of production, consumption and distribution, where individuals were "relatively free to make a range of independent, even hedonistic, consumption decisions little constrained by their productive roles."

Why do new life styles arise? Zablocki and Kanter (1976) note that new life styles emerge when members of a society cease to agree on the value of the markets in commodities and prestige or come to recognize other, independent sources of value. Thus, with a minimum basis of consensus absent, people use one of several strategies to cope with the loss of "value coherence." Sociologists have used two alternative hypotheses to explain the proliferation of life styles in the U.S. since World War II. The transitional society hypothesis argues that the growth of different life styles is associated with the breakdown of one cultural tradition and occurs prior to the emergence of a new culture (Etzioni, 1968). The consumer society hypothesis (Lewis, 1973; Bell, 1973) says that society has accumulated sufficient capital to generate enough leisure time for many people so that "alternative standards of value and alternative life styles become a permanent feature" of society.

This dispute between the two hypotheses continues, but in either case, mass media consumption is a major factor in at least two ways. First, media themselves are a primary vehicle for "creating" or aiding in the formation of many life-style collectivities by providing symbols and objects for sharing values and by legitimizing the "sharing" itself. Secondly, media consumption itself constitutes a significant portion of people's lives. Thus, newspaper reading, viewing MTV, and other media use, together with leisure behaviors, are major ingredients of current life styles (Bryand, Currier and Morrison, 1976). The question is how and what patterns of media and other leisure behaviors fit into life styles.

Efforts to explain leisure activities often center on socio-economic factors, but so far studies have detected few clear patterns. Income level is associated with the absolute amount of money spent on leisure but otherwise only shapes leisure activities by placing limits on those that are affordable. Education is positively related to strenuousness of leisure pursuits and engaging in a diversity of leisure activities (Cheek and Burch, 1976). Occupation is correlated with leisure choices; for example, high prestige occupations correlate with golf, tennis and sailing. However, socio-economic differences in type of leisure activity are "not marked" and predicting one's leisure behaviors on the basis of SES is "all but impossible" (Wilson, 1980).

So work and leisure are multidimensional, but no consensus has developed on what those dimensions are. Most recent studies have assumed that a person seeks compensation in leisure for debilitating effects of work or have assumed that work spills over into leisure. Wilson (1980) concludes that the simple compensation theory is the less tenable of these two. During leisure, people adapt to their work but they do not actively and specifically seek compensation for it.

Parker and Smith (1976) identify three ways that work and leisure are related: (1) leisure can be an extension of work so that the demarcation between the two is weak and work is the individual's primary interest; (2) leisure can be set in opposition to work, where leisure activities are deliberately counterposed to work and clearly set apart from it; and (3) the relation can be one of neutrality, where the boundary between them is not strong and the person is slightly more interested in leisure than work. In a summary of research, Wilson (1980) finds evidence for a spill over into leisure pursuits of the "kinds of activities required by work." Examples would be work-acquired skills, mental vs. physical activities, job autonomy and leisure planning, etc. The compensation vs. spillover hypothesis also has been related to work and job satisfaction, but the research does not find a clear relationship. Although there is some carryover of satisfaction from one sphere to the other, it is not clear that changes in one variable bring changes in the other (Wilson, 1980). Furthermore, the boundary between work and leisure and their relationship may not be fixed over a lifetime.

Failure to find a strong relation between leisure behaviors and SES prompts us to look at other institutional influences on "free time." Examining the choice of specific leisure activities, we see that one's immediate situation is most influential; this includes facilities available, the type of home one lives in, whether one has children or not, etc. (Kelly, 1978). An adult's leisure-time pursuits can be accounted for in large part by early family influences, Kelly notes, though not all adult leisure activities have origins in childhood certainly, as our earlier discussion of media socialization shows. The research available also suggests that spouses who share their leisure time have higher marital satisfaction.

Our definition of life style refers to a sharing of both consumption behavior patterns and the meaning, or values attributed to them. As major components of various life styles, leisure activities themselves may be engaged in for a variety of meanings. Different activities favored by different social groups may have the same meaning while a jointly popular activity may conceal a variety of satisfactions. Csikszentmihalyi (1975) found that leisure does have "intrinsic meaning," and Kelly (1978) found that people chose more than half of their most important leisure activities for such intrinsic reasons as "it's exciting," while the rest of their activities "acquired meaning as a result of their relation to work, family or community."

The intrinsic vs. extrinsic meaning of leisure pursuits is a useful way to identify whether media consumption and other leisure activities are related to work, family, etc. The "meaning" of leisure activities is another way of identifying the uses and gratifications which attract and sustain people in their media behavior patterns. Some gratifications that people derive from newspaper reading and other media are best labeled intrinsic, though they may be expressed as habit by comments such as "it makes me relax, feel good." Other uses and gratifications are extrinsic—"I read the stock market tables because it's useful at work." Thus, the uses and gratifications perspective may link media not only to needs but to other behaviors that form a coherent life style (Villani, 1975).

In summary, life styles represent a way of integrating media behaviors with individual patterns of daily activities. As culture becomes more homogenous on other dimensions and income, educational, and ethnic differences are reduced, people make themselves more "distinctive" by adopting various life styles. In the process, they join subgroups of otherwise dissimilar people in acting out patterns of consumption behaviors with distinctive meanings and goals (e.g., becoming a "yuppie" by acting like one). Though constrained by the environment and social factors, life styles emerge as either a transition to a different cultural tradition or as a more permanent expression of individuality in modern consumer societies.

Summary

In this chapter we examined audiences of the mass media. First, we looked at how big a slice of our lives is taken by the mass media (about 10%). We also outlined audience patterns for TV use, newspaper reading, radio listening, attending the cinema, and reading books and magazines. A review of media diets showed a competitive situation in which TV increasingly is pitted against the print media. Then we analyzed various ways researchers are asking the "why" question: Why do people engage in mass media behaviors? This was followed by a review of the evidence available for how people use media in specific situations and how individual patterns of media use differ. The bulk of the evidence for individual differences represents several research traditions: social categories (ascriptive and achievement-oriented factors), uses-and-gratifications, media socialization, and life style research.

Our examination of the mass media audience is a necessary step before we look at effects. The factors which are related to media consumption patterns also appear when we look at how the media affect people and their lives. For example, we shall find that people who use the media for surveillance purposes are more likely to be affected in particular ways by political campaigns than are other people. Our profile of the media consumer also is important for the content of the media. Producers, managers, editors, advertisers — a host of actors try to identify and understand their audience. And this focus on the audience affects the content offered on the media menu. In the next chapter we will take a systematic look at media content and the public's general perceptions of the media.

5

Media Content and Public Perceptions

The New York Times prides itself on its slogan, "All the news that's fit to print," and TV newscasters often label their programs "eyewitness news," implying that they provide the same direct experience people in the audience would have if they were present at news sites. However, in addition to the fact that journalists have to be selective in choosing from the huge volume of potential facts, they also obtain access to information—whether images, sounds or other symbolic form—that the average person would not have in the same situation. The "news content" of media by definition is an effort to represent some aspect of reality. However, "non-news content" is equally important in its representation of the human experience. Here the purposes are quite different: to excite, to stimulate, to focus attention, to express sentiments and convictions.

In later chapters we will find that media content of all types can have an impact on people's political perceptions, cultural tastes, and consumer preferences. Thus, we need to look at not just that part of the media which by tradition and intent "reflects" reality but those creative, "fictionalized" aspects of the media which together claim a much greater attention from audiences. Furthermore, what are the public's perceptions of media content and do they make the same distinctions often raised by critics and educated observers?

Our discussion of media *content* cannot be restricted to a single chapter because it is relevant to every other topic in the book. As noted in Chapter 2, historical trends in the media often represent changes in media content such as new definitions of news or a new medium offering different images or representations of reality. As noted in Chapter 3, operations inside media organizations are conventions or patterns of behavior that are established to cope with the demands of encoding specific types of content—newscasts, feature films, newspaper stories, radio programs or magazine articles. In Chapter 4, we found that audience attention to the media is often defined in terms of the specific contents attended to; thus, we have frequency of *news* viewing, radio *format* preferences, interest in the *sports writing*, favorite movie *genres*, and readership of *specialized* magazines (such as computers, food, business). Subsequent chapters on effects will link behaviors to particular types of content—violence and aggression on TV, news coverage of political events, advertising, and entertainment representing cultural patterns.

Clearly, we can slice up media content in a variety of ways. We do this every day when we recognize the *content structures* that media practitioners themselves use to identify and analyze their work—the "urban sound" of radio, city magazines targeted at people with a particular lifestyle, "horror" films, newspapers "op ed" pages or "lifestyle" sections, and TV formats like "Miami Vice" or mini-series. Some scholars look at media content as just more symbolic representation of our culture. Those employing this view may group TV sitcoms with clothing styles and eating patterns as representations of particular cultural forms (See Peterson, 1979; Berger, 1984).

If we apply a model that describes communication as a process of encoding and decoding of messages flowing through channels, then media content represents "messages," a unit which can be abstracted from the rest of the process (see Fisher, 1978). These messages can be subjected to content analysis, which traditionally has been conducted for one of three purposes: a) to infer something about the encoders themselves, e.g., "Are journalists biased?"; b) to find out something about the channel, either the volume carried or content differences by channel, e.g., "Which medium contains a representation of minorities most similar to that in the general population?"; or c) to find out what decoders have been exposed to, e.g., "How much violence on TV cartoons are children exposed to Saturday mornings?" These analyses may form part of a larger search for causal relationships, such as media effects (Does the amount of violence on TV make children more aggressive?)

Another purpose for analyzing media content is found in the work of structuralists and those using semiology to guide their questions. Developing out of linguistics, this perspective focuses on sign-systems and "meaning" (see Eco, 1976; Fiske and Hartley, 1978; Crowley,

1982). A sign is any image or sound that acts as a signifier of some object or concept in the world of experience. Semiology explores the nature of sign-systems, and its use in communication focuses attention on connotative meaning as well as denotative meaning, i.e., the images and links invoked and expressed by various combinations or uses of signs. This perspective supplies a different approach for helping to establish the "cultural meaning" of media content; thus, a TV program or film might be analyzed as a "text" describing the dominant images of women (Jaddou and Williams, 1981) or social class struggle.

McQuail (1984) describes the assumptions of structuralism. Though concerned with the "meanings" of media content, this approach does not offer a systematic method or any way of knowing how far one can generalize based on a particular analysis. This contrasts with those applying social science methodologies to the same conceptual area; these methods are critiqued according to whether they follow established procedures and generalizeability depends on sampling techniques. Examples of such structural content analyses include both broadcast (Fiske and Hartley, 1978) and print media (Corrigan, 1983) and communication in general (Crowley, 1982; Davis and Walton, 1983).

Though structuralists often appear at odds with those using such social science methods as surveys, experiments and traditional content analyses, that need not be the case. Ideological differences generally lie at the base of such conflicts. More recently, we are seeing mergers of the two perspectives as social scientists draw upon semiology as a conceptual area but pursue questions which can be addressed by scientific methodologies. In fact, we might argue that the real significance of structural concepts (of media content/texts) will only be achieved when they are included in audience analyses that employ various quantitative strategies. For example, "genre" is a concept used to describe a particular kind of film. Its significance is found in the fact that people have prior expectations about what a "western" is, and this can affect subsequent media seeking, information processing and understanding. These are issues for scientific research and that line of research, though growing, is still in its early stages. The research on information processing has looked at how people "process" TV news (Gunter et al., 1984; Berry, 1983a, b; Woodall, Davis and Sahin, 1983; Housel, 1984), advertising (Mitchell, 1983; Hoyer et al., 1984), educational movies (Baggett and Ehrenfeucht, 1983), colors (Lamberski and Dwyer, 1983) and print media (Jacoby et al., 1983).

The relationship between media content and social reality is a major concern of various groups critical of their media images. Often fearful of the impact media may have on society over time, these groups analyze media content to see whether it reflects those aspects of society that are important to them. Thus, we have women and ethnic groups criticizing media images and stereotypes. The criticism also comes from others who want to control how they're portrayed—including business and labor, occupations and professions, government agencies, towns, cities, and countries, and interests representing family life, children and other groups.

After an examination of content forms and images, we will look at public perceptions of the media, including the important notion of credibility.

Content Structures

Radio

Today, radio content tends to fall into two large categories: news and music. This represents a major change from the days when flipping the dial would provide you with sounds of variety programs, comedies, cops-and-robbers serials, westerns, and big band musical programs. However, when homogenization occurs on one dimension, efforts to create variety (differentiation) occur on other dimensions. Thus, since most stations offer music-and-news, distinctions are made in terms of the music content.

Radio content is structured as "formats," patterns of programming that today represent increasingly specialized musical tastes. As Routt et al. (1978) note, radio station formats are infinite in variety and subject to constant reappraisal and change. A "formula" that stresses progressive rock music today may be changed to feature rhythm and blues music tomorrow. Once a decision to adopt a format is made, it is subjected to a dozen subtle shifts and adjustments because the "execution of conceptualities is the essence of any format." Today formats are shaped by extensive audience research that extends to testing of individual songs played on the air (Hall and Hall, 1977). In the extreme, the final configuration of musical content is based on the collective reactions of designated audience targets—identified by age, sex, income, ethnic status, etc. According to the Radio Advertising Bureau (1984), 2,233 or 27.7% of all radio stations have adopted the country format. The second most popular format is "adult contemporary," which is followed by 1,933 stations representing about 24% of all radio stations in the U.S. The "Top 40/Rock" format was programmed by 809 stations and "nostalgia" by 687. More than 500 stations were following formats characterized as "beautiful music/easy listening" or "religious" programming. Figure 5-1 shows the percentage of stations programming each format.

Figure 5-1

Major Programming Formats of AM, FM Radio Stations

Format		# of Stations	% of Total
Country	************************//***	2,233	27.7%
Adult contemporary	*************************//*	1,933	23.9%
Top 40/Rock/CHR	********************	809	10.0%
Nostalgia/Middle of the Road	*****************	687	8.5%
Beautiful music/Easy Listening	*************	524	6.5%
Religious	*************	510	6.3%
Album Oriented Rock	*******	294	3.7%
Black Rhythm & Blues	*****	207	2.6%
Golden Oldies	****	173	2.1%
Diversified	****	155	1.9%
News/Talk	***	135	1.7%
Spanish	***	126	1.6%
Soft Rock	**	83	1.0%
Classical	*	58	.7%
All news	*	48	.6%
Ethnic	*	43	.5%
Urban Contemporary	*	37	.4%
Jazz	*	19	.3%
Total:	*************************//***********//** **********	8,071	100.0%

Source: *Radio Facts*. Radio Advertising Bureau, 1984, p. 33.

Following is a sample of radio formats and a description (Routt et al., 1978: 11-12):

> Pop/Adult—Hit singles, but does not include hard rock or Black/soul; no abrasive sounds.
>
> Progressive—Any piece of music that reflects new interpretation.
>
> MOR—"Middle-of-the-Road, indicating no extremes, indicating the station does not program hard rock or soft rock but something in between.
>
> Nashville Sound—Modern country music, produced in Nashville, Tenn., with a distinctive "sameness" year after year. The "Austin Sound" reflects a type of pro-

gressive country music produced first in that city.

Bluegrass — Country music performed without amplification and possessing many of the original tones and expressions; a type of music that expresses sorrow, pain, worry, longing.

AOR — Album-Oriented Rock.

Ethnic — music appealing to people with a distinctive ethnic background, e.g., Germans, Hispanics.

Good Music — generally meaning lush, highly-orchestrated, melodic music. The term differentiates a piece of music from rock or some other form of music.

Musical formats have changed through the decades. The 1920's abounded with the work of George Gershwin, Duke Ellington and genuine jazz. With the 1930's came Benny Goodman and "swing" music. Routt et al. (1978) note that programming music in the 30's and 40's was simple because popular music was not splintered; country music was played in rural areas and progressive music rarely made the airwaves. Music went from pop to rock in the 1950's as the spread of TV forced radio to rely increasingly on formats that were exclusively music and news. The late 1950's and early 1960's also saw the high water mark of folk music as represented by Joan Baez. As rock music grew in popularity and became more established, it diversified so that by the 1970's and 1980's audiences were harder to identify, capture and retain. The music was "almost everything" (Routt et al., 1978: 21). Some have analyzed musical lyrics of popular songs emphasizing romance from 1950 to 1980 showed that 89% of the songs released in the 1950s were somewhat or very emotional, compared to 71% of those released during the 1960's and 42% of those released between 1970 and 1980. Emphasis on "physical" love went in the opposite direction, from 3% in the 1950's to 11% in the 1960's and 40% in the 1970's (Fedler, Hall and Tanzi, 1982).

Current radio formats are defined in terms of music and news-talk. That was not always the case in earlier decades, though music and talk formed the bulk of early radio schedules too. For example, major network radio programs on the air in January, 1927 included: 1 general variety hour, 9 programs of concert music, 12 programs of musical variety, 4 light music programs, 4 religious talk programs, 1 news commentary, 2 other talk programs (travel and bridge), and 1 daytime homemakers talk show (see Summers, 1958). A listing of programs by format illustrates shifts that occurred through the decades (See Table 5-1). Note the growth of thriller dramas, news and commentary, and religious talk programs across the three survey points. Musical variety also retained its popularity. Some formats popular in the 1930's had disappeared two decades later—Broadway and Hollywood gossip programs, for example. Appearing somewhat later on the chart were formats like sports interviewing and broadcasts and magazine-type variety programs.

Table 5-1

Number of Radio Programs on the Air by Format

	January 1935	January 1945	January 1955
Comedy variety	13	16	3
General variety	7	10	5
Amateur hour	1	1	1
Hillbilly, minstrel	4	4	5
Semi-variety programs	10	1	2
Magazine-type variety	--	--	2
Concert music	22	22	16
Musical variety	44	30	31
Light music	27	4	13
Disc jockey program	--	--	2
Quiz shows	--	11	7
Comedy audience participation programs	--	2	1
Panel quiz or comedy programs	--	4	--
Human interest programs	4	5	4
Prestige drama	2	3	2
Informative drama	3	9	6
Light, homey or love-interest drama	13	6	3
Comedy drama	3	15	5
Thriller drama	13	26	29
Women's serial drama	3	--	--
Sports broadcasts	--	1	4
News and commentary	9	34	36
Public affairs talks, forums	8	7	14
Religious talk programs	8	14	29
Sports news, interviews	2	1	7
Broadway & Hollywood gossip	4	3	--
Miscellaneous talk programs	9	5	15

Note: Daytime programs are excluded. The figures represent the number of programs on the air in January of each year. They were compiled from programs listed by Summers (1958).

Film Structures

The commercial cinema in general is identifiable by formal and narrative elements common to all (Schatz, 1981). These include a story of a certain length focusing upon a protagonist (such as a hero, a central character), certain standards of production, a style of editing, the use of musical score, and so forth. However, the "genre film" contains not only these general film devices but also a predetermined structure in which the characters, setting, plot techniques, etc. have prior significance to the audience. This is significant because it means people have prior expectations that guide their media-seeking and information processing. Genre films are often criticized because they appeal to a pre-existing audience while the film "classic" creates its own special audience; critics have thus ignored genre films because of their prejudice for the unique (Braudy, 1976).

Films can be characterized by genre, or film type. Armour (1980) examines various film genre and their components. The genre include: adventure, comedy, crime-gangsters-and villains, detectives, suspense-&-film noir, fantasy and horror, musicals, sex-&-violence, war movies, westerns, documentaries, etc. Armour's descriptions of the genre illustrate the difficulty in identifying film "structure" or achieving a consensus about it. Adventure is a genre especially difficult to define and it can be further subdivided into various types of historical, national or religious epics; an example is "Lawrence of Arabia."

Mobile unit advertising a movie playing at a local cinema in Legaspi, the Phillippines.

No genre is more typically American than the Western. What is a Western? Traditionally, it is a setting—the American West, but also the issues and kind of men facing issues there. The characters are plentiful, including noble or ruthless Indians, strong silent gunmen, single women, powerful cattle barons and tireless soldiers. The Western genre has been so rich its elements have been translated to Japanese, Italian and German settings and retained sufficient unity to be recognizable as the same genre by audiences (Jarvie, 1970). He also attributes the popularity of the western and the gangster melodrama to the formality and simplicity of settings and action. Both frameworks allow the creators to pursue allegories and ethical explorations— heroes, trials, ordeals. He argues that the two genre do not get worn-out by over use but are renewed in the retelling much as in the days of oral story telling. Though film theorists have developed various arguments for the development of specific genre, the importance of individual genre varies as new ones emerge and older ones decline in importance. An example of the former is the popular "Star Wars"/ aliens genre of the past decade or so. An example of the latter is the Western, which returned with Clint Eastwood in the mid 1980's after a hiatus of more than a decade. Some have argued that the two genre represent different settings but similarities on other dimensions, such as the pitting of clear-cut symbols of good and evil.

TV Content Structures

Some television stations specialize in particular types of content such as religious programming, classic movies, reruns of programs originating on network TV, and so forth. Within daily schedules we also find patterns or concentrations of TV content designed to appeal to audience segments. We also could characterize TV content as "entertainment" or "actuality" programming (e.g., news, documentaries); this distinction is similar to the fiction/non-fiction division in literature. However, it is the TV program itself which is the most important content unit and the one which has some sense of coherence and unity for both the creators and the audience.

The television "format" represents a concept similar to the notion of genre in film. In fact, the latter is increasingly being applied to TV content itself. Again, the notion is that the public has prior conceptions about what constitutes a particular TV format, such as a situation comedy. This form has a limited, generally indoor setting, a small cast of characters whose interaction is the focus, and "substantive" content which, though it may be of major import in some cases, is generally mundane. Goedkoop (1983) notes that an important ingredient is the development of strong characters. Sitcoms, thus, offer predictable settings and situations that allow the audience to roleplay and vicariously enjoy somewhat exaggerated characterizations. Just as a "western" in film follows a particular structure, a sitcom and other formats do the same in TV.

The number and diversity of formats is limited only by human creativity. Most of us do not seek constant stimulation, particularly the kind that requires attention to structure in order to understand the content or to enjoy the process. Were that the case, all film would be experimental and TV content would represent public acceptance of the artist's desire to be "expressive." A format or genre reduces the need to pay close attention for understanding. It also allows the audience to plan one's behaviors, to watch a sitcom in order to laugh, to enjoy predictable characters acting out roles that make us feel good about our own lives, or to watch a news program that makes us feel we're current on world affairs. In such low-involvement situations like TV viewing, the public has certain expectations about the redundancy of content. Though we could argue that such expectations exist at some level of generality across all creative situations, it is much more evident in the case of "mass" media, those aimed at large audiences, especially television.

TV formats, like film genre, represent successful compromises between creative ideas and public expectations over time. In the cases of television, "new formats" generally represent combinations of older formats or subtle changes in the elements generally associated with an existing one. "New" also often means a return to the "old," as formats from the past appear new when recast with today's popular culture, language and problems. Though TV is a relatively new medium, its history is now long enough to suggest that formats or genre may go through cycles of popularity and acceptance. We can see some evidence of these ideas in a tabluation of the top-rated programs through the years (see Table 5-2). The format which has enjoyed the most consistent presence among the top programs is the situation comedy. Beginning with *Mama* in 1950, sitcoms have remained among the most popular programming on television. They were particularly dominant during the early 1970's when they included 15 of the top 25 programs (see Mitz, 1983). Other examples of sitcoms through the years are: *I Love Lucy* which is still running in syndication; *The Andy Griffith Show* where actor-director Ron Howard got his start as Opie; *Gilligan's Island*, also in syndication; *The Mary Tyler Moore Show* which featured one of the first independent, single women in a sitcom; *Happy Days* where Ron Howard returned as a teenager; *Alice* featuring a single, divorced mother; and *The Cosby Show* featuring popular Black actor Bill Cosby.

Some formats enjoyed immense popularity for a decade or more but

Table 5-2
Television Formats
Number of Top Rated Programs by Format

TV Formats	1950-1951	1955-1956	1960-1961	1965-1966	1970-1971	1975-1976	1980-1981	1984-1985
Variety:								
General	2	1	2	1	1	--	--	--
Musical variety	--	--	1	--	--	1	--	--
Comedy variety	2	2	2	2	4	--	--	--
Music	--	--	--	1	--	--	--	--
Talent Scouts	1	--	--	--	--	--	--	--
Situation comedies	1	4	6	12	5	15	12	7
Humor	--	--	1	--	--	--	--	--
Western	2	--	5	3	3	--	--	--
Drama:								
General drama	--	--	--	--	--	1	1	4
Drama anthology	4	3	1	--	1	--	--	2
Medical drama	--	--	--	--	2	--	1	--
Drama mini-series	--	--	--	--	--	1	--	--
Romantic drama	--	--	--	--	--	--	1	--
Anthology	--	1	--	1	1	--	--	--
Quiz/Audience								
Participation	--	3	2	1	--	--	--	--
'Crime' Shows								
Police drama	--	1	1	--	5	3	1	--
Detective	2	--	2	--	1	--	1	6
Lawyer	--	--	1	--	--	--	--	--
Adventure								
Adventure drama	--	--	--	1	--	2	2	2
Fantasy adventure	--	--	--	2	--	--	--	--
Comedy adventure	--	--	--	--	--	--	1	--
Spy spoof	--	--	--	1	--	--	--	--
Sports	1	--	--	--	--	--	1	--
Cartoons	--	--	1	--	--	--	--	--
Films/Movies	--	--	--	--	2	2	1	2
News magazine	--	--	--	--	--	--	1	1
Human interest/ audience participation	--	--	--	--	--	--	2	1
(N =)	15	15	25	25	25	25	25	25

Note: The figures represent the programs rated in the top 15 for the first two periods and in the top 25 for the other years. The data were compiled from Brooks and Marsh (1981) and Variety (May 1, 1985, p. 468).

then faded. Examples are the Western which peaked with the Cartwright family in *Bonanza*—Little Joe was played by Michael Landon—*Gunsmoke*, and *Wagon Train*. The variety program in any form has virtually disappeared from TV today after enjoying top ratings for two and a half decades. *The Ed Sullivan Show*, the longest-running example of this format, was first telecast in 1948 and ended in 1971.

We also see the blending of formats—from pure comedy and dramatic adventure to *The Dukes of Hazzard* which is classified as a comedy adventure program. The format which has grown increasingly differentiated is "drama," which is represented by medical shows, mini-series, romantic drama (*Fantasy Island*), and other formats (adventure drama—*Little House on the Priarie*; police drama—*CHIPS*). In the 1970's actuality programming provided new formats with such popular programs as *60 Minutes* and *Real People*, the former concentrating on public figures and issues while the latter celebrated offbeat professions, hobbies and interests of common people. The table misses those formats not sufficiently popular to reach the top 15 or 25 programs—such as dance contests, docudramas (Brode, 1984). It also excludes formats restricted to non prime-time evening hours, e.g., daytime soap operas, Sunday public affairs panel shows, how-to-do it/fishing/bridge/hobby/cooking shows, educational instruction, children's programs (see Woolery, 1983), local news magazines, "entertainment news," late night talk-variety programs, weather programs, *C-SPAN*, music TV and other "videos," nature programs, travelogues, musical concerts, videotex and community access programs.

It is easy to classify the same programs using different format categories, e.g., family drama; the formats listed in Table 2 are illustrative, not definitive. However, ultimately it should be possible to identify TV formats/genre by researching audience perceptions and expectations. Such research could verify and validate the general observations and theoretical schema constructed by scholars, or the converse. Though TV formats, like film genre, may have their origins in the creative minds and interactions of small groups of people, their survival depends on audience acceptance and subsequent use in seeking out and processing content. Thus, *Miami Vice* in the 1984-85 TV season married a visual style and pacing to traditional police drama, but it will not emerge as a format until: a) the public recognizes unique elements or a pattern (perhaps not articulated in the same manner as observers would expect), b) additional creative organiza-tions "produce" other TV programs which would elicit the same public response, and c) the public comes to identify those elements as a particular format (whether they like the format or not). Most of those investigating this area have followed literary and critical traditions which do not seek scientific judgment for their analysis. However, interest is growing among social scientists who see changes in TV programming stimulated by new technologies and the visual techniques they permit. Dominick and Pearce (1976) looked at fall schedules of TV networks from 1953 to 1974 and found action/adventure programs rising to a dominant position beginning in 1957, but with sharp fluctuations. Sitcoms remained at a fairly stable level. They noted mutual interdependence among program formats — as adventure rose, other types decreased. Network programming was marked by relatively regular periods of change and permanence. All three networks seldom undertook major content shifts in the same year. Peaks in diversity occurred in 1961-63 and 1969-70 but otherwise generally declined over the two decades. The three network schedules also became increasingly similar.

Public TV emphasizes different program formats from that found on commercial prime-time network television. The two major categories of programs are "informational" (24%) and "cultural" (23%). Children's programming accounts for another 22%, instructional programs for 13% and news/public affairs for 12% (Eastman, Head and Klein, 1985: 432).

Most content analyses of TV programming focus either on news or images and stereotypes, which will be discussed below. However, Henderson and Greenberg (1980) report findings about the range of activities on TV representing a normal person's day. Restricting their analysis to two TV seasons of network programs, coders identified more than 4,500 acts that were grouped into 16 major categories. Two types of behavior occurred more than 5 times per program hour — driving and media use. Three other behaviors were seen at a rate of 3-4 incidents per hour: personal grooming, eating and riding. Appearing almost as frequently were making business phone calls and entertaining. Drinking and smoking occurred about twice per hour. Other activities and rates per hour were: food preparation, 1.4; playing games, 1.36; writing, 1.11; using firearms, 1.02; social courtesies, .86; personal phone calls, .73; athletics, .71; and indoor housework, .51. Five other categories of behavior occurring infrequently (less than .02 incidents per hour) were: yard work, shopping, child care, office work and sewing.

In contrast with the focus on normal daily activities, others have examined the atypical, sensational elements that are often the focus of drama. Cassata, Skill, and Boadu (1983), for example, content analyzed life and death for 341 characters on 13 soaps during a one-year period. There was a total of 191 occurrences of health-related conditions and 43 deaths; some 13% of the characters died of some disease, accident or crime. They found 79 accidents or violent incidents (homicide, suicide, etc.); of these, 28 ended in death. There also were some 51 diseases identified by organ system — from neurological to congenital — with 9 resulting deaths. Some 61 other diseases and health-related conditions were found (psychiatric disorders, pregnancy-related problems, and undefined), with 3 deaths resulting.

Porter (1983) applied semiotics to prime tive TV programs, finding noticeable similarities among six programs (e.g., *Dukes of Hazzard, Dallas, Quincy*) in terms of the number of syntagmas found in each episode. "Syntagmas" refers to such content units as series of temporally consecutive scenes. Overall, the six TV series used comparable montage structures, though some differences also were noted.

Other observers have examined more limited aspects of TV content, e.g., the verbal language of public TV (Stevens, 1985), variety of programming on independent TV (Austin, 1982), and the dimensions of themes and topics of religious TV (Abelman and Neuendorf, 1985). The latter found that 75% of religious programming had a religious theme, with only 2% being overtly political. The most important religious topics were: 1) God, 2) Jesus; 3) faith; and 4) the Bible as a text. The social topics appearing most frequently were: 1) death and dying, 2) nonprint media; 3) education; and 4) marriage.

Print Media Content Structures

The print media themselves are differentiated as content structures. Books represent the most indepth treatment of concepts, themes or stories. Magazines are more timely but still somewhat lengthy treatment of materials, and newspapers generally represent the briefest and most current treatment. Certainly, there are lengthy newspaper articles, short magazine pieces, and book collections of little more than isolated anecdotes. Furthermore, like the visual media, we have some content structures which are found across the media forms themselves. Examples would be news articles, news magazines, and instant news books relying heavily on pictures.

The two major contents found in newspapers are advertising and news. The latter content must form at least a third of the space for a paper to obtain second-class mailing rates; however, advertising is an even more important content in shoppers and freely-distributed papers (Hunt and Cheney, 1982). Newspapers have become increasingly segmented as content is aimed at target audiences. Many large papers, for example, now publish weekly science sections that feature health, medicine, science and technology (SIPI, 1984). Like the broadcast media, some content has the intent of informing readers but it must attract attention and maintain interest at the same time. It is this marriage of factors which is partly responsible for the changing content structures found in newspapers and other print media. Walker (1983) found in a content analysis of the *Washington Post* that the editorial mix included the following proportions (newspaper columns per issue): style, 17; sports, 14; national news, 14; comics/features, 12.5; metro news, 12; financial news, 10; foreign news, 8.

In a recent survey of more than 1,310 U.S. daily newspapers, Bogart (1985) notes shifts in U.S. newspaper content. A typical weekday paper now has an average of 18 news and editorial pages with a growing use of zoned editions aimed at particular geographic regions within the circulation area. He notes that one striking change has been section-alization. For example, 25% of the daily papers added "life-style" sections between 1981 and 1983. Increases in news coverage of sports and business also were reported. A wide variety of features is now regularly found in American newspapers, as Table 5-3 illustrates. Bogart concludes that the mix of newspaper subject matter has not changed much in recent surveys, with no dramatic shifts in newspaper content devoted to crime, public health, taxes or Hollywood. Three trends which were identified are: an increase in the ratio of features to hard news content, a reduction in the number of regular standing columns and features dealing with specialized interests, and a reduction in the ratio of national-and-world news to local news.

Newspaper editorial pages continue to play vital roles with 97% of daily papers devoting at least one page a day to editorials and such related features as cartoons, columns and letters to the editor (Hynds, 1984). The amount of space devoted to editorials also seems to be growing. Most (82%) of the larger papers have "op ed" pages in addition to the editorial page that traditionally has been the voice of management or ownership. Some 29% of the dailies employ local cartoonists for these pages and 98% use syndicated cartoons (e.g., Pat Oliphant and Herbert Block). Some 91% include syndicated columnists (e.g., James Kilpatrick) and 62% have local columnists as well; the former are selected more for their ability to draw readers regardless of philosophy, according to Hynds' survey.

Today this part of the newspaper includes content that makes it a forum for the exchange of information and opinion across diverse readership groups. Editors themselves see not only a community leadership function in the editorial page content but also these goals: attracting readers to the papers, educating people on issues, sorting out important issues and stimulating the public's thoughts about them, helping people understand trends and developments, stirring the community to get a public opinion response, reflecting wants and needs of the community, allowing public access to the medium, encouraging a

Table 5-3
U.S. Newspaper Content (1983)

Percentage of Newspapers Carrying Sections of:

[% Daily/ % At Least Once a Week]

Sports	70%/	74%	Fashion	4%/	13%
Main news	70%/	71%	Food	3%/	53%
Second news	41%/	45%	Food/Home	3%/	9%
Lifestyle/Women	39%/	52%	Home	2%/	13%
TV/Radio	30%/	49%	Farm	1%/	7%
Entertainment	28%/	54%	Travel	1%/	5%
Business/Finance	25%/	43%	Science	1%/	4%

Percentage of Newspapers Carrying Features at Least Once a Week:

Spectator Sports	88%	Music, Tapes, Records	31%
TV Log	87%	Restaurants	28%
Astrology, Horoscope	84%	Fashion, Women	26%
Society/Social News	80%	Books	25%
Games, Puzzles	78%	Youth, Teenage	24%
Participant Sports	78%	Beauty	23%
Recipes	74%	Retirement, Social Security	23%
Personal Advice	71%	Home Building, Repair	22%
Business, Financial	67%	Consumers (Action Line)	21%
Weather Map	65%	Home Furnishings, Decorating	18%
Health, Medical	63%	Radio Log	16%
Bridge	55%	Fashion, Men	16%
School News	52%	Fashion, Teen	16%
TV Reviews	51%	Real Estate	16%
Best Food Buys	50%	Pets	14%
"People"	50%	Wine	14%
Religion	48%	Automotive	13%
Security, Commodity Tables	48%	Etiquette	12%
Movie Timetable	48%	Child Care	11%
Movie Reviews	46%	Travel & Resort	11%
Sewing Patterns	44%	Career Advice	11%
Outdoors, Camping, Hunting	44%	College	10%
Diet, Nutrition	44%	Science, Technology	9%
Household Hints	43%	Environment, Ecology	9%
Theater	41%	Computers	7%
Advice on Personal Finance	38%	Photography	6%
Gardening	37%	Stamps, Coins	6%
Farm and Ranch	34%		

Source: Compiled from Leo Bogart, "How U.S. Newspaper Content Is Changing," *Journal of Communication* (Spring, 1985) 35(2): 82-90.

local exchange of ideas, making people think, criticizing official mal-feasance, evaluating candidates for public office, being a "kind of public conscience in the community" and establishing the character of the paper. Clearly, the content of the editorial pages has changed to meet what editors see as an expanding range of functions, often including interpretations, guest essays, cartoonists, columnists, letters, editorials, and analyses by journalists and contributors.

The appearance of newspaper content—the "graphics"—also is increasingly important today, a fact which is illustrated by the success of Gannett's national daily *USA Today* with its use of color and charts. The "graphics" of newspapers parallel the "visual style" of TV and film. Major design changes are not new to newspapers. In the 1960's a revolution of sorts occurred as papers moved to more readable type, eliminated rules between columns and emphasized horizontal makeup (Sissors, 1965). Today more papers than ever are paying attention to their appearance and many are hiring graphics designers. The changes are not limited to large dailies but include smaller papers as well (Click and Stempel, 1979). Utt and Pasternack (1984) conducted a study of the front pages of American newspapers with daily circula-tions of 25,000 or more. They concentrated on the front page, which has become a newspaper's showcase and traditionally has reported the major stories of the day. They found that 85% of the dailies use a 6-column front page and the others 5 or 7, with varying column widths and a flexibility in their use. Most papers also include a boxed index on the front page. The "flag," or newspaper name, spans the width of the page but is not always at the top and periodically is in color. Some two thirds of the papers also use a modular format, while 30% use a horizontal layout and only 4% a vertical format. The number of stories on the front page ranges from 3 to 10, with an average of 5-6. Many of those stories conclude inside the paper, a factor readers dislike (Bain and Weaver, 1979).

Movement toward modular design is affecting the way news is emphasized on the front page. Utt and Pasternack found that papers still tend to follow the traditional practice of placing the day's main headline in the upper right corner (34%) or spanning the top of the page (26%), but 39% follow no pattern for placement of the lead story headline. Most front pages have two photographs and a third regularly use four-color photographs or other art. The impact of design elements cannot be assumed or overstated, however; Berner (1983), for example, found structural content changes such as the style of the headline and first paragraph had less impact on readers' decision-making than the story's actual relevance.

The significance of graphic design is not limited to newspapers. Moriarty (1982) looked at elements of magazine ads, concluding that those in special-interest magazines seemed to be striving for a distinctive fashionable statement in a manner which led them to risk functional problems such as legibility or readability. Those appearing in magazines aimed at general audiences tended to follow design strategies which avoided such problems.

Readability of print media has long concerned journalists. The Flesch Reading Ease formula is still the most widely used (Severin and Tankard, 1979); it is based on the average sentence length and number òf one-syllable words per 100 words. Flesch recommended that newswriters use an average sentence length of 19 words. A recent study compared the readability levels of three New York City newspapers and the Wall Street Journal (Fusaro and Conover, 1983). Findings indicated that one would have to be able to read as well as the average college freshman to comprehend the lead news stories in the *New York Times* and the *Wall Street Journal* adequately, while one would only need to read as well as the typical high school senior to comprehend those in the *Daily News* and *New York Post*.

News

The content structure often abstracted from the specific medium is "news." It can be categorized along with other "actuality" content, a distinction that is based on notions of *intent* (to convey situations for audience perception), *origin* of the situation (a separate existence in reality rather than one constructed from personal experiences or imagination), and *form* (whose conventions generally vary by medium). The concept of news was discussed in Chapter 3.

News form has been analyzed on various dimensions, e.g., soft vs. hard news (Turow, 1983). However, it is the foreign vs. domestic distinction that has been content analyzed most often. For example, a 1972-1981 sample of U.S. network TV newscasts found that each network devoted about a fourth of the news time to foreign news, falling to a low of 20% in 1973 and reaching a high of 32.5% in 1981 (Weaver, Porter and Evans, 1984). Topical content was diverse but concentrated in the following four areas: military-defense, foreign relations, domestic political activities, and crime-justice-terrorism. Similar emphases have been found on national TV newscasts and in newspapers of other countries and on international wire services (Golding and Elliott, 1979: 142; Stevenson and Shaw, 1984; Larson, 1984).

Moving to the local TV news level, Wulfemeyer (1982) divided TV newscast content into seven categories: non-news, issues, unexpected events, entertainment, banter, sports, and weather. At the San Diego station analyzed, coverage of unexpected events took up about 6 minutes of each newscast, while sports took 5 minutes and weather 4.5

minutes. Discussion between on-air personalities was less than 3 minutes per newscast and non-news items took up the largest amount of newscast time, reaching a third of one station's content. The newscasts were fast paced and averaged 28 separate stories in the "news hole."

Use of film or video, particularly in news originating abroad, has been linked to the spread of satellite technology (Larson, 1984). The percentage of nations with earth stations grew from almost 30% in 1972 to 76% a decade later; those with such international links are more likely to originate video reports for TV newscasts. A breakdown of U.S. network themes by story format shows that 36.8% of the 4,374 formats were anchor reports, while 33.7% were foreign video reports and 29.4% domestic video reports (Larson, 1984: 46).

Topical emphases and structure have changed through the decades. Shaw (1981, 1984) focused on the 1820-1860 period when new printing press technology allowed newspapers to expand their audiences and reduce prices. His content analysis of 3,000 stories from 67 newspapers found that the content did not become less political and more social; rather, the papers carried a substantial amount of social/cultural news all along.

Images and Stereotypes

Media images are central to discussions about the impact of communication on relationships between people, the sexes, age groups, ethnic groups, cities, and countries. Representatives from these groups decry what they see as unfair media images. For example, the cultural indicators project compares its findings with the demographic profile provided by U.S. census figures (Signorielli, 1983). The world of TV drama is found to have a very different demographic structure than the U.S., and is dominated by white men in traditionally powerful, important and adventurous occupations. The result of such critiques often is an effort to change the images or "kill the carrier of bad messages." However, concern with media images extends beyond the traditional categories to include those concerned with professions, diseases, social interaction, problems like drugs and alcoholism, etc. In most cases, the issue is whether media portrayals are negative or "fair" in the eyes of their proponents, and whether an adequate amount of attention is being paid. In this section we will examine the empirical research on media images and stereotypes.

Ethnic Groups. Concern with media stereotypes has long been an issue among different ethnic groups. The concern has spread across all media — from stereotypes of Chinese and American Indians in

Hollywood movies of the 1930's to charges that Arabs are stereotyped in U.S. TV programs today (Shaheen, 1980). A national survey of 1,700 adults showed that both Anglos and Hispanics believe there were more media portrayals of Mexican-Americans doing bad things than good things. Many of these groups note that some of their individual identity is tied to these "corporate entities" and, if the larger entity suffers, the individual suffers in some smaller way (see Van Dyke, 1977).

What are the images of ethnics in various mass media? The portrayal of Black Americans has received increasing attention. Berry (1980) notes that there have been three major periods in the portrayal of Blacks on TV: 1) the stereotypic age, 1948-1965, when the medium reflected and reinforced the sensibilities of the dominant Anglo culture; 2) the new awareness, 1965-1972, when TV was sensitized by the Civil Rights movement and urban unrest sought to represent Blacks as competent, positive members of society; and 3) stabilization, 1972 to the present, when there is less pressure to include a Black in every situation but more effort to be realistic and focus on universal personal concerns of specific characters.

MacDonald (1983) notes that early TV (in the 1950's) offered better roles for Blacks than any other medium, but the bright promise was unfulfilled for many years. Early TV often spotlighted Black talent on variety series; thus, Pearl Bailey, Louis Armstrong and Cab Calloway appeared on *Your Show of Shows,* the *Garry Moore Show,* and the *Jackie Gleason Show,* etc. This was a breakthrough for Black entertainers who had not been used consistently in network radio in the preceding two decades. However, blacks found few opportunities in video drama; a program with both a Black and a white detective, *Harlem Detective* lasted only three months in 1953. There were roles in such stereotyped situation comedies as *Amos 'n Andy.* The breakthrough for Black drama stars came when Bill Cosby joined Robert Culp in "I Spy" in the mid 1960's. Nat King Cole in the late 1950's was the first Black performer to host a TV show of his own.

Greenberg and Neuendorf (1980) sampled three consecutive seasons on U.S. network TV, beginning with the fall of 1975. They looked at black families' role interactions and how they compared with white TV families. The findings showed that black TV families were almost exclusively nuclear and had more children than their white counterparts. Black mothers and sons were overrepresented in comparison to black fathers and brothers. The male role in black families was generally more energetic than white male TV roles. Black family members also were more often portrayed in interpersonal conflict. A 1977 sample showed that blacks were concentrated in situation comedies (Baptista-Fernandez and Greenberg, 1980); also, half of the blacks were in virtually all-Black shows and the other half spread out one to a show in a "token fashion." Turning to print media, we find Blacks again underrepresented but in increasing numbers over the past few decades. Humphrey and Schuman (1984) looked at the occupational levels of Blacks in *Time* and *Ladies' Home Journal* advertisements during 1950 and 1980. The percentage rose considerably in that period, with a disappearance of Blacks in roles as maids or servants (also see Sentman, 1983).

The growing number of Hispanic-Americans has been matched by an increasing interest in their representation on TV. Looking at fiction and film, Petit (1980) notes that shifts in Anglo attitudes towards Mexicans have meant only variations in the already prevailing stereotypes of Mexican characters. Underrepresentation of Hispanics in news stories was noted in one analysis of six southwestern newspapers (Greenberg et al., 1983) but a cross-media study found Hispanic news presented as prominently across the media as non-Hispanic news (Heeter et al., 1983).

Coverage of Indians in North America has been examined in both the U.S. and Canada. Murphy and Avery (1982, 1983) looked at eight Alaskan newspapers and found coverage in native-owned papers was more pro-native than that in the non-native press, though attitudes toward Native peoples were positive in both. The establishment press paid relatively little attention to native Alaskan news, though the types of stories were similar to those in the Native press. In Ontario, Canada, a study found that the image of the Indian or Eskimo was based on his land claims and dependence on government support (Singer, 1982).

Seggar et al. (1981) examined TV portrayals of minorities in comedy and drama from 1971 to 1980 to see whether gains made in the 1960's were retained over time. They found that Blacks generally were slightly less frequently shown in the late 1970's than at the beginning and the black female had become almost invisible. Both Black men and women decreased in major roles while other minority men gained in role significance. Mexican-Americans, Asians, Native Americans and foreign-born ethnics dropped considerably in terms of their representation over that period.

Age. How are older persons portrayed in the media? As the American population "ages," we would expect older people to receive greater attention in the media. The Greenberg et al. (1980) sample of three TV seasons found that persons in the 65 and older age group were increasingly less visible on TV, comprising about 3% of all TV characters by the 1977-78 season. A disproportionately high number of older characters was found in situation comedies, and there was a clear male bias in portrayal of the elderly. Elderly people were increasingly cast in regular roles rather than guest roles and they were increasingly represented as lower-class. They also were presented as victims rather than perpetrators of aggressive acts. A study of 1978 soap opera characters found that 16% were judged to be 55 or older, and 52% were male. Some 90% were in good health and 75% lived in their own homes. Males tended to be professionals or managers and were community leaders (Cassata et al., 1983).

A 1981 study of 136 TV commercials found that only 11 included one or more people age sixty or older (Hiemstra et al., 1983), and two thirds were males. These figures are highly inconsistent with demographics for the general populace in the United States. In addition, the majority of older people were portrayed as youthful looking and active. Another study focused on advertisements in five magazines (*Vogue, MS, Playboy, Time, Ladies' Home Journal*) from 1960 to 1979, finding that 62% of the adults appeared to be under 30, compared with about 28% of the U.S. population. Women depicted in ads were usually younger than the men they were pictured with; only 4% of all the women were judged to be 40 or older compared to 57% in the general population. There was no major change in the portrayal of ages during the period studied (England et al., 1981). Newspaper coverage of the elderly was examined in a comparison of 10 newspapers that included the *St. Petersburg Times*, which has a concentration of elderly people. The Florida paper had the most coverage of the aged and devoted almost 5% of its space to them, almost double the average of 2.5% for all ten papers. Second highest was the *New York Times*, which devoted 3.5% of its space to the aged. The tone of newspaper stories was positive or neutral and did not support criticism that newspapers are creating negative images of the aged (Broussard, 1980).

Children and Families. Those at the other end of the age spectrum, children, also receive proportionately little media coverage (Dennis and Sadoff, 1976). The coverage received is more often institutionally-oriented rather than people-oriented, e.g., emphasizing administrative issues such as school boards and taxes. Almond (1980) also points out that while families are shrinking in size and changing their shape, the media tend to mistake these changes as signs of collapse. One recent report (Kaplan, 1984) found that 36% of families on new series in the fall of 1984 were traditional, two-parent families while 10% of all the women portrayed on TV are divorced and 9% are widows.

The Greenberg et al. (1980) study included an analysis of 73 family units depicted during one TV season. Four basic types of families were presented: the nuclear family, one parent with one child, couples without children, and the "conglomerate" of many relatives. The vast majority of TV characters portrayed had no relatives and divorce was infrequent. An analysis of family interaction showed that nuclear family males were the initiators of 50% of all family acts, with nuclear females accounting for 36%. Approaching other people in a positive fashion was the most frequent act observed in families. Offering information was the major function, but seeking information and directing others also occurred frequently. An analysis of family life in magazine advertisements from 1920 to 1978 found a significant increase in the portrayal of intimacy between spouses and between brothers and sisters, with greater emphasis on companionship in household tasks among younger couples (Brown, 1981).

Gender. With the rise of the feminist movement in the 1960's came attention to media portrayals of women. Recently, a report issued by the National Commission on Working Women (Kaplan, 1984) showed that women have begun to achieve a better image on network TV and have begun to achieve roles that show leadership and authority, e.g., in programs such as *Kate and Allie*. Some 76% of the women portrayed on TV have professions outside the home, according to the report. This is consistent with other studies over the past decade or so. TV programs are showing a less discouraging view of women pursuing a career than was the case in the early 1970's (Weigel and Loomis, 1981); in 1978, though female characters employed outside the home were less likely to be married than were employed male characters, they were just as likely to be depicted as successfully married as were their male counterparts or unemployed housewives. Studies of women on TV in the mid 1970's found that men were more likely than women to be portrayed as giving orders, and women were shown as needing emotional assistance while men needed physical assistance (Henderson, Greenberg and Atkin, 1980; Greenberg, Richards and Henderson, 1980). Public TV programming also shows that males outnumber females 2 to 1 and women rarely served as narrators (Matelski, 1985).

An analysis of prime-time TV humor showed that men were the object of humor or disparagement more than females because of their greater numbers on TV; however, males were more likely to disparage females than the reverse. Nonsexual humor was more frequent than sexual humor (Suls and Gastoff, 1981). An analysis of male-female interaction on daytime serials showed that male dominance of females occurred most often in business dyads. A pattern characterized as competitive symmetry (where both spouses try to talk) was the most common pattern in families; submissive symmetry (where neither person seeks control) was more common in exchanges between socially linked men and women (Arliss, Cassata and Skill, 1983).

Portrayal of gender has also been analyzed in print media content. Hynes (1981) looked at fiction and nonfiction short stories in the *Saturday Evening Post, Cosmopolitan, Ladies Home Journal* and *Atlantic Monthly* between 1911 and 1930, finding only 300 of the nearly 8,500 stories had at least one female character. Women were portrayed in their social roles and 24 of the 29 stories concerned with women's involvement in politics in some way portrayed them as basically uninterested in political affairs or inept. More recently, Clark (1981) looked at how five magazines treated women living alone. Some 11% of the nonfiction articles made some reference to women living alone and few of the references presented a positive view. A similar study (Loughlin, 1983) focusing on magazine fiction in 1979-81 found that the fiction mirrored some of the changes occurring in America, such as increased female education and employment, with somewhat less emphasis on romance and personal appearance than in the past.

Sex-role portrayals in advertising are seen as important because of their potential impact on uninvolved members of the audience. One study looked at changes in advertising in 22 different magazines and found small shifts between 1974-5 and 1979-80. Women appear less frequently as dependent upon men and men were less likely to be depicted in themes of sex appeal, dominance over women and as authority figures. Women were portrayed more frequently as career oriented and in non-traditional activities. However, the physical attractiveness stereotype remained prevalent and sex object themes continued to be used to sell certain types of goods (Lysonski, 1983). Another study found changes in male sex-role portrayals in ads paralleling the change in women's roles; men are increasingly portrayed in decorative roles and less often in traditional "manly" roles in magazine ads (Skelly and Lundstrom, 1981). Textbooks also have been examined and one analysis of 11 books used as introductory texts in college found that females were underrepresented in examples in every type of textbook (Bertilson et al., 1982).

Since music is the major content of radio, the portrayal of men and women in contemporary music takes on greater significance. Hyden and McCandless (1983) analyzed the lyrics of 110 songs popular from 1972-1982, finding 68% were sung by males and 26% by females; also, while men were pictured as possessing both masculine and feminine characteristics, women largely conformed to traditional stereotypic feminine attributes. Women were most frequently described as being young, childlike, passive and powerful.

Occupations and Professions. As people have invested greater personal identity into their jobs, they have become concerned about the images of their occupation or profession. A study of TV situation comedies from 1946 to 1978 found that 64% were middle class families; professionals accounted for 43% of heads of households on TV compared to 14.5% in the general population. The self-employed also were overrepresented but the largest discrepancy was in the representation of the working class which accounted for only 8% of the heads of TV households but 65% of the actual population (Butsch and Glennon, 1983). Rondina et al. (1983) found that 49% of the soap opera work force was made up of professionals, with managers shown at twice the rate they occur in the general population.

A sample of TV series from 1950 to 1980 found 240 nurses and 287 physicians portrayed; 99% of the former were female and 95% of the latter male (Kalisch and Kalisch, 1984). Four major treatments of nurse characters were identified: the nurse as nonentity (nurses in Medical Center or Ben Casey), the good nurse (Marcus Welby), the nurturing nurse (Julia Baker of Julia), and the professional nurse (Margaret Houlihan of M*A*S*H). Kalisch et al (1983: 200) conclude that the image of nursing depends exclusively upon this image of the good doctor. "A kindly nurse might keep his office tidy and make sure he gets his meals; she might keep his patients calm while they wait for him; but she will never provide the comprehensive and aggressive care his patients have come to expect." Looking at one paper's coverage of education, Ross (1983) found attention to post-secondary rather than elementary or preschool education and greater emphasis on events rather than people.

The old movie image of the mad scientist and nineteenth century newspaper exaggerations of scientific findings made the scientific community leary of media coverage and concerned about media contributions to the understandings of what scientists do. Gerbner et al. (1981) analyzed TV programming and found that science was the main focus of 4% of primetime and 9% of weekend-daytime programs. Though science was a frequent theme of TV drama, the scientist was a relatively rare dramatic character. Positive portrayals outnumbered negative ones and scientists were "smarter" but they tended to be less attractive, fair, sociable, warm or as young as other characters.

Business and labor in general have been concerned about their image. Hackett (1983) analyzed Canadian TV and CBS network TV newscasts for two months in 1980, finding business mentioned in 17% of the items and labor mentioned in 11% of the items. Overall, business people and corporations were shown in a broad range of social activities and roles. Business performance was cited as an indicator of the general economic climate (also see Gale and Wexler, 1983). Threats to business health were seen as threats to the health of the country. Unions, on the other hand, were portrayed primarily as engaged in strikes or other socially disruptive activities. Workers were sometimes shown as the victims of economic conditions but also were portrayed as causing trouble for the economy. A media monitoring project by the Machinists Union in 1979 and 1981 concluded that unions were almost invisible on TV (Rollings, 1983). TV depicted unions as violent and obstructive; workers in unionized occupations were clumsy, uneducated fools with little leadership ability. Occupational prevalence on TV was grossly disproportionate to that found in the population at large. TV tended to emphasize occupations dealing in services rather than goods production. An equally unflattering portrait was found by the Media Institute in its analysis of 50 prime-time programs of the 1979-80 season (Theberge et al., 1981). While portrayed mainly as powerful and rich, a considerable number of businessmen were from small firms and the middle or lower middle class. Some two thirds of the businessmen were portrayed as criminals, fools or greedy malevolent egotists, they concluded. Big businessmen were often portrayed as criminals involved in activities ranging from fraud to murder and they were seldom portrayed as contributing to the social or economic well-being of their communities.

Problems and Issues. When President Ronald Reagan's colon cancer dominated the news in the summer of 1985, many observers noted that the coverage might save many lives by alerting others in "at risk" categories to have checkups. Public fears of diseases or other problems have concerned many professionals. They have examined the media to see how such problems are portrayed. The National Cancer Institute conducted studies of news media coverage of cancer in 1977 and 1980 (Freimuth et al., 1984). They found that news coverage tended to emphasize dying rather than coping and fewer than 5% of the stories dealt with the support services available to cancer patients and their families. Headlines of cancer news stories were generally accurate and neutral in tone. An analysis of three major news and consumer magazines from 1959-1974 reflected significant government support of health research, the emergence of specialized care programs and a rapid escalation of health care costs (Fisher, Gandy and Janus, 1981). These print media also tended to support the introduction of expensive technology and were supportive of the medical establishment. The little criticism that existed focused on the consumer of medical services.

Drug and alcohol abuse have also received increasing examination. Some have argued that media play a part in the development or continuation of drug dependence. A content analysis of two major metropolitan newspapers found drug themes a common occurrence but most of the stories focused on the danger of drug abuse (Craig, 1981). Advertising is a major source of images portraying the use of alcohol. Strickland et al. (1982) report on a study of more than 3,100 alcohol ads in 42 magazines in 1978, finding that the majority of the themes used were product-related, about quality and tradition. Sexually-oriented themes and "lifestyle" themes were infrequent. Male models were used most frequently. The heaviest concentration of alcohol ads was in arts and sciences magazines such as *Psychology Today* and the *New Yorker*, followed by men's magazines. Black-oriented publications also had a higher than average number of alcohol ads. Most models appeared to be older than 25, contrary to recent criticisms of advertising for using young adult models under age to provide peer models (Finn and Strickland, 1982). Some sex-role stereotyping in the use of alcohol has also been noted (Litman, 1980).

Breed and De Foe (1982) report on an effort to influence the portrayal of drinking on TV by working with production personnel and within the dramatic framework of the medium. Contacts were made with studio personnel who were assisted in using more accurate and authentic material about alcohol use. They concluded that the process was most effective in increasing the authenticity of alcohol use portrayal. Recent evidence suggests that the campaign to reduce TV presentations of alcohol has been somewhat successful (Chan, 1985). Between 1982 and 1985, *Dallas* trimmed 70% of its drinking.

Crime is probably the major problem portrayed on TV and in other entertainment content because of its dramatic value and use in themes of conflict. Several analyses of TV programming show murder and robbery to be the most frequently depicted crimes. Estep and MacDonald (1983) looked at three different seasons of TV — 1976-77, 1978-79 and 1980-81 — finding murder representing 25% of all crimes while the depiction of robbery more than doubled from 8 to 19% of all crimes through that period. Violent crime was over represented as was the middle class in both suspect and victim roles. More women than men were depicted as murder victims which is inconsistent with crime data.

Lichter and Lichter (1984) content-analyzed a six-week sample of prime-time TV programs from 1980-81, finding 250 criminals who committed 417 crimes. Murder was the most common crime, averaging one every two and a half programs. TV crime was 100 times more likely to involve murder than real life crimes. Most TV crimes involved violence; businessmen were responsible for more crime than any other group besides professional criminals. Most TV criminals were caught or thwarted. Although a majority of police and government officials were shown positively, a large number were shown as either corrupt or incompetent (also see Graber, 1980). The Greenberg et al. (1980) study of three fall seasons in the 1970's looked at different types of antisocial behavior. Results showed that the major form of antisocial behavior on commercial TV was verbal aggression. The typical hour of TV contained 20 instances of verbal aggression and 14 acts of physical aggression, plus several acts of deceit. Saturday morning cartoons contained the most physical aggression and situation comedies contained most of the verbal aggression. Males committed more antisocial acts than did females, and the frequency of physical aggression increased from the youngest age group to those in their 30's and 40's, then declined among those age 50 or older.

Other Countries. Nations worry about their images, and some even advertise. A study of newspapers from three different countries (New York Times, Wall Street Journal, London Times, Financial Times, and the Times of India) showed that 2,723 ads were placed by foreign governments in the decade ending in 1980. The New York Times was used the most frequently for ads from other countries; it accounted for two thirds of all ads and had an average of 3.3 per issue. Industrialized countries placed the greatest percentage of ads of any region (43%). Pittatore (1983) looked at the image of Italy in U.S. magazine ads, finding a "sophisticated image" used in 55%, an "art image" in 14%, a "craftsmanship image" in 12% and a "sex image" in 11%. The changing image of Iran in U.S. media also has been documented (Tadayon, 1980; Altheide, 1982; Meeske and Jayaheri, 1982). The U.S. image found in China's People's Daily focuses on relations with that country and then U.S. domestic news (Lee, 1981). Although 10% of the coverage of U.S. domestic issues portrayed the U.S. as beset by social and economic crises, substantial coverage included admiring mentions of advances in science and technology. Numerous other studies have focused on news coverage of other nations (e.g., Morales, 1984); we will discuss this further in Chapter Nine.

Government Agencies. An analysis of network news stories about six federal regulatory agencies during 1980 found that news centered on social regulatory matters rather than conflicts between agencies or with Congress (Thomas and Boyd, 1984). Most of the stories were judged to be neutral (87%), while 11% depicted agencies in a negative manner and 2% in a positive light. The agencies were EPA, FDA, CAB, ICC, FTC and OSHA. An example of an event capturing media coverage and focusing public attention on a regulatory function was the Three Mile Island accident at the nuclear power plant (Nimmo and Combs, 1981; Stephens and Edison, 1982). Tone of the coverage was predominantly reassuring, although alarming statements were reported on health and safety issues. The government institutions receiving the bulk of media attention in the U.S. are the presidency and Congress. Orman (1984) found that coverage of the American president has increased over the years in the periodical press (1900-1982). Coverage of the presidency varies during election campaigns (Stempel and Windhauser, 1984).

Other Images. Interest groups of all types are concerned with media images. For example, an interest in consumer education led to an analysis of 1980-81 TV programs and the finding that consumer behaviors related to buymanship, choice-making and rights and responsibilities were portrayed in about equal numbers. All of these acts were twice as frequent as those related to financial management

(Way, 1984). Greenberg and Atkin (1983) looked at how "driving" was portrayed in prime-time TV series and found few instances of immediate legal penalties for irregular or dangerous driving acts. Such acts occurred more than seven times per hour on prime-time TV. Dangerous driving was more prevalent among males than females, among younger adults than those middle aged or older, and among whites than non-whites. Villains were portrayed as the most dangerous drivers of all. Even insects suffer a bad press, according to one analysis. Of the articles dealing with insects in 40 different magazines between 1970 and 1980 (Moore et al., 1982) found that only 20% dealt positively with insects while 80% stressed their negative aspects. They note that the overwhelming image of insects is that they are bad organisms which should be killed rather than appreciated for their aesthetic or other value.

What Do People Think about the Media?
Beliefs, Attitudes, and Impressions

People's attitudes towards the mass media often appear quite ambivalent. They generally like the U.S. media system but fear its potential control over their lives and feel guilty about how much time they spend with the media. They have what many would call a healthy skepticism about what they see or read, but it is combined with a large measure of confidence in the performance of media people.

The Gallup Poll (1977) asked a national sample of adults in 1977 whether they spend too much or too little time watching TV, reading newspapers, or reading magazines during their non-working time each day. Almost half of the sample (48%) said their TV viewing was about right, while 31% said they spent too much time and 17% too little time. More men than women feel they watch too much TV; 32% of whites feel they watch too much TV, while only 19% of nonwhites feel that way. Those with college and high school educations feel they watch too much TV in greater proportions than those with grade school backgrounds. Younger people also feel they watch too much in greater numbers than older people; 42% of those ages 18-24 feel they watch too much, compared to 39% of those ages 25-29, 35% of those ages 30-49, and 21% of those age 50 and older. In contrast, only 5% of the sample felt they spent too much time reading newspapers and 6% felt they spent too much time reading magazines. Some 47% said they spent too little time reading newspapers and 45% thought their reading time was about right. Some 49% felt they spent too little time reading magazines while 39% thought the time spent reading magazines was about right. Bower (1973) found a U-shaped relationship between attitudes toward TV and one's position in the life span. Those younger and older were more positive in their ratings of TV than those in the middle. Gantz (1985) studied 416 married adults on how TV fit into their lives. His findings indicated that most saw viewing as a shared and valued activity that generally did not disrupt activities with spouse or friends. Some 14% thought TV interfered with the amount of time they spend with their friends. Morgan (1984), on the other hand, found TV viewing associated with claims of a "lousy" life. Heavy viewers were more likely to say their lives are "intense" rather than calm, secure, peaceful, etc.

Social categories may influence attitudes towards media. One study of Black and Mexican-American adults in Texas showed both groups were negative in their media evaluations, but Blacks were more critical than Mexican-Americans (Tan, 1978). Blacks who were critical tended to have more education, be younger and have high esteem. Mexican-Americans who were younger and high on self-esteem also were more critical of the media. In a study of perceptions of media by white ethnic groups, Jeffres and Hur (1979b) found that people who saw a positive image of their ethnic group in a particular medium also tended to evaluate that medium's performance in covering the ethnic community positively.

Burgoon and Burgoon (1979) sought to find out what would predict satisfaction with newspapers using a sample of 4,000 people in four areas. The most important factor was an image of the newspaper as a fair-minded watchdog involved in the issues of the community and interested in what readers think. Another study found that editors and a sample of youth age 18-24 agreed on goals of newspapers, but the readers were not happy with the end product (Rawlings, 1979). There was strong agreement between editors and youths on several attributes one would expect in North American newspapers (such as accuracy, impartiality in reporting, investigative enterprise, and specialized staff skills), but only moderate agreement on almost two dozen editorial qualities.

The media are important actors in American communities. Janowitz (1952) found, for example, that people in smaller homogeneous communities thought local newspapers should promote social consensus. Tichenor, Donohue and Olien (1980) have demonstrated that residents of larger diverse communities are more likely to support media content which is controversial and conflict oriented. Smith (1984a,b) sought public perceptions of the media in Louisville, finding that newspapers and TV were considered the most influential of 12 community groups. Broadcast media got almost 30% of the nominations as institutions exercising the "greatest influence," followed by daily newspapers with 21%. Furthermore, most Louisville residents were satisfied with the media's role in supporting the community. More than two thirds felt that the media projected at least a positive image of the community and there was strong consensus among racial and income groups. Those who rated the quality of life highly also were more likely to feel the media conveyed a positive image of the community than those who were less satisfied with the area.

What knowledge lies behind those public attitudes? Three phone surveys in Columbus, Ohio in 1978 and 1979 sought to understand public knowledge of how the news media operate (Becker, Whitney and Collins, 1980). Results found significant gaps in public understanding. Audience members were more knowledgeable about TV stations than about newspapers, and knowledge was related to exposure. Knowledge also seemed to lead to a decrease in confidence concerning people who produce the news.

People's general attitudes and satisfaction with the media are often linked to the notions of credibility—How believable are TV news programs and newspapers?

Media Credibility

Considerable resentment of the press is found in the general public. Wolfson (1979) notes: "The road to public confidence is a long one. Journalists may see themselves as working in the public's interest, but the public doesn't. Journalists rate higher than politicians in surveys of public sentiment, but not by much. Gone is the lonely editor who was the last resort for Jimmy Stewart when the establishment bankers and politicians were bearing down on him.

Instead people often find another door that's hard to open when they need information, help and support. Wolfson says journalists should concede that they become involved in their reporting but not capitulate to the press-power harpies. "They can also say that they follow standards of fair reporting that will not allow them to slant a story to force a desired outcome. This standard clearly distinguishes journalism from the calculating, power-conscious worlds of politics, law and business—the worlds from which come the people who cry loudest about press power."

What do people think about the media's performance? A Roper Poll reported in 1985 found the media among five American institutions obtaining favorable ratings from the public. At the top were police and business/industry with 86% favorable ratings, followed by the TV-press with 77% and the print press with 76%. Congress had a 64% positive rating and labor unions 49%. Credibility seems to be linked to authority and visibility in another 1985 survey by Media Opinion Research, in which 40% of respondents gave high credibility to TV news anchors, 28% to TV reporters, 27% to newspaper editors and 18% to newspaper reporters.

Both the general public and government officials were surveyed for their perceptions of media credibility by Yankelovich, Skelly and White (1979). They found a strong majority of the public believed that TV and newspaper news was biased. Their definition of bias was not a display of favoritism to specific groups but rather a problem of emphasizing bad news over good news. In the general public no distinction was made between TV and newspaper credibility. College students believed newspapers had much more credibility than TV broadcasts. Among government officials all three media showed relatively strong credibility, but newspapers and news magazines had a slight edge over network TV news. The credibility of leading newspapers was greater among federal officials than among state and local officials. Metropolitan media were seen as more credible and accurate than the community media in a New England suburban survey (Nwankwo, 1982). Preceptions of bias and low credibility are not static. Tillinghast (1983) found increased credibility among news sources (and journalists) following two newspapers' mergers and changes in management.

Newspapers and TV news have battled for credibility at least since 1961 when, for the first time, the Roper polling organization reported that the public found TV news more believable than newspapers. Since then TV news has steadily drawn away from newspapers so that the margin is now about 53-24% (Roper, 1985). Roper's finding have been criticized from several angles. For example, the definition of credibility as believability has been questioned. That is, when people consider newspaper believability, are they thinking about coverage of a local news event while in the case of TV they associate credibility with national newscasts rather than local news? TV seems to win in direct comparisons.

Channel dimensionalities are probably strongly related to credibility. TV's ability to show events happening may give people the feeling that they have almost direct contact with the news and newsmakers. Even if they are informed enough to recognize that pictures are edited, the visual element is a powerful factor that grey print cannot match. Perhaps the most important factor is audience expectations concerning the media. Greenberg and Roloff (1975) say that audience orientation skews results of the credibility polls. People turn on the TV expecting entertainment; they go to newspapers for information rather than entertainment. TV news is a mass appeal medium— it does not cater to role interests as much as newspapers. TV news' tendency to give people what they want may be a factor in presenting too-comfortable, predictable, simple stories about the world in 30 second segments. TV builds a familiarity and is more easily digested than the complex world offered by newspapers. Mulder (1980) found that people who seek news find newspapers to be the most credible medium, while those who passively consume news thought TV news was more credible. Thus, credibility was linked to patterns of uses and gratifications.

Since research into credibility began in earnest in the early 1950's, a host of dimensions have been identified, as Singletary (1976) notes. The following have been identified in different studies as components of credibility: evaluative, dynamism, competence, trustworthiness, safety, authoritativeness, character, and honesty.

Gallup's 1980 national survey of teenagers age 13-18 sought ratings of eight professions in terms of their honesty and ethical standards. Journalists were second from last, preceding business executives but following medical doctors, clergy, college teachers, lawyers, senators and Congressmen. Some 31% said journalists have either "very high" or "high" ethical standards. Higher ratings of journalists were given by older teenagers (age 16-18), nonwhites (39%), teenagers from white-collar backgrounds, and those living in the south.

We get a longer-range view in a study by Caplow and Bahr (1979) which repeated the celebrated Middletown studies of Robert and Helen Lynd from the 1920's and 1930's. The entire high school population was surveyed in 1924 and again in 1977, more than 50 years later. There was a considerable increase in people's confidence in sources of information on public issues, one dealing with the major morning newspaper, one dealing with national mazazines, and one concerning the campaign speeches of candidates. The students showed significantly more confidence in the newspaper in 1977 than they did in 1924. Fifty years earlier, 60% said the Middletown newspaper presented a fair and complete picture of the issues in the recent election; 71% thought so in 1977. While only 5% of the students in 1924 said voters can rely on statements of fact made by political candidates in campaign speeches, 21% of the 1977 students expressed such confidence a half century later. However, there was a 9% drop in 1977 from the 50% who thought in 1924 that it was safe to assume that a statement appearing in an article in a reputable magazine was correct.

A variety of factors can affect one's media credibility, including both media characteristics and audience characteristics. For example, the sex and race of visible newscasters can affect credibility. An experiment by Balon, Philport and Beadie (1978) showed that white students perceived white male newscasters as more cheerful, less sympathetic and more extroverted than Black males. Another study of black adults found that 85% of them saw black newscasters as more attractive and 66% saw them as more believable (Johnson, 1984). Adams (1977) found that a man's criticism of TV coverage of the Vietnam War was influenced by how active he had been in combat. A veteran's background, age and TV viewing habits also influenced his criticism. An analysis of Roper poll data found three factors most related to criticism of the media's role in Watergate: support of Nixon, party affiliation, and ideology. There also was evidence that sentiments about the health of the political system and political leadership in general were related to press criticism. Political variables were the most important determinants of press criticism. Support of the press was negatively related to support of the national leadership. A TV newscaster's credibility may be affected by the camera angle and similar technical factors. McCain, Chilberg and Wakshag (1977) examined the effect of high vs. low camera angle on the credibility of televised speakers, finding that higher camera angles enhanced the speaker's perceived competence, composure and sociability.

Advertising and Commercials

Almost three fourths of Americans surveyed by the Roper organization (1973) saw commercials as a fair price to pay for TV entertainment, and 63% did not mind commercials on children's TV shows. However, advertising often is an area of intense feelings and disagreements. Zanot (1984) chronicles 38 public opinion surveys concerning advertising since the depression. The earlier studies show general satisfaction but growing disenchantment with public opinion turning negative towards advertising in the 1970's. A poll for the Ogilvy & Mather advertising agency found that 59% of the public thought Advertising did not "present an honest picture" in 1974 and the figure had grown to 70% in 1985 (Garfield, 1985). Almost three quarters of the respondents felt advertising insulted the average consumer's intelligence and made people want things they don't really need.

Rich, Owens and Ellenbogen (1978) found that 58% of their Montreal sample thought commercials were a fair price to pay for TV, but 86% thought there were too many commercials on TV and similar percentages thought commercials were too long. Some 48% said commercials were "usually" or "sometimes" helpful, while 52% said they "seldom" were. Viewing habits were related to criticism of commercials. Those who switched channels less often and those who watched between 6 p.m. and midnight expressed stronger disapproval of commercials. The researchers conclude there is much dissatisfaction with commercials. Recent Canadian Broadcast Corporation studies found that 90% of Canadian respondents were either moderately or very unfavorably disposed towards commercials on TV.

In the U.S., Sandage, Barban and Haefner (1976) found that farmers maintained a positive view of advertising as an institution since a study 16 years earlier though there was a less positive view than earlier.

The American Association of Advertising Agencies has found that opinions of advertising are primarily influenced by the advertising we see on TV. Naturally, newspaper, radio and magazine advertisements also have impact. Direct mail and billboards contribute the least to our opinions of advertising. Issues about which people are more concerned are advertising's credibility, entertainment value, advertising as a social force, and consumer benefits. People are concerned about how advertising manipulates and motivates us, its clutter and intrusiveness, its content, and media support of advertising as an institution. Negative opinions center on credibility, content, intrusiveness, and ability to manipulate and motivate us. As Grotta, Larkin and Carrell (1976) found, when people are interested in a topic or object, they do not distinguish between advertising and news content. In an analysis of 340 people in a metro area, they found agreement with these notions: there is too much advertising on TV, television commercials insult one's intelligence, TV ads represent the latest trends and newest products, and they didn't pay much attention to radio or TV commercials. There was slight disagreement with the notion that newspaper advertising is less informative than TV advertising. Other surveys have found the public questioning the informational value of advertising (Soley and Reid, 1983; Norris, 1983).

New Communication Technologies

There have been relatively few attempts to assess public attitudes towards the new communication technologies and the media they are spawning (Bowes, 1976). This is beginning to change as the new technologies diffuse more widely throughout the population. A survey of more than 1,000 Texas residents in 1984 found that 42% of the households surveyed had cable TV, 16.5% video cassette recorders, and 13.5% a home computer (Reese, Shoemaker and Danielson, 1984). More than half of the sample rejected the idea that new computer technologies will benefit only the few, a view held by such critics as Schiller (1980). Some 58% thought new technologies would give them greater control over their information consumption and 69% agreed that everyone should know about computers. On the negative side, a majority also thought the new technologies would allow the government to invade people's privacy. Differences in expectations were found by age and social status. The more well-off individuals were less concerned that high cost might limit access to the new technologies among poorer people; they were more likely to believe that the technologies would provide "the electronic equivalent of Head Start" (Reese et al., 1984: 22). Age was related to pessimistic views about the distribution and personal control of the new technologies. The researchers suggest older people may feel they won't be around long enough to realize the potential benefits of new technologies. They also are more likely to be apprehensive about the technical operation of computers, VCR's, etc., and this fear may be at the base of such negative attitudes.

Summary

In this chapter we analyzed media content structures and reviewed public perceptions. First, we discussed the various ways scholars, media professionals and the public view media content. Then content structures were examined for different media including: radio formats, film genre, TV program formats/genre, print media editorial forms and graphic design, and news distinctions.

Media images and stereotypes are central to discussions about whether the media affect or reflect society. We reviewed the literature on media images of ethnic groups, age groups, children and families, gender, occupations and professions, problems and issues, countries, government agencies, etc. In the final section we documented public perceptions of the media including attitudes towards their own media use; beliefs about mass media organizations and their influence; credibility of newspapers and TV newscasts; and attitudes toward advertising and commercials.

It was pointed out that media content is analyzed for several purposes: to make inferences about the intentions and behaviors of media professionals; to compare communication channels or gather information about the volume of messages carried; and to make inferences about media content to which people are exposed. It is the third point which is most crucial for those concerned with media effects. In the next chapter, we will look at media content considered important for social effects of the media.

Social Effects
of the Media

by
Richard M. Perloff*

It is commonly believed that the mass media wield wide and mysterious powers. An increasingly diverse number of citizens groups, including the Parent Teachers Association, the American Medical Association, the Moral Majority, Action for Children's Television and the National Organization of Women, have strongly criticized the media, particularly television. Their criticism has taken two forms. On the one hand, they have lambasted the content of the media, charging that the portrayals are fraught with biases, stereotypes, and excessive amounts of violence. At the same time, these groups have contended that media portrayals exert harmful effects on the developing attitudes and behaviors of children and adolescents. This chapter examines these criticisms in the light of scientific evidence on the content and social effects of mass media. The goal is to summarize and synthesize knowledge about the role that mass media, particularly television, plays in the socialization process.

*Richard M. Perloff is Associate Professor of Communication and Director of the Communication Research Center at Cleveland State University.

Life on the Small Screen
Stereotypes, Role Models and Psychological Effects

Children spend as much time watching television as they do listening to their teachers in school. What do children learn from all this exposure to TV? What lessons does television teach them about life? What values, myths and philosophies of life does it foster?

These questions have been the subject of considerable research over the past thirty years. As a result of these investigations, we have come to know a great deal about how television portrays ethnic groups, men and women, and the elderly, as well as how it depicts a variety of everyday behaviors including drinking, driving and debates between family members. The discussion below summarizes these findings; it focuses in large part on the painstaking work by Greenberg and his colleagues at Michigan State University and by Gerbner and his associates at the University of Pennsylvania. This section highlights those findings particularly relevant to the psychological effects of mass media (see Chapter 5 for a complete discussion of mass media content).

The Demographics of Television Characters

On television, most of the characters are white adult males in their late 30's or early 40's. And this character is more likely to be a male if he is a member of a new ethnic minority on television. After analyzing the portrayal of television's newest minority groups (Hispanic-Americans) Greenberg and Baptista-Fernandez (1980) concluded that there were relatively few Hispanic-Americans on television, even fewer female Hispanics, and noted that "If you watched 300 different television characters, say, you'd find less than a handful of Hispanics" (Greenberg, 1980, p. 11). Hispanic-American male characters also tend to have heavy accents, dark complexions, and exhibit little concern for their futures.

The only other minority group to gain visual prominence on television is Blacks. Blacks too are portrayed in a rather distinctive fashion. They are rather young; most Blacks are under 20 (unlike most non-black characters). Compared to whites on the same television shows, black characters are funnier, flashier, leaner, economically poorer and less likely to hold jobs. Nearly half the black characters appeared in situation comedies, compared to only one-fifth of the whites. Nearly half of all the black characters appeared on black-oriented programs.

Some insight on these stereotypes is provided by Clark's (1969) analysis of the development of minority groups in mass media entertainment. Clark argues that ethnic groups pass through four psychological stages of character development. The first stage is one of non-recognition or invisibility in which the minority group is not seen or heard from very often. Blacks occupied this role in the 1950's; Hispanic characters do today. The second stage is ridicule, where the ethnic group achieves recognition but largely as fall guys and objects of derision. Jewish characters fell into this role in the 1940's and 1950's (frequently self-derision, as in the case of Jack Benny). Blacks may just have completed this stage. The minority group then rises to increased stature in the third stage; here characters perform regulatory roles or those maintaining law and order functions (e.g., police, lawyer). The final stage is that of egalitarian roles in which the characters are portrayed in a wider range of occupations, exhibit ever-more differentiated psychological traits and blend increasingly into non-minority situations. It will be interesting to trace the evolution of black and Hispanic characters to determine if they progress or decline throughout televised history.

As noted in Chapter 5, television presents a familiar and stereotyped portrait of the sexes. Moreover, when women and men are placed in an emotionally stressful situation on television, men are more likely to need physical support than women while women more frequently show a need for emotional support. In general, women ask for more emotional support, are offered more of it, and receive more of it than men. Television provides dramatic evidence for the idea that women require more nurturance and emotional sustenance and, conversely, for the notion that men can function without this help or are somehow devoid of these very human needs (Henderson, Greenberg and Atkin, 1980). Finally, men and women engage in a cluster of sex-typed behaviors on television: men more frequently drive cars, participate in sports, drink, smoke and conduct business on the phone; women more often perform indoor housework, prepare and serve food and entertain others by singing or playing a musical instrument (see Henderson & Greenberg, 1980).

Sex on Television. Sex on television? Until cable appeared, there was really no sex to speak of. Although references to sexual intercourse have become commonplace, the overwhelming majority of interpersonal touching on TV is not sexual at all (Sprafkin and Silverman, 1981). Most physical contact consists of handshakes, pats to get someone's attention, and touches to make a point. And when sex is mentioned on television, it typically means heterosexual sexual intercourse (between unmarried people); sexual deviation is rarely suggested (Greenberg, 1980).

Alcohol Use. Concern about the impact of televised alcohol use on youngsters assumes that such substance abuse frequently appears on the small screen. Greenberg's studies indicate that this is indeed the case: while one had to watch TV for over an hour to see illegal drugs being consumed and for two hours to observe a character or actor smoke a cigar, pipe or cigarette, the same viewer could see alcohol being offered or consumed every 21 minutes during the 1977-78 season (Greenberg, 1980). Alcohol is most likely to be consumed on the most popular crime and comedy programs. The overwhelming majority of the boozing was done by white males, but since there are more of them shown on television anyway, that doesn't tell us as much as we'd like. Since about 33% of the users of alcohol are women, it is fair to say that both sexes consumed alcohol in proportion to their representation in the entire cast of television characters.

Is all this a lot? The best way to answer this is to view it from the perspective of the child who sits before the small screen each day. On the average, the child sees two instances of smoking and drug intake each day, and up to 10 acts of drinking each day, or about 3,000 over the course of a year. Moreover, those who drink are usually portrayed as "good" characters, and when they drink too much, they are rarely punished or censured (Breed and DeFoe, 1981).

Televised Portrayals of Health

After physicians, television is the source from which most Americans obtain their knowledge about health. How then are doctors and health-related issues portrayed on the small screen?

Television Doctors. In a typical week a viewer sees about twelve doctors and six nurses during prime time alone (Gerbner et al, 1981). Compared with other professionals, doctors are good, successful and kind. Only four percent of all TV doctors are portrayed as evil, which is half the proportion found in other professions. Moreover, doctors are a bit more fair and sociable than other characters, while they are more stable and intelligent than nurses (Gerbner et al, 1981). On television doctors also symbolize power and authority and have a remarkable ability to control the lives of others. However, doctors almost never are shown in their homes or with their families.

Demographically, 90 percent of doctors are white men, young or middle-aged, while nurses are usually young white women. When doctors interact with their female nurses (or typically female patients) they confront them from a position of daring and authority, according to Gerbner et al (1981). In fact nearly half of female patients are depicted as bed-ridden with a strong man—a husband, doctor, or lover—at their bedsides. As McLaughlin (1975) concludes, the television doctor continues to exert an almost mystical power over the physical, emotional and social life of the patient; if the doctor just followed the rules—and did not take risks to help patients or (worse yet) left matters to patients themselves—television suggests that things would simply not work out.

Nutrition and Food. During an average week of prime time programs, viewers will see people eating, drinking or talking about food on the average of nine times per hour (Gerbner et al, 1981). Thirty-nine percent of all eating or drinking episodes involve grabbing a snack; in fact on television people snack almost as frequently as they eat breakfast, lunch and dinner combined (42 percent). Moreover, as Gerbner et al note, half the food commercials concern sweets, snacks, and non-nutritious (junk) foods.

Obesity and Safety. On television, people are healthy in spite of the fact that they frequently surrender to their urge to eat and drink (Gerbner et al, 1981). They also are relatively safe from accidents, slim, hardly ever in need of glasses (only one in four persons wear them); and although obesity afflicts 25 to 45 percent of Americans, it afflicts relatively few individuals on television—approximately six percent. In the realm of safety, although highway accidents are the leading cause of violent injury and death, on television they are relatively infrequent. When characters do drive cars on television, they wear seat belts only 23 percent of the time.

Perspective. Life on television—How closely does it correspond to life in the real world? How well does TV reflect social reality? Not very well, says Greenberg (1980). He notes that:

> Television fiction provides a strong dose of tunnel vision. A steady ingestion of episodes from fictional series on the commercial networks would be as representative of life as a steady ingestion of the output of food chains would be representative of the fare offered by American restaurants. Television characterizations and interactions are narrow, contagious, and persistent. (Greenberg, 1980, p. 183).

On some level, of course, television does reflect reality—most women are less aggressive than most men (Maccoby and Jacklin, 1974), and most individuals hold stereotyped beliefs about what men, women, Blacks and the elderly are like. On the most basic level, television reflects our stereotypes, our expectations and our values. But as Greenberg notes, it offers a restricted and narrow range of possibilities.

At this point members of the television and advertising industries may complain—and quite appropriately. Their argument is that television is not designed to reflect accurately the number of Blacks or Hispanics in the American population; nor should television refuse to show material such as sex or drinking because it may offend certain segments of the audience. Instead, television is designed to entertain, to amuse, to develop programming that will attract the greatest possible audience at a given hour of the day. As advertising executives

frequently point out when confronted with evidence of sex-role stereotypes in commercials, their job is not to improve social reality or to
change it—but, instead, to promote products that people will buy. In
response to this, television critics point out that what is good for programming or advertisers may not necessarily promote psychological
well-being. And so the debate goes.

Recently, a new dimension has been added to the debate about
television content: evidence of the medium's psychological impact on
the audience. Social scientists have emphasized that it is not possible
to make conclusions about the effects that television exerts merely on
the basis of its content. Evidence that television presents a stereotype
of the sexes in no way proves that these portrayals cause children to
develop a sex-typed view of gender roles. In order to prove this latter
point—to demonstrate television effects—it is necessary to conduct
surveys, experiments and other studies that probe audience members'
perceptions of what they see. Over the past decade many studies have
investigated the influences of televised stereotypes and role portrayals
on children, adolescents and adults. Reviewing these investigations
should give us some idea of what role the media play in the socialization process.

Psychological Effects

Two major theoretical approaches have been put forward to explain
the social effects of mass media. The first, George Gerbner's cultivation theory, asserts that television acts as our society's high priest and
teaches or cultivates American society's values, myths and moral
lessons (Gerbner, 1972). Gerbner and his associates also maintain that
television may be a particularly strong—and disturbing—teacher
when its messages differ from what other socialization agents assert.
Gerbner's thesis is that heavy television viewers come away with a distorted version of life, believing among other things that there are
virtually few if any Hispanic Americans, most older people are hostile
and crotchety, few women work or hold positions of authority, most
physicians are male and help people with their problems, and that
policemen frequently use their guns when at work.

The second theoretical approach is actually quite similar and is
probably more basic. This theory is Albert Bandura's social learning
theory or theory of imitative learning or modeling (Bandura and
Walters, 1963). Through a series of experiments, Bandura showed that
children do not need to be directly rewarded or punished to learn new
attitudes or behaviors from television. Instead, they can acquire new
beliefs and behaviors simply by observing symbolic role models. Today

this proposition may not seem surprising, but 25 years ago, in an era when psychologists believed that individuals learned primarily through direct rewards or punishments, his theory constituted a radical approach. Bandura pointed out that many standard psychological theories of the day could not easily account for how children learned from mass media; contrary to what many standard learning approaches suggested, children managed to learn vast amounts of information without being directly rewarded every time they watched a television program. According to social learning theory, individuals could acquire or learn a great deal of information simply by watching others and without being directly reinforced. However, their decision to perform or enact what they had learned depended to a considerable extent on "reinforcement contingencies" — that is, rewards and punishments.

Both Gerbner's and Bandura's theories suggest that exposure to racial, sex-role and other stereotypes in the mass media will contribute to the development of stereotyped beliefs, attitudes and behaviors. Both also suggest that television plays an important part in the socialization process. We now turn to studies that more directly examine this issue.

Sex-Role Portrayals. In one of the first explorations of the impact of sex-typed TV programming on children, Beuf (1974) recounts the case of a boy who was asked what he would like to be when he grows up if he were a girl. "Oh," he exclaimed, "if I were a girl, I'd have to grow up to be nothing." In her study of preschool children, Beuf reported that 76 percent of the heavy television viewers selected stereotyped careers for themselves, while only 50 percent of the moderate viewers did so. These preliminary findings raised a number of interesting questions about the impact of televised sex-role portrayals and how it is that boys and girls identify with TV characters.

What is particularly interesting is that preschool children already have developed stereotyped images of themselves and who it is they wish to be like. Young boys and girls both prefer programs that feature characters of their own sex (Sprafkin and Liebert, 1978); and identify more with same-sex than with opposite-sex characters (Miller and Reeves, 1976).

Nonetheless, boys and girls differ in several important ways in their identification with TV characters. In one study, 100 percent of the boys identified with the male TV characters, whereas only 71 percent of the girls said that they wanted to be like female characters (Miller and Reeves, 1976). Thus, close to a third of the girls, but none of the boys, said they wanted to be like opposite-sex TV characters. Both boys and girls seemed well aware that there are more desirable male than female role models on television, while at the same time girls' choices reflected the greater freedom that is given girls to identify with individuals of the opposite sex. Boys and girls perceive television characters differently in another way. Boys describe characters more in terms of physical strength, while girls are more influenced by the character's physical attractiveness (Reeves and Greenberg, 1977).

With these findings in mind, we now turn to the intriguing question of exactly what effects stereotyped portrayals of the sexes have on children and adults. Several experiments leave little doubt that television commercials can create and reinforce sex-role stereotypes (Atkin, 1975; O'Bryant & Corder-Bolz, 1978). Traditional television fare can also exert profound effects on adults' sex-role attitudes and behavior, as a fascinating experiment by Jennings-Walstedt, Geis and Brown (1980) demonstrates. These investigators found that college-age women exposed to traditional commercials expressed fewer career aspirations than those who viewed nontraditional advertisements. Compared to the women who saw the non-traditional ads, the female subjects exposed to the traditional stereotyped portrayals exhibited less self-confidence when giving a speech and were less independent on another experimental task. These findings point to the subtle effects that traditional role portrayals can exert on young women's self-concepts.

Although these experiments suggest that televised sex-role portrayals exert direct effects on all or most viewers, the studies tend to minimize the influence of background variables, such as the individual's values or their parents' sex-role attitudes. Several studies suggest that television is most likely to increase sex-role stereotyping if the child has a low self-concept (Cheles-Miller, 1975), the mother holds a less prestigious occupation or does not work at all (Perloff, 1977), or fails to provide examples of counter-stereotypic social roles (O'Neil, Schoonover & Adelstein, 1980). For other children and young adolescents, television role portrayals may make attitudes less extreme and more homogenized—TV may, as Morgan (1982) reports, bring these children into the cultural "mainstream" which is characterized by a stereotyped view of the sexes. In a longitudinal study that occurred over a two-year period, Morgan found that TV viewing caused the most significant change in traditional sex-role attitudes among girls who had high IQ's and came from relatively affluent backgrounds. At the outset, these girls' intellectual capacities and family backgrounds placed them at society's fringes, but exposure to television with its heavy dose of stereotyped sex-role portrayals moved these girls in a more traditional direction (Also see the next section on The Cultivation Controversy).

Other studies indicate that males too can be influenced by the images of men and women that appear on television. Kenrick and

Gutierres (1980) found that after watching an episode of *Charlie's Angels,* the television show with three beautiful female detectives, college men rated a group of women as less attractive than did a control group of male subjects. This finding, in conjunction with evidence of the effects of beauty ads (Tan, 1979) suggests that televised images of beauty may influence individuals' standards of who is beautiful and attractive and who is not. If adolescents begin comparing themselves and their friends to the extraordinarily attractive role models they see on television, they may be sorely frustrated and disappointed.

In a similar fashion, stereotyped images of ethnic minorities and the elderly may also influence children's attitudes and behavior. About one fourth of the young respondents in one study reported that "most of the things I know" about Blacks come from TV viewing (Atkin, Greenberg and McDermott, 1983). Greenberg (1972) reported that white children who watched black-oriented television shows were more inclined to believe that Blacks behave in real life as they do on television. Such televised depictions may exert the greatest impact when children have little real life contact with an ethnic group, receiving their knowledge instead from television entertainment programs. Given the narrow and at times comical ways in which ethnic groups are portrayed on TV, there may be some reason to worry about these effects. At present, though, there is little hard evidence supporting this general proposition (Greenberg and Reeves, 1976); however, the idea is sensible and deserves continued research attention. (See, for example, Adoni and Druri, 1983.)

Other Types of Observational Learning. In a dramatic demonstration of the power of media suggestion, Phillips (1974) reported that suicides increase immediately after a suicide has been publicized in newspapers in the United States and Britain. In a study of suicide stories from 1947 to 1968, Phillips concluded that the more publicity devoted to a story, the larger the subsequent rise in suicides; moreover, suicides increased primarily in the geographical areas that received publicity in the stories. On the other hand, fictional suicide stories on soap operas do not seem to cause an increase in real-life fatalities (Kessler and Stipp, 1984). At the same time, there is evidence suggesting that another symbolically modeled behavior — drinking — does lead to imitative learning. There is a strong association between exposure to alcohol advertising and liquor drinking (Atkin, Hocking and Block, 1984). Furthermore, Atkin et al reported that advertising exposure was more strongly associated with both beer and liquor consumption than parental influence, age, sex, church attendance and social status.

We are just beginning to understand the processes that underlie observational learning effects. Reeves and Garramone (1983) suggest that television characterizations may activate or "prime" personality traits, causing the trait to become more mentally accessible, and therefore, more capable of influencing evaluation of individuals in real life. Symbolic interactionist theorists contend that children may take the role of their favorite television characters during viewing and nonviewing contexts and may modify their actions to conform to their imaginary evaluations of these characters (Ellis, Streeter and Englebrecht, 1983).

There is now abundant evidence that children can learn new attitudes and behaviors from exposure to symbolic role models portrayed in books, film, television entertainment programs and TV advertising. Some observers (Comstock et al, 1978) go so far as to say that there may be conditions where observations via television exert a stronger impact on imitative learning than does observation of real life.

The Cultivation Controversy. A related issue that has generated considerable controversy concerns the extent to which television cultivates distorted perceptions of social reality. This is Gerbner's (1972) thesis. Gerbner has argued that television functions as our society's storyteller, communicating our culture's values and myths and cultivating a set of beliefs in the minds of the audience. Gerbner argues that such effects may be dangerous inasmuch as television frequently presents a distorted, unrealistic view of the world—particularly the world of crime and violence. As studies have suggested, television adventure programs depict a great deal of violence between strangers, imply that police use their guns to solve most problems, suggest that there are too many restrictions on what police can do, and generally portray the world as a hostile and scary place to live. (See next section on TV violence.) If viewing television crime shows cultivates these beliefs, we should find that heavy TV viewers are more likely to feel this way than are light viewers.

Over the course of the past 10 years, Gerbner and his colleagues have obtained a great deal of evidence to support this hypothesis (Gerbner et al, 1981). For example, when heavy viewers (watching at least four hours of TV a day) and light viewers (viewing one hour or less) were asked whether one person out of every 100 is involved in some kind of violence in any given week or if the number is closer to ten out of every 100, 73 percent of heavy viewers said it is closer to ten out of 100, while only 62 percent of light viewers replied in this manner. Three times as many heavy viewers as light viewers believe that a policeman pulls out his gun more than five times a day. Substantially more heavy than light viewers say that they are afraid to walk alone in their own neighborhoods at night. Heavy viewers also say that they are more distrustful of other people and more inclined to believe that people are just looking out for themselves. The relationships between television viewing and these perceptions persisted, even after education, income and other variables were statistically controlled. (In other words, among low and high income, and among highly educated and less educated individuals, heavy viewing was associated with these distorted perceptions of reality.) Gerbner concluded that television viewing cultivates distorted views about the nature of violence in American society. In short, he concluded that TV viewing leads individuals to perceive the world as "a mean and scary" place.

One might think that such an intuitively-appealing idea would be widely accepted among researchers. Indeed for many years social scientists accepted these findings without question. However, inevitably criticism began to surface, and researchers discovered problems with Gerbner's research. First, several researchers reanalyzed Gerbner's data and found that when they used somewhat different methods, they could not find any relationship between television viewing time and perceptions of social reality (e.g., Hughes, 1980; O'Keefe, 1984; Roberts, 1981). Furthermore, when Doob and MacDonald (1979) looked at whether individuals lived in a high-crime or a low-crime neighborhood, they found that heavy viewers from low-crime areas were no more fearful or distrustful than light viewers; only individuals who lived in high-crime areas were more fearful and watched significantly more television. Doob and MacDonald concluded that living in a high-crime area was what was important: it led people to develop realistic fears of violence and caused them to stay home and watch TV to avoid violent crime. (See also Wakshlag, Vial and Tamborini, 1983.)

As if this were not enough, Paul Hirsch reanalyzed the data Gerbner himself used and found no evidence to support Gerbner's contention that television viewing was associated with perceptions of social reality. In fact, based on a somewhat different method of categorizing viewers, Hirsch concluded that "on many of these items (that Gerbner used), the scores of nonviewers are higher than those of television's light, medium, heavy, and/or extreme viewers (Hirsch, 1980, p. 419).

As you might expect, the dispute between Gerbner and his critics became very heated. Hirsch titled his first critique of Gerbner's research: "The Scary World of the Non-Viewer and Other Anomalies..." Not to be outdone, Gerbner and his colleagues wrote a rejoinder entitled: "A Curious Journey into the Scary World of Paul Hirsch." Finally, Gerbner responded to the contradictory findings and criticism by presenting a modified and refined version of his theory. He argued that television violence exerted two more specific effects called *mainstreaming* and *resonance*.

Mainstreaming is the process by which television brings various groups into the mainstream of American values. Specifically, Gebner argued, heavy viewers within various subgroups of the population develop common outlooks or viewpoints that differ from those of light viewers of the same subgroup. For example, since crime may be extremely pervasive in certain extremely low-income areas, mainstreaming would not expect low-income heavy viewers to be more likely than any other individuals from extremely low-income backgrounds to be concerned about crime. However, watching heavy doses of TV's distorted views of violence and crime might exert different effects on high-income individuals—bringing them into the mainstream: most affluent individuals have little direct experience with crime; therefore television may be the critical agent that causes these individuals to develop unrealistic fears about crime. Resonance, on the other hand, occurs when heavy viewers are more fearful than light viewers among a particular subgroup of the population; if, for instance, heavy viewers who live in a city are more distrustful than light viewers, TV, along with first-hand experiences, has dealt a double dose of violent imagery.

Since mainstreaming and resonance have been proposed just recently, there have been only a handful of studies on the topic. A study conducted by Carlson (1983) provided intriguing evidence in favor of mainstreaming. Carlson focused on the attitudes of teenagers whose parents are quite tolerant of dissent and who tend to support basic civil libertarian positions.

Gerbner's mainstreaming hypothesis suggests that heavy viewing of TV crime programs—which tend to oppose a civil libertarian point of view—should move these adolescents closer to the mainstream or archetypical American position on civil liberties (e.g., belief that there are too many restrictions on what police can do and that evidence which shows a defendant did not commit a crime should be used at his trial, regardless of how the police got the evidence). The findings indicated that mainstreaming occurred: crime show viewing exerted its greatest impact on teenagers who came from families that were predisposed to support the civil libertarian position.

Despite some of the contradictory findings, most researcher acknowledge that there is probably something to Gerbner's idea that television viewing cultivates distorted perceptions of reality. There also is evidence that television cultivates other perceptions beyond those pertaining to a mean and scary world. Buerkel-Rothfuss and Mayes (1981) reasoned that since lawyers, doctors, divorced people and illegitimate children are overrepresented in soap operas, heavy viewing of soap operas should be associated with higher estimates of the proportion of doctors, lawyers, divorced people and illegitimate children in the population. The results supported their predictions.

(Also see Hawkins and Pingree, 1981.) Carveth and Alexander (1985) showed that soap operas exerted greater effects on perceptions of social reality for individuals who viewed for ritualistic reasons (enjoyment, boredom) rather than for instrumental purposes (reality exploration, character identification). At the same time, several experiments have demonstrated that television and film can cultivate misperceptions of rape (see discussion of pornographic effects). Increasingly, research suggests that cultivation may be particularly likely to occur under certain circumstances—e.g., when viewers watch TV less critically and more ritualistically (Carveth and Alexander, 1985; Rouner, 1984).

One final point deserves mention. Gerbner and his colleagues have contended that television cultivates *distorted* perceptions of the world. But the world *is* a mean and a scary place; one might argue that rather than cultivating distorted perceptions, television encourages a realistic view of life in contemporary society. The problem with this position is that it ignores the many instances in which television crime programs depart markedly from reality (e.g., television's portrayal of the police, civil liberties and the frequency with which policemen use their guns). And it is in these areas that television does cultivate distinct perceptions of social reality.

Conclusions. If they were asked what role television plays in the socialization process, the overwhelming majority of social scientists would respond without hesitation that TV exerts a powerful impact on children's perceptions and their imitative learning. However, most would also point to gaps in our research knowledge, and would suggest that much needs to be learned about the conditions that facilitate media effects on social stereotyping.

As Catton observed back in 1969:

> People ordinarily learn in the process of being socialized that they can check doubtful impressions of the world around them which they have obtained from one source by seeking information from other independent sources. The ubiquity of television...tends to undermine the independence of anyone's alternative sources... they may "confirm" his impressions because they have been watching the same shows. But, having thus obtained the same image from several sources which seem independent to him, this viewer's impression hardens into a conviction. (Catton, 1969, p. 304.)

Television Violence: The Anatomy of Effects

Does television continue to paint a hostile and violent portrait of reality? Does TV violence incite young people to behave aggressively?

And what steps, if any, should the government take to regulate violence on television? No other set of media research questions has
caused more controversy than these. Television violence has become a
rallying cry for the PTA and the AMA and has united the networks as
no other cause has in a unanimous defense of First Amendment
Freedom. TV violence has been studied, researched, discussed and
debated by psychologists, communication researchers, citizens groups
and United States Senators. As Greenberg (1980) notes:

> No other communication research issue has been studied so often,
> nor by so diverse a collection of social scientists, therapists,
> physicians, and lay groups. More federal dollars have supported
> research on the effects of televised violence than on any other topic
> which bears on the social effects of the commercial media. It is the
> best-known question asked about television, and is likely to be the
> one about which most people have an opinion. (Greenberg, 1980,
> p. 99.)

Yet an adequate answer to the question of television violence effects
requires a response to an earlier question—how much violence is
there on TV and just what form does it take? Numerous studies have
been conducted over the past 30 years and they provide us with an
excellent idea of just how much violence there is on television and how
TV violence has changed over the years. We will discuss what we know
about violence on TV, but first we must provide a definition of
aggression.

Definition of Aggression. Just what does violence or aggression mean?
Scholars have proposed a number of definitions. Among the most
famous is the one offered by George Gerbner and his colleagues at the
Annenberg School of Communications at the University of Pennsylvania.
Their definition has guided many of the content analyses of television
violence. According to Gerbner (1974) violence is "the overt expression
of physical force (with or without weapon) against self or other, compelling action against one's will on pain of being hurt or killed or
actually hurting or killing." Gerbner, like other researchers, treats
violent and aggressive behavior equivalently. Greenberg and his
colleagues (1980) used a somewhat broader category, that of antisocial
behavior. This referred to behaviors that are psychologically or
physically injurious to another person whether intended or successful.
Included within this broad label of antisocial behaviors was physical
aggression, as well as verbal aggression, theft and deceit. Armed with
these definitions, researchers have counted the number of instances of
violence on television, as well as the setting in which they occurred, the
duration of the violent acts, as well as what types of people are most
likely to commit violent acts.

In contrast, researchers studying the effects of television violence usually emphasize that action cannot be considered violent or aggressive unless the perpetrator intended to inflict harm on an individual or object. They point out that if a flower pot falls out of a penthouse suite and strikes an unfortunate passerby, this would not necessarily be a violent or aggressive act. It could be an accident. The act would be aggressive if someone intended that the flower pot hurt a pedestrian. This definition plays a very important role in the studies of television violence effects, a topic we will discuss shortly.

How Much Violence Is There On TV? If we really want a historical perspective on this question, we have to consider the issue of violence in the mass media in general. And here it is useful to remember that the Bible (see the Books of Job, Luke or Matthew) and Shakespeare (*Macbeth* or *Julius Caesar*, for example) contain countless instances of physical aggression and verbal abuse. The mass media have always contained violence, from books to newspapers to film and comic books. Thirty years ago citizens' groups expressed grave concerns that comic book violence might incite young people to commit violence. In the current era, television and video technologies are dominant—is it any surprise that society should worry about the amount and effects of violence on television?

With respect to the amount of violence on television, the worries are justified. Research indicates that almost since the inception of the medium, television has painted a mean, hostile and violent picture of the world (Gerbner, 1972). In 1953, a typical week of television contained no less than 3,421 violent acts and threats (Smythe, 1954). In 1969, Gerbner estimated that there were approximately eight violent episodes each hour. In fact, Gerbner's studies of television violence from 1967 to 1979 indicate that about 80 percent of all programs contain violence. Although the proportion of violence fluctuates depending on the year (it dropped to 73 percent in 1973), the pattern is remarkably consistent over the 12 year period. On the average, there are five violent acts per program.

Stuides also show that certain types of characters are more likely to be victims than aggressors. These include women of all ages (particularly young adult and elderly females), nonwhites, foreigners and members of the uppermost and lowermost income strata (cf. Liebert et al, 1982). In fact, in daytime serials females are depicted more often as murder and robbery suspects than would be expected from real-world documents (Estep and MacDonald, 1985).

Gerbner's studies indicate that there are overwhelming amounts of physical aggression on television. It is important to remember, however, that he counted all acts of overt force as aggressive, regardless of whether they were intentional. Consequently, his analyses may have inflated the amount of violence that actually occurs on television. In support of this view, Greenberg and his colleagues (1980), using a somewhat different definition of aggression, found that verbal violence accounted for about 50 percent of all the antisocial acts in a television season. There was more verbal violence (e.g., insults, verbal threats, hostile words) than either physical aggression or theft or deceit. Over the course of the three years that Greenberg studied, verbal violence appeared most often in situation comedies. Although this may seem surprising at first blush, it makes a good deal of sense when one considers that witticisms are often nasty and that humor is frequently rooted in aggressive impulses (Freud, 1905/1960).

Finally, how realistic is all this violence that appears on television? Perhaps verbal violence resembles real-life arguments and real-life drama, but as for physical violence the answer that emerges from a variety of studies is: it isn't very realistic at all. Nearly nine out of 10 television crimes are solved, while data from the FBI reveal that only 23 percent of real-life crimes are solved (Dominick, 1973). Television crime shows also tend to portray police as more violent than in real life. On television crime shows, criminal activity usually results in a violent resolution, but in reality crime is more frequently resolved through legal processes (Carlson, 1983). Furthermore, shows like *Miami Vice* portray violence in a glitzy "high tech" environment, juxtaposing cars and chrome interiors with the pastel colors and art deco of the restored South Beach area of Miami. The horrific physical and emotional consequences of violence there and in such films as *Rambo* are glossed over and are even glorified by the special visual and audio effects.

Music Videos. Ever since its inception in August, 1981, Music Television (MTV) has been a hotbed of controversy. Initially critics charged that MTV depicted women in stereotyped and offensive ways; more recently, citizens groups have claimed that there is too much sex and violence in music videos. During the fall of 1985, an ad hoc group, the Parents Music Resource Center, whose leaders included the wives of several prominent senators, made their charges public at a Senate hearing. Are there in fact considerable amounts of violence in music videos? And if so, what form does the violence take? Two recent studies tackled these questions, obtaining several surprising results.

Caplan (1985) found that the overall level of violence in music videos is higher than on commercial television. According to Caplan, the number of acts of violence per hour in music videos (10.18) is almost twice that of commercial television. Baxter et al (1985), while also reporting considerable violence on music videos, contend that much of the aggression is understated and suggestive — there is more innuendo than action. Sherman and Dominick (1984) found that music videos departed in several interesting ways from conventional television portrayals. Whereas in conventional TV females are more likely to be the victims than the aggressors, in MTV the proportions are reversed: women are more likely to be shown as aggressors than as victims. Similarly, there was a time when non-whites were more likely to be victims than aggressors on most adventure shows; on Music-TV non-whites are about as likely as whites to be an aggressor or a victim. Non-whites, the authors concluded, are strongly identified with violence. In addition, in both music videos and conventional television, children and teenagers are more likely to be the victims than the aggressors. Interestingly, on MTV older adults are most likely to be cast as the aggressors, suggesting that young people are being persecuted by their elders in the world of MTV. Finally, Sherman and Dominick found tht MTV clearly associated sex and violence; more than 80 percent of the videos that contained violence also contained some sexual imagery. Taken together, these studies suggest that the world of music videos, while probably not as violent as critics charge, is a strange world indeed. When violence occurs, it is most likely to be directed against teenagers and will probably happen in a context heavily laden with sexual overtones.

Effects of Television Violence. We now turn to the knotty issues surrounding the effects of television violence on children and adults. As we discuss the many studies on this issue, the reader should try to keep in mind that we are trying to prove — much like a detective does — that TV violence causes or leads to aggressive behavior or aggressive personality traits. If we are to persuade the skeptics or convince the Federal Communications Commission to regulate television violence, our case must be air-tight. At least three conditions must be met: First, television must offer consistently violent portrayals of society; secondly, viewers must be exposed to and pay attention to this programming; and thirdly, these shows must exert various psychological effects on viewers.

There is little doubt that our first condition has been met: television offers a violent depiction of many aspects of our social life and relationships. But in and of itself this does not constitute proof. We now must turn to the second condition necessary for proving television violence effects — are individuals exposed to and pay attention to televised violent portrayals? Is there any doubt but that they do! Many children spend more time watching television than they do in school and, although television viewing dips a little in late adolescence (McLeod and O'Keefe, 1972), there is no question that teenagers spend considerable amounts of time before the television set. Many American adults report that they spend more of their leisure time watching television than doing anything else (Robinson, 1977). And, as any casual review of the Nielsen ratings over the past decade will demonstrate, violent programs (e.g., *The A-Team, Starsky and Hutch, The Untouchables*) regularly top the ratings chart. Thus, our second condition has been met—children, adolescents and adults regularly attend to television programming and to violent TV fare. The bulk of our discussion centers on the third condition, pertaining to psychological effects, for this is the most important, but, as we shall see, the most difficult to prove convincingly.

Four methods have been used to investigate the social psychological effects of television violence: (1) case studies; (2) laboratory experiments, (3) surveys and (4) field experiments.

Case Studies

There are numerous case studies of children and adults who have imitated what they saw on violent TV shows—sometimes with tragic consequences. For example, in Los Angeles a housemaid caught a seven year-old boy sprinkling glass on his parents' lamb stew to see if it "would really work as well as it did on television." In Boston a nine year old boy "suggested to his father that he send his teacher a box of poisoned candy after he received a particularly poor report card. "It's easy, Dad," he said, "they did it on television last week." A New York newspaper reported on December 22, 1960 that the police arrested an 11 year old who admitted that he burglarized Long Island homes for more than $1,000 in cash and possessions. The boy, accompanied by a seven year-old accomplice, claimed that he learned the technique from watching television (Schramm, Lyle and Parker, 1961). Finally, in 1974, a young girl, Olivia Niemi, was assaulted and raped with a bottle by three older children on a San Francisco beach. Four days prior to the attack, NBC broadcast "Born Innocent," a story depicting a girl being similarly raped with a plumber's helper. After reading these and other grizzly examples of apparent imitation of violent television, it is hard not to conclude that television is a major contributor to the level of violence in society.

Upon reflection, of course, such a conclusion would be premature. It is equally plausible to argue that these individuals developed aberrant and highly aggressive personality dispositions long before they watched a particular series of television programs. Furthermore, even if television were the cause, such cases may represent rather unusual and infrequent exceptions to the rule. Clearly, it is necessary to conduct more scientific studies with a more representative cross-section of the population. If the evidence from these more scientific investigations corroborates the case study findings, one would have stronger evidence for television violence effects.

Experiments

Social Learning Theory. The earliest experiments concerning television violence effects were spawned by Albert Bandura's social learning theory. Although the individual studies that Bandura conducted differed in various respects, they all shared a common experimental procedure. Young children watched a live or filmed version of an adult delivering a number of novel and repeated assaults against a large inflated plastic clown, a "Bobo doll." After watching these modeled behaviors, the child was observed while playing with a Bobo doll. Each time the child physically assaulted the clown or verbalized aggressive comments (e.g., "Pow," "Sockee") an observer coded it as an act of imitative aggression. Regardless of whether they saw a live or filmed version of these events, children who viewed modeled aggressive behavior performed significantly more aggressive acts themselves than subjects in a control condition who were not exposed to modeled aggressive behaviors (Bandura, Ross and Ross, 1963).

In other studies, Bandura and his students explored the impact of vicarious and direct reinforcement on aggressive responses to mass media fare. Bandura, Ross and Ross (1961) demonstrated the impact of vicariously experienced rewards and punishments: 60 percent of the children who saw an aggressive character, Rocky, rewarded for his actions said that they would like to be like Rocky. In contrast, only 20 percent of those who saw Rocky punished indicated that they would select him as a model. These studies showed that children could learn novel aggressive responses or could come to identify with aggressive characters without being directly rewarded or punished themselves. Although this finding may seem obvious today, it departed dramatically from what would have been expected from the standard theories of the day; according to most of these accounts, learning depended on the child being rewarded directly for his or her actions.

In a later study Bandura (1965) focused on the role of direct reinforcement. In a first experiment, Bandura showed that young boys and girls did not differ in how much they remembered from watching a series of novel aggressive behaviors; however, boys were significantly more likely to perform what they learned — to actually act aggressively when given the opportunity in a play situation. Interestingly, when girls were directly rewarded for behaving aggressively (they were given a small treat of fruit juice), their levels of aggressive behavior did not differ significantly from boys. These results suggested that an explanation of why males are frequently more aggressive than females and respond more aggressively to violent television fare may not be found in boys' greater knowledge of aggression; instead these sex differences in aggression are more likely due to the greater freedom that society gives males to perform what they have learned.

For a while Bandura's studies attracted widespread attention and for a time scholars accepted them without question. Soon, however, criticisms began to surface. Critics argued that what Bandura had measured in his Bobo doll studies was not really aggression, but instead some form of playfulness. As Liebert, Sprafkin and Davidson (1982) noted: "Beating on plastic dolls which are designed to be punched and kicked around does not seem shocking or anti-social behavior." Since children in those studies may not have intended to hurt the dolls, their behavior may not have been aggressive at all.

Liebert and Baron (1972) addressed this problem by devising a more valid measure of aggressive behavior — the Help-Hurt machine. In their study children were told that as part of a game, they could push either a "Help" or "Hurt" button. They were told that pushing the "Hurt" button would cause harm to a child in an adjoining room, while pushing the "Help" button would assist the other child. As social learning theory would predict, children who viewed an aggressive film (*The Untouchables*) pushed the "Hurt" button longer than subjects in a control condition. Thus, watching a violent TV program increased children's willingness to harm another child — that is, to behave aggressively.

Aggressive Cues versus Catharsis. Long before there was concern about the effects of television violence, Aristotle theorized that audience members could symbolically purge their feelings of guilt and pity by watching dramatic portrayals. Aristotle called this process catharsis. Applied to violent TV, catharsis suggested that exposure to portrayals of aggression could stimulate fantasy aggression, thereby draining off feelings of anger and hostility (Feshbach and Singer, 1971). While the catharsis hypothesis predicted that television violence should actually reduce aggressive behavior, another theory suggested precisely the opposite. According to Berkowitz's (1965) aggressive cues approach, television and film violence should be more likely to cause angered individuals to behave aggressively as the viewer increasingly associates the violent portrayals with the object of the anger. Violent films serve as a cue, reminding the angered individual about the source of his anger and helping to link his hostile feelings with the aggressive behavior he sees in the film. Both theories sounded plausible and both made sense; the only way to decide which was correct was to test them empirically. In a series of studies with college males, Berkowitz and his colleagues experimentally manipulated anger (sometimes by administering mild electric shocks to the subjects), as well as the type of film that individuals saw (aggressive or an equally arousing non-aggressive film). In general, subjects were most aggressive when they had been previously angered and watched a violent film (Berkowitz, 1965). This effect is heightened when the filmed aggression is portrayed as justified or sanctioned and when the subject perceives a strong association between the individual who angered him and the aggressor in the film (e.g., Berkowitz and Geen, 1966).

Most of the evidence argues against the catharsis hypothesis. Although Fesbach and Singer (1971) offered some evidence in favor of catharsis, one major study was marred by methodological problems: when subjects in a nonaggressive TV condition objected that they were not allowed to watch Batman (an aggressive program), the experimenters allowed them to watch portions of this show. Thus, when the investigators reported that exposure to nonaggressive television led to increased aggression, it was impossible to know whether this finding was due to catharsis, to anger on the part of the boys that they could not watch Batman, or to their dislike of the shows they watched.

In summary, the experiments on television violence tell us that young children can learn novel aggressive behaviors from watching TV, particularly if the televised behavior is rewarded or sanctioned; furthermore, exposure to certain violent television fare can increase the chances that angered men will translate their hostile feelings into aggressive behavior. There is even evidence that TV violence can harden or desensitize young children to real-life violence effects (e.g., Rabinovitch, McLean, Markham and Talbott, 1972). Although these studies tell us that television can exert various effects, they do not tell us whether TV actually exerts this impact. The generalizability of the experimental conclusions is limited to the types of stimuli that were used (frequently they were not actual TV programs but films), the ways that aggression was assessed (critics charge that the laboratory measures are clearly artificial), and the duration of the effects (the experiments provide only evidence of short-term effects, yet another real concern is long-term influences on personality development). In other words, up to this point we know that television violence has effects — but only in theory. In order to examine the influences of television violence under real-world conditions, we now turn to the surveys and field experiments.

Surveys and Field Experiments

Survey researchers have investigated whether there is a correlation between the amount of time spent watching violent television programs and aggressive behavior, as assessed by teachers, parents, peers, or the individual himself or herself. In some cases (e.g., Leifer and Roberts, 1972) survey respondents were asked to indicate how they would respond to a series of hypothetical conflict situations in which aggression was one of several possible responses.

The results from a variety of surveys conducted primarily among adolescents have been remarkably consistent: viewing violent television programs was significantly associated with aggressive behavioral tendencies. For example, Robinson and Bachman (1972) in a survey of over 1,500 older adolescents, found that violence viewing was significantly correlated with a number of self-reported measures of aggression, tapped by questions such as "When I lose my temper at someone, once in a while I actually hit them" and "Suppose someone played a real dirty trick on you, what would you do? Hit, yell, ignore or laugh at them?" Similar findings were reported by Dominick and Greenberg (1972) and Milavsky, Kessler, Stipp and Rubens (1982), among others.

Most investigators reported statistically significant, but modest, correlations between violence viewing and aggression; the correlations ranged from .2 to .3 (correlations can range from − 1 to + 1). Although the findings offer some real-world support for the hypotheses derived from social learning theory and perhaps aggressive cues theory, they are, on another level, quite problematic. The problem is, of course, that correlations show only association, but not causation, and as such they are subject to at least three different interpretations.

TV Viewing Causes Aggression. The first interpretation holds that, for several of the theoretical reasons previously suggested, exposure to television violence leads to increased aggressive behavioral tendencies. Perhaps the most widely cited survey that supports this interpretation is Lefkowitz, Eron, Walder and Huesmann's (1972) cross-lagged longitudinal study. Lefkowitz and his colleagues assessed violence viewing and aggressive behavior when their male respondents were nine years old and administered the same general questions when the boys were 19. A cross-lagged statistical procedure allowed them to compare the strength of two relationships: the correlation between amount of TV violence viewed at age nine and aggressive behavior at 19, and the association between aggressive behavior at age 9 and amount of TV violence watched at 19. The first correlation was statistically significant, while the second was not, suggesting that TV violence viewing increases aggressive behavior rather than vice versa. Additional evidence emerges from an intriguing study conducted by Phillips and Hensley (1984). These investigators found that the number of homicides in the U.S. increases following stories about prizefights, in which violence is rewarded, while it sharply decreases after stories about murder trials and executions, in which violence is punished. (Also see Phillips, 1974).

Aggressiveness leads to a preference for violent TV. According to this second equally plausible interpretation of the correlational findings, individuals naturally prefer stimuli that reflect their values and attitudes.

Aggressive individuals should gravitate to television shows (e.g. violent ones) that reinforce their feelings and their views of the world.

Indirect experimental support for this explanation is provided by Fenigstein (1979). Fenigstein found that when male subjects were angered and asked to indicate which of many fictional plots they would like to see, they chose significantly more aggressive entertainment plots than any others. This suggests that the correlation between violence viewing and aggressive behavior can indeed be explained by a tendency of aggressive individuals to prefer violent television shows.

The correlation can be explained partly or entirely by third variables. It is also possible that violence viewing and aggressive behavior are correlated because both are *themselves* caused by yet another factor (a third variable) such as income, education, intelligence, parental childrearing practices, and so forth. It is possible, for instance, that having a low income may predispose individuals both to watch violent television and to perform aggressive acts. If the correlation between viewing violence and aggression disappeared when income was statistically controlled, one would conclude that the correlation was spurious or relatively unimportant. Contrary to this interpretation, when the variety of the effects of demographic and parental variables were removed through statistical procedures, the correlation did not drop appreciably (e.g., McLeod, Atkin and Chaffee, 1972). Thus, variables like income and education do not explain why viewing television violence is associated with aggressive behavior.

Other studies suggest that a different factor — the child's prior level of aggressiveness — underlies the correlation between violence viewing and aggressive behavior. Several field studies lend some support to this view. Stein and Friedrich (1971) measured pre-school children's actual level of aggressive behavior and then assigned them to sustained (four weeks) exposure to aggressive TV programs (e.g., *Batman*) or other TV shows. They found that children who watched the aggressive television fare were more likely to behave aggressively subsequently — but only if they were above average in their initial level of aggressiveness. Parke, Berkowitz, Leyens, West and Sebastian (1977) reported similar findings in field experiments conducted with juvenile delinquents residing in minimum security institutions in the United States and Belgium. Singer, Singer and Rapaczynski (1984) also found that later aggression in children is strongly predicted by a combination of heavy viewing of violent television shows and a family that emphasizes physical discipline and assertion of power. (Also see Korzenny, Greenberg and Atkin, 1979.)

Another set of correlates of violence viewing and aggression have been reported recently by researchers at the University of Illinois at Chicago (Eron et al, 1983). In a study of children in the United States and Finland, Huesmann, Lagaerspetz and Eron (1984) found that children were most likely to be aggressive if they identified strongly with the aggressive characters in television shows, frequently have aggressive fantasies, are performing poorly in school and are unpopular with their peers. Furthermore, Eron et al (1983) reported that there is a sensitive period around age 8-9 years during which the effects of television violence are particularly influential. Prior to age nine, children believe that much of what they see on TV is realistic and they do not distinguish fantasy and reality very well.

Perspectives. Clearly, all three interpretations of the relationship between violence viewing and aggressiveness command empirical support. And, of course, one's interpretation of the evidence influences the position one takes on whether to regulate the television industry. Those who believe that TV violence should be restricted or regulated tend to favor the first (TV effects) explanation, while those who work for the television networks and the film industry are more sympathetic with the second and third interpretations. Thus, for a variety of reasons, the individuals who study television violence have strong (one might even say violent) positions on the issue—and this has generated intense debate.

Proponents of each of the varying positions interpret the *same* evidence differently—sometimes very differently. When a study reports findings that dispute their position, researchers find fault with the study. The reaction to Milgram and Shotland's (1973) study provides one case in point. Milgram and Shotland sought to provide a more realistic test of the effects of television violence (and of social learning theory in general). With the help of CBS, they developed several versions of an actual television program, *Medical Center,* that showed an orderly stealing money from a charity drive and receiving one of several consequences. A sample of adults, recruited from the newspapers, watched the programs and in some cases were frustrated by not receiving the gifts they were promised for participating in the study. Next, like the character in the TV program, they were tempted by the presence of money contained in a charity box. How many subjects subsequently stole money and broke into the charity box? Did the antisocial television shows increase their willingness to burglarize? Milgram and Shotland found that on the average about eight percent of the subjects actually stole money or goods from the charity box; more importantly, they discovered that men in the various anti-social television treatment groups were not more likely to commit antisocial acts than subjects not exposed to the *Medical Center* programs. This "real-world" test seemed to provide little evidence that television violence increased antisocial behavior.

The results presented an important challenge to the researchers who believed that TV violence increases aggressive behavior. Rather than conclude that the findings were valid and their theories were wrong, these researchers maintained that the study represented a poor test of the television violence hypothesis. Liebert, Sprafkin and Davidson (1982), for example, pointed out that only about five percent of the subjects recruited from newspapers actually showed up for the study and that, therefore, they may not have been particularly representative of the general population. Liebert et al also argued that it was unrealistic to expect relatively normal individuals, even if they were angered and watched an episode of violent television, to break into a *charity* box, of all things. In Liebert et al's view, the pressure *not* to steal was too great and they regarded the Milgram study as an overly-stringent test of the TV violence hypothesis.

In the same way, researchers who believe that television exerts few effects on aggressive behavior have found a variety of flaws in the studies that purport to find TV violence effects. Recently, Freedman (1984) reviewed the many field experiments and surveys of television violence effects and concluded that there were a host of methodological flaws in the analysis and execution of the research projects. For example, he argued that the correlational studies failed to demonstrate that the amount of violent television, as opposed to the hours spent watching TV in general, contribute to aggressive behavior. He pointed to a variety of inconsistent findings on the effects of prior aggressiveness, suggesting that some studies find that viewing television violence affects the highly aggressive most, while others report that TV violence exerts the most impact on the less aggressive. Freedman also argued that there is little convincing evidence that television exerts a cumulative impact over time since there is weak evidence that the correlation between aggressiveness and violence viewing increases with the age of the child, and there are mixed results from longitudinal studies of television's impact.

In summary, after 30 years of research on television violence effects, researchers still disagree about the nature and effects of TV violence. So, although the question of television violence may seem simple and straight-forward to many members of the American public, the fact of the matter is that the question is far more complex and is subject to very different interpretations by a number of very intelligent scholars and researchers. However, given how important it is to find ways to understand and to reduce aggressive behavior, it behooves us to make a concise determination of just what the effects of TV violence are. In my view, there is reason to believe that television violence has a causal impact on aggressive behavior. Although critics like Freedman (1984) and Cook, Kendzierski and Thomas (1983) are correct that the evidence is not entirely consistent, they tend to minimize the case for television effects. There is simply too much evidence from a variety of research methodologies to reach any conclusion other than one favoring television effects.

The surveys show a consistent pattern of association between violence viewing and aggressive behavior (as even the critics acknowledge), while the field experiments generally provide additional evidence that TV exerts a causal impact on aggressive behavior in the real-world. At the same time, laboratory experiments demonstrate that TV *can* exert powerful effects on aggressive behavior under certain conditions. Finally case studies graphically remind us that these effects do occur. Even critics like Cook et al (1983), asking themselves if the association between violence viewing and aggressiveness is causal, say: "If we were forced to render a judgment, it would be: Probably Yes." (Cook et al, 1983: 192). (For a stronger statement of television violence effects, see the 1982 Surgeon General's Report on this issue.) It would be nice if our findings were as clear and unambiguous as critics like Freedman would like; unfortunately, social science research rarely provides us with this luxury.

Now that we have reached a verdict in the case of television violence, can the case be finally closed? Not quite. Social science research demands precise answers, and we still need to determine the types of effects that television exerts, as well as the types of individuals who are most likely to be affected.

It seems clear that television violence will exert the greatest impact on those who have already developed aggressive predispositions. These individuals tend to prefer violent television programs (Fenigstein, 1979). Social learning theory tells us that they should be most likely to remember what they see and, given the appropriate situation, to perform it. Television violence provides attractive aggressive role models to individuals whose temperaments, personalities and peer groups already predispose them to behave violently. In so doing, TV undoubtedly strengthens their belief that aggression is an appropriate and acceptable method to solve problems. Thus, for this small and (largely male) portion of the population, television violence viewing increases the chances that anger and hostility will become translated into aggressive behavior.

Television will not exert this impact on most individuals. As Milgram and Shotland demonstrated, exposure to antisocial television programs is not sufficiently powerful to overcome normal inhibitions against stealing and violence. Nevertheless, television violence leaves its mark on those who watch it; for most people, the effects are smaller and more subtle. Gerbner is fundamentally correct that television news and entertainment programs cultivate certain myths and perceptions, leaving viewers with unrealistic and exaggerated ideas about the nature of violence in the real world and their own chances of being harmed. The time-honored themes of television crime shows—particularly those that minimize the importance of civil liberties—do influence American viewers' attitudes toward crime and civil liberties. In some cases television may serve to homogenize attitudes, bringing them into the mainstream of American life; in other cases, TV may harden attitudes, perhaps desensitizing individuals to the effects of real-life violence. Not every heavy viewer of television will be affected in this way, as Hirsch's and Hughes' research makes clear. However, we can expect that television violence will exert a small, but subtle, impact on the attitudes and perceptions of a large proportion of the viewing public. In addition, as Huesmann et al (1983) have persuasively demonstrated, the more viewers identify with aggressive characters, the more likely it is that they will behave aggressively.

What Can Be Done Now? We now can address the larger policy questions involving television violence. For example, even if TV violence viewing increases the aggressive behavior tendencies of only a very small number of individuals, aren't the effects of their actions serious enough to justify some type of regulation of television violence? Given that most countries — including the nations of Western Europe and Israel — place strict regulations on the amount of violence shown, why shouldn't the U.S. do the same? On the other hand, is any such interference with First Amendment freedoms in the best interest of the American public?

These are interesting and important questions, worthy of debate. They raise deeper questions about the types of harm that society is willing to tolerate to protect freedom of speech and press. However, questions of policy are rarely answered by philosophy alone; instead, they hinge on a variety of legal, economic and political considerations. In the case of television violence, these considerations are paramount. Crime and adventure shows are too popular — they bring in too many advertising dollars — for the networks to take them off the air. Moreover, even when the networks voluntarily agreed not to broadcast violent programs from 7 to 9 p.m., the courts declared this policy — Family Viewing Hour — to be unconstitutional, in large part because it violated the First Amendment. In the end, the broadcast industry is too powerful politically to allow the FCC to impose strict regulations. If federal regulations are not the answer, then what is? Perhaps nothing at all should be done; some critics argue that, like it or not, violence is part of life, and individuals should be exposed to it. There is some merit to this position; however, if one wishes to teach young people about violence, there are probably better sources than television. Literature, art and even newspapers provide more insightful and accurate accounts. Moreover, too much exposure to television violence is a bad thing. The research leaves little doubt about this. In their efforts to counteract the effects of television violence, researchers and activists have turned increasingly to parents and children themselves.

Some schools have begun to teach short courses that are designed to increase children's "critical viewing skills" (Abelman and Courtright, 1983). These courses try to teach children that much of the violence they see on television is not real, and that there are other ways than violence to solve real-life problems. Perhaps the greatest onus rests on parents themselves. Children whose parents emphasize harmony and "going along" with what parents believe, to the exclusion of independent thinking, tend to watch more television (and probably more violent TV as well) (McLeod and O'Keefe, 1972). Television violence seems to exert a greater impact on adolescents whose parents don't strongly oppose their use of force (Dominick and Greenberg, 1972). And parents who use physical or verbal discipline, rather than moral explanations, are apt to find that television is reinforcing their children's aggressive behavior (Korzenny, Greenberg and Atkin, 1979). Still other studies suggest that parents would be well advised to consider the manner in which violence is portrayed. Programs that do not depict the graphic physical and emotional consequences of violence may leave viewers with the impression that violence has few negative side effects, perhaps causing some to believe that the benefits of aggression exceed the costs (Goranson, 1970). These studies of parental intervention are a hopeful sign. They provide a viable middle ground between two extreme positions: those who, on the one hand, would restrict violent programming and those who, on the other hand, would do nothing to discourage children from viewing violent shows. An important task for future research is to identify other such strategies to reduce the impact of violent television programs.

Arousal and Sexual Aggression
The Case of Pornography

When the Commission on Obscenity and Pornography concluded in 1970 that there was no evidence that pornography had antisocial effects, many social scientists regarded the issue as closed. However, a number of other researchers and feminist leaders increasingly found fault with this assessment; their criticisms coincided with the rise in aggressive pornography in the 1970's and 1980's—after the Commission's report was issued. Both researchers and activists suspected that aggressive pornography might have the most serious effects on men's behavior patterns. To examine this idea, communication researchers have conducted numerous experiments over the past decade—in fact, more experiments have been published in the last five years than in the 20 years the Obscenity Commission surveyed before writing its report. As we shall see, the accumulated findings from these recent studies lead to a much different conclusion about the impact of pornography and they reopen the issue of government regulation.

Aggressive pornography involves situations in which a woman (or man) is physically coerced into having sex; such portrayals frequently involve the use of weapons, torture, or bondage. In contrast, non-aggressive erotic films or media portrayals do not fuse sex and physical violence. The amount of aggressive pornography in books, films and television also has rapidly increased during the 1970's and 1980's. With these distinctions in mind, we now turn to a discussion of the focus of this section — the psychological effects of pornography on sexual arousal and aggressive behavior.

Arousal Erotic films arouse both men and women sexually, although more men than women are likely to engage in sexual activity after viewing an arousing film (Wilson and Liedtke, 1984). More interestingly, the reactions of the victim of a sexual act powerfully influence the amount of arousal experienced by men and women. When the female victim is depicted as becoming aroused involuntarily by an assault, male subjects became as sexually aroused as when they are shown portrayals in which both partners have mutually consented to engage in sex (cf. Malamuth and Donnerstein, 1982). Other evidence indicates, however, that male college students are less aroused by depictions of sexual assault than by portrayals of mutually consenting sex. In general, when a woman is shown experiencing pleasure from a sexual assault men are more likely to be aroused than if the rape victim is depicted as continuously abhoring the experience (Malamuth and Donnerstein, 1982).

However, there is disturbing evidence that a sizable number of male subjects are more stimulated by rape than by depictions of mutually consenting sex (Malamuth and Check, 1981). For example, men who report that power is a motive for engaging in sex and men who score high in psychoticism, are particularly likely to be aroused by rape portrayals. Furthermore, recent research indicates that although women are most aroused when a rape victim is depicted as experiencing an orgasm and no pain, men are most aroused when they see a victim experience an orgasm and pain (Malamuth, Heim and Feshbach, 1980). Malamuth and his colleagues suggest that one reason why these portrayals may arouse men is that men come to identify with the rapist, and "identification" with a powerful assailant may be stimulating to individuals reared with "macho" ideals of the male sex role (Malamuth et al, 1980).

Taken together, these experiments suggest that pornographic films that fuse sex and violence can sexually arouse heterosexual men.

Myths and Misperceptions. Pornography also may have more subtle effects: it may desensitize men to the horrors and consequences of rape. Zillman and Bryant (1982) found strong support for this notion. They exposed college males and females to varying doses of pornographic films over a period of six weeks. Students who watched massive doses of pornography over this period believed that rather uncommon sexual practices (such as sadomasochism and bestiality) were significantly more common than subjects in the control group. In addition, massive exposure to pornography caused the subjects to recommend shorter sentences for rapists and led them to descrease their support for the Women's Liberation Movement.

Similarly, Malamuth and Check (1981) have found that subjects who listened to a rape portrayal that suggested that the victim became aroused later believed that a larger proportion of women would derive pleasure from being raped, as compared to subjects listening to rape depictions emphasizing the woman's disgust. Taken together, these findings suggest that pornography influences men's perceptions of rape and rape victims.

Effects of Pornography on Aggressive Behavior

From peep shows to erotic fiction to films that are increasingly making their way to cable television, there has been a dramatic rise over the past decade in the amount of aggressive pornography (e.g., Malamuth & Donnerstein, 1982). Previously, we've discussed the effects that such films may have in arousing men sexually. But what impact do they have on aggressive behavior? Under what types of conditions do such portrayals cause men to behave more aggressively toward both men and women? A series of intriguing experiments conducted by Edward Donnerstein and Leonard Berkowitz have explored these issues.

In an experiment published in 1980 Donnerstein explored the impact of aggressive and non-aggressive pornography on aggressive behavior. Half of the male subjects were treated in a neutral manner by a male or female confederate. However, the other half of the male subjects were angered by a male or female confederate who delivered a series of electric shocks following the subject's performance on an essay task. Some subjects then saw a neutral film concerning a talk show that contained no sex and no violence, while the others saw one of two pornographic movies that differed only in their level of aggressiveness. The non-aggressive film portrayed a couple making love, the aggressive erotic film portrayed a man raping a woman by breaking into her house and forcing her into sexual contact at the point of a gun. In order to ensure that these films differed only in terms of the amount of aggression, the experimenters made certain that both the aggressive and non-aggressive pornographic movies elicited the *same* amount of *physiological arousal* (as measured by blood pressure). After watching the films, subjects had the opportunity to deliver a series of electric shocks to the male or female confederate.

Donnerstein found that when male subjects were given the opportunity to aggress against another male, both the aggressive and non-aggressive pornographic films produced more aggression than the neutral movie; however, the aggressive pornographic film did not produce more aggression than the less violent film. The critical finding occurred when male subjects were given the chance to aggress against a female. Under these conditions, males who saw the aggressive-pornographic film inflicted the greatest amount of aggression against a female. Thus, this study showed that aggressive pornography increases aggression, but only against females. Apparently, viewing a film in which a man behaves aggressively in a sexual context served to loosen male subjects' inhibitions against directing physical aggression against a female.

This finding receives even more support from other studies which compared the effects of aggressive-pornographic films with aggressive non-pornographic films (e.g., ordinary violent movie fare). In one study (Donnerstein and Berkowitz, 1981), in which male subjects were angered by a female, the aggressive-pornographic film caused the highest level of aggression; although the aggressive non-pornographic film increased aggression, it did not have as significant an impact as the film that was both aggressive and pornographic. Other studies find that non-aggressive pornography may stimulate aggressive behavior — provided that the erotic films are highly displeasing or cause male viewers to react very negatively (e.g., Zillmann, Bryant and Carveth, 1981). In Zillmann's study, the investigators found that male subjects who watched depictions of sexual bestiality — such as an unattractive woman masturbating with a live snake — were especially likely to behave aggressively against another male.

Finally, what impact does the film victim's reaction to a sexual assault have on aggressive behavior? Are men more likely to behave aggressively if the film depicts the woman enjoying the attack or if it portrays her as suffering? Good arguments can be made for either of these predictions. In the first case, the female victim's pleasure could be interpreted to mean that she is making the act even more pleasurable for the aggressor; when angered males watch depictions such as this, they may come to believe that they too will derive gratification from sexual aggression. By the same token, angry men may also be made more aggressive by watching films in which the woman is shown to be suffering. Since angry people want to harm others, information that someone has been hurt would be rewarding. When these same male subjects are then given the opportunity to aggress against a female who earlier provoked them, they may remember the vicarious pleasure the male protagonist received in the film when the victim's suffering gratified his aggressive urges. Thus, these subjects may be more likely to behave aggressively against the females in the laboratory experiment. It turns out that both the positive and negative outcomes—depictions of the woman enjoying the attack and of her clearly suffering—heightened angered male viewers' attacks against a female target (cf. Malamuth and Donnerstein, in press).

Understanding Why: Theoretical Explanations

Researchers usually are not content to describe the effects that mass media exert; they also are interested in understanding why. Scholars have proposed several theories to help explain the impact of pornography on sexual aggression.

"It's only arousal." Zillmann and his colleagues originally argued that pornographic films instigate aggression primarily because of their arousing, exciting content: the films physically excite and energize viewers' existing aggressive impulses (e.g., Tannenbaum and Zillmann, 1975). According to this view, erotic films should increase males' aggressive behavior, regardless of whether they contain scenes of sexual aggression against women. However, the evidence does not provide much support for this theory. Many studies find that it is aggressive pornography—rather than simply highly arousing erotic films—that produces the greatest increase in aggressive behavior. However, if arousal is not the major factor underlying the effects of pornographic films, it is clearly important. Donnerstein and his colleagues emphasize that aggressive pornography is particularly harmful because it fuses two potent psychological forces—arousal and aggression. Zillmann and Tannenbaum's theory suggests that when men are feeling angry, the arousing effects of pornographic films may heighten their hostility, leading to more intense aggressive responses (Tannenbaum and Zillmann, 1975).

"If it feels bad, then retaliate." The second approach, also offered by Zillmann and his colleagues, emphasizes the role of both arousal and hedonic valence, or how pleasing or displeasing the sexual stimuli are. Pornographic films that arouse viewers, but also contain a great deal of displeasing or upsetting stimuli, should lead to the highest levels of aggression. Consistent with this view, there is evidence that pornographic movies that contain bestial imagery or very ugly and displeasing sexual activities may actually increase aggressive behavior; apparently, when men feel sexually aroused and are at the same time displeased, disgusted or irritated at what they see, they translate these feelings into aggression, and behave aggressively toward other males.

This theory does not explain why some types of pornographic films should cause men to behave more aggressively against a female aggressor than a male tormentor.

"Anger by Association." The third explanation, based on Berkowitz's (1974) aggressive cues approach, accounts for the role that the victim's gender plays in research on pornography. Several experiments found that aggressive pornography caused angered men to behave particularly aggressively toward a female who had previously provoked them. This is quite consistent with aggressive cues theory which emphasizes that individuals will elicit aggressive responses to the extent that they have been associated with filmed violence. In this case, the male viewer, already angry at a female confederate for needlessly provoking him, sees a film in which a woman is sexually assaulted. The film connects the female in the laboratory experiment with the sexual aggression in the film, and this causes the male to feel increased hostility toward the female confederate. Of course, aggressive pornography will only exert such effects if subjects are sufficiently angered and sexually aroused (e.g., Donnerstein, Donnerstein and Evans, 1975).

In summary, these experiments strongly suggest that there is reason to be concerned about the effects of the increasing amounts of aggressive pornography. Aggressive erotic films can arouse men sexually (particularly men who are already predisposed to behave aggressively). More importantly, aggressive pornography can cause men to behave aggressively toward women who the men perceive have inflicted harm on them. These effects can be heightened if the film suggests that the woman is enjoying the act (as many films strongly imply or directly suggest).

How seriously should we take these findings? On the one hand, these studies generally took place in laboratory settings and their generalizability to the real world is therefore somewhat limited. An important counterargument to this criticism is that, however unrealistic the experimental procedures must appear to observers, they are quite realistic to the subjects: the male subjects believed that the confederate meant to harm them, and they believed they were actually inflicting harm on a woman (Berkowitz and Donnerstein, 1982). Moreover, unlike the early laboratory studies on television violence, there is evidence that the laboratory measures of aggression validly tap real-world desires to hurt a particular woman (see Malamuth and Donnerstein, 1982). Nonetheless, pornography, like television violence, probably will not cause most men to commit sexual or other types of aggression against women; their psychological inhibitions are too strongly developed, and most situations make it difficult to act on these impulses. Pornography probably exerts a stronger impact on most men's attitudes and perceptions than on their behaviors. But even if pornographic films will not cause most men to commit sexual assaults, the experiments leave us with a good deal of concern. They demonstrate the powerful effects that films which fuse anger and arousal can exert. After all, if reasonably well-adjusted college males can be provoked to aggression, one can only imagine the effects that pornography exerts on men who have been subjected to frustration, anger and a history of aggressive behavior.

Pornography: Ethical and Legal Issues

The issues surrounding pornography and censorship are steeped in controversy. Two dimensions of the controversy are worthy of some discussion: research ethics and legal efforts to restrict pornography.

Research Ethics. Critics have questioned two aspects of the social science research on pornography. First, they have criticized the practice of experimentally manipulating anger and aggression (i.e., making subjects angry by insulting them and then asking them to deliver electric shocks to a confederate of the experimenter); although no shocks are actually delivered, the subject thinks that he is inflicting harm and critics charge that this causes psychic damage to the subject. Secondly, critics question the ethics of studies which expose male subjects to depictions of sexual assault and rape (see Sherif, 1980). The argument is that if rape portrayals have harmful effects, why expose hundreds of college males to these stimuli?

The social scientists who do this research offer several counter-arguments to manipulating aggression. Researchers point out that subjects are asked to sign a consent form which informs them of the general nature of the experimental procedures. If a student feels that procedures are objectionable, he is free to decline to participate in the study. Researchers also point out that subjects are debriefed after the study; and they note that when the procedures are explained, most subjects do not show any evidence of short-term psychological harm. Debriefing also helps to nullify the effects of pornographic films, the concern of the critics' second objection. For example, Malamuth and Check (1981) reported that subjects who viewed aggressive erotic films and were debriefed subsequently showed less acceptance of standard rape myths. Debriefing (and the study as a whole) therefore, had beneficial effects. In the end, researchers strongly regret the need to make subjects feel angry or hostile; however, they justify the experiments on the grounds that pornography and film aggression in general are important problems—problems that require scientific facts rather than opinion and conjecture.

Changing the Law. Just what is obscenity? Does pornography extend to books like James Joyce's Ulysses, or does it just refer to filmed depictions of sexual aggression? Should pornography be somehow regulated, even if this restricts the ability of consumers to watch erotic films? Legal scholars and philosophers have been debating these issues for years; only recently, however, have feminists and civic groups sought to take legal action against pornography.

Recently, the Minneapolis' City Council narrowly passed legislation aimed at limiting pornography, but the mayor vetoed it, claiming that censoring pornography is unconstitutional. Soon after the Minneapolis action, Indianapolis passed an ordinance that made any portrayal of sexual aggression a violation of civil rights laws. The Indianapolis ordinance defined pornography as "sexually explicit subordination of women, presenting women as sexual objects who experience sexual pleasure being raped...as sexual objects tied up, cut up (or mutilated)."

Less than two hours after the Council passed the ordinance, a complaint was filed in U.S. District Court seeking a permanent injunction against the law on the grounds that it violated the First Amendment. City Council representative Beulah Coughenour, who worked to pass the ordinance, cited research evidence that indicates pornographic films have harmful effects. Asked by a reporter whether she thought that a movie like Alfred Hitchcock's Psycho or a book like James Joyce's Ulysses also might be banned under the ordinance, she responded, "All you have to do is read the ordinance to know how ridiculous that is... And even if they were (ruled pornographic), if you can prove that watching movies like that or reading those books cause harm, shouldn't the chips fall where they may?" However, Michael Bamberger, a New York lawyer who represented the book companies challenging the ordinance, argued that "Even if the motives are good, what you have is an unconstitutional statue." The court agreed, ruling the ordinance unconstitutional.

The future for such ordinances looks bleak. Civil libertarians oppose these laws, the courts are not likely to restrict freedom of speech, despite the evidence that pornography has harmful effects. And this is probably a good thing. If the law prohibited some types of pornographic films, it might also ban works of art (like Ulysses) that contain obscene language or even describe sexual aggression. Besides, what evidence do we have that changing the law will actually deter sexual aggression? It might have the opposite effect. In fact, in Denmark, the high availability of hard-core pornography seems to have contributed to a decline in at least one type of sexual crime: child molestation.

In summary, although most researchers are reluctant to conclude that government regulations are the best solution for the problem of pornographic effects, they clearly agree that something should be done. It is likely that there will be increased efforts to resocialize individuals about the harmful impact of certain types of erotic films.

Living and Growing with Television
A Cognitive Developmental Approach

When a mother asked her sixth grade son what he thought about television commercials, he shook his head and said, "You can't trust them. The things you buy always break. They don't work like they do on TV."

The boy's four year-old sister nodded and her mother half-expected to hear a similar response. "What do you think TV commercials are there for?", the mother asked.

Her daughter didn't wait a second. "They're there to give the actors a chance to change their clothes.

This conversation, adapted from actual comments children have made to interviewers (see Ward, Wackman and Wartella, 1977), illustrates the central theme of this section: how children's comprehension of television develops as they grow older and become more emotionally mature. This orientation differs from what has been discussed previously in an important way: the review of stereotypes, violence and pornography all emphasized what children and adults *learned* from television. In this section we shall discuss how children's understanding of television *develops*—that is changes, matures, becomes more sophisticated as children grow older.

Much of the research in this area has evolved out of Jean Piaget's (1936/1952) theories of child development. According to Piaget, children not only go through various stages of physical maturity, they also pass through several stages of mental maturity, developing an ever-more abstract and complex view of the world. Piaget identified four stages of cognitive development: sensiomotor, preoperational thought, concrete operations and formal operations.

During the early 1970's media researchers began to realize that Piaget's theory had a lot to say about how children perceive and comprehend television. Beginning with studies of children's attention to TV, and moving through television advertising, aggression, sex roles and frightening films, we will review what we know about how children's understanding of mass media develops with age.

Attention to TV. For better or for worse, even infants attend to television. In a systematic series of studies of young children's attention to TV, Anderson and his colleagues have discovered that children between one and five years of age are apt to "lock in" to what they happen to be watching on TV (Anderson, 1977). The longer that a very young child has been watching TV, the greater the chances that he or she will continue to look. Conversely, the longer that a child has not been looking at the screen, the less likely that he will begin looking. Anderson and his colleagues (e.g., Anderson, Alwitt, Lorch and Levin, 1979) have termed this pattern *attentional inertia*. In addition, studies of children's attention to commercials reveal that about 78 percent of younger children (5-7) continue to pay full attention to television when the commercial comes on; in contrast, barely more than half (57%) of the older children continue to devote their full attention when the ads come on the screen.

Researchers also have begun to investigate factors that cause young children to pay more attention to commercial and educational television programs. These factors include: peculiar voices, auditory changes, animation, movement, camera cuts and lively music. Attributes that tended to cause children to look away from the screen include extended zooms and pans, animals, inactivity and still drawings (Anderson and Levin, 1976; Levin and Anderson, 1976). However, certain techniques like rapid camera action may stimulate attention, but may interfere with comprehension or learning.

In a recent review of the literature on these formal features of television, Wright and Huston (1983) noted that commercial programs, especially cartoons, contain very high levels of perceptually salient features (e.g., high action and rapid pace). Educational programs use some of the same techniques, but use more language and other features that may encourage thoughtful processing. Wright and Huston concluded that children's attention to TV is primarily governed by these formal features (rather than by the content of what is shown). They point out that these features are more important determinants of attention than is violent content, emphasizing (in a McCluhanesque vein) that such features as rapid action, pacing and zooming function as the syntax and the language of television.

Comprehension. Young children recall remarkably little information that is central to the plot of a story. Second and third graders recall about 65 percent of the essential or central content of a plot, while eighth graders retain over 90 percent of the essential information (Collins, 1970; Newcomb and Collins, 1979). Younger children's difficulty stems in large part from their inability to differentiate what is central to the plot from what is simply peripheral. Another barrier hindering younger children's comprehension is their limited experience and social knowledge; consequently, young children have difficulty understanding plots in which the characters come from different economic backgrounds than their own (Newcomb and Collins, 1979) or in which the characters have personalities that differ vastly from what young children have come to know and expect. The lesson to producers is that they need to keep the child's age and mental stage in mind when they design and refine programs. For example, in one study when the main or central content of a plot was presented with salient formal features, like action and visual special effects, kindergartners were particularly likely to recall the central or key information in the plot (Calvert et al, 1979). This lesson has not been lost on the architects of *Sesame Street*, who have continued to pay close attention to matching program content to the child's mental skills.

Advertising. Concern about the impact of television advertising on children helped promote a series of studies of how children perceive TV advertisements. These investigations found striking age differences in children's understanding of the purposes of commercials (Ward, Wackman, and Wartella, 1977). Kindergartners have virtually no understanding that the purpose of commercials is to sell products or intentions of the advertiser. Kindergartners typically exhibit confused responses, or they may say "commercials are there to help and entertain you" or "Commercials are there to give actors a chance to change their clothes." Second graders, showing some recognition of advertisers' motives, believe that commercials are there "to make you buy the toy," and "so they can get more money for their factories." As children progress through elementary school they show even more understanding of the selling motive, until at around sixth grade, children have a clear understanding of selling and profit motives (e.g., "ads get people to buy products and that pays for the programs"). While preschool children show little or no understanding of what advertising is trying to achieve, by the time that they have completed fourth or fifth grade most children have begun to develop a realistic (if somewhat cynical) attitude toward commercials. Several explanations of young children's difficulty understanding the purpose of advertising have been put forth, including an inability to "get beyond perceptual appearances to underlying realities" (Ward, Wackman and Wartella, 1977) or an inability to take others' perspectives, including the perspective of the advertiser (Faber, Perloff and Hawkins, 1982). Other studies suggest that the effectiveness of advertising containing premium offers and disclaimers (e.g., "some assembly required") depends on the child's age and cognitive developmental stage (e.g., Liebert, Sprafkin, Liebert and Rubinstein, 1977).

Soon after this research appeared, the Federal Trade Commission became increasingly concerned about the possible deceptive effects of advertising directed to children. Basically, the Federal Trade Commission acknowledges that a certain amount of puffery or exaggeration is necessary to sell a product. The FTC allows advertisers to engage in such practices, guided in part by the assumption that a "reasonable individual" knows that the advertiser is trying to sell a product or is using persuasive gimmickry to get a message across. This logic breaks down in the case of young children who do not yet grasp the purpose of advertising or understand the advertiser's intent.

Activist groups were also concerned that advertising for certain products, particularly sugared foods, might encourage children to develop unduly favorable attitudes toward these goods. Several studies provide correlational evidence in support of this possibility. Ninety percent of young children exposed to a cereal commercial said they wanted to eat that cereal, compared to 66 percent in a control group who did not view that advertisement (Atkin and Gibson, 1978). Among fourth to seventh graders, 49 percent of the children who frequently saw an advertisement for a candy bar said that they ate the candy a lot, as against 32 percent of the less frequent television viewers (Atkin, 1975). There also is some evidence that heavy television viewers are more likely than lighter viewers to report that they like foods that are frequently advertised (Atkin, Reeves and Gibson, 1979). Heavy viewers also are less knowledgeable about nutritional dimensions of food (Atkin et al, 1974) and are more inclined to believe that sugared cereals are high in nutritional value (Atkin et al, 1979).

The FTC held hearings to consider the possibility of restricting TV advertising directed at children. Although the Commission considered further regulating and even banning such advertisements, it stopped short of such action, deciding in favor of a hands-off policy on children's advertising. Some of the reasons for the FTC's decision can be traced to the difficulty in deciding just how to limit commercials (Should ads before a certain hour be limited? Should ads directed at only very young children be banned, and if so, how?); reluctance to interfere with First Amendment proscriptions; and political pressures (the Reagan Administration frowned upon interference with the private sector, while the cereal industry opposed regulations for obvious reasons).

Aggression. Collins and his associates have reported several intriguing instances of age differences in observational learning of televised aggression. In one study Collins, Berndt and Hess (1974) found that younger children (kindergartners and second graders) remembered only the consequences of an aggressive act, while older subjects (fifth and eighth graders) recalled the motivations for the act, as well as its consequences. Younger children also evaluated the aggressive character solely in terms of the consequences of his actions — while older children assessed the actor in terms of both the character's intentions or motives, as well as the consequences of his act. Collins et al argued, based on Piaget's theories, that younger children tend to focus on the immediate, graphic and "here and now" aspects of a character's actions — i.e., whether it causes harm or benefit. They have difficulty getting beyond the brute immediacy of the consequences to the inner mental motivations that underlie the act. Collins (1973) also found that when four minutes of commercials separated the motivations for an aggressive act from the action itself, third grade children had difficulty linking up the motivations with the aggressive activity. Compared to older children, third graders actually became more aggressive in this condition; apparently, the commercials led the younger children to forget that "bad" motives were responsible for the actions.

Sex and Sex Roles. Mass media provide children and adolescents with a host of same-sex models to learn from and emulate. But at what point do children begin caring about how models of their gender behave? When do they start attending to same-sex television role models? A key determinant is children's knowledge that their gender identity is fixed and stable. Preschool children still believe that their gender identity may change if they put on clothing worn by the opposite sex or if they play sports that are associated with the opposite sex. Slaby and Frey (1975) maintain that once children recognize that their gender identity is stable and invariant, they will begin to imitate the activities and behaviors exhibited by same-sex models on TV.

Once children begin focusing on models of the same sex, they can be expected to perceive them in somewhat stereotyped ways. Age should make a difference in how children perceive TV characters: younger children should focus more on the physical aspects of a character (such as whether he is strong), whereas older children, having acquired more interpersonal sophistication, should be additionally concerned with psychological attributes (like psychological strength, courage, and grace under pressure) (see Perloff, Brown and Miller, 1982; Durkin, 1984; see Hoffner and Cantor, 1985).

The effects of televised portrayals of sex also should vary with the viewer's age. As Greenberg (1980) notes:

> Shown a man and woman in bed together, with suggestive verbal interaction, accompanied by initial embracing, and the inevitable fade-out, what does the viewer think is happening, or about to happen? (Greenberg, 1980: 135)

Clearly, it is reasonable to expect that a child's cognitive level influences his/her interpretations of televised sex, although few studies have yet tested this notion.

Frightening Films and TV Shows. As scary films like Halloween and frightening television shows like The Incredible Hulk and That's Incredible have proliferated over the past several years, parents have expressed increasing concern about the effects that these movies and TV shows exert on young children. Parents are understandably concerned that exposure to these stimuli exerts psychological discomfort that may evolve into more persistent fears. Recently, researchers have begun to probe the effects of frightening media fare, focusing on how children of different ages and cognitive-developmental stages react to these films and television programs. Cantor and Sparks (1984) tested several hypotheses about the impact of scary media fare that were based on Piaget's theories. They reasoned that scenes or people that look frightening, such as a visually grotesque figure, would be more frightening to a young child than evil intentions or the apparent ability to harm others. These young children were expected to fixate or "center" on a striking visual feature of an object and have difficulty getting beyond this to understand the potential harm resulting from the character's evil intentions. In contrast, older children (who had presumably passed through Piaget's stage of concrete operations) should be capable of "decentering" their attention from the visual cues and be more mentally able to consider more subtle aspects of the situation. They also argued that young children should have particular difficulty understanding aspects of television and film fare (such as *The Incredible Hulk*) in which a character undergoes a physical metamorphosis or change of appearance. Particularly frightening to young children, they argued, was a scene in which a pleasant-looking character takes on an ugly and grotesque appearance.

In a survey of Madison, Wisconsin parents, Cantor and Sparks (1984) obtained support for their ideas. They reported that younger preschool children were more frightened by programs with grotesque fantasy characters (such as *The Incredible Hulk* and *The Wizard of Oz*), programs in which the characters *looked* scary. On the other hand, older children were frightened by shows that featured things that could happen, regardless of the frightening appearance. "What seems to distinguish these media offerings from the ones that are less frightening to older children is that they are realistic, or, if fictional, involve events that for the most part *could* happen." (Cantor and Sparks, 1984, p. 96).

Their findings also suggested that preschool children do indeed have difficulty understanding how David Banner becomes metamorphosized into the Hulk, and that the various facets of the transformation scare them. Finally, parents of younger preschool children more frequently reported that fantasy material caused their children to be frightened than did parents of older elementary school children (i.e., fourth grade children). Apparently, older children, who are more aware of the difference between fantasy and reality, recognize that the threats depicted in fantasy programs will not cause any actual or palpable harm. On the other hand, frightening events that could happen scared older children more than younger children. Cantor, Wilson and

Hoffner (in press) reported that *The Day After,* the television program that dramatized the after-effects of nuclear war, frightened older children much more than younger children. Interestingly, many parents feared the program would have the opposite effect.

"And Now for Some Good News?" Prosocial Effects of TV

There is one final aspect of mass media effects that deserves our consideration. This too is an area in which children's age and cognitive level influences what they take away from the small screen, as well as from other mass media fare. This facet of mass media effects—educational and prosocial portrayals—represents the flip side of the anti-social programming and effects that have been discussed in such detail up to this point. Both media representatives and critics agree that the American media, particularly television, have great potential to improve our quality of life. But are the media living up to their potential? What does the research tell us about this final arena of media effects?

Over the past decade there has been an increasing amount of pro-social programming directed at children. In response to criticism, the television industry has sought to increase its educationally-oriented programming. Thus, we now have Big Bird and the colorful cast of characters on *Sesame Street,* the indefatigable Mr. Rogers (*Mister Rogers' Neighborhood*), the quick-paced *Electric Company,* as well as a number of other Saturday morning programs including *Fat Albert* and *The Cosby Kids, Shazam* and *Isis* which tried in varying ways to incorporate behaviors such as helping, sympathy and sharing.

A number of experiments have demonstrated that these programs exert positive effects, increasing such behaviors as sharing, cooperation, resistance to temptation, as well as reducing such behaviors as verbal aggression and stereotyping (e.g., Bryan and Walbek, 1970; Stein and Bryan, 1972; Wolf, 1972; Freidrich and Stein, 1975; Sprafkin, Liebert and Poulos, 1975; Collins and Getz, 1976; Baran, Chase and Courtright, 1979; Sprafkin and Rubinstein, 1982; Johnston, Ettema and Davidson, 1980). Many of the early studies (e.g., Bryan and Walbek, 1979), although they persuasively demonstrate that television can cause children to imitate prosocial behaviors, do not tell us about real-world media effects because they either examined only one television program at one point in time or used rather arti-ficial behavioral measures. Several later studies remedied these problems and still found that television could exert prosocial effects (Sprafkin and Rubinstein, 1982; Freidrich and Stein, 1975). However, as Greenberg (1980) notes, it is not clear whether exposure to prosocial themes or behaviors on television nullifies antisocial portrayals or precisely how the child integrates in his or her own mind the multitude of prosocial and antisocial behaviors that s/he views.

Similarly, early research demonstrated that educational programs like *Sesame Street* exerted remarkably positive effects on a host of verbal and quantitative skills (Ball and Bogatz, 1970; Bogatz and Ball, 1972; Liebert, Sprafkin and Davidson, 1982). Subsequent studies suggested that the positive effects of *Sesame Street* may be somewhat exaggerated. Cook et al (1975) concluded that children in advantaged families are probably more likely to watch *Sesame Street* and will be more likely to be encouraged by their parents to watch and to practice what they learn. Therefore, *Sesame Street* may widen—rather than reduce—already existing intellectual gaps between children from advantaged and disadvantaged families. In addition, several researchers have suggested that other educational programs (i.e., *The Electric Company*) may overstimulate children, causing them to be excessively active. Furthermore, the "showbiz" "high-tech" aspects of these programs may cause children to expect that school and educational experiences must be entertaining and glitzy in order to be effective (Postman, 1985). Despite these limitations, most scholars acknowledge that educational programs like *Sesame Street* have exerted many positive effects on children's knowledge and cognitive skills.

One other potentially harmful television effect deserves mention at this juncture. Ever since the inception of television, observers have worried that TV viewing might reduce reading and intellectual skill development. Over the past several years, a growing number of studies have pursued these questions. Pierce (1983) reported that primary school children's writing ability was positively associated with the number of books read per month, while it was negatively correlated with TV viewing hours. Fetler (1984) found that students who viewed more than six hours of television per day had sharply lower achievement test scores. There is also evidence that, for children from professional families, heavy television viewing is significantly associated with lower achievement test scores, as Gerbner's mainstreaming hypothesis would predict (see Fetler, 1984; Morgan and Gross, 1981). A variety of explanations for these effects have been offered, including Salomon's (1981) hypothesis that television does not demand as much "invested mental effort" as does reading. As always, the effects of TV viewing on achievement are likely to be heavily mediated by third variables such as socioeconomic status (Briller and Miller, 1984) and cognitive level (Roberts et al, 1984).

Increasing Television Prosocial Effects. In recent years researchers and citizens groups have adopted a variety of strategies to encourage more prosocial uses of television. One strategy has been to encourage children to develop "critical viewing skills," such as teaching children that much of what appears on television is not realistic, that programs are broadcast to make money, that incidents are fabricated and that characters are actors (Dorr, Graves & Phelps, 1980; see also Singer and Singer, 1983). Although schools can encourage children to become both more critical of antisocial fare, and to get the most out of educational programming, the major onus falls on parents and children themselves.

In addition to restricting time spent with television, and encouraging other more "active" uses of leisure time, parents can intervene while children are watching television. Dorr and her colleagues have suggested a variety of strategies that parents can employ to make children more critical of television entertainment programs and advertising. Parents also can encourage children to watch educational shows, trying wherever possible to discuss the material and reward children for attending to those programs.

Finally, parents can encourage children to devote their energies to other mass media — such as newspapers and books. Beyond this, trite as it may sound, parents (and peers) exert influence on what children learn from television simply by example. We know, for example, that when parents tend to ignore children's development of aggressive attitudes, television seems to exert a more powerful effect on aggressive behavior (Dominick and Greenberg, 1972). Parents who are more concerned with harmony and with the child going along with their ideas, at the expense of the child's mental development, are apt to cause their children to watch violence to escape an oppressive home life (see McLeod and O'Keefe, 1972). Violence viewing also may be higher among children whose parents tend to resort to physical or verbal punishment rather than explanations of why the child's actions were wrong (Korzenny et al, 1979).

All of these suggestions tend to have a moralistic tone, as if there is something dastardly wrong with watching TV. Many critics seem to believe that unless parents actively intervene, children will grow up violent, or with irreparably distorted views of the world. This is most unlikely. Furthermore, children actually can benefit from watching TV — television does entertain and it increasingly teaches novel visual codes. But a medium as ubiquitous as television is bound to affect some people quite negatively.

We began the chapter noting that many groups are critical of the mass media for such reasons. We should not be surprised that people attribute large negative effects to the media. Individuals have done so since the time that the Greeks discovered the "kill the messenger" phenomenon. Inevitably, people exaggerate the negative effects that the media — particularly television — exert, while minimizing the positive influences and failing to recognize that the media operate in concert with other socialization agents, such as parents, peers and teachers. But if critics exaggerate the media's impact, spokesmen for the television networks and major newspapers clearly minimize their role in shaping children's attitudes and social behaviors. Under some conditions, and for some individuals, the mass media are powerful stimulants for imitative learning. For other individuals, and for other behaviors, the media are relatively insignificant. Specifying the conditions that facilitate harmful effects, pinpointing the circumstances under which prosocial influences are most likely to occur, and identifying the mechanisms by which these effects are achieved remains a most important and engaging task for the decades to come.

Summary

Children spend as much time watching TV as they do listening to their teachers in school. What do children learn from TV exposure and what lessons does television teach them? This chapter examined these issues and scientific evidence on social effects of mass media.

Content analyses document that most television characters are white adult males in their late 30's or early 40's, and other stereotypes abound. In addition, other TV depictions such as those concerning obesity and safety do not correspond to reality. In response, TV network executives have pointed out that television is not intended to reflect accurately the number of blacks, females and doctors but is designed to entertain and attract a large audience.

Studies of televised role portrayals leave little doubt about television's effect. Research on sex-role socialization indicates that boys are more likely to identify with same-sex characters than are girls, and that conventional portrayals of the sexes may have particularly strong effects on girls who had high IQ's and came from somewhat affluent backgrounds. Thus, TV exposure moves these girls into the cultural mainstream where conventional attitudes predominate.

There is still some controversy concerning the pervasiveness of these effects. Originally, Gerbner and his colleagues reported that heavy TV viewers were more likely than light viewers to perceive the world as a mean and scary place. Other researchers challenged these conclusions and subsequent research has pointed to a milder view of TV's perceptual effects. Several studies provide evidence of *mainstreaming* or bringing elite or "fringe" groups into the cultural mainstream — and of *resonance*, a reinforcement effect typified by the finding that heavy viewing urban dwellers are more affected by TV than their light viewing counterparts.

The largest amount of research has focused on the question of TV violence effects. Today, even music-videos contain some violent imagery. Guided by Bandura's and Walter's social learning theory, experiments have documented that TV acts as a powerful stimulant to imitative learning. Some of the early laboratory experiments were particularly artificial and contrived, but later experiments demonstrated more convincingly that children could indeed learn and perform novel aggressive responses from watching television. Studies with adolescents also have demonstrated that violent films serve to intensify anger rather than to reduce it.

Extending these findings to more real-world settings, surveys indicated that there is a modest association between watching TV violence and aggressive behavior. The issue is complicated by questions of cause and effect. There is evidence that TV violence exerts a causal impact on aggressive behavior, but there is also reason to believe that these individuals who are already aggressive gravitate to violent television. The question of causation has aroused intense debate as researchers and many parent groups have interpreted the evidence as indicating television effects, while network executives and a smaller number of researchers have maintained that TV reflects rather than causes aggressive behavioral tendencies.

Attention in recent years has gravitated to the impact of another type of aggressive mediafare—pornography. With studies indicating that increasing amounts of erotica are violent, researchers have explored the effects of these films on adult male viewers. Research demonstrates that aggressive pornography increases male aggression against females. There is compelling evidence that erotica cultivates myths about rape and sex roles in general. Several theoretical explanations have been advanced to account for these findings.

The final arena of research centers on how children's comprehension of television increases with age. Guided by Piaget's theories of child development, researchers have found that young children have difficulty grasping the central elements of fictional plots, do not understand the purposes of TV advertising, focus on concrete rather than abstract features of men and women's characters, and tend to be more frightened by television fantasies—rather than by events that could happen. Other studies, focusing on educational TV, leave little doubt that shows like "Sesame Street" improve children's cognitive skills. As a whole, the research on media effects presents a brighter picture of television's effects than critics usually paint. Much needs to be learned about how prosocial (as well as antisocial) mediafare interact with other socialization agents, and the processes by which entertainment media effects occur.

7

Political Effects of the Media

Politics is the pursuit and exercise of power and the mass media are effective actors in both processes. Power has many bases. In a democracy, media organizations and individuals operate with a certain amount of independence that allows them to affect the daily activities of government. Davison (1965) points out that many of the characteristics associated with democracy depend on free access of all groups in a population to communication channels—both as senders and receivers. These include nonviolent competition for political power among various groups in the country, the ability of those outside the government to influence its actions, and the reliance of the government more on persuasion and less on force to accomplish its domestic policies. What are the political effects of the mass media and how do they occur? That's what we'll discuss in this chapter.

The question of how mass media affect the political life of Americans can be broken into two parts. First, what are the consequences of mass media in the on-going political process, the election campaigns and daily political events? Here, we ask how and whether the media are successful in conveying political information, setting the agenda for political debate and competition, forming and altering candidates' images, changing voters' attitudes and feelings, and persuading people to vote for one candidate rather than another. In this section, we assume the basic outlines of the American political system and seek to trace media effects within that system.

Increasingly, critics and observers are raising questions about whether the communication media have or are in the process of changing the nature of the political system here and elsewhere (Meadow, 1985). As mass media have grown into a powerful institution, they have attracted the attention of observers who question whether the media are undermining public support for political institutions, changing basic attitudes toward politics, altering power relationships withing the electorate, changing the nature of the campaign process that allocates power, or passing on the political culture to subsequent generations. For example, the cumulative impact of media may alter basic norms and values concerning the political process. In recent yars, Americans have grown more cynical about their government, and some people credit the media with some of that change. Thus, in the second section we will look at the arguments and evidence bearing on how the media affect the nature and structure of the political system itself.

Media Effects in the Political Process

The people who vote, the electorate, also make up the media audiences. Thus, when we talk about the media effects on individual voters, we're concerned with how people's media use influences their political perceptions and behaviors. Mass media involvement in the daily political process is not limited to elections but includes a host of activities extending from news media coverage of routine government actions to entertainment-oriented television programs with political messages and themes. However, the time period scrutinized most carefully for media effects is the election campaign.

Election Campaigns

The past several decades have produced a substantially revised view of how election campaigns affect people and what people do with campaigns. First, the environment itself has changed substantially; this has altered the relationship between the media and political institutions. Since the 1940's, we have seen the emergence of different life styles, generational differences, declining significance of major institutions such as religion and the family, the rise of new powerful interest groups, and consequences stemming from international events such as Vietnam. Furthermore, several factors seem to converge as researchers have revised their thinking from early survey work conducted in the 1940's through the 1960's. Especially important is the fact that party loyalties and organizations have declined drastically as voters split their tickets between parties. Voters have increasingly based their voting decisions on issues and images rather than party affiliations. At the same time, television grew to dominate the political scene when it reached saturation coverage in U.S. homes, expanded its news coverage, and paid increasing attention to political affairs. The position of media has undergone such substantial change that the potential for media effects seems to have increased greatly (O'Keefe and Atwood, 1981).

How the media influence voters during campaigns has also emerged as a more complex process than many once thought. No single factor appears paramount. Rather, we are finding that the media affect some people in some ways under particular conditions during particular stages of political campaigns. Before considering these more complex models of how the media affect voters, we will examine the evidence for media impact on individuals in specific ways: cognitive (knowledge, information), affective (feelings, evaluations, interest), and behavioral (voting).

Learning from the Media

How effective are the media in conveying political information to the public during election campaigns? Patterson (1980) found that amount of news coverage given the various candidates in the 1976 primaries was strongly related to gains in voter knowledge about them during that period. For example, Carter received the most coverage and went from being "known" by 20% of the public in February to 81% in June. Newspapers seem to be generally superior to TV news in conveying campaign-related information to the general public. Researcher Rebecca Quarles (1979) found that newspaper-use among first-time voters predicted the accuracy of their knowledge about campaign issues, but TV news viewing was unrelated. In 1976, a national study found that regular exposure to newspapers had more impact on increasing voters' knowledge about candidates than did TV news exposure. However, both TV and newspapers had about equal influence on increasing awareness among the least interested members of the electorate.

A variety of media content may act to increase political knowledge. Several researchers have found that political TV and radio advertising raised levels of political information about both candidates and issues in recent presidential elections. Even children seem to learn about candidates from political advertising. Some people think that political advertising may have direct effects on information gain because voters find the cost of acquiring information via advertising to be quite low, especially TV spot ads. Viewing the party conventions and the debates between presidential candidates also increases knowledge of candidates' stands on the issues. The link between media use and political knowledge also has been documented in other countries from Great Britain and Germany to Mexico and Ghana.

Numerous other studies confirm the success of the media in teaching people about candidates and issues (Garramone, 1983; McLeod and McDonald, 1985; McLeod, Bybee and Durall, 1979; Almond and Verba, 1963; Atkin and Heald, 1976; Hill and Dyer, 1981; Becker and Dunwoody, 1982). However, people often forget what they see in TV broadcasts and one study found barely 5% of the viewers could remember the content of an election broadcast on behalf of one political party not long after they had seen it. However, some of the information may be recalled with the appropriate cuing, which means many stories are understood and stored in some manner.

The nature of the media system and communication environment means that some people will gain more information than others. Hill and Dyer (1981) compared those who watched local TV news with those who watched a distant signal brought by cable TV and found that those diverted to the station from out of town lagged in political knowledge about the local situation. Thus, the introduction of cable TV to non-metropolitan areas is likely to decrease the local political information held by many residents.

When do people learn the most about politics from the mass media? The learning that occurs is greatest when voters' information needs are greatest — when there is difficulty in deciding on candidates (Atkin and Heald, 1976; Mendelsohn and O'Keefe, 1976). In the case of the 1976 presidential debates and party conventions, learning about candidates' stands on the issues was greatest among the moderate and low interest voters. Also, the better educated are better equipped to process new political information because of their background knowledge of the system; this is particularly evident for older voters. However, people learn even when there is little interest. Zukin and Snyder (1984) looked at two groups of people during the 1980 election, those with no interest in the election but who lived in a media-rich environment and those uninterested cohorts living in a media-poor environment. The former were 40% more likely to have acquired information than the latter. Thus, even in the absence of active motivations, people learned about the election campaign.

When people process information from the mass media during an election campaign, they are also being exposed to a set of priorities. This brings us to another cognitive effect of the media, agenda-setting.

Agenda Setting

The media are quite successful in focusing public attention on specific issues, events, and persons. By presenting more and more information about abortion, for example, the media elevate the importance of that issue in people's minds. Similarly, by ignoring a topic, the media suggest that it does not deserve the public's attention. This ability to tell the public "what to think about" is called the Agenda-Setting function of the media. By focusing attention the media tell people what is worth thinking about, what is "salient" or important.

Though agenda-setting can occur any time, election campaigns are ideal times to view the process because campaigns traditionally contain an "agenda" of issues and candidates. In simple terms, the media in the process of selecting some things and not others construct a political agenda which tells people what issues should be on their personal agendas and in what order. One researcher took data from the Gallup poll on what people said were most important problems and compared that with media coverage over a seven year period; the two "agendas" were similar, which is consistent with the notion of agenda setting.

In a panel study conducted throughout 1976, Dave Weaver and his colleagues found the influence of both newspapers and television was significant, particularly during the primaries when the shape of the political year begins to emerge and personal interest in politics begins its rise. The agenda-setting influence of both media was less during the summer and least during the traditional fall campaign. The agenda-setting impact of TV appeared to be short-range, spotlighting key issues, while newspapers were the prime movers in setting the public agenda across a longer span of time.

Strong evidence of agenda setting also comes from recent experiments using TV newscasts (Iyengar, Peters and Kinder, 1982). Viewers who were exposed to reports alleging U.S. military vulnerability grew more concerned about defense during the six-day experiment. Furthermore, comparisons of public ranking of issues with agendas found in newspapers, TV news and political TV commercials showed evidence of agenda setting in the 1984 elections (Lasorsa, 1985; Ghorpade, 1985).

What is the time frame for agenda-setting? In other words, how long does it take for media attention to build up public significance for an issue? Eyal (1980) found that the average time frame for significant agenda-setting was a 14-week period during the spring of 1976 for newspapers but only 6 weeks for television. By late summer the agenda-setting impact of both media showed up across 6-8 week periods. Shorter time spans have been found in other studies. Clearly, the characteristics of events are important. For example, one nuclear power plant explosion would likely elevate the safety of nuclear power to the top five issues in one day. Lang and Lang (1981, 1983) argue that issues can be categorized as either low threshold—readily identified with by everyone—or high threshold. Economic problems such as unemployment are low threshold topics. To have an agenda-setting impact, the media must establish linkages from high threshold problems to other symbols and ideas such as the general credibility of a president. For such topics, frequency of coverage is sufficient.

The characteristics and situations of media consumers and voters also act as contingent conditions in the agenda-setting process. Clearly, not everyone's personal list of issues matches that of the media they use. Grunig (1979b) suggests that we focus on the need for political orientation and voters' involvement in the election. According to one study, media coverage did have greater impact on people who are sensitive to the issues—crime and unemployment, for example— and almost none on the rest of the audience. Agenda-setting seems to occur for voters who need information prior to making a decision but who lack the commitment and interest in politics that might interfere with absorbing the media agenda (O'Keefe and Atwood, 1981). Agenda setting may be absent when audiences are engaged in substantial discussions about politics, especially if new information is made available. Membership in political interest groups also tends to counteract media agenda-setting because the political groups supply their own agendas, though Asp (1983) found media more powerful than parties in agenda setting in Sweden. The fact that audience and issue characteristics are important is illustrated by the numerous studies which sought but failed to identify an agenda-setting function of the media.

Agenda setting is not limited to issues. And the media agenda is not simply a duplicate of the candidate's agendas. Just because the candidates stress particular issues does not mean the same ones will receive heavy coverage by the media. The media also focus on issues the candidates prefer to ignore. Looking at the 1976 election, Patterson (1980) conducted a panel survey of 1,200 people and content analyzed major papers, the TV networks, and news magazines. He found that the media emphasized the race rather than policy or leadership, and it was the race that people thought of when asked about the election's "most important aspect." Though matters of policy and leadership were at the top of people's lists before the campaign, they sank to the bottom during the campaign as people's mental maps reflected the press' interest more than the candidates. Broh (1980) also notes journalists' emphasis on the competition but concludes that the "horse-race" metaphor is beneficial because it enhances the public's interest in the electoral process and reduces the possibility that reporters can settle on an early winner and turn the campaign into a self-fulfilling prophecy. Graber (1976), reporting on the content analysis of 10,000 stories from network TV news and 20 daily newspapers, found a pattern of heavy stress on personal characteristics and daily campaign events in all sources. In this campaign reportage, parties themselves also can be affected. Weaver, Graber, McCombs and Eyal (1981) found that the press plays a major role in setting the agenda of candidate image qualities or attributes.

Agenda-setting is considered important because of its impact on other government processes. In addition to the public agendas, we have institutional agendas to consider. Political authorities have their own sets of priorities and they often decide to handle issues on the public agenda only when they reach the top. Furthermore, Congress stalls on what experts think are critical problems if the same problems are not high on the public agenda. One researcher looked for consistency between popular opinion and public policy in several areas (economics, defense, energy, civil rights, etc.) over a 16-year period, concluding that the poll data representing popular opinion about the importance of issues was quite consistent with policy outcomes. Monroe (1979) concluded that the "political process at the national level does tend to respond to public preference, but in a decidedly imperfect way." Furthermore, those decisions which have to make it through the most hurdles are least responsive to popular opinion, perhaps because special interests and groups have more opportunities to exercise their influence.

The media's agenda is not simply a product of newspaper, radio and TV organizations and their newsmaking conventions. Although a comparison of media, candidate and audience agendas shows that the media do make an independent contribution, they too are influenced by other actors in this political process. As Weaver, Graber, McCombs and Eyal (1981: 84) note, more information is needed to identify "whether the candidates were important agenda-setters of issues for the media or vice versa, whether the process was reciprocal or whether some other sources (e.g., public opinion poll reports or pressure groups activities) were setting the agenda for both candidates and the news media." Others have found weak effects or no effects of the media as agenda setters (Sohn and Sohn, 1983; Gadziala and Becker, 1983; Culbertson and Stempel, 1984).

Image Formation

With the decline in party affiliations, voters are seen as turning to either candidate images or issues for criteria on which to make voting decisions. As noted above, one of the cognitive consequences of media use in campaigns is learning about issues and the candidates. Another is the formation of candidate's images (Hofstetter and Strand, 1983). Kenneth Boulding (1971) sees the media as forming images, which in turn are the keys to voting decisions. A national survey analyzed by Hofstetter, Zukin and Buss (1978) found that TV exposure was associated with increases in the amount but not the kind of images. The 1960 presidential debates effectively changed the image of the candidates while failing to alter the audience's attitude toward the debate topics; in this era of the tube the electorate has been persuaded more by projected images of candidates than by their positions on political issues.

That impact is not limited to the national or presidential level. One study found candidate image the overwhelmingly dominant factor in predicting the outcome of 23 Texas mayoral races. Maddox and Nimmo (1981) analyzed the survey data from 1952 through 1976 and concluded that ticket-splitting—voting for candidates from both parties—was related to attention to candidate images, late vote decisions and lack of strong party identification. The emphasis on images in campaign politics also is not limited to the U.S. Increased emphasis on image politics has also been noted in Japan where voters are floating between parties, and party identification has dropped as voters focus on candidate image.

While the media are clearly the major vehicles for disseminating information which goes into image-building, their ability to change images is certainly limited. Patterson and McClure (1976) and Hofstetter et al. (1978) found little change in candidate images resulting from exposure to the 1972 presidential TV ads. Kinder (1978) suggests that voters construct images of candidates which reinforce and support their own opinions about politics. Some evidence supports the view. In one study, voters who admired a candidate saw him as supporting policies they favored, while candidates they opposed were seen as being more distant. Experiments also show that there are limitations on how much a voter can be manipulated by politician's ads and their images. Clearly, however, those voters who are uncommitted or have little "image" to begin with should be most affected by media portrayals of candidates and other political figures. The ability of media to mold candidate images seems to be greatest in the early stages of the campaign or between elections.

Mendelsohn and O'Keefe (1976) argue that the dispute over whether candidate image or issue positions is more important is a moot point. They found that both were highly related to vote decisions among those who decided early in the campaign, while both were less important among late deciders. Weaver, Graber, McCombs and Eyal (1981) agree with this position that both images and issue stands are important determinants of the overall evaluation of political candidates. The two often seem inseparable. In their study, voters seemed able to learn about candidate images more easily than about issue positions. Both the mass media and interpersonal communication were important in providing raw material for the formation of candidate's images. They also concluded that the image agendas for Carter and Ford in the *Chicago Tribune* had an influence on the voters' image agenda in their 1976 Illinois sample, and they suspect the same is true for other media and other communities.

People's images are based on knowledge about political events that largely comes from the mass media. How does news of current events spread throughout the country? In the next section, we'll look at how information about important events diffuses into a social system.

News Diffusion

In addition to political campaigns, people learn most of what they know about current events through the mass media. In fact, once people leave their formal schooling, they are dependent upon the mass media for updating their knowledge about a host of topics, ranging from changes in technology to scientific discoveries, and from economic trends to foreign affairs. Some types of information are of little immediate significance, but even here people learn from the media. For example, the ability of adults to describe the purposes of satellites doubled within a short period after they first appeared and figured prominently in the media (McLeod and Swinehart, 1960). Robinson (1972) also found that heavier TV viewers were more knowledgeable about principles of weather forecasting, information apparently gained from watching that segment of news broadcasts.

Efforts to increase the public's awareness about public topics are often made in information campaigns that utilize both mass media and interpersonal communication (Katz, Gurevitch and Haas, 1973). Freimuth and Van Nevel (1981) found that an asbestos awareness campaign in 16 markets was moderately successful in raising the level of knowledge about asbestos among two select targeted groups: manual laborers and those age 50 or older. Jones and Saunders (1977) found that a five-week multimedia campaign involving heavy use of TV had a moderate impact on the public's knowledge about the issue of privacy, a fairly abstract concern. And Bogue, Bursik and Mayo (1979) reported some success in a venereal disease campaign that used public service announcements on radio and TV coupled with follow-up communication in clinics. However, many information campaigns also have failed (Star and Hughes, 1950; Jobes, 1973). O'Keefe (1985) examined the impact of "Taking a Bite Out of Crime," a public information campaign, concluding that more recent campaigns may have more efficacy than research of previous decades suggested. This campaign used data from a national survey and a three-city panel survey. Findings suggest the campaign influences people's cognitions, attitudes and behaviors regarding crime prevention.

The ability of mass media to inform people is more crucial in times of crisis, when people are most uncertain and dependent upon the media for learning about critical events (Ledingham and Masel-Walters, 1985). Recent years have witnessed a rash of critical events threatening the stability of both countries and international institutions. How does news about such events as assassinations and shootings spread throughout a social system? Substantial research has looked at questions of news diffusion, and major studies are summarized in Table 7-1. Generally, we can say the following (Jeffres and Quarles, 1983; Quarles and Jeffres, 1983; Bantz et al., 1983). The medium through which people learn about critical events depends on where they're located, and that factor is largely determined by the timing of events. Thus, when major events occur during the working hours of the day, larger numbers of people will be at work or in public places where they will learn the news from other people—interpersonal communication. Those at home are more likely to learn through the mass media. However, even the news passed on to other people can be traced back to the media at some point. The speed of diffusion depends on the significance of the event, so the more important the event, the faster the news will spread. Gantz and Trenholm (1979) found four reasons people pass on news about critical events: 1) to establish social status (show they're "superior" to others in some manner); 2) to satisfy informational and interest needs; 3) to express affection; and 4) to initiate social contact—to talk with others. The speed with which major news diffuses may vary across countries, but the basic trends are the same. Thus, the death of a Malaysian King was first learned through interpersonal communication by 52% of people surveyed in that country (Idid, 1981) while the attempted assassination of Pope John Paul II was first learned by 40% of Americans in one study (Jeffres and Quarles, 1983). A survey of tourists and residents in Honolulu shortly after the Reagan shooting (Hudson and Miller, 1983) found some 93% of the tourists and 95% of local residents were aware of the shooting, and both groups obtained initial information from similar sources: 26% of tourists and 31% of local residents, from radio; 16% of tourists and 10% of residents, from TV; 58% of tourists and 59% of residents, from other people. Local residents also were more likely to learn earlier than tourists, and 79% knew within an hour of its initial announcement by the media, compared to 37% of tourists.

Table I
Diffusion of News about Five Critical Events

Person & Event	Date	Study	Location	Time	Percentage Aware within			First Source (in Percentages)			
					30 min.	60 min.	90 min.	Radio	TV	People	Other
Franklin D. Roosevelt's death	April 13, 1945, Friday	Miller (1945)	Kent State University students (N = 143)	4:50 p.m. ET news flashed	83	94	99	11	–	87	1.4
		NORC study (1945) reported in Sheatsley & Feldman (1964)						47 (radio & press)		53	
Dwight Eisenhower's stroke	Nov. 25–26, 1957, Tuesday	Deutschman and Danielson (1960)	Lansing, Mich. (N = 205)	3 p.m ET heart attack announcement	20	26	31	32	38	18	12
John F. Kennedy's assassination	Nov. 22, 1963, Friday	Hill and Bonjean (1964)	Dallas, Texas (N = 212)	12:30 p.m. CST	84	93	95	17	26	57	
		Greenberg (1964)	San Jose, Calif. (N = 419)	10:30 a.m. PST	61	79 (within 45 min.)		26	21	53	
		Mendelsohn (1964)	State of Colorado (N = 200)	11:40 a.m. MST				39	17	32	1
		Banta (1964)	Denver, Colo. (N = 114; 36% students)	11:40 a.m. MST		82 (by time JFK died an hour later)		13	9	76	4
		Spitzer and Spitzer (1965)	Iowa City (N = 151)	12:30 p.m.	68			25	19	55	1
		Sheatsley & Feldman (1964)	National US survey (N = 1,384)	10:30 a.m.–1:30 p.m.			92	47 (TV & radio)		49	4
Ronald Reagan, attempted assassination	March 30, 1981, Monday	Jeffres and Quarles (1981)	Cleveland, Ohio (N = 261)	2:30 p.m. ET	70		90	25	34	40	1
		Sanchez & Neuwirth (1981)	Monterrey, Mexico (N = 255)	1:30 p.m.	.5	10	25	27	42	29	2
Pope John Paul, attempted assassination	May 13, 1981, Wednesday	Quarles and Jeffres (1981)	Cleveland, Ohio (N = 174)	11:30 a.m. EST	42	53	65	26	32	41	1
		Sanchez and Neuwirth (1981)	Monterrey, Mex. (N = 193)	9:20 a.m. (within) 40 min. 70 min. 100 min.	22	32	45	27	38	22	11
			Monterrey, Mex., students (N = 329)		15	21	30	32	29	34	3

Changes in Affect

In addition to its impact on cognitions, media use can lead to changes on the affective dimension by, for example, increasing interest in the campaign or lowering evaluations of candidates. A national study during the 1972 presidential election found that TV exposure was associated with increased interest in both personalities and issues. Kraus and Davis (1981) conclude that the presidential debates most likely will serve those people who are only moderately interested in politics and whose interest is stimulated by campaign events. Such voters also tend to have weak party affiliations and make up their minds late in the campaign. For this group, the debates can provide a catalyst to increase their concern about the election, and the hoopla surrounding televised debates may serve that purpose. The timing of the debates usually is ideal for such voters because the party conventions usually come too early and last minute advertising campaigns too late for them to get involved and still learn much about the candidates. This group seems to be increasing in size and institutionalization of debates might strengthen this trend, Kraus and Davis argue.

Although the evidence is more tentative, some results show that media can have an impact on evaluations. Becker and Whitney (1980) found that people dependent on TV news for public affairs information are more likely to have negative attitudes toward government than those dependent on newspapers; thus, the media may work in different directions. Brunk and Fishkin (1982) found that the level of media attention given candidates before the 1976 nominating conventions corresponded to candidate's popularity, one measure of people's preferences. Two studies found that people exposed to political ads on radio or TV had more positive evaluations of lower-level candidates than those not exposed to the political advertising. However, Becker and Doolittle (1975) found that diminishing returns could eventually set in, followed by a drop; in other words with rising frequency, evaluations went up but beyond some point greater frequency of the advertising actually led to a drop in feelings toward the candidate. Satiation may occur when subjects become bored with highly redundant ads. Also, negative political ads can boomerang and evoke negative affect (Merritt, 1984; Garramone, 1984).

A decade ago there were wild claims that marketing strategies applied by media campaign specialists could work magic on unsuspecting voters. However, there is no evidence to support those claims. While political advertising can have some impact, it is not the only factor. In one national study of voters' attitudes towards the presidential candidates in 1972, political commercials were found to have practically no influence because voters were selective in what they watched and what they recalled. The voters having the most difficulty in making a decision and those most dependent on TV for political information tended to report more influence. However, even slight changes may be significant in close elections. Furthermore, advertisements also serve party workers who tend to pay more attention to political ads than does the average voter. They report that such ads bolster their morale and confidence while providing substantive information on their candidate and his qualifications. Expenditures for advertising have been on the rise. In 1956 both parties spent a combined total of more than $9 million on radio and TV time in the presidential campaign. In 1984 the two presidential campaigns alone spent an estimated $50 million on commercial TV advertising and one senate race cost $20 million. The key element sought by candidates in political advertising is the right to control message form and content. Patterson and McClure (1979) reported that political commercials on TV contained about five times as much issue information as did the network news programs. Joslyn (1980) examined 156 political commercials used between 1960 and 1976 and found that, although 75% mentioned issues, only 20% contained specific issue positions. Shyles (1983) identified issues in the 1980 campaign commercials and concluded they held some informational value for the political system. And a study of radio, TV and newspaper ads for a governor's race found that newspaper ads contained substantially more political issues than those found in the broadcast media (Elebash and Rosene, 1982).

The political parties also appear as almost daily media images. How are they affected by that coverage? Todd and Brody (1980) examined the possibility that the media play an active role in the variation of party affiliations between elections. In a panel study covering the 1972, 1974 and 1976 elections, they found no evidence that higher levels of media exposure were related to either strength of party affiliation or changes in party identification.

Charges of partisan bias have been levied at the media ever since they moved toward a more informational role rather than acting as partisan vehicles. Hofstetter (1978) analyzed TV network news coverage of the 1972 presidential campaign and found little basis for asserting the existence of partisan bias. Malaney and Buss (1979) analyzed Associated Press (AP) wire reports of the 1972 presidential campaign and compared it with a similar analysis of CBS TV coverage, finding that both were neutral in covering candidates and parties. An examination of 551 floor interviews recorded live during the 1972 Democratic National Convention found that 99% of the themes originating with reporters were neutral while 64% of those originating from other sources were neutral. However, the potential of bias in broadcasting was found in a European study which looked at camera positions and interviewed cameramen and journalists. Kepplinger (1982) found that the conservative candidate, Kohl, was more frequently shot from perspectives which cameramen said emphasized weakness, antipathy and clumsiness. In general, though individual stories or treatments of candidates or parties may appear incomplete or biased to some observers, the evidence suggests that in the overall campaign media reports show relatively little candidate preference. However, this does not mean that campaign coverage will not end up favoring a particular candidate.

Interpersonal communication networks and other factors play a more significant part in determining party choice, although the media may be important in providing information that changes the images of parties and the public's subsequent reaction to them in the long run.

Behavioral Changes — Voting

Of course, one of the most significant influences that media can have in an election campaign is changing people's voting decisions. The impact on cognitions (learning, knowledge) and on affect (interest, feelings) are preparatory to the voting decision. There is evidence, however, that the three are connected. Researchers Lee Becker and Sharon Dunwoody (1982) found that media use led to knowledge gain, which in turn led to voter behavior. The more knowledgeable a voter was about a candidate, the more likely he was to vote for that candidate.

Again, there are many sources of influence that push voters in one direction or another. Prior party affiliations, interpersonal communication with family and friends, and personal values all go into the mix of factors affecting the final voting decision, which may be a decision not to vote at all. Rust et al. (1984) found magazine and newspaper readership positively related to voting participation, but TV viewing was negatively associated.

Media content which can affect final voting decisions include not only the news columns, but political advertising, editorial endorsements and other content. Numerous studies have found a relationship between the amount of advertising expenditures and election outcomes, particularly in primaries and elections other than the presidency. The evidence is strongest for television advertising (Luttbeg, 1983b; Nowlan and Moutray, 1984). Hofstetter and Buss (1980) found late campaign exposure to TV spots and longer paid-TV programs led to higher vote turnout and changing candidate preferences in the 1972 presidential election. That seemed to occur more among voters with low levels of involvement. Those voters who were highly involved in the election campaign were less affected by their attention to political advertising in the media. Joslyn (1981) found that political broadcast advertising was influential in voters' decisions to defect from their traditional political parties in an election. There has been relatively little study of the impact of newspaper advertising.

Media endorsements of candidates is a direct attempt to influence the public's voting decisions. Several studies suggest that newspaper editorial endorsements have an impact, but the influence is greater in local elections than national ones (McCleneghan, 1983). The influence also is greatest among the undecided voters rather than those who have already made up their minds. Researcher John Robinson's (1972, 1974) national study of Americans led him to conclude that the overwhelming editorial support Richard Nixon received from newspapers in 1968 and 1972 significantly boosted his share of the vote and accounted for a 3% voting difference. Less impact was found in a similar analysis of 1980 data by Hurd and Singletary (1984) who concluded that newspaper endorsements are unlikely to be a major factor in most U.S. national elections.

Two other media influences are the televised presidential debates and the results of election polls reported by the media. The 1960, 1976 and 1980 presidential debates were extraordinary events which attracted almost all voters to watch for at least a limited amount of time. In 1976 the debates encountered substantial prior preference, with about 55% of the voters having definite preferences before the debates and most others leaning toward a candidate. Decisions as to who won the debates split along partisan lines. Thus, vote intentions did not seem to be affected very much, and the debates served to reinforce the public's prior decisions. Kraus and Davis (1981) conclude that among the voters most likely to be served by the debates are ticket-splitters — who have strong political interests — and the party faithful. The former use the debates to confirm or reinforce their voting predispositions and the latter can use the debates as a brief, well-organized summary of pertinent information to help them draw some final conclusions or rethink conclusions already reached.

The impact of published and private polls on political candidates and voters is hard to predict. In 1972, for example, the polls of Democratic candidate George McGovern confirmed the gloomy message of the Gallup polls but there was little significant change in the candidate's stance. However, in 1968 polls showed Humphrey trailing but the outcome uncertain, and this information stimulated a major shift in Humphrey's stance on Vietnam, one which almost brought him victory (Weiner, 1976-77). Ceci and Kain (1982) concluded that knowledge of polling results affected both the strength of attitudes towards candidates and the actual candidate preference in a study of students. The students reacted against the dominant candidate, but did not become more favorable to the underdog. For many years, there has been concern that poll results would lead to either a "bandwagon" effect— where undecided voters go with the apparent front runner—or the "underdog" effect—where voters root for the losing candidate. Atkin (1981) notes that pre-election poll reports in the news media appear to influence some voters in terms of preferences and turnout motivation, but election night coverage of projections and vote tabulations seem to have inconsequential bandwagon effects but may depress turnout (Worcester, 1980).

A Model of Mass Media Political Effects
Context, Contingencies, and Limitations

In our discussion of how the media have an impact on people's political cognitions, affective relations and behaviors, we often noted limitations. Some media effects occur only when people are undecided or interested, for example. Throughout the history of mass media, there have been debates about the nature of their impact: Are they powerful "hypodermic needles" injecting ideas into people or are they simply handmaids to other institutions? Nowhere has this controversy over the effects of mass media been more important than it has in the political arena.

The debate traced over several decades can be characterized as following two basic themes. One line of argument and evidence says that the media have largely indirect or limited effects and generally act to reinforce existing beliefs, attitudes and behaviors. In this model, media do not change people's political ideas but simply allow voters to fill in the blanks with information that is consistent with existing beliefs and preferences. This view of political effects of the media has appeared under a variety of labels—indirect effects, null/limited effects, and a reinforcement model.

A second approach sees the media as having direct consequences among the electorate, constructing a political reality that is not merely a reproduction of the views and positions of the political candidates, but one which reflects the structure and perogatives of the media institutions themselves. In this scenario, the media are responsible for forming political images, emphasizing some issues over others because they fit the media's needs, and directly changing some people's political cognitions, beliefs, feelings and behaviors. This approach also has appeared under different labels, most often as a direct effects model or strong effects model.

More recently, scholars have opted for a view which recognizes the evidence supporting each approach. Thus, the media are seen as having some direct effects and some indirect effects. The media impact is also seen as being multi-dimensional, occuring in the cognitive, affective and behavioral realms. A number of different terms have appeared to describe this emerging view of media political effects— a dependency model, a contingency model, a transactional model. We will discuss the ingredients of this approach in a series of models.

The first model examines the potential sources of influence on people's political behaviors, and sees them as falling into two categories: internal influences and external influences (see Figure 7-1). The former include personal growth and changes in life style and life cycle. As people mature, they develop an interest in politics and an expanded view of the world. Changes in personal circumstances also may mean changes in political behaviors—marriage or divorce, unemployment, a new home, etc. The external influences include the outside environment that we learn about through other people, mass media, or personal observation and experience within the community. Thus, people observe local conditions and see their political figures and candidates. In small towns, you may even be acquainted with the local candidates. But in most political contexts, what we learn comes not through personal observations but through communication with other people or mass communication.

Several questions can be asked about media effects by comparing components of the first model. First, are the media and other people simply neutral vehicles linking people with other actors and institutions that can affect one's political beliefs and behaviors? Second, what is the relationship among the three links to the external environment, particularly that between mass and interpersonal communication?

Figure 7-1

Model 1: Potential Influences on Political Behaviors

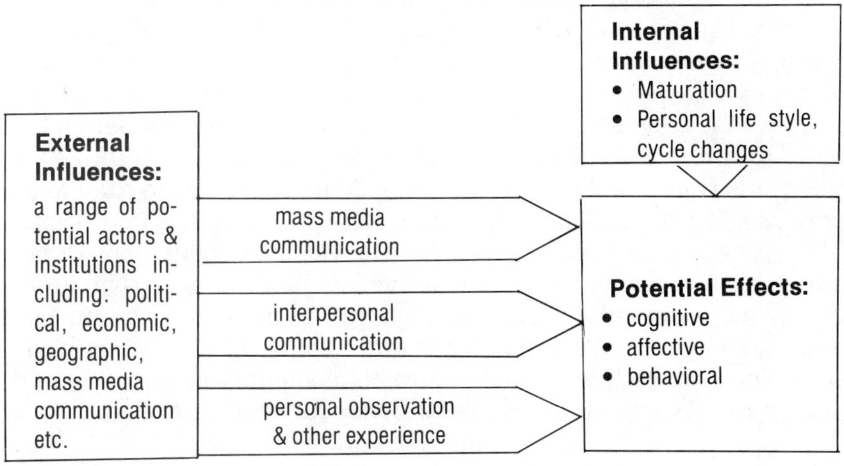

The first question can be rephrased as follows. Are the media neutral—having no direct consequences—or are the media external influences in the same manner as the political, economic and other institutions that affect people's political behaviors? Nimmo and Combs (1980) note that myth is so common in American politics and myth-making so pervasive that the creation and communication of mythical accounts goes on with people not even realizing it happens. Myth refers to the dramatic representation of past, present, or future events that people come to believe. Key myth makers are not only political press agents, politicians, political scientists and pollsters, but also popular entertainers and journalists. The term "myth" has some negative connotations, but we can use "constructed reality" or "political images and beliefs" to refer to essentially the same thing. We will return to this question in the second half of this chapter, since the relationship between the media and other institutions concerns long-range effects.

The second question is a long-standing concern about the signifi-cance of mass media and personal influence. Two areas of research have centered on whether the mass media or other people (interper-sonal communication) are more successful in persuading people. One stems from classical research conducted some 40 years ago in Erie County, Ohio when Paul Lazarsfeld and his colleagues, expecting to find people reporting great influence by the media, found instead that voters claimed little influence from the media. The external source of influence was other people, and the researchers posited what became known as the "Two-Step Flow Hypothesis." According to this view, the mass media are consumed in greater quantities by opinion leaders, generally more highly educated, wealthier, and high status individuals. Being more informed and politically astute, these opinion leaders influenced the less active, lower status individuals through interper-sonal communication. This communication took place in generally informal settings—over coffee or during informal chats, for example. Subsequent research has raised numerous questions. Opinion leaders in American society and most other settings are not leaders on all topics but tend to specialize. Thus, you may be an opinion leader on the latest rock music but not on politics or sports. In addition, if influence were to flow from high to low status individuals, there would have to be opportunity for such communication. And research shows that people tend to associate with those from the same social groups, though not exclusively, of course. Thus, the influence that occurs from inter-personal communication occurs within the same social strata: one middle-class individual influencing another voter with the same back-ground. Opinion leaders precede others in collecting information and changing their views; this occurs in diverse cultural settings (Muis, -

1983). Black (1982) studied opinion leaders between 1975 and 1978 and found that they changed their attitudes earlier than others in their group on six government activities including health, defense, product safety, expanding employment, and space exploration.

Researcher John P. Robinson (1976) suggested revising the original two-step flow model to account for interaction among the media, opinion givers and opinion receivers. He also noted that many people are "non-discussants," and do not discuss politics with anybody. These are the people who are particularly open to media influence because of their relative isolation from other external influences (see Figure 7-2).

Figure 7-2

Model 2: Relationship between Interpersonal & Mass Media Effects

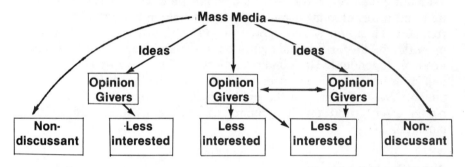

A recent survey of adults in a Florida senate race compared political opinion leaders with nonleaders. Andersen and Garrison (1978) found that opinion leaders hear more about candidates from all media as well as from other people. Political opinion leadership did not depend on age, though males were more likely to be such leaders than women.

The other research tradition focusing on the influence of media vs. people is the diffusion of innovations. Here, we are concerned with how a new innovation, such as digital recording or personal computers, diffuses or spreads throughout a population. Clearly, both the media and people play important parts in diffusion processes.

When we ask whether the media have an impact on voters, we are treating the electorate as a collection of similar individuals. Yet we know that people differ greatly in terms of their information, beliefs, values and preferences. The original "Hypodermic Needle Model" viewed people as naive if not defenseless individuals open to influence by the media. Clearly, however, people differ in terms of a variety of characteristics and patterns of behavior which may account for similar differences in media effects. Some view the question of whether media effects are direct or indirect as turning on the relationship between media behaviors and these individual differences, and this is where most of the research has been conducted by mass communication scholars in the past decade or so.

When people watch political ads on TV or read the newspaper, two sets of mechanisms may be at work. One set activates the individual— propelling the consumer to act on his or her environment. Thus, you may be motivated to seek particular content or expect particular gratifications associated with media use. Once the actual media use begins, a second set of mechanisms acts to filter the media content. Here you use existing mental categories to process incoming ideas, and you interpret new information about political candidates in terms of your personal values and existing attitudes and political preferences.

There is another restriction on media effects. As we noted in examining the first model, mass media compete with personal observation and interpersonal communication in linking people to their environment. Thus, we would expect people who are more "dependent" upon the media for this linkage to be influenced more than those who are less dependent. The nondiscussants in Figure 7-2 are more media dependent than opinion receivers who talk about politics with other people. We will examine the evidence for a "dependency model" of media effects and for the impact of both activating and filtering mechanisms.

Activating Mechanisms

Some people are more motivated to follow election campaigns than others. Audience motives may produce effects indirectly through stimulation of media use which then turns out to have political effects (McLeod and Becker, 1981; Garramone, 1984a). Several studies over the past two decades have found citizens saying they use the media for surveillance of the political environment or for political guidance. Voters use media to "judge what the candidates are like" or "to see what they would do if elected" (McLeod and Becker, 1974; Becker, 1979; Blumler and McQuail, 1969). Other reasons often given for public affairs media use are to "decide about candidates" and "see where candidates stand on the issues." There also does not appear to be much difference in motivations across different levels of political involvement (McLeod and Becker, 1974; O'Keefe and Mendelsohn, 1978). Several studies provide support for the view that differences in people's motivations to use media lead to differences in political effects (McLeod and McDonald, 1985; McLeod, Luetscher and McDonald, 1980). For example, people who are motivated to use the media for political surveillance (i.e., to learn candidates' positions on issues and their performances) are also more likely to become more informed about issues such as the state of the economy, inflation, etc. In one study, audience members motivated by information seeking were generally less likely to show an agenda-setting effect than those without such motivation. The less motivated were more likely to pick up the newspaper's agenda (McLeod, Becker and Byrnes, 1974).

For several decades, people were viewed as selectively exposing themselves to supportive information which agreed with their opinions. In other words, Democrats watched their party's TV programs and advertisements because they had a conscious preference for the supportive material. As we noted above, party workers often say they find the political ads a boost to their morale. However, there is relatively little evidence for the view that many people are actually motivated to consume media content because they want the support (Garramone, 1985; Sears and Freedman, 1967). If this were the case, then media effects would generally reinforce existing views and opinions. Ziemke (1980) suggests that the more certain voters are about their decision, the more likely they will select supportive information. It appears that people generally turn to supportive political material because it has some utility or is useful, not just because they feel the need for support (Cf. Erbring et al., 1980).

Filtering Mechanisms

In the Audience chapter we noted that much media use occurs because people want to escape boredom, to be entertained, and/or it is a habitual activity. In such cases, people's defenses may be down and media might be consumed with little conscious evaluation. At other times, people may be quite involved. Such involvement operates like interest and can trigger any one of a set of filtering mechanisms that mediate content effects (Perloff, 1984). Researchers have focused on how people are selective in processing incoming information, interpreting it so it is consistent with existing preferences.

People with low political interest are more likely to be influenced by the media to change political attitudes (Kazee, 1981). And McCombs and Weaver (1973) found agenda-setting occurring only for people who were unsure about their voting decision and highly interested in the election campaign. Roberts (1981) found that voters' feelings about candidates developed early in the campaign and these differences in attitudes toward the candidates affect voters' subsequent gathering and interpreting of campaign materials.

Focusing primarily on political TV commercials during the past decade, researchers have compared high and low involvement voters in terms of media effects. Hofstetter and Buss (1980) found that when voter involvement was low, paid advertising stimulated turnout and caused changes in candidate preference during the 1972 campaign. Political TV spot ads are thought to be particularly effective because they are not predictable and are encountered by viewers while occupied with other concerns. For example, TV is effective in exposing Democrats to Republican ads and Republicans to Democratic commercials.

Party affiliation and ideology can be important filtering mechanisms. Chaffee and Choe (1980) concluded that partisan precommitment was sufficient to preclude campaign effects, but without such commitment, those exposed to the campaign made their decisions primarily on the basis of campaign-specific information. Those not exposed to the campaign made their decisions on the basis of weak cues, such as loose ties with political parties. Analysis of data from a 1976 national election study indicates that people use their ideology to sort and structure their political attitudes. In this case, TV news was found to be generally helpful to viewers' formation of political opinions, particularly among those with low ideological utility—having difficulty placing themselves on a liberal-conservative continuum (Reese and Miller, 1981).

Numerous other filtering mechanisms have been identified as significant to the electorate's processing of political information. One set of filters, generally called "social categories," refers to achievement-oriented factors such as education, income and social status (Gaziano, 1984; Lovrich and Pierce, 1984), and ascriptive factors such as sex (Newman and Sheth, 1984), race, and ethnicity. Several decades of evidence show that education is particularly important. People with more education have more highly developed information-processing skills, tend to be more print oriented (and thus, are subject to influence from those sources), tend to be more interested in news and public affairs topics (and thus, engage in more informa-tion-seeking and less avoidance of such material), and also tend to discuss politics more (and thus, have a more diverse set of influences on their political behaviors). Evidence for the "knowledge gap hypothe-sis" shows that increases in media publicity lead to widening dispari-ties in knowledge between high and low socioeconomic status groups in some circumstances (Tichenor et al., 1970, 1980; Gaziano, 1983, 1984). However, the gap depends on the issue and the nature of the campaign (Miyo, 1983; Ettema, Brown and Luepker, 1983; Lovrich and Pierce, 1984; Brantgarde, 1983).

Ascriptive filters also may be significant for processing information about some particular topic. For example, Jeffres and Hur (1979) found that Eastern European ethnics surveyed in Cleveland, Ohio were sensi-tive to President Gerald Ford's statement during the televised 1976 debates that Eastern Europe was not dominated by the Soviet Union. They were also more likely to hear about the statement than other ethnics in the sample.

Filtering mechanisms are particularly important in today's campaign because voters have minimal control over what they watch, read and hear during an election campaign. News media focus on campaigns with the same criteria used to evaluate other events and situations. Thus, though you may be concerned with long-range issues such as the environment or world health, media messages are likely to focus on the "horse race" aspect of the election and other factors which appear on the agenda for various reasons.

Media Dependency

The importance of mass media for people's political perceptions is captured by the concept of media dependency. This idea refers to the extent people rely on the media, or a particular medium, for their campaign coverage and other political information. Fry and McCain (1983), for example, found that community leaders were more dependent on interpersonal sources and newspapers for information about a civic issue. The potential significance of a diverse environment is found in a study which contrasted communities served by competing newspapers with those in monopoly situations. Greater diversity in political opinions about public questions was found in the competitive situation (Chaffee and Wilson, 1977). The same notion of diversity can be applied to people's own sources of influence. Erbring et al. (1980) found that citizens integrated into everyday networks of social inter-action—by talking politics with others—are less likely to be affected by media content. Miller and Reese (1982) found that reliance on a particular medium improved the medium's ability to influence political efficacy and activity. Political efficacy refers to people's trust that they have a say in their government, that the system is responsive and cares about its citizens. Becker and Whitney (1980) found that newspaper-dependent people seem more knowledgeable about local affairs, think they understand local government more and are more trusting than are television-dependent people. They note that people depend on a partic-ular medium because it satisfies their needs and that dependency does not exist without inherent consequences. Audience members dependent on a given medium for their information about the world may end up viewing the world quite differently from those dependent on another medium or a more diverse set of sources. McLeod and McDonald (1985) found reading newspapers for public affairs predicted higher levels of economic knowledge and political participa-tion while TV exposure was related to low levels of both measures.

The origins of channel dependence may be found in several places: opportunities for personal contact, people's skills in using the media, the quality and nature of the media available, individual motivations, and so forth. Reliance on particular media also depends on the rest of the environment. Pettey (1985), for example, finds that people's dependence on particular media for political information is linked to the expectations of their primary/reference group. This suggests that people learn from their friends and peers what constitutes an appropriate strategy for keeping up with political affairs — depending on TV or on newspapers.

Researchers Melvin DeFleur and Sandra Ball-Rokeach (1982) posit that as a social system becomes more complex and the informal channels of communication more disrupted, people become more dependent on the mass media. Thus, people in modern, urban, industrialized societies are becoming almost totally dependent on the media for much information. That media dependency, they argue, is likely to be heightened during periods of structural conflict and change within societies. An examination of how the media uses and gratifications change during war and peace was conducted in Israel in 1973-74. Dotan and Cohen (1976) found that cognitive needs (information) were most important and escapist needs least important during both periods; thus, people's use of the media for information did not change in times of stress. There was, however, a shift towards radio due to its greater speed in disseminating information during war time. Control over communication channels is also important. The greater the monopoly by either individual private interests or government of com-

Figure 7-3

Model 3: Nature & Process of Media Political Effects

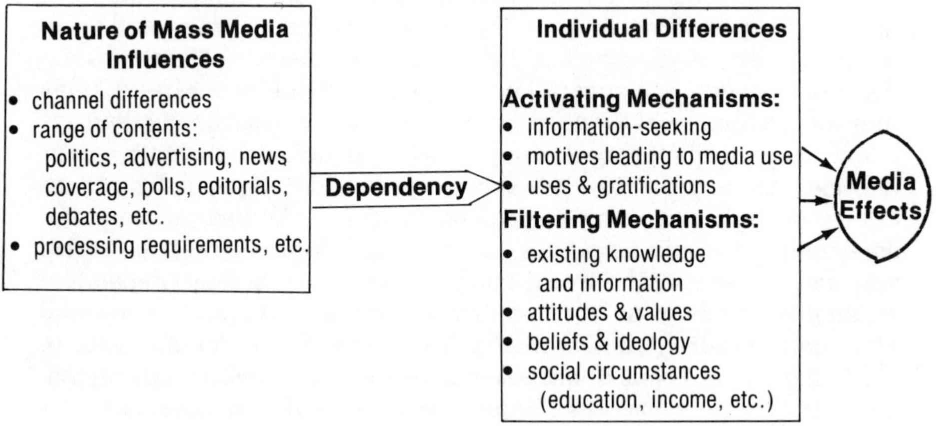

munication channels, the more centralized the control over the political symbols and images that affect people.

Media dependency during election campaigns has become more important because of several factors including the decline in significance of one filtering mechanism: party affiliation. There has been a slow but steady decline in the number of partisan identifiers since the mid-1960's with a movement away from the party as the basis for campaign organization and shift to hired professionals (research firms, public relations agencies, etc.); the latter change also means a shift from interpersonal influence attempts to extensive media campaigns. Overall, the changes concentrate influence in media communication channels and create greater dependency than was the case several decades ago.

Media Impact on the Political System

In only a relatively small percentage of the world's countries is the impact of media during the political process significant. In the prior section, we paid particular attention to media effects during election campaigns because the peaceful competition for power is so basic to the American political system and other democracies. However, in many countries, open competition through election campaigns is rare and the elections that do occur are efforts to legitimize or gain public ratification of prior decisions. Media participation in those cases reflects the differences between democracies and closed political systems.

Because democracies are such inherently complex and messy arrangements for governing people and sharing power, there is built-in concern over threats to political stability. Such concerns are manifest during periodic election campaigns but their focus is long-term. There are a number of different perspectives on this matter. Threats are seen as taking various forms but most appear as imbalances in the political system. Those imbalances in the eyes of Marxists, for example, are inherent in capitalist systems and stem from economic divisions. In Marxist ideology and other materialistic perspectives, the mass media necessarily support the power structure and reflect its goals and interests. However, in democratic theory there also is the potential for mass media to have consequences quite irrelevant to their economic interests. Democratic theorists look for threats from a more diverse set of sources, and the mass media have become central to many critiques.

What are the long-range effects of the mass media for the political system? The evidence for such effects is scanty at best, but some of the arguments make intuitive sense. Furthermore, some of the research on media impact during the on-going political process is suggestive of long-range consequences.

Long-term effects of the media are rooted in basic media — government relationships. Within those relationships, political figures affect the media and media people affect the government. We will examine these relationships and then discuss how changes may lead to imbalances in the political system in the long term.

Two basic themes run through current thoughts about the relationships between mass media and government. According to one view, the mass media are a subsystem of the larger social system and, as a consequence, reflect the size and diversity of that system. This is the systems perspective taken by researcher Phil Tichenor and his Minnesota team (Tichenor et al., 1980). Though their research has looked at how media operate within communities rather than countries, their assumptions about the relationship between media and other subsystems are applicable at the national level as well. According to the Minnesota team, the media's operation as a separate "fourth estate" is doubtful at best. The media are strongly linked with other components that impinge upon them as much as they impinge upon other subsystems, such as government. Extrapolating from the Minnesota research, we would expect the American media to reflect the concerns of the dominant power groupings of the country. Media, thus, demonstrate the consensus or diversity of opinions present, though that representation is neither total nor an undistorted reproduction of current events and institutions. The term "reflects" is ambiguous in that it's simply another way of saying "effect." In other words, the diversity of the country and the conflict present affect the manner in which the media report social problems and handle conflict. One generalization of Tichenor et al. (1980) is that media performance and media use differ according to what are called structural characteristics of the general social system. Thus, in small traditional rural communities, the local weekly paper tends to be dominated by local news and citizens are less likely to read a daily paper than are those of larger urban areas served by dailies. The media content reflect the size and diversity of the city and, by inference, the country.

A major assumption of the Minnesota research is that media reinforce or operate to maintain the larger social system. Thus, the media tend to "reflect" the perspectives of organizational power centers such as business and other power groups. When there is disagreement about a particular problem among the powerful groups, the media represent that disagreement, as is usually the case in diverse urban areas. When there is local consensus, as in small towns, the media tend to avoid conflict.

Another theme runs counter to the assumptions made by the

Minnesota team. Also based on research conducted during the 1960's and 1970's, this view sees fundamental changes in the media leading to changes in its supportive relationship with the larger social system. One of its more articulate spokespersons has charged the media, in particular television, with undermining the public trust that is crucial to the survival of the democratic system. While Tichenor and his colleagues have focused on how media operations are affected by the social structure, these critics focus on how the media affect the political system. The mechanisms include not only direct impact on political structures but indirect influences through manipulation of public opinion. Differences between the two views reflect the "chicken-and-egg" problem of media effects discussed earlier.

Relations Between Media and the Government

In the short-run, we can describe relations between the media and government as an "exchange model." Each gives something and gets something else in return. Each affects the other and no one is totally independent. Newsmaking during election campaigns is a product of each interaction between two organizations as Sigal (1973) noted: one composed of news people, the other of either campaigners or politicians. Both groups have their goals and priorities which often conflict but accommodations are generally arrived at one way or another. Day to day coverage of the government follows a similar path. The wire services, TV networks and major national publications have the most national influence. Thus, they get the most attention at the White House or on the campaign trail when space and other facilities are allocated. In return, the government and political candidates get access to the national media audience. Newspaper reporters complain about the preferential treatment given to television reporters (Massing, 1981), but the allocation does solve the government's logistics problem.

Legislators, both elective and appointive officials, seek to recruit members of the press into active, participatory roles when it suits them (Morgan, 1978; Sigal, 1973). Reporters gain access, sometimes exclusive access, to important information; politicians and officials secure their access to the public. Reporters also receive personal recognition that parallels their political relationships. Alter (1981) suggests that reporters who followed President Reagan on the campaign trail avoided asking tough questions and "rooted" for him to increase their chances of receiving prestigious assignments. Thus, reporters who follow the "winning" candidate get better assignments than those who cover the "loser." Martindale (1984) did not find evidence of the "pack journalism" phenomenon often associated with journalists covering candidates over time.

Officials, politicians and candidates all seek to manage their presentation through the media. Florida journalists, for example, found it difficult to avoid the gimmickry that dominated a 1978 gubernatorial campaign in which one candidate worked a full day at each of 100 different jobs. The gimmick was mentioned in several hundred stories (Fedler, 1981). As Hilderbrand (1981) notes, such presidents as McKinley, Theodore Roosevelt, Taft and Wilson grasped the usefulness and necessity of widening their control of popular opinion long before television and current campaigns. They did so through changes in their routine relationships with the press. McKinley pioneered the press release and provided advance copies of his speeches to reporters. Roosevelt personalized the process begun by McKinley by inviting reporters to his office for little chats; these foreshadowed the press conference. Taft felt there was something undemocratic about a president attempting to manage public opinion and as a consequence, he received bad publicity because reporters were forced to turn elsewhere for foreign affairs information. Over time, as presidents since Franklin D. Roosevelt have taken greater efforts to reach people directly, they have increasingly lost the control earlier presidents exercised over the news generated in their press conferences. The press has evolved as a force in its own right and the press conference has become the American version of the British Prime Minister's stand to answer questions and criticism before Parliament (French, 1982). Brzezinski and Huntington (1963) note that political pressure is funneled upward by the press in the United States. In contrast, the Soviet Union funnels pressure in the reverse direction. Such pressure emerges in press conferences, the media themselves, and in opinion polls distributed through the media.

The beginning of the modern era of political broadcasting has been traced to the 1948 presidential campaign between Harry Truman and Thomas E. Dewey. Most modern campaign techniques were used or anticipated in that campaign (Carroll, 1980). Since that time, candidates have turned to professional public relations firms, research organizations, and pollsters to run their campaigns. Daniel Boorstin (1962) notes that candidates long ago learned how media news organizations work and the values used to identify and to process news. That information has been used to gain access to media by staging "pseudoevents." Press meetings, stunts and confrontations are staged by candidates as well as protestors and other political groups who inform the media of the events in advance so they can schedule their "cameras" and reporters to cover them. The essential ingredient is that the events be staged, planned or planted rather than spontaneous creations with a purpose other than being reported by the news media. Though reporters are somewhat cynical about such "manufactured news," such events do get reported quite often and they represent efforts to control the media. Apparently this attitude can slip over into the rest of the campaign. Ostroff (1980) found an almost cynical attitude by TV news personnel toward the reputed news value of most campaign activities during Ohio's 1978 election. Nimmo and Combs (1983) argue that news people and political advertisers concoct a representation of reality that is clearly fantasy, simplified and often designed to sell a story rather than to enlighten the public.

Polls and public relations firms are important in the conduct of politics and election campaigns today (Strand et al., 1983). Manheim and Lammers (1981) looked at the impact of popularity polls on altering presidential behavior in the scheduling and conduct of news conferences. They find that opinion polls do influence scheduling but not the president's verbal behavior. Sudman (1982) notes that presidents also use opinion polls to get elected and as guides for formulating politics; that use has also included abuses through mis-representation of poll results.

Though other influences may be significant, it is television which many believe is responsible for changing the nature of American election campaigns (Bonafede, 1981; Hart, 1984). Edwin Emery (1976) notes that even the whistle stop technique, while still basic to political campaigning, is now designed to entice the TV cameras. The apparent emphasis on "image" by TV is another factor that may eliminate some contendors from political consideration.

Since 1952, when extensive TV coverage began, cooperation between the TV networks and political parties in covering presidential campaigns has developed into a strong reciprocal relationship. The parties receive free national exposure and the networks have an opportunity to present live, emotional programming, to promote their news departments, and to demonstrate the latest communication tech-nologies (Fant, 1980). An examination of 15 federal elections between 1867 and 1925 suggests that TV's emphasis on image may merely heighten something that began long ago. Nolan (1981) argues that the organizational structure for mid-twentieth century election campaigns was laid when the advertising agent replaced the newspaper editor as a principal strategist at election time. During the period investigated, campaigns became more skillfully organized as party leaders were relieved of election-time burdens and campaign specialists began to oversee the leader's tour and plan campaign strategy. Style had already triumphed over content in election campaigns and the projec-tion of the leader's personality was as important then as it is now, Nolan argues. If that is the case, what TV adds is a visual emphasis and requirements for public appearance and speaking that pre-TV candidates could handle with less difficulty. Streitmatter (1985) analyzed newspaper coverage of six presidents and concluded that presidential personality has far more impact on media coverage than historians or other observers have recognized. More robust presidents get more general and more personal coverage.

Government officials also are dependent upon the media for much of their information. Hesse (1981) suggests that state senators in urban areas depend too much on media coverage to understand the needs and views of their constitutents. He suggests they should emphasize interpersonal contact with constituents more, as rural legislators do.

Two long-term consequences for the political system seem to emerge from the government-media relationship during campaigns and the day-to-day political process. First, although both the media and government benefit from the exchange relationship, the net effect has been to augment greatly the power of the executive branch. As Grossman and Rourke (1976) note, "The media provide the president with a linkage to public opinion, and it is upon this tie that a president's power ultimately rests." Second, with the growth of mass media and ancillary organizations, election campaigns depend more on media and less on political parties than they did in the past. The shift to media campaigns has also been linked to an emphasis on issue voting rather than the enactment of party loyalties. Thus, in the long-run party loyalties may suffer.

Long-Range Effects

Long-range effects of the mass media on the political system can occur in several ways. First, the media can affect the electorate's support for the system and its effectiveness. Second, the media can affect political structures by altering the relationship between power contenders or weakening particular institutions. Third, the media can indirectly affect government policies through their impact on public opinion. Fourth, the media can help or hinder in "socializing" subsequent generations to American political culture. One of the major functions attributed to the mass media is passing on the political norms and values from one generation to the next. We will examine the arguments and evidence for each of these long-range effects.

"Videomalaise" and Media Support for the System

All political systems at bottom depend on public support or acquiescence, and some fear that the mass media's emphasis on "bad news" — such things as political corruption and inefficiency — will eventually undermine the electorate's faith in the American democratic system (Gergen, 1984). Becker and Whitney (1980) found people dependent on

TV news for public affairs information held more negative attitudes toward the government than those dependent on newspapers. Robinson (1975, 1976) also found that TV dependence was associated with political cynicism. Another small study looked at the impact of the film, *All the President's Men*, on political attitudes of alienation, trust, etc. Though the party affiliation was also a factor, viewing the film was associated with political alienation (Elliott and Schenck-Hamlin, 1979).

American values have changed markedly in the past two decades and have reached a point where a majority of the public now expresses fundamental doubts about the performance of government and other institutions. A 1979 New York Times-CBS News survey found 86% of the public agreeing that there is a "moral and spiritual crisis" or a "crisis of confidence" in the country. Though the percentage was inflated by a presidential speech using the same words just before the poll, it does reflect the high dissatisfaction with government. Some say this stems from disappointment over government performance in policy areas—whether that be failure to eliminate poverty, racial discrimination, inflation, or abortion (Zukin, 1981). Social conflict associated with the Vietnam war is also a factor. Lunch and Sperlich (1979) associate the war with public skepticism regarding government claims, more resistance to government plans and considerable popular alienation from symbols of the American political system. Though some of this changed in later years, attitudes and predispositions such as these make presidential leadership difficult.

One popular view of this rise in political disaffection is Michael Robinson's (1976) notion of "videomalaise." He argues that the growing political malaise and decline in political efficacy can be linked to the media, particularly television. He sees several factors as significant: inadvertent, or unmotivated, TV news viewing (when filtering defenses are down), high credibility attributed to the television networks by the public, the interpretive character of TV news coverage, TV news's emphasis on the negative, its emphasis on conflict and violence, and the anti-institutional theme of network news programs. Paletz et al. (1980) did find that polls reported by the New York Times, NBC and CBS featured predominantly negative themes. Looking at campaign coverage, Graber (1980) found that the proportion of negative comment about candidates in the press rose from 41% for Hubert Humphrey in 1968 to 58% for both Gerald Ford and Jimmy Carter in 1976. Robinson believes that the disaffection between government and the public began growing at about the same time the TV networks expanded their nightly news broadcasts from 15 to 30 minutes. Arguing that the two occurrences are not simply coincidental, Robinson sees TV news portraying social and political institutions in a state of perpetual conflict, fostering cynicism and distrust of officials and institutions, and promoting frustration and low efficacy.

Robinson's scenario is based on observations and evidence gathered during the 1960s and the first half of the 1970s. Zukin (1981) notes that "the relationship between television dependency and malaise held in the 1960s but is no longer true today." During that period, TV news coverage was more certainly negative and not supportive of government than has been the case more recently (see Patterson, 1984a,b; Hallin, 1984). Survey evidence gathered by Becker et al. (1979) found TV dependency to be related to distrust of local officials, but not national government officials. Becker and Whitney (1980) also found TV dependency negatively related to trust and the perceived complexity of politics at the local level, but not at the national level. Since Robinson's thesis is cast at the national level, this evidence is inconsistent with his notion of videomalaise. Sharp (1984) found no support for the videomalaise hypothesis. However, Miller et al. (1979) did find a link between critical media content and public feelings of malaise. As Zukin (1981) notes, the question of whether the mass media contributed to the growth of political malaise over the past several decades is one that probably will never be satisfactorily answered. Even if TV did promote such malaise but has since diversified to include more supportive content, the past effects of public distrust may persist for some time.

Media Impact on Political Structures

Since parties are such crucial political institutions in a democracy, any potential impact on their operation deserves our attention. A central question is whether the media have contributed to or helped accelerate the decline of party affiliation and the rise of greater volatility or instability among the electorate. The United States is not alone in experiencing such changes. The electorates of Western democracies in Europe and elsewhere have become more volatile. In the U.S. the volatility has taken several forms as fewer people vote, party loyalties decline, citizens split their votes among the parties, and trust in political institutions and organizations has declined. Accompanying the decline in parties has been a rise in issue voting. The mass media seem to have inherited an expanded role in election campaigns at the expense of the political parties. Media coverage, particularly TV news, also is seen as contributing to lower party loyalties and instability.

Carl Bybee and his colleagues (1981) sought to test the notion that use of television for political news contributes to electoral instability. Even after controlling for other factors such as education and political interest, media use did not predict voter volatility. In fact, TV exposure actually predicted lower levels of volatility. Trying to get at the question in another way, Wattenberg (1982) compared the level of campaign media expenditures with the salience of attitudes about parties and candidates held by voters in the 1978 national election. He found that when media expenditures were higher, the salience of parties was lower and the salience of candidates higher. Thus, when more money was poured into the media, voters thought more about the individual candidates and less about the political parties they represented.

Political parties are one mechanism for allocating power within a society. Saldich (1979) argues that television is the "great democratizer" and has become a corridor to power for people normally excluded from the political system. This has revitalized the political process. At the same time, TV teaches a politics of violence, that physical assault and property damage attract TV cameras; thus, authorities often ignore more orderly petitions. The media may have altered the way Americans attempt to influence their government by shifting petitioning efforts from parties to elected representatives and increasing emphasis on communication and persuasion through public opinion.

Deviant political groups also use protests to obtain attention. Shoemaker (1982) suggests that the U.S. media contribute to the support of centrist parties by reporting on the activities of fringe political groups so that they appear ridiculous. A former president of the Students for a Democratic Society (SDS) suggests that the media disparage social and political movements not because they conspire to do so but because editors and reporters take for granted that political demonstrations are disturbances of a legitimate social order. Simultaneously, elements of the radical ideology are absorbed by the mainstream (Gitlin, 1980) and the group fades away. Echoing a similar theme, George Gerbner and his colleagues (1982) believe that television blurs traditional differences among political factions and brings conservatives, moderates and liberals together. Among Republicans, heavy TV viewers tended to be more liberal than light viewers. Among Democrats, heavy TV viewers tended to be more conservative than light viewers. TV viewing is seen as blurring traditional differences, blending them into a more homogeneous mainstream. The "television mainstream" may be the true twentieth-century melting pot of the American people, they suggest. In an analysis of several national surveys, Gerbner et al. (1984) found that those who watch more TV are more likely to call themselves "moderate" and to avoid the labels of "liberal" or "conservative." Heavy newspaper readers were more likely to say they are "conservative" and heavy radio listeners more "liberal," strengthening their contention that television is fundamentally different from other media.

Affecting Public Opinion

Mass media and public opinion are inevitably tied together in both the short-run and long-run. As Zukin (1981) notes, the central role accorded the public in a liberal democracy requires information on which judgments about leadership may be made. Thus, the central question of democratic theory—How are public preferences transmitted to decision makers?—focuses on communication.

Though political parties and pressure groups act to link public opinion with government policies, the media also serve this function in contemporary politics. In the United States, public preferences reach decision makers through several routes: voting decisions, media coverage of public activities and private actions, dissemination of opinion poll results, government officials' personal observations and communication about the electorate's desires.

First, what is public opinion? Probably the example that comes to most people's minds is the Gallup Poll or similar efforts to tap public perceptions. However, the popular opinion registered through surveys may be quite different from that expressed in groups or organizations. Nisbet (1975) distinguishes between public opinion and popular opinion. "Fundamentally, this is the difference between organized community on the one hand and the mass or crowd on the other." Public opinion is based on consensus and unifying tradition, common ends and acceptable means. Popular opinion refers to the aggregated views of the moment. Nimmo (1978) identifies three different concepts of public opinion. Popular opinion refers to basic beliefs and evaluations and is expressed in the relative privacy of the voting booth, letters to congressmen, responses to opinion pollsters, etc. Mass opinion is the generally diffuse, unorganized expression of views frequently symbolized as culture, consensus and what is often glibly referred to as "public opinion." And group opinions are those expressed during the give-and-take of private opinions within social groups.

As Zukin (1981) notes, the relationship between mass and popular opinion is important for several reasons. Leaders responding to what they see as mass opinion may arrive at policy decisions which anticipate electoral consequences (losing the next election). Policy makers are thus responsive to mass opinion rather than popular opinion. Polling results are increasingly important indicators of mass opinion (Niemi et al., 1983). Much of that polling today is an extension of journalism (Cantril, 1976; Ismach, 1984).

Crespi (1980) examined a quarter century of public opinion polls to identify the strengths and weaknesses of their links to journalism. He concludes that journalism has affected polls positively in four areas: 1) journalists place a high value on factual documentation of poll results;

2) subjective editorializing is devlaued in reporting results; 3) attention is focused on opinions about specific real-life events and issues; and 4) there is sensitivity to changes in public opinion resulting from current events. At the same time, ties to journalism have resulted in four weaknesses in polling as well: 1) there is a preoccupation with reporting numbers and less interest in their underlying meaning; 2) superficiality and lack of analysis of complex issues; 3) emphasis on topics that are expected to create front page headlines; and 4) limited coverage of long-term trends. (Also see Lang and Lang, 1984; Stovall and Solomon, 1984).

The differences between concepts of public opinion rest on several important distinctions. One is the difference between basic values and preferences; the other incorporates more transitory views about current topics. The former include the electorate's basic trust and political efficacy; the latter include people's opinions about a proposed tax bill or how good a job the president is currently doing in foreign policy. Another distinction focuses on the organized vs. unorganized nature of opinions. As noted above, the media give expression to special interest groups and protest groups wishing to have an impact on public policy.

A third distinction centers on the private vs. public setting in which opinions are expressed. This classic distinction has found expression most recently in a theory of public opinion that comes from Germany. Elizabeth Noelle-Neumann (1974, 1977), director of the Allensbach Institute, has posited a "spiral of silence" in which people gradually perceive which opinions are in the ascendancy and which are losing ground. These perceptions are based on media coverage as well as personal experience. If people believe that their opinions are in accordance with the dominant or growing trend, they feel reassured and express their convictions openly and publicly outside their primary sphere of family and friends. If they believe the opposite (that their opinions are in a minority or have become a minority), they reconsider and feel less certain of their position. Regardless, they are less likely to discuss their opinion except with friends. When adherents of majority views express themselves and minority adherents remain silent, this influences the individual's assessment of the opinion environment. The losing position appears weaker than it actually is and in a spiral-like process becomes increasingly suppressed because fewer people will risk expressing opinions which might result in negative judgments from others. Noelle-Neumann (1974) found some support for hypotheses based on the theory in surveys conducted in 1972 and 1974 in Germany. In the United States, Glynn and McLeod (1984) found support for the "spiral of silence" proposition; individuals perceiving support for a certain candidate were more likely to express a preference for that candidate. Lang and Lang (1983) note that a determined, vocal minority may have an impact on those without strong convictions if the group can make its view appear to be that of a majority. In those cases, a minority opinion becomes dominant without commanding an actual majority. However, to have influence, an opinion has to be visible and gain the attention of those responsible for making policy. Yet, how much public opinion can be said to lead those delegated as leaders and how much that presumed "public" opinion was in fact manipulated by policymakers remains an open question (Lang and Lang, 1983).

As Zukin (1981) notes, it is "difficult to pinpoint what effects the media have on public opinion," and the question will likely persist for some time to come. Beniger (1976) concludes that winning the presidential nomination depends much more on national public opinion and less on state primary elections than many had thought. Comparing more than 200 Gallup polls and 248 state primary elections from 1936 through 1972, he found there was no greater advantage than strength in the early polls for winning the presidential nomination because major changes in national public opinion are usually glacial in speed. Although primaries did influence polls, the strongest relations were of national opinion polls on both state primary elections and the presidential nomination. Wagner (1983) also found that different radio exposure produced consistent differences in public opinion even when education, class and interest in public affairs were taken into account.

Quite different views are held on how media affect the performance of government officials. Cotteret (1972) argues that communication today has, in a sense, replaced the notion of direct representation because the governed form a heterogeneous group and media must seek a common denominator. But Fitchen (1980) believes media will not supplant parliaments in their legislative or deliberative roles because they do not have the same responsiblity for upholding reason in political debate. However, since legislators in the modern era are swamped with demands on government, the media do provide an alternative avenue for public debate that can ease this burden. Thus, the media provide a forum of public information and debate beyond any which congresses and legislators could create, yet they are functionally linked together in a common transactional network. Members of legislative bodies also are media consumers and must depend upon the media for some information. Cohen (1963) found that the more narrow an official's specialization in the State Department, the greater his dependence on the media for his larger view of the world.

The potential impact of mass media on public opinion in other countries is noted by Fox's (1984) analysis of the Argentine media during the Falkland/Malvinas war. Argentine TV audiences received, almost exclusively, the government's version of the war. That coverage consisted almost entirely of army training films, high command communiques and commercials. There were no direct shots of battles, no independent correspondents and no record of the hardships faced by the civilian population for over two months. Fox concludes that TV and radio kept people from thinking rationally about the possibility of an Argentine victory or defeat by playing on patriotism and nationalism in a war that was far off at sea and which represented no danger to the civilian population. Coverage was similar to the propaganda that had been used by the government since 1976.

Political Socialization: Do Media Pass on the Culture?

Continuity within all countries requires transmission of the political culture from one generation to the next. This process is called "socialization," and one of the chief agents serving to pass on this political culture is the mass media (Kraus, 1973). Certainly, other agents are important including the family, peer groups, schools, and churches, but the media provide an abundance of content and capture the attention of children for periods often surpassing that spent with teachers or parents. The opportunity for teaching children about the political system occurs not just in the explicit news media, but also in the entertainment programming of TV and other popular media such as comic books and radio's top 40 hits.

What do children learn about their political system from the media and how does media use affect their support for the political system? Most scholars agree that political orientations acquired in preadult years have important implications for later adult behavior (Sears, 1975). As chilren move into adolescence, they develop a more rational view and knowledgeable conception of political processes, one which depends less on individual personalities. At the same time some distrust and cynicism also develop (Greenstein, 1965, 1968). Young people themselves believe that the media are "more influential than parents, teachers or peers" (Chaffee, Ward and Tipton, 1970). Dominick (1972) found junior high students rating the media as their primary source of information about the president; newspapers were first and television was second. The "best place to go for information about candidates and issues" was newspapers — cited by one-half of those polled followed by television — mentioned by 20%, and then parents — cited by 12%. Children from low-income homes were more reliant on TV and less dependent on parents compared to children from middle-income families. Rubin (1976) found similar results among seventh graders, where 58% said they received most of their information about politics from TV but 78% named TV as their chief source for information about the federal government and the president.

Media Use Patterns. Newspaper reading rises sharply through elementary school to junior high and high school. A recent national survey found that 33% read newspapers in early elementary school, 61% in late elementary school, 75% in junior high and 82% in high school (Gollin and Anderson, 1980). Among those reading a newspaper, the comics are read most often, followed by the front page. Sports, entertainment and soft news features follow with only 16% reading national news, 10% foreign news and 4% the editorial page. TV and radio use also rises sharply. About a third of the students reported watching TV news "most days," including 13% of early elementary school children, 23% late elementary school, 40% junior and senior high school. Listening to radio news "yesterday" rose from 12% in early elementary school to 26%, 43% and 55% across the four age levels. Other studies also report considerable media consumption and trends rising with age (Atkin, 1978, 1981; Jennings and Niemi, 1974; Drew and Reeves, 1980; Jeffres, 1980). There is also considerable evidence that children and adolescents pay some attention to politics during election campaigns. More than half of junior and senior high school students watched the 1976 presidential debates on TV in one study (Hawkins, Pingree, Smith and Bechtolt, 1979). The latest and least consumed medium is news magazines, which are read at least monthly by a fourth of junior high school students and a third of high school students. In addition to the explicit public affairs news content, entertainment— particularly TV programming—exposes children and adolescents to political values. And youth spend much more of their media time with TV programming than public affairs materials.

Passing on Knowledge. Both newspaper reading and TV news viewing successfully transmit political information to youths. A number of studies have related such media use to knowledge gains among elementary school age children (Atkin and Gantz, 1978; Hawkins et al., 1975; Conway et al., 1975) and junior and senior high school youths (Chaffee et al., 1970; Chaffee, 1977; Hawkins et al., 1975). Atkin and Neuendorf (1980) found children who watched national TV news were better able to recognize such figures as Iran's Ayatollah Khomeini, President Reagan and British Prime Minister Margaret Thatcher. Learning about politics from news and campaign advertising is greater among older children whose information-processing skills and cognitive abilities are more advanced than younger children (Atkin, 1981; Hirsch, 1971; Johnson, 1973; Tolley, 1973; Rubin, 1976, 1978; Hawkins et al., 1979; Jackson-Beeck, 1979). One study found that youths who watched crime shows on TV were more knowledgeable about a suspect's arrest rights (Dominick, 1974), and another found young people's images of lawyers and judges corresponding to TV stereotypes of these roles (Jeffries-Fox and Signorielli, 1979).

Interest and Feelings. As Atkin (1981) notes, the media have a significant influence on youths' affective orientations, their interest and feelings about government. The areas most affected by exposure to media news are interest, attitude towards leaders, and opinions about issues. In one study, elementary students who watched .TV news showed greater interest in the president's activities and major news events (Atkin and Neuendorf, 1980). Elementary and high school students who watch local and national network news show greater interest in city, state and national affairs (Drew and Reeves, 1980). In Israel, daily exposure to newspapers was related to an interest in political and social problems of that country. Tan (1981) notes that media use and political interest mutually affect each other as children develop. As youths become more interested in politics, they turn to the media for more of such content, which stimulates even greater interest.

More basic dispositions such as political trust and party identification appear to be more resistant to change, but they also have been linked to media use. Rubin (1978) found that youths who watched more public affairs and news programming on TV were more likely to show support for government. Byrne (1969) also linked TV news to government support, but Chaffee (1977) found print news media associated with feelings of political efficacy among high school seniors. Entertainment programming also has been related to young people's feelings about government. A survey of adolescents found those who watched adult entertainment such as *M*A*S*H* or *Fantasy Island* had more negative feelings toward the government while viewing juvenile shows such as *Happy Days* or *Wonder Woman* was related to positive feelings (Atkin, 1981). Sandell and Ostroff (1981) concluded that information about the American political system is often inaccurate or negative on TV entertainment programs likely to be seen by children. However, Marshall's (1981) content analysis of children's TV programs and books found media depicting characters as heros who are benevolent and competent and seldom involved in controversy. Elementary children who watched TV news viewing are more likely to identify with a political party, according to one study (Conway et al., 1975).

Media are not alone in their influence on youth's political feelings and evaluations. A survey of junior high school students the day after viewing the first televised presidential debate between Ford and Carter in 1976 found that youths reported more influence from parents than the media on decisions about who won the debate (Desmond and Donohue, 1981).

Stimulating Political Behaviors. Though children and other youths have limited opportunities to get involved in politics, some activities are open to them. They can discuss political topics with friends and parents. Such conversations seem to be more frequent among those youths who are exposed to more news in the media (Atkin and Greenberg, 1974; Roberts et al., 1975; Lewellen, 1976; Atkin and Gantz, 1978; Egan, 1978; Drew and Reeves, 1980). In one study, high school seniors who consumed more public affairs content from the media also engaged in such partisan activities as attending rallies, wearing buttons and campaign work (Lewellen, 1976).

Clearly, the political images and feelings about government held by children and adolescents are affected by mass media. However, most of the evidence so far is based on the short-term rather than long-range studies of political socialization. Though we would expect an accumulation of information acquired through media use, the influence of media on party identification, government support and other feelings is likely to interact with influences from other socializing agents, particularly parents and schools.

Summary

The evidence suggests that mass media have significant political effects during the routine political processes' such as election campaigns. However, the media are not blunt instruments used to influence the electorate at will, but rather complex vehicles that have some direct and indirect impact. So far, the media seem most successful in passing on political information and creating political images, and these cognitive effects are more direct. The media also help set the political agenda and have some influence on people's affective links and political behaviors. However, both activating mechanisms and filter mechanisms operate in conjunction with the media. The emerging perspective of political effects that seems most consistent with current knowledge is a contingency model which recognizes the direct impact of media as well as the individual differences and influence felt through other sources.

Media institutions also have the potential for longer-term effects, but evidence for such consequences is scanty and philosophical differences clutter the area. Certainly, the media do not act independently, and one line of inquiry emphasizes the ways in which the larger social structure affects media organization and performance. However, no institution operates in a vacuum and those who argue that the media cannot have "direct effects" on the electorate because they too are affected by the larger social structure beg the issue. The same logic would say democratic political institutions cannot operate independently on the electorate because their existence in the present form necessarily requires accommodation with such institutions as the communication media. The term "effects" can get in the way of our discussion.

A second line of inquiry posits that basic changes in media institutions and the growth of mass media have altered the political system in several ways, perhaps even undermining public trust and confidence in the government. Again, we argue that media structure and operations certainly are affected by other social institutions, but the reverse is also a clear possibility. The emergence of new communication technologies from sources "unknown" (serendipity) may enable new, different patterns of social organization. Arguing about which came first is less productive than trying to understand both the short and long term relationships between mass media and our political institutions.

Economic Effects
of the Media

In earlier chapters, we focused on the social and political effects of the mass media. Often economic constraints such as annual income appeared to limit media effects on individuals. At the national level, most observers have taken a "materialistic view," in which economic factors are the prime movers in determining social and political realities. However, the media also have an impact in the economic realm, chiefly through the advertising they carry. What are these economic effects of the mass media, and how do they operate to influence the production, distribution and consumption of material goods—the essence of economics? We'll try to answer those questions in this chapter.

Advertising has been surrounded by controversy almost from its first appearance. The criticism has grown rather than subsided, particularly with the arrival of television and fears that it would over emphasize material values to the exclusion of cultural, aesthetic and spiritual values. At the same time, advertising has been the subject of admiration for its function as a modern image maker and perceived capacity to accomplish great feats.

Our survey of the economic effects of the media raises some of the same questions faced in the chapter on political effects. First, are we explaining economic effects of the media on individuals or on "society?" We will examine the economic impact of media on individuals as well as on the marketplace and society. At both levels

289

we have the familiar "chicken-and-egg" problem of effects. At the individual level, do the media merely reinforce existing dispositions of the consuming public or does media advertising create wants and desires? And at the national level, does advertising merely reflect power divisions within society or does advertising produce further concentration and monopoly? Again we find that researchers are rephrasing the question to allow for both direct media effects as well as indirect effects, particularly at the individual level.

To sort out media economic effects, we will first look at the "advertising controversy" and the different ideological positions bearing on these questions. Then we will look at the impact of advertising on individual consumers. Here we will review the evidence for effects on people's cognitions (such as brand awareness), affective links to products (attitudes toward products), and behaviors (from intentions to actual purchases). Then we will see what intervening variables operate here. Considerations will include both characteristics of products and advertising as well as individual factors such as social categories and motivations. Next we will examine models of advertising effectiveness at the individual level and see how direct and indirect effects are handled.

After a discussion of the "advertising controversy" and research on how individual consumers are affected, we will move up to higher levels of analysis — the marketplace and society. Our last section will evaluate the arguments and evidence for advertising and media impact in the marketplace. It is at this level that our discussion turns on questions studied more frequently by economists than communication, business or sociological researchers.

The Advertising Controversy

Advertisers are accustomed to criticism. Although 17th century publications regarded the desire of someone to buy or sell something as news much like reports of war and other events, there were early signs of alarm. "Promise, large promise, is the soul of an advertisement," wrote Dr. Samuel Johnson, English author and critic, in the 18th century. That criticism has continued up through the present century. A review of 38 public opinion surveys between 1930 and 1980 shows changing attitudes by the American public and growing disenchantment with advertising in the recent decades (Zanot, 1981). There is some evidence of even more negative attitudes toward advertising among different subgroups such as the educated (Anderson, Engledow and Becker, 1978). Peebles and Ryans (1978) note there is evidence of declining public support and a deteriorating public image of advertising not only in the U.S. but in other countries as well. They assign some of the responsibility to increased government regulation and aggressive consumer movements. Stupening (1982) points to a similar concern over TV advertising in West Germany.   At the same time, other surveys have noted more support for advertising from the American public. Aaker and Norris (1982) studied viewers' evaluations of more than 500 prime time TV commercials and found that 40% were described as informative by a fifth of the viewers. Apparently some of the public see advertising as another factor providing balance in the marketplace. Adults in one metropolitan area were asked whether doctors should be allowed to advertise. More than half felt that advertising would force physicians to be more responsive to consumers' needs and would assist consumers in selecting physicians. Although only a fifth of the respondents felt the ads would be completey truthful, advertising was not believed to contribute negatively to professionalism. Younger and lower-income people were more positive about physician advertising (Vanier and Sciglimpaglia, 1981). This suggests that Americans are more supportive of the functions played by advertising than they are of the forms it frequently takes.

This split personality toward advertising also has some research to back it up. One model of attitude change distinguishes between generalized and personalized beliefs (Fishbein, 1975). Reid and Soley (1982) applied this to adults' perceptions of advertising, finding that people feel others are more susceptible to the social effects of advertising than they are. Thus, advertising is seen as insulting other people's intelligence, persuading others to buy unnecessary products, and misleading and deceiving *other* people. People were also asked about the economic effects of advertising. Again, there was a distinction made between general and personalized attitudes. People felt that advertising lowers rather than raises product prices but that the lower prices benefit other people more than themselves. They also thought that advertising results in better products, but other people were seen as benefiting more than themselves. No distinction in attitudes was found on whether advertising raises the standard of living.

The public's somewhat mixed feelings about advertising reflects the questions being asked both by supporters and by critics as well as the different value systems that often serve as the starting point when arguments are presented. The growth of advertising in communist countries also illustrates this ambiguous status. In the 1941 edition of the Great Soviet Encyclopedia, advertising was characterized as follows: "Hullabaloo, speculation and a mad race for profits have made advertising a means of swindling the people and of foisting upon them goods frequently useless or of dubious quality." Some three decades later, advertising in the U.S.S.R. was defined as "the popularization of goods with the aim of selling them, the creation of demand for these goods, the acquaintance of consumers with their quality, particular features and the location of their sales, and explanation of the methods of their use." During that same period the Soviet Union moved closer to a consumer society and advertising increased to become a multi-million dollar industry. In 1979 Chinese authorities decided to use advertising not only to sell Chinese goods abroad but to sell both foreign and Chinese goods at home (Anderson, 1981). Since China has been viewed as one model for development in the Third World, its introduction of advertising is likely to intensify interest in the arguments and evidence for the economic and other effects of advertising.

Some critics simply dislike advertising and demonstrate their antipathy in discussing its effects. Thus, we find that advertising: "manipulates" consumer consciousness (Ewan, 1976; Willis, 1970), creates "artificial" tastes (Janus, 1981) or "distorts" existing tastes (Littlechild, 1982), "violates" consumer autonomy (Arrington, 1982), "obstructs" competition and promotes monopoly (Janus, 1981), and has "distorting" effects on the media (Curran, 1981). However, if we can put the rhetoric aside, we find the critics constructing particular images of consumers and how they are affected by media advertising.

How malleable are consumers and how successful are advertisers in their efforts to control consumer behaviors? In the last chapter, we noted that some saw the voter as greatly affected by the media while others emphasized the activating and filtering mechanisms that inter-vene. A similar dichotomy exists in the economic arena, but the individual "role" is that of "consumer" rather than "voter." We will construct two ideal types reflecting different images of the consumer and see how the contrasting views fit in with national models of media advertising effects.

According to one image, the consumer is a pliable creature. Although not necessarily defenseless, individual behaviors almost certainly comply with the designs of larger social forces. The decisions individuals make are not particularly important. "When consumers do decide to buy one brand rather than another, for example, the result is seen as wasteful, with no gain in total sales or other significant benefits (Littlechild, 1982). Such an image of the consumer is included in Ewan's (1976) portrait of advertisers as the "captains of conscious-ness." He sees the American advertising industry manipulating consumer desires and enabling corporations to channel discontent into purchasing behaviors where it is neutralized. No real social change is possible with such corporate control over consciousness, the argument goes. Thus, advertisers have defused opposition from the Left, fem-inists and others by appropriating their language and style but not the substance of dissent. Schudson (1981) notes that Ewan claims too much on too little evidence, but the arguments do illustrate how the image of a malleable consumer is crucial to arguments about advertising control at the societal level: if the individual is easily affected, then influence shifts to those who control advertising and the media. At this level, then, the question is recast to ask how media advertising is affected by other institutions, A materialist interpretation sees media advertising as simply operating to meet the marketing needs of the capitalist system and reflecting class inequalities (Curran, 1981). In this process corporations and other elites alter media forms to suit advertising-marketing needs. Janus (1981:15) posits a direct correspondence where "the patterns of production determine, to a significant degree, the patterns of consumption." Advertising also is seen as a force promoting monopolies because it raises profits of corporations and makes it more difficult for new firms to enter the competition; thus, advertising supports the continued growth of existing corporate forces according to this view.

What is it about consumer behavior that is so easily affected in this scenario? Some suggest that advertising can control consumer "consciousness" by creating images out of whole cloth. Thus, cognitive effects are attributed to advertising. However, it is on affective dimensions that the most controversial effects are envisioned. Schudson (1981) notes that one proposition put forth by critics sees advertising shaping or creating human needs and desires, artificially constructing various wants. Willis (1970: 76) wrote that "the most widely accepted tenet of the movement ideology...is the idea that we are psychically manipulated by the mass media to crave more and more consumer goods." The same assumption is made by economist John Kenneth Galbraith (1967) who sees this "ability" of advertising as ensuring that the public will continue to need more material goods and have an incentive to work toward unlimited horizons. Advertising is also seen as altering consumer behaviors in addition to cognitive images and desires, wishes, wants (Janus, 1981). Through such manipulation of consumers, advertising and the media are seen as necessarily promoting and reinforcing values and visions of Western capitalist society (Schudson, 1981).

Another image of the consumer portrays an individual who engages in at least some rational decision-making regarding his or her economic interests and personal needs and desires (Arrington, 1982; Littlechild, 1982). Arrington cites two defenses of advertising that reflect this view of the consumer. First, individual preferences should count: when consumers use advertising to reflect personal interests in the open market, those purchasing decisions become preferences which affect the producers. Influence flows up rather than down. Advertising, thus, allows industry to provide consumers with what they want. Clearly, by attributing free will and some ability to make individual choices, the influence attributed to corporate elites is reduced and shifted downward in part. A second defense is that "pre-advertising" preferences are not the only "genuine" ones. In one sense, critics of advertising would have to locate pre-industrial situations in order to identify "pure" needs and desires untainted by modern images which have influenced the range of alternatives on which people base their desires. Duesenberry (1949) argued that consumers are not manipulated by advertising but that consumer tastes are relative to those of other consumers. Thus, people see goods around them superior to what they own and believe high quality goods to be desirable and important. We would add that even when goods are not immediately perceptible, advertising makes the range known, and this could have the same effect. While this is not a totally rational model, it does give the individual some autonomy to stymie efforts of advertisers to manipulate one's cognitions, affect, and behavioral intentions. In this process, advertising is also viewed as having not only persuasive intentions for industry but also informational value for consumers. Evidence indicates that consumers prefer abundant information when they buy (Patton, 1984). Most of the discussions and research on advertising have been conducted by sociologists, business researchers and economists rather than communication scholars. Thus, advertising has been treated as a "commodity" rather than mass communication content much of the time. However, Beales, Craswell and Salop (1981) examine advertising as a form of consumer information that is important to efficient markets in which consumers are seen as somewhat rational creatures but still subject to potential deception or information failures. This second image of the consumer clearly supports a more benign view of advertising in society—one with both informational benefits for consumers and persuasive consequences for producers. Most demand for product information is derived from the demand for products themselves. To satisfy this demand, a diverse set of information sources has arisen in the modern industrial economy. This includes past experience and purchased information from such sources as journalists, attorneys and consultants (Beales et al., 1981: 502). The economic incentive for consumers to gather information is strong since it increases the efficiency of purchase decisions. Sellers also have a substantial economic incentive to disseminate information to consumers since, without it, all brands would be viewed as equivalent.

This second image of the consumer more closely approximates the current view of media effects among communication scholars. It's also more consistent with the way advertising is treated in most democratic societies. Recently, in striking down a state law restricting the dissemination of consumer information, the U.S. Supreme Court brought "commercial speech" at least partly within the protection of the First Amendment (see Beales et al., 1981: 493). At the same time, the Federal Trade Commission actively seeks informational remedies for market information failures in the belief that such adjustments still leave consumers free to make their own choices and introduce less rigidity into the market. "Such remedies leave the market free to respond as consumer preferences and production technologies change over time" (Beales et al., 1981: 513). This perspective on advertising as communication also reflects a somewhat "agnostic" stance toward how much we understand about the relationships between media advertising, consumer decisions, and other social forces. In other words, rather than try to answer the "chicken-and-egg" problem, we will allow for several possibilities — that advertising has direct effects on consumers, that consumers can affect the marketplace through their decisions and processing of advertising, that advertising reflects the economic structure in some fashion, and that the emergence of new technologies may upset existing relationships regardless of historical precedent.

In the next section, we will examine the evidence bearing on the question of how and whether advertising affects individual consumer decisions. Note how the research clarifies our view of the consumer.

How Does Advertising Affect the Individual Consumer?

Media advertising can affect consumers in several ways (See Lipstein and McGuire's massive bibliography, 1978). Advertising contains at least a minimum of information about products and services available. By providing such information, advertisers hope to fill in people's cognitive maps. Advertisers also try to create favorable attitudes toward their products and specific brands and to link such products to existing needs. Lastly, advertisers hope to stimulate actual purchase behaviors. Thus, media advertising can have cognitive, affective and behavioral effects on consumers.

Cognitive Effects

Recall of advertisements is widely used as a measure of advertising effectiveness because recall is seen as a necessary condition for a change in attitude (affect) and behavior. Advertisers hypothesize that if the purpose of advertising is to sell, it must communicate. Ads that communicate best are the ones that will produce the greatest memory impression (Perry and Perry, 1976). The need for on-going programs of advertising is supported by evidence that unaided recall of the content starts to decline sharply once advertising stops (Zielske and Henry, 1980). Reekie (1982) refers to empirical studies which show that advertising can increase consumer awareness and acquaint them with both available choices and additions to that range. Increased awareness through advertising also has been linked to advertising in all the media. For example, a study of advertising by the Bell System found that the more time people spent listening to the radio, the greater the probability they became aware of an advertised message. Cognitive effects also have been achieved by advertising aimed at specialized audiences. Leffler (1981) found that pharmaceutical advertising informs physicians about the existence and characteristics of new products while also producing brand name recall effects that favor established products. However, as Faber and Storey (1984) note, free recall of advertising can also be quite low; they found that a third of the people surveyed failed to recall anything of election advertising.

Agenda-setting is a cognitive effect of the media which has generally been restricted to the political arena. However, Sutherland and Galloway (1981) have suggested applying the process to the area of advertising effects. Accordingly, prominence of products or ideas in the media (primarily through advertising) should increase the salience of the brand, and that should lead to such behavioral outcomes as purchasing. In the first of these two links, frequent ad exposure would produce greater brand salience. They note that products heavily advertised would have a status conferred upon them and are seen as the "most popular" products. Just as the "ordinary person" does not appear on TV, neither does the "ordinary product" (Sutherland and Galloway, 1981: 27). Sissors (1978) also notes the media's ability to disseminate information about the majority's value systems to a large audience, creating what Sutherland and Galloway call perceived popularity or "climate of opinion." Many of those in the audience are unaware of the majority's values or the cognitive effects achieved through the communication. To test their notion that media advertising can engage in such agenda setting and produce images that the advertised products are superior, Sutherland and Galloway (1981) surveyed homemakers on their use of a variety of products from toothpaste to TV and disposable diapers. They also asked which brands the respondents thought were used by the greatest number of people, and why that was the case. A fourth of the respondents included in their reply something about the brand's frequency or quality of advertising. The brand thought to be most popular also was related to brand awareness, the first brand recalled being the one seen as most popular.

In summary, advertising does appear quite successful at teaching people about the range of brands available, as well as other product information. Such cognitive effects parallel those found in the political arena.

Advertisement for "bear brand" canned milk and other products in the public market, Baguio city, the Philippines.

Impact on Attitudes

Through the years, efforts to change people's attitudes have met limited success if any, whether in product marketing, politics, or other areas. Two decades ago researcher Joseph Klapper's (1960) classic statement that the media had minimal effects was based largely on evidence that attempts to change attitudes and opinions were largely unsuccessful in the short run because of a variety of filtering mechanisms. To be sure, there are different models of persuasion and opinion or attitude change (see Roloff and Miller, 1980), but it is the affective dimension — liking or disliking a brand, for example — which has garnered the most attention. And there is some evidence that media and advertising can have at least a limited impact on the affective dimension. For example, Payne and Caron (1982) found exposure to American media related to more favorable attitudes toward U.S. products in a Canadian sample. Messmer (1979) found evidence that exposure to TV advertising influenced people's brand attitudes, with the greatest gain obtained at the first exposure. However, prior attitudes mediated the effects of exposure. The impact of corrective advertsing required by the Federal Trade Commission is another opportunity to detect changes in attitude. As Beales et al. (1981) note, the FTC uses a variety of information remedies to correct what are identified as "deceptive advertising" practices. These include requirements to disclose additional information and corrections of past information. Both have the potential to change not only basic beliefs about products but also people's evaluations of them. Armstrong, Gurol and Russ (1979) found support in an experiment for the proposition that corrective ads can have a significant effect on reducing deception. Armstrong, Franke and Russ (1982) examined changes in Warner-Lambert's image over the course of the Listerine corrective campaign. Four national probability samples of adult mouthwash users showed changes in perceived trustworthiness, although the changes were slight. The company's image decreased initially but attitudes of trustworthiness and success rose again by the time of the fourth survey wave. Thus, the affective consequences of the corrective advertising were only temporary.

Both affect and cognition are viewed with interest because they are seen as precursors to the focal behavioral change—product purchasing.

Affecting Behavior

The "bottom line" is generally the purchase of products advertised, although other types of overt behaviors also may be the target in some advertising campaigns. Peretti and Lucas (1975) found that reading newspaper advertising was linked to increased purchases of advertised items. The frequency of advertising exposure sufficient to produce desired purchasing behavior varies with product and other circumstances. Naples (1981) concluded that a single exposure of an ad to a target group during a purchase cycle (for example, weekly grocery shopping for items purchased each week) has little effect in most situations, but an exposure frequency of three was effective and efficient. Some evidence shows advertising having a reinforcing rather than a brand-switching impact. Raj (1982) conducted an experiment which split cable TV viewers into two groups for reception of varying amounts of advertising. He found that increased advertising about a frequently-purchased grocery item—Brand A—seemed to protect loyal buyers from drifting to competing brands. However, those loyal to other brands—such as Brand B—did not switch to Brand A but merely decreased their purchases of Brand B.

Although adults' retail shopping is the major focus of advertising efforts, other audiences and other behaviors also merit attention. As noted in Chapter Six, children's purchase behaviors and consumption patterns can also be affected by advertising. Gorn and Goldberg (1982) conducted an experiment with children ages 5-8, exposing them to 14 consecutive days of TV food and beverage messages. The children saw a different half-hour videotaped Saturday morning cartoon each after-noon just before making their snack choices. The TV programs contained either candy commercials, fruit commercials, public service announcements on nutrition, or no commercial messages at all. Results indicated that children's snack choices were affected by exposure to the different food messages during the two week period. Children who viewed candy commercials picked candy over fruit as snacks. Elim-inating the candy commercials proved as effective in encouraging the selection of fruit as did exposing the children to fruit commercials or the nutrition-oriented public service announcements. Another group, physicians, as examined in one study which found that the doctor's awareness of medical journal ads enhanced prescribing the products advertised. This link occurred despite the physicians' acknowledged skepticism toward ads directed at them and their view of themselves as being unaffected by such commercial advertising appeals.

Efforts at achieving lifestyle behavioral changes through advertising have proven quite difficult. Hutton (1982) notes that motivating consumers to conserve energy has proven a difficult task in the U.S., and the Department of Energy has used paid advertising on a limited basis as part of its program. A more optimistic conclusion is drawn from a large-scale field experiment which showed a 20-minute cable TV program dramatizing simple conservation strategies. Winett et al. (1984) conclude that significant savings on electricity resulted even without intensive face-to-face contact. Rice and Paisley (1981) also report on successful public communication campaigns. The effects of the anti-cigarette advertising required by the FCC and the subsequent federal ban in 1971 on all broadcast cigarette ads were small when compared to the large impact occurring as a result of other communi-cation and persuasive efforts (Schneider, Klein and Murphy, 1981).

In summary, although some evidence links advertising exposure to product purchasing, the support is limited and behaviors other than purchasing seem more resistant to such media persuasion. As we found in the last chapter, direct effects of the media are constrained by a variety of activators or filter mechanisms which will be examined in the following section.

Filters and Activators

Between advertising and prescribed effects (cognitive, affective and behavioral) lie both activating and filtering mechanisms that may alter the impact or direction of media influence. Included here are: individual characteristics (social categories), people's motivations and past experience with the products advertised (uses and gratifications), situational factors, and so forth. Those who conduct advertising campaigns are certainly aware of the importance of these mediating variables (Korgaonkar et al., 1984).

Prior Attitudes and Experiences. The prior experience people have with products and their attitudes towards brands affect the way information from advertising is processed. The consumer's mind is not a blank slate on which advertisers write. A new McDonald's commercial, for example, is interpreted in terms of such familiar categories as fast-food restaurants and hamburgers. Gronhaug (1975) found, for example, that the inexperienced buyer tends to see advertising information as difficult to handle. Messmer (1979) found that people's prior attitudes mediated the effects of exposure in an experiment, and Olson, Schlinger and Young (1982) found that consumers are more skeptical of the claims for new products than for existing brands. Thus, they tend to "counterargue" more when watching commercials for new brands. In counterarguing, people mentally engage in the process of arguing back, attempting to refute the persuasive appeal. This acts as a filter which reduces the impact of the advertising. Schlinger (1982) also found evidence that attitudinal responses to TV commercials are influenced by brand usage and preferences.

The advertising industry was quick to realize the importance of findings that consumers' attitudes, needs and values influenced purchasing decisions (Horowitz and Kaye, 1975). Today, advertisers promote not only their product but its symbolism to the consumer's self concept and striving for social recognition. Personal factors such as values and motives serve to modify the message communicated by the advertisment. Dolich (1969) found that preferred brands were evaluated as more consistent with people's self concept than were other brands.

People's Uses and Gratifications. People's preferences for media as consumer information vehicles vary, and this also affects the impact achieved by advertising. The public's use of media advertising as a source of consumer information has been documented in national surveys (Opinion Research Corp., 1979). Hirschman and Mills (1980) found a high incidence of newspaper use as an information source for major shopping trip decisions. Lynn (1981) found all audience segments exposed to advertising in nonmetro newspapers. One three-city survey found that the extent to which audiences find ads useful varies with the media in which they appear as well as individual orientations and demographic characteristics (O'Keefe, Nash and Liu, 1981). Ads in newspapers were seen as more useful than those in other media.

Furthermore, the more exposure a person had to a given medium, the more useful the ads in that medium were considered and the greater the utility ascribed to them, particularly for print. Thus, people who spent more time reading a newspaper or who read a paper more often found newspaper advertising more useful and paid greater attention to it. Uses and gratifications serve to activate consumers, so we would expect the use of particular media for consumer information would enhance the ability of advertising in those media to affect consumers' decision-making. Advertising credibility of the media also differs. One small study found that the credibility of media advertising varies by product category (Durand, Teel, and Bearden, 1979). For example, while newspapers were found most credible for grocery advertising, television was most credible for furniture advertising and radio was rated low on all of the five product categories except furniture. The categories were automobiles, furniture, groceries, political candidates, and public service ads. People's preference for the TV program and degree of involvement also have been found to enhance product recall from the accompanying advertising (Burke, 1978, Yuspeh and Kover, 1979; Yuspeh, 1980). Thus, since people tend to be less "involved" in their viewing of TV newscasts than of programs such as action-adventure shows, we would expect them to do a poorer job of recalling commercials imbedded in news programs.

In summary, people's uses and gratifications of media advertising serve as activators while existing attitudes, prior experience, perceived credibility and other factors act as filtering mechanisms.

Consumer Characteristics. Numerous individual characteristics act as filters in consumers' processing of advertising messages. Generally, advertisers are interested in social categories for two purposes. One, they indicate purchasing power, and two, they serve as "locating" devices for targeting messages. Most important are age, an ascriptive factor, sex, and three achievement-oriented factors: education, income, and occupational status. Sex is important because a dispro-portionate share of the most highly-advertised consumer products (for example, groceries, household products, personal grooming products) are purchased by women. Age indicates people's life-cycle position and the types of products most appropriate to them (for example, child care in the 20's and 30's). The three indicators of social class are useful to advertisers because they indicate wealth and consuming ability. All of these variables in varying combinations represent media use patterns and content preferences that aid advertisers in targeting advertising messages. Thus, because consumer characteristics have such obvious utility to advertisers, they often have not been viewed as filtering mechanisms which alter media advertising effects but rather as simple locators of people subject to persuasive attempts. Research relating such consumer characteristics to advertising and persuasive communication is abundant. A massive bibliography of communication processes published by the Advertising Research Foundation (Lipstein and McGuire, 1978) lists almost a thousand citations under demographic characteristics. Here are a few examples of how such characteristics may act as filters in the processing of media advertising (Schlinger, 1982). Some studies show that recall of TV commercials declines with rising age (Burke, 1978; Young, 1972). Evidence on education and family income is mixed, with some reports that ad recall is unaffected by the two variables (Burke, 1978) and others showing a positive relationship (ARS, 1978). Looking at effects on behaviors rather than recall, Peretti and Lucas (1975) found that lower class consumers were affected by newspaper advertising more than middle class consumers. However, Bowen (1982) found that lower-income groups were more critical of advertising in general and preferred pertinent consumer information in their favorite medium, television. He argues for a model of communication effects in which information is the major mediator influencing the affective relationship between the consumer and the product. Munson and Spivey (1981) survey a number of studies that identify differences in consumption between social classes. Their own study also found differences in brand perceptions that seem to reflect their ability to communicate symbolically. Women interviewed were asked to use 15 different scales (such as successful-unsuccessful, informed-uninformed, etc.) in evaluating "a person who owns or prefers" each of a series of brands that included such highly expressive products as automobiles and magazines and low value-expressive products as brassieres, deodorants and laundry detergents. Significant differences in brand-user stereotypes were found between upper and lower social class women for seven of the value expressive brands (such as Chrysler, Ford, Vogue, Playboy), but only two of the three utilitarian product brands were seen differently (Right Guard deodorant and Salvo detergent). Clearly, social status differences may act as filters in processing advertising messages, but more research is needed to substantiate that social status differences actually mediate cognitive, affective or behavioral effects.

What Advertising Works?

Advertisers use a variety of techniques to achieve the desired cognitive, affective and behavioral effects already discussed. Although research does play an increasing part, successful advertising often depends on intuition, creative hunches and serendipity. Ogilvy and Raphaelson (1982) argue that advertising would be more effective if creative people used accumulated research data to learn which techniques are most likely to work.

Many of the ingredients of successful advertising represent appeals to consumers' desires for gratification or information, tastes or preferences based on self-images and goals, and a hierarchy of needs ranging from physical needs like food and sex to secondary needs representing self-fulfillment. We will examine some of the evidence on advertising puffery, comparative ads, time-size-&-placement, appeals to sex and humor, and the human images presented.

Puffery. The legal assumption is that consumers expect exaggerated claims in advertising—called "puffery'"—and, therefore, they know certain statements are not to be believed as facts. There is some evidence that people discount puffery (VandenBergh and Fink, 1983). But in one study, literal puffery claims in five commercials were communicated to some 80% of the members of community groups, while implied puffs were successfully communicated to 45%; such evidence casts doubt on the current legal logic that advertising claims considered to be puffery are not deceptive because they are not believed (Rotfeld and Rotzoll, 1980, 1981). After a review of the literature on advertising puffery, Oliver (1979) concludes that puffery achieves its intended impact through a combination of pre-exposure and post-purchase effects. Puffed claims create high expectations used in attitude and intention formation prior to purchase. The nature of those claims is such that many cannot be disconfirmed after purchase. How, for example, do you confirm that a toothpaste has made you sexier? Other claims are repressed because consumers are reluctant to acknowledge the discrepancy. In a similar vein are qualifying statements and disclaimers accompanying ads. Moore and Pride (1980) found that qualifying statements in newspaper ads reduced readers' confidence in the claim, but Lovil and Padderud (1981) found TV viewers not very successful at recalling video disclaimers accompanying commercials. Certainly, the research on puffery cautions us from assuming that we can make easy distinctions between hard facts and soft images.

Comparative Ads. Some of the earliest research on persuasion and propaganda compared the impact of different message structures. Which is more persuasive, a message giving only one side or one which compares your arguments with another's? Advertisers have increasingly used comparisons in advertising, and researchers are asking similar questions about commercial messages. An analysis of almost 2,400 magazine ads found comparative ads contained more information than noncomparative ads (Harmon et al., 1983). Murphy and Amundsen (1981) compared three different ads using comparative appeals in an experiment—a direct comparison between two brands, a Brand X reference to the dominant brand, and a non-comparative appeal. There was no difference in brand recall, but the non-comparative appeal was seen as more believable than either the direct comparison or Brand X appeal. In another experiment, a comparative ad was rated as more informative than a non-comparative ad, but recall of product features was not aided by the comparative format. Students in this experiment thought both ads were equally informative about the product (Earl and Pride, 1980). And yet a third experiment found that a two-sided comparative appeal yielded more positive attitudes toward a new brand being introduced than did the more traditional, one-sided comparison appeal. In this case, the two-sided ad incorporated both positive and negative arguments about the product, a technique called immunization (Etgar and Goodwin, 1982). Smith and Hunt (1978) also demonstrated that advertisements with two-sided product claims were seen as more truthful than one-sided claims. Certainly, there are many distinct message formats and probably different effects depending on the nature of the product and the audience (Demirdjian, 1983). The research on comparative advertising illustrates the pitfalls of trying to generalize from a single study or relying on intuition. Successful advertising must take into account the product, audience characteristics, the medium used, the type of effects desired (cognitive, affective, behavioral), the consuming environment and the competitive environment (other brands).

Time, Size and Placement. A popular TV commercial for Federal Express featured a fast-talking, fast-moving salesman who managed to condense an incredible amount of sorting/filing/stamping/cutting and talking into a brief commercial that provoked laughter and positive consumer reactions. MacLachlan and LaBarbera (1978) found that time-compressed commercials elicited more interest and recall than those played at normal speed, although their findings were not based on the exaggerated speeds of the Federal Express commercial. An experiment using business students found that the faster spokesperson in a commercial was rated more favorably on 13 of 16 scales but there was no difference in terms of friendliness. The faster talker was considered more enthusiastic and knowledgeable (MacLachlan, 1982), but other evidence suggests that time compression may suppress emotional involvement (Schlinger et al., 1983). Lautman and Dean (1983) conclude that time compression does not produce gains promised in recall or other factors.

Size and location of advertising can also be determining factors (Houston and Scott, 1984), although not necessarily so. Soley (1982) analyzed advertising readership in a dozen different daily newspapers. He found that ads in the front section and the "women's section" were read more often than those in the sports section. Placement also affected whether men or women read them, but increases in newspaper ad size did not give the larger advertiser an incremental competitive advantage over the smaller advertiser. Size in print and time in broadcasting are equivalent measures, just as location within the programming schedule and position within the newspaper represent similar targeting efforts. Location on the page can also be a factor. Recent research uses eye-movement monitoring techniques which measure the number of eye fixations on different parts of the page. Such research suggests that textual elements positioned in the top half of an ad are acquired by readers more than those in the lower half. Copy receives the most attention in the upper left and the least attention in the lower left section, which is consistent with previous studies (Kroeber-Riel and Barton, 1980). Decisions to glance at an ad are made quickly and the amount of time people devote to a particular advertisement, either print or broadcast, is brief indeed. Thus, such technical research as that monitoring eye movements may prove fruitful for advertisers focusing on how to capture the attention of readers, viewers or listeners for a matter of seconds. Sparked by competition from other media, newspapers also are resorting to the use of more color today, both in editorial and advertising copy. Two experiments which compared the effectiveness of color vs. black-and-white ads found that color ads produced higher sales on reduced price items than did the other ads (Sparkman and Austin, 1980).

Appeals: Sex, Humor, and Music. Appeals would seem to be a relatively easy ingredient to feature in advertisements. One merely selects the pertinent need (such as food) and appeal linking the need and product to the target consumer. However, there are a variety of advertising effects and anticipated consequences may not be forthcoming. Joseph (1982) notes that studies have shown people make more favorable evaluations of ads and their products when attractive models are used, but opinion change studies indicate that attractive sources are not seen as trustworthy, honest, expert or intelligent. Furthermore, the evidence on message recall consistently and clearly shows that model attractiveness does not enhance message recall, although it may facilitate recognition of the ad. Carrying appeals to attraction a bit further, Alexander and Judd (1978) looked at the impact of nudity in ads on male university students. They used five nudity levels that ranged from the pastoral scene to a full frontal view exposing the model's face, breasts, pubic area and legs. More brand names were recalled for ads containing nonsexual pastoral scenes than any of those with varying levels of nudity. Although the amount of nudity was not important, brand recall did not decrease as the explicitness of nudity in the ad increased. Sex can have an impact on affect, however. Friedman and Dripple (1978) found sex-linked brand names having an impact on product reactions. A cigarette labeled "April" received better evaluations from women while the same cigarette called "Frontiersman" received more positive evaluations from men. Women reacted more strongly than men to the brand name influence. Gender differences in reactions to ads with sexual content also have been found (Bello, Pitts and Etzel, 1983).

Humor evokes different emotions in people, and these can affect the consumer's processing of advertising content. In one experiment, Cantor and Venus (1980) found that people recalled more of a radio ad when they heard it in a serious version than when they heard it in a humorous version. Working with another medium, Madden and Weinberger (1982) found that humor worked better for men than for women in attracting attention to magazine advertising. Humor seemed to decrease attention levels for readers of black-oriented magazines such as *Ebony*. Moving from cognitive effects to affect, we find that mild humor can be a more effective device than mild fear in developing favorable responses to such products as tooth brushes and vaccines (Brooker, 1981). Ads following a humorous message were more favorably received than those following a non-humorous one. Music also is used to create an affective link between consumers and products. Gorn (1982) found that hearing music which was liked or disliked while being exposed to a product in a commercial affected product preferences. In general, advertising practitioners discount the effectiveness of humor or find it harms recall (Madden and Weinberger, 1984; Sutherland and Middleton, 1983).

People, Models, and Images. In recent years, women, minorities, the aged, and ethnic groups have sought to improve both their image and representation in TV commercials in the expectation that the impact would be favorable for their constituencies. At the same time, Lee Iacocca of Chrysler Corp. has popularized commercials featuring chief executives. Assorted celebrities have peddled everything from denture cleaners (Martha Raye) to soft drinks (Michael Jackson, Joe Montana). How successful are these human images in advertising messages? Kerin and Barry (1981) found that the presence of a chief executive officer improved identification and recall in one experiment. Friedman and Friedman (1979) also found that celebrity endorsement was effective in sustaining brand-name recall for several different products including cookies, costume jewelry, and a vacuum cleaner. Analyzing past research, Ogilvy and Raphaelson (1982) note that TV commercials built around celebrities are not very successful in changing brand preferences but are recalled better than other types of commercials. In contrast, slice-of-life commercials have been shown to be markedly better at changing brand preferences than are those featuring celebrities. There also is some evidence that commercials with unusual casting perform above average in changing brand preference. Whipple and Courtney (1980) measured the influence of sex role depictions on the effectiveness and irritation of advertising. Commercials which portrayed female product representatives, showed working housewives, depicted men participating in household tasks, and used female voice-overs were all rated as effective when matched with commercials employing more traditional portrayals. But exaggerated presentations of the sexes, whether traditional or nontraditional, caused significant consumer irritation. Continued research on reactions to roles and ethnic images in advertising are needed because of changes in audience attitudes. Early research in the 1960s, for example, found some resistance to ads featuring minorities, but that reaction has faded.

Changing the Question on Advertising Effects
Not *Whether* but *How* Are Effects Achieved?

The advertiser is interested in the ad and the response it evokes. The "bottom line" is that advertising sells products, with relatively little interest in learning why. However, with rapidly changing audiences and complex environments, what worked today may not work tomorrow. Thus, lists of yesterday's "effects" are insufficient for handling tomorrow's problems. In recent years, an important development in media effects research has been the rise of models and theories which attempt to explain why various effects occur. The focus in advertising is the consumer and how he processes information from advertisements. This information-processing has consequences for the subsequent effects on people's behaviors. Although there are numerous models attempting to integrate research in this area, we will discuss only three: cognitive structures and the hierarchy of effects; cognitive processing; and the well-known models on subliminal effects.

Cognitive Structures and the Hierarchy-of-Effects

Throughout our discussions of effects we have referred to three types of variables affected by the media: cognitive, affective, and conative (or behavioral intention). These three categories are the traditional components used to represent attitudes. An attitude refers to a tendency or predisposition to respond in a consistent manner regarding some object. Thus, you may think, feel and act favorably toward a major department store or computer game. Though advertisers are interested in overt purchase behaviors in the final analysis, they target their commercial messages at the other goals as well—changing people's cognitive maps by shaping or changing beliefs about products, intensifying or altering the positive or negative feelings people have about brands, and influencing the intent to purchase (conative). How are these antecedent goals linked to the final purchase behavior? Is there any order in which changes occur? What individual characteristics affect this change process?

Lavidge and Steiner (1961) summarized previous work on how consumers process information with a six-stage model which Palda (1966) labeled a hierarchy of effects because each step was considered a necessary but insufficient condition for each succeeding step: awareness, knowledge, liking, preference, conviction, purchase. The steps were later summarized under the following response sequence:

$$Cognition \longrightarrow Affect \longrightarrow Conation$$

Though there was some support for the stages, the causal ordering was criticized and seldom observed in the research. Instead, the ordering which appeared more often was: cognition $\longrightarrow$ conation $\longrightarrow$ affect. A conceptual framework was developed to reconcile the different orderings.

The key concept introduced to explain the different sequences is individual involvement. The concept is particularly significant for advertisers with the growing importance of TV commercials. Newspaper reading is believed to require greater involvement than TV viewing which is seen as a more passive behavior (Klein, 1981). With low involvement, people "learn" the cognitive images, though advertising appears limited to the formation of lower order, less important beliefs. Since people are not very involved, they do not evaluate the incoming advertising messages. Thus, attitudes are not formed until later, generally after someone has actually purchased the product advertised. The actual purchasing behavior occurs because the individual has learned about the brand or product from the advertising and decides to try it out based on the advertising claims. The actual development of an attitude is based on personal experience. Certainly, even with this scenario, all TV viewing would not be low on the involvement scale (Soldow and Principe, 1981), but would depend on the individual and other circumstances. Witek (1981) argues that direct response advertising will become world-wide with interactive TV; the relationship between viewers and their TV's will become personal and active, and involvement will characterize consumption of TV advertising.

With high involvement, the sequence of people's responses to advertising would remain in the original order, cognitions developing from exposure to advertising, followed by the formation of attitudes and subsequent behaviors acted out as the third stage. For most people, the purchase of big-ticket items such as an automobile or home are important and relatively risky decisions not made lightly (Traylor, 1981). In those cases, according to the hierarchy-of-effects model, we would expect people's cognitions to change first. People would engage in considerable information seeking and acquire both lower-order and higher-order beliefs. The formation of attitudes comes next, and here we might expect our first-time car buyer to develop an attitude toward the vehicle make (for example, Ford or Chrysler). Lastly, the actual purchase intention develops (See Lehman, 1977, for an example). There also is a third response sequence, in which an individual's behavioral intention or actual decision comes first, followed by a change of attitude to bolster the decision and then selective learning that supports the other two stages. This is called the "dissonance-attribution" hierarchy; it is the exact reverse of the high involvement, learning hierarchy. We would expect to find this occurring when product alternatives are seen as almost indistinguishable and the consumer is forced to make a choice before there is time to collect much information or to develop an attitude. Once the product has been purchased and a commitment made, the individual develops an attitude and then reduces dissonance or "rationalizes" the decision, sometimes by adding new supportive beliefs. However, if the product is a rather inexpensive one, then there is no need to make a major commitment and the actual purchase becomes an efficient method for collecting information. Thus, in addition to the need to know about an individual's involvement, we need to know whether the individual's behavior reflects a trial or actual adoption (Smith and Swinyard, 1982). There is some research which supports the hierarchy of effects, but there also are questions. More work will be required to integrate the different strains of theory and research. (For criticism and an elaboration of the hierarchy of effects model, see Perloff, 1984, Smith and Swinyard, 1982; Ray, 1973; Houston and Rothschild, 1977; Greenwald and Leavitt, 1984).

Smith and Swinyard (1982) provide a model which integrates the key concepts of involvement, commitment, and response order (see Figure 8-1). The top line in Figure 8-1 represents exposure to advertising which normally generates a minimal acceptance of the message. This is usually seen as a vested interest source which is discounted, rejected, negatively evaluated. As a consequence, advertising normally generates only lower order beliefs. In the model, involvement is referred to as information acceptance. As a consequence, people have little information and are uncertain about the product's characteristics. They may simply fail to collect additional information to avoid the associated risk, or they may seek out more information from advertising, other people, or direct experience gained from a trial. This moves us to the bottom line where actual experience leads to the devel-

Figure 8-1

Smith and Swinyard's Integrated Information Response Model

Summary Labels

cognition - - - ►trial- - - ► affect- - - ► commitment

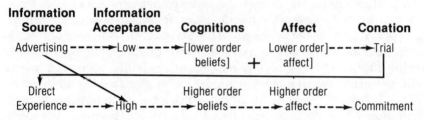

Detailed Sequence

Information Source	Information Acceptance	Cognitions	Affect	Conation
Advertising - - - - ►Low - - - - ►		[lower order beliefs] **+**	Lower order] - - - - ►Trial affect]	
Direct Experience - - - - ► High - - - - - ►		Higher order beliefs - - - - ►	Higher order affect - - - ►	Commitment

Source: Robert E. Smith and William R. Swinyard, "Information Response Models: An Integrated Approach," *Journal of Marketing* (Winter, 1982) 46(1): 85. Used with permission.

opment of more important beliefs and stronger feelings about the product. At the end a commitment is made, and this may appear as "brand loyalty," a desirable outcome from the point of view of most advertisers.

The integrated response model posits the same sequence based on consumer involvement, but it distinguishes between behaviors which are a trial run and those representing commitment. This distinction seems particularly useful in the consumer area because the bulk of the products advertised in the media represent little risk or thought prior to purchase. Additional sequences can be developed from the information response model. Its authors use the model for organizing studies dealing with advertising of products ranging from food to household items, cars, consumer durables, mouth wash, political issues and candidates, and Red Cross donations (Smith and Swinyard, 1982: 87-89). While the integrated model appears promising, more research is needed before its utility is recognized.

Others subjecting the hierarchy of effects model to critical scrutiny have suggested more substantial changes. Moriarty (1983) proposes replacing hierarchy and process-oriented approaches with a model based on three domains of message effects: perception, education and persuasion. These three domains are seen as equally important, inter-dependent and operating simultaneously. Continuing the debate, Preston and Thorson (1984) argue that hierarchy models still provide the best way to guide organization of advertising plans because they provide an outline of points that should be covered in an advertising plan and guide measurement, control and review of the advertising program.

Cognitive Processing Models

The hierarchy-of-effects has several limitations. First, as Perloff (1984) notes, the research supporting the low-involvement sequence is limited and what does exist is not very compelling. A second problem is the failure of the hierarchy model to explain how voters process advertising messages under conditions of high and low involvement and how these lead to behavioral change. Perloff (1984) directs us to focus on "how" media content leads to the various sequences identified. One model which does that is called the Cognitive Response model. Its basic premise is that spontaneous thoughts (cognitive reponses) are elicited by exposure to media advertising (or other media content) and these thoughts act as direct mediators of attitude formation or change. The cognitive response model of effects may be characterized as follows:

Ad Exposure ⎯⎯→ Cognitive Responses ⎯⎯→ Attitude Change
(or formation)

From this point of view, understanding the impact of media content, including advertising, requires attention to the thoughts that run through people's heads when they watch TV commercials or read ads in magazines and newspapers. Several common types of cognitive responses are: counterarguments — where one literally thinks of arguments that run counter to the ones being presented ("He says it's inexpensive, but it's probably poorly built too."); supportive arguments — adding supportive ideas ("And it's cheap too!"); source derogations — questioning the credibility of the messenger ("She's paid to give that personal testimony."); and curiosity statements — queries and musings ("I wonder if it does taste as good as it looks?").

According to this model, cognitive responses such as counterarguing mediate the effects of an advertisement on beliefs (cognitions), attitudes (affect) and behavioral intention (conation). Perloff (1983) argues for a cognitive response model in understanding people's processing of political content from the media. Olson, Toy and Dover (1982) argue for a combined cognitive response-cognitive structure model for understanding the effects of advertising content.

To test their notions, Olson et al. (1982) set up an experiment in which advertisements were created to vary types of information about a low-involvement product, a ball-point ink pen. Students were told the experimenters wanted their reactions to some promotional material. Their general knowledge of and purchase behavior towards the product was obtained at the outset. Then they were exposed to varying versions of the ads for a new ball-point pen and asked almost immediately to write down "all the things that come to mind as you read the ad." This was done for each ad, and the comments later categorized as being one of a set of cognitive responses, including counterarguments and support arguments. Other measures tapped the elements of cognitive structure—student's beliefs about the pen, their evaluation of its qualities across a set of scales, and their intention to buy one for personal use on the next shopping trip.

As expected, the manipulated information in the advertisements did have effects on beliefs about such things as price, value for money, etc. Thus, there were cognitive effects of the advertising. There also were effects on students' evaluations (affect) and intentions to purchase the item (conation). Given that the advertising was effective, the next question is whether the students' cognitive responses (such as counter-arguing or support arguing) mediated all or some of that impact. Results show that both types of responses—counterarguing (CA) and support arguing (SA)—had mediating effects for all three cognitive structural elements—beliefs, evaluations and intentions. Thus, people who generated supportive thoughts about price and other character-istics of the pen were more likely to give positive evaluations and exhibit intentions to purchase the pen later. However, direct effects also were found for the advertising, so that cognitive responses did not eliminate the media influence.

The next logical step is to trace out the origins of people's cognitive responses. If advertising and other media content trigger various thoughts, their origins are likely to be based at least partially on existing knowledge. Little is known about the impact of existing know-ledge structures, but Toy (1982) does examine the impact of belief dis-crepancy on cognitive responses. Belief discrepancy is the difference between one's prior beliefs and the statement encountered in adver-tising or other media material being processed. Thus, past information which disagrees with an advertisement creates a discrepancy which should produce more counterarguing and less support arguing as cog-nitive responses. Since the former is negatively related to the adver-tisers goals—positive beliefs, evaluations and intentions—we would expect the discrepancy to reduce the advertising's impact. Results of their experiments do support the model. The level of discrepancy between prior beliefs and those in the ad had a strong impact on the production of couanterarguing and support arguing. However, again, though the cognitive responses mediated some of the advertising impact on cognitive structure, direct effects also persist.

Subliminal Advertising

You are probably familiar with media accounts of attempts to manipulate consumers through "subliminal advertising." For example, a Seattle radio station for a short time broadcast subaudible messages such as "TV is a bore," and movie houses have shown "eat popcorn" and other messages superimposed on a movie in progress (Moore, 1982). Reports of subliminal advertising have raised fears that a Brave New World was being ushered in by advertisers and others who would manipulate consumer's minds. However, the accounts are greatly exaggerated and the subliminal phenomenon a fairly minor factor.

Subliminal perception is a bona fide phenomenon, and there are three means by which it has been claimed to achieve strong behavioral effects. One involves briefly-presented visual stimuli which are flashed so quickly that the viewer is unaware of their presence, but the stimulation does register subconsciously. A second method is the use of accelerated speech in low volume auditory messages where the message is unintelligible and unnoticed at a conscious level but is processed subconsciously. The third procedure consists of embedding sexual imagery or words in pictoral advertisements so that they are not available to conscious perusal (Moore, 1982; Dixon, 1971).

Taken literally, subliminal means "below threshold," but there is no absolute cut-off point below which stimulation is imperceptible and above which it's always detected. It varies with the individual and circumstances. There are ample illustrations that weak stimuli can influence behavior, but studies show that in general such stimuli are overwhelmed by the things we consciously process above the threshold level. Some of the subliminal effects are achieved only when virtually no other stimulation is present. Furthermore, there is no research demonstrating that people draw out the meaning of subliminal words, but there are studies which cast doubt on the possibility (Moore, 1982; Heilbrun, 1980; Severance and Dyer, 1973). There also is no evidence that subaudible messages of the type envisioned by subliminal advertising are possible; thus, subliminal radio ads seem to be ruled out as well. The third procedure for achieving subliminal effects — erotic images or words embedded in advertising — has been popularized by Key (1973, 1976, 1980). He describes the high-speed photography and airbrushing techniques through which subtle appeals to subconscious sex drives are hidden. Intriguing examples show Ritz crackers with the word sex baked into them. Again, there is no evidence for the unconscious perception of such stimuli outside the range of our receptor organs. Whether such erotic imagery has been deliberately planted is irrelevant to the question of whether they have any traceable effects. Under typical circumstances, advertisements' most salient characteristics receive the bulk of one's perceptual activity. If you do not actively search for the hidden images or words, "what you see is what you get" (Moore, 1982:45). In summary, the literature on subliminal perceptions shows that the most clearly documented effects are achieved only in highly contrived and artificial situations. Subliminal directives simply have not been shown to have the power ascribed to them by their advocates.

How Does Advertising Affect the Marketplace?

The last section demonstrated the direct and indirect impact that advertising has on consumers. In the process of influencing consumer perceptions, brand attitudes and purchase intentions, advertising functions as a distributive mechanism in society. One of the media's four major functions is coordination of the different parts of society in the political, economic, and social realms. Advertising manages to "get buyers and sellers together" and thus achieves economic coordination —matching consumers with goods and services. However, as noted earlier, advertising is also envisioned as having somewhat controversial effects in the marketplace itself. In this section, we will examine the arguments and questions bearing on advertising's influence at higher levels of analysis.

Although a large number of economic effects has been attributed to advertising, three will receive most of our attention. First, does advertising affect consumption in society? Put another way, does advertising successfully promote materialism and the consumption of goods? Second, does advertising promote competition or concentration of ownership? And third, does advertising raise or lower the prices paid by consumers?

Does Advertising Promote Consumption?

There are really two different questions about the effect of advertising on consumption. The first focuses on whether advertising can increase consumption for a particular industry, shifting resources from other areas. For example, can advertising increase consumption of all automobiles or all magazines? The second question focuses on total consumer consumption (aggregate consumption). Here the question is whether advertising can shift money from savings to consumption.

Though firms such as Jello and Campbell's soup have tried to increase "primary demand" for their industry's products through advertising campaigns, relatively little research has focused on the question. Underlying social and environmental conditions are the major determinants of product demand (Borden, 1942; Albion and Farris, 1981), and changes in the demographics of a country can lead to the rise of some products and the decline of others. For example, currently the population of the United States is "aging," which produces a demand for health care products serving older groups, while baby-care products rise and fall with the birth rate. However, within reason, there is some elasticity in the consumption of individual products. What is the evidence? Albion and Farris (1981) conclude from their review that the effect of advertising on consumer spending across industries was "severely limited" by other social and economic forces. Market by market studies have found relationships in some cases, but not in others (Lancaster, 1984). For example, advertising has been found to have a positive effect on consumption of magazines, tea, oranges, fresh cream, gasoline, refrigerators and dentifrices, but not for sugar, walnut and shoe industries, with mixed evidence on the cigarette industry (see Albion and Farris, 1981, for full citations). Advertising operates within the large framework of the marketing mix in the industry, and its function changes through the product cycle.

The second question is whether advertising raises aggregate consumption, not within industries, but overall consumption, at the expense of savings. In other words, does advertising convince people to spend money on goods and services that they would save in the absence of such persuasion? Economists have long speculated that such a relationship may occur. Galbraith (1967) had little doubt that the effects of advertising go beyond simply shifting market shares in an industry—the distributive function. He saw advertising as "relentless propaganda in behalf of goods in general." Thus, advertising is seen as promoting materialism, the need for more material goods. Galbraith (1967) says that advertising stimulates the workforce to strive for goods which fulfill needs and desires that can never be fully satisfied. So advertising creates wishes and desires that can only be met by goods produced by the industrial system. In a never ending cycle, people work harder to obtain goods that satisfy wants and desires created by advertising. The creation of material desires and their consumption continue endlessly. In Galbraith's (1967) view, advertising is primarily a societal response to the needs of highly-specialized technologies that require heavy investment and cannot be converted to other uses easily. A good example today would be the automobile industry, where empty plants represent capital investment not easily converted to other uses. Advertising's job is to manage the total consumer demand of a nation to fit the needs of the industrial system.

Advertising expenditures in 1982 totaled more than $66 billion, 33 times the $2 billion figure spent in 1935. The number of advertisers, the amount of advertising and the size of the audience grew correspondingly but the costs of advertising to the economy went from only 2% of the gross national product (GNP) to some 2.9% of consumer expenditures in 1975, a fairly constant rate. Simon (1970) plotted per capita income against advertising as a percentage of GNP and concluded that the richer a country was, the higher the proportion of income spent on advertising. Simon (1970) cited a dozen economic and noneconomic reasons for the relationship, including a decline in custom, fatalism and superstition, the differentiation of wants (so there are many more distinct ones), individualism, etc. Certainly, environmental and socio-demographic influences play a critical role—technological changes, demographics, personal income, tastes, and lifestyle shifts. Advertising is a more controversial factor than other things affecting consumer demand because it is more controllable (Albion and Farris, 1981:81). We might add that advertising is also controversial because, unlike many of the other environmental factors, it seems to be concentrated in the hands of corporations and large business interests.

Albion and Farris (1981: 84) note that our ability to make meaningful generalizations about advertising and total consumption is greatly limited. Several have found a positive relationship between total consumption and advertising (Cowling et al., 1975; Taylor and Weiserbs, 1972; Yancey, 1957), but Schmalensee (1972) found the reverse, that consumption causes advertising. Much of the evidence attempts to look at changes in the business cycle to show that firms that did not cut advertising in a recession fared better in sales volumes and profits than those which did reduce advertising. Such evidence does not tell why some firms cut their advertising budgets while others didn't. In general, the empirical evidence is inconclusive and scanty.

Quarles and Jeffres (1983) examined data for more than 50 nations to test relationships between advertising and consumption. Their project pitted the Galbraithian notion that advertising raises consumption with the competing argument that advertising plays a solely distributive function and is caused by consumption rather than the reverse. The competing models are described in Figure 8-2. Income and industrial development are seen as factors also affecting advertising and consumption. Their evidence tends to support Galbraith's critics that advertising is caused by consumption rather than the reverse. They conclude: "We find little evidence for Galbraith's view of advertising as a high priest of materialism with the persuasive force to alter the spending and savings habits of people and nations. Instead, our analysis yields a picture of spending severely constrained by disposable income—a world where advertising has little room to maneuver in any efforts to draw spending from savings" (Quarles and Jeffres, 1983:13). "Our analysis, along with those that have gone before, gives us no reason to believe that advertising is the high priest of such a cult. Its role appears to be more like that of an acolyte who follows and assists in the rituals of the greater culture."

Figure 8-2

Competing View on the Relationship between Advertising & Consumption

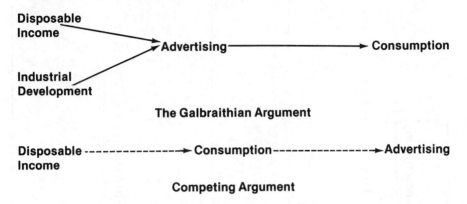

The Galbraithian Argument

Competing Argument

Does Advertising Promote Competition or Concentration?

Two schools of thought have raged in battle over the question of whether advertising promotes competition or leads to concentration of market power. As Albion and Farris (1981) note, the arguments have often turned into ideological warfare more than anything else. Here we will try to summarize some of the many pertinent relationships which are examined as evidence of one side or the other (see Figure 8-3).

The traditional view maintains that advertising is a form of persuasion that creates product differentiation (Makes them appear distinct, different); this allows firms to exercise market power at the consumer's expense. According to this approach, advertising makes the demand curves less elastic, and this leads to higher prices. Elasticity refers to how responsive consumers are to price changes; thus, if there is low elasticity, firms can raise prices without reducing demand. Advertising is seen as establishing a brand loyalty among buyers which allows firms to raise prices without losing customers. This also creates barriers to entry because new competitors have to bear the heavy costs of advertising to gain a share of the market. As a consequence, concentration of market power is achieved through advertising.

A more recent approach views advertising as information, an inexpensive way to communicate with massive numbers of consumers. In this model, advertising informs buyers of the range of substitutes available, and this increases the price elasticity of demand and lowers prices. Producers cannot raise prices at will because consumers know of substitutes through advertising. By allowing previously unknown

Figure 8-3
Two Models on the Impact of Advertising on Concentration

Market Power Model

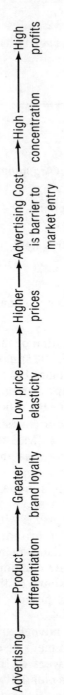

Information Model

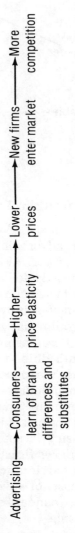

products to gain rapid market acceptance, advertising allows new entrants into the marketplace and this reduces monopoly power; thus, advertising is less a barrier to market entry and more a promoter of competition. Advertising serves consumers by increasing variety and allowing firms to exploit economies of scale in production and distribution; these in turn yield lower prices.

Price Elasticity of Demand. Many economists believe that the true measure of market power is the price elasticity of demand. However, since it is so difficult to measure this factor, economists concentrate on the profit rates of manufacturers. A firm's ability to earn monopoly rates of return (profit margins about the industry norm) has been used as an indicator. Callahan (1982) analyzed 17 consumer goods industries and the retail chain service industry from 1969 to 1978, finding that heavy advertising led to higher profits across the 80 companies. Albion and Farris (1981:55) conclude that the empirical studies offer no overwhelming evidence to substantiate either the market power or competition models, though a majority of the studies do find a positive relationship between advertising and profitability.

Advertising and Concentration. One approach has involved studying direct relationships between advertising and industry concentration. The evidence is somewhat mixed. Ayanian (1983) argues that new evidence suggests advertising is a long-lived investment which is unrelated to rates of return and, furthermore, the theory that heavy advertising expenditures create entry barrier is not supported by the facts. Nagle (1981) argues that advertising positively affects the competitiveness of an industry. Scherer (1970) concludes that advertising may destabilize market shares initially but then lead to an increase in product differentiation that helps the larger manufacturers and increases concentration. Some support for this view is found in the U.S. where overall industry concentration in the country has remained quite stable in this century but has increased for differentiated consumer products. The emergence of TV advertising as a power tool has also attracted interest. Mueller and Rogers (1980) looked at industry concentration and TV advertising, concluding that advertising has prevented highly concentrated industries from becoming less concentrated and that television advertising has been particularly effective in discouraging entry because of its limited availability and escalating costs. Lancaster and Miracle (1978) find evidence that network TV advertising "is the most important advertising media affecting market share." The emergence of cable TV may make TV more like radio. With the audience more segmented, TV would be more accessible to smaller firms. Albion and Farris (1981:66) conclude that advertising is positively related with concentration and profitability, but other factors are also involved and more research is needed on consumers' responsiveness to advertising. In 1985, Coca-Cola tried to change the taste of Coke and to maintain customer loyalty with a powerful advertising campaign. But, as Rukeyser (1985) notes, "Coke's immense market power was not enough to put across a product decision that large numbers of customers rejected."

Brand Loyalty and Product Differentiation. One of the issues is whether advertising leads to greater brand loyalty and product differentiation, as the market power model suggests. The notion of product differentiation is that consumers facing two brands with similar characteristics but different prices often pick the more expensive one. For example, aspirin products have been characterized as physically identical yet national brands have 95% of the market. Unfortunately, there is almost no agreement on how to measure product differentiation and, thus, there is little research bearing on the topic. Haefner et al. (1983) found that total brand advertising in 63 consumer product categories was positively related to the number of brands in the category and to the number of brands consumers usually buy. However, as advertising becomes skewed (concentrated) in the direction of the top brands in the category, it appears to be associated with decreases in the number of available brands and the number of brands consumers usually buy.

Brand loyalty is the tendency of consumers to purchase the same brand rather than switching from one brand to another. Papazian (1982) analyzed a survey of 2,500 adults on their brand loyalties in various categories. He found that brand loyalty is lowest when products are nearer to being commodities (for example, potatoes, onions) and highest when the consumer feels switching is risky (such as automobiles). The 1980 Simmons Market Research survey data reveal that the most popular-selling brands also tend to have higher loyalty ratios. The significance of brand loyalty is that it is viewed as creating a buffer for large firms because it requires substantial advertising expenditures by new firms entering the market. Schmalensee (1974) argues that brand loyalty created by advertising is a barrier only if it cannot be changed easily. Furthermore, brand loyalty also occurs because of personal experience. The ability of advertising to create brand loyalty in one industry also may not be duplicated in a different industry. Albion and Farris (1981:115) conclude that advertising effectiveness depends on other parts of the marketing mix, particularly product quality; however, though the "singular power of advertising has often been overestimated," advertising can be quite effective when coupled with other marketing tools and recognition of such factors as competition, life cycle stage of the product, and other market characteristics.

Advertising and Prices

For the consumer, the key question is whether advertising makes the things he buys more expensive. The two models maintain different positions. The market power model says that advertising leads to industry concentration and higher prices, while the information model argues that advertising allows new entries to the market and subsequent competition that eventually reduces prices to the consumer.

Albion and Farris (1981:153) argue that we need to look at the question from a different perspective. First, they distinguish the factory price of the manufacturer from the consumer price of the retailer. Most evidence found by supporters of both models is consistent with the view that less price sensitivity at the factory level is consistent with more price sensitivity at the retail level. Also, higher prices for advertised brands may be consistent with lower absolute prices for the whole product category.

The question is whether products would cost more if there were no advertising. To answer that we need a standard for comparison. Simply comparing advertised and unadvertised brands doesn't work. The absolute prices of all brands might be higher or lower without advertising.

What are the arguments for higher prices? A simplistic notion is that a company which spends money for advertising has to pass on the costs in the form of higher prices to consumers; in this case, advertising is seen in isolation from the communication strategies available to firms and the information needs of consumers. Moving to the market level, one argument says that all firms in a market would benefit if they could reduce their advertising costs and avoid competitive waste. The ban on TV cigarette advertising, for example, may have helped the manufacturers increase profits, reduce costs and reduce the absolute price to consumers.

What are the arguments for lower prices? The most commonly cited argument is that advertising lowers the product price by increasing market efficiency (Ferguson, 1982). Advertising is the cheapest and most efficient way of letting consumers know about a product, particularly at the national level. Advertising allows the price of a product category to be lower than if less efficient marketing tools were used.

Albion and Farris (1981: 159) note that most of the evidence shows that advertising increases price sensitivity at the consumer level but decreases price sensitivity at the factory level. Thus, while advertising increases the market power for the manufacturer, it decreases any monopoly power the retailer might have in selling the product to consumers. Retailers must compete on price because consumers are knowledgeable about the brand's price and product characteristics.

However, translating price elasticities into actual prices is not easy; businesses don't behave as economic theory predicts. The ability to raise prices doesn't always lead to that outcome. The evidence does show that highly advertised products tend to have higher prices than the less advertised or unadvertised competing products. The difference may be due, in part at least, to differences in quality (Albion and Farris, 1981: 162). This evidence refers to "relative" rather than absolute prices which might be different without any advertising.

Advertising may reduce costs in three ways. One is through economies of scale (Hazard et al., 1983). Business people believe that advertising has made possible the large national markets that permit large-scale production and reduced manufacturing costs. Though there are examples, it is difficult to separate out advertising from other economies of scale. A second way for advertising to reduce costs is as a substitute for other marketing tools. Again, although evidence is meager, advertising may shift communication costs among firms in an industry. Third, advertising may reduce consumers' costs for information searches; the system of self-service retail stores would probably not exist in its current developed form without advertising of brand products. The clerks would have to perform some of the functions accomplished by advertising.

These are the arguments for the impact of advertising on absolute price, but what is the evidence? Albion and Farris (1981: 167) note that only a few studies have been conducted where a standard of comparison was available. Retail advertising was associated with lower market prices in the eyeglass, gasoline and prescription drug industries (Maurizi, 1972; Maurizi, Moore and Shepard, 1981; Benham, 1972; Cady, 1976). This was based on investigations which compared market areas with and without advertising. The markets with advertising had lower retail prices. Similar research in England found manufacturer advertising led to lower market prices in chocolate, cocoa mixes, and detergents. In the United States, Steiner (1978) found dramatic reductions in the retail price of bicycles with the growth of advertising. An examination of toy advertising in France showed that the price dropped quickly when a ban of advertising was lifted. And a report by the FTC suggests that advertising promoted competition and lower prices among lawyers (Ricks, 1984).

Albion and Farris (1981: 168) conclude that advertising decreases price sensitivity at the manufacturer level allowing firms to charge higher prices. They also found that advertising increases price sensitivity at the retail level reducing prices paid by consumers. Thus, while advertising appears to shift market power between manufacturers and retailers, it does benefit consumers at their "bottom line."

Economic Effects of the Media: Some Notes

Media advertising appears to have economic effects on both individual consumers and the marketplace. However, many other economic consequences have been attributed to the media. Some have noted that improved communication reduces travel and transportation costs. Coupled with the personal computer, improved communication may even change where and how people work (Williams, 1983; Evans, 1979; Dizard, 1985). Advertising has also been linked with product innovation. In fact, there is evidence that network TV advertising is linked with product innovation among consumer goods (Albion, 1976; Porter, 1978). At a more macro level, some claim that television has had more impact on the business of sports — professional, collegiate, and Olympics — than almost any other single factor (Schneider, 1985). One example often cited is the Super Bowl which attracts more than 100 million viewers annually. Others have noted that TV was responsible for the creation of the American Football League in 1960 by providing the economic justification. Longer-range economic effects of the media may be particularly difficult to forecast, but they clearly deserve attention along with social and political consequences.

Summary

In this chapter we examined economic effects of the media on individuals and "society," focusing primarily on the impact of advertising. After a discussion of the "advertising controversy," we reviewed the evidence for effects on people's cognitions (such as brand awareness), affective links to products (attitudes toward products), and behaviors (from intentions to actual purchases). Between advertising and prescribed effects lie both activating and filtering mechanisms. We examined the literature on these, looking at prior experiences, people's uses and gratifications, and consumer characteristics. A review of "what advertising works" examined puffery, comparative ads, time/size/placement, appeals (sex, humor, music), and models. An additional section evaluated some models constructed to explain how effects are achieved including: the hierarchy of effects, cognitive processing, and subliminal effects. Then we moved up to higher levels of analysis to see how advertising affects the marketplace. Three major questions were considered: Does advertising affect consumption in society? Does advertising promote competition or concentration of ownership? Does advertising raise or lower the prices paid by consumers? Available evidence was presented in an effort to answer these questions.

Cultural Effects of the Media

The mass media have been portrayed as great educators, capable of bringing culture to the masses and assisting in efforts to bridge cultural gaps and reach national developmental goals. At the same time, the media's accusers see them as representatives of foreign cultures and the local power structure, helping to destroy traditional values and to promote "modern" popular culture while intensifying disparities between the rich and the poor. Like most arguments drawn to their extremes, the truth probably lies somewhere in the middle. In this chapter we will discuss the arguments on how mass media operate within the "cultural arena," and examine evidence for cultural effects of the media.

Questions over media impact on different cultures are posed at both the national and international levels. Within countries, we are concerned with how media influence indigenous, local cultures and how media operate to stimulate social, economic and political development. At the international level, we focus on how mass media operate as links between countries and as vehicles for cultural influence.

We will examine cultural effects of the media through the following questions: 1) What is "culture" and what is its relationship to mass communication? 2) How do news and information flow around the world from one culture to another? 3) What does "media imperialism" mean and what is its impact? How do the new communication technologies affect news flow and do they facilitate additional media effects on national cultures? 5) How do the mass media operate in national development?

How Is *Culture* Related to Mass Communication?

If we're going to discuss "cultural effects" of the media, then we first need to clarify the concept of "culture"—one of those elusive terms that means almost anything. In daily conversations, "culture" might refer to artistic tastes or different customs practiced by a new immigrant. Indeed, Kroeber and Kluckholn (1952) collected well over a hundred definitions. Some scholars have virtually abandoned the concept, preferring instead to focus on its more recognizeable components. Traditionally culture has been viewed as consisting of four elements: norms, values, beliefs, and expressive symbols. Values indicate what we think people and things are worth (for example, "I value my 'independence.'"), and norms refer to the values accepted by most people in a society ("Most Americans put great stock in the rights of individuals."). Beliefs represent our conviction about how the world operates and expressive symbols refer to all aspects of material culture—from primitive huts to modern media. Most social scientists have insisted that the four elements of culture fit together in patterns: a certain set of norms is compatible with a given set of values, beliefs and expressive symbols. Recent works have shifted the weight given to each of the four elements, and one of the newer tendencies has been to focus on expressive symbols as portraying fundamental beliefs (Williams, 1976; Peterson, 1979). Even when the concept of culture has been fuzzy and of little scientific use, it has persisted in dialogues and debates. The concept has been revitalized in recent years, in large part because of the interest in communication and mass media.

Peterson (1979) identifies four perspectives on culture. The first is called the "mirror metaphor." Here, culture mirrors society and researchers have examined media content, patriotic celebrations or other forms of symbolism because they expressed less visible aspects of social relations. This tradition has been expressed by media professionals for several generations—"We merely report what's there—We don't create the sex and violence." In this tradition the media are seen as "reflecting" culture rather than having an impact on culture. Those who accept this view would focus on the material presented in Chapters 2 and 3, the media industries and their relationships to other social institutions. However, even those who accept the "mirror metaphor" need to provide evidence that media behaviors reinforce existing culture. A second view asserts that expressive symbols constitute the code for creating and recreating society from generation to generation. This view stresses the potency of symbols and focuses on how systems of expressive symbols (such as those found in the media) are linked to people's beliefs and social action. Researchers here have looked, for example, at how elements of popular culture (mass media, TV programs) influence aspects of group life. Studies have looked at life styles, public taste groups, consumer groups, cultural classes, and various symbolic communities. The traditions of this second view have favored the methods of anthropologists and other scholars who do not use the term "effects" and prefer to analyze media and symbol systems for "structure."

However, the conceptual thrust is not inconsistent with the notion of "cultural effects" of the media. Lyle (1978) notes that the diverse ethnic and racial groups in American society increasingly attempt to use TV and other media to establish what they see as their rightful place in society and to readdress past inequities. Thus, media symbols are seen as having an impact on social perception and interaction. Lichty (1981) notes that in many countries like the U.S., television and the central government are the only national institutions. As a consequence, TV possesses a peculiar, implacable kind of stability for people. One group of communication scholars sees culture as being composed of patterns that reflect communicative responses to the environment (Kim, 1982). A more process-oriented approach than that described by Peterson (1979), this communication research sees acculturation as the process of developing communication competence in a host system. Thus, immigrants "take on" the elements of a new culture through their communication. There is a shift in levels downward from the societal level, but communication scholars working with this view do assert the potency of what Peterson (1979) notes would be called symbolic behavior.

A third view of culture accepts the significance of symbols and emphasizes how they perpetuate what are seen as fundamental splits between dominant and dominated elements of society: the rich and the poor, for example. Here we find Marxists who see media symbol systems representing and recreating the class system. Scholars in this tradition have examined media content as "cultural capital" used by the "capitalist elite" to further their interests. Carey (1975) notes that communication passes on a tradition which perpetuates society over time and binds status groups into society by coopting their expressive culture forms and substituting standardized mass media forms and content. This is the view which most directly serves as the basis for those who see U.S. media spreading American cultural values throughout the world (Schiller, 1969; Tunstall, 1977). Another example is found in the view that TV acts to dissolve social bonds and to create alienation (Ozersky, 1977); TV here homogenizes culture not by bringing people together but by erasing distinctions between fact and fiction and implying that all experience is equal. TV is seen as reducing people's tolerance for ambiguity and increasing the need for immediate satisfaction. The fourth view on culture focuses on how it is produced. Studies here examine the tasks of those who teach, communicate, disseminate the "cultural code." This view also is represented in Chapter 3.

We add a fifth perspective to the four noted by Peterson (1979). Though loosely-defined, it takes the form of assuming that communication — including the mass media — may have an influence on "culture" independent of the social structure. Thus, new communication technologies and derivative communication patterns enable new systems of organization and influence that alter existing cultural values, beliefs, and norms. We will return to this notion in the section on new communication technologies.

The Flow of News and Information

Though it would be difficult to measure, clearly the amount of communication linking people from different cultures around the world is growing rapidly. Some of that takes the form of tourists and globe-trotting business people from one country talking with their hosts (Cherry, 1971). But most of the information we receive about people from other cultures arrives through the mass media. Within the short span of a single generation we have seen two broadcast media — radio and TV — spread around the globe. One Unesco study of Africa, Latin America and Asia found that the demand for news in those areas in 1975 was three and one-half times that of only 20 years earlier (Robinson, 1977:66). At the same time, international structures have developed to collect and distribute news on a massive scale. Thus, five international wire services (the Associated Press, United Press International, Britain's Reuters, Agencie France Press and TASS from the Soviet Union) are supplemented by a growing number of regional services and more than 120 national news agencies located in almost every country. Except for TASS, whose influence is generally restricted to the Soviet bloc, the wire services are Western and most are Anglo-American. In addition, two firms (Visnews — owned largely by Reuters and British broadcasting Corp. — and UPITN — a combined effort of UPI from the U.S. and Britain's Independent Television News organization) distribute film coverage of major events to TV systems around the world. In addition to these efforts, the *International Herald Tribune* circulates throughout world capitals, international editions of the news magazines are distributed widely, and world radio services are provided by the BBC from Britain, the Voice of America, and external broadcasting services of other nations.

Most of the increase in global news flow is of recent vintage. The past several decades have seen a growth in the number of international organizations and exchange agreements. Western European nations have exchanged TV programs through an organization called Eurovision since 1954, and Eastern Bloc nations set up Intervision to do the same thing in 1960. In 1971, the two exchanges entered into an agreement which allows any news event covered by one member to be used by other systems the same evening (Le Duc, 1981). Asian nations also exchange TV programming, regional news exchanges have grown stronger (Arbee, 1983; Giffard, 1985, 1985), and Third World countries dissatisfied with coverage of their regions by the international wire services have set up a Non-Aligned News Agencies Pool (Hachten, 1981:107); Robinson, 1977).

Conflicting Views. The international news system is largely an outgrowth of the Western news media, and that has led to increasing dissatisfaction in recent years among Third World nations. Developing nations have become increasingly critical about how well media are performing their job and whether the international system should be restructured to correct deficiencies or imbalances. What are the different perspectives?

Third World nations consider themselves as victims of a one-way flow of communication which originates in the industrialized nations of the West (plus Japan), and then flows through news services and distribution systems they control to audiences in developing nations. This international news system is seen as simply an extension of the old colonial system and represents a virtual news monopoly that perpetuates an inequality in information resources. What appears as "free flow" to the West is unrestricted access by the wealthier countries to the less powerful. Thus, developing audiences are exposed to news gathered with the values and concerns of the West in mind. This means an overemphasis on such topics as conflict between the West and Soviet power blocs. Little attention is given to such things as development programs and problems facing impoverished nations of Asia, Africa, and Latin America. Furthermore, the imbalance created by the international news system is matched by Western control of major advertising agencies that serve multinational corporations. Together with the news media, these "foreign messages" are seen as an alienating influence that produces a distorted and negative picture of developing nations (see, for example, Hachten, 1981; MacBride, 1980; Gunaratne, 1978; Makagiansar, 1977).

Western countries see themselves as the depositories of freedom and liberty. As Hachten (1981) notes, the world's ability to know the news about itself depends on what gets into the news flow in the 15 or 20 open societies with highly developed media systems. These are the same countries responsible for four of the five major international wire services. Western observers accept several criticisms but also point to major problems. They acknowledge the thin network of correspondents covering the world (There were only 435 American correspondents abroad in 1975, for example). This is a consequence of rising costs and inflation; one foreign correspondent is estimated to cost some $150,000 a year. The distribution of correspondents is also uneven, with more than half of those abroad stationed in 19 European countries. This means that journalists with little background and preparation are flown into trouble spots to cover emerging crises, returning to European capitals and other major cities to await the next assignment. Western journalists also express frustration and wish the amount of foreign news coverage could be expanded. A somewhat disinterested public and inflation are cited as chief culprits for the situation. Western observers also note that their news media tend to report foreign news from the viewpoint of their country's foreign policy concerns, despite their relative independence from governments. Thus, when the U.S. developed relations with the People's Republic of China, U.S. media coverage was soon to follow. However, Western journalists also cite roadblocks to the collection of news, primarily from governments of Communist countries and an increasing number of Third World nations. The growing hostility and antagonism toward Western reporting has produced rules and restrictions limiting the movement of foreign correspondents, as well as subtle restraints and attempts to persuade or influence actual reporting through such things as press junkets, distractions, etc. As more and more nations close themselves off from critical inquiry, the picture portrayed by world media becomes increasingly fragmented and incomplete. Ironically, each nation's leadership wants "full and complete information" about the rest of the world for making decisions, but they want only positive pictures of their nations reaching other peoples (see Fascell, 1979; Hachten, 1981; Gunter, 1979).

These conflicting views have clashed in the United Nations and a series of conferences held in the past decade to discuss what has been called a "New World Information Order" (Mehan, 1981). Up through the 1960's, Unesco supported efforts to break down barriers to the "free flow of ideas," building up media professionalism, arranging for low customs duties for books and papers, sponsoring training centers and copyright conventions (Knight, 1976). However, in the 1970's Unesco became a forum for vehement debate about the nature and function of mass communication media. Having acquired a numerical majority in the UN and its specialized agencies, developing nations have sought changes in the news system which would protect their national sovereignty from both the capitalist West and Soviet-dominated bloc. While radical states attribute to the developed countries a conscious ideological hostility, more moderate developing nations believe that industrialized nations unwittingly support a system which perpetuates social and economic injustice (Nowell, 1980). Mustapha Masmoudi (1979), former Tunisian secretary of state for education, articulated what has become the defining statement of the New World Information Order. He issued a seven-point complaint:

1. The current media system enshrines the old colonial system and represents its values.
2. A de facto hegemony and a will to dominate—the Western media are indifferent to the concerns and problems of developing countries and simply sell them news like other commercial products.
3. There is an inequality in news resources; the five international news agencies dominate the flow of news, while Visnews and UPITN dominate the distribution of TV news film, and so forth.
4. There is an imbalance between North and South in the volume and flow of news, with more news flowing south than north.
5. International news media are poorly designed for the audiences of developing nations because the news is designed for the reading, viewing and listening public of the industrialized West.
6. There is a lack of information on developing countries, and the transnational media emphasize negative images of developing nations, stressing strikes, crime, putsches, street demonstrations, disasters, etc.
7. International news media are an alienating influence in the economic, social and cultural spheres.

Some of these points we will see again when we examine "media imperialism."

Masmoudi's (1978) statement was followed by *Many Voices, One World* (1980), a report by Unesco's International Commission for the Study of Communication Problems. Subsequently named after its chair, Sean MacBride, the report recommended that journalists have free access to all news sources and that all censorship be abolished. It also supported Third World concerns about the "colonial domination" of news distribution and had some harsh comments about commercial influences and suggested that attention be devoted to obstacles stemming from the concentration of ownership, public or private. Singh and Gross (1981) argue that the most innovative part of the MacBride report is its endorsement of the "democratization of communication," where the commission unanimously endorsed alternative information systems such as community and local media movements, which are seen as means to resist undemocratic political influences. The MacBride report was roundly criticized by both sides and coverage of the issue was sometimes strident and provocative (see, for example, Roach, 1982).

The debate over a "New World Information Order" has already produced changes. At the 1980 Belgrade conference, the International Program for Development of Communication (IPDC) was established as a clearinghouse for communication development needs, resources and priorities (Harley, 1981). Power (1981) says that the U.S. response has followed several paths: trying to work with the moderate developing nations on pragmatic, noncontroversial goals; blurring North-South divisions; isolating the Soviets and Third World radicals; and supporting the IPDC. Block (1982) notes that the January 1982 meeting of the IPDC was a welcome change from the sort of posturing that has occurred in the past. And the non-aligned news pool working through the Tanjug agency has continued. The Non-Aligned News Agency was established in 1976 by 85 nations which wanted a news service independent of those located in the large, industrialized nations. The Yugoslav news agency Tanjug coordinates the news pool (Nasser, 1983). Manekar (1981) notes that Western fears that their news agencies would not be able to operate as freely once the non-aligned pool was set up were ill founded. On the other hand, Nordenstreng (1982) sees the Western response as essentially a propaganda campaign coupled with gentle blackmail that trades a little assistance for cooperation. Others also see the continuing North-South dialogue as an effort to "buy time" for the industrialized nations to make good on their pledges to assist Third World news media and contain movement toward state control of news organizations. Agee (1979) reports on the diverse efforts of U.S. and other countries' journalism organizations, wire services and individual media who have pledged to help develop the media infrastructures of developing nations. Anderson (1979) notes that the U.S. stands to lose the most in any "new order" because the concept does much more than challenge America's generally privileged position and its ability to trade software freely (movies, news, TV, books, music, etc.) and hardware (satellites, telephones, computers, telecommunication equipment). Such a "new order" also could threaten the nation's strong historic commitment to the philosophy that media should be privately owned and free and independent.

Observers with long memories might feel they are experiencing *deja* vu. The current debate over the flow of news around the world is reminiscent of the 1930's when there was an objection to the partitioning of the world according to the interests of a few large transnational wire services. This led to calls for a free flow of information which meant largely freedom from control by the European agencies. Since the 1970's, Third World nations have believed that freedom of information can exist only when all parties concerned have equal access to the channels or a free flow will lead to de facto control by the most powerful (Cuthbert, 1980).

Masmoudi's (1978) seven-point indictment contains a mixture of both values and beliefs that can be subjected to scientific inquiry. Stevenson and Cole (1984a) point out that the charges center on questions about cultural sovereignty and government responsibility. We will examine each of the seven points. Most observers would agree with the first point, that the current system reflects the colonial heritage. Tunstall (1977) carefully lays out the history of American and European involvement in setting up institutions that are now part of the international news system. At one point, 90% of the world news distributed by the press and radio in Africa, Latin America and Asian countries other than Japan or China was distributed from new York, Paris or London (Fontgalland, 1976).

The second point, that the West has a will to dominate and lacks concern for developing nations is essentially a charge about the "intentions" of Western media; such charges are value judgements and an effort to assign responsibility. One indication of interest is found by Schramm (1980), who studied the Asian "prestige" press and four wire services in Asia. Results showed the Asian papers were local in fheir focus, catering to the needs and interests of their audiences. They devoted about three quarters of their space to domestic news and showed no greater interest in developmental topics than do Western mass media. If other developing regions show a similar pattern, then the charge of disinterest in topics pertinent to developing countries can be levied at both the media of industrial nations as well as those serving the Third World. Giffard (1984) looked at the AP and UPI Asian wires and found more Asian news on those wire services than news of any other region. Also, reports from the developing nations were on the average longer than those from developed countries, contradicting the notion that Third World events are covered only sketchily in comparison with those of the West.

Claims that developing and industrial nations have unequal news resources — the third point — are accepted by both parties and the IPDC clearinghouse is an effort to respond to this need.

The fourth charge is that news flows in a predominantly North to South pattern rather than the reverse (a metaphor used because most industrialized nations are in the north and most developing countries are in the south.) This is also generally supported when we view news as a commodity distributed by the international wire services. A study of four newspapers in nine Asian countries and all of the major wire services showed that three fourths of all non-local Third World news came to the Asian papers from one or more of the four major international wire services (Schramm et al., 1978). However, the uneven nature is not necessarily bad. As observers have noted, much of that information flow from the West consists of technical data and other content useful in national development.

The North-South flow pattern is one of dependence and several studies note unequal patterns of news flow. Sparkes (1978) compared U.S. and Canadian newspapers and found the average Canadian daily devoting 273 column inches to American news, compared to 5.12 column inches of Canadian news in American papers. Nnaemeka and Richstad (1980) found the old colonial networks are still important factors in understanding the flow of news into the Pacific region and between the islands. Kressley (1978) found an imbalance in the flow of TV programs between Eastern and Western Europe, with much more news flowing from West to the East than was traveling in the other direction. Breen (1981) notes that the Australian government was successful in promoting local programs over imported TV fare. And Keller and Roel (1979) note that Americans receive less exposure to other cultures through their media than most other people in the world, although the United States is being forced to reshape its system of communication because of a growing interdependence with other nations. The latter observation is based on American network TV, and, as Stevenson and Cole (1984a: 19-20) note, a list of foreign TV programming available from cable and public TV in the U.S. shows more international fare presented than is generally the case elsewhere in the world. There also is evidence that following harsh Third World criticism during the 1970's, elite U.S. dailies now devote more attention to the Third World. An examination of the *New York Times,* the *Washington Post* and the *Christian Science Monitor* (Mazharul, 1983) found that 44% of the front page stories were international and the Third World accounted for 82% of them.

Skurnik's (1981) results bear on the fifth point, that news distributed through Western agencies reflects the interests and values of the west rather than the audiences of developing countries. Although the international wire services distribute news and information to individual countries, much of this is redistributed by national news agencies and all of it must pass through local media gatekeepers. Certainly, the media of developing countries cannot distribute what is not received, but they can shift emphases for their audiences. A variety of studies has shown that the U.S. dominates foreign news around the world, in such places as Nigeria (Nwuneli and Udoh, 1982), Japan (Kitatani, 1981; Iwao, 1981), Yugoslavia (Becker, Underwood and Lemish, 1981), and Canada (Sparkes, 1978). Thus, the criteria for news identified by Hester (1973) and others (Galtung and Ruge, 1965; Rubin, 1977) appear to be common practice in both developing and industrialized countries —power, proximity, cultural affinities, economic ties, conflict, etc. News emphasis is generally the same around the world, with national and international politics receiving the most attention; a survey of 15 papers in seven African nations found the major categories of news coverage were international and domestic politics, economics and sports, in that order (Ume-Nwagbo, 1982). Furthermore, cross-cultural comparisons suggest that the rules by which newsworthy events are identified, selected and routinely transformed into items of news are more similar across countries than anticipated (Davis and Walton, 1983). However, looking only at domestic news, Lang (1984) found that less developed nations give greater emphasis to cooperation stories than do their more developed counterparts, despite a strong similarity in general news values. The countries examined were: South Africa, Rhodesia, Kenya, Zambia, Ghana and Uganda.

The sixth point charges the West with emphasizing negative stories about developing countries who are sensitive about their images, for a variety of reasons. Stevenson and Smith (1984) compared coverage of Mexico and Lebanon in American newsmagazines, finding strong positive cultural images, a somewhat less strong but still positive image of power and a neutral image of those nations on an "activity" dimension. They conclude that "we find no evidence to support the argument that the Third World is covered in mostly negative ways." Looking at the reverse relationship, Rubin (1979) notes that during the 1963-73 decade the American image in the European and Third World press was extremely poor and in part reflected the influence of those nations' foreign policies.

Most of the evidence introduced so far has relied on studies within one or two countries, but comparisons of media in several countries at the same time are ideal for testing some of the notions about media performance in developing and industrial countries. Recently, the International Association for Mass Communication Research (IAMCR) authorized a project to analyze international news in the media of 29 countries; major national daily papers and TV newscasts were sampled for a total of 12 days in March-June, 1979. Results are summarized by Stevenson and Shaw (1984) and debated in several places (Nordenstreng, 1984; Stevenson, 1984). Key findings included: 1) politics dominated the international news reporting both in terms of the topics covered and the actors presented, in all the media systems, including both developed and developing nations. The four hard news categories accounting for the bulk of the news, particularly in the developing world, were: international politics, domestic politics, military/defense, and economics; 2) In all of the national systems, most attention was paid to events happening within and actors belonging to the immediate geographic region; 3) In almost all nations, news was defined as the exceptional event, so that coups and catastrophes were considered newsworthy wherever they occurred (Screberny-Mohammadi, 1982); 4) News flows respond to cultural, linguistic and geographic determinants rather than simply to economic factors such as investment and trade relationships (Haynes, 1984; Ahern, 1984).

Stevenson and Cole (1984) note that the assertion that Western agencies ignore the Third World in regional services to those parts of the world is simply not true. Proximate countries get more attention, (Sreberny-Mohammadi, 1984), followed by Europe and then North America. The invisible part of the world is the Socialist Second world. The gaps in existing news, such as development and regional news, are ideal for concentration by the new national and regional news agencies, which they argue should try to supplement rather than supplant the large international news agencies.

The argument that the Third World is singled out for special treatment also is not supported by data, because political news is the standard around the world. This emphasis and narrow definition of news is a problem of journalism rather than Western coverage of the Third World (Stevenson and Cole, 1984a,b). In the U.S. sample which was part of the 29-nation project, Wilhoit and Weaver (1982) found that coups and earthquakes did not make up the bulk of foreign news, despite the common view. However, their data did support the claim that Western news agencies focus on conflicts and crises when covering less developed countries. Newspaper editors also tend to select news in roughly the same proportions as it is delivered by the wire services; thus, given the opportunity to select a larger or smaller percentage of foreign news, editors stick to the "agenda" set by the Associated Press and United Press International. Economic matters, social services, culture, scientific and medical achievements and ecological issues were all but neglected in the coverage of both developing and industrialized nations (Wilhoit and Weaver, 1982).

Stevenson and Thompson (1984) compared five countries from the international sample — the U.S., the Soviet Union, Brazil, Algeria and Zambia — they found little evidence to support Third World complaints that they are singled out for negative coverage in the western media and in the trans-national news agencies (also see Stevenson and Smith, 1984). However, there was support for the argument that national media editors often over-select bad news (Stevenson and Gaddy, 1984).

In general, editors use a higher percentage of political bad news than the wire services supply and the over-selection is somewhat greater in news of the Third World. Interestingly, both the U.S. and Soviet media were similar in reporting much bad news from the Third World, both emphasizing political bad news. Stevenson and Gaddy (1984) note another interesting similarity between two former British colonies, Kenya and Zambia. Zambian media are "mobilized" to support the government and are highly political, while Kenyan media are strikingly similar in their coverage of bad news from other countries. A comparison of coverage in free, pluralistic nations like the U.S. and those which are not free (the Soviet Union, for example) showed that the more closed, stable systems are less likely to emphasize political or civil conflict, especially at home (Shaw and Stevenson, 1984). This suggests that even when there are major differences between the social structures or media systems, we may still find similar patterns of news. Such evidence flies in the face of the "reflection hypothesis," that media mirror the social structure.

A serious reservation to the discussion about news flow is the model being used. Communication here is seen as a mechanistic model in which a communicator "does something" for somebody else (see Fisher, 1978, for a discussion of communication perspectives). As discussed in earlier chapters, while the media can have direct effects, a number of individual filters and activators stand between the media and a whole range of effects. In the international context, audiences in developing countries are activated to seek out both indigenous and imported media content, and they use a host of filters in processing the news and other media messages. At a higher level of analysis, Skurnik (1981) found that journalists in the Ivory Coast and Kenya were far from the "helpless consumers" of world news that current rhetoric depicts. He argues that national interests, personal factors of African journalists and the positions of their governments are dominant factors in their selection of news.

The last point on Masmoudi's agenda attributes cultural effects to the trans-national media organizations, and this takes us to the next section on "media imperialism." The question of cultural effects is broader than the issue of news flow, although it is based on some of the same concerns and incorporates many of the same arguments.

"Cultural Imperialism" and Cultural Effects of the Media

Notions of "imperialism" are offensive to many people encountering the charges of "cultural/media imperialism" for the first time. Simply put, imperialism is the practice and policy of seeking to dominate the affairs of underdeveloped areas. Increasingly, the concept of "hegemony" is being used to focus on the same issue (Altheide, 1984). Hegemony refers to the domination of a way of life and thought, and it's generally based on a Marxist perspective. Such efforts have negative connotations to most people in a world which has enshrined ideas of equality, fraternity and liberty. The offense taken stems from belief that the concept infers actual intent by people in the United States and other industrial nations to dominate the Third World's media system and cultural life. For the moment, we'll suspend discussion about whether there is "intent" or not, and move to a similar concept encountered earlier.

We can draw a parallel between the concept of imperialism at the international level and the idea of media dependency at the individual level (see Chapter 7). People are dependent on particular media for most of their information. By comparison, one country may be dependent on several other countries for much of the content that is distributed through its media system — importing films from Hollywood, TV programs from Britain, news from France, radio dramas from mexico, and so forth (Jussawalla, 1983). Individuals in the U.S. have some freedom to alter their pattern of media dependency by adding newspaper and magazine subscriptions, buying books or switching the TV channel. In this manner one enriches the news diet and is less dependent on a narrow filter. However, developing nations often feel they have relatively little freedom to engage in such diversifying tactics. Instead, they see themselves as dominated by economically-powerful countries with highly-developed media systems which can overwhelm local, indigenous efforts to produce both hardware (such as communication technology, TV sets, etc.) and software (TV programs, radio music, feature-length films). Unable to compete with the imported "culture," the media of developing countries distribute the inexpensive foreign products through their systems. It is this exposure which many fear will alter indigenous cultures and such effects are at the base of charges about "cultural imperialism."

Probably the most vocal and strident proponent of notions of "cultural imperialism" is U.S. Marxist Herbert I. Schiller (1971, 1976), who started presenting his ideas in the late 1960's. Building on the general notion of imperialism, Schiller sees the great expansion of U.S. media and cultural products as part of a general effort of the U.S. military-industrial complex to subject the world to military control, electronic surveillance and a homogenized American commercial culture. Schiller (1976) sees the United States as the core of a world capitalist system which uses media along with other tactics to dominate the peripheral developing regions. Schiller is particularly concerned with the "commercial" nature of exported media, ranging from international advertising agencies to technology and the values implicit in TV programs. He argues that commercial values almost necessarily accompany the adoption of foreign American or European media technology (see Still and Hill, 1984; Aydin et al., 1984). Schiller also attacks the notion of "free flow" (of news, other media content or hardware) as simply a doctrine which means elimination of the weaker countries in a "laissez-faire market" (See Fejes, 1983). Schiller (1980) sees a worsening of the situation with the introduction of advanced electronic information systems. Television comes in for the largest share of attention in this debate. Latin American critic Luis Beltran (1978) believes the TV images shown residents of those countries portray elements of "individualism, elitism, racism, materialism, adventurism, conservatism, conformism, self-defeatism, providentialism, authoritarianism, romanticism and aggressiveness," which is contrary to the aspirations for autonomous, democratic national development in the region. Clearly, such laundry lists of charges reflect the emotion which has been invested in the "cultural imperialism" thesis. It should be pointed out that many non-Marxists share some of the same concerns as Schiller and his colleagues.

Schiller's thesis was examined by British researcher Jeremy Tunstall (1977) in a book whose title makes a major point: *The Media Are American.* Essentially, the argument is that modern mass media are "American" because so many media forms and technologies originated in the United States prior to their eventual diffusion and eventual modification throughout the world. Tunstall points out that Schiller's figures are unreliable and, more importantly, they concentrate on the high point of American TV exports in the mid-1960's and do not take into account changes in American influence.

That influence by the United States is so pronounced because American firms benefited from their early introduction of media products. However, media software and technology, like other products, go through life cycles which eventually limit the control of their creators. Lee (1980: 48-49) outlines this "product life cycle theory" which non-Marxists have offered as an alternative to notions of "capitalism imperialism." First, products are developed in the U.S. as a response to the country's high per capita income, availability of production factors, a large internal market demand, and swift communication system. Second, the media products are exported throughout the world. Once introduced, the monopoly is upset as competition arises from the rapid spread of research and development. Third, there is a slowdown in foreign expansion by U.S. corporations as other industrialized nations use the exported technologies and challenge American firms. Fourth, the American enterprises can no longer protect their "oligopolistic" advantage and foreign industries become competitive. At this point, American parent companies lose their cost advantage and either abandon some products, invest in cost-saving developing nations, launch aggressive marketing campaigns, or change products. This completes the cycle.

The early influence of American products is well documented by Tunstall (1977). Long before the United States became the dominant international power, it was influencing other nations through the development of novel media forms and products and the use of successful business practices. For example, the popular, mass audience newspaper now found around the world owes its debt to the American "penny press" started in New York City in the mid-19th century. And Hollywood films dominated Chinese movie screens in the 1930's, while the actual operation and management of the first commercial radio station in China was under the direction of an American (Tunstall, 1977:193). American newspapers in the last century, Hollywood films in the 1920's and U.S. TV in the 1950's were widely copied by other countries. Being early with the technology, Americans "fixed" the format and successfully exported products based on a large domestic market which enables media industries to achieve some cost efficiencies and then sell abroad at rates which undercut other countries' media industries. Tunstall notes that the U.S. practice in all media fields was to undercut the opposition initially through price competition, based on the huge size of the U.S. market.

However, the American advantage eventually erods for most media products as other countries enter the market. The U.S. influence as a model has remained because it was "first." Thus, the media are "American" in the sense that many of the modern forms accepted around the world were first developed in the United States. Media are "American" in the same sense that opera is "Italian" or European. Early American influence also occurred because governments thought they could control things more easily than it turned out. Other governments also believed that, while news was inherently political, not all films or TV programs were political and certainly not advertising. Thus, other countries' governments put few road blocks in the way of American media exporters.

Tunstall adds, however, that Schiller's thesis also is too weak and could be strengthened by recognizing the empires and influences of such European nations as Britain, France, Belgium, Portugal, and the Netherlands. The impact of these European countries on other nation's media systems and the international flow of media products has been well documented (Tunstall, 1977; Boyd-Barrett, 1980). Furthermore, the American and European influence on other nations' media systems has a parallel among communist nations. The Soviet Union has exported its media system throughout Eastern Europe and has been used as a model in other Marxist countries, setting up a dependency relationship that resembles that explained by Schiller between the industrialized West and developing nations. Schiller believes that "going socialist" and abandoning ties with the capitalist West would enable developing nations to avoid cultural/media imperialism. As Lee (1980) notes, evidence from China, Cuba and Eastern Europe provides little support for the claim that such action would guarantee an authentic indigenous cultural expression. Furthermore, the economic dependence on the West would likely be replaced by political and some economic dependence on dominant socialist nations.

The dialogue over media imperialism and cultural dependence essentially pits two models against each other, one an "economic dependency model" and the other a "media diffusion model." Lee's (1980) discussion of the diffusion model focuses on the spread of media influence through the export of TV programs, the transfer of broadcasting systems, and actual foreign ownership of media. American media firms did attempt to gain control or ownership of media outlets in some foreign nations, particularly Latin America, but those ventures proved unprofitable and the U.S. companies withdrew. However, American advertising and public relations agencies continue a strong presence abroad (Fejes, 1980). American and European broadcasting systems have been used as models around the world, with British and French models employed by former colonies of those nations and the U.S. model dominating in Latin America. Katz and Wedell (1977) note that American and European influences in broadcasting are most visible in the early phases of media adoption that developing nations pass through. At first, a U.S., British, or French model of broadcasting is adopted. In a second phase the system is adapted to the local society and in a third stage a new sense of direction is given as the remaining vestiges of direct foreign control are removed. In addition to the structure of broadcasting systems, TV programs exported by the U.S. and other industrialized nations constitute a major influence. These programs may not fit the "product life cycle theory" because other countries do not offer competitive advantages such as low labor costs and raw materials. About 47 of the 57 Third World nations examined import at least 40% of their TV programs, with the U.S. the most important exporter followed by the United Kingdom, France and West Germany (Lee, 1980). According to the Motion Picture Export Association of New York, sale of American TV series and movies for foreign TV brings in about $575 million a year (also see Caranicas, 1984). In 1983, the popular series *Dallas* was being shown in 90 countries from Bangladesh to Zimbabwe, while *Little House on the Prairie* was seen in 102 nations and *M*A*S*H* was broadcast in about 100. The U.S. receives two thirds of its TV film sales profits from seven other industrialized nations including Canada, Australia, Japan, England, Brazil, France and West Germany. This does not conflict with the concern of Third World nations for media autonomy and cultural expression.

Some recent evidence shows a diminishing impact of American TV programming and a more mixed view of its influence. Antola and Rogers (1984) found that U.S. exports of TV programs are still significant in Latin America but less so than in the early 1970s. Furthermore, the imported U.S. programs produced lower audience ratings than those imported from other Latin American nations. Mexico was the main gatekeeper for TV program flow from the U.S. to Latin America. Together with Brazil, it was a major exporter of TV programs to other countries in the region. Focusing on Brazil, Straubhaar (1984) also concluded that American influences had diminished in recent years as the country's large market supported quality programming. The past 20 years have seen the growth of two private TV systems in Latin America that rank in size just behind the three U.S. commercial networks (Mattos, 1984). One is Mexico's Televisa and the other is TV Globo in Brazil. Both have had success in exporting TV programs. In fact, Televisa owns Spanish International Network (SIN), a U.S. network that imports TV programs from Mexico and totally dominates the Spanish-language TV market in the U.S. Gutierrez and Schement (1984) note that this questions previous analyses of cultural domination. Although the TV program "Sesame Street" was once cited as an example of American influence when it was introduced in Latin America, little long-range effect is discernible today; Mayo et al. (1984) note that the programs attracted huge audiences in Mexico and Brazil but the joint productions ceased after several seasons when viable local organizations to support the program were not developed.

Non-Marxists see this flow of media content as largely a function of supply and demand. They also argue that there are internal constraints that can limit foreign influence, and some of the foreign media influence is positive. Third World nations can and do take actions to restrict the importation of foreign films and TV shows. Ceilings have been set on foreign films in Canada, Thailand, Malaysia, Taiwan, Australia and many European countries. The amount of TV air time or screen time devoted to imported media also has been limited. Brazil's efforts to restrict foreign influence date back to 1939 when theaters were required to show Brazilian films 7 days a year, a figure that increased to 56 in 1963 and 84 in the mid 1970's (de Camargo and Noya Pinto, 1975). In the early 1970's, Malyasia applied a 50% surcharge on the showing of foreign-made TV commercials (Adhikarya, 1977). Other remedies put forth by non-Marxists are regional cooperatives for producing or exchanging media products, grounding media practices in native cultures, diversifying the source of imported products to include more countries, and using group efforts at the local community level to assist in education and development. Some of these remedies can turn the influence of foreign products into positive effects (Lee, 1980).

Most of the literature on economic dependency at the bottom reduces to class conflict. Lenin argued that imperialism is the necessary result of advanced monopoly capitalism, with its concentration on production and capital. International cartels would be organized to sustain advantageous positions for the outlets of their capital. A failure to separate economic dependency from political dependency is a serious flaw (Lee, 1980). The model also neglects other noneconomic variables, such as the military, and is insensitive to the different types of dependence. World communication patterns do somewhat correspond with the international power structure, but this has more to do with the relative political and economic strength of individual countries than with the conventional Marxist dichotomy of economic capitalism vs. Marxist socialism.

There are thriving regional media centers in specific nations. Mexico and Argentina produce radio and TV dramas that circulate throughout the region while Egypt occupies a similar spot in the Arab world and Sweden among Nordic countries. India exports films and records to many nations in Africa and Asia, Hong Kong is a film production center for much of Asia, and the Soviet Union has a strong media market in Eastern Europe. Thus, we find a pattern of "regional dependency" and media dependency linked to political domination. Lee (1980) notes that radical writers are good at diagnosis but poor at therapy. Thus, Marxists sensitize Westerners to the problems of developing regions but they undermine their case by overstatement and forcing the data to fit their ideology.

Above we noted that "intent" to dominate is inferred from some of the rhetoric. Tunstall (1977) notes there is much room for disagrement over the "motives" surrounding media exporters, as well as those of importers and audiences. If American multi-national companies are regarded as instruments of neo-imperialism, then a company like RCA-NBC, also a defense contractor, is such an instrument. If the fact that people in New York City or Washington plan world-wide sales strategies constitutes media imperialism, then this also is a frequent, almost daily occurrence. However, as Reed (1972) points out, the expansion of American communication industries is motivated by profit rather than by attempts to manipulate the minds of peoples in the Third World. Nor is there a need to since most of the profit from exports is derived from other industrialized nations. After interviewing 30 media and corporate executives in the U.S., Nair (1980) concluded that news from international media can influence investment decisions of corporations when they question their sense of social responsibility or create an adverse impact in the firm's home country. Thus, corporations themselves are dependent upon local reception and response. Dagnino (1973) says that the effects of cultural dependence on the lives of Latin Americans are not a consequence of "an invasion led by a foreign enemy, but of a choice made by their own ruling class."

Lee (1980) points out the simplicity of an argument which focuses on local elites as participants in a class conflict, where the wealthy cooperate with international capitalist interests in dominating the working classes. There are many different elites within countries, and coalitions have formed around different communication policies. For example, religious elites fought television for moral reasons in Israel and Saudi Arabia. In Taiwan, the government and media commercial elites joined to diminish foreign dependence despite demands by intellectuals for foreign programs. And in India intellectuals saw TV as an unnecessary luxury but urban elites wanted TV for their lifestyles. Lee (1980) suggests it is more useful looking at how local elites coalesce around efforts to develop local media and restrict foreign influence than simply viewing them as local capitalist agents of the international capitalist system.

Audience interests and tastes for foreign products reflect the growing interdependence among all nations. Many American intellectuals flock to their TV sets to watch programs produced by the British Broadcasting Corporation, and take in the French cinema at local art houses. Certainly the United States also is not immune to foreign media influence. However, American films and TV programs have received a more positive reception from the general public than the media products of most other nations. Shaheen (1980) notes, for example, that young viewers in many Arab states prefer to watch American TV shows, especially violent crime/adventure shows, or to watch European dramas. Tunstall (1977) notes that the alternative to media imperialism is unclear. Should Third World communicators give audiences more local fare even if it is more costly or less popular? Most of the imported media products represent popular culture. As such, they are the culture of urban, industrial society, exhibiting the widest appeal, excluding the fewest people and requiring the least training or background to enjoy. This is what separates them from elite culture.

The argument over media/cultural imperialism rests, in the final analysis, not on patterns of media dependency. Those are not debated but illustrated through historical documentation. The core to the argument is the anticipated negative consequences of this dependency, and this takes us to the evidence for cultural effects of the media.

Evidence on Cultural Effects of the Media

The "cultural imperialism" thesis claims that traditional and local culture in many parts of the world is being battered out of existence by the indiscriminate dumping of large quantities of slick commercial and media products that come primarily from the United States and other industrialized nations. This is the crux of assertions by Third World countries which are seeking cultural autonomy in an increasingly interconnected world economy. Those who make this argument most forcibly tend to favor imposing restrictions on media imports similar to those described above plus the deliberate preservation of traditional culture (Tunstall, 1977: 57).

However, the concern over cultural effects of the mass media is not restricted to the international debate. Within countries, ethnic groups and minorities struggle to survive in the face of the dominant culture. Even between industrial nations, there is concern over the potential impact of foreign culture. The nature of "cultural effects" also needs clarification. Most of the conventional evidence refers to popular tastes in such things as popular music, TV or film stars, styles of dress, and so forth. Do such effects extend beyond simple tastes to more significant things, such as people's values, self-concepts, or images of others? We will discuss each of these issues and the available evidence.

Perhaps the starting point for our examination of the evidence is simpler, "primitive" civilizations which have the least experience with modern media and are more vulnerable because they have the fewest defenses which would mediate cultural effects. One of the most chilling accounts of how modern media can influence people is found in Edmund Carpenter's (1973) observations of how film was introduced to a village called Sio in New Guinea. The natives in this remote mountain village were visited only by missionaries, soldiers or government agents up to the time of their visit. The natives were still using stone axes when Carpenter and his students arrived.

> We gave each person a Polaroid shot of himself. At first there was no understanding. The photographs were black and white, flat, static, odorless — far removed from any reality they knew. They had to be taught to "read" them: I pointed to a nose in a picture, then touched the real nose, etc. Often one or more boys would intrude into the scene, peering intently from picture to subject, then shout "It's you!"
>
> Recognition gradually came into the subject's face. And fear. Suddenly he covered his mouth, ducked his head and turned his body away. After this first startled response, often repeated several times, he either stood transfixed, staring at his image, only his stomach muscles betraying tension, or he retreated from the group, pressing his photograph against his chest, showing it to no one, slipping away to study it in solitude.

We recorded this over and over on film, including men retreating to private places, sitting apart, without moving, sometimes for up to twenty minutes, their eyes rarely leaving their portraits.

When we projected movies of their neighbors, there was pandemonium. They recognized the moving images of film much faster than the still images of photographs.

Seeing themselves on film was quite a different thing. It required a minor logistic feat to send our negative out, get it processed, then returned, but it was worth the effort.

There was absolute silence as they watched themselves, a silence broken only by whispered identification of faces on the screen.

We recorded these reactions, using infrared light and film. In particular, we recorded the terror of self-awareness that revealed itself in uncontrolled stomach trembling.

The tape recorder startled them. When I first turned it on, playing back their own voices, they leaped away. They understood what was being said, but didn't recognize their own voices and shouted back, puzzled and frightened.

But in an astonishingly short time, these villagers, including children and even a few women, were making movies themselves, taking Polaroid shots of each other, and endlessly playing with tape recorders. No longer fearful of their own portraits, men wore them openly on their foreheads.

When we returned to Sio, months later, I thought at first we had made a wrong turn in the river network. I didn't recognize the place. Several houses had been rebuilt in a new style. Men wore European clothing. They carried themselves differently. They acted differently. Some had disappeared down river toward a government settlement, "wandering between two worlds/one dead, the other powerless to be born."

In one brutal movement they had been torn out of a tribal existence and transformed into detached individuals, lonely, frustrated, no longer at home — anywhere.

I fear our visit precipitated this crisis. Not our presence, but the presence of new media. A more isolated people might have been affected far less, perhaps scarcely at all. But the people of Sio were vulnerable. For a decade they had been moving imperceptibly toward Western culture. Our demonstration of media tipped the scales. Hidden changes suddenly coalesced and surfaced.

The effect was instant alienation. Their wits and sensibilities, released from tribal restraints, created a new identity: the private individual. For the first time, each man saw himself and his environment clearly and he saw them as separable.

Source: Edmund Carpenter, *Oh, What a Blow that Phantom Gave Me!* (New York: Holt, Rinehart and Winston), 1973. Reprinted with the author's permission.

In this context the media were the catalyst for change, but such cultural effects cannot be generalized to relationships between modern countries or relationships between ethnic cultures and host societies. In these cases, most people are literate in media forms and have developed various filters and activators which limit the direct effects described in Sio. For example, Coledvin (1979) found that Eskimo adolescents were influenced more by two years of expsoure to "foreign" TV programs than were adults, who were more attached to traditional norms. Credibility of a new medium also is another example of a potential filter. Granzberg (1982) studied the Algonkina Indians in Central Canada and found they attributed high credibility to television because it fit in with their story telling and other traditions.

In earlier chapters we found that cognitive effects of the media were more pronounced than those having to do with affect (feelings, evaluations, values, goals) or behavioral goals. We would expect a similar pattern here, with media having more impact on images and information than basic values or attitudes. The evidence seems to provide some support for this expectation. Payne (1978) looked at TV viewing among Canadian-U.S. border communities, finding that viewing TV from the opposing country did increase knowledge levels. Only minor attitudinal changes were noted and those were in a direction opposite to that predicted by the "cultural/media imperialism" hypothesis. Those Canadian viewers who watched American TV had more favorable attitudes toward their own country than did those who watched only Canadian TV. Payne suggests that local newscasts in an open, democratic society like Canada expose viewers to national problems and a diet of criticism. This can help form negative attitudes toward Canadian institutions. American newscasts, on the other hand, tend to ignore Canadian politics and focus on more positive aspects of Canadian life.

Another study of Canadian students sought to test the impact of U.S. TV programs on Canadian knowledge about their legal system (Tate and Trach, 1980). At the time of the study Canadian TV was dominated by programs about the U.S. legal system. Since the Canadian court system is quite different from the U.S. system portrayed on TV, they expected Canadian viewers to be affected by the American programming. They found that people who said they relied on TV as a source of information about the law did have more inaccurate perceptions about the Canadian court system than those not relying on the medium. In this instance, people's personal media dependency for this purpose (uses and gratifications) acted as an intensifier of media effects.

One of the potentially most significant cognitive consequences of exposure to media from other cultures is changing people's self-perceptions and their images of other groups. Tsai (1970) found that exposing Formosan children to American TV programming did not affect the children's images of their own cultural group, although it did have an impact on how they saw Americans. Caron (1979) looked at the effects of first-time TV exposure on Eskimo children ages 8-13 and found that cultural programs from a number of different countries had an effect on the children's images of other cultural groups, but the impact was most pronounced on groups closest to their own and less on those with which they were least familiar. Tan (1982) found that heavy TV viewing among a sample of Chineses foreign students in the U.S. was related to their perception of Americans as materialistic and pleasure loving. Roberts et al. (1974) found that showing a TV series called the "Big Blue Marble," which was designed to encourage international awareness in children, successfully created a more positive view of other cultural groups.

Changes in evaluations, feelings and attitudes also have been associated with media originating in other cultures. Isolation and simply avoiding exposure to communication channels which would allow access to foreign culture can reduce outside influence (Engelmayer, 1984). Murphy (1978) notes that Dutch Calvinists in North America see the mass media as working to undercut personal responsibility and personal discipline by giving those who control them a power over the masses and the ability to supplant the Scriptures as the source of life's direction. They see it as a threat to the socializing of children into Calvinism and they believe that interpersonal communication and literature should be the primary tools in such socialization. One indication of attitude was found in a sample of children in five Nordic countries, who were asked where they would move if forced to leave and where they got most of their information about the country of destination. Children consistently chose countries they considered larger and richer than their own. The sources of information cited most often were school, TV and personal experience. Television was mentioned as the most important source of information by those who selected the United States (Werner, 1981). TV thus prompted a positive evaluation and some feelings of attachment. The "Big Blue Marble" study (Roberts et al., 1976) and the Formosan project (Tsai, 1970) mentioned earlier both found changes in affect among children and those changes also concerned evaluations of other people, not self images. However, attitudes toward local institutions were the focus in a survey conducted in Windsor, Ontario, near Detroit. Winter and Baer (1982) found that Canadians who spent more time with the U.S. media identified more closely with anti-government sentiment, and they argue this is more consistent with American than Candian culture. Only minimal effects were attributed to foreign TV programs in an Icelandic study. Payne and Peake (1977) found that watching U.S. television programs had little impact on Icelandic children's attitudes toward the U.S. and no effect on increasing such feelings as fear, anger or sadness, which Icelanders commonly associate with American culture.

One of the more threatening consequences of foreign media, including advertising, is the inflation of people's expectations about their future life. If such expectations are not met, people can grow frustrated and angry. Halad (1978) notes that the media of industrialized nations export a materialistic life style which, when introduced to countries still riddled with poverty and social inequality create an identity crisis and accelerate the rising frustrations of the masses. O'Connell (1977) found that there was an increased desire for social change among Eskimo communities exposed to a year of foreign television. There also was greater desire to travel. Hornick, (1977) found a link between rising education and growing occupational aspirations and a desire to live in urban areas among El Salvadorean junior high school students. He also found early mass media use linked to changes in social expectations. Coldevin (1976) found that the major effect of frontier TV on Canadian Eskimos was to raise aspirations about employment, etc.; however, there was also a desire to return to traditional ways.

It is matters of taste which have most easily been linked to popular media, particularly those portraying Western lifestyles. Jorgensen and Karlin (1980) found Romanian adolescents imitating American tastes as portrayed in U.S. media imports — from slang to blue jeans and personal habits such as smoking. Many Romanian youths in their mid to late teens expressed the desire to "be like Americans" but this attitude seemed to change with age. They conclude that American media are not radically eroding the cultural heritage of the young in Romania. Skipper (1975) compared American and Canadian college students' musical tastes and found considerable influence of American music on the Canadian youths. In fact, 80% of the Canadian sample chose non-Canadians as their favorite musical artists and half of these were American.

Almost all countries around the world are polyglot in the sense they are multilingual, multiracial, multi-religious, or multinational (Van Dyke, 1977). Various strategies are used to integrate diverse ethnic groups. One strategy is assimilation which eliminates distinctive cultural traits of minority communities; another is establishing national loyalties without eliminating subordinate cultures — "unity in diversity" (Jeffres, 1981). Regardless of the national policies, members of ethnic groups struggle to maintain their distinctive cultures in the face of national and international pressures (Bevan, 1984). Those pressures include both mass and interpersonal communication. At the same time ethnics use their specialized ethnic media and other ethnic communication channels to strengthen ties within groups (Fathi, 1973). Although the "cultural effects" of media are occurring within countries rather than between them, the processes may be quite similar.

Jeffres and Hur (1978, 1983) looked at communication patterns among members of 13 different ethnic groups in Cleveland, Ohio, ranging from Irish to Romanian, Hispanic and Slovene. They found that ethnic media use (listening to ethnic radio programs, reading ethnic newspapers, books and magazines) predicted ethnic identification and other ethnic behaviors such as observing ethnic holidays. Focusing on interpersonal communication, Kim (1982) underscores the significance of communication. She sees culture as being composed of patterns that reflect communicative responses to the environment. When immigrants arrive in a new culture, they must acquire the cultural rules of communication in order to function effectively. In her view, acculturation becomes the process of developing communication competence in the host sociocultural system. One learns this by communicating. This scenario on communication and culture concerns immigrants in host countries. We might ask whether local people react in a similar fashion when their own media system confronts them with an abundance of foreign content. Certainly, there is not the need to develop "communication competence" from such content in order to operate within one's social system, but some abbreviated version of competence may be called for in social interaction.

Ethnics who are indigenous to a country find a similar situation in that they face cultural pressure from several quarters. Olmedo (1980) argues that ethnics have a range of responses to such cultural pressure, and one is to adopt what we might call a hybrid culture that incorporates the best of the traditional culture and elements of the "foreign" cultures faced through both mass media and interpersonal communication. Reversing the direction of the influence from the minority ethnic group to the cultural majority, we do find evidence that mass media can have some impact on cultural perceptions of minorities by the majority. Within the United States, researchers have looked at the impact of Roots, two TV mini-series which traced the origins and history of slavery in America. A review of the literature shows that viewing the series did provoke feelings of sympathy and sadness for Blacks among Whites. However, there was little evidence that actual attitudes changed very much (Surlin, 1978; Ball-Rokeach, Grube and Rokeach, 1981; Goldberg, 1979). Hur and Robinson (1978) suggest that the program might have had greater impact on Blacks' self-images than it did among other people.

However, other studies have linked cultural effects to such media use. Goldberg and Gorn (1979) studied English-Canadian kindergartners from upper middle-class homes. Some were assigned to watch "Sesame Street," an integrated educational TV program directed at preschoolers and others remained in a control group. They found that those who watched the program were more likely to choose non-whites as playmates than those who didn't watch the TV show. However, the impact diminished greatly over time. DeBock and van Lil (1981) found that viewing the *Holocaust,* an American-produced TV show on the Nazi extermination of Jews in World War II, combined with interpersonal factors to produce significant long-term effects by increasing both knowledge of the history of World War II atrocities and disapproval of anti-semitism.

There is little hard, scientific evidence available to address the most controversial issue: Can local cultures persist in the face of strong national and international forces, and, if so, how? Those most concerned with the issue provide us with strong feelings about the desirability of maintaining "authentic cultures" but no rationale for how that is to be achieved other than some form of isolation (inhibiting communication between local citizens and outsiders by restricting travel, interpersonal communication, or mass communication). Somehow, there is the belief that local development will occur along some unique line if left alone. In Canada, for example, those concerned with the maintenance of French-speaking culture have argued that it will succeed only if its proponents are "productive," if they produce original films, plays, books, and so forth. The minority culture will slowly be overwhelmed if its members become dependent on imports from the "mother country," France.

The only "positive" proposals have been some form of government support for local cultural efforts. Numerous examples of this were outlined in chapter one, e.g., Brazil's local film quota for theaters, Malaysia's tax on foreign-produced commercials, and Ireland's efforts to increase use of the local language; such efforts have met with limited success. In addition to theoretical and practical concerns about the relationship between communication and cultural forms, we have debates stemming from different values. Often we find that people supporting national cultures and the "suppression" of local, ethnic cultures argue for quotas on foreign cultural imports. Thus, for example, we might find someone arguing that India has too many languages for national development and Hindi should be promoted to a place of favor, but restrictions should be placed on foreign-language imports from other countries. The debate often can be reduced to the issue of nationalism.

At other times, the value is not nationalism but ideology; cultural influence is unacceptable because it occurs through an exchange in commercial markets. Exchanges occuring between governments are seen as acceptable, according to one line of argument. In this case, the debate often is reduced to struggles between capitalism and various forms of Marxism. We are unlikely to see an end to the cultural debate as long as nationalism and contemporary ideologies remain at the center of conflicts, but we can hope future theoretical developments and scientific research provide for a more rational debate by gnawing away at untested assumptions and vague concepts.

In summary, when we consider the cultural effects of mass media, we need to specify the context in which the influence occurs, whether the relationship is between two countries, a primitive society and foreign culture, or between an ethnic culture and the larger host culture. Certainly the media do have cultural effects, but these effects are also constrained by various filters and activators — familiarity with foreign cultures, media literacy, media credibility, etc. There is some evidence that foreign media can increase people's knowledge and have an impact on images, although the impact appears to be greatest on images of foreign peoples and least on self-images. Some affective changes also were noted but there is only scanty empirical evidence of such long-range cultural effects stemming from imported media products. Media are successful, however, in changing popular tastes that range from music to clothing and ideas of beauty. Clearly, we need more research before we can conclude that the cultural effects attributed to the media in the debates over news flow and media imperialism are of the magnitude envisioned or feared.

Enter the New Communication Technologies
What Impact Will They Have on the Cultural Debate?

The world is entering what some people have called the "information age." We might as easily call it the "communication age," because the central questions over economic power, political autonomy and cultural integrity center on communication issues. The new communication technologies have merged with the computer to create new possibilities of social organization and influence. Those possibilities also have intensified the debates over "cultural/media imperialism" and the flow of news and information around the world. The political question is whether international communication networks will respect national political boundaries. The economic question is whether the industrialized nations will get richer and the developing world poorer because of the new technological innovations. And the cultural question is whether the new technologies will provide even greater access by other countries to local cultures. Most of these questions will be debated for years to come, but the rapid advance of technology provides the stimulus for nations to cooperate and try to solve disagreements before it's too late. There is an additional incentive in that the new technologies achieve their impact only through the development of "international" systems; thus, they create interdependence between nations by their very existence. For example, you can't have an effective phone system unless most people are hooked into the system. Similarly, international communication netwroks via satellite, the spread of data and information banks, and other systems require the cooperation and participation of people from different countries and cultures.

Rapid Growth and Change

Dizard (1985) lays out the new information age as one in which the world is crisscrossed by an integrated grid which allows messages to move in any form over a network of wire or wireless channels. There are several ingredients to this grid. Coaxial cable will remain a part of the system but not in its current form. The first transatlantic coaxial cable began in 1956 with 36 phone circuits and the Bell research labs have now developed one with a 40,000 capacity. The newest cable technology, fiber optics, promises even more radical changes. The other channel is wireless communication technology which uses the radio spectrum, or radiant energy in the form of invisible waves that move through time, space, and matter to satellites, radios and your TV set. The useable part of the spectrum extends from 10 kilohertz (the lowest limit of human hearing) to 275 gigahertz (a frequency which approaches that of light waves). Scientists are busy trying to pack as many channels as possible into that space. Given the current usage, the question is one of allocating the frequencies to users, and this is one of the political questions we'll touch on later.

Another ingredient of this grid is the communication satellite, which is linked by microwaves to ground switching stations. Satellites have line-of-sight capacity that allows them to cover a third of the earth when they travel at the speed of the earth's rotation and appear "geostationary." In this manner, the satellites appear to float 22,300 miles above the equator, their speed synchronized with that of the earth. In less than 20 years satellites have gone through several generations of technology. The current Intelsat V can transmit a combination of two TV signals and 12,000 phone calls simultaneously, compared to one TV station and 250 phone circuits for the first generation satellite. One of the most recent additions to the grid is the direct broadcast satellite, which can transmit signals directly to TV sets rather than relaying them through the local TV station.

Future growth is likely to be in computer-links, with people talking to computers or computers linked to computers. One study predicted an annual growth rate of 28% in such communication traffic. Pipe (1979) notes that the "computer has introduced boundless possibilities for storage, integration, transfer and accessibility of vast quantities of information." Polcyn (1981) predicts that by the 1990's there will be highly sophisticated communication satellites capable of meeting any communication need, with a total integration of media and computer technology.

Since the first broadcast of a presidential election in the U.S. in 1920, the speed and mechanics of delivering the news have changed dramatically. The most recent additions are satellites and computer-based methods of moving information, which represent a quantum jump in the ability of people to communicate.

Potential Consequences

This rapid change in communication technologies has intensified the debate over information flow and the cultural impact of media around the world. Several observers have noted that the outcome of these debates will eventually hinge on who controls the new technologies, who uses them and what laws are made and abided by globally to ensure that those possessing the technologies do not bombard those who do not with their values and philosophy (Mitchell, 1978; Langdale, 1982). Mitchell (1978) argues that the Third World must consolidate its information media and receive assistance from the developed Western countries. In general, this is the position of most industrialized nations who recognize that their future is linked together with the developing nations and cooperation is the only approach likely to succeed.

However, another critic sees a dark side to this transfer of technology. Schiller (1980) argues that the Third World should be leary of the new technologies. He argues that the transfer of electronic information systems by giant conglomerates and organizations will merely lead to increased dependency by developing nations on industrialized countries. Schiller does not provide a solution to technological needs other than those cited earlier.

Information has become the cutting edge of technological advancement and economic growth. As a consequence, the way in which governments view information is changing. Increasingly, they see information as a commodity that governments must control or tax for economic reasons (Hamelink, 1979). Spero (1982) notes that this conflicts with the U.S. acceptance of the principle of free flow of information, and he argues that the U.S. government must recognize that some of the opposition represents these economic interests rather than political or ideological values; otherwise, protectionism will continue to grow and U.S. economic and political interests will suffer. Read (1979) also notes that America's information resources have been neglected by U.S. foreign policy because communication matters have long been regarded as simply environmental factors rather than basic resources that are central to the conduct of international relations.

The central argument is one of national sovereignty. Jacobson (1979) argues that the merger of computers and satellites has serious implications for the sovereignty of nation states because individuals and other enterprises will no longer be reliant on national postal, telegraph or telephone systems for any of their information needs. This removes the last link in making transnational businesses and organizations subject to national governmental scrutiny. The noted scientist and science fiction writer Arthur C. Clarke, who began writing about space exploration long before the first satellite was launched, noted the 1983 World Telecommunications Day with a forecast that national boundaries will effectively turn into sieves as national governments lose control. In the coming decade more and more well-heeled tourists, most reporters and many businessmen will carry attache-sized units allowing them two-way communication with their homes or offices through satellite connections.

> The implications of this are profound—and not only to media news gatherers who will no longer be at the mercy of censors or inefficient (sometimes non-existent) postal and telegraph services. It means the end of closed societies and ultimately...to unification of the world. (Clarke, 1983:4)

Clarke argues that national governments will not take the steps necessary to control such communication because they would be "committing economic suicide," discouraging tourists and businessmen but having no impact on spies who would have no difficulty concealing the powerful new tools. The debate over the free flow of information will soon be settled, he argues, not by politicians but by engineers. Clarke sees a rather positive future in this because governments will be less able to conceal such things as major crimes or atrocities for very long. He suggests that the new information system will have a powerful influence for civilized behavior and in the long run everyone will benefit from the exposure of scandals and political abuses in a more open international society.

Malik (1984) advances the thesis that the appearance of inexpensive electronic information technology is a fundamental challenge to the survival of the Soviet system and its associated countries which cannot survive the large-scale introduction of information technology in any meaningful way. The main reason is that the infrastructure necessary for the USSR to reap the benefits cannot be created without a massive administrative restructuring of the entire Soviet bloc, which is difficult ideologically. The problem facing the Soviet bloc is that to breed a competitive society, it must breed not just an educated society but an informed society.

The basis of national sovereignty in this area depends on the view that the airwaves belong to "the public" because they are limited. In the United States, this is the basis for the regulation of American broadcasting by the Federal Communication Commission. Extending this to the international arena, where communication takes place between people from different nations and cultures, it is an "international public." This complicates the question of regulation, which falls to international organizations and transnation cooperation (See Mitchell, 1978). Just as there are limits to the number of radio or TV signals that can be carried, there are limits to the number of parking spaces available to satellites girding the center of the globe. Several international organizations are responsible for both debates and negotiations between countries over trans-national communication questions, including Unesco, the International Telecommunications Union (ITU), the Universal Postal Union, and others.

The ITU sponsors the World Administrative Radio Conference, a meeting held every few years to allocate the radio spectrum for new services and to solve specific problems such as allotting space for satellites. The ITU performs the increasingly complex and politically sensitive task of allocating bandwidths and registering each individual nation's frequency usage (Smith, 1980). As conflict between the industrialized and developing nations built up through the 1970's, many expected the 1979 WAR conference to be an explosive situation as the Third World nations fought for their piece of the economic pie, whether they could use it now or not (Kroloff, 1979). As Clippinger (1979) has noted, the most important issue of the "new world information order" is the slotting of satellites because it sets a precedent for other issues. However, rather than an acrimonious debate, the conference arrived at a compromise which gives priority to the requirements of developing nations without dividing up the radio spectrum into priorities (Berrada, 1981). A series of technical conferences to be conducted in the ensuing decade is to sort out the touchy issues. The 1985 WAR conference marked the return of charges about "obstructionist tactics" and struggles over political issues but some progress as well ("WARC 1985: The Politics of Space").

This is not the first time nations have had to cooperate through such arrangements. Uses of the radio spectrum had become so varied by the 1920's that they had to be adjusted through international conferences just a couple decades into the radio age (Hawkins, 1979); they have been held regularly since then and have turned into a forum for debate and conflict because communication questions themselves have turned out to be keys to political, economic and cultural questions.

One of the oldest and most successful international organizations dealing with communication questions is the International Telecommunication Satellite Organization, known as Intelsat. Started by the

U.S. and managed by it through the Communications Satellite Corporation (Comsat) for a dozen years, Intelsat is based on a usage system, where countries with higher usage have more control. Through the years, the American voting share has dropped from 60% in 1965 to less than 25% in the early 1980's. Dizard (1985) believes that Intelsat was a unique creation of its time, "involving a technology that would not work without a high degree of political cooperation." Moreover, the technology was the monopoly of one country, the U.S., which had the "resources, the imagination, and the will to allow its monopoly to erode gradually in the interests of a long-term viable world system." Such a situation is not easily replicated in other areas. Intelsat has more than 100 members, including Mainland China, South Africa, the Vatican State, and all major countries except the USSR. The first commercial communication satellite, "Early Bird," was placed in orbit in 1965. That was the first generation, and today Intelsat has been joined by regional systems such as the European Space Agency in satellite communication. PALAPA satellites serve Indonesia, MOLNIYA links Eastern European countries, and more are planned for the Arab countries and other regions.

Not everyone sees conflict or exploitation in the new technologies. Jussawalla (1981) notes that developing countries have the least invested in existing technologies and, as a consequence, they have relatively more freedom to invest in newer satellite technology. Polcyn (1981) points out that communication satellites will help emerging nations reach remote and rural areas previously inaccessible. Island nations also should benefit from the new technologies (Pool, 1981). Nimetz (1980) argues that the impeded flow of information goods and services is essential for several reasons, primarily because competition and open markets seem to provide the strongest incentives for innovation, creativity, formation of capital and risk-taking.

Pool (1979) also argues that developing countries have the most to gain from a free flow of international telecommunications, and he recommends the effective use of satellite TV and radio, satellite telephone, computers and other systems as well suited for developing nations. The new technologies could be used to solve many of the problems identified by Third World nations. For example, satellites make it possible to develop inexpensive news networks which is one solution to concerns over lack of alternative news sources. We have already seen more regional exchanges of broadcasting because of advancing technology.

What are the implications of these new technologies? The systematic evidence collected so far is quite meager, although general observations and arguments abound. In Brazil a satellite-based tele-education system broadcast 15 minutes a day for students and a half hour daily for teachers (McAnany and Oliveira, 1980). The experiment was conducted to demonstrate the cost effectiveness of satellite-provided education. The media in this case did not increase enrollments in rural areas and the project suffered from being too traditional and not using the technology's capabilities. In the mid-1960's, one of the most publicized educational TV broadcasting systems began beaming core instruction into the public schools of American Samoa. By 1980, however, TV played only a minor supplementary role in instruction (Thomas, 1980). Over that 15-year period, however, the introduction of educational TV did play a major role in advancing the level of education (Schramm, Nelson and Betham, 1981). Pool (1975) says the U.S. should fight censorship but also try to make satellites into channels that allow developing countries to express their views to Americans.

Tehranian (1981) notes that the new communication technologies may be a "double-edged sword, allowing not only large-scale organization and centralization but also making it possible for individual self-expression and social protest movements to launch effective counter-attacks on the power establishments. For example, although satellite technology facilitates trans-national organization, the portable cassette played an important part in the recent Iranian revolution by allowing dissidents to smuggle in tapes that could be widely distributed within the country and bypass the "big" technology of the ruling government. A similar situation is occuring with video cassette recorders which have spread more rapidly through developing nations than industrialized countries. VCR's allow elites and members òf the middle class to by-pass governmental restrictions and seek out either foreign content or regional/ethnic cultural offerings; the growth of VCR "theaters" and neighborhood viewing extends this opportunity to the population at large.

The newer communication technologies also have stimulated debate over the place occupied by communication in national development. In the next section, we will briefly examine developmental questions.

Communication and Development
What's the Relationship?

Most of the Third World is concerned with national development, a concept which generally has emphasized economic growth but is now undergoing changes. At times change at the individual level has been called "modernization" while change at the national level has been termed "development." (For a discussion of concepts see Bendix, 1966; Schramm and Lerner, 1976; Rogers, 1983; Schramm, 1964).

Many models and theories have been proposed for relating communication and other factors to development. Schramm (1964) noted the positive correlation between economic growth and communication services and suggested that the level of investment in communication be a bit ahead of that in other institutions of developing countries. Schramm (1964) identified several functions of the mass media in national development including: acting as watchmen to broaden horizons, helping the decision process by discussing policies, and training the population. Others have elaborated on media functions in development and found evidence of them in a variety of contexts (see, for example, Farace, 1966; Frey, 1966; Rao, 1966; McNelley, 1968).

Frey (1973) outlined four areas in which theories of development have occurred: economics, psychology, political science, and communication. Even within the first three areas, communication variables are important. Economic theories include those emphasizing stages of economic growth and the accumulation of capital for "takeoff" into self-sustaining growth (Todaro, 1981; Rostow, 1960, 1978). Psychological theories focus at the individual level and include McClelland's concept of the "n/Ach," or achievement factor, which refers to an individual's motivation to establish and meet demanding standards of excellence — to strive for achievement (see Freeman, 1976, and Tekiner, 1980, for evidence supporting this concept). Hagen's (1962a,b) theory of social change points to the need for certain types of personalities in national development. Political theories focus on national integration and note that modern societies demand more communication for integration and decision making (See Frey, 1973, Pye, 1963, 1965, 1966; Deutsch, 1953; Deutsch and Merritt, 1970). Among the explicitly communication theories are Lerner's (1958) classic theory about the passing of traditional society (see Frey, 1973; Winham, 1970; Lerner, 1977), and the voluminous literature on the diffusion of innovations (Rogers, 1983). Diffusion is the process by which an innovation is communicated through certain channels over time among members of a social system. See Figure 9-1 for steps in the process.

Recently, there has been a re-examination of models of development and the part played by communication. This was stimulated in part by growing frustration over what is seen as insufficient progress in economic development, shifting goals, and ideological debates. Older economic models emphasized urban, capital-intensive industry that led to a draining of the rural areas and failing agricultural development, among other negative consequences. Developing countries also have become leary of foreign aid and are emphasizing self-reliance and independence in development. Another element is recognition of a threat to traditional symbols and an interest in returning to the use of traditional, folk media (Lent, 1980, 1982; Wang and Dissanayake, 1982; Ranganath, 1982). Interest in non-western models also has grown, e.g., China and its use of interpersonal communication (small groups) to pull up the laggards (Durdin, 1976; Oshima, 1976), and India with its village emphasis and use of radio forums (Dikshit et al., 1979; Dube, 1976). Recently, with a more open-door policy, China's development policies have taken on a different look to outsiders in this continual process of assessing development programs (see Butterfield, 1983; Mosher, 1983; Stevenson, 1985).

An important element of the emerging development model is growing popular participation in both planning and execution, and decentralization of activities (Rogers, 1978; Rosario-Braid, 1983). This means that communication patterns should reflect a more "bottom-up" and less "top-down" flow of ideas and control. Journalists and the media have been urged to focus on development goals in Third World countries and there is some evidence that such news is becoming more common (see Quebral, 1975; Smart, 1978; Madjri, 1977; Banarjee, 1978; Chalkey, 1980; Kaur and Mathur, 1981; Ogan, 1982; Ogan and Swift, 1982; Ogan and Fair, 1984).

Figure 9-1
Steps in the Diffusion Process

Knowledge	Persuasion	Decision	Implementation	Confirmation
Person is exposed to innovation's existence.	One forms a favorable or negative attitude toward the innovation.	One engages in activities that lead to a choice to adopt/reject innovation.	One puts the innovation into use.	One seeks reinforcement of an innovation decision already made.

Two factors are emphasized in recent views about development. Both reflect a shift in economic goals from focusing only on absolute growth to also striving for a more equal distribution of wealth. One factor points to the internal social structure, which must be changed or taken into account in development programs. For example, the diffusion of innovations can mean that the rich get richer and the poor poorer because of initial advantages in skills and resources. Rogers (1976) calls this a "communication effects gap." However, recent research shows that a ceiling effect can occur and gaps closed with carefully-constructed communication campaigns (Roling, Ascroft, and Chege, 1976; Shingi and Mody, 1976; Galloway, 1977).

The second factor links development within countries to their position in the international economic structure. In short, this neo-Marxist, neocolonial view attributes problems of the Third World to policies of the industrial, capitalist and socialist countries of the North and their extensions via small elites within developing countries. This view emphasizes "dependency theory" (Fejes, 1980) and reiterates the need for self-reliance and national control. The debate here parallels that encountered in our discussion of news flow. This debate, like others, occurs on shifting sands as patterns of industrial wealth change and the "center" is challenged by newly industrialized nations in Asia. Like so many debates of the past, we may find the situation discussed in dependency theory is contravened at the very time the theory becomes most popular (see Dizard, 1985; Parker, 1978).

Disputes over development strategies often parallel controversies about the New World Information Order or use of the new communication technologies. An anti-West theme runs through much of the rhetoric. Here we find an emphasis on disengagement from western organizations and systems — technological, economic, or political. Third World nations are encouraged to avoid dependence on western wire services for news, or dependence on western institutions for economic development. Furthermore, they are encouraged to reduce western control over organizations that must be international in order to administer a world telecommunication system. Even westerners who share some of the concerns raised by developing nations characterize the dispute as largely one of protest about the distribution of political and economic power. Beyond the appeal to national interests, any statement of positive development is vaguely one of self reliance or, in the case of Marxist proponents, shifting dependence from the West to the East. Countries which were cited as examples of alternative development in the 1970's have either changed strategies (e.g., China shifting toward use of more capitalist incentives) or experienced breakdowns and instability (e.g., Tanzania's economic bankruptcy). Those countries currently cited as examples of successful economic development have followed western economic models and traditions (e.g., South Korea, Singapore).

Summary

In this chapter, we examined the evidence and debate over cultural effects of the mass media. After a discussion of the ways "culture" and "communication" are currently being related, we discussed the flow of news and information around the world. Currently, the Third World and industrialized countries are engaged in a debate over control of international news organizations and the impact news has on developing countries. These differences also are reflected in the debate over "cultural imperialism" and the influence of American media around the world. Here, the dialogue pits the "economic dependency model" against the "media diffusion model." A summary of the evidence on cultural effects shows that foreign media can increase people's knowledge and have an impact on images but the impact is greatest on images of others rather than self-image. Although media can change tastes for various products, evidence of long-range cultural effects is scanty.

The arrival of new technologies has fueled the international debate; some fear inequality between nations will be heightened rather than reduced, although some positive assessments also have emerged. The debate has turned on questions of national sovereignty over the "airwaves" used by satellites and radio waves. The international debate also has extended to questions of national development and the position occupied by communication. Several models and theories relate communication and development, some emphasizing economic, psychological or political factors. Among those emphasizing communication and the media is the diffusion model. In a reexamination of develoment models, we find an increasing emphasis on social structure, international dependency and the combined use of inter-personal and mass communication in development programs.

CONCLUDING COMMENTS

Modern communication systems are inextricably linked with the rise of a world culture based on western technology and influence. But the relationship, once viewed with promise, now is often evaluated with suspicion. In the years following the end of World War II, most people seemed to welcome the prospects for a world culture in the belief that some elements of national uniqueness were worth sacrificing for the promise of reduced international conflict and greater cooperation among peoples and nations. This optimism was quite consistent with the hopes and desires of former colonies in Africa and Asia that obtained their independence in the 1940's and 1950's. But statehood did not produce the economic independence or cultural cohesion leaders of many new countries expected. They sought assistance from a variety of institutions and experts including economists, political scientists and communication scholars. Lerner in the 1950's presented a scenario in which communication would lead to a more mature, stable political system, and researchers like Schramm (1964) showed how communication could be used for internal economic and social development.

By the 1970's, disillusionment had set in on many fronts, and Third World nations sought explanations for their failure to develop further by looking to the international arena for answers. There are a variety of academic trends that could be invoked to explain the shift (e.g., the spread of Marxist notions, the emergence of different philosophical interpretations and a shift by economists toward analysis of a world economic system), but these are probably less significant than the reality of what countries themselves faced. Disappointment with current programs and fears about national stability led to a pragmatic program of experimentation based on the prospect for progress using different models such as Mao's China, Castro's Cuba, and Julius Nyerere's Tanzania.

The communication system was no less important in this pespective, but it was seen as part of the problem as well as part of the solution. Media and interpersonal communication remained important in national development programs, but communication links with other cultures and nations were seen as evidence of foreign control. The central theme now was self-reliance and independence. Internal economic development and the lack of cultural cohesion were hindered by a reliance on foreign TV programs, foreign films, foreign news services, foreign music, and foreign advertising.

Increasingly, the concept of dependency was extended to all dimensions—economics, political power, and communication. Integration into the world culture, world economy, and world political arrangements were now viewed as involvement in inherently unequal relationships. This is the scenario that has buttressed the New World Information Order and paralleled charges of cultural imperialism.

This scenario has evolved using a rather simplistic model of communication, one which sees communication as something "done" by one nation or person "to" another. The "relational aspects" of communication have been ignored except for economic notions of equality. The significance of communication in international relationships has been lost in largely defensive nationalistic rhetoric. Communication represents the opportunity for stimulation and growth as well as the threat of external influence. Indeed, personal development is impossible without the self-evaluation and reflection that comes from interaction or communication with others. The same concept should be applied to larger systems; isolated nations and national cultures are less likely to develop far or be very creative without the stimulation that comes from contact with representatives of other nations and their cultures.

What is novel to the modern era is the end of isolation and the reality of an international communication system. We are not talking about building such a system—it has existed for more than a century. The new communication technologies have simply made the international system more visible and obtrusive and its consequences more immediate, evidence, perhaps, of Toffler's (1971) "future shock." Just as nations are no longer self-sufficient in any political or economic sense—"No nation is an island"—few countries are independent of the emrging international culture or the world communication system. Isolation is still a possibility for countries (e.g., Albania), but the price is high.

A simple application of cybernetics/information theory points out the disadvantages of isolation (e.g., stagnation, no stimulation for development economically, culturally, politically, or otherwise). It is doubtful if most countries or peoples of the world are willing to delay the potential economic or psychological rewards stemming from communication with others in order to gain the short-term advantages of security and certainty. We are already seeing countries reject the 1960's/1970's scenario painted earlier. This rejection appears to stem from experience with self-reliance, and the success of more classic capitalist models that involve considerable integration with other economies and extensive involvement in international cultural exchanges (e.g., Taiwan, South Korea, Singapore).

The issue then is not isolation vs. contact, but the nature of international communication exchanges and their consequences for both national and international cultural forms. An interaction view of communication points out that both participants are affected in the process of cross-cultural communication. The encoders are affected in two ways. First, they take their "audience" into account in their own encoding process. For mass communication, it means the professional encoders, like film producers, take into account the international (other cultural) market as they construct messages, or films in this case. Secondly, they are impacted by that audience when it accepts, rejects, evaluates, feeds back information in the ongoing process. Thus, the "exporting" culture is affected by the contact, or cross-cultural communication and over time we would expect it to incorporate elements of the value system of the audiences with which it interacts. Similarly, the audiences themselves learn about other people and use them as a point of reference for evaluating their own culture. Clearly, in this scenario, cross-cultural communication involves "changes" in representatives of all cultures involved. What emerges as the "international culture" are the most successful efforts at anticipation and accommodation within international communication exchanges.

Over time this leads to the development of an international cultural system, one which today has a disproportionate Western input, but one which is increasingly integrating influences from African and Asian nations. Following World War II, the possibility of a World culture was viewed with hope and desire rather than the suspicion and envy that characterize today's reactions. In one sense this reflects a lack of faith in progress and disappointing experience with government intervention and man's own efforts to construct reality via political constraints. The question is whether nations of the world will find methods for participating in but not being overwhelmed by world culture. And this means we must be more adept at conceptualizing relationships between the international communication system and other systems of interdependence.

References

Aaker, David A. and Donald Norris. "Characteristics of TV Commercials Perceived as Informative," *Journal of Advertising Research* (April/May, 1982) 22(2): 61-70.

Abel, J.D. "Female Ownership of Broadcast Stations," *Feedback* (Spring, 1984) 25(4): 15-18.

Abel, John D. and Frederick N. Jacobs, "Radio Station Manager Attitudes Toward Broadcasting Graduates," *Journal of Broadcasting* (Fall, 1975) 19(4): 439-451.

Abelman, Robert and John Courtright. "Television Literacy: Amplifying the Cognitive Effects of Television's Prosocial Fare through Curriculum Intervention," *Journal of Research and Development in Education* (1983) 17(1): 46-57.

Abelman, Robert and Kimberly Neuendorf. "How Religious Is Religious Television Programming?" *Journal of Communication* (Winter, 1985) 35(1): 98-110.

Adams, Anthony A. "A Study of Veteran Viewpoints of TV Coverage of the Vietnam War," *Journalism Quarterly* (Summer, 1977) 54: 248-253.

Adhikarya, R. *Broadcasting in Penisular Malaysia.* Boston: Routledge & Kegan Paul, 1977.

Adler, R.P., B.Z. Friedlander, G.S. Lesser, L. Meringoff, R. S. Robertson, R.S. Rossiter, S. Ward, R. Faber and D. Pillemer. *Research on the Effects of Television Advertising on Children.* Washington, D.C.: Government Printing Office, 1978.

Adoni, Hanna. "The Function of Mass Media in the Political Socialization of Adolescents," *Communication Research* (January 1979) 6: 84-106.

Agee, Warren K. "Drying Streams of International News: Journalism Organizations Respond to Threats to World Press Freedom," paper presented to the International Communication division of AEJ, Houston, Texas, August 7, 1979.

Ahern, T.J. Jr. "Determinants of Foreign Coverage in U.S. Newspapers," *Foreign News and the New World Information Order,* ed. Robert L. Stevenson and Donald Lewis Shaw. Ames: Iowa State University Press, 1984, pp. 217-236.

Albion, Mark S. and Paul W. Farris. *The Advertising Controversy: Evidence on the Economic Effects of Advertising.* Boston: Auburn House Publishing Company, 1981.

Alexander, M. Wayne and Ben Judd Jr. "Do Nudes in Ads Enhance Brand Recall?" *Journal of Advertising Research* (February, 1978) 18(1): 47-50.

Allen, Richard L. and William T. Bielby. "Blacks' Attitudes and Behaviors Toward Television," *Communication Research* (October, 1979) 6: 437-462.

Allen, Richard L. and David E. Clarke. "Ethnicity and Mass Media Behavior: A Study of Blacks and Latinos," *Journal of Broadcasting* (Winter, 1980) 24(1): 23-34.

Allen, Richard L. and Benjamin F. Taylor. "Media Public Affairs Exposure: Issues and Alternative Strategies," *Communication Monographs* (June, 1985) 52: 186-201.

Almond, Gabriel A. and Sidney Verba. *The Civic Culture: Political Attitudes and Democracy in Five Nations.* Princeton: Princeton University Press, 1963.

Almond, P.O. "What We Were Up Against: Media Views of Parents and Children," *Child Abuse: An Agenda for Action,* ed. George Gerbner et al. New York: Oxford University Press, 1980, pp. 225-238.

Alter, Jonathan. "Rooting for Reagan," *The Washington Monthly* (January, 1981) 12: 12-17.

Altheide, David L. "Media Hegemony: A Failure of Perspective," *Public Opinion Quarterly* (Summer, 1984) 48: 476-490.

367

Altheide, David L. "Three-in-one News: Network Coverage of Iran," *Journalism Quarterly* (Fall, 1982) 59(3): 482-486.

Altschull, J. Herbert. "What Is News?" *Mass Comm Review* (December, 1974) 2(1): 17-23.

Amaize, O. and R.J. Faber, "Advertising by National Governments in Leading United States, Indian and British Newspapers," *Gazette* (1983) 32(2): 87-101.

Andersen, Peter A. and John P. Garrison. "Media Consumption and Population Characteristics of Political Opinion Leaders," *Communication Quarterly* (Summer, 1978) 26: 40-50.

Anderson, D.R. "Children's Attention to Television," paper presented at the biennial meeting of the Society for Research in Child Development, New Orleans, Louisiana, March, 1977.

Anderson, D.R., L.F. Alwitt, E.P. Lorch and S.R. Levin. "Watching Children Watch Television," *Attention and the Development of Cognitive Skills*, ed. G. Hale and M. Lewis. New York: Plenum, 1979.

Anderson, D.R. and S.R. Levin. "Young Children's Attention to 'Sesame Street,'" *Child Development* (1976) 47(3): 806-811.

Anderson, D.R., E.P. Lorch, D.E. Field and J. Sanders. "The Effects of TV Program Comprehensibility on Preschool Children's Visual Attention to Television," manuscript, University of Massachusetts, 1979.

Anderson, Michael H. "An Overview of the Wide, Wide World of Advertising and the 'New World Information Order' Debate," paper presented to the International Division, Association for Education in Journalism, Houston, Texas, August 5-8, 1979.

Anderson, Michael H. "China's Great Leap' Toward Madison Avenue," *Journal of Communication* (Winter, 1981) 31(1): 10-22.

Anderson, Ronald D., Jack L. Engledow and Helmut Becker. "How Consumer Reports Subscribers See Advertising," *Journal of Advertising Research* (December, 1978) 18(6): 29-34.

ANPA '85 Facts About Newspapers. Washington, D.C.: American Newspaper Publishers Association, 1985.

Antola, Livia and Everett M. Rogers. "Television Flows in Latin America," *Communication Research* (April, 1984) 11(2): 183-202.

Arbee, Rejal. "Bernama in the Asean News Exchange-1982," *Media Asia* (1983) 10(1): 22-26.

Arliss, L., Mary Cassata and Thomas Skill, "Dyadic Interaction on the Daytime Serials: How Men and Women Vie for Power," *Life on Daytime Television*, ed. M. Cassata and T. Skill. Norwood, N.J.: Ablex Publishers, 1983, pp. 147-156.

Armour, Robert A. *Film: A Reference Guide*. Westport, Conn.: Greenwood Press, 1980.

Armstrong, Gary M., George R. Franke, and Frederick A. Russ. "The Effects of Corrective Advertising on Company Image," *Journal of Advertising* (1982) 11(4): 39-47.

Armstrong, Gary M., Martin N. Gurol and Frederick A. Russ. "Detecting and Correcting Deceptive Advertising," *Journal of Consumer Research* (December, 1979) 6(3): 237-246.

Armstrong, Gary M. and Laurence P. Feldman. "Exposure and Sources of Opinion Leaders," *Journal of Advertising Research* (August, 1976) 16(4): 21-27.

Arrington, R.L. "Advertising and Behavior Control," *Journal of Business Ethics* (February 1982) 1(1): 3-12.

ARS. *Factors Affecting Measurements of Related Recall*. Evansville, Ind.: Research Systems Corp., 1979.

Asp, Kent. "The Struggle for the Agenda: Party Agenda, Media Agenda, and Voter Agenda in the 1979 Swedish Election Campaign," *Communication Research* (July, 1983) 10(3): 333-355.

Atkin, Charles K. "Mass Media Effects on Voting: Recent Advances and Future Priorities," *Political Communication Review* (1981), pp. 13-19.

Atkin, Charles K. "Broadcast News Programming and the Child Audience," *Journal of Broadcasting* (1978) 22: 47-61.

Atkin, Charles K. "Effects of Television Advertising on Children—First Year Experimental Evidence," Report No. 1 and Report No. 2, East Lansing, Mich.: Michigan State University, 1975.

Atkin, Charles. "Instrumental Utilities and Information Seeking," *New Models for Communication Research*, ed. Peter Clarke, Vol. 2, Sage Annual Reviews of Communication Research. Beverly Hills: Sage Publications, 1973, pp. 205-242.

Atkin, Charles K. "Communication and Political Socialization," *Handbook of Political Communication*, ed. Dan D. Nimmo and Keith R. Sanders. Beverly Hills: Sage, 1981, pp. 299-328.

Atkin, Charles K. and Walter Gantz. "Television News and the Child Audience," *Public Opinion Quarterly* (1978) 42: 183-198.

Atkin, Charles K. and W. Gibson. "Children's Nutrition Learning from Television Advertising," unpublished manuscript, Michigan State University, 1978.

Atkin, Charles and Bradley Greenberg. "Public Television and Political Socialization," *Congress and Mass Communication*. Appendix to hearings before the Joint Committee on Congressional Operations. Washington, D.C.: Government Printing Office, 1974.

Atkin, Charles, Bradley Greenberg and Steven McDermott. "Television and Race Role Socialization," *Journalism Quarterly* (Autumn, 1983) 60(3): 407-415.

Atkin, C.K. and G. Heald. "Effects of Political Advertising," *Public Opinion Quarterly* (1976) 40: 216-228.

Atkin, Charles, John Hocking and Martin Block. "Teenage Drinking: Does Advertising Make a Difference?" *Journal of Communication* (Spring, 1984) 34(2): 157-167.

Atkin, Charles and M. Mark Miller. "The Effects of Television on Children: Experimental Evidence," paper presented to the Mass Communication Division at the annual convention of the International Communication Association, Chicago, April, 1975.

Atkin, Charles K. and Kimberly Neuendorf. "Television News Exposure and Children's Knowledge about Political Figures," unpublished manuscript, 1980, available from Department of Communication, Michigan State University, East Lansing, Mich.

Atkin, Charles, Byron Reeves and W. Gibson. "Effects of Television Food Advertising on Children," paper presented at the annual convention of the Association for Education in Journalism, Houston, Texas, 1979.

Atwater, Tony. "Product Differentiation in Local TV News," *Journalism Quarterly* (Winter, 1984) 61(4): 757-762.

Austin, Bruce A. "Portrait of an Art Film Audience," *Journal of Communication* (Winter, 1984) 34(1): 74-87.

Austin, Bruce A. "Motivations for Television Viewing among Deaf and Hearing Students," *American Annals of the Deaf* (February, 1984) 129 (1): 17-22.

Austin, Bruce A. *The Film Audience: An International Bibliography of Research*. Metuchen, N.J.: The Scarecrow Press, 1983.

Austin, Bruce A. "Prime-Time TV Programming Following Introduction of Independent Broadcaster," *Journalism Quarterly* (Winter, 1982) 59(4): 627-632, 637.

Austin, Bruce A. and John W. Myers, "Hearing-Impaired Viewers of Prime-Time Television," *Journal of Communication* (Autumn, 1984) 34(4): 60-71.

Avery, Robert K. "Adolescents' Use of the Mass Media," *American Behavioral Scientist* (September/October, 1979) 23(1): 53-70.

Ayanian, Robert. "The Advertising Capital Controversy," *Journal of Business* (July, 1983) 56(3): 349-364.

Aydin, N., V. Terpstra and A. Yaprak. "The American Challenge in International Advertising," *Journal of Advertising* (1984) 13(4): 49-57.

Bagdikian, B.H. "The Media-Conglomeration Concentration," *The AFL-CIO American Federationist* (March, 1979) 86(3): 14-33.

Baggett, Patricia and Andrzei Ehrenfeucht. "Encoding and Retaining Information in the Visuals and Verbals of an Educational Movie," *Educational Communication and Technology* (Spring, 1983) 31(1): 23-32.

Bain, Chic and Dennis H. Weaver. "Readers' Reactions to Newspaper Design," *Newspaper Research Journal* (1979) 1: 48-59.

Baldwin, Elizabeth. "The Mass Media and the Corporate Elite: A Re-analysis of the Overlap Between the Media and Economic Elites," *Canadian Journal of Sociology* (1977) 2(1): 1-27.

Ball, S. and G. Bogatz. *The First Year of Sesame Street: An Evaluation*. Princeton, N.J.: Educational Testing Service, 1970.

Ball-Rokeach, Sandra J., J.W. Grube, and M. Rokeach. "'Roots: The Next Generation' — Who Watched and With What Effect?" *Public Opinion Quarterly* (Spring, 1981) 45(1): 58-68.

Balon, Robert E., Joseph C. Philport and Charles F. Beadie. "How Sex and Race Affect Perceptions of Newscasters," *Journalism Quarterly* (1978) 55(1): 160-164.

Banarjee, Sumanta. "Report on the Three Community-Originated Radio Programmes," *Media Asia* (1978) 5(1): 34-36.

Bandura, Albert. "Influence of Models' Reinforcement Contingencies on the Acquisition of Imitative Responses," *Journal of Personality and Social Psychology* (1965) 1: 589-595.

Bandura, Albert and Richard Walters. *Social Learning and Personality Development.* New York: Holt, Rinehart and Winston, 1963.

Bandura, Albert, Dorthea Ross and Sheila A. Ross. "Transmission of Aggression through Imitation of Aggressive Models," *Journal of Abnormal and Social Psychology* (1961) 63: 575-582.

Bandura, Albert, Dorthea Ross and Sheila A. Ross. "Imitation of Film-Mediated Aggressive Models," *Journal of Abnormal and Social Psychology* (1963) 66: 3-11.

Banta, Thomas J. "The Kennedy Assassination: Early Thoughts and Emotions," *Public Opinion Quarterly* (1964) 28: 225-232.

Bantz, Charles R., Suzanne McCorkle and Roberta C. Baade. "The News Factory," *Communication Research* (January, 1980) 7(1): 45-68.

Bantz, Charles R., Sandra G. Petronio and David L. Rarick, "News Diffusion After the Reagan Shooting," *Quarterly Journal of Speech* (1983) 69: 317-327.

Baptista-Fernandez, Pilar and Bradley S. Greenberg. "The Context, Characteristics and Communication Behaviors of Blacks on Television," *Life on Television: Content Analyses of U.S. TV Drama,* ed. Bradley S. Greenberg. Norwood, N.J.: Ablex, 1980, pp. 13-21.

Baran, Stanley J., Larry J. Chase and John A. Courtright. "Television Drama as a Facilitator of Prosocial Behavior: 'The Waltons,'" *Journal of Broadcasting* (1979) 23(3): 277-284.

Barrett, Grace H. "Job Satisfaction Among Newspaperwomen," *Journalism Quarterly* (Autumn, 1984) 61(3): 593-599.

Bauer, Raymond A. "The Audience," *Handbook of Communication,* ed. Wilbur Schramm, Nathan Maccoby and Edwin B. Parker. Chicago: Rand McNally, 1973.

Baxter, Richard L., Cynthia De Riemer, Ann Landini, Leslie Larry, Michael W. Singletary. "Content Analysis of Music Videos," *Journal of Broadcasting & Electronic Media* (1985) 29(3): 333-346.

Beales, Howard, Richard Craswell, and Steven C. Salop. "The Efficient Regulation of Consumer Information," *Journal of Law & Economics* (December, 1981) 24: 491-539.

Becker, Lee B. "Measurement of Gratifications," *Communication Research* (1979) 6: 54-73.

Becker, Lee B. and J.C. Doolittle. "How Repetition Affects Evaluations of Information-Seeking about Candidates," *Journalism Quarterly* (1975) 52: 611-617.

Becker, Lee B. and Sharon Dunwoody. "Media Use, Public Affairs Knowledge and Voting in a Local Election," *Journalism Quarterly* (Summer, 1982) 59(2): 212-218.

Becker, Lee B., Sharon Dunwoody and Sheizaf Rafaeli, "Cable's Impact on Use of Other News Media," *Journal of Broadcasting* (Spring, 1983) 27(2): 127-140.

Becker, Lee B., I. Sobowale and W. Casey. "Newspaper and Television Dependencies: Effects on Evaluations of Public Officials," *Journal of Broadcasting* (1979) 23: 465-475.

Becker, Lee B., P.S. Underwood and D. Lemish. "Western Wire Services and News of the USA in the Yugoslav Press," *Gazette* (1981) 28(2): 105-116.

Becker, Lee B. and D. Charles Whitney. "Effects of Media Dependencies: Audience Assessment of Government," *Communication Research* (1980) 7: 95-120.

Becker, Lee B., D. Charles Whitney, and Erik L. Collins, "Public Understanding of How the News Media Operate," *Journalism Quarterly* (Winter, 1980) 57(4): 571-578.

Bell, Daniel. *The Coming of Post-Industrial Society: A Venture in Social Forecasting.* New York: Basic Books, 1973.

Bello, Daniel C., Robert E. Pitts and Michael J. Etzel. "The Communication Effects of Controversial Sexual Content in Television Programs and Commercials," *Journal of Advertising* (1983) 12(3): 32-42.

Beltran S., Luis Ramiro. "Alien Premises, Objects, and Methods in Latin American Communication Research," *Communication Research* (April, 1976) 3(2): 107-134.

Beltran S., Luis Ramiro. "TV Etchings in the Minds of Latin Americans: Conservatism, Materialism, and Conformism," *Gazette* (1978) 24(1): 61-85.

Bendix, Reinhard. "Tradition and Modernity Reconsidered," *Comparative Studies in Society and History* (1966) 9: 292-346.

Benham, Lee. "The Effect of Advertising on the Price of Eyeglasses," *Journal of Law and Economics* (October, 1972) 15: 337-352.

Beniger, James R. "Winning the Presidential Nomination: National Polls and State Primary Elections, 1936-1972," *Public Opinion Quarterly* (Spring, 1976) 40(1): 22-38.

Berger, Arthur Asa. *Signs in Contemporary Culture: An Introduction to Semiotics.* New York: Longman, 1984.

Berkowitz, Leonard. "Some Determinants of Impulsive Aggression: Role of Mediated Associations with Reinforcements for Aggression," *Psychological Review* (1974) 81: 165-176.

Berkowitz, Leonard, "Some Aspects of Observed Aggression," *Journal of Personality and Social Psychology* (1965) 2: 359-369.

Berkowitz, Leonard and Edward Donnerstein. "External Validity Is More Than Skin Deep: Some Answers to Criticisms of Laboratory Experiments," *American Psychologist* (1982) 37: 245-257.

Berkowitz, Leonard and Russell G. Green. "Film Violence and the Cue Properties of Available Targets," *Journal of Personality and Social Psychology* (1966) 3: 525-530.

Berner, R. Thomas. "Commentary: The Narrative and the Headline," *Newspaper Research Journal* (Spring, 1983) 4(3): 33-40.

Berrada, Abderrazak. "International Radio Regulations Resulting from WARC 1979," *Media Asia* (1981) 8(3): 133-135 + .

Berry, Colin. "Learning from Television News: A Critique of the Research," *Journal of Broadcasting* (Fall, 1983a) 27(4): 359-370.

Berry, Colin. "A Dual Effect of Pictoral Enrichment in Learning from Television News: Gunters Data Revisited," *Journal of Educational Television* (1983b) 9(3): 171-178.

Berry, G.L. "Television and Afro-Americans: Past Legacy and Present Portrayals," *Television and Social Behavior: Beyond Violence and Children*, ed. S.B. Withey and R.P. Abeles. Hillsdale, N.J.: Lawrence J. Erlbaum Associates, 1980, pp. 231-248.

Bertilson, H.S., D.K. Springer and K.M. Fierke. "Underrepresentation of Female Referents as Pronouns, Examples and Pictures in Introductory College Textbooks," *Psychological Reports* (December, 1982) 51(3): 923-931.

Bevan, D. "The Mobilization of Cultural Minorities: The Case of Sianel Pedwar Cymru," *Media, Culture and Society* (April, 1984) 6(2): 103-117.

Beuf, Ann H. "Doctor, Lawyer, Household Drudge," *Journal of Communication* (Spring, 1974) 24(2): 142-145.

Bierig, Jeffrey and John Dimmick. "The Late Night Radio Talk Show as Interpersonal Communication," *Journalism Quarterly* (Spring, 1979) 56(1): 92-96.

Black, Joan C. "Opinion Leaders: Is Anyone Following?" *Public Opinion Quarterly* (Summer, 1982) 46(2): 169-176.

Blankenburg, William B. and Ruth Walden. "Objectivity, Interpretation and Economy in Reporting," *Journalism Quarterly* (Autumn, 1977) 54: 591-595.

Block, Clifford H. "Promising Step at Acapulco: A U.S. View," *Journal of Communication* (Summer, 1982) 32(3): 60-70.

Blumler, Jay G. "The Role of Theory in Uses and Gratifications Studies," *Communication Research* (January, 1979) 6(1): 9-36.

Blumler, Jay G. and Elihu Katz (eds.). *The Uses of Mass Communications: Current Perspectives on Gratifications Research.* Vol. 3, Sage Annual Reviews of Communication Research. Beverly Hills: Sage Publications, 1974.

Blumler, Jay G. and Denis McQuail. *Television in Politics.* Chicago: University of Chicago Press, 1969.

de Bock, Harold and Jan van Lil. "'Holocaust' in the Netherlands," *Mass Communication Review Yearbook*, Vol. 2, ed. G.C. Wilhoit and H. deBock. Beverly Hills: Sage, 1981, pp. 639-646.

Bogart, Leo. "How U.S. Newspaper Content Is Changing," *Journal of Communication* (Spring, 1985) 35(2): 82-90.

Bogart, Leo. *Press and Public: Who Reads, What, When, Where, and Why in American Newspapers*. Hillsdale, N.J.: Lawrence Erlbaum Associates, Publishers, 1981.

Bogart, Leo and Al Gollin. "How Do Your Papers Rate with Readers?" presented at the American Society of Newspaper Editors Convention, Denver, Colorado, May 9, 1983.

Bogatz, G.A. and S. Ball. *The Second Year of Sesame Street: A Continuing Evaluation*. Princeton, N.J.: Educational Testing Service, 1972.

Bogue, Donald J., Robert Bursik and Judith Mayo. *Communicating to Combat VD: The Los Angeles Experiment*. Vol. 1. Chicago: Community and Family Study Center, University of Chicago, 1979.

Bonafede, Dome. "The Press and the Hollywood Presidency," *Washington Journalism Review* (January/February, 1981) 3: 27-31.

Boorstin, Daniel J. "Advertising and American Civilization," *Advertising and Society*, ed. Yale Brozen. New York: New York University Press, 1972.

Boorstin, Daniel J. *The Image*. New York: Atheneum, 1962.

Borden, Neil H. *The Economic Effects of Advertising*. Chicago: Richard D. Irwin, 1942.

Boulding, Kenneth E. *The Image*. Ann Arbor: University of Michigan Press, 1971.

Bowen, Lawrence. "Advertising and the Poor," *Journalism Monographs* (February, 1982) No. 75.

Bower, Robert T. *Television and the Public*. New York: Holt, Rinehart & Winston, 1973.

Bowes, John E. "Media Technology: Detour or Panacea for Resolving Urban Information Needs?" *Journal of Broadcasting* (1976) 20: 333-343.

Bowker Annual of Library & Book Trade Information. New York: R.R. Bowker Co., 29th edition, 1984 (Julie Ehresmann, ed.)

Boyd-Barrett, Oliver. *The International News Agencies*. Beverly Hills, Calif.: Sage, 1980.

Brantgarde, Lennart. "The Information Gap and Municipal Politics in Sweden," *Communication Research* (July, 1983) 10(3): 357-373.

Braudy, Leo. *The World in a Frame: What We See in Films*. Garden City, N.Y.: Anchor/Press/Doubleday, 1976.

Brazaitis, Thomas J. "Chief Librarian Refuses to Bury Books," *Plain Dealer*, Dec. 11, 1984.

Breed, Warren and James R. De Foe. "Effecting Media Change: The Role of Cooperative Consultation on Alcohol Topics," *Journal of Communication* (Spring, 1982) 32(2): 88-99.

Breed, Warren and James R. De Foe. "The Portrayal of Drinking Processes on Prime-Time Television," *Journal of Communication* (Winter, 1981) 31(1): 58-67.

Breen, Myles P. "The Flow of Television Programs from America to Australia," *Journalism Quarterly* (Fall, 1981) 58(3): 388-394.

Briller, B. and S. Miller. "Assessing Academic Achievement: Television at the Crossroads," *Society* (September/october, 1984) 21(6): 6-9.

Broadcasting magazine, "Summary of Broadcasting as of April 31, 1985," June 17, 1985, p. 76.

Brode, D. "Video Verite: Defining the Docudrama," *Television Quarterly* (1984) 20(4): 7-26.

Broh, C. Anthony. "Horse Race Journalism: Reporting the Polls in the 1976 Presidential Election," *Public Opinion Quarterly* (1980) 44: 514-529.

Brooks, Tim and Earle Marsh. *The Complete Directory to Prime Time Network TV Shows: 1946-Present*. New York: Ballantine Books, 1981, rev. ed.

Broussard, E. Joseph, C. Robert Blackmon, David L. Blackwell, David W. Smith and Sarah Hunt. "News of Aged and Aging in 10 Metropolitan Dailies," *Journalism Quarterly* (Summer, 1980) 57(2): 324-327.

Brown, Ben. "Our TVs Are on 7 Hours a Day," *USA Today* (April 29, 1985), p. 1.

Brown, Ben. "We're More Picky about Our TV Fare," *USA Today* (April 25, 1983a), pp. 1-2A.

Brown, Ben. "How our TV-Watching Patterns Change," *USA Today* (April 27, 1983b) p. 5D.

Brown, Bruce W. *Images of Family Life in Magazine Advertising: 1920-1978.* Praeger Studies on Changing Issues in the Family. New York: Praeger, 1981.

Brown, J.R. "Children's Uses of Television," *Children and Television,* ed. Ray Brown. Beverly Hills: Sage Publications, 1976, pp. 116-136.

Brown, J.R., J.K. Cramond, and R.J. Wilde. "Displacement Effects of Television and the Child's Functional Orientation to Media," *The Uses of Mass Communications,* ed. Jay G. Blumler and Elihu Katz. Beverly Hills: Sage, 1974.

Browning, Ned, Don Grierson and Herbert H. Howard. "Effects of Conglomerate Take-over on a Newspaper's Coverage of the Knoxville World's Fair: A Case Study," *Newspaper Research Journal* (Fall, 1984) 6(1): 30-38.

Brunk, Gregory G. and James A. Fishkin. "Media Coverage of Presidential Candidates: A Study of Popularity Prior to the 1976 National Nominating Conventions," *Communication Research* (October, 1982) 9: 525-538.

Bryan, James H. and Nancy Hodges Walbek. "Preaching and Practicing Generosity: Children's Actions and Reactions," *Child Development* (1970) 41: 329-353.

Bryand, Barbara E., Frederick P. Currier and Andrew J. Morrison. "Relating Life Style Factors of Person to His Choice of a Newspaper," *Journalism Quarterly* (Spring, 1976) 53: 74-79.

Bryant, Jennings and Dolf Zillmann. "Using Television to Alleviate Boredom and Stress: Selective Exposure as a Function of Induced Excitational States," *Journal of Broadcasting* (Winter, 1984) 28(1): 1-20.

Brzezinski, Zbigniew and Samuel P. Huntington. *Political Power USA/USSR.* London: Chatto & Windus, 1963.

Buerkel-Rothfuss, N.L. and S. Mayes. "Soap Opera Viewing and the Cultivation Effect," *Journal of Communication* (1981) 31(3): 108-115.

Burgoon, Judee K., James M. Bernstein and Michael Burgoon. "Public and Journalist Perceptions of Newspaper Functions," *Newspaper Research Journal* (Fall, 1983) 5(1): 77-85.

Burgoon, Judee K., James M. Bernstein, Michael Burgoon, and Charles K. Atkin. "Journalists' Perceptions of the Future of the Newspaper Industry," *Newspaper Research Journal* (Spring, 1984) 5(3): 13-25.

Burgoon, Michael and Judee K. Burgoon. "Predictive Models of Satisfaction with the Newspaper," *Communication Yearbook 3,* ed. Dan Nimmo. New Brunswick, N.J.: Transaction Books, 1979, pp. 271-281.

Burke Marketing Research, Inc. *The Effect of Environmental and Executional Variables on Overall Memorability.* Cincinnati, Ohio: September, 1978.

Butler, D. and D. Stokes. "The National Press and Partisan Change," *Political Change in Britain,* ed. Jeremy Tunstall, 1970, pp. 479-498.

Butler, Jacalyn Klein and Kurt E.M. Kent. "Potential Impact of Videotext on Newspapers," *Newspaper Research Journal* (Fall, 1983) 5(1): 3-12.

Butsch, Richard and Lynda M. Glennon. "Social Class: Frequency Trends in Domestic Situation Comedy, 1946-1978," *Journal of Broadcasting* (Winter, 1983) 27(1): 77-81.

Butterfield, Fox. *China: Alive in the Bitter Sea.* London: Coronet, 1983.

Bybee, Carl R., Jack M. McLeod, William D. Luetscher and Gina Garramone. "Mass Communication and Voter Volatility," *Public Opinion Quarterly* (Spring, 1981) 45(1): 69-90.

Byrne, G. "Mass Media and Political Socialization of Children and Preadults," *Journalism Quarterly* (1969) 46: 40-52.

Cady, John F. "Advertising Restrictions and Retail Prices," *Journal of Advertising Research* (October, 1976) 16(5): 27-30.

Callahan, Francix X. "Does Advertising Subsidize Information?" *Journal of Advertising Research* (August, 1978) 18(4): 19-22.

Callahan, Francis X. "Advertising and Profits 1969-1978," *Journal of Advertising Research* (April/May, 1982) 22(2): 17-22.

Calvert, S., B. Watkins, J.C. Wright and A. Huston-Stein. "Recall of Television Content as a Function of Content Type and Level of Production Feature Use," paper presented at the biennial meeting of the Society for Research in Child Development, San Francisco, March, 1979.

de Camargo, Nelly and Virgilio B. Noya Pinto. *Communication Policies in Brazil.* Paris: The Unesco Press, 1975.

Cantor, Joanne and Pat Venus. "The Effect of Humor on Recall of a Radio Advertisement," *Journal of Broadcasting* (Winter, 1980) 24(1): 13-22.

Cantor, Joanne and Glenn G. Sparks. "Children's Fear Responses to Mass Media: Testing Some Piagetian Predictions," *Journal of Communication* (Spring, 1984) 34(2): 90-103.

Cantor, Joanne, Barbara J. Wilson and Cynthia Hoffner. "Emotional Responses to Holocaust Film," *Communication Research* (in press).

Cantril, Albert H. "The Press and the Pollster," *The Annals of the American Academy of Political and Social Science* (September, 1976) 427: 45-52.

Cantril, Hadley. *The Invasion from Mars: A Study in the Psychology of Panic.* Princeton, N.J.: Princeton University Press, 1940.

Caplan, Richard E. "Violent Program Content in Music Video," *Journalism Quarterly* (Spring, 1985) 62(1): 144-147.

Caplow, Theodore and Harold M. Bahr. "Half a Century of Change in Adolescent Attitudes: Replication of a Middletown Survey by the Lynds," *Public Opinion Quarterly* (Spring, 1979) 43(1): 1-17.

Caranicas, Peter. "American TV Tightens Its Grip on the World," *Channels* January/February, 1984), p. 27-34.

Carlson, James M. "Crime Show Viewing by Preadults: The Impact of Attitudes Toward Civil Liberties," *Communication Research* (October, 1983) 10(4): 529-552.

Caron, Andre H. "First-Time Exposure to Television: Effects on Inuit Children's Cultural Images," *Communication Research* (April, 1979) 6(2): 135-154.

Carpenter, Edmund. *Oh What a Blow that Phantom Gave Me!* New York: Holt, Rinehart & Winston, 1973.

Carroll, Raymond L. "The 1948 Truman Campaign: The Threshold of the Modern Era," *Jôurnal of Broadcasting* (Spring, 1980) 24(2): 173-188.

Carter, Richard F. "The Journalistic Function," unpublished paper. University of Washington, Seattle, 1967.

Carveth, Rodney and Alison Alexander. "Soap Opera Viewing Motivations and the Cultivation Process," *Journal of Broadcasting* (Summer, 1985) 29(3): 259-273.

Cassata, Mary, Thomas Skill and Samuel Osei Boadu. "Life and Death in the Daytime Television Serial: A Content Analysis," *Life On Daytime Television: Tuning-in American Serial Drama,* ed. Mary Cassata and Thomas Skill. Norwood, N.J.: Ablex Publishing Company., 1983.

Cassata, Mary, P.A. Anderson and Thomas Skill. "Images of Old Age on Day-time," *Life on Daytime Television,* ed. Mary Cassata and Thomas Skill. Norwood, N.J.: Ablex Publishers, 1983, pp. 37-44.

Catton, William R. Jr. "Violence in the Media," contributed paper, National Commission on the Causes and Prevention of Violence, 1969.

Ceci, Stephen J. and Edward L. Kain. "Jumping on the Bandwagon with the Under-dog: The Impact of Attitude Polls on Polling Behavior," *Public Opinion Quarterly* (Summer, 1982) 46(2): 228-242.

Chaffee, Steven H. "Mass Communication in Political Socialization," *Handbook of Political Socialization,* ed. S. Renshon. New York: Free Press, 1977.

Chaffee, Steven H. "The Interpersonal Context of Mass Communication," *Perspectives in Mass Communication Research,* ed. F. Gerald Kline and Phillip J. Tichenor. Beverly Hills, California: Sage Publications, 1972, pp. 95-120.

Chaffee, Steven H. and S.Y. Choe. "Time of Decision and Media Use during the Ford-Carter Campaign," *Public Opinion Quarterly* (1980) 44: 53-69.

Chaffee, Steven H. and Albert R. Tims. "Interpersonal Factors in Adolescent Television Use," *Journal of Social Issues* (1976) 32(4): 98-115.

Chaffee, Steven, Scott Ward and Leonard Tipton. "Mass Communication and Political Socialization," *Journalism Quarterly* (1970) 47: 647-659.

Chaffee, Steven H. and Donna G. Wilson. "Media Rich, Media Poor: Two Studies of Diversity in Agenda-Holding," *Journalism Quarterly* (1977) 54(3): 466-476.

Chalkey, Alan. "Development Journalism — A New Dimension in the Information Process," *Media Asia* (1980) 7(4): 215-217.

Chan, Mei-Mei. "TV is on the Wagon to Set Good Example," *USA Today,* March 21, 1985, p. 11a.

Cheek, Neil H. and William R. Burch Jr. *The Social Organization of Leisure in Human Society.* New York: Harper & Row, 1976.

Cheles-Miller, Pamela. "Reaction to Marital Roles in Commercials," *Journal of Advertising Research* (August, 1975) 45-49.

Cherry, Colin. *World Communication: Threat or Promise?* London: Wiley-Interscience, 1971.

Christians, Clifford G. "Fifty Years of Scholarship in Media Ethics," *Journal of Communication* (1977) 27(4): 19-29.

Clark, Cedric C. "Television and Social Controls: Some Observations on the Portrayal of Ethnic Minorities," *Television Quarterly* (1969) 8: 18-22.

Clark, Rebecca L. "How Women's Magazines Cover Living Alone," *Journalism Quarterly* (Summer, 1981) 58(2): 291-294.

Clarke, Arthur C. "Beyond the Global Village," *Chronicle of International Communication* (June, 1983) 4(5):4.

Click, J.W. and Guido H. Stempel III. "Rate of Adoption of Modern Format to Daily Newspapers," *ANPA News Research Report,* No. 22, Sept. 28, 1979.

Cline, Carolyn Garrett. "The Myth of the Monolith," *Newspaper Research Journal* (Winter, 1979) 29(1): 197-203.

Clippinger, John H. "The Hidden Agenda: The U.S. Faces WARC," *Journal of Communication* (Winter, 1979) 29(1): 197-203.

Coen, Robert J. "Final Figures: 1984 Ad Spending Up 16%," *Advertising Age,* May 6, 1985, p. 47.

Cohen, Akiba A., Hanna Adoni and Gideon Drori. "Adolescents' Perceptions of Social Conflicts in Television News and Social Reality," *Human Communication Research* (Winter, 1983) 10(2): 230-225.

Cohen, Bernard C. *The Press, the Public and Foreign Policy.* Princeton: Princeton University Press, 1963.

Coldevin, Gary O. "Satellite Television and Cultural Replacement among Canadian Eskimos: Adults and Adolescents Compared," *Communication Research* (April, 1979) 6(2): 115-134.

Coldevin, Gary O. "Some Effects of Frontier Television in a Canadian Eskimo Community," *Journalism Quarterly* (Summer, 1976) 53: 34-39.

Collins, Janay, Joey Reagan and John D. Abel. "Predicting Cable Subscribership: Local Factors," *Journal of Broadcasting* (Spring, 1983) 27(2): 177-183.

Collins, W. Andrew. "Effect of Temporal Separation between Motivation, Aggression and Consequences: A Developmental Study," *Developmental Psychology* (March, 1973) 8(2): 215-221.

Collins, W. Andrew. "Learning of Media Content: A Developmental Study," *Child Development* (1970) 41: 1133-1142.

Collins, W. Andrew, Thomas J. Berndt and Valerie L. Hess. "Observational Learning of Motives and Consequences for Television Aggression," *Child Development* (Sept.-Dec., 1974) 45: 799-802.

Compaine, Benjamin M. (ed.) *Who Owns the Media? Concentration of Ownership in the Mass Communications Industry.* New York: Harmony Books, 1979.

Comstock, George. *Television and Human Behavior: The Key Studies.* Santa Monica, Calif.: Rand Corp., 1975.

Comstock, George, Steven Chaffee, N. Katzman, Max McCombs and Donald Roberts. *Television and Human Behavior.* New York: Columbia University Press, 1978.

Consoli, John. "1982: Review of Year's Events," *Editor & Publisher* (Jan. 1, 1983), pp. 12, 14.

Conway, M.A. Stevens and R. Smith. "The Relation Between Media Use and Children's Civic Awareness," *Journalism Quarterly* (1975) 52: 531-538.

Cook, Thomas D., H. Appleton, R.F. Conner, A. Shaffer, G. Tabkin and J.S. Weber. *Sesame Street Revisited.* New York: Russell Sage, 1975.

Cook, Thomas D., Deborah A. Kendzierski and Stephen V. Thomas. "The Implicit Assumptions of Television Research: An Analysis of the 1982 NIMH Report on Television and Behavior," *Public Opinion Quarterly* (Summer, 1983) 47(2): 161-201.

Corrigan, Dennis M. "News as Symbolizing Activity," paper presented at annual convention of the Association for Education in Journalism and Mass Communication, Corvallis, Oregon, August, 1983.

Cotteret, Jean-Marie. "Communication and Society," *Revista del Institute de Ciencias Sociales* (1972) 20: 45-51.

Cowie, E. "Viewing Patterns Within the UK Population," *Annual Review of BBC Broadcasting Research Findings* (1981/1982) No. 8: 27-39.

Cowling, Keith, John Cable, Michael Kelly and Tony McGuiness. *Advertising and Economic Behavior*. London: The Macmillan Press, Ltd., 1975.

Craig, Richard J. "Drug Themes in Metropolitan Newspapers: Review and Analysis," *The International Journal of the Addictions* (1981) 16(6): 1087-1093.

Crespi, Irving. "Polls as Journalism," *Public Opinion Quarterly* (Winter, 1980) 44(4): 462-476.

Crowley, D.J. *Understanding Communication: The Signifying Web*. New York: Gordon & Breach Science Pub., 1982.

Csikszentmihalyi, M. *Beyond Boredom and Anxiety*. San Francisco: Jossey-Bass, 1975.

Culbertson, Hugh M. "Three Perspectives on American Journalism," *Journalism Monographs* (June, 1983) No. 83.

Culbertson, Hugh M. "Specialized Journalism — A Structural View," *Mass Com Review* (Spring, 1978) 5(2): 2-3.

Culbertson, Hugh M. "Gatekeeper Coorientation — A Viewpoint for Analysis of Popular Culture and Specialized Journalism," *Mass Com Review* (Winter, 1975/76) 3(1): 3-7.

Culbertson, Hugh M. and Nancy Somerick. "Quotation Marks and Bylines — What Do They Mean to Readers?" *Journalism Quarterly* (Autumn, 1976) 53: 463-467 + .

Culbertson, Hugh M. and Guido H. Stempel III. "Possible Barriers to Agenda Setting in Medical News," *Newspaper Research Journal* (Spring, 1984) 5(3): 53-60.

Curran, James. "The Impact of Advertising on the British Mass Media," *Media, Culture and Society* (1981) 3: 43-69.

Cuthbert, M. "Reaction to International News Agencies: 1930's and 1970's Compared," *Gazette* (1980) 26(4): 99-110.

Cutler, Neal E. and James A. Danowski. "Process Gratification in Aging Cohorts," *Journalism Quarterly* (Summer, 1980) 57(2): 269-276.

Dagnino, Evelina, "Cultural and Ideological Dependence: Building a Theoretical Framework," *Struggles of Dependency*, ed. F. Bonilla and Robert Girling. Stanford, Calif., 1973.

Davis, Howard H. and Paul A. Walton. "Sources of Variation in News Vocabulary: A Comparative Analysis," *International Journal of the Sociology of Language* (1983) 40: 59-75.

Davis, Richard H. "Television and the Older Adults," *Journal of Broadcasting* (Spring, 1971) 15: 153-159.

Davison, W. Phillips. "Diplomatic Reporting: Rules of the Game," *Journal of Communication* (Autumn, 1975) 24(4): 138-146.

Davison, W. Phillips. *International Political Communication*. New York: Praeger, Publishers, 1965.

DeFleur, Melvin L. and Sandra Ball-Rokeach. *Theories of Mass Communication*. New York: Longman, 1982, 4th ed.

Demirdjian, Z.S. "Sales Effectiveness of Comparative Advertising: An Experimental Field Investigation," *Journal of Consumer Research* (December, 1983) 10(3): 362-364.

Dennis, Everette E. and Michal Sadoff. "Media Coverage of Children and Childhood: Calculated Indifference or Neglect?" *Journalism Quarterly* (Spring, 1976) 53(1): 47-53.

Desmond, Roger Jon and Thomas R. Donohue. "The Role of the 1976 Televised Presidential Debates in Political Socialization of Adolescents," *Communication Quarterly* (Fall, 1981) 29: 302-308.

Deutsch, Karl W. *Nationalism and Social Communication*. New York: Wiley, 1953.

Deutsch, Karl W. and Richard L. Merritt. *Nationalism and National Development*. Cambridge, Mass.: MIT Press, 1970.

Deutschmann, Paul J. and Wayne A. Danielson. "Diffusion of Knowledge of a Major News Story," *Journalism Quarterly* (1960) 37: 345-355.

Dewey, John. *The Quest for Certainty: A Study of the Relation of Knowledge and Action.* New York: G.P. Putnam's Sons, Gifford Lectures, 1929. Capricorn Books Edition, 1960.

Dikshit, K.A. et al. (ed.) "Rural Radio: Programme Formats," *Monographs on Communication Technology and Utilization,* No. 5, Paris: Unesco, 1979.

Dimmick, John W. "The Gatekeepers: Media Organizations as Political Coalitions," *Communication Research* (April, 1979) 6(2): 203-222.

Dimmick, John. "Family Communication and TV Program Choice," *Journalism Quarterly* (Winter, 1976) 53: 720-723.

Dimmick, John W., Thomas A. McCain and W. Theodore Bolton. "Media Use and the Life Span," *American Behavioral Scientist* (September/October, 1979) 23(1): 7-31.

Dixon, Norman F. *Subliminal Perception: The Nature of a Controversy.* London: McGraw Hill, 1971.

Dizard, Wilson P. Jr. *The Coming Information Age.* New York: Longman, 2nd ed., 1985.

Dolich, Ira J. "Congruence Relationships Between Self Images and Product Brands," *Journal of Marketing Research* (1969) 6: 80-83.

Dominick, Joseph R. *The Dynamics of Mass Communication.* Reading, Mass.: Addison-Wesley, 1983.

Dominick, Joseph R. "Children's Viewing of Crime Shows and Attitudes on Law Enforcement," *Journalism Quarterly* (1974) 51: 5-12.

Dominick, Joseph R. "Television and Political Socialization," *Educational Broadcasting Review* (1972) 6: 48-55.

Dominick, Joseph R. and Bradley S. Greenberg. "Attitudes Toward Violence: The Interaction of Television Exposure, Family Attitudes and Social Class," *Television and Social Behavior. Vol. III: Television and Adolescent Aggressiveness,* ed. George A. Comstock and Eli A. Rubinstein. Washington, D.C.: U.S. Government Printing Office, 1972, pp. 314-335.

Dominick, Joseph R. and Millard C. Pearce. "Trends in Network Prime-Time Programming, 1953-1974," *Journal of Communication* (Winter, 1976) 26(1): 70-80.

Donnerstein, Edward. "Aggressive Erotica and Violence Against Women," *Journal of Personality and Social Psychology* (1980) 39(2): 269-277.

Donnerstein, Edward and Leonard Berkowitz. "Victim Reactions in Aggressive-Erotic Films as a Factor in Violence Against Women," *Journal of Personality and Social Psychology* (1981) 41: 710-724.

Donnerstein, Edward, M. Donnerstein and R. Evans. "Erotic Stimuli and Aggression: Facilitation or Inhibition," *Journal of Personality and Social Psychology* (1975) 32: 237-244.

Donsbach, W. "Journalists' Conceptions of Their Audience: Comparative Indicators for the Way British and German Journalists Define Their Relations to the Public," *Gazette* (1983) 32(1): 19-36.

Doob, Anthony N. and Glenn E. MacDonald. "Television Viewers and Fear of Victimization: Is the Relationship Causal?" *Journal of Personality and Social Psychology* (1979) 37: 170-179.

Dorr, Aimee. "Children's Advertising Rule Making Comment," testimony to the Federal Trade Commission's Rulemaking Hearings on Television Advertising and Children, San Francisco, November, 1978.

Dorr, Aimee, Sherryl Browne Graves and Erin Philps. "Television Literacy for Young Children," *Journal of Communication* (1980) 30(3): 71-83.

Dotan, Judith and Akiba A. Cohen. "Mass Media Use in the Family During War and Peace," *Communication Research* (October, 1976) 3(4): 393-402.

Dougherty, Philip H. "Advertising Spending Could Top $100 Billion," *New York Times,* July 18, 1985, p. 41.

Dreier, Peter and Steve Weinberg. "Interlocking Directories," *Columbia Journalism Review* (November/December, 1979), pp. 51-68.

Drew, Dan G. "Reporters' Attitudes, Expected Meetings with Source and Journalistic Objectivity," *Journalism Quarterly* (Summer, 1975) 52: 219-224 + .

Drew, Dan and Byron Reeves. "Children and Television News," *Journalism Quarterly* (1980) 57: 45-54.

Drew, Dan and Byron Reeves. "Learning from a Television News Story," *Communication Research* (1980) 7: 121-135.

Dube, S.C. "Development Change and Communication in India," *Communication and Change: The Last Ten Years — and the next,* ed. Schramm and Lerner. Honolulu: University Press of Hawaii, 1976, pp. 98-118.

Duesenberry, James S. *Income, Saving, and the Theory of Consumer Behavior.* Cambridge: Harvard University Press, 1949.

Dunn, Edward W. Jr. "Mexican-American Media Behavior," *Journal of Broadcasting* (Winter, 1975) 19(1): 3-10.

Dunwoody, Sharon and Michael Ryan. "Scientific Barriers to the Popularization of Science in the Mass Media," *Journal of Communication* (Winter, 1985) 35(1): 26-42.

Durand, Richard M., Jesse E. Teel Jr. and William O. Bearden. "Racial Differences in Perceptions of Media Advertising Credibility," *Journalism Quarterly* (Autumn, 1979) 56(3): 562-566.

Durdin, F. Tillman. "How Durable Is Mao's Policy?" *Communication and Change: The Last Ten Years — and the Next,* ed. Schramm and Lerner. Honolulu: University Press of Hawaii, 1976, pp. 134-137.

Durkin, K. "Children's Accounts of Sex-Role Stereotypes in Television," *Communication Research* (July, 1984) 11(3): 341-361.

Dyer, Carolyn Stewart and Oguz B. Nayman. "Under the Capital Dome: Relationships Between Legislators and Reporters," *Journalism Quarterly* (1977) 54(3): 443-453.

Dzinic, Firdus. "Regional Differences in the Contact of Citizens with Mass media," *Sociologica* (1974): 16: 131-139.

Earl, Ronald L. and William M. Pride. "The Effects of Advertisement Structure, Message Sidedness, and Peformance Test Results on Print Advertisement Informativeness," *Journal of Advertising* (1980) 9(3): 36-45.

Eastman, Susan Tyler, Sydney W. Head and Lewis Klein. *Broadcast/Cable Programming.* Belmont, Calif.: Wadsworth Publishing Company, 1985, 2d ed.

Eco, Umberto. *A Theory of Semiotics.* Bloomington: Indiana University Press, 1976.

Editor & Publisher 1984 International Yearbook. New York: Editor & Publisher, 1985.

Egan, Lola. "Children's Viewing Patterns for Television News," *Journalism Quarterly* (1978) 55: 337-342.

Einsiedel, Edna. "Comparisons of Subscribers and Non-Subscribers," *ANPA News Research Report* (Dec. 27, 1983) No. 39. Washington, D.C.: American Newspaper Publishers Association.

Einsiedel, E.F. and Namjun Kang. "Civic Attitudes Among Non-Readers and Non-Subscribers," *Newspaper Research Journal* (Summer, 1983) 4(4): 37-42.

Eisendrath, Charles R. "Back to the People with the Mom-and-Pop Press," *Columbia Journalism Review* (November/December, 1979), pp. 72-74.

Elebash, Camille and James Rosene. "Issues in Political Advertising in a Deep South Gubernatorial Race," *Journalism Quarterly* (Autumn, 1982) 59: 420-523.

Elliott, Philip. "Media Organizations and Occupations: an Overview," *Mass Media and Society,* ed. James Curran, Michael Gurevitch and Janet Woollacott. London: Edward Arnold in association with The Open University Press, 1977, pp. 142-173.

Elliott, William R. and Cynthia P. Quattlebaum. "Similarities in Patterns of Media Use: A Cluster Analysis of Media Gratification," *Western Journal of Speech Communication* (1979) 43: 61-72.

Elliott, William R. and William J. Schenck-Hamlin. "Film, Politics and the Press: The Influence of 'All the President's Men'," *Journalism Quarterly* (Autumn, 1979) 56(3): 546-553.

Ellis, G.J., S.K. Streeter and J.D. Englebrecht. "Television Characters as Significant Others and the Process of Vicarious Role Taking," *Journal of Family Issues* (June, 1983) 4(2): 367-384.

Emery, Edwin and Michael Emery. *The Press and America.* Englewood Cliffs, N.J.: Prentice-Hall, Inc., 1978, 4th ed.

Engelmayer, Paul A. "Island Off Virginia Is So Remote It Has Its Own Dialect," *The Asian Wall Street Journal,* July 19, 1984.

England, Paula, Alice Kuhn and Teresa Gardner. "The Ages of Men and Women in Magazine Advertisements," *Journalism Quarterly* (Fall, 1981) 58(3): 468-471.

Epstein, Edward J. *News from Nowhere.* New York: Random House, 1973.

Erbring, Lutz, Edie N. Goldenberg and Arthur H. Miller. "Front-Page News and Real-World Cues: A New Look at Agenda-Setting by the Media," *American Journal of Political Science* (February, 1980) 24(1): 16-49.

Eron, Leonard D., Rowell Huesmann, Patrick Brice, Paulette Fischer and Rebecca Mermelstein. "Age Trends in the Development of Aggression, Sex Typing, and Related Television Habits," *Developmental Psychology* (1983) 19(1): 71-77.

Estep, Rhoda and Patrick T. Macdonald. "Crime in the Afternoon: Murder and Robbery on Soap Operas," *Journal of Broadcasting* (Summer, 1985) 29(3): 323-331.

Estep, Rhoda and Patrick T. Macdonald. "How Prime Time Crime Evolved on TV, 1976-1981," *Journalism Quarterly* (Summer, 1983) 60(2): 293-300.

Etgar, Michael and Stephen A. Goodwin. "One-Sided versus Two-Sided Comparative Message Appeals for New Brand Introductions," *Journal of Consumer Research* (March, 1982) 8(4): 460-465.

Ettema, James S., James W. Brown and Russell V. Luepker. "Knowledge Gap Effects in a Health Information Campaign," *Public Opinion Quarterly* (Winter, 1983) 47(4): 516-527.

Etzioni, Amitai. *The Active Society.* New York: Free Press, 1968.

Evans, Christopher. *The Micro Millennium.* New York: Washington Square Press, 1979.

Ewen, Stuart. *Captains of Consciousness.* New York: McGraw-Hill, 1976.

Eyal, C. "Time Frame in Agenda-Setting Research: A Study of the Conceptual and Methodological Factors Affecting the Time Frame Context of the Agenda-Setting Process." unpublished doctoral dissertation, Syracuse University, 1980.

Faber, Ronald J., Richard M. Perloff and Robert P. Hawkins, "Antecedents of Children's Comprehension of Television Advertising," *Journal of Broadcasting* (1982) 26(2): 575-584.

Faber, Ronald J. and M.C. Storey. "Recall of Information from Political Advertising," *Journal of Advertising* (1984) 13(3): 39-44.

Fant, Charles H. "Televising Presidential Conventions, 1952-1980," *Journal of Communication* (Autumn, 1980) 30(4): 130-139.

Farace, R. Vincent. "A Study of Mass Communication and National Development," *Journalism Quarterly* (Summer, 1966) 43: 305-313.

Farris, Paul and Mark S. Albion. "Determinants of the Advertising-to-Sales Ration," *Journal of Advertising Research* (February, 1981) 21(1): 19-26.

Farris, Paul W. and Mark S. Albion. "The Impact of Advertising on the Price of Consumer Products," *Journal of Marketing* (Summer, 1980) 44: 17-35.

Fascell, Dante B. *International News: Freedom Under Attack.* Beverly Hills: Sage Publications, 1979.

Fathi, A. "Mass Media and a Moslem Immigrant Community in Canada," *Antrhopologica* (1973) 15: 201-230.

Fedler, Fred. "'100 Jobs' Dominate News During Florida Election," *Journalism Quarterly* (Summer, 1981) 58: 302-305.

Fedler, Fred, Joe Hall and Lawrence A. Tanzi. "Popular Songs Emphasize Sex, De-Emphasize Romance," *Mass Com Review* (Spring and Fall, 1982) 9(2/3): 10-15.

Fejes, Fred. "The U.S. in Third World Communications: Latin America, 1900-1945," *Journalism Monographs* (November, 1983) No. 86.

Fejes, Fred. "The Growth of Multinational Advertising Agencies in Latin America," *Journal of Communication* (Autumn, 1980) 30(4): 36-49.

Felson, Marcus. "The Differentiation of Material Life Styles: 1925 to 1966," *Social Indicators Research* (1976) 3: 397-421.

Fenigstien, A. "Does Aggression Cause a Preference for Viewing Media Violence?" *Journal of Personality and Social Psychology* (1979) 37(12): 2307-17.

Ferguson, J.M. "Comments on 'The Impact of Advertising on the Price of Consumer Products,'" *Journal of Marketing* (Winter, 1982) 46(1): 102-105.

Feshbach, Seymour and Robert D. Singer. *Television and Aggression.* San Francisco: Jossey-Bass Inc., Publishers, 1971.

Fetler, Mark. "Television Viewing and School Achievement," *Journal of Communication* (Spring, 1984) 34(2): 104-118.

Fico, Fred. "Search for the Statehouse Spokesman: Coverage of the Governor and Law-makers," *Journalism Quarterly* (Spring, 1985) 62(1): 74-80, 94.

Fico, Fred. "How Lawmakers Use Reporters: Differences in Specialization and Goals," *Journalism Quarterly* (Winter, 1984) 61(4): 793-800, 821.

Finn, T. Andrew and Donald E. Strickland. "The Advertising and Alcohol Abuse Issue: A Cross-Media Comparison of Alcohol Beverage Advertising Content," *Communication Yearbook 6,* ed. Michael Burgoon. Beverly Hills, Calif.: Sage Publications, 1982, pp. 850-872.

Fishbein, M.S. and I. Ajzen. *Beliefs, Attitudes, Intention and Behavior: An Introduction to Theory and Research.* Reading, Mass.: Addison-Wesley, 1975.

Fisher, B. Aubrey. *Perspectives on Human Communication.* New York: Macmillan Publishing Co., Inc., 1978.

Fisher, Harold A. "Broadcast Journalist's Perceptions of Appropriate Career Preparation," *Journalism Quarterly* (1978) 55(1): 140-144.

Fisher, J., O.H. Gandy Jr. and N.Z. Janus. "The Role of Popular Media in Defining Sickness and Health," *Communication and Social Structure,* ed. E.G. McAnany et al. New York: Praeger Publishers, 1981, pp. 240-257.

Fiske, John and John Hartley. *New Accents: Reading Television.* London: Methuen & Co., Ltd., 1978.

Fitchen, R. "Parliaments and Media-Extension or Bypass," *Communication* (1980) 5(2): 339-351.

Fontgalland, Guy de, "Newspool: Background to the Controversy," *Media Asia* (1976) 3(3): 147.

Fox, E. "Mass Communications in the Falklands/Malvinas War," *Media, Culture & Society* (January, 1984) 6(1): 45-51.

Foxall, Gordon. "The Meaning of Marketing and Leisure: Issues for Research and Development," *European Journal of Marketing* (1984) 18(2): 23-32.

Frank, Ronald E. and Marshall G. Greenberg, "Zooming in on TV Audiences," *Psychology Today* (October, 1979) 13(4): 92-103 + .

Freedman, Jonathon L. "Effect of Television Violence on Aggressiveness," *Psychological Bulletin* (September, 1984) 96(2): 227-246.

Freeman, Katherine B. "The Significance of McClelland's Achievement Variable in the Aggregate Production Function," *Economic Development and Cultural Change* (July, 1976) 24(4): 815-824.

Freimuth, Vicki S., Rachel H. Greenberg, Jean DeWitt, and Rose Mary Romano. "Covering Cancer: Newspapers and the Public Interest," *Journal of Communication* (Winter, 1984) 34(1): 62-73.

Freimuth, Vicki S. and J. Paul Van Nevel. "Reaching the Public: The Asbestos Awareness Campaign," *Journal of Communication* (Spring, 1981) 31(2): 155-167.

French, Blaire A. *The Presidential Press Conference: Its History and Role in the American Political System.* Lanham, Md: University Press of America, 1982.

Freud, Sigmund. "Jokes and Their Relation to the Unconscious," *Standard Edition,* Vol. 8. London: Hogarth Press, 1905/1960.

Frey, Frederick W. "Communication and Development," *Handbook of Communication,* ed. Ithiel de Sola Pool, Wilbur Schramm and others. Chicago: Rand McNally, 1973, pp. 337-461.

Frey, Frederick W. "The Mass Media and Rural Development in Turkey," Report No. 3, Rural Development Research Project. Cambridge, Mass.: Center for International Studies, Massachusetts Institute of Technology (cited in Frey, 1973, "Communication and Development").

Friedman, Hershey H. and Linda Friedman. "Endorser Effectiveness by Product Type," *Journal of Advertising Research* (October, 1979) 19(5): 63-71.

Friedman, Hershey H. and William S. Dripple Jr. "The Effect of Masculine and Feminine Brand Names on the Perceived Taste of a Cigarette," *Decision Sciences* (1978 9(3): 467-471.

Fry, Donald L. and Thomas A. McCain. "Community Influentials' Media Dependence in Dealing with a Controversial Local Issue," *Journalism Quarterly* (Fall, 1983) 60(3): 458-463.

Fusaro, Joseph A. and Willis M. Conover. "Readability of Two Tabloid and Two Non-tabloid Papers," *Journalism Quarterly* (Spring, 1983) 60(1): 142-144.

Gaddy, G.D. "The Power of the Religious Media: Religious Broadcast Use and the Role of Religious Organizations in Public Affairs," *Review of Religious Research* (June, 1984) 25(4): 289-302.

Gadziala, Stephen M. and Lee B. Becker. "A New Look at Agenda-Setting in the 1976 Election Debates," *Journalism Quarterly* (Spring, 1983) 60(1): 122-126.

Galbraith, John K. *The New Industrial State.* Boston: Houghton Mifflin, 1967.

Gale, J.L. and M.N. Wexler. "The Image of Business on Canadian-produced Television," *Canadian Journal of Communication* (Spring, 1983) 9(2): 15-36.

Galloway, John J. "The Analysis and Significance of Communication Effects Gaps," *Communication Research* (October, 1977) 4(4): 363-386.

Gallup, George. The Gallup Youth Survey 1980. Reported in "Top Evening: Visiting Friends: The Gallup Youth Survey," *Plain Dealer* (Dec. 7, 1980), p. 11C.

Gallup, George. The Gallup Youth Survey 1980. Reported in "Doctors, Clergy Rate Highest: The Gallup Youth Survey," *Plain Dealer* (Nov. 30, 1980).

Gallup, George. *The Gallup Poll.* Dec. 9-12, 1977 poll on attitudes toward media use, pp. 40-42.

Galtung, J. and M. Holmboe Ruge. "The Structure of Foreign News," *Journal of Peace Research* (1965) 2.

Gans, Herbert. *Popular Culture and High Culture: An Analysis of Taste and Evaluation of Taste.* New York: Basic Books, Inc., Publishers, 1974.

Gantz, Walter. "Exploring the Role of Television in Married Life," *Journal of Broadcasting & Electronic Media* (Winter, 1985) 29(1): 65-78.

Gantz, Walter and Susan Tyler Eastman. "Viewer Uses of Promotional Media to Find Out about Television Programs," *Journal of Broadcasting* (Summer, 1983) 27(3): 269-277.

Gantz, Walter and S. Trenholm. "Why People Pass on News: Motivations for Diffusion," *Journalism Quarterly* (Summer, 1979) 56(2): 365-370.

Gantz, Walter et al. "Gratifications and Expectations Associated with Pop Music Among Adolescents," *Popular Music & Society* (1978) 6(1): 81-89.

Garfield, Robert. "If You're Skeptical About Ads, You Have Plenty of Company," *USA Today,* May 15, 1985.

Garnham, Nicholas. "Toward a Theory of Cultural Materialism," *Journal of Communication* (Summer, 1983) 33(3): 314-329.

Garramone, Gina M. "Motivation and Selective Attention to Political Information Formats," *Journalism Quarterly* (Spring, 1985) 62(1): 37-44.

Garramone, Gina M. "Audience Motivation Effects: More Evidence," *Communication Research* (January, 1984a) 11(1): 79-96.

Garramone, Gina M. "Voter Responses to Negative Political Ads," *Journalism Quarterly* (Summer, 1984b) 61(2): 250-259.

Garramone, Gina M. "TV News and Adolescent Political Socialization," *Communication Yearbook 7,* ed. R.N. Bostrom and B.H. Westley. Beverly Hills, Calif.: Sage Publications, 1983, pp. 651-669.

Gaziano, Cecilie. "Neighborhood Newspapers, Citizen Groups and Public Affairs Knowledge Gaps," *Journalism Quarterly* (Autumn, 1984) 61(3): 556-566, 599.

Gaziano, Cecilie. "The Knowledge Gap: An Analytical Review of Media Effects," *Communication Research* (October, 1983) 10(4): 447-486.

Gaziano, Cecilie and Jean Ward. "Citizen-Developed Neighborhood Press," *Mass Com Review* (Spring, 1978) 5(2): 14-18.

Gentry, James W. and Mildred Doering. "Sex Role Orientation and Leisure," *Journal of Leisure Research* (Second Quarter, 1979) pp. 102-111.

Gerbner, George. "Violence in Television Drama: Trends in Symbolic Functions," *Television and Social Behavior. Vol. 1: Media Content and Control,* ed. George A. Comstock and Eli A. Rubinstein. Washington, D.C.: U.S. Government Printing Office, 1972, pp. 28-187.

Gerbner, George, Larry Gross, Michael Morgan and Nancy Signorielli. "Scientists on the TV Screen," *Society* (May/June, 1981) 18(4): 41-44.

Gerbner, George, Larry Gross, Michael Morgan and Nancy Signorielli, "Political Correlates of Television Viewing," *Public Opinion Quarterly* (Spring, 1984) 48: 283-300.

Gerbner, George, Larry Gross, Michael Morgan and Nancy Signorielli, "Charting the Mainstream: Television's Contributions to Political Contributions," *Journal of Communication* (Spring, 1982) 32(2): 100-127.

Gerbner, George, Larry Gross, Michael Morgan and Nancy Signorielli. "Health and Medicine on Television," *The New England Journal of Medicine* (Oct. 8, 1981) 305(15): 901-904.

Gergen, David R. "How Television Weakens the Presidency," *Channels* (March/April, 1984), p. 63.

Gertner, Richard (ed.) *1985 International Television Almanac.* New York: Quigley Pub. Co., Inc., 1985.

Gertner, Richard (ed) *International Motion Picture Almanac.* New York: Quigley Pub. Co., Inc., 1985.

Ghorpade, Shailendra. "Political Spots: Setting the Agenda for Voter Decisions," paper presented to the Advertising Division at the annual convention of the Association for Education in Journalism and Mass Communication, Memphis, Tenn., August, 1985.

Giffard, C. Anthony. "The Inter Press Service: New Information for a New Order," *Journalism Quarterly* (Spring, 1985) 62(1): 17-23, 44.

Giffard, C. Anthony. "Inter Press Service: News from the Third World," *Journal of Communication* (Autumn, 1984) 34(4): 41-59.

Giffard, C. Anthony. "Developed and Developing Nation News in U.S. Wire Service Files to Asia," *Journalism Quarterly* (Spring, 1984) 61(1): 14-19.

Gitlin, Todd. *The Whole World Is Watching: Mass Media in the Making and Unmaking of the New Left.* Berkeley, Calif.: University of California Press, 1980.

The Glasgow Media Group, "Bad news," *Theory and Society* (Fall, 1976) 3(3): 339-363.

Glasser, Gerald J. and Gale D. Metzger. "Radio Usage by Blacks," *Journal of Advertising Research* (October, 1975) 15: 39-45.

Glynn, Carroll J. and Jack M. McLeod. "Public Opinion du Jour: An Examination of the Spiral of Silence," *Public Opinion Quarterly* (Winter, 1984) 48(4): 731-740.

Goedkoop, R.J. "Elements of Genre in Television Situation Comedy," *Feedback* (Summer, 1983) 25(1): 3-5.

Goldberg, M.A. "'Roots': The Next Generations — A Study of Attitude and Behavior," *Television Quarterly* (Fall, 1979) 16(3): 71-74.

Goldberg, Marvin E. and Gerald J. Gorn. "Television's Impact on Preferences for Non-White Playmates: Canadian 'Sesame Street' Inserts," *Journal of Broadcasting* (Winter, 1979) 23(1): 27-32.

Golding, Peter and Philip Elliott. *Making the News.* London: Longman, 1979.

Gollin, Albert E. "The Daily Diet of News: Patterns of Exposure to News in the Mass Media," New York: Newspaper Advertising Bureau, July, 1978.

Gollin, Albert and T. Anderson. *America's Children and the Mass media.* New York: Newspaper Advertising Bureau, 1980.

Gollin, Albert E. and Nicolas A. Bloom. *Newspapers in American News Habits: A Comparative Assessment.* New York: Newspaper Advertising Bureau, 1985.

Goranson, Richard E. "Media Violence and Aggressive Behavior: A Review of Experimental Research," *Advances in Experimental Social Psychology,* Vol. 5, ed. L. Berkowitz. New York: Academic Press, 1970.

Gormley, William T. Jr. *The Effects of Newspaper-Television Cross-Ownership on News Homogeneity.* Chapel Hill: University of North Carolina, Institute for Research in Social Science, 1976.

Gorn, Gerald J. "The Effects of Music in Advertising on Choice Behavior: A Classical Conditioning Approach," *Journal of Marketing* (Winter, 1982) 46(1): 94-101.

Gorn, Gerald J. and Marvin E. Goldberg. "Behavioral Evidence of the Effects of Televised Food Messages on Children," *Journal of Consumer Research* (September, 1982) 9(2): 200-205.

Graber, Doris A. *Crime News and the Public.* New York: Praeger, 1980.

Graber, Doris A. *Mass Media and American Politics.* Washington, D.C.: Congressional Quarterly Press, 1980.

Graber, Doris A. "Press and TV as Opinion Resources in Presidential Campaigns," *Public Opinion Quarterly* (Fall, 1976) 40(3): 285-303.

Gramsci, Antonio. *Prison Notebooks.* New York: International Publishers, 1971.

Grannis, Chandler B. "Title Output and Average Prices, 1982 Preliminary Figures," *Publishers Weekly* (March 11, 1983) 223 (10): 44.

Granzberg, Gary. "Television as Storyteller: The Algonkian Indians of Central Canada," *Journal of Communication* (Winter, 1982) 32(1): 43-52.

Greenberg, Bradley S. "Children's Reactions to TV Blacks," *Journalism Quarterly* (1972) 49: 5-14.

Greenberg, Bradley S. "Diffusion of News of the Kennedy Assassination," *Public Opinion Quarterly* (1964) 28: 225-231.

Greenberg, Bradley S. (ed.) *Life on Television: Content Analyses of U.S. TV Drama.* Norwood, N.J.: Ablex, 1980.

Greenberg, Bradley S. et al. *Mexican-Americans and the Mass Media.* Norwood, N.J.: Ablex Publishers, 1983.

Greenberg, Bradley S. and Charles K. Atkin. "The Portrayal of Driving on Television, 1975-1980," *Journal of Communication* (Spring, 1983) 33(2): 44-55.

Greenberg, Bradley S., Nancy Buerkel-Rothfuss, Kimberly A. Neuendorf and Charles K. Atkin. "Three Seasons of Television Family Role Interactions," *Life on Television: Content Analyses of U.S. TV Drama,* ed. Bradley S. Greenberg. Norwood, N.J.: Ablex, 1980, pp. 161-172.

Greenberg, Bradley S., Nadyne Edison, Felipe Korzenny, Carlos Fernandez-Collado and Charles K. Atkin. "Antisocial and Prosocial Behaviors on Television," *Life on Television,* ed. Bradley S. Greenberg. Norwood, N.J.: Ablex, 1980, pp. 99-128.

Greenberg, Bradley S., Carrie Heeter, Judee K. Burgoon, Michael Burgoon and Felipe Korzenny. "Local Newspaper Coverage of Mexican Americans," *Journalism Quarterly* (Winter, 1983) 60(4): 671-676.

Greenberg, Bradley S., Mary Hines, Nancy Buerkel-Rothfuss and Charles K. Atkin. "Family Role Structures and Interactions on Commercial Television," *Life on Television,* ed. Bradley S. Greenberg. Norwood, N.J.: Ablex, 1980, pp. 149-160.

Greenberg, Bradley S., Felipe Korzenny and Charles K. Atkin. "Trends in the Portrayal of the Elderly," *Life on Television,* ed. Bradley S. Greenberg. Norwood, N.J.: Ablex, 1980, pp. 23-33.

Greenberg, Bradley S. and Kimberly A. Neuendorf. "Black Family Interactions on Television," *Life on Television,* ed. Bradley S. Greenberg. Norwood, N.J.: Ablex, 1980, pp. 173-181.

Greenberg, Bradley S. and Byron Reeves. "Children and the Perceived Reality of Television," *Journal of Social Issues* (Fall, 1976) 32: 86-97.

Greenberg, Bradley S., Marcia Richards and Laura Henderson, "Trends in Sex-Role Portrayals on Television," *Life on Television,* ed. Bradley S. Greenberg. Norwood, N.J.: Ablex, 1980, pp. 65-87.

Greenberg, Bradley S. and M.E. Roloff. "Mass Media Credibility: Research Results and Critical Issues," *News Research for Better Newspapers,* ed. Galen Rarick. Vol. 7. Washington, D.C.: American Newspaper Publishers Association Foundation, 1975.

Greenberg, Bradley S., Katrina W. Simmons, Linda Hogan and Charles K. Atkin. "The Demography of Fictional TV Characters," *Life on Television: Content Analyses of U.S. TV Drama.* Norwood, N.J.: Ablex, 1980, 35-46.

Greenstein, Fred I. "Political Socialization," *International Encyclopedia of the Social Sciences.* New York: Macmillan/Free Press, 1968.

Greenstein, F. *Children and Politics.* New Haven, Conn.: Yale University Press, 1965.

Gronhaug, Kjell. "How New Car Buyers Use Advertising," *Journal of Advertising Research* (February 1, 1975) 15(1): 49-53.

Grossman, M.B. and F.E. Rourke. "The Media and the Presidency: An Exchange Analysis," *Political Science Quarterly* (1976) 91: 455-470.

Grotta, Gerald L. and Anantha S. Babbili. "Daily Newspaper Subscribing Behavior: 'Atypical' Segments Key to Circulation," *Newspaper Research Journal* (Winter, 1983) 5(2): 3-8.

Grotta, Gerald L., Ernest F. Larkin, and Bob L. Carrell Jr., "News vs. Advertising: Does the Audience Perceive the Journalist Distinction?" *Journalism Quarterly* (Autumn, 1976) 53: 448-456.

Grotta, Gerald L., Ernest F. Larkin and Barbara De Plois. "How Readers Perceive and Use a Small Daily Newspaper," *Journalism Quarterly* (Winter, 1975) 52: 711-715.

Grunig, James E. "Time Budgets, Level of Involvement and Use of the Mass Media," *Journalism Quarterly* (Summer, 1979a) 56(2): 248-261.

Grunig, James E. "A Simultaneous Equation Model for Intervention in Communication Behavior," paper presented at the meeting of the Association for Education in Journalism, Houston, Texas, 1979b.

Gunaratne, Shelton A. "The Background to the Non-Aligned News Pool: Pros and Cons and Research Findings," *Gazette* (1978) 24(1): 20-35.

Gunaratne, Shelton A. "Media Subservience and Developmental Journalism," *Communications and Development Review* (Summer, 1978) 2(2): 3-6.

Guimary, Donald L. "Ethnic Minorities in Newsrooms of Major Market Media in California," *Journalism Quarterly* (Winter, 1984) 61(4): 827-830, 834.

Gunter, B., A. Furnham and J. Jarrett. "Personality, Time of Day, and Delayed Memory for TV News," *Personality and Individual Differences* (1984) 5(1): 35-40.

Gunter, Jonathan F. *The United States and the Debate on the World 'Information Order'.* Washington, D.C.: Academy for Educational Development, Inc., 1979.

Gutierrez, Felix F. and Jorge R. Schement. "Spanish International Network: The Flow of Television from Mexico to the United States," *Communication Research* (April, 1984) 11(2): 241-258.

Hachten, William A. *The World News Prism.* Ames: Iowa State University Press, 1981.

Hackett, R.A. "Decline of a Paradigm? Bias and Objectivity in News Media Studies," *Critical Studies in Mass Communication* (September, 1984) 1(3): 229-259.

Hackett, R.A. "The Depiction of Labor and Business on National Television News," *Canadian Journal of Communication* (Winter, 1983) 10(1): 5-50.

Haefner, James E., Kent M. Lancaster and Spencer F. Tinkham. "How Amount of Brand Advertising Is Related to Consumer Buying Behavior," *Journalism Quarterly* (Winter, 1983) 60(4): 691-699.

Hage, George S., Everette E. Dennis, Arnold H. Ismach and Stephen Hartgen. *New Strategies for Public Affairs Reporting.* Englewood Cliffs, N.J.: Prentice-Hall, Inc., 1983, 2nd ed.

Hagen, Everett E. *On the Theory of Social Change.* Homewood, Ill.: The Dorsey Press, 1962a.

Hagen, Everett E. "A Framework for Analyzing Economic and Political Change," *Development of the Emerging Countries, ed.* Robert E. Asher et al. Washington, D.C.: Brookings Institution, 1962B.

Hagner, Paul R. "Newspaper Competition: Isolating Related Market Characteristics," *Journalism Quarterly* (Summer, 1983) 60(2): 281-287.

Halad, Ismid, "Media and International Misunderstanding," *Phaedrus* (1978) 5(1): 17-19.

Hall, Claude and Barbara Hall. *The Business of Radio Programming.* New York: Billboard Pub., Inc. 1977.

Hall, Stuart. "Culture, the Media and the 'Ideological Effect'" *Mass Communication and Society,* ed. James Curran, Michael Gurevitch and Janet Woollacott. London: Edward Arnold Publishers Ltd., in association with The Open University Press, 1977, pp. 315-348.

Hamelink, Cees J. "Informatics: Third World Call for New Order," *Journal of Communication* (Summer, 1979) 29(3): 144-148.

Handberg, Roger and Milan D. Meeske. "Controversial Programming on Educational Television," *Mass Comm Review* (Winter, 1978) 5(1): 18-23.

Harley, William G. "The U.S. Stake in the IPDC," *Journal of Communication* (Autumn, 1981) 31(4): 150-158.

Harmon, Robert R., Nabil Y. Razzouk and Bruce L. Stern. "The Information Content of Comparative Magazine Advertisements," *Journal of Advertising* (1983) 12(4): 10-19.

Louis Harris & Associates, Inc. *A Survey of Citizen Views & Concerns about Urban Life.* Final report, Par 1, conducted for HUD, Dec. 1977-Jan., 1978. released February, 1978.

Louis Harris and Associates, Inc. *The Harris Survey Yearbook of Public Opinion, 1973.* New York, 1976, p. 401.

Hart, R.P. "The Language of the Modern Presidency," *Presidential Studies Quarterly* (Spring, 1984) 14(2): 249-264.

Hartman, John K. "How 21-34 Year Olds Perceive Competing Newspapers in a Small-to-Medium Sized Market," *Newspaper Research Journal* (Fall, 1983) 5(1): 91-100.

Hartman, Paul. "News and Public Perceptions of Industrial Relations," *Media, Culture and Society* (July, 1979) 1(3): 255-270.

Hartman, Paul. "The Use of Entertainment: Some Findings and Suggestions," *Media Asia* (1978) 5(3): 154-158.

Harwood, K. "Women in Broadcasting 1984-1990," *Feedback* (Spring, 1984) 25(4): 18-21.

Hawkins, Robert P. and Suzanne Pingree. "Some Processes in the Cultivation Effect," *Communication Research* (1980) 7: 193-226.

Hawkins, Robert Suzanne Pingree and Donald Roberts. "Watergate and Political Socialization, 1" *American Politics Quarterly* (1975) 3: 406-422.

Hawkins, Robert, Suzanne Pingree, Kim Smith and Warren Bechtolt. "Adolescents' Responses to Issues and Images," *The Great Debates: Carter vs. Ford, 1976,* ed. Sidney Kraus. Bloomington: Indiana University Press, 1979.

Haynes, Robert D. Jr. "Test of Galtung's Theory of Structural Imperialism," *Foreign News and the New World Information Order,* ed. Robert L. Stevenson and Donald Lewis Shaw. Ames: Iowa State University Press, 1984, pp. 200-216.

Hazard, G.C. Jr., R.G. Pearce and J.W. Stempel. "Why Lawyers Should Be Allowed to Advertise: A Market Analysis of Legal Services," *New York University Law Review* (November, 1983) 58(5): 1084-1113.

Head, Sydney W. *World Broadcasting Systems.* Belmont, Calif.: Wadsworth Publishing Co., 1985.

Head, Sydney W. *Broadcasting in America: A Survey of Television and Radio.* Boston: Houghton Mifflin, 1976, 3rd ed.

Heeter, Carrie, Bradley S. Greenberg, Bradley E. Mendelson, Judee K. Burgoon, Michael Burgoon and Felipe Korzenny. "Cross Media Coverage of Local Hispanic American news," *Journal of Broadcasting* (Fall, 1983) 27(4): 395-402.

Heilbrun, K.S. "Siverman's Subliminal Psychodynamic Activation: A Failure to Replicate," *Journal of Abnormal Psychology* (1980) 89(4): 560-566.

Henderson, Laura, Bradley S. Greenberg and Charles K. Atkin. "Sex Differences in Giving Orders, Making Plans, and Needing Support on Television," *Life on Television,* ed. Bradley S. Greenberg. Norwood, N.J.: Ablex, 1980.

Henderson, Laura and Bradley S. Greenberg. "Sex-Typing of Common Behaviors on Television," *Life on Television,* ed. Bradley S. Greenberg. Norwood, N.J.: Ablex, 1980, pp. 89-85.

Henke, Lucy L., Thomas R. Donohue, Christopher Cook and Diane Cheung. "The Impact of Cable on Traditional TV News Viewing," *Journalism Quarterly* (Spring, 1984) 61(1): 174-178.

Henningham, J.P. "Comparisons Between Three Versions of the Professional Orientation Index," *Journalism Quarterly* (Summer, 1984) 61(2): 302-309.

Henningham, J.P. "Comparisons Between Australian and U.S. Broadcast Journalists' Professional Values," *Journal of Broadcasting* (Summer, 1984) 28(3): 323-331.

Henningham, J.P. "Kyodo Gate-keepers: A Study of Japanese News Flow," *Gazette* (1979) 25(1): 23-30.

Herzog, H. "Professor Quiz: A Gratification Study," *Radio Research, 1941,* ed. Paul F. Lazersfeld and F.N. Stanton. New York: Duell, Sloan & Pearce, 1942.

Hess, Beth B. "Stereotypes of the Aged," *Journal of Communication* (Autumn, 1974) 24: 79.

Hesse, M.B. "Strategies of the Political Communication Process," *Public Relations Review* (Spring, 1981) 7(1): 32-47.

Hester, Al. "International Information Flow," *Gazette* (1973) 19(4).

Hiemstra, R. et al. "How Older Persons Are Portrayed in Television Advertising: Implications for Educators," *Educational Gerontology* (March-June, 1983) 9(2-3): 111-122.

Hilderbrand, R.C. *Power and the People: Executive Management of Public Opinion in Foreign Affairs, 1897-1921.* Chapel Hill: University of North Carolina Press, 1981.

Hill, David B. "Qualitative Dimensions of Exposure to Political Television," *Social Science Quarterly* (September, 1983) 64(3): 614-623.

Hill, David B. and James A. Dyer. "Extent of Diversion to Newscasts from Distant Stations by Cable Viewers," *Journalism Quarterly* (Winter, 1981) 58(4): 552-555.

Hill, Richard J. and Charles M. Bonjean. "News Diffusion: A Test of the Regularity Hypothesis," *Journalism Quarterly* (Summer, 1964) 41: 336-342.

Himmelweit, Hilde and Betty Swift. "Continuities and Discontinuities in Media Usage and Taste: A Longitudinal Study," *Journal of Social Issues* (1976) 32(4): 133-155.

Hirsch, Paul M. "On Not Learning from One's Own Mistakes: A Reanalysis of Gerbner et. al.'s Findings on Cultivation Analysis," *Communication Research* (1981) 8(1): 3-37.

Hirsch, Paul M. "The 'Scary World' of the Nonviewer and Other Anomalies: A Reanalysis of Gerbner et al.'s Findings on Cultivation Analysis," *Communication Research* (1980) 7(4): 403-456.

Hirschman, Elizabeth C. and Michael K. Mills. "Sources Shoppers Use to Pick Stores," *Journal of Advertising Research* (February, 1980) 20(1): 47-51.

Hoffner, Cynthia and Joanne Cantor. "Developmental Differences in Responses to a Television Character's Appearance and Behavior," *Developmental Psychology* (November, 1985) 21(6): 1065-1074.

Hofstetter, C. Richard. "Perception of News Bias in the 1972 Presidential Campaign," *Journalism Quarterly* (1979) 56: 370-374.

Hofstetter, C. Richard and T.F. Buss. "Politics and Last-Minute Political Television," *Western Political Quarterly* (1980) 33: 99-114.

Hofstetter, C. Richard and Paul J. Strand. "Mass Media and Political Issue Perceptions," *Journal of Broadcasting* (Fall, 1983) 27(4): 345-358.

Hofstetter, C. Richard, Cliff Zukin and Terry F. Buss. "Political Imagery and Information in an Age of Television," *Journalism Quarterly* (1978) 55: 562-569.

Hornick, Robert C. "Mass Media Use and the 'Revolution of Rising Frustrations,' A Reconsideration of the Theory," *Communication Research* (1977) 4(4): 387-414.

Horowitz, Irwin A. and Russell S. Kaye. "Perception and Advertising," *Journal of Advertising Research* (June, 1975) 15(3): 15-21.

Housel, Thomas J. "Understanding and Recall of TV News," *Journalism Quarterly* (Autumn, 1984) 61(3): 505-508, 741.

Houston, F.S. and D. Scott. "The Determinants of Advertising Page Exposure," *Journal of Advertising* (1984) 13(2): 27-33.

Howard, Herbert H. "An Update on TV Ownership Patterns," *Journalism Quarterly* (Fall, 1983) 60(3): 395-400.

Howard, Herbert H. "The Contemporary Status of Television Group Ownership," *Journalism Quarterly* (1975) 53: 399-405.

Hoyer, W.D., R.K. Srivastava and J. Jacoby. "Sources of Miscomprehension in Television Advertising," *Journal of Advertising* (1984) 13(2): 17-26.

Hudson, David D. and Michael Miller. "The Impact of News of the Reagan Shooting on Two Diverse Populations," *Communication* (Journal of the Communication Association of the Pacific) (December, 1983) 12(3): 77-79.

Huenergard, Celeste. "Ad Linage in Recession as Circulation Gains," *Editor & Publisher* (Jan. 1, 1983), p. 21.

Huesmann, L. Rowell, Kirsti Lagerspetz and Leonard D. Eron. "Intervening Variables in the TV Violence-Aggression Relation: Evidence from Two Countries," *Developmental Psychology* (1984) 20(5): 746-775.

Humphrey, Ronald and Howard Schuman. "The Portrayal of Blacks in Magazine Advertisements: 1950-1982," *Public Opinion Quarterly* (1984) 48: 551-563.

Hunt, Todd and Michael Cheney. "Content Comparison of Free and Paid Circulation Weeklies," *Journalism Quarterly* (Spring, 1982) 59(1): 134-137.

Hur, Kenneth K. and John P. Robinson. "The Social Impact of 'Roots,'" *Journalism Quarterly* (1978) 55(1): 19-24.

Hurd, Robert E. and Michael W. Singletary. "Newspaper Endorsement Influence on the 1980 Presidential Election Vote," *Journalism Quarterly* (Summer, 1984) 61(2): 332-338.

Hutton, R. Bruce. "Advertising and the Department of Energy's Campaign for Energy Conservation Program," *Journal of Advertising* (1982) 11(2): 27-39.

Hyden, C. and N.J. McCandless. "Men and Women as Portrayed in the Lyrics of Contemporary Music," *Popular Music & Society* (1983) 9(2): 19-26.

Hunds, Ernest C. "Editorials, Opinion Pages Still Have Vital Roles at Most Newspapers," *Journalism Quarterly* (Autumn, 1984) 61(3): 634-639.

Hynes, Terry. "Magazine Portrayal of Women, 1911-1930," *Journalism Monographs* (May, 1981), No. 72.

Idid, Syad Arabi. "The Death of the King — How One Malaysian Society Knew About It," *Media Asia* (1981) 8(3): 162-166.

Idsvoog, Karl A. and James L. Hoyt, "Professionalism and Performance of Television Journalists," *Journal of Broadcasting* (Winter, 1977) 21(1): 97-109.

IMS/Ayer Directory of Publications. Fort Washington, PA.: IMS Press, 1985.

Ismach, Arnold H. "Polling as a News-Gathering Tool," *The Annals of the American Academy of Political and Social Science* (March, 1984) 472: 106-118.

Iwao, S. "Study of the International TV News in Japan," *KEIO Communication Review* (March, 1981) 2: 3-16.

Iyengar, Shanto, Mark D. Peters and Donald R. Kinder. "Experimental Demonstrations of the 'Not-So-Minimal' Consequences of Television News Programs," *American Political Science Review* (December, 1982) 76(4): 848-858.

Jackson, Kenneth M. "Local Community Orientations of Suburban Newspaper Subscribers," *Newspaper Research Journal* (April, 1981) 2(3): 42-49.

Jackson, Miles M. "A Comparison of Newspaper Use by Lower-Income and Middle- and Upper-Income Blacks," *ANPA News Research Report* (May 24, 1978) No. 11. Washington, D.C.

Jackson-Beeck, Marilyn. "Interpersonal and Mass Communication in Children's Political Socialization," *Journalism Quarterly* (1979) 56: 48-53.

Jackson-Beeck, Marilyn. "The Nonviewers: Who Are They?" *Journal of Communication* (Summer, 1977) 27: 65-72.

Jacobson, R.E. "Satellite Business Systems and the Concept of the Dispersed Enterprise: An End to National Sovereignty?" *Media, Culture & Society* (July, 1979) 1(3): 235-253.

Jacoby, J., W.D. Hoyer, and M.R. Zimmer. "To Read, View, or Listen? A Cross-Media Comparison of Comprehension," *Current Issues & Research in Advertising 1983*, ed. J.H. Leigh and C.R. Martin Jr. Ann Arbor: Graduate School of Business Administration, University of Michigan, 1983, pp. 201-213.

Jaddou, L. and J.A. Williams. "A Theoretical Contribution to the Struggle Against the Dominant Representations of Women," *Media, Culture & Society* (April, 1981) 3(2): 105-124.

Jalbert, Paul L. "Some Constructs for Analyzing News," *Language, Image, Media, ed.* Howard Davis and Paul Walton. New York: St. Martin's Press, 1983, pp. 282-299.

Janowitz, Morris. *The Community Press in an Urban Setting.* Glencoe, Ill.: Free Press, 1952.

Janowitz, Morris. "Professional Models in Journalism: the Gatekeeper and the Advocate," *Journalism Quarterly* (Winter, 1975) 52: 618-626 + .

Janus, Noreene Z. "Advertising and the Mass Media: Transnational Link Between Production and Consumption," *Media, Culture and Society* (1981) 3: 13-23.

Jarvie, I.E. *Movies and Society.* New York: Basic Books, Inc., 1970.

Jeffres, Leo W. "Media Use for Personal Identification: Linking Uses and Gratifications to Culturally Significant Goals," *Mass Comm Review* (Fall, 1983) 10(3): 6-12.

Jeffres, Leo W. "Ethnicity, Communication and National Integration," paper delivered at Linguistics and Communication Session of the International Conference held at Cleveland State University as part of a program of cooperation between CSU and the Universidade Gama Filho, Rio de Janeiro, Brazil, March 12, 1981.

Jeffres, Leo W. "Socialization for Mass Media Consumption," *Participation in Social and Political Activities,* ed. David Horton Smith, Jacqueline Macaulay and Associates. San Francisco: Jossey-Bass, Inc., 1980, pp. 244-256.

Jeffres, Leo W. "Cable TV and Viewer Selectivity," *Journal of Broadcasting* (Spring, 1978a) 22(2): 167-177.

Jeffres, Leo W. "Cable TV and Interest Maximization," *Journalism Quarterly* (Spring, 1978b) 55(1): 149-154.

Jeffres, Leo W. "Consequences of the Television of Abundance," paper presented to the Theory & Methodology Division of the Association for Education in Journalism, College Park, Maryland, August, 1976.

Jeffres, Leo W. "Functions of Media Behaviors," *Communication Research* (April, 1975) 2(2): 137-161.

Jeffres, L.W. "A Study of Similarities in the Use of Print Media by Fathers and Sons," Unpublished master's thesis, Department of Communication, University of Washington, 1968.

Jeffres, Leo W. and Mildred Barnard. "Communication and the Persistence of Ethnicity," CRC Monographs (May, 1982) No. 5. Cleveland State University: Communication Research Center.

Jeffres, Leo W. and K. Kyoon Hur. "Communication & Perspectives on Ethnicity," paper presented at the Conference on Culture and Communication, Temple University, Philadelphia, PA., March 25, 1983.

Jeffres, Leo W. and K. Kyoon Hur. "The Forgotten Media Consumer — The American Ethnic," *Journalism Quarterly* (Spring, 1980) 57(1): 10-17.

Jeffres, Leo W. and K. Kyoon Hur. "Impact of Ethnic Issues on Ethnic Voters," *The Great Debates: Carter vs. Ford 1976,* ed. Sidney Kraus. Bloomington, Indiana University Press, 1979a, pp. 437-445.

Jeffres, Leo W. and K. Kyoon Hur. "White Ethnics and Their Media Images: Ethnic Studies in Black and White," *Journal of Communication* (Winter, 1979b) 29(1): 116-122.

Jeffres, Leo W. and K. Kyoon Hur. "Ethnic Communication in Cleveland," *CRC Monographs* (1978) No. 3. Cleveland: Cleveland State University, Communication Research Center in conjunction with the Ethnic Heritage Studies Center.

Jeffres, Leo W..and Rebecca Quarles. "A Panel Study of News Diffusion," *Journalism Quarterly* (Winter, 1983) 60(4): 722-724.

Jeffries-Fox, S. and N. Signorielli. "Television and Children's Conceptions of Occupations," *Proceedings of the Sixth Annual Telecommunications Policy Research Conference,* ed. H. Dordick. Lexington, Mass.: D.C. Heath, 1979.

Jennings, M. Kent and Richard Niemi. *The Political Character of Adolescence.* Princeton: Princeton University Press, 1974.

Jennings-Walstedt, Joyce, Florence Geis and Virginia Brown. "Influence of Television Commercials on Women's Self-Confidence and Independent Judgment," *Journal of Personality and Social Psychology* (1980) 38: 203-210.

Jobes, Patrick. "An Empirical Study of Short-Term Mass Communication Saturation and Perception of Population Problems," *The Journal of Sex Research* (November, 1973) 9(4): 342-352.

Johnson, Norris R. "Television and Politization: A Test of Competing Models," *Journalism Quarterly* (1973) 50: 447-455.

Johnston, J., J. Ettema and T. Davidson. *An Evaluation of 'Freestyle': A Television Series Designed to Reduce Sex Role Stereotypes.* Ann Arbor, Mich.: Institute for Social Research, 1980.

Johnstone, John W.C., Edward J. Slawski and William W. Bowman. *The News People: A Sociological Portrait of American Journalists and Their Work.* Urbana: University of Illinois Press, 1976.

Jones, E. Terrence and Joan Saunders. "Persuading an Urban Public: The St. Louis Privacy Campaign," *Journalism Quarterly* (Winter, 1977) 54(4): 669-673.

Jorgensen, Rebekah and Allen J. Karlin, "The Influences of American Films and Television Programs on the Adolescents of a Romanian Community," paper presented at ICA, May, 1980.

Joseph, W. Benjoy. "The Credibility of Physically Attractive Communicators: A Review," *Journal of Advertising* (1982) 11(3): 15-24.

Joslyn, Richard A. "The Impact of Campaign Spot Advertising on Voting Defections," *Human Communication Research* (Summer, 1981) 7: 347-360.

Joslyn, Richard A. "The Content of Political Spot Ads," *Journalism Quarterly* (1980) 57: 92-98.

Jussawalla, Meheroo. *The Future of the Information Economy.* AMIC Occasional Paper 16, Singapore: Asian Mass Communication Research and Information Centre, 1983.

Jussawalla, Meheroo. "Policy Outcomes of WARC '79: Their Impact on Developing Countries," *Media Asia* (1981) 8(1): 7-12.

Kahalas, Harvey and William B. Carper. "Anti-Business Bias and Television: A National Survey of Confidence in Business Leadership," *Business and Society* (Spring, 1978) 18(2): 21-30.

Kalisch, Philip A. and Beatrice J. Kalisch. "Sex-Role Stereotyping of Nurses and Physicians on Prime-Time Television: A Dichotomy of Occupational Portrayals," *Sex Roles* (April, 1984) 10(7/8): 533-553.

Kalisch, Philip A., Beatrice J. Kalisch, and Margaret Scobey. *Images of Nurses on Television.* New York: Springer Pub. Co., 1983.

Kaplan, Peter W. "Women Upgrade Image on TV's Network Shows," *Plain Dealer,* Dec. 16, 1984, p. 15p.

Kapoor, Suraj. "Perception of and Conformity to Policy in Indian Newspapers," *Journalism Quarterly* (Summer, 1979) 56(2): 388-391.

Katz, Elihu, Jay G. Blumler, and Michael Gurevitch. "Utilization of Mass Communication by the Individual," *The Uses of Mass Communications,* ed. Jay G. Blumler and Elihu Katz. Beverly Hills: Sage Publications, 1974.

Katz, Elihu, Michael Gurevitch, and Hadassah Haas. "On the Use of the Mass Media for Important Things," *American Sociological Review* (April, 1973) 38(2): 164-181.

Katz, Elihu and Paul F. Lazarsfeld. *Personal Influence.* Glencoe, Ill.: Free Press, 1954.

Katz, Elihu and G. Wedell. *Broadcasting in the Third World: Promise and Performance.* Cambridge: Harvard University Press, 1977.

Kaur, D.K. and P.N. Mathur. "Developing Criteria for an Effective Farm Magazine," *Journalism Quarterly* (Summer, 1981) 58(2): 296-300.

Kazee, Thomas A. "Television Exposure and Attitude Change: The Impact of Political Interest," *Public Opinion Quarterly* (Winter, 1981) 45(4): 507-518.

Keller, Edward and Ronald Roel. "Foreign Languages and U.S. Cultural Policy: An Institutional Perspective: The Politics of Language," *Journal of Communication* (Spring, 1979) 29(2): 102-111.

Kelly, John R. "Leisure Styles and Choices in Three Environments," *Pacific Sociological Review* (April, 1978) 21(2): 187-207.

Kenrick, Douglas T. and Sara E. Gutierres. "Contrast Effects and Judgments of Physical Attractiveness: When Beauty Becomes a Social Problem," *Journal of Personality and Social Psychology* (January, 1980) 38(1): 131-140.

Kepplinger, Hans Mathias. "Visual Biases in Television Campaign Coverage," *Communication Research* (July, 1982) 9(3): 432-446.

Kerin, R.A. and T.E. Barry. "The CEO Spokesperson in Consumer Advertising: An Experimental Investigation," *Current Issues & Research in Advertising 1981,* ed. J.H. Leigh and C.R. Martin Jr. Ann Arbor: Graduate School of Business Administration, University of Michigan, 1981, pp. 135-147.

Kessler, R.C. and H. Stipp. "The Impact of Fictional Television Suicide Stories on U.S. Fatalities: A Replication," *American Journal of Sociology* (July, 1984) 90(1): 151-167.

Key, Wilson B. *Subliminal Seduction.* Englewood Cliffs, N.J.: Signet, 1973.

Key, Wilson B. *Media Sexploitation.* Englewood Cliffs, N.J.: Prentice-Hall, 1976.

Key, Wilson B. *The Clamplate Orgy.* Englewood Cliffs, N.J.: Prentice-Hall, 1980.

Kielbowicz, Richard B. "Newsgathering by Printers' Exchanges before the Telegraph," *Journalism History* (Summer, 1982) 9(2): 42-48.

Kiesel, Diane, June Nicholson, John Henkel and Geri Fuller-Col. "Washington Neglected," *The Quill* (May, 1978), pp. 19-26.

Kim, Y.Y. "Communication and Acculturation," *Intercultural Communication: A Reader,* ed. L.A. Samovar and R.E. Porter. Belmont, Calif.: Wadsworth, 1982.

Kinder, Donald R. "Political Person Perception: The Asymmetrical Influence of Sentiment and Choice on Perceptions of Presidential Candidates," *Journal of Personality and Social Psychology* (August, 1978) 36(8): 859-871.

Kitatani, Kenji. *Assessment of the New World Information Order: A Content Analysis of International Affairs Coverage by the Primary Western Television Networks.* Hosa Bunka Foundation, Inc., 1981.

Klapper, Joseph. *The Effects of Mass Communication.* New York: Free Press, 1960.

Klein, G. "Relative Advertising Channel Effectiveness: A Test of Learning vs. Involvement Orientations," *Current Issues & Research in Advertising 1981*, ed. J.H. Leigh and C.R. Martin Jr. Ann Arbor: Graduate School of Business Administration. University of Michigan, 1981, pp. 71-84.

Knight, Robert P. "Unesco's International Communication Activities," *International Communication*, ed. Heinz-Dietrich Fischer and John C. Merrill. New York: Hastings House, 1970, pp. 219-226.

Korgaonkar, P.K., G.P. Moschis and D.N. Bellenger. "Correlates of Successful Advertising Campaigns," *Journal of Advertising Research* (February/March, 1984) 24(1): 47-53.

Korzenny, Felipe, Bradley Greenberg and Charles K. Atkin. "Styles of Antidisciplinary Practices as a Mediator of Children's Learning from Antisocial Television Portrayals," *Communication Yearbook* (1979) 3: 282-294.

Korzenny, Felipe, Kimberly Neuendorf, Michael Burgoon, Judee K. Burgoon and Bradley S. Greenberg. "Cultural Identification as Predictor of Content Preferences of Hispanics," *Journalism Quarterly* (Winter, 1983) 60(4): 677-685.

Kotz, Nick. "The Minority Struggle for a Place in the Newsroom," *Columbia Journalism Review* (March/April, 1979) 17(6): 23-31.

Kraus, Sidney. "Mass Communication and Political Socialization," *Quarterly Journal of Speech* (December, 1973) 59(4).

Kraus, Sidney and Dennis K. Davis. "Political Debates," *Handbook of Political Communication*, ed. Dan D. Nimmo and Keith R. Sanders. Beverly Hills: Sage, 1981, pp. 273-296.

Kressley, Konrad, "East-West Communication in Europe — The Television Nexus," *Communication Research* (1978) 5(1): 71-86.

Kroeber, A.L. and Clyde Kluckhohn. *Culture: A Critical Review of Concepts and Definitions*. Cambridge: Harvard University, No. 1, Papers of the Peabody Museum of American Archaeology and Ethnology, 1952.

Kroeber-Riel, W. and B. Barton. "Scanning Ads — Effects of Position and Arousal Potential of Ad Elements," *Current Issues & Research in Advertising 1980*, ed. J.H. Leigh and L.R. Martin Jr. Ann Arbor: Graduate School of Business Administration, University of Michigan, 1980, pp. 147-163.

Kroloff, George M. "The View from Congress: The U.S. Faces WARC," *Journal of Communication* (Winter, 1979) 29(1): 165-169.

Kumar, Krishan. "Holding the Middle Ground: the BBC, the Public and the Professional Broadcaster," *Sociology* (1975) 9: 67-68.

Kuo, E.C.Y. "Mass Media and Language Planning: Singapore's 'Speak Mandarin' Campaign," *Journal of Communication* (Spring, 1984) 34(2): 24-35.

Lachenbruch, David. "The VCR Is Changing the Whole TV Picture," *Channels*, March/April, 1984, p. 16.

Lacy, Stephen and David Matustik. "Dependence on Organization and Beat Sources for Story Ideas: A Case Study of Four Newspapers," *Newspaper Research Journal* (Winter, 1983) 5(2): 9-16.

Laliberte, Raymond, "Concerning the Journalist and Various Powers," *Communication et Information* (Autumn, 1976) 3: 231-242.

Lamberski, R.J. and F.M. Dwyer. "The Instructional Effect of Coding (Color and Black and White) on Information Acquisition and Retrieval," *Educational Communication & Technology* (Spring, 1983) 31(1): 9-21.

Lancaster, Kent M. "Brand Advertising Competition and Industry Demand," *Journal of Advertising* (1984) 13(4): 19-30.

Lancaster, Kent M. and Gordon E. Miracle. "Advertising and Market Concentration: Some Empirical Evidence on Selected Product Categories," *1978 Proceedings of the Annual Conference of the American Academy of Advertising*, ed. Stephen E. Permut. Columbia, S.C.: American Academy of Advertising, 1978, pp. 41-47.

Lang, Gladys Engel and Kurt Lang. *The Battle for Public Opinion*. New York: Columbia University Press, 1983.

Lang, Gladys E. and Kurt Lang. "Watergate: An Exploration of the Agenda-Building Process," *Mass Communication Review Yearbook*, ed. G.C. Wilhoit and H. deBock. Vol. 2. Beverly Hills: Sage Publications, 1981, pp. 447-468.

Lang, Kurt and Gladys E. Lang. "The Impact of Polls on Public Opinion," *The Annals of the American Academy of Political and Social Science* (March, 1984) 472: 129-142.

Lang, J.C. "National Development and News Values: The Press in the Third World and the West," *Gazette* (1984) 33(2): 69-86.

Langdale, J. "Competition in Telecommunications," *Telecommunications Policy* (December, 1982) 6(4): 283-299.

Larkin, Ernest F. and Gerald L. Grotta. "A Market Segmentation Approach to Daily Newspaper Audience Studies," *Journalism Quarterly* (Spring, 1979) 56(1) 31-37 + .

Larson, James F. *Television's Window on the World: International Affairs Coverage on the U.S. Networks.* Norwood, N.J.: Ablex Pub. Co., 1984.

Larson, Timothy L. "The U.S. Television Industry: Concentration and the Question of Network Divestiture of Owned and Operated Television Stations," *Communication Research* (January, 1980) 7(1): 23-44.

Lasorsa, Dominic L. "Cognition and Affect Early in the 1984 Presidential Campaign: The Role of the Press," paper presented to the Theory and Methodology Division at the annual convention of the Association for Education in Journalism and Mass Communication, Memphis, Tenn., August, 1985.

Lasswell, H. "The Structure and Function of Communications in Society," *The Communication of Ideas,* ed. L. Bryson. New York: Harper, 1948.

Lautman, M.R. and K.J. Dean. "Time Compression of Television Advertising," *Advertising and Consumer Psychology,* ed. L. Percy and A.G. Woodside. Lexington, Mass.: D.C. Heath, 1983, pp. 219-236.

Lavidge, Robert J. and Gary A. Steiner. "A Model for Predictive Measurements of Advertising Effectiveness," *Journal of Marketing* (October, 1961) 25: 59-62.

Lazarsfeld, Paul F., Bernard Berelson, and Hazel Gaudet. *The People's Choice.* New York: Duell, Sloan and Pearce, 1944.

Ledingham, John A. and Lynne Masel-Walters. "Written on the Wind: The Media and Hurrican Alicia," *Newspaper Research Journal* (Winter, 1985) 6(2): 50-58.

Le Duc, Don R. "East-West News Flow 'Imbalance': Qualifying the Quantifications," *Journal of Communication* (Fall, 1981) 31(4): 135-141.

Lee, Chin-Chuan. "The United States as Seen Through the People's Daily," *Journal of Communication* (Autumn, 1981) 31(4): 92-101.

Lee, Chin-Chuan. *Media Imperialism Reconsidered: The Homogenizing of Television Culture.* Beverly Hills: Sage, 1980.

Leffler, K.B. "persuasion or Information? The Economics of Prescription Drug Advertising," *The Journal of Law & Economics* (April, 1981) 24(1): 45-74.

Lefkowitz, M.M., Leonard D. Eron, L.O. Walder and L.R. Huesmann. "Television Violence and Child Aggression: A Followup Study," *Television and Social Behavior. Vol. III: Television and Adolescent Aggressiveness,* ed. George A. Comstock and Eli A. Rubinstein. Washington, D.C.: U.S. Government Printing Office, 1972, pp. 35-135.

Lehman, Donald R. "Responses to Advertising a New Car," *Journal of Advertising Research* (1977) 17(4): 23-27.

Leifer, Aimee D. and Donald F. Roberts. "Children's Response to Television Violence," *Television and Social Behavior. Vol. II: Television and Social Learning,* ed. Eli A. Rubinstein and George A. Comstock. Washington, D.C.: U.S. Government Printing Office, 1972.

Lent, John A. "Grassroots Renaissance: Folk Media in Third World Nations," *Folklore* (1980) 1: 78-91.

Lent, John A. "Grassroots Renaissance: Folk Media in the Third World," *Media Asia* (1982) 9(1): 9-17.

Lerner, Daniel. "Modernization Revisited — An Interview with Daniel Lerner," *Communications and Development Review* (1977) 1 (2/3): 4-6.

Lerner, Daniel. *The Passing of Traditional Society.* New York: Free Press, 1958.

Levin, Stephen R. and Donald R. Anderson. "The Development of Attention," *Journal of Communication* (1976) 26(2): 126-135.

Levine, D.N. "Cultural Integration," *International Encyclopedia of the Social Sciences,* ed. D.L. Sills, Vol. 7, pp. 372-380. New York: Macmillan & Free Press, 1968.

Levy, Mark R. "The Time-Shifting Use of Home Video Recorders," *Journal of Broadcasting* (Summer, 1983) 27(3): 263-268.

Levy, Mark R. "Experiencing Television News," *Journal of Communication* (1977) 27(4): 112-117.

Levy, Mark R. and Edward L. Fink. "Home Video Recorders and the Transience of Television Broadcasts," *Journal of Communication* (Spring, 1984) 34(2): 56-71.

Levy, Mark R. and Sven Windahl. "Audience Activity and Gratifications: A Conceptual Clarification and Exploration," *Communication Research* (January, 1984) 11(1): 51-78.

Lewellen, J. "Mass media and Political Participation," *Social Education* (1976) 40: 457-461.

Lewis, Russell. *The New Service Society.* London: Longman, 1973.

Lichtenstein, Allen and Lawrence Rosenfeld. "Normative Expectations and Individual Decisions Concerning Media Gratification Choices," *Communication Research* (July, 1984) 11(3): 393-413.

Lichter, Linda S. and S. Robert Lichter. *Prime Time Crime: Criminals and Law Enforcers in TV Entertainment.* Washington, D.C.: The Media Institute, 1984.

Liebert, Diane E., Joyce N. Sprafkin, Robert M. Liebert and Eli A. Rubinstein. "Effects of Television Commercial Disclaimers on the Product Expectations of Children," *Journal of Communication* (1977) 27(1): 118-124.

Liebert, Robert M. and Robert A. Baron. "Short-Term Effects of Televised Aggression on Children's Aggressive Behavior," *Television and Social Behavior. Vol. II: Television and Social Learning,* ed. John P. Murray, Eli A. Rubinstein and George A. Comstock. Washington, D.C.: U.S. Government Printing Office, 1972.

Liebert, Robert M. and R.W. Poulos. "Television and Personality Development: The Socializing Effects of an Entertainment Medium," *Child Personality and Psychopathology: Current Topics,* Vol. 2, ed. A. Davids. New York: John Wiley & Sons, 1975, pp. 61-97.

Liebert, Robert M., Joyce N. Sprafkin and Emily F. Davidson. *The Early Window: Effects of Television on Children and Youth,* 2nd ed. New York: Pergamon Press, 1982; 1st ed., 1972.

Lipstein, Benjamin and William J. McGuire. *Evaluating Advertising.* New York: Advertising Research Foundation, 1978.

Litman, Barry R. "Is Network Ownership in the Public Interest?" *Journal of Communication* (Spring, 1978) 28(2): 51-59.

Litman, G.K. "Women, Alcohol and Cultural Stereotyping: Updating the Myth," *Women's Studies International Quarterly* (1980) 3(4): 347-354.

Littlechild, S.C. "Controls on Advertising: An Examination of Some Economic Arguments," *Journal of Advertising: The Quarterly Review of Marketing Communications* (Jan.-March, 1982) 1(1): 25-37.

Loevinger, Lee. "Media Concentration: Myth and Reality," *The Antitrust Bulletin* (Fall, 1979), pp. 479-498.

Logan, Robert and Bruce Garrison. "Factors Affecting News Coverage: Two Florida Papers and the Mariel Refugee Influx," *Newspaper Research Journal* (Fall, 1983) 5(1): 43-52.

Lometti, Guy E., Byron Reeves and Carl R. Bybee. "Investigating the Assumptions of Uses and Gratifications Research," *Communication Research* (July, 1977) 4(3): 321-338.

Loughlin, Beverly. "The Women's Magazine Short-Story Heroine," *Journalism Quarterly* (Spring, 1983) 60(1): 138-142.

Lovrich, Nicholas P. Jr. and John C. Pierce. "'Knowledge Gap' Phenomena: Effect of Situation-Specific and Transsituational Factors," *Communication Research* (July, 1984) 11(3): 415-434.

Lovil, Daniel D. and Allan B. Padderud. "Video Disclaimers in Television Advertising: Are They Effective?" *Journal of Communication* (Spring, 1981) 31(2): 72-77.

Lowery, Sharon and Melvin L. DeFleur. *Milestones in Mass Communication Research.* New York: Longman, 1983.

Lull, James T., Lawrence M. Johnson and Carol E. Sweeny. "Audiences for Contemporary Radio Formats," *Journal of Broadcasting* (Fall, 1978) 22: 439-453.

Lunch, William L. and Peter W. Sperlich. "American Public Opinion and the War in Vietnam," *Western Political Quarterly* (March, 1979) 32(1): 21-44.

Luttbeg, Norman R. "News Consensus: Do U.S. Newspapers Mirror Society's Happenings?" *Journalism Quarterly* (Fall, 1983a) 60(3): 484-488.

Luttbeg, Norman R. "Television Viewing Audience and Congressional District Incongruity: A Handicap for the Challenger?" *Journal of Broadcasting* (Fall, 1983b) 27(4): 411-417.

Luttbeg, Norman R. "Proximity Does Not Assure Newsworthiness," *Journalism Quarterly* (Winter, 1983c) 60(4): 731-732.

Lyle, Jack. *Broadcasting and Urban Problems: Television and the Organization of the Contemporary American Scene.* Hoso-Bunka Foundation, Symposium on the Cultural Role of Broadcasting: Summary Report (October, 1978) Tokyo, pp. 62-69.

Lyle, Jack and H.R. Hoffman. "Children's Use of Television and Other Media," *Television and Social Behavior* Vol. 4, *Television in Day-to-Day Life: Patterns of Use,* ed. E.A. Rubinstein, G.A. Comstock and J.P. Murray. Washington, D.C.: National Institute of Mental Health, 1971, pp. 129-256.

Lynn, J.R. "Newspaper Readership and Proximity to Metropolitan Markets," *ANPA Research Report* (June 18, 1982) No. 34. Washington, D.C.: American Newspaper Publishers Association, pp. 7-9.

Lynn, Jerry R. "Newspaper Ad Impact in Nonmetropolitan Markets," *Journal of Advertising Research* (August, 1981) 21(4): 13-20.

Lysonski, S. "Female and Male Portrayals in Magazine Advertisements: A Re-examination," *Akron Business and Economic Review* (Summer, 1983) 14(2): 45-50.

MacBride, Sean (president, International Commission for the Study of Communication Problems). *Many Voices, One World.* New York: Unipub, Unesco, 1980.

Maccoby, Eleanor E. and Carol Nagly Jacklin. *The Psychology of Sex Differences.* Stanford, Calif.: Stanford University Press, 1974.

MacDonald, J. Fred. *Blacks and White TV.* Chicago: Nelson-Hall, Publishers, 1983.

MacLachlan, James. "Listener Perception of Time-Compressed Spokespersons," *Journal of Advertising Research* (April/May, 1982) 22(2): 47-51.

MacLachlan, James and Priscilla LaBarbera. "Time-Compressed TV Commercials," *Journal of Advertising Research* (August, 1978) 18(4): 11-15.

Madden, Thomas J. and Marc G. Weinberger. "Humor in Advertising: A Practitioner View," *Journal of Advertising Research* (August/September, 1984) 24(4): 23-30.

Madden, Thomas J. and Marc G. Weinberger. "The Effects of Humor on Attention in Magazine Advertising," *Journal of Advertising* (1982) 11(3): 8-14.

Maddox, William S. and Dan Nimmo. "In Search of the Ticket Splitter," *Social Science Quarterly* (September, 1981) 62: 401-408.

Maddox, Lynda M. and Eric J. Zanot. "Suspension of the NAB Code and Its Effect on Regulation of Advertising," *Journalism Quarterly* (Spring, 1984) 61(1): 125-130.

Madjri, John Dovi "Audience and Impact of a Rural African Medium: The Togo Newspaper 'Game Su,'" *Communication et Information* (Winter, 1977) 2(1): 127-134. [French].

Magazine Fact Book. New York: Magazine Publishers Association, 1982.

Magazine Newsletter of Research. New York: Magazine Publishers Association, No. 46, August, 1984.

Magazine Publishers Association. (1983) Surveys reported in *Magazine Newsletter of Research.* New York: MPA, August, 1984, No. 46.

Makagiansar, Makaminan, "Unesco & World Problems of Communication," *Unesco Courier* (April, 1977) p. 6.

Malamuth, Neil and Jonathon Check. "The Effects of Exposure to Aggressive-Pornography: Rape Proclivity, Sexual Arousal and Beliefs in Rape Myths." paper presented at the annual convention of the American Psychological Association, Los Angeles, Calif., August, 1981.

Malamuth, Neil M. and Jonathon Check. "Debriefing Effectiveness Following Exposure to Pornographic Rape Depictions," paper presented at the annual convention of the Canadian Psychological Association, Toronto, Ontario, June, 1981.

Malamuth, Neil M. and Edward Donnerstein. "The Effects of Aggressive-Pornography Mass Media Stimuli," *Advances in Experimental Social Psychology,* ed. Leonard Berkowitz. New York: Academic Press, 1982.

Malamuth, Neil M., Maggie Heim and Seymour Feshbach. "Sexual Responsiveness of College Students to Rape Depictions: Inhibitory and Disinhibitory Effects," *Journal of Personality and Social Psychology* (1980) 38(3): 399-408.

Malaney, Gary D. and Terry F. Buss. "AP Wire Reports vs. CBS TV News Coverage of a Presidential Campaign," *Journalism Quarterly* (Autumn, 1979) 56: 602-610.

Malik, R. "Communism vs. the Computer: Can the Soviet Union Survive Information Technology?" *InterMedia* (May, 1984) 12(3): 10-23.

Manekar, D.R. "A Background to Alternative News Services: History and Development," *Media Development* (1981) 28(1): 3-6.

Manheim, Jarol B. and William W. Lammers. "The News Conference and Presidential Leadership of Public Opinion: Does the Tail Wag the Dog?" *Presidential Studies Quarterly* (Spring, 1981) 11: 177-188.

Manning, Willard G. and Bruce M. Owen. "Television Rivalry and Network Power," *Public Policy* (Winter, 1976) 24(1): 33-57.

Marshall, Thomas R. "The Benevolent Bureaucrat: Political Authority in Children's Literature and Television," *Western Political Quarterly* (September, 1981) 34: 389-398.

Martin, L. John and Anju Grover Chaudhary. *Comparative Mass Media Systems.* New York: Longman, 1983.

Martin, Ralph R., Garrett J. O'Keefe, and Oguz B. Nayman. "Opinion Agreement and Accuracy Between Editors and Their Readers," *Journalism Quarterly* (Autumn, 1972) 49: 460-468.

Martindale, Carolyn. "Newspaper and Wire-Service Leads in Coverage of the 1980 Campaign," *Journalism Quarterly* (Summer, 1984) 61(2): 339-345.

Masmoudi, Mustapha. "The New World Information Order," *Journal of Communication* (1979) 29(2): 172-185.

Masmoudi, Mustapha. *The New World Information Order.* Paris: Unesco International Commission for the Study of Communication Problems, 1978.

Massing, Michael. "Reshuffling the White House Press Pack," *Columbia Journalism Review* (March/April, 1981) 20: 36-40.

Mastroianni, Tony. "Movie Attendance Up," *Cleveland Press* (Nov. 5, 1980) p. 4B.

Matelski, Marilyn J. "Image and Influence: Women in Public Television," *Journalism Quarterly* (Spring, 1985) 62(1): 147-150.

Mattos, Sergio. "Advertising and Government Influences: The Case of Brazilian Television," *Communication Research* (April, 1984) 11(2): 203-220.

Maurizi, Alex R. "The Effect of Laws against Price Advertising: The Case of Retail Gasoline," *Western Economic Journal* (September, 1972) 10: 321-329.

Maurizi, Alex R., Ruth L. Moore and Lawrence Shepard. "The Impact of Price Advertising: The California Eyewear Market After One Year," *Journal of Consumer Affairs* (Winter, 1981) 15(2): 290-300.

Mayo, John K., Joao Batista Araujo E. Oliveira, Everett M. Rogers, Sonia Dantus Pinto Guimaraes, and Fernando Morett. "The Transfer of Sesame Street to Latin America," *Communication Research* (April, 1984) 11(2): 259-280.

Mazharul Haque, S.M. "Is U.S. Coverage of News in Third World Imbalanced?" *Journalism Quarterly* (Fall, 1983) 60(3): 521-524.

McAnany, Emile G. (ed.) *Communications in the Rural Third World: The Role of Information in Development.* New York: Praeger, 1980.

McAnany, E.G. and J.B.A. Oliveira. "The SACI/EXERN Project in Brazil: An Analytical Case Study," *Reports and Papers on Mass Communication.* No. 89. Paris: Unesco, 1980.

McCain, Thomas A., Joseph Chilberg and Jacob Waskshlag. "The Effect of Camera Angle on Source Credibility and Attractions," *Journal of Broadcasting* (1977) 21(1): 35-46.

McClelland, David C. *The Achieving Society.* Princeton, N.J.: D. Van Nostrand Co., 1961.

McCleneghan, J. Sean. "New Mexico Newspapers and Mayoral Elections," *Journalism Quarterly* (Winter, 1983) 60(4): 725-728.

McCombs, Max and Dave Weaver. "Voters' Need for Orientation and Use of Mass Media," paper presented to the International Communication Association, Montreal, Canada, 1973.

McDonald, Daniel G. and Carroll J. Glynn. "The Stability of Media Gratifications," *Journalism Quarterly* (Autumn, 1984) 61(3): 542-549, 741.

McIntosh, Toby J. "Why the Government Can't Stop Press Mergers," *Columbia Journalism Review* (May/June, 1977) 16(3): 48-50.

McLaughlin, James. "The Doctor Shows," *Journal of Communication* (1975) 25(3): 182-184.

McLeod, Jack M., Charles K. Atkin and Steve H. Chaffee. "Adolescents, Parents, and Television Use: Adolescent Self-Report Measures from Maryland and Wisconsin Samples," *Television and Social Behavior. Vol. III: Television and Adolescent Aggressiveness*, ed. George A. Comstock and Eli A. Rubinstein. Washington, D.C.: U.S. Government Printing Office.

McLeod, Jack M. and Lee B. Becker. "The Uses and Gratifications Approach," *Handbook of Political Communication*, ed. Dan D. Nimmo and Keith R. Sanders. Beverly Hillls: Sage, 1981, pp. 67-99.

McLeod, Jack M. and Lee B. Becker. "Testing the Validity of Gratification Measures Through Political Effects Analysis," *The Uses of Mass Communications: Current Perspectives on Gratification Research*, ed. Jay G. Blumler and Elihu Katz. Beverly Hills: Sage, 1974.

McLeod, Jack M., Lee B. Becker and J.E. Byrnes. "Another Look at the Agenda Setting Function of the Press," *Communication Research* (1974) 1: 131-166.

McLeod, Jack M., Carl R. Bybee and J. Durall. "Equivalence of Informed Political Participation: The 1976 Presidential Debates as a Source of Influence," *Communication Research* (1979) 6: 436-487.

McLeod, Jack M. and Sun Yuel Choe. "An Analysis of Five Factors Affecting Newspaper Circulation," *ANPA News Research Report* (1978) No. 10.

McLeod, Jáck and S. Hawley Jr. "Professionalism among Newsmen," *Journalism Quarterly* (Autumn, 1964) 41: 529-538.

McLeod, Jack M., W.D. Luetscher and D.G. McDonald. "Beyond Mere Exposure: Media Orientations and Their Impact on Political Processes," paper presented at the Association for Education in Journalism annual convention, Boston, 1980.

McLeod, Jack M. and Daniel G. McDonald. "Beyond Simple Exposure: Media Orientations and Their Impact on Political Processes," *Communication Research* (January, 1985) 12(1): 3-34.

McLeod, Jack M. and Garrett J. O'Keefe Jr. "The Socialization Perspective and Communication Behavior," *Current Perspectives in Mass Communication Research*, ed. F. Gerald Kline and Phillip J. Tichenor. Beverly Hills, Sage, 1972, pp. 121-168.

McLeod, Jack and J. Swinehart. "Satellites, Science and the Public," Ann Arbor, Mich.: Survey Research Center, 1960.

McLuhan, Marshall. *Understanding Media*. New York: McGraw-Hill, 1964.

McNelly, John T. "Mass Communication in the Development Process," *Mass Communication and the Development of Nations*, ed. David K. Berlo. East Lansing: Michigan State University International Communication Institute, 1968.

McQuail, Denis. *Mass Communication Theory: An Introduction*. Beverly Hills, Calif.: Sage, 1984.

McQuail, Denis. "With the Benefit of Hindsight: Reflections on Uses and Gratifications Research," *Critical Studies in Mass Communication* (June, 1984) 1(2): 177-193.

McQuail, Denis. *Review of Sociological Writing on the Press*. Working Paper No. 2, Royal Commission on the Press. London: Her Majesty's Stationery Office, 1976.

McQuail, Denis, Jay G. Blumler and J.R. Brown. "The Television Audience: A Revised Perspective," *Sociology of Mass Communications*, ed. Denis McQuail. Harmondsworth: Penguin, 1972.

Meadow, Robert G. "Political Communication Research in the 1980s," *Journal of Communication* (Winter, 1985) 35(1): 157-173.

Media Opinion Research. 1985 survey of 1,000 people, "How We Rate Media's Ethics," *USA Today*, June 13, 1985, p. 1D.

Mediamark Research. Reported in *Magazine Newsletter of Research*. New York: Magazine Publishers Association, August, 1984, No. 46, p. 4.

Meeske, Milan D. and Mohamad Hamid Javaheri. "Network Television Coverage of the Iranian Hostage Crisis," *Journalism Quarterly* (Winter, 1982) 59(4): 641-645.

Mehan, Joseph A. "Unesco and the U.s.: Action and Reaction," *Journal of Communication* (Fall, 1981) 31(4): 159-163.

Mendelsohn, Harold. "Comment on Spitzer's...A Comparison of Six Investigations," *Journal of Broadcasting* (1964-65) 9: 51-54.

Mendelsohn, Harold and Garrett J. O'Keefe. *The People Choose a President: Influences on Voter Decision Making.* New York: Praeger, 1976.

Merrill, John C. *Global Journalism.* New York: Longman, 1983.

Merrill, John C. *The Imperative of Freedom.* New York: Hastings House, Publishers, 1974.

Merrill, John C. and Ralph L. Lowenstein. *Media, Messages and Men.* New York: David McKay Co., Inc., 1971.

Merritt, S. "Negative Political Advertising: Some Empirical Findings," *Journal of Advertising* (1984) 13(3): 27-38.

Messmer, Donald J. "Repetition and Attitudinal Discrepancy Effects on the Affective Response to Television Advertising," *Journal of Business Research* (1979) 7: 75-93.

Metzger, G.D. "Cable Television Audiences," *Journal of Advertising Research* (August/September, 1983) 23(4): 41-49.

Meyer, Philip and Stanley T. Wearden. "The Effects of Public Ownership on Newspaper Companies: A Preliminary Inquiry," *Public Opinion Quarterly* (Fall, 1984) 48: 564-577.

Milavsky, J.R., R. Kessler, H. Stipp and W.S. Rubens. "Television and Aggression: Results of a Panel Study," *Television and Behavior: Ten Years of Scientific Progress and Implications for the 80s.* Washington, D.C.: U.S. Government Printing Office, 1982.

Milgram, Stanley and R. Lance Shotland. *Television and Antisocial Behavior: Field Experiments.* New York: Academic Press, 1973.

Millar, Frank and Edna Rogers. "Relational Dimensions of Interpersonal Dynamics," *Further Explorations in Interpersonal Communication,* ed. Gerald Miller and M. Roloff: Beverly Hills: Sage Publications, in press.

Miller, Arthur H., Edie N. Goldenberg and Lutz Erbring. "Type-Set Politics: Impact of Newspapers on Public Confidence," *American Political Science Review* (1979) 73: 67-84.

Miller, Delbert C. "A Research Note on Mass Communication," *American Sociological Review* (1945) 10: 691-694.

Miller, M. Mark and Byron Reeves. "Linking Dramatic TV Content to Children's Occupational Sex-Role Stereotypes," *Journal of Broadcasting* (1976) 20: 35-50.

Miller, M. Mark and Stephen D. Reese. "Media Dependency as Interaction: Effects of Exposure and Reliance on Political Activity and Efficacy," *Communication Research* (April, 1982) 9(2): 227-248.

Miller, Susan Heilmann. "Reporters and Congressmen: Living in Symbiosis," *Journalism Monographs* (1978) 53: 25.

Mitchell, A.A. "Cognitive Processes Initiated by Exposure to Advertising," *Information Processing Research in Advertising,* ed. R.J. Harris. Hillsdale, N.J.: Lawrence Erlbaum Associates, 1983, pp. 13-42.

Mitchell, J.L. "Seeking a New International Order of Information: A Stalemate," *Media Asia* (1978) 5(1): 14-19.

Miyo, Y. "The Knowledge-Gap Hypothesis and Media Dependency," *Communication yearbook 7,* ed. R.N. Bostrom and B.H. Westley. Beverly Hills: Sage Publications, 1983, pp. 626-649.

Mobley, G.M. "The Political Influence of Television Ministers," *Review of Religious Research* (June, 1984) 25(4): 314-320.

Mohr, Phillip J. "Parental Guidance of Children's Viewing of Evening Television Programs," *Journal of Broadcasting* (Spring, 1979) 23(2): 213-228.

Monroe, Alan D. "Consistency Between Public Preferences and National Policy Decisions," *American Politics Quarterly* (January, 1979) 7(1): 3-19.

Monti, Daniel J. "Biased and Unbiased News: Reporting Racial Controversies in the *New York Times,* 1960-July 1964," *The Sociological Quarterly* (Summer, 1979) 20: 399-409.

Moore, Carlos W. and William M. Pride. "Selected Effects of Qualifying Statements Regarding Technical Performance Claims: An Experimental Investigation," *Journal of Advertising* (1980) 9(2): 20-28.

Moore, Timothy E. "Subliminal Advertising: What You See Is What You Get," *Journal of Marketing* (Spring, 1982) 46: 38-47.

Morales, Waltraud Queiser. "Latin America on Network TV," *Journalism Quarterly* (Spring, 1984) 61(1): 157-160.

Morgan, Michael. "Heavy Television Viewing and Perceived Quality of Life," *Journalism Quarterly* (Autumn, 1984) 61(3): 499-504, 740.

Morgan, Michael. "Television and Adolescents' Sex Role Stereotypes: A Longitudinal Study," *Journal of Personality and Social Psychology* (1982) 43(5): 947-955.

Morgan, Michael and Larry Gross. "Television Educational Achievement and Aspirations," In *Television and Behavior: Ten Years of Scientific Progress and Implications for the 80's.* Washington, D.C.: National Institute of Mental Health (1981).

Moriarty, S.E. "Beyond the Hierarchy of Effects: A Conceptual Framework," *Current Issues & Research in Advertising 1983,* ed. J.H. Leigh and C.R. Martin Jr. Ann Arbor, Mich.: School of Business Administration, University of Michigan, 1983, pp. 45-55.

Moriarty, Sandra Ernst. "Trends in Advertising Typography," *Journalism Quarterly* (Summer, 1982) 59(2): 290-294.

Morris, Roger. "Reporting the Race War in Rhodesia," *Columbia Journalism Review* (March/April, 1979) 17: 32-34.

Mosher, Steven W. *Broken Earth.* New York: Free Press, 1983.

Motion Picture Association. Survey of Moviegoers Age 12 and Over. "How Often We Go to the Movies," *USA Today,* March 29, 1985, p. 1D; "Movie Attendance by Age," *USA Today,* March 8, 1985, p. 1D.

Mueller, Willard F. and Richard T. Rogers. "The Role of Advertising in Changing Concentration of Manufacturing Industries," *Review of Economics and Statistics* (February, 1980) 62: 89-96.

Muis, Abdul. "Some Implications of Television Exposure among Traditional Peasants: A Case from South Sulawesi Island," *Media Asia* (1983) 10(2): 92-100.

Munson, J. Michael and W. Austin Spivey. "Product and Brand-User Stereotypes among Social Classes," *Journal of Advertising Research* (August, 1981) 21(4): 37-46.

Murdock, Graham and Peter Golding. "Capitalism, Communication and Class Relations," *Mass Communication and Society,* ed. James Curran, Michael Gurevitch and Janet Woolacott. London: Edward Arnold Publishers, Ltd., in association with The Open University Press, 1977, pp. 12-43.

Murphy, John H. II and Mary S. Amundsen. "The Communications-Effectiveness of Comparative Advertising for a New Brand on Users of the Dominant Brand," *Journal of Advertising* (1981) 10(1): 14-20.

Murphy, James E. and Donald R. Avery. "A Comparison of Alaskan Native and Non-Native Newspaper Content," *Journalism Quarterly* (Summer, 1983) 60(2): 316-322.

Murphy, James E. and Donald R. Avery. "A Study of Favorability Toward Natives in Alaskan Newspapers," *Newspaper Research Journal* (Fall, 1982) 4(1): 39-45.

Murphy, T. "Calvinism and the Mass Media," *Canadian Journal of Communication* (Fall, 1978) 5(2): 30-40.

Nagle, Thomas T. "Do Advertising-Profitability Studies Really Show that Advertising Creates a Barrier to Entry?" *Journal of Law and Economics* (October, 1981) 24: 333-349.

Nair, B. *Mass Media and the Transnational Corporation.* Singapore: Singapore University Press, 1980.

Naples, M.J. *Effective Frequency: The Relationship Between Frequency and Advertising Effectiveness.* New York: Association of National Advertisers, 1981.

Nasser, Munir K. "News Values Versus Ideology: A Third World Perspective," *Comparative Mass Media Systems,* ed. L. John Martin and Anju Grover Chaudhary. New York: Longman, 1983, pp. 44-66.

Nayman, Oguz, Blaine K. McKee, and Dan L. Lattimore, "PR Personnel and Print Journalists: A Comparison of Professionalism," *Journalism Quarterly* (1977) 54(3): 492-497.

Newcomb, A.F. and W.A. Collins. "Children's Comprehension of Family Role Portrayals in Televised Dramas: Effects of Socioeconomic Status, Ethnicity and Age," *Developmental Psychology* (1979) 15(4): 417-423.

Newman, B.I. and J.N. Sheth. "The 'Gender Gap' in Voter Attitudes and Behavior: Some Advertising Implications," *Journal of Advertising* (1984) 13(3): 4-16.

Newspaper Advertising Bureau. "Newspaper Readership Project: Patterns of Exposure to News in the Mass Media," New York: NAB, July, 1978.

Niemi, Richard G., Grace Iusi and William Bianco. "Pre-Election Polls and Turnout," *Journalism Quarterly* (Fall, 1983) 60(3): 530-532.

Nimetz, M. "Fundamental Principles for International Telecommunications and Informatics Policies," *Transnational Data Report* (December, 1980) 3(8): 9-11.

Nimmo, Dan. *Political Communication and Public Opinion in America.* Santa Monica, California: Goodyear, 1978.

Nimmo, Dan and J.E. Combs. *Mediated Political Realities.* New York: Longman, 1983.

Nimmo, Dan and J.E. Combs. "'The Horror Tonight': Network Television News and Three Mile Island," *Journal of Broadcasting* (Summer, 1981) 25(3): 289-293.

Nimmo, Dan and J.E. Combs. *Subliminal Politics: Myths and Myth Makers in America.* Englewood Cliffs, N.J.: Prentice-Hall, 1980.

Nnaemeka, Tony and J. Richstad. "Structured Relations and Foreign News Flow in the Pacific Region," *Gazette* (1980) 26(4): 235-257.

Noelle-Neumann, Elizabeth. "The Spiral of Silence: A Theory of Public Opinion," *Journal of Communication* (1974) 24: 43-51.

Noelle-Neumann, Elizabeth. "Turbulences in the Climate of Opinion: Methodological Applications of the Spiral of Silence Theory," *Public Opinion Quarterly* (1977) 41: 143-158.

Nolan, M. "Political Communication Methods in Canadian Federal Election Campaigns 1867-1925," *Canadian Journal of Communication* (March-May, 1981) 7(4): 28-46.

Nord, D.P. "The Evangelical Origins of Mass Media in America, 1815-1935," *Journalism Monographs*, No. 88, May, 1984.

Nordenstreng, Kaarle. "Bitter Lessons: The 'World of the News' Study," *Journal of Communication* (Winter, 1984) 34(1): 138-142.

Nordenstreng, Kaarle. "U.S. Policy and the Third World: A Critique," *Journal of Communication* (Summer, 1982) 32(3): 54-59.

Nordlund, Jan-Erik. "Media Interaction," *Communication Research* (1978) 5: 150-175.

Norris, Vincent P. "Consumer Valuation of National Ads," *Journalism Quarterly* (Summer, 1983) 60(2): 262-268.

Nowell, Bob. "The Role of the International Organization of Journalists in the Debate about the 'New International Information Order,' 1958-1978," paper presented to International Communication Division, Association for Education in Journalism, Boston, August, 1980.

Nowlan, James D. and Mary Jo Moutray. "Broadcast Advertising and Party Endorsements in a Statewide Primary," *Journal of Broadcasting* (Summer, 1984) 28(3): 361-363.

Nwankwo, Robert L. "Community Information Source Usage and Community Opinion," *Mass Comm Review* (Spring/Fall, 1982) 9(2/3): 17-22.

Nwuneli, O.E. and E. Udoh. "International News Coverage in Nigerian Newspapers," *Gazette* (1982) 29(1/2): 31-40.

O'Bryant, Shirley L. and Charles R. Corder-Bolz. "The Effects of Television on Children's Stereotyping of Women's Work Roles," *Journal of Vocational Behavior* (April, 1978) 223-243.

O'Connell, Sheldon. "Television and the Canadian Eskimo: The Human Perspective," *Journal of Communication* (1977) 27(4): 140-149.

Ogan, Christine L. "Life at the Top for Men and Women Newspaper Managers: A Five-Year Update of Their Characteristics," *Newspaper Research Journal* (Winter, 1983) 5(2): 57-68.

Ogan, Christine L. "Development Journalism/Communication: The Status of the Concept," *Gazette* (1982) 29 (1/2) 3-13.

Ogan, Christine and Clint Swift. "Is the News About Development All Good?" paper presented to the International Communication Division, Association for Education in Journalism, annual convention, Ohio University, Athens, Ohio, July, 1982.

Ogan, Christine L. "Development Journalism/Communication: The Status of the Concept," paper presented to the International Division of·the Association for Education in Journalism, Boston, August, 1980.

Ogan, Christine L. and J.E. Fair. "'A Little Good News': The Treatment of Development News in Selected Third World Newspapers," *Gazette* (1974) 33(3): 173-191.

Ogilvy, David and Joel Raphaelson. "Research on Advertising Techniques that Work — and Don't Work," *Harvard Business Review* (July/August, 1982) 60(4): 14-19.

O'Guinn, T.C. and T.P Meyer. Segmenting the Hispanic Market: The Use of Spanish-Language Radio," *Journal of Advertising Research* (December, 1983/January, 1984) 23(6): 9-18.

O'Keefe, Garrett J. "'Taking a Bite Out of Crime': The Impact of a Public Information Campaign," *Communication Research* (April, 1985) 12(2): 147-178.

O'Keefe, Garrett J. and L. Erwin Atwood. "Communication and Election Campaigns," *Handbook of Political Communication,* ed. Dan D. Nimmo and Keith R. Sanders. Beverly Hills: Sage, 1981, pp. 329-357.

O'Keefe, Garret J. and Harold Mendelsohn. "Nonvoting: The Media's Role," *Deviance and Mass Media,* ed. C. Winick. Beverly Hills: Sage, 1978.

O'Keefe, Garret J., Kathaleen Nash and Jenny Liu. "The Perceived Utility of Advertising," *Journalism Quarterly* (Winter, 1981) 58(4): 534-542.

O'Keefe, M. Timothy and Kenneth G. Sheinkopf. "Advertising in the Soviet Union: Growth of a New Media Industry," *Journalism Quarterly* (Spring, 1976) 53: 80-87.

Oliver, R.L. "An Interpretation of the Attitudinal and Behavioral Effects of Puffery," *Journal of Consumer Affairs* (Summer, 1979) 13(1): 8-27.

Olmedo, E.L. "Quantitative Models of Acculturation: An Overview," *Acculturation: Theory, Models and Some New Findings,* ed. A.M. Padilla. Boulder, Colo.: Westview, 1980, pp. 27-45.

Olson, D., M.J. Schlinger, and C. Young. "How Consumers React to New-Product Ads," *Journal of Consumer Research* (June/July, 1982) 22(3): 24-30.

Olson, Jerry C., Daniel R. Toy and Philip A. Dover. "Do Cognitive Responses Mediate the Effects of Advertising Content on Cognitive Structure?" *Journal of Consumer Research* (December, 1982) 9:245-262.

O'Neil, Nora, Sandra Schoonover, and Lisa Adelstein. "The Effects of TV Advertising on Children's Perceptions of Roles," summarized in "Children and Television: A Report to Montessori Parents," ed. Thomas W. Whipple. Mimeographed. Cleveland: Cleveland State University, 1980.

Opinion Research Corporation. *A Study of Media Involvement.* Research conducted for the Magazine Publishers Association, 1979.

Opinion Research Corporation, "Public Still Overestimates Corporate Profits," Feb. 10-March 9, 1975, reported in *Current Opinion* (July, 1975) 3:65.

Orman, J. "Covering the American Presidency: Valenced Reporting in the Periodical Press, 1900-1982," *Presidential Studies Quarterly* (Summer, 1984) 14(3): 381-390.

Oshima, Harry T. "Development and Mass Communication — A Re-Examination," *Communication and Change: The Last Ten Years — and the Next,* ed. Schramm and Lerner. Honolulu: University Press of Hawaii, 1976, pp. 17-30.

Ostroff, David H. "A Participant-Observer Study of TV Campaign Coverage," *Journalism Quarterly* (1980) 57: 415-419.

Otwell, Ralph. "Big, Bad Business In the Hands of the Devil Press," *Quill* (April, 1977) 65(4): 15-18.

Owen, Bruce M. "The Economic View of Programming," *Journal of Communication* (Spring, 1978) 28(2): 43-47.

Ozersky, Dick "Television: The Isolating Medium" *Et Cetera* (March, 1977) 34(1): 100-103.

Palda, Kristian S. "The Hypothesis of a Hierarchy of Effects: A Partial Evaluation," *Journal of Marketing Research* (February, 1966) pp. 13-24.

Paletz, David L., Jonathan Y. Short, Helen Baker, Barbara Cookman Campbell, Richard J. Cooper, and Rochelle M. Oeslander, "Polls in the Media: Content, Credibility and Consequences," *Public Opinion Quarterly* (Winter, 1980) 44(4): 495-513.

Palmgren, Philip and J.D. Rayburn II. "Uses and Gratifications and Exposure to Public Television: A Discrepancy Approach," *Communication Research* (April, 1979) 6(2): 155-180.

Papazian, E. "Brand Loyalty: Effects of Real-World Factors," *Ad Forum* (January, 1982) 3(1): 12-16.

Park, Robert E. "News as a Form of Knowledge," *American Journal of Sociology* (March, 1940) 45: 667-686.

Parke, R.D., Leonard Berkowitz, J.P. Leyens, S.G. West and R.J. Sebastian. "Some Effects of Violent and Nonviolent Movies on the Behavior of Juvenile Delinquents," *Advances in Experimental Social Psychology*, Vol. 10. New York: Academic Press, 1977.

Parker, Edwin B. "An Information Based Hypothesis: New Approaches to Development," *Journal of Communication* (1978) 28(1): 81-83.

Parker, S. and M. Smith. "Work and Leisure," *Handbook of Workbook Organization and Society*, ed. R. Dubin. Chicago: Rand McNally, 1976, pp. 37-64.

Parsons, Malcolm B. "A Political Profile of Newspaper Editors," *Journalism Quarterly* (Winter, 1976) 53: 700-705.

Pasternack, Steve and Sandra H. Utt. "A Study of America's Front Pages: How They Look," paper presented to the Visual Communication Division at the annual convention of the Association for Education in Journalism and Mass Communication, April 1, 1983.

Patterson, Oscar III. "An Analysis of Television Coverage of the Vietnam War," *Journal of Broadcasting* (Fall, 1984) 28(4): 397-404.

Patterson, Oscar III. "Television's Living Room War in Print: Vietnam in the News Magazines," *Journalism Quarterly* (Spring, 1984) 61(1): 35-40.

Patterson, Thomas E. *The Mass Media Election.* New York: Praeger, 1980.

Patterson, Thomas E. and Robert D. McClure. *The Unseeing Eye: The Myth of Television Power in National Elections.* New York: Putnam, 1976.

Patton, W.E. III. "Brand Choice and Varying Quantity of Information," *Journal of Business Research* (March, 1984) 12(1): 75-85.

Payne, David E. "Cross-National Diffusion of Canadian TV on Rural Minnesota Viewers," *American Sociological Review* (October, 1978) 43: 740-756.

Payne, David E. and Andre H. Caron. "Anglophone Canadian and American Mass Media: Uses and Effects on Quebecois Adults," *Communication Research* (January, 1982) 9(1): 113-114.

Payne, David E. and Christy A. Peake, "Cultural Diffusion: The Role of U.S. TV in Iceland," *Journalism Quarterly* (1977) 54(3): 523-531.

Peebles, Dean M. and John K. Ryans Jr. "Advertising as a Positive Force," *Journal of Advertising* (1978) 7(2): 48-52.

Peretti, Peter O. and Chris Lucas. "Newspaper Advertising Influences on Consumers' Behavior by Socioeconomic Status of Customers," *Psychological Reports* (1975) 37(3): 693-694.

Perloff, Richard M. "Political Involvement: A Critique and a Process-Oriented Reformulation," *Critical Studies in Mass Communication* (June, 1984) 1(2): 146-160.

Perloff, Richard M. "Political Involvement Revisited: A Critique and a Process-Oriented Reformulation," paper presented to Symposium on Political Communication at annual convention of the International Communication Association, Dallas, Texas, May 27, 1983.

Perloff, Richard M. "Some Antecedents of Children's Sex-Role Stereotypes," *Psychological Reports* (1977) 40: 463-466.

Perloff, Richard M., Jane D. Brown and M. Mark Miller. "Mass Media and Sex-Typing: Research Perspectives and Policy Implications," *International Journal of Women's Studies* (1982) 5(3): 265-273.

Perloff, Richard M., Rebecca C. Quarles and Marla Drutz. "Loneliness, Depression and the Uses of Television," *Journalism Quarterly* (Summer, 1983) 60(2): 352-356.

Perry, Michael and Arnon Perry. "Ad Recall: Biased Measure of Media?" *Journal of Advertising Research* (June, 1976) 16(3): 21-25.

Peterson, Richard A. "Revitalizing the Culture Concept," *Annual Review of Sociology*, ed. Alex Inkeles (1979) 5: 137-166.

Peterson, R.A. and R.B. Davis Jr. "The Contemporary American Radio Audience," *Popular Music & Society* (1978) 6(2): 169-183.

Peterson, Robert A., Gerald Albaum, George Kozmetsky and Isabella C.M. Cunningham, "Attitudes of Newspaper Business Editors and General Public Toward Capitalism," *Journalism Quarterly* (Spring, 1984) 61(1): 56-65.

Peterson, Theodore. *Magazines in the Twentieth Century*. Urbana: University of Illinois Press, 1964, 2nd ed.

Petit, Arthur G. *Images of the Mexican-American in Fiction and Film*. College Station, Texas: Texas A&M University Press, 1980.

Phillips, David P. "The Impact of Mass Media Violence on U.S. Homicides," *American Sociological Review* (August, 1983) 48(4): 560-568.

Phillips, David and John E. Hensley. "When Violence is Rewarded or Punished: The Impact of Mass Media Stories on Homicide," *Journal of Communication* (Summer, 1984) 34(3): 101-116.

Piaget, Jean. "The Stages of the Intellectual Development of the Child," *Readings in Child Development and Personality*, ed. P.H. Mussen. New York: Harper & Row, 1970.

Piaget, Jean. *The Origins of Intelligence in Children*. New York: Yale University Press, 1936/1952, 2d ed.

Picard, Robert G. "Revisions of the 'Four Theories of the Press' Model," *Mass Comm Review* (Winter/Spring, 1982/1983) 10(1,2): 25-28.

Picard, Robert G. and James P. Winter. *Press Concentration and Monopoly: A Bibliography*. Mass Communication and Society Division, Association for Education in Journalism and Mass Communication, 1985.

Pierce, Thurman. "New Values in Print," *Marketing & Media Decisions* (March, 1983) pp. 121-132.

Pingree, Suzanne and Robert Hawkins. "U.S. Programs on Australian Television: The Cultivation Effect," *Journal of Communication* (1981) 31(1): 97-105.

Pipe, G. Russell. "National Policies, International Debates," *Journal of Communication* (Summer, 1979) 29(3): 114-123.

Pittatore, Oddina. "The Image of Italy in Ads in Five U.S. Magazines," *Journalism Quarterly* (Winter, 1983) 60(4): 728-730.

Polcyn, K.A. "The Role of Communication Satellites in Education and Training: The 1990's," *Programmed Learning & Educational Technology* (November, 1981) 18(4): 230-244.

Pool, Ithiel de Sola. "The Future Role of Telecommunications in the Pacific," *Computer Networks* (May, 1981) 5(3): 194-203.

Pool, Ithiel de Sola. "The Influence of International Communication on Development," *Media Asia* (1979) 6(3): 149-156.

Pool, Ithiel de Sola. "Direct-Broadcast Satellites and Cultural Integrity," *Trans-Action* (September-October, 1975) 12(6): 47-56.

Porter, Michael E. "Optimal Advertising: An Intra-Industry Approach," *Issues in Advertising: The Economics of Persuasion*, ed. David G. Tuerck. Washington, D.C.: American Enterprise Institute for Public Policy Research, 1978, pp. 91-115.

Porter, Michael J. "Applying Semiotics to the Study of Selected Prime Time Television Programs," *Journal of Broadcasting* (Winter, 1983) 27(1): 69-75.

Postman, Neil. *Amusing Ourselves to Death: Public Discourse in the Age of Show Business*. (Elisabeth Sifton Books, 1985.

Power, Sarah Goddard. "The U.S. View of Belgrade," *Journal of Communication* (Autumn, 1981) 31(4): 142-158.

Preston, I.L. and E. Thorson. "The Expanded Association Model: Keeping the Hierarchy Concept Alive," *Journal of Advertising Research* (February/March, 1984) 24(1): 59-66.

Prisuta, Robert H. "The Adolescent and Television News: A Viewer Profile," *Journalism Quarterly* (Summer, 1979) 56(2): 277-282.

Prisuta, Robert H. "The Impact of Media Concentration and Economic Factors on Broadcast Public Interest Programming," *Journal of Broadcasting* (Summer, 1977) 21(3): 321-332.

Prisuta, Robert H. "Broadcast Economics and Public Interest Programming," *Journalism Quarterly* (Winter, 1977) 54(4): 782-785.

Pye, Lucian W. (ed.) *Communications and Political Development*. Princeton, N.J.: Princeton University Press, 1963.

Pye, Lucian W. "Introduction: Political Culture and Political Development," *Political Culture and Political Development*, ed. Lucian W. Pye and Sidney Verba. Princeton, N.J.: Princeton University Press, 1965.

Pye, Lucian W. *Aspects of Political Development.* Boston: Little, Brown, 1966.

Quarles, Rebecca C. "Mass Media Use and Voting Behavior: The Accuracy of Political Perceptions among First-Time and Experienced Voters," *Communication Research* (October, 1979) 6(4): 407-436.

Quarles, Rebecca C. and Leo W. Jeffres. "Advertising and National Consumption: A Path Analytic Re-examination of the Galbraithian Argument," *Journal of Advertising* (1983) 12(2): 4-33.

Quarles, Rebecca C., Leo W. Jeffres, Carlos Sanchez I. and Kurt Neuwirth. "News Diffusion of Assassination Attempts on President Reagan and Pope John Paul II," *Journal of Broadcasting* (Fall, 1983) 27(4): 387-394.

Quebral, Nora C. "Development Communication: Where Does It Stand Today?" *Media Asia* (1975) 2(4): 197-202.

Rabinovitch, M.S., M.S. McLean Jr., J.W. Markham and A.D. Talbott. "Children's Violence Perception as a Function of Television Violence," *Television and Social Behavior. Vol. 5. Television's Effects: Further Explorations,* ed. George A. Combstock, Eli A. Rubinstein and John P. Murray. Washington, D.C.: U.S. Government Printing Office, 1972.

Radio Advertising Bureau (RAB). *Radio Facts.* New York: Radio Advertising Bureau, Inc., 1984.

Radolf, Andrew. "Newspaper Experts Upbeat on Business' Prospects," *Editor & Publisher* (Jan. 1, 1983), p. 18.

Raj, S.P. "The Effects of Advertising on High and Low Loyalty Consumer Segments," *Journal of Consumer Research* (June, 1982) 9(1): 77-89.

Ranganath, H.K. "Adaptability of Indian Folk Forms to Contemporary Themes," *Media Asia* (1982) 9(1): 18-20.

Rao, Y.V. Lakshmana. *Communication and Development: A Study of Two Indian Villages.* Minneapolis: University of Minnesota Press, 1966.

Rarick, Galen. "Differences Between Daily Newspaper Subscribers and Non-Subscribers," *Journalism Quarterly* (1973) 50: 265-270.

Rawlings, E. "What Editors and Young People Think of Newspapers: Testing a Method for Measuring Reader Expectations," *Newspaper Research Journal* (April, 1979) prototype edition, pp. 23-29.

Rayburn, J.D. II, Philip Palmgreen and Tawney Acker. "Media Gratifications and Choosing a Morning News Program," *Journalism Quarterly* (Spring, 1984) 61(1): 149-156.

Read, William H. "Information as a National Resource: The U.S. Faces WARC," *Journal of Communication* (Winter, 1979) 29(1): 172-178.

Reagan, Joey. "Effects of Cable Television on News Use," *Journalism Quarterly* (Summer, 1984) 61(1): 317-324.

Reed, William H. *America's Mass Media Merchants.* Baltimore: John Hopkins University Press, 1972.

Reekie, W.D. "Advertising and Price," *Journal of Advertising* (April-June, 1982) 1(2): 131-141.

Reese, Stephen D. and M. Mark Miller. "Political Attitude Holding and Structure: The Effects of Newspaper and Television News," *Communication Research* (April, 1981) 8: 167-188.

Reese, Stephen D., Pamela J. Shoemaker, and Wayne A. Danielson. "Social Correlates of Public Attitudes Toward the New Communication Technologies," paper presented at the 10th annual conference of the Midwest Ass'n for Public Opinion Research, Chicago, Ill., 1984.

Reeves, Byron and G.M. Garramone. "Television's Influence on Children's Encoding of Person Information," *Human Communication Research* (Winter, 1983) 10(2): 257-268.

Reid, Leonard N. and Lawrence C. Soley. "Generalized and Personalized Attitudes Toward Advertising's Social and Economic Effects," *Journal of Advertising* (1982) 11(3): 3-7.

Rice, Ronald E. and William J. Paisley (ed.) *Public Communication Campaigns.* Beverly Hills, Calif.: Sage Publications, 1981.

Rich, Tom, David Owens and Irving Ellenbogen. "What Canadians Dislike About TV Commercials," *Journal of Advertising Research* (December, 1978) 18(6): 37-44.

Richards, Barbara. "More on How Reporters Judge Reporters," *Journalism Quarterly* (Autumn, 1977) 54: 607-609.

Ricks, W. Stevens. "U.S. Report Says Lawyers' Ads Can Cut Fees," *Plain Dealer*, Dec. 7, 1984, p. 6a.

Ridley-Johnson, R., H. Cooper and J. Chance. "The Relation of Children's Television Viewing to School Achievement and I.Q.," *The Journal of Educational Research* (May/June, 1983) 76(5): 294-297.

Rivet, Jacques. "Writing and the Journalist—from 'Opinion-Event' to 'Opinion-Document,'" *Communication et Information* (Winter, 1976) 1(2): 75-96.

Roach, C. "Mexican and U.S. News Coverage of the IPDC at Acapulco," *Journal of Communication* (Summer, 1982) 32(3): 71-85.

Roberts, Churcheill L. "The Cultivation Effects of Television Violence: Further Testing," manuscript, University of West Florida, 1985.

Roberts, Churchill L. "Attitudes and Media Use of the Moral Majority," *Journal of Broadcasting* (Fall, 1983) 27(4): 403-410.

Roberts, Churchill L. "From Primary to the Presidency: A Panel Study of Images and Issues in the 1976 Election," *Western Journal of Speech Communication* (Winter, 1981) 45: 60-70.

Roberts, Churchill L. and Sandra H. Dickson. "Assessing Quality in Local TV News," *Journalism Quarterly* (Summer, 1984) 61(2): 392-398.

Roberts, D., R. Hawkins and S. Pingree. "Do the Mass Media Play a Role in Political Socialization?" *Australian and New Zealand Journal of Sociology* (1975) 11: 37-43.

Roberts, D. et al. "Earth's Big Blue Marble: A Report on the Impact of a Children's Television Series on Children's Opinions," *Stanford University, unpublished*, 1974; cited in Caron (1979).

Roberts, Donald F., Christine M. Bachen, Melinda C. Hornby and Pedro Hernandez-Ramos. "Reading and Television: Predictors of Reading Achievement at Different Age Levels," *Communication Research* (January, 1984) 11(1): 9-49.

Robinson, Gertrude Joch. *Tito's Maverick Media*. Urbana: University of Illinois Press, 1977.

Robinson, John P. "Culture Indicators from the Leisure Activity Survey," *American Behavioral Scientist* (March/April, 1983) 26(4): 543-552.

Robinson, John P. *How Americans Use Time: A Social-Psychological Analysis of Everyday Behavior*. New York: Praeger, 1977.

Robinson, John P. *Changes in Americans' Use of Time: 1965-1975, A Progress Report*. Cleveland, Ohio: Communication Research Center, Cleveland State University, August, 1977.

Robinson, John P. "Interpersonal Influence in Election Campaigns: Two Step-Flow Hypotheses," *Public Opinion Quarterly* (Fall, 1976) 40(3): 304-319.

Robinson, John P. "The Press as King-Maker: What Surveys from Last Five Campaigns Show," *Journalism Quarterly* (1974) 51: 587-594, 606.

Robinson, John P. "Perceived Media Bias and the 1968 Election: Can the Media Affect Behavior After All?" *Journalism Quarterly* (Summer, 1972) 49: 239-46.

Robinson, John P. "Toward Defining the Functions of Television," *Television and Social Behavior*, ed. Eli Rubinstein, George Comstock and John Murray, Vol. 4, Television in Day-to-Day Life: Patterns of Use. Washington, D.C.: U.S. Government Printing Office, 1972.

Robinson, John P. and Jerald Bachman. "Television Viewing Habits and Aggression," *Television and Social Behavior. Vol. III: Television and Adolescent Aggressiveness*, ed. George A. Comstock and Eli A. Rubinstein. Washington, D.C.: U.S. Government Printing Office, 1972, pp. 372-382.

Robinson, John P. and P. E. Converse. "The Impact of Television on Mass Media Usage," *The Use of Time: Daily Activities of Urban and Suburban Populations in Twelve Countries*, ed. A. Szalai et al. The Hague, Netherlands: Mouton, 1972.

Robinson, John P. and Leo W. Jeffres. "The Great Age Readership Mystery," *Journalism Quarterly* (Summer, 1981) 58(2): 219-224, 231.

Robinson, John P. and Leo W. Jeffres. "The Changing Role of Newspapers in the Age of Television," *Journalism Monographs* (September, 1979) No. 63.

Robinson, John P. and Haluk Sahin. "Beyond the Realm of Necessity: Television and the Colonization of Leisure," *Media, Culture and Society* (January, 1981) 3(1): 85-95.

Robinson, Michael J. "Public Affairs Television and the Growth of Political Malaise: The Case of 'The Selling of the Pentagon,'" *American Political Science Review* (1976) 70: 409-432.

Robinson, Michael J. "American Political Legitimacy in an Age of Television," *Television as a Social Force*, ed. D. Cater and R. Adler. New York: Praeger, 1975.

Rogers, Everett M. "New Perspectives on Communication and Development," *Communication Research* (April, 1976) 3(2): 99-106.

Rogers, Everett M. "The Rise and Fall of the Dominant Paradigm: New Approaches to Development," *Journal of Communication* (1978) 28(1): 64-69.

Rogers, Everett M. "Communication and Development: The Passing of the Dominant Paradigm," *Communication Research* (1976) 3: 213-240.

Rogers, Everett M. *Diffusion of Innovations.* New York: Free Press, 1983, 3rd ed.; 1962, 1st ed.

Rogers, Everett M. and F. Floyd Shoemaker. *Communication of Innovations.* New York: Free Press, 1971.

Rogers, Everett M. and Ronny Adhikarya. "Diffusion of Innovations: An Up-to-Date Review and Commentary," *Communication Yearbook 3,* ed. Dan Nimmo. New Brunswick, N.J.: International Communication Association, 1979.

Roling, Niels G., Joseph Ascroft, and Fred Wa Chege. "The Diffusion of Innovations and the Issue of Equity in Rural Development," *Communication Research* (1976) 3: 155-170.

Rollings, J. "Mass Communications and the American Worker," *The Critical Communications Review,* ed. V. Mosco and J. Wasko. Vol..1. Norwood, N.J.: Ablex Publishers, 1983, pp. 131-152.

Roloff, Michael E. and Gerald R. Miller. *Persuasion: New Directions in Theory and Research.* Beverly Hills: Sage, 1980.

Romanow, W.I. and W.C. Soderlund, "The Southam Press Acquisition of the Windsor Star: A Canadian Case Study of Change," *Gazette* (1978) 24(4): 255-270.

Rondina, M.L., Mary Cassata and Thomas Skill. "Placing a 'Lid' on Television Serial Drama: An Analysis of the Lifestyles, Interpersonal Management Skills, and Demography of Daytime's Fictional Population," *Life on Daytime Television: Tuning American Serial Drama,* ed. Mary Cassata and Thomas Skill. Norwood, N.J.: Ablex Publishers, 1983, pp. 3-21.

Roper Organization, Inc. *Public Attitudes Toward Television and Other Media in a Time of Change.* New York: Television Information Office, May, 1985.

Roper Organization, Inc. *What People Think of Television and Other Media 1959-1972.* New York: Elmo Roper & Associates, 1973.

Roper Organization, Inc. *The 1980 Virginia Slims American Women's Opinion Poll.* 1980.

Roper Organization, Inc. Roper Poll of 2,000 adults, "Police, Business Rate High," cited in *USA Today,* July 5, 1985, p. 1.

Rosario-Braid, Florangel. *Communication Strategies for Productivity Improvement.* Tokyo: Asian Productivity Organization, 1983.

Rosengren, Karl E. "Uses and Gratifications: A Paradigm Outlined," *The Uses of Mass Communication: Current Perspectives on Gratifications Research,* ed. Jay G. Blumler and Elihu Katz. Beverly Hills: Sage Publications, 1974, pp. 269-286.

Roshco, Bernard. *Newsmaking.* Chicago: University of Chicago Press, 1975.

Rositi, Franco. "Televised Information: The Cutting and Recomposition of the Image of Society: A Study of the News Broadcasts of Four European Networks," *Studies of Radio-Television* (November, 1977) 24: 123-148.

Ross, Bonnie Lou. "Education Reporting in the Los Angeles Times," *Journalism Quarterly* (Summer, 1983) 60(2): 348-352.

Rostow, Walt W. *The World Economy.* Austin: University of Texas Press, 1978.

Rostow, Walt W. *The Stages of Economic Growth.* London: Cambridge University Press, 1960.

Rotfeld, H.J. and K.B. Rotzoll. "Puffery vs. Fact Claims — Really Different?" *Current Issues & Research in Advertising 1981,* ed. J.H. Leigh and C.R. Martin Jr. Ann Arbor: Graduate School of Business Administration, University of Michigan, 1981, pp. 85-103.

Rotfeld, Herbert J. and Kim B. Rotzoll. "Is Advertising Puffery Believed?" *Journal of Advertising* (1980) 9(3): 16-20.

Rothenbuhler, Eric W. "Programming Decision Making in Popular Music Radio," *Communication Research* (April, 1985) 12(2): 209-232.

Rouner, Donna. "Active Television Viewing and the Cultivation Hypothesis," *Journalism Quarterly* (Spring, 1984) 65: 168-173.

Routt, Edd, James B. McGrath and Frederic A. Weiss. *The Radio Format Conundrum.* New York: Hastings House, 1978.

Rubin, Alan M. "Ritualized and Instrumental Television Viewing," *Journal of Communication* (Summer, 1984) 34(3): 67-77.

Rubin, Alan M. "Television Uses and Gratifications: The Interactions of Viewing Patterns and Motivations," *Journal of Broadcasting* (Winter, 1983) 27(1): 37-51.

Rubin, Alan M. "Television Use by Children and Adolescents," *Human Communication Research* (Winter, 1979) 5(2): 109-120.

Rubin, Alan M. "Child and Adolescent Television Use and Political Socialization," *Journalism Quarterly* (1978) 55: 125-129.

Rubin, Alan M. "Television Usage, Attitudes and Viewing Behaviors of Children and Adolescents," *Journal of Broadcasting* (Summer, 1977) 21(3): 355-369.

Rubin, Alan M. "Television in Children's Political Socialization," *Journal of Broadcasting* (1976) 20: 51-60.

Rukeyser, Louis. "Coke Pops Myth of Powerful Multinational," *Plain Dealer,* July 21, 1985, p. 2d.

Rust, R.T., M. Bajaj, and G. Haley. "Efficient and Inefficient Media for Political Campaign Advertising," *Journal of Advertising* (1984) 13(3): 45-49.

Ryan, Michael. "Attitudes of Scientists and Journalists Toward Media Coverage of Science News," *Journalism Quarterly* (Spring, 1979) 56(1): 18-26 + .

Saddler, Jeanne. "Newest TV Stations Are Low in Power, High in Local Color," *Wall Street Journal,* Oct. 23, 1984, p. 1.

Salomon, Gavriel. "Introducing AIME: The Assessment of Children's Mental Involvement with Television," *Children and the Worlds of Television,* ed. H. Gardner and H. Kelly. San Francisco: Jossey-Bass, 1981.

Salomon, Gavriel. *Interaction of Media, Cognition and Learning.* San Francisco: Jossey-Bass Publishers, 1979.

Salomon, Gavriel and Akiba A. Cohen. "On the Meaning and Validity of Television Viewing," *Human Communication Research* (Spring, 1978) 4: 265-270.

Salomon, Gavriel and Tamar Leigh. "Predispositions about Learning from Print and Television," *Journal of Communication* (Spring, 1984) 34(2): 119-135.

Sandage, C.H., Arnold M. Barban and James E. Haefner, "How Farmers View Advertising," *Journalism Quarterly* (Summer, 1976) 53: 303-308.

Sandell, Karin L. and David H. Ostroff. "Political Information Content and Children's Political Socialization," *Journal of Broadcasting* (Winter, 1981) 25: 49-59.

Schatz, Thomas. *Hollywood Genres.* Philadelphia, Pa: Temple University Press, 1981.

Scherer, Frederic M. *Industrial Market Structure and Economic Performance.* Chicago: Rand McNally, 1970.

Schiller, Herbert I. "Whose New International Economic Information Order?" *Communication* (1980) 5(2): 299-314.

Schiller, Herbert I. *Communication and Cultural Domination.* New York: International Arts and Sciences Press, 1976.

Schiller, Herbert I. *Mass Communications and American Empire.* Boston: Beacon Press, 1971.

Schiller, Herbert I. *Mass Communication and American Empire.* Boston: Beacon, 1971; New York: Kelly, 1969.

Schlinger, Mary Jane Rawling. "Respondent Characteristics That Affect Copy-Test Attitude Scales," *Journal of Advertising Research* (February/March, 1982) 22(1): 29-35.

Schlinger, M.J.R. et al. "Effects of Time Compression of Attitudes and Information Processing," *Journal of Marketing* (Winter, 1983) 47(1): 79-85.

Schmalensee, Richard. *On the Economics of Advertising.* Amsterdam: North-Holland Publishing Co., 1972.

Schmalensee, Richard. "Brand Loyalty and Barriers to Entry," *Southern Economic Journal* (April, 1974) 40: 579-589.

Schmid, Randolph E. "Are You a Newt Nut? Check Newt News," *Plain Dealer*, Sept. 16, 1984, p. 12e, AP dispatch.

Schneider, Lynne, Benjamin Klein and Kevin M. Murphy. "Governmental Regulation of Cigarette Health Information," *Journal of Law & Economics* (December, 1981) 24(3): 575-612.

Schneider, Russell. "Sports Through the Looking Glass," series on television and sports, *Plain Dealer*, beginning Jan. 27, 1985, p. 1b.

Schramm, Wilbur. *Mass Media and National Development: The Role of Information on Developing Countries.* Stanford: Stanford University Press, 1964.

Schramm, Wilbur. "Circulation of News in the Third World: A Study of Asia," *Mass Communication Review Yearbook*, ed. G. Cleveland Wilhoit and Harold de Bock, Vol. 1. Beverly Hills and London: Sage Publications, 1980, pp. 589-619.

Schramm, Wilbur. *Men, Messages and Media.* New York: Harper & Row, Publishers, 1973.

Schramm, Wilbur. "Channels and Audience," *Handbook of Communication*, ed. Ithiel de Sola Pool and Wilbur Schramm. Chicago: Rand McNally, 1973, pp. 116-140.

Schramm, Wilbur. "Aging and Mass Communication," *Aging and Society*. Vol. 2: Aging and the Professions, ed. J. Riley and M. Johnson, New York: Russell Sage, 1969.

Schramm, Wilbur and E. Atwood. *Circulation of News in the Third World: A Study of Asia.* Hong Kong: Chinese U. Press, 1981, available through the University of Washington Press, Seattle, Wash.

Schramm, Wilbur and Daniel Lerner (ed). *Communication and Change: The Last Ten Years — and the Next.* Honolulu: The University Press of Hawaii: East-West Center Book, 1976.

Schramm, Wilbur, Jack Lyle and Edwin B. Parker. *Television in the Lives of Our Children.* Stanford: Stanford University Press, 1961.

Schramm, Wilbur, L.M. Nelson and M.T. Betham. *Bold Experiment: The Story of Educational Television in American Samoa.* Palo Alto, Calif.: Stanford University Press, 1981.

Schramm, Wilbur, and William E. Porter. *Men, Women, Messages, and Media.* New York: Harper & Row, 1982, 2nd ed.

Schramm, Wilbur et al. "International News Wires and Third World News in Asia," *Communications and Development Reviews* (Summer, 1978) 2(2): 32-39.

Schudson, Michael. "Criticizing the Critics of Advertising: Towards a Sociological View of Marketing," *Media, Culture and Society* (1981) 3: 3-12.

Schwartz, Stuart H. "Inner-Directed and Other-Directed Values of Professional Journalists," *Journalism Quarterly* (Winter, 1978) 55(4): 721-725 + .

Screberny-Mohammadi, A. "More Bad News than Good: International News Reporting," *Media Information Australia* (February, 1982) 23: 87-90.

Sears, David. "Political Socialization," *Micropolitical Theory*, ed. F. Greenstein and N. Polsby. Reading, Mass.: Addison-Wesley, 1975.

Sears, David O. and J.L. Freedman. "Selective Exposure to Information: A Critical Review," *Public Opinion Quarterly* (1967) 31: 194-213.

Seggar, John F., Jeffrey K. Hafen, and Helena Hannonen-Gladen. "Television's Portrayals of Minorities and Women in Drama and Comedy Drama, 1971-80," *Journal of Broadcasting* (Summer, 1981) 25(3): 277-288.

Selnow, Gary W. and Hal Reynolds. "Some Opportunity Costs of Television Viewing," *Journal of Broadcasting* (Summer, 1984) 28(3): 315-322.

Sentman, Mary Alice. "Black and White: Disparity in Coverage by Life Magazine from 1937 to 1972," *Journalism Quarterly* (Fall, 1983) 60(3): 501-508.

Severance, L.J. and F.N. Dyer. "Failure of Subliminal Word Presentations to Generate Interference to Color-naming," *Journal of Experimental Psychology* (1973) 101(1): 186-89.

Severin, Werner J. and James W. Tankard Jr. *Communication Theories: Origins, Methods, Uses.* New York: Hastings House, 1979.

Shaheen, J.G. "The Arab Stereotype on Television," *The Link* (1980) 13(2): 1-3.

Shanks, Bob. *The Cool Fire: How to Make It in Television.* New York: Vintage Books, 1976.

Shapiro, Mitchell and Wenmouth Williams Jr. "Civil Disturbance in Miami: Proximity and Conflict in Newspaper Coverage," *Newspaper Research Journal* (Spring, 1984) 5(3): 61-69.

Sharp, Elaine B. "Consequences of Local Government under the Klieg Lights," *Communication Research* (October, 1984) 11(4): 497-517.

Shaw, Donald Lewis. "News About Slavery from 1820-1860 in Newspapers of South, North and West," *Journalism Quarterly* (Autumn, 1984) 61(3): 483-492.

Shaw, Donald L. "At the Crossroads: Change and Continuity in American Press News, 1820-1860," *Journalism History* (Summer, 1981) 8(2): 38-50.

Shaw, Donald L. and Robert L. Stevenson. "Leaders and Conflict in the News in 'Stable' vs. 'Pluralistic' Political Systems," *Foreign News and the New World Information Order*, ed. Robert L. Stevenson and Donald L. Shaw. Ames, Iowa: Iowa State University Press, 1984, pp. 133-147.

Shaw, Donald L. and Robert L. Stevenson, "World of Conflict-World of Peace: Foreign Affairs News in Newspapers from Stable vs. Pluralistic Political Systems," paper presented to the International Communication Division, AEJ, Athens, Ohio, July, 1982.

Sheatsley, Paul B. and Jacob J. Feldman. "The Assassination of President Kennedy: A Preliminary Report on Public Reactions and Behavior," *Public Opinion Quarterly* (1964) 28: 189-215.

Sherif, Carolyn Wood. "Comment on Ethical Issues in Malamuth, Heim and Feshbach's 'Sexual Responsiveness of College Students to Rape Depictions: Inhibitory and Distributory Effects'" *Journal of Personality and Social Psychology* (1980) 38(3): 409-412.

Sherman, B.L. and Joseph R. Dominick. "Guns, Sex and Rock and Roll: A Content Analysis of Music Television," paper presented at the annual meeting of the Speech Communication Association, Chicago, Ill., November, 1984.

Shingi, Prakash M. and Bella Mody. "The Communication Effects Gap: A Field Experiment on Television and Agricultural Ignorance in India," *Communication Research* (April, 1976) 3(2): 171-190.

Shoemaker, Pamela J. "Media Treatment of Deviant Political Groups," *Journalism Quarterly* (Spring, 1984) 61(1): 66-75, 82.

Shoemaker, Pamela J. "The Perceived Legitimacy of Deviant Political Groups: Two Experiments on Media Effects," *Communication Research* (April, 1982) 9: 249-286.

Shyles, Leonard C. "Defining the Issues of a Presidential Election from Televised Political Spot Advertisements," *Journal of Broadcasting* (Fall, 1983) 27(4): 333-343.

Siebert, Fred S., Theodore Peterson and Wilbur Schramm. *Four Theories of the Press.* Urbana: University of Illinois Press, 1956, 1963.

Sigal, Leon V. *Reporters and Officials: The Organization and Politics of Newsmaking.* Lexington, Mass.: D.C. Heath & Co., 1973.

Signorielli, Nancy. "The Demography of the Television World," *Proceedings from the Tenth Annual Telecommunications Policy Research Conference,* ed. O.H. Gandy Jr., P. Espinosa and J.A. Ordover. Norwood, N.J.: Ablex Publishers, 1983, pp. 53-73.

Simon, Julian L. *Issues in the Economics of Advertising.* Urbana: University of Illinois Press, 1970.

Singer, Benjamin D. "Minorities and the Media: A Content Analysis of Native Canadians in the Daily Press," *Canadian Review of Sociology and Anthropology* (August, 1982) 19(3): 348-359.

Singer, Jerome L. and Dorothy G. Singer. "Psychologists Look at Television: Cognitive, Developmental, Personality and Social Policy Implications," *American Psychologist* (July, 1983) 38(7): 826-834.

Singer, Jerome L., Dorothy G. Singer, and W. Rapaczynski. "Family Patterns and Television Viewing as Predictors of Children's Beliefs and Aggression," *Journal of Communication* (Spring, 1984) 34(2): 73-89.

Singh, Kusum and Bertram Gross. "'MacBride': The Report and the Response," *Journal of Communication* (Autumn, 1981) 31(4): 104-117.

Singletary, Michael W. "Components of Credibility of a Favorable News Source," *Journalism Quarterly* (Summer, 1976) 53: 316-319.

Singletary, Michael W., Col. Giles Bax, and Col. Warne Mead. "How Editors View Accuracy in News Reporting," *Journalism Quarterly* (Winter, 1977) 54: 786-789.

Singeltary, Michael W. and Richard Lipsky. "Accuracy in Local TV News, 1" *Journalism Quarterly* (Summer, 1977) 54: 362-364.

SIPI (Scientists' Institute for Public Information). "Newspaper Science Sections: Testing for the Mass Audience," *SIPIscope* (Autumn, 1984) 12(4): 1-17.

Sissors, Jack Z. "Another Look at the Question: Does Advertising Affect Values," *Journal of Advertising* (1978) 7(3): 26-30.

Sissors, Jack Z. "Some New Concepts of Newspaper Design," *Journalism Quarterly* (1965) 42: 236-242.

Skelly, Gerald U. and William J. Lundstrom. "Male Sex Roles in Magazine Advertising, 1959-1979," *Journal of Communication* (Fall, 1981) 31(4): 52-56.

Skipper, James K. Jr. "Musical Tastes of Canadian and American College Students: An Examination of the Massification and Americanization Theses," *Canadian Journal of Sociology* (1975) 1(1): 49-59.

Skurnik, W.A.E. "Foreign News Coverage in the Ivory Coast: A Statistical Profile of Fraternite-Matin," *Gazette* (1978) 24(4): 271-281.

Skurnik, W.A.E. "A New Look at Foreign News Coverage: External Dependence or National Interests?" *African Studies Review* (March, 1981) 24: 99-112.

Slaby, Ronald G. and Karin S. Frey. "Development of Gender Constancy and Selective Attention to Same Sex Models," *Child Development* (December, 1975) 46(4): 849-856.

Smart, M. Neff, "A School/Community Newspaper's Effect on Literacy Development in Ghana," *Journalism Quarterly* (1978) 55(1): 119-124.

Smith, Anthony. *The Geopolitics of Information: How Western Culture Dominates the World.* New York: Oxford University Press, 1980.

Smith, Kim A. "Community Perceptions of Media Impressions," *Journalism Quarterly* (Spring, 1984) 61(1): 164-168.

Smith, Kim A. "Perceived Influence of Media on What Goes on in a Community," *Journalism Quarterly* (Summer, 1984) 61(2): 260-264, 338.

Smith, Robert Rutherford. "Mythic Elements in Television News," *Journal of Communication* (Winter, 1979) 29(1): 75-82.

Smith, Robert E. and Shelby D. Hunt. "Attributional Processes and Effects in Promotional Situations," *Journal of Consumer Research* (December, 1978) 5: 149-158.

Smith, Robert E. and William R. Swinyard. "Information Response Models: An Integrated Approach," *Journal of Marketing* (Winter, 1982) 46: 81-93.

Smythe, Dallas W. "Reality as Presented by Television," *Public Opinion Quarterly* (1954) 18: 143-156.

Sohn, Ardyth B. and Harold L. Sohn, "The Relationship of Newspaper Issue Agendas to the Current and Anticipated Issue Agendas of Community Leaders, Non-leaders and Newspaper Staffers," *Mass Comm Review* (Winter/Spring, 1982-83) 10(1,2): 15-20.

Soldow, Gary F. and Victor Principe. "Response to Commercials as a Function of Program Context," *Journal of Advertising Research* (April, 1981) 21(2): 59-66.

Soley, Lawrence C. "Predicting Display Ad Readership," *Newspaper Research Journal* (July, 1982) 3(4): 6-13.

Soley, Lawrence C. and Leonard N. Reid. "Advertising Article Productivity of the U.S.," *Advertising Research* (October/November, 1983) 23(5): 67-72.

Soley, Lawrence C. and Leonard N. Reid. "Satisfaction with the Informational Value of Magazine and Television Advertising," *Journal of Advertising* (1983) 12(3): 27-31.

Sosanie, Arlene K. and George J. Szybillo. "Working Wives: Their General Television Viewing and Magazine Readership Behavior," *Journal of Advertising* (1978) 7(2): 5-13.

Sparkes, Vernone M. "Public Perception of and Reaction to Multi-Channel Cable Television Service," *Journal of Broadcasting* (Spring, 1983) 27(2): 163-175.

Sparkes, Vernone M. "The Flow of News between Canada and the United States," *Journalism Quarterly* (Summer, 1978) 55(2): 260-268.

Sparkman, Richard Jr. and Larry M. Austin. "The Effect on Sales of Color in Newspaper Advertisements," *Journal of Advertising* (1980) 9(4): 39-42.

Spero, J.E. "Information: The Policy Void," *Foreign Policy* (Fall, 1982) 48: 139-156.

Spitzer, Stephen P. "Mass Media vs. Personal Sources of Information about the Presidential Assassination: A Comparison of Six Investigations," *Journal of Broadcasting* (1964-65) 9: 45-50.

Spitzer, Stephen P. and Nancy S. Spitzer. "Diffusion of the News of the Kennedy and Oswald Deaths," *The Kennedy Assassination: Social Communications in Crisis,* ed. Bradley S. Greenberg and Edwin B. Parker. Calif.: Stanford University Press, 1965.

Sprafkin, Joyce and Robert M. Liebert. "Sex-Typing and Children's Television Preferences," *Home and Hearth: Images of Women in the Mass Media,* ed. Gaye Tuchman et al. New York: Oxford University Press, 1978, pp. 228-239.

Sprafkin, Joyce, Robert M. Liebert and R.W. Poulos. "Effects of a Prosocial Televised Example on Children's Helping," *Journal of Experimental Child Psychology* (1975) 20: 119-126.

Sprafkin, Joyce N. and E.A. Rubinstein. "Using Television to Improve the Social Behavior of Institutionalized Children," *Prevention in Human Services,* 1982.

Sprafkin, Joyce N. and L. Theresa Silverman. "Update: Physically Intimate and Sexual Behavior on Prime-Time Television: 1978-79," *Journal of Communication* (1981) 31(1): 34-40.

Sprafkin, Joyce N., L. Theresa Silverman and Eli A. Rubinstein. "Reactions to Sex on Television: An Exploratory Study," *Public Opinion Quarterly* (1980) 44: 303-315.

Stamm, Keith R. and Lisa Fortini-Campbell. "The Relationship of Community Ties to Newspaper Use," *Journalism Monographs* (August, 1983) No. 84.

Stanford, Serena Wade. "Predicting Favorite TV Program Gratifications from General Orientations," *Communication Research* (October, 1984) 11(4): 519-536.

Stanford, Serena Wade and Betsy Riccomini. "Linking TV Program Orientations and Gratifications: An Experimental Approach," *Journalism Quarterly* (Spring, 1984) 61(1): 76-82.

Star, Shirley A. and Helen MacGill Hughes. "Report on an Educational Campaign: The Cincinnati Plan for the United Nations," *American Journal of Sociology* (January, 1950) 55: 389-400.

Starck, Kenneth and John Soloski. "Effect of Reporter Predisposition in Covering Controversial Story," *Journalism Quarterly* (Spring, 1977) 54: 120-125.

Statistical Abstract of the United States. Washington, D.C.: U.S. Department of Commerce, Bureau of the Census, 1985.

Stein, Aletha H. and Lynette K. Friedrich. "Television Content and Young Children's Behavior." In John P. Murray, Eli A. Rubinstein, and George A. Comstock (Eds.), *Television and Social Behavior. Vol. 2: Television and Social learning.* Washington, D.C.: United States Government Printing Office, 1972.

Stein, Gerald M. and James H. Bryan. "The Effect of a Television Model Upon Rule Adoption Behavior of Children," *Child Development* (1972) 43: 268-273.

Steiner, Robert L. "Learning from the Past — Brand Advertising and the Great Bicycle Craze of the 1890's," *1978 Proceedings of the Annual Conference of the American Academy of Advertising,* ed. Steven E. Permut. Columbia, S.C.: American Academy of Advertising, 1978, pp. 35-40.

Stempel, Guido H. III and John W. Windhauser. "The Prestige Press Revisited: Coverage of the 1980 Presidential Campaign," *Journalism Quarterly* (Spring, 1984) 61(1): 49-55.

Stephens, Mitchell and Nadyne G. Edison. "News Media Coverage of Issues During the Accident at Three-Mile Island," *Journalism Quarterly* (Summer, 1982) 59(2): 199-204.

Sterling, Christopher H. "Trends in Daily Newspaper and Broadcast Ownership, 1922-1970," *Journalism Quarterly* (Summer, 1975) 52(2): 247-256.

Sterling, Christopher H. and Timothy R. Haight. *The Mass Media: Aspen Institute Guide to Communication Industry Trends.* New York: Praeger Publishers, 1978.

Sterling, Christopher and John Kittross. *Stay Tuned: A Concise History of American Broadcasting.* Belmont, Calif.: Wadsworth, 1978.

Stevens, Kathleen C. "The Verbal Language of Public Television," *Reading Horizons* (Winter, 1985) 25(2): 83-86.

Stevenson, Robert L. "Third World Communication Development in the 1970's" paper presented in the Intercultural and Development Communication Division at the annual convention of the International Communication Association, Honolulu, Hawaii, May 25, 1985.

Stevenson, Robert L. "The 'World of the News' Study: Pseudo Debate," *Journal of Communication* (Winter, 1984) 34(1): 134-138.

Stevenson, Robert L. and Richard R. Cole. "Issues in Foreign News," *Foreign News and the New World Information Order*, ed. Robert L. Stevenson and Donald Lewis Shaw. Ames: Iowa State University Press, 1984a, pp. 5-20.

Stevenson, Robert L. and Richard R. Cole. "Patterns of Foreign News," *Foreign News and the New World Information Order*, ed. Robert L. Stevenson and Donald Lewis Shaw. Ames: Iowa State University Press, 1984b, pp. 37-62.

Stevenson, Robert L., Richard R. Cole and Donald Lewis Shaw, "Patterns of World News Coverage: A Look at the Unesco Debate on the 'New World Information Order'" paper presented to the Association for Education in Journalism, Boston, Mass. 1980.

Stevenson, Robert L. and Gary D. Gaddy, "Bad News and the Third World," *Foreign News and the New World Information Order*, ed. Robert L. Stevenson and Donald Lewis Shaw. Ames: Iowa State University Press, 1984, pp. 88-97.

Stevenson, Robert L. and J. Walker Smith. "Cultural Meaning of Foreign News," *Foreign News and the New World Information Order*, ed. Robert L. Stevenson and Donald Lewis Shaw. Ames: Iowa State University Press, 1984, pp. 98-105.

Stevenson, Robert L. and Kirsten D. Thompson. "'Contingencies' in the Structure of Foreign News," *Foreign News and the New World Information Order*, ed. Robert L. Stevenson and Kirsten D. Thompson. Ames: Iowa State University Press, 1984, pp. 71-87.

Still, R.R. and J.S. Hill. "Adapting Consumer Products to Lesser-Developed Markets," *Journal of Business Research* (March, 1984) 12(1): 51-61.

Stone, Gerald. "Community Commitment: A Predictive Theory of Daily Newspaper Circulation," *Journalism Quarterly* (1977) 54: 509-514.

Stone, Gerald C. and Elinor Grusin. "Network TV as the Bad News Bearer," *Journalism Quarterly* (Autumn, 1984) 61(3): 517-523, 592.

Stovall, James Glen and Jacqueline H. Solomon. "The Poll as a News Event in the 1980 Presidential Campaign," *Public Opinion Quarterly* (Fall, 1984) 48: 615-623.

Strand, P.J. et al. "Campaign Messages, Media Usage and Types of Voters," *Public Relations Review* (Winter, 1983) 9(4): 53-63.

Straubhaar, Joseph D. "Brazilian Television: The Decline of American Influence," *Communication Research* (April, 1984) 11(2): 221-240.

Streitmatter, Rodger. "The Impact of Presidential Personality on News Coverage in Major Newspapers," *Journalism Quarterly* (Spring, 1985) 62(1): 66-73.

Strickland, D.E., T.A. Finn and M.D. Lambert. "A Content Analysis of Beverage Alcohol Advertising," *Journal of Studies on Alcohol* (1982) 43(7): 655-682.

Stroman, Carolyn A. and Lee B. Becker. "Racial Differences in Gratifications," *Journalism Quarterly* (Winter, 1978) 55(4): 767-771.

Stupening, Eduard. "Detrimental Effects of Television Advertising on Consumer Socialization," *Journal of Business Research* (1982) 10: 75-84.

Sudman, Seymour. "The Presidents and the Polls," *Public Opinon Quarterly* (Fall, 1982) 46: 301-310.

Suggs, Henry Lewis (ed.) "The Black Press in the South 1865-1979," *Contributions in Afro-American and African Studies*, No. 74, Westport, Conn.: Greenwood Press, 1984.

Suls, J. and J.W. Gastoff. "The Incidence of Sex Discrimination, Sexual Contents and Hostility in Television Humor," *Journal of Applied Communication Research* (Spring, 1981) 9(1): 42-49.

Summers, Harrison B. (ed.) *A Thirty-Year History of Programs Carried on National Radio Networks in the United States 1926-1956*. New York: Arno Press and the New York Times, 1971 reprint edition (first published, January, 1958).

Surlin, Stuart H. "'Roots' Research: A Summary of Findings" *Journal of Broadcasting* (1978) 22(3): 309-320.

Surlin, Stuart H. and Hermann H. Kosak. "The Effect of Graphic Design in Advertising on Reader Ratings," *Journalism Quarterly* (Winter, 1975) 52: 685-691.

Sutherland, J.C. and L.A. Middleton. "The Effect of Humor on Advertising Credibility and Recall," *Proceedings of the 1983 Convention of the American Academy of Advertising*, ed. D.W. Jugenheimer. Columbia, S.C.: University of South Carolina, 1983, pp. 17-21.

Sutherland, Max and John Galloway. "Role of Advertising: Persuasion or Agenda Setting?" *Journal of Advertising Research* (October, 1981) 21(5): 215-29.

Swank, C. "Media Uses and Gratifications: Need Salience and Source Dependence in a Sample of the Elderly," *American Behavioral Scientist* (September/October, 1979) 23(1): 95-117.

Swanson, David L. (ed.) "The Uses and Gratifications Approach to Mass Communications Research," *Communication Research* (January, 1979) 6(1): (issue devoted to uses and gratifications research).

Tadayon, M. "The Image of Iran in the New York Times," *Gazette* (1980) 26(4): 217-233.

Tan, Alexis S. "Television Use and Social Stereotypes," *Journalism Quarterly* (Spring, 1982) 59(1): 118-122.

Tan, Alexis S. "Political Participation, Diffuse Support and Perceptions of Political Efficacy as Predictors of Mass Media Use," *Communication Monographs* (June, 1981) 48: 133-145.

Tan, Alexis S. *Mass Communication Theories and Research.* Columbus, Ohio: Grid Publishing, 1981.

Tan, Alexis S. "TV Beauty Ads and Role Expectations of Adolescent Female Viewers," *Journalism Quarterly* (1979) 56: 283-288.

Tan, Alexis S. "Evaluation of Newspapers and Television by Blacks and Mexican-Americans," *Journalism Quarterly* (1978) 55: 673-681.

Tan, Alexis S. "Why TV Is Missed: A Functional Analysis," *Journal of Broadcasting* (Summer, 1977) 21(3): 371-380.

Tan, Alexis S. "Public Media Use and Preference for Obtaining Weather Information," *Journalism Quarterly* (Winter, 1976) 53: 694-700.

Tannenbaum, Percy H. and Dolf Zillmann. "Emotional Arousal in the Facilitation of Aggression through Communication," *Advances in Experimental Social Psychology,* ed. Leonard Berkowitz, Vol. 8, New York: Academic Press, 1975.

Tanney, J.B. and S.D. Johnson. "Religious Television in Middletown," *Review of Religious Research* (June, 1984) 25(4): 303-313.

Tate, Cassandra. "Conflict of Interest: A Newspaper's Report on Itself," *Columbia Journalism Review* (July/August, 1978) pp. 44-47.

Tate, E.D. And L.F. Trach. "The Effects of United States' Television Programs Upon Canadian Beliefs about Legal Procedure," *Canadian Journal of Communication* (Spring, 1980) 6(4): 1-17.

Taylor, Lester D. and Daniel Weiserbs. "Advertising and the Aggregate Consumption Function," *American Economic Review* (September, 1972) 62: 642-656.

Tehranian, Majid. "The Fetish of Identity: Communication Revolutions and Fundamentalist Revivals," *Media Asia* (1981) 8(1): 35-39.

Tekiner, Ahmet C. "Need Achievement and International Differences in Income Growth: 1950-1960," *Development and Cultural Change* (1980) 28: 293-320.

Television and Behavior: Ten Years of Scientific Progress and Implications for the 80s. Washington, D.C.: U.S. Department of Health and Human Services, National Institute of Mental Health, 1982.

Television Digest. May, 1985.

Theberge, L.J. (ed.) *Crooks, Con Men and Clowns: Businessmen in TV Entertainment.* Washington, D.C.: The Media Institute, 1981.

Thomas, Larry W. and Laslo V. Boyd. "Television News Coverage of Six Federal Regulatory Agencies," *Journalism Quarterly* (Spring, 1984) 61(1): 160-164.

Thomas, R. Murray. "The Rise and Decline of an Educational Technology: Television in American Samoa," *Educational Communication and Technology (ECTJ)* (Fall, 1980) 28(3): 155-167.

Thorn, J. Dale. "Television in the Lives of the Class of 1980," *LSU School of Journalism Research Bulletin* (1978) 2(1): 1-8.

Thrift, Ralph R. Jr. "How Chain Ownership Affects Editorial Vigor of Newspapers," *Journalism Quarterly* (1977) 54: 327-331.

Tichenor, Phillip J., George A. Donohue and Clarice N. Olien. *Community Conflict & the Press.* Beverly Hills: Sage, 1980.

Tichenor, Phillip J., George A. Donohue and Clarice N. Olien. "Mass Media Flow and Differential Growth of Knowledge," *Public Opinion Quarterly* (1970); 34(2): 159-170.

Tillinghast, William A. "Slanting the News: Source Perceptions after Changes in Newspaper Management," *Journalism Quarterly* (Summer, 1984) 61(2): 310-316, 418.

Tillinghast, William A. "Changes in Bias Perceptions: A Case Study of the San Jose Mercury and News after the Knight-Ridder Merger," paper presented to the Mass Communication and Society Division at the annual convention of the Association for Education in Journalism and Mass Communication, Corvallis, Oregon, August, 1983.

Todaro, Michael P. *Economic Development in the Third World.* 2nd ed. New York: Longman, 1981.

Todd, Rusty and Richard A. Brody. "Mass Media and Stability of Party Identification: Are There Floating Partisans?" *Communication Research* (July, 1980) 7(3): 275-294.

Toffler, Alvin. *Future Shock.* New York: Bantam Books, 1971.

Tolley, Howard. *Children and War: Political Socialization to International Conflict.* New York: Teachers College Press, Columbia University, 1973.

Towers, Wayne M. "Weekday and Sunday Readership Seen Through Uses and Gratifications," *Newspaper Research Journal* (Spring, 1985) 6(3): 20-32.

Toy, Daniel R. "Monitoring Communication Effects: A Cognitive Structure/Cognitive Response Approach," *Journal of Consumer Research* (June, 1982) 9: 66-76.

Trayes, Edward J. "Managing Editors and Their Newsrooms: A Survey of 208 APME members," *Journalism Quarterly* (Winter, 1978) 55(4): 744-749.

Traylor, Mark B. "Product Involvement and Brand Commitment," *Journal of Advertising Research* (December, 1981) 21(6): 51-56.

Tsai, Michael Kuan, "Some Effects of American Television Programs on Children in Formosa," *Journal of Broadcasting* (1970) 14: 229-38.

Tuchman, Gaye. *Making News.* New York: Free Press, 1978.

Tuchman, Gaye. "The News Net," *Social Research* (Summer, 1978) 45(2): 253-276.

Tuchman, Gaye. "Professionalism as an Agent of Legitimation: Social Research on Broadcasting," *Journal of Broadcasting* (1978) 28(2): 106-113.

Tuchman, Gaye. "Objectivity as Strategic Ritual: An Examination of Newsmen's Notions of Objectivity," *American Journal of Sociology* (January, 1972) 77: 660-679.

Tunstall, Jeremy. *The Media Are American: Anglo-American Media in the World.* New York: Columbia University Press, 1977.

Turow, Joseph. "Local Television: Producing Soft News," *Journal of Communication* (Spring, 1983) 33(2): 111-123.

Ume-Nwagbo, E.N. "Foreign News Flow in Africa: A Content Analytical Study on a Regional Basis," *Gazette* (1982) 29(1/2): 41-56.

Unger, Lynette S. "The Effect of Situational Variables on the Subjective Leisure Experience," *Leisure Sciences* (1984) 6(3): 291-312.

United States Bureau of the Census. *Statistical Abstract of the United States: 1982-1983.* 103rd ed. Washington, D.C.: U.S. Government Printing Office, 1982.

Utt, Sandra H. and Steve Pasternack. "Front Pages of U.S. Daily Newspapers," *Journalism Quarterly* (Winter, 1984) 61(4): 879-884.

Van Dyke, Vernon. "The Individual, the State, and Ethnic Communities in Political Theory," *World Politics* (April, 1977) 29(3): 343-369.

Vandenbergh, Bruce and Nancy Fink. "Is Believability of Puffery Affected by Brand Credibility," *Journalism Quarterly* (Summer, 1983) 60(2): 334-348.

Vanier, D. and D. Sciglimpaglia. "Consumer Attitudes Toward Advertising by Professionals: The Case of the Medical Profession," *Current Issues & Research in Advertising* 1981.

Vidmark, Neil and Milton Rokeach. "Archie Bunker's Bigotry: A Study in Selective Perception and Exposure," *Journal of Communication* (1974) 24(1): 36-47.

Villani, Kathryn E.A. "Personality/Life Style and Television Viewing Behavior," *Journal of Marketing Research* (November, 1975) 12: 432-439.

Von Feilitzen, C. "The Functions Served by the Media," *Children and Television,* ed. R. Brown. Beverly Hills: Sage, 1976, pp. 90-115.

Wackman, Daniel B., Donald M. Gillmor, Cecilie Gaziano and Everett E. Dennis, "Chain Newspaper Autonomy as Reflected in Presidential Campaign Endorsements," *Journalism Quarterly* (1975) 52: 411-420.

Wade, Serena E. "Interpersonal Discussion: A Critical Predictor of Leisure Activity," *Journal of Communication* (December, 1973) 23(4): 426-445.

Wagenberg, Ronald H. and Walter C. Soderlund. "The Effects of Chain Ownership on Editorial Coverage: The Case of the 1974 Canadian Federal Election," *Canadian Journal of Political Science* (December, 1976) 9(4): 682-689.

Wagner, Joseph. "Media Do Make a Difference: The Differential Impact of Mass Media in the 1976 Presidential Race," *American Journal of Political Science* (August, 1983) 27(3): 407-430.

Wakshlag, Jacob J., Donald E. Agostino, Herbert A. Terry, Paul Driscoll and Bruce Ramsey. "Television News Viewing and Network Affiliation Changes," *Journal of Broadcasting* (Winter, 1983) 27(1): 53-68.

Wakshlag, Jacob J. and Bradley S. Greenberg. "Programming Strategies and the Popularity of Television Programs for Children," *Human Communication Research* (Fall, 1979) 6: 58-68.

Wakshlag, Jacob, V. Vial and R. Tamborini. "Selecting Crime Drama and Apprehension about Crime," *Human Communication Research* (Winter, 1983) 10(2): 227-242.

Wang, Georgette. "Information Utility as a Predictor of Newspaper Readership," *Journalism Quarterly* (1977) 54(4): 791-794.

Wang, Georgette and Wimal Dissanayake. "The Study of Indigenous Communication Systems in Development: Phased Out or Phasing In?" *Media Asia* (1982) 9(1): 3-8.

Ward, Scott. "Children's Reactions to Commercials," *Journal of Advertising Research* (1972) 12(2): 37-45.

Ward, Scott, Daniel B. Wackman and Ellen Wartella. *How Children Learn to Buy.* Beverly Hills: Sage Publications, 1977.

Wartella, Ellen (ed.) *Children Communicating: Media and Development of Thought, Speech, Understanding.* Beverly Hills: Sage Publications, 1979.

Wattenberg, Martin P. "From Parties to Candidates: Examining the Role of the Media," *Public Opinion Quarterly* (Summer, 1982) 46(2): 216-227.

Way, W.L. "Using Content Analysis to Examine Consumer Behaviors Portrayed on Television: A Pilot Study in a Consumer Education Context," *The Journal of Consumer Affairs* (Summer, 1984) 18(1): 79-91.

Weaver, David H. and J.M. Budeenbaum. "Newspapers and Television: A Review of Research on Uses and Effects," *ANPA News Research Report* (April 20, 1979) No. 19. Washington, D.C.: ANPA.

Weaver, David, Dan Drew and G. Cleveland Wilhoit. "A Profile of U.S. Radio and Television Journalists," paper presented at the annual convention of the Association for Education in Journalism and Mass Communication, Memphis, Tenn., August, 1985.

Weaver, David and Virginia Dodge Fielder. "Civic Attitudes and Newspaper Readership in Chicago," *Newspaper Research Journal* (Summer, 1983) 4(4): 11-18.

Weaver, David H., Dorris A. Graber, Maxwell E. McCombs and Chaim H. Eyal. *Media Agenda-Setting in a Presidential Election.* New York: Praeger Special Studies, 1981.

Weaver, David H. and John B. Mauro. "Newspaper Readership Patterns," *Journalism Quarterly* (Spring, 1978) 55: 84-91, 134.

Weaver, David H. and L.E. Mullins. "Content and Format Characteristics of Competing Daily Newspapers," *Journalism Quarterly* (Summer, 1975) 52(2): 257-264.

Weaver, David H. and G. Cleveland Wilhoit. "Foreign News in the Western Agencies," *Foreign News and the New World Information Order,* ed. Robert L. Stevenson and Donald Lewis Shaw. Ames: Iowa State University Press, 1984, pp. 153-185.

Weaver, David H., G. Cleveland Wilhoit and P. Riede. "Personal Needs and Media Use," *ANPA News Research Report* (July 20, 1979) No. 21. Washington, D.C.: American Newspaper Publishers Association.

Weaver, James B., Christopher J. Porter and Margaret E. Evans. "Patterns in Foreign News Coverage on U.S. Network TV: A 10-Year Analysis," *Journalism Quarterly* (Summer, 1984) 61(2): 356-363.

Weber, Larry J. and Dan B. Fleming. "Media Use and Student Knowledge of Current Events," *Journalism Quarterly* (Summer, 1983) 60(2): 356-358.

Webster, James G. "Program Audience Duplication: A Study of Television Inheritance Effects," *Journal of Broadcasting & Electronic Media* (Spring, 1985) 29(2): 121-133.

Webster, James G. "Cable Television's Impact on Audience for Local News," *Journalism Quarterly* (Summer, 1984) 61(2): 419-422.

Webster, James G. "The Impact of Cable and Pay-Cable Television on Local Station Audiences," *Journal of Broadcasting* (Spring, 1983) 27(2): 119-126.

Webster, James G. and Jacob J. Wakshlag. "A Theory of Television Program Choice," *Communication Research* (October, 1983) 10(4): 430-446.

Weigel, Russell H. and James W. Loomis. "Televised Models of Female Achievement Revisited: Some Progress," *Journal of Applied Social Psychology* (January/February, 1981) 11(1): 58-63.

Weiner, Sanford L. "The Competition for Certainty: The Polls and the Press in Britain," *Political Science Quarterly* (Winter, 1976-1977) 91(4): 673-696.

Werner, A. "Television and Attitudes Toward Foreign Countries: A Report on a Survey of Scandinavian Children," *Political Communication and Persuasion* (1981) 1(3): 307-314.

Westerstahl, Jorgen. "Objective News Reporting: General Premises," *Communication Research* (July, 1983) 10(3): 403-424.

Whipple, Thomas W. and Alice E. Courtney. "How to Portray Women in TV Commercials," *Journal of Advertising Research* (April, 1980) 20(2): 53-59.

White, Robert A. "Mass Communication and Culture: Transition to a New Paradigm," *Journal of Communication* (Summer, 1983) 33(3): 279-301.

Whitney, D. Charles, Marilyn Fritzler, Steven Jones, Sharon Mazzarella and Lana Rakow. "Geographic and Source Biases in Network Television News, 1982-1984," paper presented at the annual convention of the Association for Education in Journalism and Mass Communication, Memphis, Tenn., August, 1985.

Wilhoit, G. Cleveland and David Weaver, "Foreign News Coverage in Two U.S. Wire Services: Study Number 2 — 1981," paper presented to the International Communication Division, AEJ, Athens, Ohio, July, 1982.

Williams, Frederick. *The Communications Revolution.* New York: New American Library, 1983, rev. ed.

Williams, Raymond. "Developments in the Sociology Culture," *Sociology* (September, 1976) 10(3).

Willis, E. "Consumerism and Women," *Socialist Revolution* (May-June, 1970).

Wilson, John. "Sociology of Leisure," *Annual Review of Sociology* (1980) 6: 21-40.

Wilson, W. and V. Liedtke. "Movie-Inspired Sexual Practices," *Psychological Reports* (February, 1984) 54(1): 328.

Winett, Richard A., Ingrid N. Leckliter, Donna E. Chinn and Brian Stahl. "Reducing Energy Consumption: The Long-Term Effects of a Single TV Program," *Journal of Communication* (Summer, 1984) 34(3): 37-50.

Winham, Gilbert R. "Political Development and Lerner's Theory: Further Tests of a Causal Model," *American Political Science Review* (1970) 64: 810-818.

Winter, James and Douglas Baer, "U.S. Media Imperialism in a Canadian Community: the Inculcation of Anti-Government Sentiment," paper presented to MAPOR, Nov. 4, 1982.

Witek, John. *Response Television: Combat Advertising of the 1980's.* Chicago: Crain Books, 1981.

Wolf, T.M. "A Developmental Investigation of Televised Modeled Verbalizations of Resistance to Deviation," *Developmental Psychology* (1972) 6: 537.

Wolfson, Lewis W. "The Power of the Press," *The Quill* (April, 1979) pp. 23-24.

Wolseley, Roland E. *The Changing Magazine.* New York: Hastings House, 1973.

Wood, James Playsted. *Magazines in the United States.* New York: Ronald, 1956, 2nd ed.

Woodall, Gill, Dennis K. Davis and Haluk Sahin. "From the Boob Tube to the Black Box: Television News Comprehension from an Information Processing Perspective," *Journal of Broadcasting* (Winter, 1983) 27(1): 1-23.

Woolery, George W. *Children's Television: The First Thirty-Five Years, 1946-1980.* Metuchen, N.Y.: Scarecrow Press, 1983.

Worcester, Robert M. "Pollsters, the Press, and Political Polling in Britain," *Public Opinion Quarterly* (Winter, 1980) 44(4): 548-566.

Wright, Charles R. *Mass Communication: A Sociological Perspective.* New York: Random House, 1975, 2nd ed.

Wright, John C. and Aletha C. Huston. "A Matter of Form: Potentials of Television for Young Viewers," *American Psychologist* (July, 1983) 38(7): 835-843.

Wright, John S. and John E. Mertes. *Advertising's Role in Society,* St. Paul, Minn.: West, 1974.

Wulfemeyer, K. Tim. "Perceptions of Viewer Interests by Local TV Journalists," *Journalism Quarterly* (Summer, 1984) 61(2): 432-435.

Wulfemeyer, K. Tim. "The Interests and Preferences of Audiences for Local Television News," *Journalism Quarterly* (Summer, 1983) 60(2): 323-328.

Wulfemeyer, K. Tim. "A Content Analysis of Local Television Newscasts: Answering the Critics," *Journal of Broadcasting* (Winter, 1982) 26(1): 481-486.

Yancey, Thomas A. "Some Effects of Quality and Effort in a Dynamic Macro-Economic Model," Ph.D. Thesis, University of Illinois, 1957.

Yankelovich, Skelly and White, Inc. "Tracking the Attitudes of the Public Towards the Newspaper Business," *ANPA News Research Report* (April 20, 1979) No. 19. Washington, D.C.

Young, Shirley. "Copy Testing without Magic Numbers," *Journal of Advertising Research* (1972) 12: 3-12.

Yuspeh, Sonia. "The Medium Versus the Message," *A Look Back, a Look Ahead,* ed. G.B. Hafer. Chicago: American Marketing Association, 1980.

Yuspeh, Sonia and Arthur J. Kover. "On-the-Air Test Scores May Not Be Telling All," *Advertising Age* (Feb. 19, 1979) pp. S-16-S-17.

Zablocki, Benjamin D. and Rosabeth Moss Kanter. "The Differentiation of Life-Styles," *Annual Review of Sociology* (1976) 2: 269-298.

Zanot, E.J. "Public Attitudes Toward Advertising: The American Experience," *International Journal of Advertising* (1984) 3(1): 3-15.

Zanot, E. "Public Attitudes Toward Advertising," *Advertising in a New Age,* ed. H. Keith Hunt. Provo, Utah: American Academy of Advertising, 1981, pp. 142-146.

Zielske, Hubert A. and Walter A. Henry. "Remembering and Forgetting Television Ads," *Journal of Advertising Research* (April, 1980) 20(2): 7-13.

Ziemke, Dean A. "Selective Exposure in a Presidential Campaign Contingent on Certainty and Salience," *Communication Yearbook 4,* ed. Dan Nimmo. New Brunswick, N.J.: Transaction Books, 1980, pp. 497-511.

Zillmann, Dolph and Jennings Bryant. "Pornography, Sexual Callousness and the Trivialization of Rape," *Journal of Communication* (1982) 32(4): 10-21.

Zillmann, Dolph, Jennings Bryant and Rodney Carveth. The Effect of Erotica Featuring Sado-Masochism and Bestiality on Motivated Inter-Male Aggression," *Personality and Social Psychology Bulletin.* (1981) 7: 153-159.

Zukin, Cliff. "Mass Communication and Public Opinion," *Handbook of Political Communication,* ed. Dan D. Nimmo and Keith R. Sanders. Beverly Hills: Sage, 1981, pp. 359-390.

Zukin, Cliff and Robin Snyder. "Passive Learning: When the Media Environment Is the Message," *Public Opinion Quarterly* (Fall, 1984) 48: 629-638.

Index